1815

THE ROADS TO WATERLOO

Gregor Dallas

RICHARD COHEN BOOKS · London

Endpapers: "Protagonists in a dance" places the three Sovereigns of Austria, Russia and Prussia in centre-stage, while the Ministers of France and Britain mark their steps to the left, and the King of Saxony and the Republic of Genoa join in on the right

British Library Cataloguing in Publication Data:
A catalogue record for this book is available from the British Library

Copyright © 1996 by Gregor Dallas

ISBN 1 86066072 X

First published in Great Britain in 1996 by
Richard Cohen Books
7 Manchester Square
London W1M 5RE

1 3 5 7 9 8 6 4 2

Designed by Margaret Fraser

Typeset in Linotron Garamond Stempel by
Banbury Pre-Press

Printed in Great Britain by
Biddles Ltd, Guildford

To Christine

Contents

VIENNA, Autumn 1814

VIENNA, Winter 1814-1815

ELBA and PARIS, Winter 1814-1815

WATERLOO, Spring 1815

PARIS, Summer 1815

EUROPE, EUROPE

Preface

Some ten years ago, a friend of mine in Paris told me I should drive to Berlin. "In twenty-four hours you'll be facing the Red Guard," he said, "and you will understand what Europe is all about." A week later, I was on the flat fast road to Berlin; over a stretch of seven hundred miles nature had erected no obstacles apart from the Rhine. And, sure enough, by nightfall my car was being inspected by a tall customs official of the German Democratic Republic. On the approach to the checkpoint between East and West all one could see in an evening were piles of rubble, a few unadorned modern square blocks, and the yellow haze of burnt cheap petrol.

No visitor could fail to be impressed by the way a new Berlin had grown out of the ruins. No one who passed through Checkpoint Charlie could ignore the sudden change in the urban landscape; the architects of East Berlin still practised a gigantism that had long been abandoned by the West. And nobody crossing Berlin for the first time could avoid thinking of war. It was in East Berlin that I started to reflect on this book. There was that flat plain I had just driven across; the old debris of war; and a city regenerated but divided against itself.

It was the transition from war to peace that intrigued me. What I had in front of me was a living document, a city that had experienced – and experienced horrifically – that transition. Berlin set me thinking of different cities in different wars.

Berlin itself was a statement on war and peace in the twentieth century and could, as one wandered through its streets, be read like a book. The road from Paris to Berlin, on the other hand, was a statement on every century. In Berlin, one thought of 1945 and 1918; on the road to Berlin, one thought of 1815 – I had driven, in a summer's morning, across the plains of Belgium.

That strange story of a British commander from Ireland, who, at the head of a European army, defended the town of Brussels, clung to my imagination when I was in Berlin. It was the story behind the story of the ruins before me; a story, moreover, that had not been entirely recounted before.

Of course, there existed plenty of books on the Battle of Waterloo. But not many of them related the battle to the reorganisa-

tion of Central Europe, which took place that same year. Very few
told how Wellington's European army had been recruited. Virtually
none spoke of the mutinies of May 1815 and what had caused them.
Most books on Waterloo concentrated either on the military manœuvres of June or on the fall of Napoleon Bonaparte. But there were
other roads to Waterloo and I wanted to write about them.

Many books had also been written on the peace settlement of
1814-15. They were nearly all diplomatic histories, which reduced the
military history to a paragraph and completely ignored the life of the
cities where most of the diplomatic events had occurred.

In both the military histories of Waterloo and the diplomatic
histories of the European peace, there was, in addition, the almost
unavoidable problem of national prejudice. The works of C.K.
Webster and Harold Nicolson were quintessentially English. Henry
Houssaye was unashamedly French. Henry Kissinger and Enno E.
Kraehe – Central Europeans who had adopted America – of course
made Metternich their hero. The list of examples was very long.

No book is written in a vacuum. No history can be entirely objective. I have a few prejudices myself. I think immediately of one. I have
an abiding interest in local history; that is, I am convinced that where
things happened shaped how they happened (no doubt, this is why
Berlin so impressed me). It does not appear to be the view of the
majority of historians today. For several decades now, theory and
abstract reasoning have overridden the role of place in our history
books; the people who write them describe and analyse events as
though they could have happened anywhere in the world. Here,
places will play a major part in our story.

Another influence on my thought – prejudice is, perhaps, too
strong a word – has been the work of French historians. Fernand
Braudel taught that there were three levels of history: the short-term
history of events; the middle term of *conjonctures*, of cycles, of
generations replacing each other; and finally the history of the *longue
durée*. Because he wrote mostly about the latter, Braudel has been
characterised, and criticised, as a historian of structures. But Braudel
was also a great storyteller. One might even suspect that it was his
profound sense of history as a grand story that led him to think of
these three levels. The idea, in fact, was not all that original. The same
three levels are to be found, for instance, in Tolstoy's *War and Peace*:
the drama of 1812; the cycle of the seasons and of life (is there a more
exquisite depiction of life and death than in Tolstoy?); and, beneath all
this, the old permanences of Russia. Tolstoy majestically shifts from
one level to another; it is what he called his "cloud of joy" and his
"image of the sky;" it is what makes his novel work.

So a voyage across Northern Europe and a collection of ideas are at
the origin of this book. If, in writing it, I made one major discovery,

it was Talleyrand, the French Foreign Minister in 1815. I was astonished to find that Talleyrand also viewed history in terms of three levels: the "turbulence" of revolution and war, the cycle of the generations, and the old permanences of "civilisation." Talleyrand, one is tempted to say, is Tolstoy; Talleyrand is Braudel in 1815.

But Talleyrand could not be the thread of the story of 1815 because he never reached the centre of action. That thread was surely Viscount Castlereagh, the British Foreign Secretary, who travelled from city to city in search for peace. Castlereagh was no hero. Sometimes he got things hopelessly wrong. Sometimes he had to pull back in full retreat. He was anguished, disoriented; he was not even sure of what public he represented. Often he was overcome by forces greater than he. Those forces were determined by other threads – by the personalities around him, the societies he didn't always understand, the various movements of peoples displaced by the long war.

Castlereagh, an islander, could afford to take an impartial, but somewhat mechanical view of these developments – London's view. Talleyrand showed more of a sense of geography and history; he dug down into the strata of time – Paris's view. Tsar Alexander, in contrast, was an idealist and his opinions were altogether of a higher, more spiritual order – the Russian view. For the Austrian Foreign Minister, Metternich, Europe was a playing board for power, it was a complex game – Vienna's view.

Talleyrand, Castlereagh, and Metternich followed ways that were fashioned by their cities: old revolutionary Paris, the great metropolis of Regency London, and baroque Vienna. Talleyrand was Parisian to the core. Castlereagh and Metternich had adopted their respective towns and this would lead to certain personal tensions. Alexander, on the other hand, belonged to no city; between December 1812 and December 1815, he only spent one month in his capital. He had the voice of disembodied ideology and, in this sense, might be heard as a harbinger of our own century. He resembled, in many ways, Napoleon, who likewise spoke for no city – Napoleon's audience was his army, continually on the march. Recognising what they had in common, Alexander and Napoleon actually referred to each other as "friends," even when they were at war.

Behind the cities, where the decisions were made, lay that great northern plain of Europe. The Battle of Jena was fought on a plain, Borodino was fought on a plain, Leipzig was fought on a plain. *"Morne plaine"* : that would be the site of Waterloo. All these battles were fought on the same plain, across which the soldiers marched, the refugees migrated, and the power of the Powers ebbed and flowed. Metternich, in Vienna, spoke of the "devouring Powers," Napoleon's France and Alexander's Russia, which competed for the European centre. The ebb and flow of these flanking Powers across the northern plain is essentially the story of my book.

"Poland is the key to the vault," said Napoleon, banging a finger on the map: Poland was a focal point for the competitors. The activities of the diplomats and life in the cities depended to a large degree on the balance of the flanking Powers and on various efforts to strengthen Europe's weak centre.

The first half of the book deals with the developing threat of the Russian flank following the defeat of France in 1814. The second half concentrates on the unexpected resurgence of the French flank. "Germany," a composite of sovereign states, was caught in the middle.

Does any of this sound familiar? The story of 1815 is no metaphor of our times; it resonates of our times. A fallen empire, a revolutionary ideal gone sour, allies divided among themselves for lack of a common enemy, politicians distrusted, statesmen ignored, a howling press, royalty disgraced, old political parties disintegrating, unemployment and economic recession; all these are part of the story, but they are not the whole story.

No European or American can hear that story without picking out some recognisable theme. In 1815, leading minds on both sides of the Atlantic were wondering what kind of political order their world was entering. After the war with Britain was concluded in the winter of 1814-15, the United States entered the so-called "Era of Good Feelings;" but an old debate on Federation and Confederation simmered within America's fragile union. In Europe, too, one spoke of Federation and Confederation. Federal plans for Europe were put forward, a Congress was proposed, a Council of Ministers was actually set up. Against all this could be heard the voices of those who refused to be organised – stubborn voices, a permanent undertow, an opposition that had a pattern and a geography of its own.

Each city experienced some loss of direction when the generation of war ended. In London and Paris, there were serious social disturbances; in Vienna, there developed a popular political climate that had never existed before. Only in contrasting their differing perspectives, their various views across Europe, can one begin to feel the deeper cycle of life and the permanences lying under the whole grand drama of 1815.

And I do mean "feel." A bare analysis of all Europe would either be too reductionist or too complicated. It would insulate the events in their time and erase the effect of their memory on our own lives. This is the problem, I think, of most historical analysis today: it solidifies everything. Once one has created a "world system," one cannot get out of it; the dogma of function and the restraint of reason become one's walls; all ornaments, all scenery, all life beyond them appear parasitic and useless to these self-imprisoned analysers. Local history –

which is so much less restrictive – is, on the final count, more truly universal: it speaks for and from its place of origin.

What was that extraordinary thrill that I had felt in Berlin? Analyse it and you will kill it. What was London, Paris, or Vienna in 1815? Analyse it and you will never *see* it. "When the unconscious is made conscious, art ceases to exist," remarked Otto Rank, a psycho-analyst who resisted the stubborn orthodoxies of his day. It is a thought one must relate to his very last breath of life: *"Komisch,"* he muttered and died.

History is surely an art and it is frequently *komisch*. It is the art of taking an image from memory and honouring it by giving it a con-temporary new life. It is the art of holding up a narrative – comical, strange, and peculiar *("komisch")* – as it opens itself to a hundred different levels of understanding.

Through seasons of drought, rain, snows, and strikes I have always found a helpful hand among the staff of the Bibliothèque Nationale, the Bibliothèque Historique de la Ville de Paris, and the Deutsches Historisches Institut in Paris. The British Library and the Guildhall Library in London have been equally cooperative. A visit to Belfast proved highly productive thanks to Dr A.P.W. Malcolmson and his efficient staff at the Public Record Office of Northern Ireland; it was memorable thanks to Lesley Rainey and Harry Hutchman, who took me round the rooms and the grounds of Mount Stewart.

Gisela Kaufmann, at her "Buchladen" in Montmartre, supplied me with books from Germany, many of which were out-of-print. Pascale Le Tersec helped me track down titles in English and French.

I am grateful to my agent, Caroline Dawnay, who has been un-failing in her support for this project and, in a troubled publishing world, has built up the stable professional structure we first sought. As a result, the book has benefited from not just one fine editor, but two. Marian Wood, in New York, encouraged me along my path and upbraided me when I strayed. Richard Cohen, in London, stood always visible on the side, wielding his sabre. Margaret Fraser did the wonderful work in book design. Pat Chetwyn kept us all together.

I dedicate this book to my wife, Christine, because a book on the age of Beethoven, Friedrich, and Chateaubriand is so obviously hers.

G.D.
Anet
1993-6

Il danse terre
à terre.

Ils saute pou.
le roi de Sardaigne

Roi de
Saxe

République de Gênes

LONDON
Spring 1814

Previous page: Thomas Rowlandson evokes the Miseries of London

The Dover Road

Just seventy-two miles separated the old stone jetty of Dover from London; but the way was narrow, hilly, and sometimes dangerous. Slogging up hills on foot, sinking in mud to one's ankles, repeated delays at the toll gates – not to mention of the threat of robbery – were inconveniences anyone travelling it had to expect. But then what magnificent views there were of the valleys, the mansions, the old oast houses, the new inns, the sheep walks over the Downs. No other road in England evoked more forcefully the fact that Great Britain was an island; from one's carriage one could not only smell the sea, from the hills one could see it.

War and peace dictated the names of those distant waters. That dark blue line to the north and east was called the German Ocean; it was from over there that Britain had supplied herself with Protestant kings, allies and most of her soldiers. To the south lay another shimmering grey line: the English or British Channel – never French, never foreign.

When it was war the plain behind Barham Downs was the site of military encampments, and the only vehicles one was likely to encounter were the carriers of artillery and baggage. Traffic was more varied at times of peace; one would notice the fresh tracks spreading out beyond the edges of the road, too narrow for the rapid passage of chaises, crowded coaches and mails. And, with peace, the whole atmosphere was transformed in the narrow, crooked town at the beginning or the end of the line, Dover. The shopkeepers found more business, the two hotels were booked solid, gentlemen with top hats and ladies in white muslin frocks sprained their ankles on the heaps of stone that passed for a beach, and younger adventurers clambered up the covered winding staircase leading to the Governor's castle on the cliff. There was more noise in the market, a greater clatter of salvers and dishes in the hotels and the coffee houses, more pipes were smoked, more papers read, the porter flowed like nectar and the waiters could again charge foreigners eighteen shillings for eggs and tea.

How novel it all seemed then, just after the news arrived in the little

3

port, during the Easter weekend of April 1814, that Paris had fallen and the Emperor of France had abdicated. A generation of war was over.[1]

Two regiments of cavalry due to join Lord Wellington's army in the south of France were countermanded. The French prisoners, recently arrived from Dunkirk, were released and sent back across the Channel. Three packets were ordered round to do duty between Dover and Calais; they began sailing within five days.

But news of an even more extraordinary forthcoming event soon spread from Dover to London and from there to all England: for the first time since the reign of Henry VIII, European royalty was going to visit the island.[2] The significance of this escaped no one. There was something feverish in the newspaper reports, read aloud in the public houses, about the "princely strangers", "Our Illustrious Visitants", "these august Personages", the "Allied Sovereigns". Their visit spelt victory for Britain; but, even more than that, it symbolised the end of two decades of isolation.

"We now, on a sudden, not only abound with Ambassadors, but the Continent sends out their masters to come and see us," wrote the anonymous editor in *The Examiner*. He explained why they were coming: to admire Britain's "general independence of spirit, which has been kept alive from century to century by domestic patriots and the press, which has outstripped even the progress of corruption, and brought us once more under the shadow of older, loftier, and truer laurels, than craft or conquest know how to plant."[3]

In London, the apartments of the Duke of Cambridge were prepared for the Emperor of Russia, those of the Duke of Cumberland for the Emperor of Austria, and those of the Duke of Clarence for the King of Prussia. The climax of their visit would be a royal wedding. In early May it was announced that Princess Charlotte, daughter of the Prince Regent, grand-daughter of the King, would marry, in the presence of the Crowned Heads, William, the Hereditary Prince of Orange. William had already arrived in Harwich, travelling under the pseudonym "Captain H. George."

Yet the whole month of May went by and there was still no sign of the Sovereigns. King Frederick William III of Prussia was supposed to arrive in Dover on 12 May. His ship never docked. Emperor Francis II of Austria was expected with Emperor Alexander I of Russia on the 15th. Neither came. In the last week of May it was reported that the Austrian Emperor would not be visiting England at all, while Alexander's voyage was inexplicably delayed.

The cause of the problem was diplomatic; the expected Sovereigns had been kept in Paris, negotiating what was known simply and portentously as "the Treaty". In May the British public was told only to expect the preliminaries, but by the end of the month it was clear that something more solid was on its way.

The men of the press were uncomfortable. Rumour spread that France was being let off too lightly, that the interests of the free nations of Europe were not being respected, that Britain was selling out her hard won independence, and the independence of others. There was an undercurrent of anger. "It perhaps would be ultimately better for Europe if it was never signed," wrote the editor of *The Examiner* on 22 May; "almost every clause seems to be a violation of principle." How did he know? Not a copy of the Treaty was yet available.[4]

It was only murmur. On Friday, 3 June, something much more exciting was announced. The British Foreign Secretary, Viscount Castlereagh, had landed in Dover to carry to London not the preliminaries but "the Definitive Treaty of Peace". The guns of the port were fired in his honour and he was hailed in every village he passed on his way to the capital.

Castlereagh also brought news that the Allied Sovereigns could be expected in town on Monday. The public debate on the Treaty was thus postponed. In London and along the whole road to Dover were scenes of popular turmoil. Britain was first going to celebrate the Peace.[5]

The Allied Sovereigns enter

In London, the owners of houses on Parliament Street and Bridge Street – as well as of the homes of the porkmen, cow-keepers, and the myriad ale-houses stretching down the Kent Road to Shooter's Hill – started setting up the wooden stages shortly after Castlereagh's arrival: renting seats on the roadside was a profitable business. Banners were unfurled, gentlemen wore brilliant waistcoats and frockcoats while the ladies were in silks and sarsenets, despite the cold weather. As for the people, they wore what they could, and went where they could. Women and children sold pottles of strawberries, one could buy grapes out of a basket and the hot-potato man – with his huge cans – was doing a thriving trade.

Further down the Dover Road the crowds arrived by horse, by foot, and in vehicles decorated with ribbons and laurel. Branches of oak, elm, and laurel festooned the fronts of houses. Austrian, Russian, and Prussian flags rippled in the easterly wind. The Bourbon *fleur de lys* was brandished but so was the Union Jack. And there was native ingenuity, too. One white flag contained the image of a whole plum-pudding, a bee-hive, the horn of abundance, a pot of porter, a sirloin of beef, and the word "Peace" written under the lot. The occupants of another small house, bedecked in flags and laurel, had plastered on their front a huge paper poster reading, "Thanks Royal Strangers for your valiant aid in the general cause. You have fought and conquered.

We may now sit down in Old England and eat roast beef and plum-pudding in peace."[6]

Thus Monday came and went. The crowds waited. Still no sign of the Sovereigns.

It was known that a small party of Don Cossacks had landed at Dover to act as the Russian Emperor's bodyguard. Word also spread of the arrival of some Illustrious Persons, like Prince Oldenburg Holstein and the Austrian General Colloredo. Prince Metternich, the Austrian foreign minister, had stepped ashore late on Sunday. The heroes of 1812 and the German campaign of 1813 – Count Barclay de Tolly, Count Tolstoy and Count Platov – sailed into Dover on the *Sparrow* sloop early on Monday morning. Brave Platov, *hetman* of the Don Cossacks, so enjoyed the short trip across the Channel that he set promptly off to sea once more for a coastal cruise, and wasn't seen again until that afternoon.

The sun had already set when the rumour spread that the Emperor of Russia and the King of Prussia had arrived in Dover. This was confirmed by an official bulletin from London the next morning. "A message will go down to both Houses of Parliament, in the course of a few days," it added, "to announce the intended nuptials between the Hereditary Prince of Orange and the Princess Charlotte of Wales." So three long-expected events were at last being realised – the Treaty, the Sovereigns' visit, and the Royal Marriage.[7]

The Prince Regent did not, as had been earlier announced, leave town for Deptford to meet the Sovereigns. Instead, early on Tuesday morning he sent twelve of his most beautiful bay horses, with grooms and outriders, to Shooter's Hill for the purpose of drawing the Sovereigns to town. A party of the Fourteenth Dragoons, astride their thundering chargers, escorted them up to the Bull Tavern on the hill's summit.

All the beauty and fashion of London seemed to be there. The nobility and gentry of England stationed their carriages in double ranks. Poorer classes clambered up the decaying triangular brick tower memorial.

Twelve o'clock passed; no Sovereigns.

One o'clock passed; still no Sovereigns.

The east wind seemed colder. Then telescopes picked up a body of horsemen coming in the direction of Northfleet and, at about half past one, they cantered into full view, escorting an open carriage.

"The veteran Blücher!" exclaimed the horsemen, "the gallant Blücher!" A loud huzza echoed across the dark mass of humanity. Ladies waved their handkerchiefs. Gentlemen stood up. Inside the carriage Blücher, the Prussian marshal, was distinctly recognisable in his white locks and lacquered moustachios; he bowed, replying in his magnificent English, "Me ferry tankvoll! ferry, ferry tankvoll!"

But two o'clock passed and the Sovereigns had not yet been sighted.

At three o'clock Sir Charles Stewart, Castlereagh's younger brother, drew up in a plain travelling carriage near a tavern in Welling, stood up on the footplate and announced: "They are already in London!" Gradually the patriotic crowds of England dispersed like clouds in heaven.

On the forecourt of Cumberland House, where the building works in preparation for Emperor Alexander's reception had lasted over a month, two military bands performed all Tuesday afternoon. The Sergeants of Arms with their maces and collars, the Sergeant Trumpeter with his mace and collar, the trumpets, the drum-major and drums struck up a grand and hearty "See the Conquering Hero Comes" and a booming "God Save the King." The two bands seemed to be in competition. While the din of brass and drums of one would grow then fade with a barely recognisable "To Arms! To Arms!" a still less coherent "Britannia!" – rising and falling – belched from the other. It was hardly counterpoint, it was certainly not syncopation; it was palpitating noise.

A royal standard drooped forlornly from a nearby tower and a Russian eagle, like Janus, cast its puzzled eyes in both directions. On the steps, in formal attire, their four necks bulging above their tight stiff collars, stood the Lord Chamberlain and the Lord Steward.

They stood; the bands pounded; and they stood and stood. The Emperor did not arrive.

But His Imperial Highness's lofty figure had been sighted on a balcony of the Pulteney Hotel in Piccadilly, where a new crowd began to swarm. For a moment one might have looked down that long straight road to Piccadilly and watched it ebb and flow, a heaving tide of men and women – something impermanent, perishable, something not quite real, like the coloured objects in an old optical box. The sound of myriad feet on cobbles was joined by the distant boom of confused military bands, waxing and waning, and the voice of a mad old woman heckling the clients of a corner tavern. The metropolis of London: immense, heavy, stupefying. The old woman spat out her words, "God save the King! God save our King!"

An insane and patriotic King

The King? It had been his seventy-sixth birthday the previous Saturday, the day Castlereagh had entered London. The Park and Tower guns had boomed out their ritual salute and the guards of the palaces were dressed in white gaiters. His Majesty's ministers and great officers of state gave dinners "at their separate houses." But few that cold, wind-swept day had turned out on the streets.[8]

It was nearly fifty-four years since he had acceded to his grand-father's throne and been proclaimed, "George the Third, by the Grace of God King of Great Britain, France, and Ireland, Defender of the Faith, and so forth." Time had nibbled away at both title and Sovereign. Among the miscellaneous domains "and so forth" he had been deprived of his claim on the American colonies and, four and a half centuries after Edward III had stood up for his rights, he had dropped – with royal relief – his claim on France. In the last two decades he faced the threat of republican revolution on the continent, upheaval at home, and the most destructive war the world had yet known. But in June 1814 George III was unaware of the victory, unconscious of the arrival of the foreign Sovereigns; he did not even know it was his birthday.[9]

The King was living in the state apartments at Windsor Castle, overlooking the North Terrace and the playing fields of Eton. This had been his favourite spot in the world; his world, which stretched from Cheltenham, Weymouth and Plymouth all the way up to Worcester (he had never travelled on the continent, he had seen neither Scotland, Wales, nor Ireland). "I am myself an Etonian," he told the masters and boys of the College opposite; but they never saw him now.

It was a heavy mass of stone, this Windsor, without the gothic fantasy of bay windows and balconies, their columns, cornices and architraves squeezing stuffy volume out of the thick medieval walls – all that came later, with the son. No building in Europe had so long a record of habitation by a ruling family. It was under-financed, this Windsor; the masonry was crumbling, the plaster was cracked, the high doors rattled and every corridor and chamber bore a sustained smell of English Renaissance drains. The King occupied three compartments, two of which formed one sitting-room, having an arched open communication between them. In the third compartment was his bed, once described as resembling an officer's camp bed with only a simple mattress, one bolster and no pillow. No sun ever entered the rooms. No carpets were on the floors, because the King had always argued that carpets harboured dust. There was the whispering beat of a clock, an occasional creak on the broken parquet, a still rarer whiff of fresh air, and every now and again the sudden appearance of darkly dressed phantoms – the King's constant companions, his daily tormentors, his permanent prison guard: the three brothers Willis.[10]

Since the onset of his final illness in November 1810 few others saw the King. Louis Simond, a French *émigré*, had sighted him on the North Terrace on a March day in 1811 when rumours abounded that his health had improved. "His Majesty was dressed in a plain blue coat," wrote Simond in his diary, "his hat flopped over his eyes, – stooped a little, – looked thin, and walked fast; talking continually,

Rowlandson's *Doctor Willis at home*. The brothers Willis were keepers of the King and, among their remedies for madness, they advocated "inculcating salutary fear"

and with an appearance of earnestness. We could at times distinguish his voice at twenty yards distance; – this does not look like recovery."[11]

Nobody would have seen the King walking on the terrace in 1814. The only news the public received of their King were the brief, non-committal bulletins exhibited at St James's Palace at the beginning of every month. The one posted on 4 June 1814 – the King's birthday – read: "The King's health has been uninterruptedly good, and His Majesty has been very tranquil throughout the last month, though His Majesty's disorder continues without any sensible alteration."[12]

History is left with the record of a select few who did make it past the two main barriers to the monarch, the Queen's Council and then the Willises. They tell us that at times the King was silent, and his attendants, amazingly fearful of breaching court etiquette, would not break that silence by addressing him a question. At other times he would talk endlessly, rambling on, on one occasion "for nineteen hours without scarce any intermission." "I am nervous; I am not ill, but I am nervous," he cried out once in a hoarse, exhausted voice. "If you would know what is the matter with me, I am nervous."

His language was full of "strategem & project," his looks wild and vehement, his eyes coloured "like black currant jelly," the veins in his face red and swelling. He was incapable of "maintaining any steadiness in his ideas and conversation for more than an instant," his speech "seemed more like the detail of a dream in its extravagant confusion" as he delved into "the inexhaustible resources of his distempered imagination." In his most extreme moments of delirium he reportedly spoke in Latin.[13]

Nobody said in public that the King was mad, or even insane. Doctor Robert Willis spoke of his derangement as "more nearly allied to delirium, than insanity." Doctor Matthew Baillie said "his memory seems to be impaired." Doctor Henry Revell Reynolds decided the illness "came from the anxiety of his mind." Doctor William Heberden junior spoke of paroxysm. Doctor John Monro admitted a "degree of mental disorder" but he found "no symptoms of fatuity." The closest anyone came to saying that the King was actually mad was Doctor John Willis who told a parliamentary committee in 1812 that His Majesty's "very great degree of derangement" had "very much the symptoms of insanity," but he qualified this by adding that the King showed "at the same time rather unusually... delirious characters."[14]

The physical nature of the King's disease is still debated. It would have required someone who was *not* a doctor to grasp the full calamity that had struck that snowy bearded monarch in his purple dressing-gown, blind and nearly deaf, banging out on old Handel's harpsichord the tragic melodies of *Samson Agonistes* and the lamentations of Jephthah; someone more sensitive than the brothers Willis may have comprehended the terrible, morbid, intimate and, in the end, poetic world that bore the Sovereign away. The "detail of a dream," an "extravagant confusion," a "distempered imagination"; King George III of Great Britain and so forth stared into his own little optical box.

A European Prince Regent

The Prince Regent remained in his palace too, not out of reasons of health, but because, in London, he was not popular. He did not ride to Shooter's Hill to greet the Sovereigns and, when he learnt that Alexander was at the Pulteney Hotel, he refused to descend the streets to meet him. Instead, Alexander, the hero of 1812, the first of the Allies to enter Paris, was obliged to make the short trip himself. The people, chagrined and humiliated on Tuesday, blamed the Regent for keeping the Illustrious Sovereigns hidden from view, an accusation the Regent immediately and formally contradicted.[15]

"Prinny," "Florizel," the "Pig of Pall-mall," the "Prince of Whales," the "Voluptuary under the Horrors of Digestion," "Adonis, Prince of Modern Macaronis" had not struck the same happy chord with his people as his father. The campaigns against him in the press – and not just the penny and pauper press – had descended to new depths by the spring of 1814. Every movement he made was noted and analysed. "The Prince Regent left town yesterday for Windsor, in

George,
H.R.H. the Prince Regent
and "First Gentleman
of Europe"

the most private manner," reported *The Examiner* on 5 June, "*through the back entrance* of Carlton House."

His father had led a blameless domestic life with Queen Charlotte, producing fifteen children, nine sons and six daughters, all but two of whom miraculously lived to adulthood – the first time a ruling English monarch had had so many surviving children since the reign of Edward III. He was kind, religious, sober – and boring; yet the English loved him, even after reason had completely abandoned him. In that reign of over half a century, he had made no great contribution to the arts; and the English loved him even more. His favourite painter was Benjamin West, not because of the quality of his works but because of the lessons in virtue his large flat canvases taught. He did not like "mountains and other romantic scenery"; nor "the fine wild beauties of nature"; he objected to nude women, bucolic surroundings, lovers, sartorial frills, and idle gestures; "His Majesty," the connoisseur Sir William Hamilton once remarked, "has never arrived at being sensible of what is properly called the sublime in the arts."[16]

His eldest son did, and thereby put his royal reputation at risk. It was sublimity washed down with a bowl of punch, a bacchanalian perspective on the arts; for if Good King George's reign had been the age of virtue, Prinny's was the age of drinking. The Prince, who weighed over seventeen stone and wore a belt more than fifty inches long, enjoyed the company of the most famous society wastrels, the most dissipated dukes and earls – the Lades, the Barrymores, Norfolk, Queensberry, the Hon. George Hanger, and the highest spending gambling lady of London, the Duchess of Devonshire. The Prince's appreciation of the arts had been acquired in drawing rooms and taverns, Devonshire House and the Pantheon, the theatre green-rooms and Brooks's. How he was hated for it. When he was in his early twenties pamphlets and newspapers were already making a scandal about his "companions and confidential intimates," the "very *lees* of society." Those who actually met him might have been capti-vated by his perverted charm. When he was a young man, it was said by one of his attendants, "Louis XIV himself could scarcely have eclipsed the son of George III." But this hardly endeared him to the freeborn Briton; he behaved like a European monarch.[17]

The "lees of society" were in fact far from nonentities, and the Prince himself could be brilliant. He loved Greek and Latin literature, he enjoyed music, he was an impressive bass singer, a cellist (even Joseph Haydn said he played "quite tolerably"), one of the greatest connoisseurs of painting in the world, and the most important art collector in Britain since Charles I. He was one of the greatest patrons of British architecture, too. It was the Prince Regent, rather than John Nash (more a shrewd opportunist than a grand planner), who was the main force behind the radically changing face of London at this time. June 1814 was one of his great opportunities: the Prince wanted to introduce the Allied Sovereigns to a new European capital.[18]

But London was not a court culture, it had no taste for majestic architectural projects, for grand vistas or imposing monuments; London was impatient with art. Architects in the tradition of Chambers, Adam, Soane, and Nash understood this better than the Prince Regent; what they designed was generally small, sometimes diminutive, and frequently – if one listened to the comments of foreign visitors – mean in concept.

Commerce was the only king. The City had contempt for the Regent and his gingerbread gauds in Carlton House, his visual whim-sies, his sense of fun. The honest artisans of London – those of the respectable associated trades, the first enemies of "old corruption" – hated, and hated to distraction, Prinny, the dissipated Regent.[19]

Was he even English? "Born and educated in this country, I glory in the name of Britain," Good King George had once proclaimed. The son styled himself as the "First Gentleman *of Europe*." This was not a title to win one friends in London.[20]

But if one had asked the Regent's enemies in June 1814 why they hated him so much, they would have denied it was his continental tone, his love of art, his drinking "debauches" even. They would have all spoken with one voice: it was the way he treated his wife.

The women in his life: Caroline and Charlotte

She was no beauty, Caroline. Even the most flattering portraits confirm the picture left by contemporaries of her being short, "very full chested," with jutting hips; Joseph Farington, for one, described her as "very large and coarse, exhibiting nothing of feminine dignity." Her manner of dress didn't help; she gartered below the knee and attired herself in garments "shewing too much of her naked person." Her ample figure in 1814 convinced Lady Charlotte Campbell that the Princess was pregnant (she was then forty-six), until someone assured her that this was due to her penchant for leaving off her stays. She was always asking embarrassingly personal questions, making outrageous comments, blurting out remarks that were offensive, sarcastic and pert – a "rattling, affecting raillery" it was described as by an attendant. Her mother, the old Duchess of Brunswick, sister of George III, had told Lord Redesdale before she died, "She is not quite right *here*," touching her sad old head and bursting into tears. Caroline's receptions at Montague House, in Blackheath, and later at Kensington Palace, were infamous. If her dancing partner didn't move fast enough she would cry out, *"Vite! Vite!"*, sometimes leading him all over her apartments to a dance of her own invention. If she got bored she would disappear with a gentleman to the Blue Room upstairs, or simply walk out and take her place in a reserved box at the opera. Lady Hester Stanhope called her "a downright whore" and indeed her taste in men was wide and varied, the goal of her flamboyant if clumsy flirtatiousness never in doubt. "I have a bedfellow whenever I like," she told Lady Douglas as she munched fried onions and potatoes in bed, washing the lot down with ale. London was rife with rumours of who her lovers were: Captain Thomas Manby of the Royal Navy, Admiral Sir Sidney Smith, Sir Walter Scott, Sir William Scott, Thomas Lawrence, the Duke of Cumberland, George Canning. She liked both pot-bellied lawyers and handsome young officers, and seemed undeterred by the fact that adultery by a Princess of Wales was still considered high treason in England, punishable by death. Young men were less keen on the idea. "I had much rather be the bellows than the poker," remarked John William Ward to William Henry Lyttelton after a chase across the ballroom floor. Others were less fussy. Roberts, her footman at Montague House, declared the Princess was "very fond of fucking."[21]

Why did the Prince Regent marry her, a first cousin, to begin with?

Because of money and the need for an heir. In 1795 the Prince was so shot through with debts and his brothers so tied up with their mistresses and left-handed marriages that he had no choice. The Duke of York was the only regularly married son, and his duchess could bear no children. It was frequently said that the marriage was a plot foisted on the Prince by Lady Jersey, his mistress at the time, who thought that disgust for the wife would assure constancy to her. If so, the first half of the scheme proceeded smoothly. "Harris, I am not well," said the Prince on being introduced to the Princess, "pray get me a glass of brandy." "Sir, had you not better have a glass of water?" replied Harris. "*No,*" said the Prince. "*Mein Gott!*" exclaimed Caroline. "Does the Prince always act like this?" The Prince climbed drunkenly into bed with her on the morning after a disastrous wedding night, and nine months and a day later Princess Charlotte was born.[22]

Not surprisingly, when it came to Charlotte's turn to help pair off the states of Europe through marriage, she hesitated.

By nearly all accounts she was better looking than her mother and also better behaved, even if she did wear her petticoats too short and showed her drawers and legs when getting in and out of carriages – well, it was said, her legs were rather pretty. She had blond hair, blue eyes, and her skin was marked by smallpox. There was an element of romanticism about her (in tune with the times), an emotional storm within her: she was excitable, impudent, hot-tempered, warm-hearted, "innately affectionate," and for long periods desperately depressed. Some described her laugh as brash, her talk unending. Others said it was perhaps a taint in the blood both her mother and father had passed on to her, in their single encounter, from their ancient royal race.[23]

Men were attracted to her. She had enjoyed the company of the Duke of Devonshire, and her father said she had spent too much time with Gloucester. Her relationship with Captain Charles Hesse of the 18th Hussars had been, in 1812, a cause of scandal, though her father had not yet learnt about it. Her mother had given them the use of her own bedroom at Kensington, turning the key and saying, "*A présent je vous laisse, amusez-vous.*" Charlotte was not amused at all, and interpreted this "scrape" as an intention of her mother to disgrace her and bring forward as heir to the throne the boy who was rumoured to be Caroline's son, William Austen or "Willikin."[24]

She far preferred her father to her mother, whose behaviour and "war with the royal family" deeply embarrassed her. One gets the impression that the Regent's strict rules of visitation were quite a relief for Charlotte, who spoke of her visits to Kensington as a "duty," though her mother of course complained of being deprived of her "ever beloved Charlotte," her "only happiness."[25]

She now lived most of her time at Warwick House, a dark and

gloomy mansion in much need of repair which was next door to Carlton House; there was even a communicating door between them (the Regent had forbidden Caroline to see Charlotte at her home because of a "possibility of my meeting the Princess were she to come here.") She considered her father "very kind," enjoyed the brisk rides in his phaeton and dined with him frequently. Even so, she found the restrictions on her movements oppressive and had been furious when the Regent refused to let her set up her own household the previous year – her father had ruled no household before marriage.[26]

So Charlotte would get married.

The candidate, William, the Hereditary Prince of Orange, had been chosen by the government, endorsed by the Regent and, at first, refused by Charlotte. "I think him so ugly," she remarked after her first encounter with him in the autumn of 1813, "that I am sometimes obliged to turn my head away in disgust when he is speaking to me." But the Regent's private messenger and doctor, Sir Henry Halford, somehow persuaded her that he could be a husband after all – this gallant prince had served in the Peninsula, he was adored in the army (where he had been known as "Slender Billy"), he had spent two years at Oxford, and in the prints he didn't look *so* ugly.

A walk in the grand fan-vaulted conservatory of Carlton House seemed to seal the matter, Charlotte pale but hiding her fears, William small, frail and in a state of abject terror – the portly Prince Regent marched between them. After some tortuous conversation the father guided the daughter into a gothic niche: "Well, it will not do, I suppose." "I did not say that," she answered, flushing. "I like his manner very well, as much as I have ever seen it." The Regent was apparently overwhelmed with joy; arm in arm he brought his daughter silently back – just their feet echoing on the polished tiles – to the diminutive Hereditary Prince Sovereign of Orange, standing perplexed in the centre of the hall, and there he joined their hands. Charlotte spoke of the whole scene as "a dream."[27]

A dream or a nightmare? If she were to marry a foreign prince, where would she live? And what would happen to her claim to the throne? Charlotte remained depressed, troubled and shut up in her own black world.

The politics of a drawing room

For Caroline, the visit of the conquering Sovereigns marked the beginning of open warfare. The press was mobilised – *The Morning Chronicle*, *The Examiner*, *The Pilot* and *The News* for the Princess, *The Morning Herald* and *The Morning Post* for the Prince. The political parties were rallied – Whigs and Radicals for the Princess,

Tories for the Prince. The foreign Sovereigns themselves got embroiled. Next to their own busy agenda of banquets and balls, it was the major news story in London. In parliamentary reports, debates on "the Princess of Wales" pushed aside the unfinished business of madhouses, the Slave Trade and the Corn Laws.

The opposition Whigs badly needed an issue like this. Their reputation as a peace party stood them no good in 1814. They were divided and lacked leaders. Indeed, there was talk in 1814 that the party system no longer existed, that Tories and Whigs merely denoted those who were in power and those who were out.[28]

Two prominent Whigs, Henry Brougham and Samuel Whitbread, were determined that this would not be so, and they latched on to the Caroline affair as a means of reviving their party. It has to be said Brougham was not the sort of person one would expect to find championing a lady's rights. He had a notoriously bad manner with women and he treated his own wife with total contempt; she was eventually locked up in a madhouse. A man of many interests, and many opinions indeed. Torch-bearer of the Scottish Englightenment, both engineer and architect, Brougham's first vocation was that of a wily lawyer in search of rich clients and famous cases. In other years he would have just as willingly supported the Man, but this was the Year of the Woman.[29]

Mr Samuel Whitbread, on the other hand, actually believed in what he said. He really should have been leader of the Whigs, but Whitbread was a business man, a rich brewer, and the Whigs, in addition to supporting the noble issues of reform, peace, abolition of the slaves, and justice for the sexes, were a party of the landed interests. So they put the nonentity George Ponsonby at the head of their party in the Commons, not Whitbread. Whitbread was a master of oratory. Lord Byron considered Whitbread "the Demosthenes of bad taste," Wilberforce said he spoke as if he had "a pot of porter to his lips and all his words came through it," Thomas Barnes of *The Times* thought his appearance was as English as his mind; what everybody admired in him – his opponents included – was his sincerity. It was Barnes again who said that in Whitbread you felt a man "where the naked soul may yet walk abroad and feel no shame." Whitbread was "the promoter of every liberal scheme for improving the condition of mankind, the zealous advocate of the oppressed, and the undaunted opposer of every species of corruption and ill-administration," as his fellow Whig parliamentarian, Sir Samuel Romilly, observed, and not a soul alive in 1814 would have denied it.[30]

Liberal souls had enemies. Whitbread had one in particular. His pacifism brought him into conflict with the Foreign Secretary, Lord Castlereagh. His campaign for electoral reform opened up a long running battle with the Tory leader of the Commons, Lord Castlereagh.

His action in favour of Caroline caused an open rift with the nephew of the Regent's mistress, Lord Castlereagh. Somehow, whenever an issue of justice was to be fought he was always crossing swords with Lord Castlereagh.

The great issue that June concerned a drawing room. The Queen's Drawing Room was a vestige of the old court society, when the Monarch was the centre of all social, administrative and political life and all major business – from international diplomacy, war and peace, to official appointments, investitures, and leaves to marry – was conducted in his palace. Since the King's illness the receptions and ceremonies of the court had fallen into rapid decline. Yet the Queen still held a Drawing Room at Buckingham House, formally every Thursday, though even these were frequently cancelled. But in the spring of 1814 the Queen signified her intention "to hold several Drawing-rooms this season." The Drawing Room thus became a litmus test of those who mattered at the moment the foreign Sovereigns arrived in London.[31]

Efforts had been made by the Prince Regent and his government to prevent his wife from causing trouble. Not only was she forbidden from attending the official functions but every possible precaution had been taken to prevent her from even meeting the Sovereigns in private. This included a letter from the Regent addressed to Caroline in which he reaffirmed his "fixed and unalterable determination" never to meet her "upon any occasion, either in public or private." The Regent had been counselled by the government, which was by now convinced the Russians were working on Caroline to defeat the marriage between her daughter and the Hereditary Prince of Orange – and thus sabotage the Anglo-Dutch alliance, a keystone in the new peace.[32]

There followed a flurry of letters between Princess Caroline (with Brougham's backing) and Queen Charlotte (receiving advice from the Regent and his government) – all published in the press. Caroline's letters invoked noble family sentiments, which struck an emotive chord with the middle classes and with the honest tradesmen and artisans of London. In the first place, there was the old King, still alive, who had been "so kind as to honour me";[33] Caroline (i.e. Brougham) argued that since his "indisposition" she had found herself in the unenviable position of being "without appeal or protector." The royal family had lost a father figure. Second, a mother's rights were about to be denied. In a letter to the Prince Regent she asked, "Has your Royal Highness forgotten the approaching marriage of our daughter, and the possibility of our coronation?" So a mother would not be allowed to attend the marriage of a daughter? A Queen would not be crowned with a King?[34]

Brougham had laid the ground well; now Whitbread had to play his turn in Parliament.

Parliament debated the correspondence on Friday, 3 June, three days before the Sovereigns landed at Dover. The House of Commons sat in St Stephen's Chapel, a tiny, stifling Elizabethan chamber in old Westminster Palace. Thomas Carlyle, the historian, described the House shortly before it was burnt down in 1834 as "hardly larger than some drawing rooms"; he compared the Speaker's chair to his bedroom wardrobe. It could only seat half its members, despite the architectural "improvements" of 1800, which had added a fourth bench to either side of the assembly and another four feet to the room's original width of twenty-nine feet. Thermometers had been introduced and an "air machine" was installed in the attic above the flat roof to draw off the bad air.[35]

It was standing-room only in the candle-lit Commons that Friday evening. The Speaker rapped his gavel and shook his curly wig; the assembly fell to near silence.

The Speaker then announced that he had just received a letter from Princess Caroline complaining that the Regent's decision not to meet her "in public or private" was based on "advice" he had been given to prevent her from appearing in court. Whose "advice"? Before the government had time to demand that the House stick to the order of the day – the slave trade and the Corn Laws – Mr Methuen, a prominent Whig, moved that "a humble address be presented to the Prince Regent" praying him to inform the House who had been advising him never to meet the Princess.[36]

Bragge Bathurst, for the government, argued that the House had no right to discuss the case because this would be interfering both in the etiquette of a Drawing Room and in the Regent's own "sentiment."

Samuel Whitbread responded that Bathurst was being "irresolute, wavering and contradictory." He recalled that in the Delicate Investigation of 1807 – which had inquired into the Princess's private affairs – Caroline had been acquitted and, on these grounds, had a right to appear in any Court function. Moreover, the acquittal had been read aloud in the Commons by "a noble lord who is now daily expected but who is not in this country"; Lord Castlereagh's frigate had, in fact, just arrived in Dover.

The motion was momentarily withdrawn, for neither Methuen nor Whitbread had the full support of the Whigs. But over the next two weeks – with the celebrations over the Sovereigns' presence in full course – Methuen kept on threatening to re-introduce his motion "unless something should be done to ameliorate the situation of the Princess of Wales."

The press also kept up the pressure. *The Examiner* asserted that the Regent's outrageous declaration was not merely "a private matter affecting none but private persons and private feelings, ... it is a case in which the public man says to his consort 'I will publicly disgrace you. ...' The Royal Visitors might well be surprised." "There is no reflecting person who does not commiserate with the situation of the Princess of Wales," affirmed *The Sunday Monitor*. "In contending for the just rights of a defenceless female," it proposed, "we are supporting the cause of morality."

Morality – and their circulation too. Papers which supported the Princess sold; the papers which did not, like *The Times*, saw their circulation plummet.[37]

Queen Charlotte diffused some of the tension simply by cancelling her Drawing Rooms and receiving the Sovereigns in private. It was not enough to satisfy Whitbread and his friends. On Thursday, 23 June, Methuen had risen again to say that something really should be done "to ameliorate the situation of the Princess of Wales." "Hear! hear!" roared out the honourable gentlemen. Methuen knew the lines that would seize their honourable hearts. "Let them legislate with the feelings of fathers or brothers," he said; "let them suppose that their daughters or sisters were made to endure a similar dignity and degradation." "Hear! hear!" responded the moral fathers of the land. Methuen moved: "That this House do, on Tuesday next, take into consideration the correspondence communicated to this House by her Royal Highness the Princess of Wales." What righteous soul could refuse this?

The Foreign Secretary, Viscount Castlereagh, was sitting just opposite; he rose to speak. As usual, it was not a speech that electrified souls; it was long, wordy and sometimes confusing. But that speech turned the fortunes of the Whigs into reverse almost as effectively as had the French Revolution of 1789 and the defeat of Napoleon by Alexander in 1812.

Methuen himself unintentionally opened the way for Castlereagh's counter-offensive. To prove the Princess's unhappy condition, he had noted she was "obliged to live on a less income than when she resided at Carlton House:" she had to reduce the number of her horses; she had to give up seeing company. "Is that a situation for the Princess of Wales, for our future Queen to be placed in?" "Hear! hear!" cried the shocked gentlemen.

Well yes, responded Lord Castlereagh, "but this is the first occasion in which it has been openly avowed in Parliament that an extended provision for the Princess of Wales is the object sought after."

Castlereagh must have secretly smacked his hands. Whitbread bowed his head. If – Castlereagh continued – "there should appear to be a disposition in Parliament to put the establishment of her Royal Highness on a more liberal footing, I do not hesitate to say that I believe there will be found no obstacle." No obstacle at all! Castlereagh knew our lady: she would take the money and go. It was a first step along the lines of the disastrous scenario outlined by

Brougham: Princess Caroline might leave England, and that would end all debate, along with the prospects of a Whig revival.

Whitbread tried desperately to return the discussion to the moral issue, where he knew Castlereagh was weak: "I do not know what money could be to her any sort of compensation for the mortifications that she has of late been subject to." He "utterly disclaimed" that the object of her Royal Highness had ever been "the obtaining of money."

But all the elegance of Whitbread could not redress Methuen's blunder. From that time onwards the parliamentary debates on the Princess of Wales focused on the question of placing her establishment "on a more liberal footing," on money.

It has been argued that this new political dimension of the Caroline affair was a landmark on the road to British democracy – it brought power to the press, it encouraged party political organisation, and it gave a significant first boost to women. It certainly mobilised the London mob. "Where's your wife?" cried out the butchers of Fleet Market as the Regent's yellow carriage, its maroon blinds half closed, scuttled by. Caroline always got the applause. "Three cheers for an *injured woman!*" they clapped when she appeared at Covent Garden. But this was hardly a political programme and, once the debate had turned against the Whigs in parliament, Brougham's resources were pushed to their limit.

Caroline herself felt increasingly isolated. She was tired of playing the role of the injured woman, she was tired of the Whigs, and most especially she was getting tired of Henry Brougham. Old "Wicked-shifts" was forced to give more attention to Charlotte, who very well knew what her mother would do if she got too piqued and weary – she would leave England, she would leave England without consulting her. The relationship between the two had not improved. Lady Charlotte Lindsay said they were irreconcilable.

Meanwhile Lord Liverpool's government had become absolutely convinced of a Russian plot to wreck the royal marriage. That gave Brougham one more card, a European card, to play. He warned Charlotte she must never consent to leave the country after her marriage; for once she left, her mother would almost certainly go as well. It just so happened that Charlotte was receiving the same advice from her "great favourite," the Duchess Oldenburg Holstein, the Grand Duchess Catherine of Russia, "sister of our magnanimous Ally, the Emperor of Russia."

Divine inspiration: Tsar and his sister

As the former Ambassador to St Petersburg, Sir Charles Whitworth, used to say, "Wherever there are three Russians at least one must be a spy." But Whitworth of all people – such a grand intriguer, such a man of learning and enlightenment, who was perhaps involved in Paul I's murder – should have known better than that. Two were enough: the Tsar and his sister.[38]

The government was determined to keep the number of high-ranking Russians visiting Britain that June to a minimum, and most especially marriageable Russians. In early May Lord Liverpool, the Prime Minister, had warned Castlereagh in Paris that members of the Russian Embassy in London were intriguing "to break off the Marriage with the Prince of Orange and to form a Connection between the Princess and one of the Grand Dukes of Russia." It was consequently "of the utmost Importance to prevent the Grand Dukes who are [in] Paris from coming over to England." The message was put to good effect; the Grand Dukes never came. But nobody was going to stop the Tsar.[39]

What sort of liberator was this, this Little Father of Russia who was implicated in the murder of his own father? "Will I have the strength to reign?" he despairingly questioned his wife on that fateful March night, 1801. "I can't. I'll turn over my power to whomever wants it!"[40]

His apartments in the Mikhailovsky Palace were only doors away from the chamber in which Crazy Paul was murdered. Alexander most surely heard the feet rushing about, the shouts of the guard (his own Siemionovsky regiment), the screams of the victim. "My God, how he screams!" exclaimed one of the assassins as Paul was gradually throttled by Captain Skariatyn's scarf.[41]

The murder of his own father. A terrible storm cloud hung permanently over Tsar Alexander: a profound secret, an intimate mystery. Many, many times would he lisp in the ear of his Polish tutor, minister and friend, Adam Czartoryski, "No, it is impossible, there is no remedy to that; I must suffer; how do you want me to stop suffering? Nothing can change." Frequently with Alexander Arakcheev – inspector of General Artillery and the only faithful companion Paul had ever had – he knelt in the golden Grouzino chapel beneath the icons and the gilt inscription that crossed the wall: "My soul is pure before Thee and my spirit is justified."

Pure and justified? Alexander Pavlovich was Emperor by assassination. Every year, when Russia celebrated the anniversary of the accession of Alexander I, Alexander Pavlovich hid himself in his apartments, abandoned himself to his torment and let out sighs and torrents of tears.[42]

Murder had made him head of the Romanov dynasty. He had never wanted to be head, nor wanted to be Emperor, and he rejected in his youth the very idea of a hereditary monarchy. "I do not feel myself at all made for the place that I occupy now, and still less suited for the one fated for me tomorrow," he told his companion Kochubey when he was still only a Grand Duke of nineteen. And, in truth, the dynastic link was questionable, for, as it was frequently whispered at the time, when a Princess Anhalt-Zerbst – Grandmother Catherine – mates with a Colonel Saltykov, do they beget a Romanov?[43]

His inheritance was cast in doubt and his children appeared damned, as though cursed by the murdered father. "*Maman, je suis bien malheureuse,*" Empress Elizabeth had written to her German mother when her only daughter succumbed to "fever" in 1808. That same year, the daughter of Maria Naryshkin, his mistress, had also died. "God does not love my children," Alexander mournfully told his doctor.[44]

Not surprisingly, his relationships with women were fleeting. Of all the women in his life, only one exercised a lasting influence on him – "governed him absolutely, uniquely," said Countess Lieven. That was his younger sister, the Grand Duchess Catherine.[45]

It was a passionate, binding relationship; some even spoke of incest. They had never known each other as children because they had been raised separately; it was after the murder of his father that Alexander discovered the affection he had for Catherine.

Letters passed constantly between them. "I also love my dear Bissiam with all my heart, *oh! cela, Dieu le sait*, and everything that comes from her touches me beyond all expression." Alexander wrote in a round strong hand, though in pencil: "*Le Monarque Magnanime à Biskis Bissiamovna salut!*" It was a romantic love: "Adieu, charm of my eyes, adoration of my heart, lustre of the century, phenomenon of Nature, or better than all that, Bissiam Bisiamovna with the flat nose." There was physical attraction: "I cannot say how much I miss you, and the need that I feel to see you, to hold you in my arms." Catherine's early letters were distinctly cooler; they were addressed to "cher Alexandre" or "cher et bon ami" or simply "mon cher" and were frequently accompanied with a request for a favour.[46]

She was eleven years younger than her brother (who was thirty-seven when he visited London in 1814) and, unlike the imperial-looking Alexander, she seems to have inherited the physical traits of her father rather than those of her goddess-like Württemberg mother, Maria Fyodorovna (whose features belonged entirely to Alexander). Catherine had Paul's squatness, the bulging eyes, the large lips. But historians have been unfair about her looks, as they have about her manners in general. The British press adored her: "The Duchess is a very elegant woman, of the most affable and pleasing manners, and speaks English extremely well." Countess Lieven, the Russian Ambassador's wife and not exactly a sympathetic witness, said she had "great seduction in both her look and manners, an assured bearing, a proud air, but gracious, physical features hardly classical, but dazzling glamour and freshness of complexion, a sparkling eye and the most beautiful hair in the world." Her small, bonneted figure in Thomas Phillips's painting of Lord Egremont's reception of the Sovereigns at Petworth House (Alexander bowing as far as his bad back would permit) puts one in mind of Catherine Morland in a Jane Austen novel – "Catherine grows quite a good-looking girl, she is almost pretty today."[47]

It was the prettiness of intention, acquired from a hard inner will rather than nature. Many noticed how good she was at languages. She spoke fluent French, German and English, like most members of the imperial circle. But what astonished people was that she not only spoke Russian, she could read and write it as well – unlike her brother.

"The greatest regret in my life is not having been a man in 1812!" she would exclaim. No Englishman could have understood that. England in 1814 was absolutely ignorant of the drama Russia had lived through two years before. It was not just the break up of Napoleon's Grande Armée, the loss of hundreds of thousands of lives, the destruction of Smolensk, the burning of Moscow which had marked this turn in Napoleon's fortunes. When in late June, 1812, Napoleon crossed the Nieman he had brought down on himself and his army the religious wrath of Russia. "God Almighty!" the Holy Synod of Russia ordered the clergy to read in prayer, "the enemy who subverts Thy land and intends to turn the universe into a desert has risen against us. Bring us Thine aid! That shame and confusion should attain those who wish us Evil! That Thine Angel outrage them and chase them away!" Catherine understood what this meant.[48]

Deprived of the security of her lands – for Napoleon controlled all Europe – invaded, violated Russia turned more and more to her God. A howling religious campaign was launched against Napoleon "the Antichrist" who would finally be vanquished by "the return of God", the "Angel", the "Elect", the "Blessed".

Alexander would be Russia's "Angel". Five days after Moscow had fallen, Alexander wrote to Catherine, "I place my hope in God, in the admirable character of our nation and in the perseverance I have decided to put into not bending beneath the yoke.'[49]

Catherine would supply the political means, for in the summer and autumn of 1812 the party in power in Russia was her party. Catherine had married, in 1809, a first cousin, Duke George of Oldenburg, whom Alexander named Governor of Novgorod, Iaroslavl, and Tver (for the Duke had lost his own lands to Napoleon). In their cold ugly old castle at Tver, about a day's ride from Moscow, Catherine surrounded herself by people who were soon being called the "Slavophiles," because of their opposition to the "Westerners" in St Petersburg. In Catherine's salon one would find Rostopchin, Bagration, Kutuzov – names that would ring in 1812.[50]

1812 was a personal trauma for Catherine. In April she lost her first child; in December she lost her husband. But Catherine was not one to complain. Throughout August and early September she attacked her brother for a lack of courage, a "failure of nerve," indecisiveness and even betrayal. She warned him that every class in Russia believed him responsible for the misfortunes of the Empire. "The feeling of shame which follows the loss of Moscow gives birth to that of the desire for vengeance. They are complaining of you, and loudly so. I believe it my duty to say this to you, my dear friend, for it is so important. What you have to do, it is not in my province to show you, but save your honour which is under attack."[51]

Alexander answered with prayer. In a letter of over three thousand words written a fortnight after the fall of Moscow he said to his sister, "What can a man do more than follow his best conviction? It is that alone which has guided me."

Alexander was not weak. His resolution was unshakable – "I would rather cease being what I am than come to terms with the monster who has created the misery of the world" – and it was based on faith. Another long letter, probably written around the same time, tells his sister of the secret societies he has joined, the lessons he has learnt and it lists the dozens of works he has been reading, theological works, biblical commentaries, mystical and inspired works from Germany and Sweden, metaphysicists from France, quietists from Moravia, freemasons from Scotland. The only religious sect which he did not seem to read about was that of his own formal faith, Russian Orthodoxy. "There is still today," he told his sister, "as there always has been, an interior Church and an exterior Church." Alexander, wandering alone in his palace woods, dreamed of conquering the Antichrist and bringing that "interior Church" to the world.[52]

A European Christian world, which would combine the republican virtues La Harpe had taught him in his youth with the new religious truths he had learnt from his advisers, Alexander Galitsyn and Rodion Kochelev. "It is simply to say to you *Christos Voskresse* ['Christ is risen'] that I write to you these lines, dear friend," he had told Catherine. "The fire of Moscow lit up my soul," he said to the Lutheran Bishop Eylert once the War of Liberation was under way in Germany, "and the judgment of the Lord, which manifested itself on our frozen plains, filled my heart with an ardent faith I had never felt before." Evidently, in 1812 the Emperor Alexander had undergone – and there are no other words for it – a religious conversion.[53]

It brought Catherine and Alexander yet closer together. As Alexander's armies marched victoriously westwards, Catherine moved to Germany, to Holland and, from there, to England. The news of the fall of Paris and the abdication of Napoleon led her to think her brother really was an "Angel." As Napoleon was escorted to Elba, Catherine signed off a long letter to Alexander in Paris, "to love you more than I do is an impossible thing, keep for me a little friendship and, believe me, I am all yours for life." "Dear good friend," replied Alexander, "Blessed a thousand times be the Supreme Being for all the countless benefits he has bestowed on us! This surpasses the most exaggerated hopes! Finally the great end is attained, and Napoleon no longer tyrannises Europe and France... I hope in a fortnight to hold you in my arms in London. What joy! What happiness! The idea alone transports me. . ."[54]

So the arms of Catherine awaited him, the crowds of England longed to cheer him, royalty had decorated its palace chambers, the City had laid out its turtled tables, and the whole world glowed in triumphant anticipation of an encounter between West and East, between the two extremes of Europe, between the commercial power of London and the sacred sword of Russia; between two profoundly illusioned mortals, two Sovereigns, the divine Alexander and the sublime Prince Regent.

Catherine, imperial herald

"Handsome as he is, the Regent is a man visibly used up by debauchery and is rather disgusting," the Grand Duchess Catherine reported to her brother after her first two meetings with Britain's Prince. The British government, through Castlereagh's insistence, had gone out of the way to please her – in fact, too much so. Having been held up in the Hague for several days because the small cutter in port was not thought sufficient for Her Imperial Highness, she finally made the crossing to Sheerness on 31 March aboard a frigate under the command of the Duke of Clarence, brother of the Regent. Catherine would have preferred the cutter and its good captain.[55]

Outriders and a party of light horse escorted her to London. As her carriage bounced along the old Kent Road, she looked out of her window to admire what she described as "one continuous garden" – "it's not at all exaggerated what you see in the prints, but on the contrary, it is perfectly exact." But she wasn't impressed with London ("there are not many grand palaces," she grouched). She got down from her carriage at the Pulteney Hotel on the corner of Piccadilly, overlooking Green Park. The whole building, certainly one of the most majestic in London, had been rented by the Russian Embassy for 210 guineas a week. But besides what she was wearing and a few other oddities, the Emperor's sister had no clothes; they were all on the cutter, still at sea.[56]

Early the next day the Prince Regent sent a message that he was going to pay her a visit at the hotel. Catherine planned to stand dignified at the head of the staircase as the Prince entered the hall and cast him Russian imperial glances. However, since her clothes had not yet arrived, it was the Lievens – the Russian Ambassador and his wife – who met His Highness at the entrance. They led him across the hall, past the wide and empty staircase, on into a large living room, where they sat for long minutes in silence. Finally, flushing and half dressed, the Grand Duchess came bustling through the tall doors. "She did not have her usual aplomb," remembered the Ambassador's wife. She asked the Prince to join her in her *cabinet*, where they spent quarter of an hour alone. Then out they came, Catherine first, the Regent second, both with a "barely satisfied air." On their way to the wide staircase the Regent managed to whisper to the Ambassadress, "Your Grand Duchess is not beautiful." Once the Regent had disappeared through the door, the Grand Duchess said to the Ambassadress, "Your Prince has bad manners."[57]

That evening the Prince Regent held a grand dinner at Carlton House – the usual multi-course meal with teams of servants in livery rushing about, and several Italian musicians to add tones of merriment.

The Grand Duchess wore black, for she was still mourning her husband's loss. Perhaps it was the previous embarrassment at the hotel; for whatever reason, the Regent seemed to think the Grand Duchess was putting on an act and immediately started to make fun of her dress and solemn looks. Catherine maintained a haughty silence. The Italian musicians continued to pipe away in the background.

"Music makes me *sick*," she suddenly announced. The Regent signalled and the Italians filed out. There was a polite mutter here and there, the tinkle of glass and plates, and the patter of servants' feet; Catherine remained silent. It was clear to all who attended that between the Regent and the Grand Duchess there was only "mutual hatred."[58]

"His much vaunted friendliness is of the most licentious, I would even say the most filthy tone I have ever heard in my life," Catherine wrote to Alexander three days later. She said he made her feel stiff and she had no idea what to do with either her eyes or ears. He had "a brazen way of looking where eyes should not go, and I can't see how to put up with it."[59]

The memory of the popular "national war" in Russia led Catherine to ignore Britain's uncrowned, unblessed Sovereign and place her faith in the people. In England she saw plenty of them. "The workers owe you a new existence, while earlier they were dying of hunger," she wrote to Alexander, "the merchants owe you their new riches in the place of a flagging trade, all the classes bless you and all worship your *private character*..." Private, like Alexander's "interior Church," and mystical, as in Alexander's vision of the liberating world Sovereign and his people: "You should rejoice, and nobody, no, nobody more than you can recognise the generosity of this Providence, the source of your fine soul." Catherine knew it was God's Providence. This was proven by the enthusiasm of the people: she was followed by crowds everywhere she went.[60]

These were the people of London, however, and London was not England. The Prince had a following in the country and, though he might not have been the finest Gentleman of Europe, Catherine made a serious political error in insulting him.

She was cold with the government ministers and markedly impolite with the Regent's mistress, Lady Hertford, reserving all her charm for Whigs and anyone with a reputation of being opposed to the court. She was most popular as she did the rounds of London society. People found her lively, witty and gracious; all the great houses of London vied for the honour of having her to dinner (though she would never accept a *soirée*). Yet her very success only deepened her belief in God's Providence and her total misunderstanding of English life and politics.

Catherine knew there was one person in London who would fully agree with her assessment of the Regent's character, and that was of course Caroline, "deprived of her natural and acquired parents and protectors," as Whitbread would say.[61] Catherine knew all about the role of parentage and was quite an artisan at sisterly protection as well.

So, as often as she could, she would signal a wish to make the acquaintance of the Princess of Wales. Count Lieven warned her that this was impossible; it would lead to an open break with the Regent at the moment Alexander was about to set foot in England. Catherine persisted. Lieven threatened to resign. Finally Catherine yielded, but she never forgave Lieven; and, though at every dinner in the Pulteney Hotel the Count would meet her at the famous staircase and lead her to the table, she never addressed him another word until the day of the Emperor's arrival.

But Warwick House was not off-bounds. Where was Catherine when news of the fall of Paris arrived? Or when it was announced that Emperor Napoleon had abdicated? She could be found at Warwick House, with Charlotte.

Both ladies were eligible for marriage. Catherine had stories to tell, advice to give. "Oh no-oh, I could never think of marrying *him*," she said of Charlotte's uncle, the Duke of Clarence, for the idea of becoming "Madame Clarence" appalled her. As for "Madame Sussex," she thought it was a magnificent joke and, once that duke (another of Charlotte's uncles) had made a bumbling profession of love, she refused to see him again. The uncles didn't know it, but they were in hopeless competition; the Archduke Charles, the Austrian Emperor's brother, was the subject of some serious romantic talk; and, though she never told Charlotte, Catherine had also developed an interest in the Hereditary Prince of Orange.[62]

Catherine proved her role as Charlotte's protector in another infamous dinner with the Regent. It was held in Lord Liverpool's London home, Fife House. Catherine found herself on one side while Countess Lieven was placed on the other side of the Prince Regent, his eyes again darting to where they should never dart, the servants again rushing about, the bands again notably absent.

"Why then, Your Highness," the Grand Duchess asked the Regent, "do you hold your daughter under lock and key? Why is she nowhere with you?"

"My daughter is too young, Madam, to go out into the world," the Prince Regent replied, in as haughty a manner as the Grand Duchess.

"She is not too young for you to have chosen her a husband," said the Grand Duchess, adding grapeshot to haughtiness.

"She will only be married in two years" (either the Regent was making major news, or the Countess's ears were not quite in tune).

"Well," riposted the Grand Duchess, "when she is married I do hope she will be fully compensated for her present gaol sentence."

"When she is married, Madam," replied the Regent, wiping his ruby lips with a silken napkin, "she will do as her husband pleases" – and he placed the napkin on the table – "for the present she does as I wish."

It was time to bring in the cannon. The Grand Duchess distanced herself, made a cast iron Russian look, and fired: "Yes, Your Highness, between a husband and wife there can be only one will." The insinuation was clear. The Regent turned brusquely to Countess Lieven and exclaimed, "This is intolerable!"[63]

Catherine gave a description of her royal protégée to Alexander: "She is slightly smaller than I, broad, a bit too much so in the hips, pale, fresh, quite delectable, beautiful arms, pretty feet, large clear blue humorous eyes, though she sometimes has the stare of the House of Brunswick, blond, beautiful nose, delicious mouth and beautiful teeth ... She goes to every man, young or old, it's just the same; or, better put, the latter are her preference ..." This was a description of an open candidate for marriage, not of an English princess solemnly engaged to a Dutch prince.[64]

The Liberator steps ashore

The same easterlies that chilled the crowds on the road to Dover had kicked up a rough sea in the Channel. At the first lurch of HMS *Impregnable* Emperor Alexander retired to his cabin and he was not seen again until the end of the five-and-a-half-hour crossing. In the meantime King Frederick William III of Prussia, his sons, and the

Tsar Alexander I had
dreams of liberating all
Europe

accompanying princes, marshals and counts of Europe enjoyed "magnificent entertainment" at the Duke of Clarence's flagship table. At a
quarter to five, Monday, 6 June, the whole fleet – about a dozen ships,
frigates and yachts in all – dropped anchor about a mile and a half
from the shore, nearly opposite the entrance to Dover harbour. A
barge was sent out to ascertain the best point for landing and, after
one effort failed because of the rapidly falling tide, a wooden platform
was set up on the beach. When the Allied Sovereigns appeared on
deck, they were greeted by loud huzzas from the manned riggings,
the sailors dressed in new blue jackets and white trousers. On land,
the acclamation of "thousands of the British people" rent the air. The
guns of the *Impregnable* and other ships of war fired a salute as the
Sovereigns left ship, and they fired again on the landing, along with a
full discharge from the heavy batteries on shore. Alexander, pale and
trembling, was met by Count Lieven and they cantered off in an
unmarked green travelling coach to the private home of J.M. Fector,
Esq. The other royal guests were put up at the York Hotel.[65]
    The Russian Emperor knew exactly what he was going to do the

following morning. "If you lodge at the Palace we will be separated and you won't be at your ease," Catherine had written; "if you prefer freedom, I offer you my hotel." On Tuesday morning Alexander and Count Lieven drove in the green carriage straight through the crowds of Kent, unnoticed; they left the main road at Greenwich and crossed the Battersea Bridge to Piccadilly where, at two o'clock, they arrived at the hotel unannounced. They could just about hear the bands thumping away at Cumberland House.[66]

Alexander was an extraordinarily elegant and even seductive Sovereign. He stood over six foot; he could look down on the Prince Regent. Napoleon, when he first met Alexander at Tilsit in 1807, thought that in comparison to the lacklustre Austrian Emperor and the King of Prussia this was somebody of "veritable imperial race." This impression was based entirely on his physique and charm, not his dress, for he was the first Russian Emperor to dispense with im- perial pomp and instead wear a military uniform, his natural blond hair exposed. In a ballroom or salon he liked to wander around and speak as an ordinary gentleman, not an emperor; "will you permit me to remark . . .," "I am so sorry . . .," "I hope you don't mind . . ." were the phrases of Alexander. There was such a tenderness in his face that even the most sceptical could admit that he could be "the Angel." Yet he was deaf in one ear, short sighted, had a slight limp, and a bad back gave him a stoop, so that after the first enthusiasm one might sud- denly get the feeling that the man was lost. This was what led Herzen to call him "crowned Hamlet," why Czartoryski said his soul was "all the colours of the rainbow," and what brought Napoleon to remark, "It would be difficult to have more intelligence than Emperor Alexander, but something is missing and I haven't discovered what it is."[67]

Paris and his sister's letters had now convinced him of his role as world liberator. The people belonged to him. There were never less than ten thousand milling in the park, standing in the streets around his hotel, waiting to catch a glimpse of the man who looked like a Sovereign, the vanquisher of Napoleon. He had utter contempt for the Regent, who could not, on the day of the arrival, even leave his own palace. Alexander went round to Carlton House and only stayed there for half an hour. On leaving he remarked, "A poor Sire!" Count Lieven added diplomatically, "Who has helped you make a war and a glorious peace."[68]

Alexander was not, at the time, very concerned with diplomacy. As Countess Lieven observed, he treated his London visit as a vacation, a moment to benefit from the company of his sister and rebuild his energy, a period of spiritual renewal cultivated in fields of cheering people. Catherine, looking out from her hotel window at the London crowds and the bright night lights of celebration, ruminated, "undoubtedly never has there been so sudden a transition as the one from this awful and bloody war to this perfect peace." This perfect peace. This sudden peace.[69]

And the people; Alexander had placed so much his faith in the people. He told Lord Lonsdale, "The high state to which England had advanced was not solely owing to the excellence of Her constitution and the perfection of Her laws, but also to something inherent in the people." Lonsdale agreed. He said, "Though the People are sometimes carried away by a violent impulse of feeling, it is not long before the Publick mind is again restored to reflection."[70]

The people; these were the other actors, the other coloured pieces of the show.

London lights up

The first impression foreigners got of London was nearly always the same: the place was dull and disappointing. Louis Simond, for one, said that "London does not strike with admiration; it is regular, clean, convenient (I am speaking of the best part) but the site is flat; the plan monotonous; the predominant colour of objects dingy and poor. It is altogether without great faults and without great beauties." A.A. Feldborg, a Danish visitor, after passing Greenwich and the docks by boat landed in London feeling "considerable disappointment." Against "the chequered gaiety of Copenhagen," he remarked, "the gloomy solemnity in the houses of London presented a very ungrateful contrast;" his eye was wearied by "the sameness of colossal piles of brick and mortar." Richard Rush, the American Ambassador, expressed as much when he arrived in 1817; "I am disappointed in the general exterior of the dwelling-houses," he said, "I had anticipated something better." Londoners themselves complained of the monotony.[71]

One of the main culprits for London's tedious arsenal appearance of brick and mortar was the Building Act of 1774, which limited construction to four standard types of house (from "first rate" to "fourth rate"); it virtually abolished external ornaments, it restricted bayed shop-windows to a ten-inch projection, and forced window joinery to be concealed in recesses behind the wall face. The comments of foreigners suggests how boring and lonely this made whole districts of London.[72]

The fogs were no help. In winter, said Simond, "smoke increases the general dingy hue, and terminates the length of every street with a fixed and grey mist, receding as you advance." Early in 1814, as the military campaign was raging in France, London experienced its worst fog since November 1755, the month of the earthquake at Lisbon as *The Times* (in a rare apocalyptic mood) reminded its readers. All the mails were held up, carriages were overturned; a few hackney coaches ventured out at walking pace, an assistant leading the horses; lanterns moved in all directions and cries resounded in every street, "Mind! Take care! Where are you?" That was followed by three months of ice and snow.[73]

Some people were astonished to look out of their window on a summer's morning and actually see the end of the street. J.P. Malcolm, a painter, remembered getting up early one August morning and going outside as the sun rose: "Then lengthened the perspective, and enabled the eye to penetrate depths unfathomable at eight o'clock, and shewed retiring houses at distances I had never seen them before. The fanciful decorations of shop windows, doors, and the fresh-painted fronts, had each their relief; and the brazen appearance of the gilt names [that] had vanished with the smoke, now darted with due lustre."[74]

Those "fanciful decorations of shop windows" fascinated every visitor, even in winter. Drapers, stationers, confectioners, pastry-cooks, seal-cutters, silversmiths, booksellers, print-sellers, hosiers, fruiterers, china-sellers, all close to one another, without intermission: "a shop to every house, street after street, and mile after mile." All witnesses agreed that, after the first disappointment, the eyes were opened to the "opulence and splendour" of London's shops.[75]

Foreigners were also impressed by the comfort of people's homes. The French lived horizontally, in apartments, and every other continental capital imitated them. In London the inhabitants insisted on a verticality, they lived in houses; only bachelor lawyers lived in "chambers." The narrow houses with their staircases going up two or three floors might have given Louis Simond the impression of "a cage with its sticks and birds" but even he admitted they had their advantages over the French system: "Instead of the abominable filth of the common entrance and common stairs of a French house, here you step from the very street on a neat floor-carpet, the wall panelled or papered, a lamp in its glass bell hanging from the ceiling, and every apartment in the same style."[76]

And if the homes looked comfortable, so did the people. "I have heard no cries in the streets," said Simond, "and seen few beggars." Though he might have thought "the human race is here rather of mean stature," he didn't *see* poverty. Like most visitors, he thought London working people were well dressed and had a sturdy and healthy look.[77]

London was the largest metropolis in the world (it had just passed one million), but its people were better off than the faster growing towns to the north, they were better housed and better fed than their suffering country cousins, and they were infinitely richer than any population, urban or rural, on the continent. There was of course poverty, a grinding poverty, but it was tucked away in a band of dilapidated courts, alleys and crumbling tenements that surrounded the City – a product of Elizabethan and Stuart policy to restrict the growth of London by refusing new construction. Poverty had been further scattered by the Irish unskilled labourers who settled where they could – in the rookeries of the "Caribee Islands," between St Martin's Lane and Bedford Street, and noted for their cook-shops and violence; or in Thieving Lane and the Sanctuaries in the older part of Westminster. Petty France, not far from the Houses of Parliament, was not a healthy place to take a stroll. And as Madame d'Avot discovered after a performance of *Don Giovanni* at the Haymarket, the lanes between the theatre and St James's Market were not designed for princesses.[78]

However, even the "respectable trades" were beginning to feel the pinch of hard times in 1814. London was not an industrial city of factories; its workers were artisans. The twenty years of war with France had been a boon for them, especially for the largest associated group of them all, the shipwrights. The demand for their labour was high, their wages went up. But after 1812 everything went in the opposite direction. There was a glut of labour in London, new firms refused to recognise the old artisan qualification of apprenticeship and began to farm out, and even relocate, for the cheaper untrained provincial labour.[79]

The bitterness of the men of the "respectable trades" got mixed up with politics – neighbourhood politics, urban politics, national politics. Geography gave the politics of London its colour.

The elemental fact of Britain's capital was the ancient cleavage between east and west. Louis Simond spoke of a "line of demarcation" running north and south through Soho Square: "Every minute of longitude east is equal to as many degrees of gentility *minus*, or towards west, *plus*. This meridian line north and south, like that indicated by the compass, inclines west towards the north, and east towards the south, two or three points in such a manner as to place a certain part of Westminster on the side of fashion." Sovereignty, wealth, and fashion flowed west of that line; business, finance, and the artisanry lay to the east, in the City.

The City was all movement. In *A Tale of Two Cities*, Charles Dickens had Mr Jeremiah Cruncher sitting on his stool in Fleet Street watching that movement – "Who could sit upon anything in Fleet Street during the busy hours of the day, and not be dazed and deafened by two immense processions, one ever tending westward with the sun, the other ever tending eastward from the sun, both ever tending to the plains behind the range of red and purple where the sun goes down." Robert Southey, Richard Rush, and Simond described the same phenomenon. "The crowd, the carriages, and the mud increase rapidly as you advance from west to east," noted Simond. Some of the draught horses were gigantic, "perfect elephants!" If he had turned left towards the Newgate Prison he could have encountered bullock as well. In January 1814 Mr Crowder, accountant, had one of them in his house in Warwick Square. The animal "nearly got up one pair of stairs, and in his retreat demolished the panel of the door of the counting-house."[80]

It was in the City that one found the Ironmongers' Hall, the Merchant Taylors' Hall, the Drapers' Hall and the other thirty-six halls of the Incorporated Companies of Traders and Artizans, Citizens of London. Yet, if some of these halls were very rich, the real wealth of the City – the wealth that marched westwards – belonged to the bankers (who were no longer goldsmiths), and to stockbrokers and commission agents (who had nothing to do with mercers, drapers, stationers, tailors, apothecaries, or even cattle drovers). The new wealth, which had grown so remarkably during the twenty years of war, was utterly divorced from the old administrative Corporation of London; its leading figures did not even have a vote and – a galling fact – they made no effort to gain it.

Thus the Corporation turned inwards to its traditional "freemen," the artisans, the shopkeepers. All this gave the artisans a powerful political voice; they had common councillors in the City, they had members of parliament at Westminster and a big toe in the press. That artisan voice, proud and bitter, was the Radical voice of London: Radical and isolated.[81]

In the West End, fashionable gentlemen referred to crowds that crossed the "line of demarcation" as the "mob." But the "mob" in 1814 was rarely violent and, from its looks, it wasn't recruiting from the rookeries and the down-and-out corners like Thieving Lane. The men would be dressed in coats, jackets and hats, many were even cravatted; there were small masters, shopkeepers, and professional men among them.

They might not have been members of the City's guilds, but they shared the ideals of the guilds. They believed that the possession of a skill, valuable to the community, was a man's property, it defined his station in life, and had to be defended. They had as much contempt for the poor Irish as any West End gentleman – in fact, probably even more so. They were not thieves, they were not ignorant; what they performed for the metropolis and for Britain was *useful* and *valuable* labour. They formed the moral pillar of old England. So, if they hated the poor Irish, they held the ruling classes in equal contempt, those parasites in power, that small group of corrupt courtiers, civil servants, lawyers and politicians: the country could well do without them. Many in the Radical crowd subscribed to the "Norman theory" which traced the blackguard rulers back to the foreign brigands and freebooters who came over with William the Bastard in 1066 to sub-jugate the freeborn Briton. Their rulers were not really English.[82]

They cheered Alexander because he was a conqueror of the same sort of foreign tyranny, a defender of English-style liberty, a true ally – like good, sick King George – of the Union Jack. They hated the Prince Regent because he was immoral, he sat in his palace with his whores and his baubles, he was a parasitic "European" courtier.

"Where's your wife?" the butchers cried as the Regent's coach racketed past. And "Hurrah for Alexander! Hurrah for English liberty!"

As respectable as it might have appeared to foreigners, there was fear of the London crowd in 1814, a fear which had some foundation. People knew what a crowd of artisans could do in Paris, less than three hundred miles away. Many people, not so old, would have remembered the Gordon Riots, thirty-four years before, when over 285 rioters had been killed (many of them honest artisans), over a hundred houses destroyed and the whole of London seemed ablaze. Added to that was a more general fear of crime which, if on the decline, always seemed present.

To drive alone in one's curricle across Hounslow Heath, or take a short cut through the Kensington gravel-pits, was to put one's life at risk; there are several accounts, in the spring of 1814, of such fool-hardy travellers, pistols held to their heads, being forced to deliver their watches and pocket-books. The previous January, the Buckingham stage coach had been robbed in Oxford Street in broad daylight. The Strand was reportedly infested with "day street robbers" and in mid-February a whole gang was committed to trial. Public houses were frequently robbed, often in the presence of help-less clients.[83]

One of the problems was that London wasn't policed. This amazed foreigners. "No armed watch, *guet*, or *maréchaussée*, is ever met patrolling the streets or the highways," observed Simond, though he added in wonderment that there was "no apparent want of police; nothing disorderly." A leading guide of the time gave the comforting information that "watch houses are placed at convenient distances in all parts, where a parochial constable attends in rotation, to see that order prevails, to receive offenders, and deliver them the next morning to the sitting Magistrate." The guide then explained what to do in case attack: "A cry of *'watch'* three or four times repeated will instantly bring by the assistance of several of the watchmen, and it is a ten to one if the thief or assailant makes his escape." Who were these watchmen? The guide said, "a few old men, mostly without arms." Southey remarked that their principal occupation was "to inform the good people of London every half hour of the state of the weather." They also cried out the time, through the night, so that Southey got no rest.[84]

Perhaps Londoners didn't need a police force, perhaps violent crime really was on the decline (despite a Piccadilly knifing or two), perhaps all the crowds were polite, and the only problem was a handful of corrupt courtiers and politicians. Perhaps nobody should have feared anything at all. Perhaps Master Francis Place was right when he wrote in 1815 that a million Londoners were less gross, more civilised than half a million Londoners a century before.[85]

But London's laws were not civilised. It was no longer the custom to display the heads of traitors on the spikes of Temple Bar, but the law was still in the books. For several years, Sir Samuel Romilly had been leading a campaign to define crime and punishment on a more equable basis, to limit the arbitrary power of judges, and commute most cases of capital punishment to banishment and imprisonment. "The ancient criminal code of England," he said, "is the most sanguinary in existence." In April 1814 the Commons was again debating the merits of drawing a traitor's guts and severing his head after the hanging; and the honourable members came to no conclusion.[86]

Punishments inflicted in 1814 were sometimes savage. The military set an example. In January, Private Martin Hogan was conveyed from Newgate in a cart, conducted by a number of City officers, and, "in the presence of a few spectators," hanged at low tide at Execution Dock for the murder of Lieutenant Johnson. That same month Thomas Beckworth was court-martialled for deserting the 45th Regiment and lacerating the tendons of his heels. He was condemned to one thousand lashes. At his barracks, without uttering a word, he received five hundred and fifty "when the surgeon stepped in and stopped the infliction."[87]

With the opening of the "fashionable season" of 1814 came the season of civil public executions. In late March J. Buckley, quack doctor, was hanged for the death of his pregnant mistress, Dolly Rosthorp, following an attempted abortion. William Botteril was hanged in front of the Debtors' Doors of Newgate in May for "uttering a forged Bill of Exchange." He was aged twenty-three years, eight of which had been spent in the navy. "I have prayed to my God for fortitude," he said to the spectators from his scaffold; "you see he has given it to me." On the same day in April when the Grand Duchess Catherine dined for the first time with the Regent, seven men were publicly hanged in front of the Debtors' Doors.[88]

Public executions were just a very small part of the circus, the show, the great informal exhibitions of London. Some of them were loved, some hated, but one had to admit that they brought the people out of their houses, they made the classes mix, they broke down old barriers, old hierarchies; they prepared the country for a great social and political levelling.[89]

One of the shows was the weather. The last months of the war – it was a pertinent curtain-raiser to spring's show of peace – were the coldest months since the Great Freeze of 1739-40 when a frost fair was held on the frozen River Thames. And so it was again in the first week of February 1814. The Thames watermen placed notices and wooden arrows on the City-side pointing out the cindered footways ("The High Road to the Fair") that had been prepared across the river. Booths were set up with streamers, flags and signs, where those favourite luxuries of London – gin, beer and gingerbread – were sold. Thousands wandered around and about the rugged white plains separating Blackfriars from London Bridge, the Feathers pub at Queenhithe from Brooks' Wharf in Southwark.[90]

But the main show of 1814 was of course the Peace. Alexander was huzza'd by the people every moment he was seen. On the second day of the Emperor's visit even Joseph Farington, of the Royal Academy, abandoned his painting room in the middle of the afternoon to see what all the noise was about. "I walked to Piccadilly & found that street crowded with people, & Horses and carriages, waiting to see the Emperor of Russia and the Duchess of Oldenburgh go to Carlton House." By that time quite a ceremony had been established at the Pulteney Hotel. The people would cheer, the Emperor and the Grand Duchess would come to the balcony, the cheers grew louder, the Emperor would repeatedly bow, and after three minutes disappear. Trains of foreign carriages, carrying the princes and the heroes of 1812, 1813 and 1814, would receive the same applause. Blücher's carriage was held up at the Horse Guards, his own horses were taken, and he was drawn down Whitehall by the people. "Me ferry tankvoll! ferry, ferry tankvoll!" he repeated, opening his arms and shaking his uncovered grey head.[91]

There was a grand military review at Hyde Park. The Emperor was on time, the King of Prussia was ready; the Prince Regent was an hour late. The Surrey Yeomanry had no way of controlling the people, who were soon mixing with the infantry and cavalry lined up in the park. They clambered up the trees. The branch of one elm, thirty feet up, gave way under the weight of twenty men; four were killed in the fall. But when the Regent and his party finally arrived the troops managed to clear a way, the bands struck up the royal anthem, numerous regiments passed in review order, and then fired a *feu-de-joie*.[92]

The real fire of joy, however, were the night-time illuminations. Gentlemen who had toured Europe might say the illuminations in Rome were better managed, that when the vast dome of St Peter's was covered with large lamps, all kindled at the same moment, when the fireworks roared from St Angelo, spectators were awestruck – but they were not involved; and the show was over in an hour. The London illuminations were put on by individuals, by enterprise and commerce. Westminster Abbey, that June, remained in darkness; only the moon caressed her gothic pinnacles and ornaments. In London, the most spectacular illuminations were those of the Bank of England. Fifty thousand lamps were arranged in rows and columns, bordering the windows and pediments. In the midst was a huge transparency representing the "genius of France reviving" – her right hand clasping the bust of "beloved Louis," surmounted on a pillar, while her left was supported by proud Britannia.[93]

But it was not only the public buildings, the commercial buildings and the counting houses which were illuminated. Every house of London was lit up. Preparations had gone on for weeks. Oxford Street formed two long parallel lines of light, narrowing towards each other in the distance. The rumble of tens of thousands of feet on the flagstones and cobbles sounded like a rolling thunder. Men were wedged to men; they had little choice in where they went. The coaches were immoveably locked together; people crossing the street passed under the horses' bellies without fear and danger.[94]

Joseph Farington was drawn to the streets again. He walked past India House, the Excise Office, the Bank, Somerset Palace and Drury Lane and Covent Garden Theatres. "The illuminations were very splendid, but I was most struck with the *appearance of the people*," the old Tory painter emphasised. "The streets were crowded in many parts to excess, but there was not the least disorder, – a child might have gone on without injury, and all the masses of people well or decently clad, so as to exhibit an immense population moving under a general feeling of order and mutual consideration of respect. . ." It was peace, a people's peace. No one ever forgot it.[95]

You could buy your own transparencies and set them up in the window. Pictures of famous heroes, allegorical sketches, "Gothic Window Blinds," calm landscapes; they were all advertised in the papers. These pictures, made with translucent paints on materials like calico, linen, or oiled paper and lighted from behind – some of them several feet high – were common commodities during the June of peace, that June of the people.

Carlton House was illuminated with green and yellow flares that glowed between the high palm trees in their painted tubs. But only a few peeped through the colonnades at the Regent's Palace. The crowds were at Piccadilly, admiring the plainly lighted Pulteney Hotel, with its motto held high on the balcony: "Thanks to God."[96]

On the third night of the illuminations the easterly winds picked up again. The whole range of buildings on the north side of Whitehall were blacked out, save a few circles of lamps on the summit of the Horse Guards and traces of light at the Treasury. A walk that night on Westminster Bridge might have conjured up thoughts, the pennants streaming westwards, newspapers, yellow printed bills, red notices of quack doctors' remedies, pink announcements of the next fair, white pronouncements of peace carried up by the wind and blown to the waters. The City glowed in the distance. Nothing was dull, nothing was dingy then. It was an Arabian Night's entertainment.

Sam Whitbread's house was all lit up; there was a transparency to "Peace" surrounded by laurels at the summit, and lamps were grouped downwards to the ground in deep crimson.

And there were throngs of people gathered around the high iron fences of St. James's Square, protecting a new statue of William III, a Prince of Orange who had been made King. They looked up, they looked west, at the transparency of a Dove with an olive branch in its beak, at the illuminations of Number 18, on the corner of King Street, the house of Viscount Castlereagh.[97]

Castlereagh's lonely journey

And Lord Castlereagh looked out. But, as he stared out of his window, he really looked in – for Castlereagh was always at the periphery, seeking the centre; at the exterior, in search of the interior. He came from an offshore island, off an offshore island, yet he yearned to be a part of the main; he was an Irishman, who became an Englishman, who wanted to be a European. He was baptised a Presbyterian; he became an Anglican. He was an Irish Volunteer, who eventually abolished the Irish parliament; he was the author of the Union, the United Kingdom of Great Britain and Ireland. He was a Whig and Independent, who became a Pittite Tory; now he talked of a Concert of Europe. He had once shunned foreign politics and, in 1812, would have handed the job over to his old rival, George Canning; now, as British Foreign Secretary, he was recognised by every major statesman on the continent as the author of the European Peace of 1814.

Castlereagh passed frontiers (he knew the road to Dover). Castlereagh moved inwards (he had travelled the continent at war). This made him a lonely man.

South of Belfast stretches the Ards peninsula; to its east lies the Irish Sea, swirling and white-crested; to its west the calm waters of Strangford Lough. Castlereagh's home was on that peaceful western side, at a place once called Mount Pleasant; his grandfather had renamed it Mount Stewart. Some way to the south, on the other side of the lough, one could just catch the grey outline of the Mourne Mountains. To the west lay the rugged Dromara Hills. And, closer, just to the north, on this side of the lough, was Mount Scrabo, where the Irish yeomen gathered in the Rebellion of '98 – another reminder of roughness, of violence.[98]

"Every visit to this place rivets my affections more closely to it," wrote Castlereagh six years before the Rebellion, when he was twenty-three. He imagined he would spend his lifetime improving the land and that this would be the life of his children as well. But Castlereagh would have little time for plantations, he would have no children, and he would live most of his years in England, though long letters from his father would inform him of the farming at Ards in County Down. Castlereagh went instead into politics. After the Rebellion, he became one of the most hated men of Ireland, "bloody Castlereagh," a traitor who had sided with the English and Pitt. "A high gallows and a windy day," sang the rebels, "For Bill Pitt and Castlereagh."[99]

Rumour had it that the first Stewart to leave Scotland for Ireland was a peddlar named MacGregor. Rob Roy and the clan MacGregor were branded outlaws in Scotland and many MacGregors thought it a good idea to become Stewarts. At any rate, Colonel William Stewart made up for the sins of his cousins by raising his own cavalry and in 1689 playing a heroic role in the siege of Londonderry; he was rewarded with an estate in Donegal. Thereafter the rise, through marriage and money, of the Irish Stewarts to the peerage was meteoric, even by eighteenth-century standards. It was Alexander Stewart who had bought up the lands along Strangford Lough; his son, the elder Robert Stewart, married Lady Sarah Seymour-Conway, a daughter of the first Marquess of Hertford, Ireland's Lord Lieutenant. Five years after her death, he married Miss Frances Pratt, eldest daughter of Lord Camden, the former Lord Chancellor of England. Through the influence of Lord Hertford and Lord Camden, the elder Robert Stewart was raised to the peerage as the Baron of Londonderry in 1789, the year of the Revolution. In 1796 he became the Earl of Londonderry, while his eldest son, already active in politics, received the courtesy title of Viscount Castlereagh. In 1816, in recognition of his son's achievements, he would become the first Marquess of Londonderry. It was an incredible voyage upwards for the original Mr Robert Stewart; his promotion in Ireland was due entirely to English marriage, war, and revolution on the continent. While the French were undoing their aristocracy, the British were still busy fabricating theirs.[100]

So it was that Castlereagh, the younger Robert Stewart, was born a commoner in Ireland in 1769, the same year that Napoleon was born a commoner in Corsica. Moreover, Castlereagh was born on 18 June, a date that would have some significance for both men. His mother, the lovely Lady Sarah Seymour-Conway, died of a prenatal complication in 1770 when Robert was a year and a month old. He was the only surviving child of that marriage; for the remainder of his life he carried locks of his mother's hair in a golden brooch inscribed with the word "Irreparable." His father's second marriage brought him eleven half brothers and sisters, but the eldest of them was eight years younger than he, so they were hardly siblings. The long and affectionate correspondence between him and his eldest half-brother, Charles – "Fighting Charlie", they called him in the family – reads like letters between a father and a son; there were nine years between them.[101]

Despite the loss of his mother, Castlereagh's childhood does not appear to have been lonely. He regarded his step-mother as his own mother, and his step-grandfather, Lord Camden, was his introduction to England and the Pittite Tories. But his dead mother also played a role in his political formation and, perhaps, in his personality too. In 1776 her brother, the second Marquess of Hertford, married Isabella, daughter of the ninth Viscount Irvine. This was one of the most dedicated Tory families in England; they were a very rich and very beautiful people.

In 1806 the Prince of Wales fell passionately in love with Isabella, though she was by then nearly fifty and had been a grandmother "for more than twelve or fourteen years." After fits of fever, illnesses, numerous bloodings, attempted suicides and many letters to *"la bella e grassa Donna che lo signoreggia ora"* (she had apparently become very *grassa*), the Prince became her lover.

Once he was Regent, the aimiable and cuckolded Marquess of Hertford, formerly Master of the Horse, was named Lord Chamberlain, which gave him control of the whole new court. His son, the Earl of Yarmouth (Tory MP and close friend of cousin Castlereagh), was named Warden of the Stannaries. It seems that Thackeray created his mad Marquess of Steyne in *Vanity Fair* by combining the father Hertford with the son Yarmouth. Yarmouth, at any rate, was to become one of the most notoriously bad-living aristocrats of the kingdom – "there has been, so far as I know, no such example of undisguised debauchery exhibited in the world," remarked Charles Greville. As it was said of the House of Brunswick and Hanover, so it was said – by Henry Hobhouse and by the comtesse de Boigne, among others – of the House of Hertford, the Seymour-Conways: the taint of madness was running in their blood.[102]

Though his tutor, the Reverend James Cleland, described him at ten as a "sickly and enfeebled child," there was nothing sickly and enfeebled about Castlereagh, now a noble of forty-five, in 1814. Like Emperor Alexander he stood over six foot and, again like the Emperor, his physical presence created a certain awe. He had been the only diplomat in Paris without decoration – no stars, ribbons, fleeces or garters for Lord Castlereagh – but, *"Ma foi, il a l'air bien distingué,"* exclaimed a lady after this had been observed. Castlereagh followed the new English decorum, black-and-white dress with Brummel boots. Awe, fascination, wonder... Emma, Lady Edgecumbe, his wife's niece who was with Castlereagh in Paris, said, "The calm dignity of his manner gave an impression that he was cold, but no one who has seen his kindly smile, or been greeted by his two hands stretched out in welcome, could have thought him so." But who ever saw his smile and his out-stretched hands? Castlereagh worked alone. He built Britain's foreign corps up from scratch (for there were hardly any embassies to fill in Europe before 1812); but though he gave his subordinates the consideration that was their due, it was Castlereagh himself who wrote all the despatches, conducted the negotiations, even drafted the treaties. The baron de Vitrolles, self-appointed agent of the French royalist cause, recalled meeting Castlereagh, in his white cape, in the courtyard of the château de Vandœuvre during the late winter campaign of France; Vitrolles said he was "non-committal, handsome, very cold."[103]

What a contrast there was between those formal dispatches to Liverpool in the winter of 1814, and the letters he wrote at the same time to his wife, "Dearest Em": "I have laid in a stock of silks and old Sevres china for you here, but you must come for it, or else I will give it *en dépit* to some belle at Paris. God bless you dearest friend, I am a bad boy but you will forgive me when we meet which I trust will be in the fewest days possible." Like Doctor Faust, Castlereagh was inhabited by two souls.[104]

On rare occasions the tension overwhelmed him. One such was in the spring of 1801, immediately following Great Britain's union with Ireland. Another was in the autumn of 1813, immediately preceding Castlereagh's voyage to the continent and his direct involvement in the European discussions for peace.[105]

We also find Castlereagh curiously absent for three important days during the Sovereigns' visit. He failed to turn up at the huge Guildhall dinner of 18 June (perhaps he had premonitions) and he wasn't seen again until the following Tuesday, 21 June, when he accompanied Liverpool and the duc d'Orléans in an audience with the Regent. The official explanation given to the press was that he was "confined from indisposition." Given the government's and court's exasperation with Alexander and his sister, this could well have been a diplomat's cold.[106]

Few, at any rate, thought Castlereagh "indisposed" in June 1814. At his first appearance in the Commons since his return, on Monday, 6 June, the debate on the Corn Laws was interrupted and the whole House gave him a standing ovation. On 12 June his father wrote him a long letter from Mount Stewart. "Oh, that I could at this moment embrace you, and holding you close clasped in my arms give full vent to all that parental ardour and effusion of affection and joy which dilate, at this blessed era, my heart, but which no language or pen are [*sic*] competent to express! Is there anything on earth which approaches nearer to Elysian enjoyment?...When I hear your

Robert Stewart,
Viscount Castlereagh.
Contemporaries
described him as
handsome but distant

Sovereign and the nation greet your arrival with unbounded acclamations and applause, and all Europe joins in acknowledgments. . .and after my son has been so successful, I trust I may without sinning exult a little and be proud of of his deeds." Old Londonderry may have been just as wordy as his son, but there is no doubt of the father's affection, and the pleasure this must have given his son when he received the letter on 18 June, his forty-fifth birthday.[107]

Pitt's engine, Castlereagh's peace

One cannot exaggerate the political influence exercised on Castlereagh by William Pitt the Younger, who died "of a general wearing-out of the body" in January 1806 at the age of forty-six.[108] It was thanks to Pitt that Castlereagh was able to realise his project of the union of Great Britain and Ireland. It was Pitt who gave Castlereagh his main ideas about Europe. Their relationship is often described as one of master and pupil.

But behind Pitt lay a century-long tradition of British foreign policy. Good King George had defined it as concisely as anyone back in 1771: "I confess my political creed is formed on the system of King

William. England in conjunction with the house of Austria and the republic [of Holland] seems the most secure barrier against the Family Compact." Castlereagh would be reminded of Britain's late seventeenth-century Dutch king, William III, every time he looked out of his window. It was an empirical, hardly ideological and mostly negative policy. It was *against* France – "that dangerous and faithless nation," said King George; the "Family Compact" essentially referred to anything that France arranged in Europe. It was *against* entanglement in the affairs of the continent, which most Englishmen regarded as a sink of Popery and despotism best left to itself. It was *against* the dominance of the continent by any single power – a mortal threat to Britain's commercial interests. Thus even the most positive features of the "system of King William," the maintenance of a Balance of Power and the defence of the Low Countries, were derived from a negative though, from eighteenth-century Britain's view, perfectly justifiable attitude.[109]

But the policy became self-contradictory. So many things was Britain *against* that she found herself, in the Revolutionary Wars, totally isolated. That was the problem Pitt the Younger had to resolve.

The solution itself was negative. It was not an initiative, but a response to a fantastic plan for European federation, proposed in the autumn of 1804 by Russia through a secret agent, Novosiltsev: Tsar Alexander, convinced of his personal powers in matters of diplomacy, pursued what Louis XV and Louis XVI used to call *le Secret du Roi*, the exchange of political views between Sovereigns through secret envoys; Pitt preferred to work with the Ambassador, the very old-fashioned, wig and powdered Count Vorontsov, and he initially dismissed Novosiltsev as "Mr Weathervane" and his plan as "a piece of daydreaming and visionary nonsense." But, within months, Pitt was having second thoughts.[110]

The Russian plan had actually been drafted by Prince Adam Czartoryski, who was somewhat of a dreamer himself. A leader in a Polish rising against Russia in 1794, he had been imprisoned in the SS Peter and Paul fortress before he managed, through charm and intelligence, to get hired as a tutor for Alexander; in 1804, he was Alexander's Acting Foreign Minister, though he remained a good patriotic Pole. His plan called for a treaty that would end the war in Europe and would lay down "the right of peoples" (*"le droit des gens"*). "Feudalism" was be replaced by liberal governments and constitutions; a "code of the right of peoples" would be established; the states of Europe were be organised in a "league" that would guarantee the "positive law of nations" and would abolish war except as a last resort after "all the means offered by a third mediating party had been exhausted." Any state which defied this new "positive law of nations" could expect an immediate response from a coalition of all the others. Britain and Russia were to act together, through a separate treaty, as the protectors of the new Europe, because they were the only Powers "free from conflicting desires and interests [and] will never trouble this happy tranquillity."

The plan also made concrete territorial suggestions: the King of Sardinia was to regain Piedmont, the Italian republics would be freed from the French, the independence of Switzerland and Holland was to be guaranteed, and the smaller German states would be organised in a confederation. Nothing was said about the interests of Austria and Prussia, and, curiously, the fate of Poland was not mentioned either.[111]

It was the territorial suggestions that eventually intrigued Pitt because they accorded with his own idea, which he had developed in the 1790s, of "barrier" states (he was thinking, in particular, of the Low Countries); they also complemented nicely the old English notion of a Balance of Power. The fact that Britain was, in 1804, alone in her war with France incited further thought. In the spring of 1805, Pitt at last responded to the Russians with his own plan.[112]

Pitt's "draft" of 1805 was the basis of an Anglo-Russian Treaty that April and of the Third Coalition in August. It was a work that was achieved almost single-handed, for the Foreign Secretary was sick and his stand-in was not the brightest spark in the Cabinet. The only person with whom he discussed the plan in any detail was the young President of the Board of Control, Viscount Castlereagh.[113]

Pitt stripped the original Russian plan of all its ideological ornaments, leaving a naked, shiny engine designed to defeat France and, subsequently, to control her. Two new pistons were added in the form of alliances with Austria and Prussia. This required a few adjustments to the cogs and shafts hidden inside the Russian plan: Pitt had to appeal to Austrian and Prussian interests. Like the old-fashioned Whig he was, accustomed to "the system of King William," he had not the slightest interest in the internal domestic affairs of Europe, so to blazes with constitutions and "the right of peoples" – he would use Russia's territorial suggestions as compensations and rewards for the new pieces in his engine, Austria and Prussia. France would be reduced to her "former limits as they stood before that time [the Revolution]." The "territories recovered" would constitute "a more effectual barrier in future against encroachments on the part of France." His idea of "barriers" was attached to the Russian suggestions on a united Sardinia and Piedmont, and, to strengthen the "independence of Holland" he made the revolutionary suggestion of attaching to it the former Austrian Netherlands, the Catholic "Belgic provinces." But the rest of northern "Italy" he held out as a compensation for Austria's loss of the Netherlands, and "Germany" – the German states, he contended, were too "jealous" ever to become a union – west of the Rhine would be a reward for hesitant Prussia. The engine did receive a little paint in the recognition of Russia's call for a system of collective security; Pitt called it "a general agreement and guarantee for the mutual protection and security of different Powers, and the re-establishing [of] a general system of public law in Europe." He also agreed that Russia and Britain, as disinterested Powers, would guarantee the lot.

But Prussia was more tempted by Napoleon's offer of Hanover, and she never joined. Austria was defeated at the Battle of Ulm, Russia was defeated at the Battle of Austerlitz, and Alexander came to the conclusion that constitutions and the "right of peoples" had more of a chance through an agreement with the Corsican Ogre – he duly signed one at Tilsit. These were dark and lonely years for Britain.

Things began to improve after 1812. That was the year Russia defeated Napoleon. That was the year Castlereagh became Foreign Secretary in the Earl of Liverpool's new government. He revived the Pitt plan.

When he learned in April 1814 that Russia had signed a treaty with Prussia, he forwarded a copy of the old plan to the Russian Court, which was then following its army in Germany; "the Emperor of Russia probably has not this interesting document at headquarters," wrote Castlereagh in a note to his Ambassador. But the Emperor of Russia did not respond.[114]

It was only in January 1814 that Castlereagh discovered what was wrong: Russia was not, as he and Pitt had assumed, a disinterested Power; she was expanding westwards into Europe, through Poland. Alexander might have clung to his ideas of "leagues" and "confederations," his appeal to the liberated "peoples" was probably sincere, he was convinced God was his guide ("Here's our motto," he said when signing his treaty with Prussia, "Hope in God, courage, and perseverence!"); but somehow all this always corresponded to immediate Russian territorial interests. Castlereagh's voyage into the centre of Europe shattered his illusions. On 18 January 1814, in Bâle, Switzerland, he met the Austrian Foreign Minister, Prince Clemens von Metternich. He was absolutely delighted with this new acquaintance; "I get on with him as if we had spent our lives together," he wrote immediately back to Liverpool. Within hours he came to the realisation that Austria was Britain's natural ally, not Russia. Within days he had experienced a conversion; Castlereagh had become a European.[115]

On his route across frosty Germany to Bâle, Castlereagh had been having long conversations with the Earl of Ripon. He talked more about Europe and less about British interests; in fact, he couldn't separate the two. Britain's role, he thought, – *his* role – was to mediate continental disputes, iron out the differences between Austria and

Prussia, get the Powers of the continent talking to one another, create harmony between the rival parties. He told Ripon he wanted "an habitual confidential and free intercourse between the Ministers of the Great Powers *as a body*." He would talk of "concert" and "confederation," of "European unity"; his ideas, once married to those of Metternich's, would give birth to the notion of regular meetings of the Foreign Ministers. It was a revolution in European thought. Ripon looked back on those conversations, the windows of the carriage frozen over, twenty-five years later. "No man was ever better calculated so to transact business himself," he said. "The suavity and dignity of his manners, his habitual patience and self-command, his considerate tolerance of difference of opinion in others, all fitted him for such a task."[116]

Between that January and the Sovereigns' visit to Britain in June, Castlereagh was involved in three major diplomatic events; the Châtillon Conference, which attempted a negotiated peace with Napoleon, the Treaty of Chaumont, which established an alliance between the four Powers at war with Napoleon, and the Peace of Paris, which settled French frontiers once Paris had fallen.

France was on the way down, Russia was on the way up. The essence of Castlreagh's conversion lay in this understanding. No longer was he content to play the part of a disinterested mediator; now he actively defended, with Metternich, the notion of a European equilibrium. "Isolated states exist only as the abstractions of so-called philosophers," Metternich had once mused. "In the society of states each state has interests which connect it with the others."[117] That was Castlereagh's view, too. If he still sought to impose limits on France, he was equally willing now to impose limits on Russia, and was ready to negotiate with Napoleon himself to insure that those limits were imposed. Thanks largely to Castlereagh, as the Allies moved on France, Russia found herself increasingly isolated.

But Castlereagh's new European ideas came into conflict with British "public opinion" – as it was beginning to be called at the time – which was outraged to learn, in late February 1814, of the Châtillon Conference and the possibility of a negotiated peace with Napoleon. "Liddel spoke of the disposition of the People of London generally with respect to making Peace," recorded Farington in his diary on the 24th, after one of his long political conversations. "He said should Lord Castlereagh return from the Congress at Châtillon and proclaim that Peace was made with Buonaparte He would be *hooted*." But Castlereagh remained firm, undeterred by the hooting; he had had the same attitude about opinion in Ireland when he organised the new United Kingdom.[118]

Napoleon, proud and confident to the end, in fact failed to come to any agreement. Castlereagh's crowning achievement was the Treaty of

Chaumont, signed on 4 March. '*My* treaty,' he called it. Not only did it formalise the alliance of the Four Powers (Britain, Austria, Prussia and Russia) in the name of Europe – "to *concert* together on the conclusion of a peace with France" – but it bound the Four Powers together for a period of twenty years. It was a first step in the direction of regular European meetings.[119]

The Peace of Paris was essentially limited to a definition of the position of the new Bourbon France within the new Europe, though the latter remained to be determined. This Peace, signed on 30 May 1814, was the "Definitive Treaty" that the British press got so excited about in early June. After the rumours about Châtillon, there was a residue of anger in Britain. It was unwarranted. The Peace was perhaps more lenient to France than many in Britain would have wished. But this was almost wholly due to the fact that the Four Powers could not agree on what else to do. It was easier to define France's limits than to dispose of her old continental empire and set up the machinery that would enforce them. The "German question" was left open. Russia still refused to discuss Poland. The Netherlands remained disunited and undefined. Plans for Italy remained vague. It was decided that an international congress would be held in Vienna on 15 July, immediately following the Sovereigns' visit to London. But many, including Castlereagh, held out the hope that the new Europe would be defined in London.

It proved impossible to fulfil. Castlereagh was too busy with the politics of drawing rooms, royal marital problems, dinners, and receptions; he did at least receive a compensation, the Order of the Garter, from his Sovereign. "It is hardly possible to give any idea of all the duties which fall to him," wrote the Bavarian Ambassador to his King. Then there was the problem of Alexander, who still refused to talk about Poland and was intent on basking in the crowds.

The only topic that was discussed in London, and discussed with some passion, was the future of the Netherlands, Britain's key to the continent. The press focused on the impending marriage between Princess Charlotte and the Hereditary Prince; it was, after all, a symbol of Britain's commitment to the new barrier state. But another issue was beginning to emerge. The Netherlands was not just a "barrier" or a cog in an engine; a lot of people were living there too. And the people were suffering. News was coming in of horrors being committed in the Netherlands.

How the Belgic provinces were liberated

Those history textbooks on the bottom shelf, which make our past so neat, tell us that a certain war ended on a certain date. But did the guns really fall silent across all Europe on 11 November 1918? Was

Europe's Second World War really finished for good on 8 May 1945? What day did the Franco-Prussian War end? On what afternoon did the world lay down its arms in the Seven Years War? When was the English Civil War over? Was Hastings the end of the armed Norman invasion? Wars rarely end on a single day.

Paris capitulated to the Allied armies on 31 March 1814. Napoleon abdicated and the Senate offered the French throne to Louis XVIII on 6 April. But the war went on in the Netherlands.

General Lazare Carnot, the Great Carnot, the Organiser of Victory of 1793, was in 1814 the Governor of Antwerp. He refused to surrender. Several isolated fortified towns held out. The last to fall was Maastricht, where the River Meuse becomes the River Maas, where the river banks form one frontier and language forms another. The Flemish-speaking people, the French-speaking people, and the German-speaking people all had a claim on Maastricht; they had been fighting over it for centuries. Louis XIV lost an empire there, d'Artagnan died there. Maastricht fell to a Swedish army on 19 April 1814.

The Swedes were close allies of the Russians and were not welcomed as "liberators" in what were called the "Belgic provinces" of the Netherlands. Letters of April and May from Lord Clancarty, Britain's Ambassador at the Hague, explained to Castlereagh why: "Since their rapid and heroic passage of the Rhine," said Clancarty of the Swedes, "their 'governing principle' seems to be to do as little good and as much mischief as possible; and more especially to lean heavy upon any country which either formerly belonged to the Dutch, or might be likely to form an addition to the territories of the Prince of Orange." From Maastricht the Swedish armies spread westwards across the rural but densely populated province of Brabant, imposing "enormous requisitions." Clancarty wondered if anything could be more calculated "to fortify an already sufficiently prevalent desire in this people to place themselves under the French." These rolling fertile plains south of Brussels were of considerable significance to the British and Clancarty recommended that the Swedes be immediately replaced by the Hanoverians, the British, and the Dutch.[120]

They eventually were. But the replacement was slow, not immediate. When, in May, the British finally disembarked at Nieuport and Ostend and marched towards Brussels they came in for a surprise; they found the area already occupied by the Prussians. General von Bülow had forty thousand troops in Flanders and Brabant. Kleist was marching into the provinces, and Yorck was on the other side of the Rhine just waiting to follow. "I never dreamt that the Prussian troops were to be poured in such torrents, or indeed at all, upon us," exclaimed Clancarty astonished. He warned Castlereagh that the current provisional civilian governor of the area was surrounded by "an overwhelming military force, over which he has no control, and the commandants of which have no interest in common with him, or any other, than to squeeze the people to their last stiver."

Clancarty was more than worried; he thought the French could one day take advantage of the apalling treatment the "suffering people" of the Belgic provinces were receiving from their liberators. "The nature of the free quarters to which they are exposed," he said, "presses more severely than four times the exactions imposed on them by the French." On 7 June, the day the victorious Sovereigns arrived in London, Clancarty wrote again to Castlereagh, pointing out that the Prussians, far from evacuating the area, were demanding "an additional requisition." "I should hope measures will be taken to prevent this," Clancarty solemnly concluded, "for, in truth, these countries have already been sufficiently pillaged."[121]

Castlereagh must have been already aware that there would be no general agreement about the new Europe in London. But more troubling still were these signs that not only Russia, but also Prussia, was not behaving the way a good Ally should.

A royal jilt

Charlotte's Dutch fiancé, Prince William, had attended all the major social events that season and – it was reported to the Princess – was repeatedly getting drunk. On Friday, 10 June, he had gone to the Ascot Races and had come back to London hanging onto the outside of a stage coach. Brougham spoke of him being made "remarkably drunk" by the Princess's cousin, the wild Prince Paul of Württemberg. Prince William's dress was riotous; plenty of jokes were passed around the English court about "the ruddy hue of his gulligaskins." Charlotte sent notice to the Prince that she would like to see him immediately he returned from the following week's celebrations at Oxford.[122]

For the last three months she had been put under considerable pressure from Grey, Brougham, Madame de Tatischev (a Russian diplomat's wife), and the Grand Duchess herself to remain "complete mistress" of her own actions and, particularly, not to accept any requirements to leave England without her consent. She was continually reminded of the possibility of her mother's departure for the continent and a new variation on Brougham's nightmare scenario: divorce proceedings for her mother, remarriage of the Regent, a new son and heir, Charlotte's exclusion from the throne. Earnest discussions over Charlotte's marriage contract with William went on through April and May, with Charlotte insisting on a clause that she leave and return to England "at her own pleasure." Just as the Sovereigns were arriving in England, this clause was accepted.

But, as the marriage preparations continued, the idea of "living in Holland amongst the fogs and dykes" became less and less appealing. Her Prince went everywhere; she was invited nowhere, apart from a boring reception at her grandmother's and one of those deadly dinners at Carlton House. She had been driven around in her carriage to see the crowds and the decorations, to watch "with perfect sang froid" the guards of honour salute the arriving and departing dignitaries – she was never among them. All the Sovereigns visited her at Warwick House, but they didn't even stay for tea.

Others did. Wild Prince Paul put in a call, much to the chagrin of Charlotte's father. He was joined by the two Prussian princes, Augustus and Frederick, whom the Regent held in equal contempt. Then there was the mild, fine looking Prince Leopold, third son of the Duke of Saxe-Coburg-Saalfield, who had accompanied the Russian suite to England and whom the Regent actually thought "a most honourable young man." He not only stayed for tea, he also had breakfast at Warwick House. There were rumours about a possible interest in the Prince of Mecklenburg, but it was Prince Leopold who had caught Charlotte's eye.

So before he had even gone to Oxford Prince William's prospects were doomed. As Charlotte had requested, he presented himself at Warwick House on his return. The Princess, looking very royal and determined, insisted that her lady-in-waiting, Lady Charlotte Lindsay, remain in the room during the interview. The speech was so well prepared that it could have been mimed, with Brougham himself speaking from a corner. Charlotte declared it was utterly impossible for her to leave England now and, because of that, she was going to avail herself of "the discretionary power" promised in the contract. The reason, she said, for being so bound to England was the situation of her mother, the Princess of Wales. William, who was evidently "very unhappy," told the Princess that if she insisted on this "the marriage must be off," for he was "already engaged to the Dutch to take the Princess among them for a short time"; but he pledged, as a man of honour, that he would return with her to England "after her first introduction to his nation." Lady Charlotte Lindsay reported immediately to Brougham that the poor man left the house "in much agitation." That evening, 16 June, the Princess wrote to William informing him that she considered their engagement "to be totally and for ever at an end."

So now the die was cast: politicians, princes, and sovereigns were poised to take their winnings. It was one of the great ironies of 1814 that the victorious Powers of Europe, the defenders of monarchy, had to place so much hope in the consensus of adolescents. Indeed, the biggest loser of the war, Napoleon himself, had learnt that marriage (in his case, to the Austrian Emperor's daughter) did not make a very solid base for an international alliance.

Prince William looked very much a loser. He left London "full of grief" on Tuesday, 21 June; his baggages and horses went off two days later. Castlereagh's niece, Lady Edgcumbe had seen him at a ball in Devonshire House that Monday night. "Goodbye, God bless you, Lady Emma" – he wrung her hand, tears in his eyes –"I am off to-morrow." His father still entertained hopes. The Sovereign Prince of Orange, according to Clancarty in the Hague, was so anxious "to continue the negociation" that "there was scarcely any sacrifice which he might not be induced to make for the satisfaction of the Princess Charlotte."[123]

Castlereagh knew it was too late. "I think nothing ought to be done to close this door," he wrote back to Clancarty; "yet it would be unwise to hope too much." But Castlereagh could turn a loss into a gain. "I have not been idle," he boasted. In fact, sensing trouble, he had got the Foreign Ministers of the Four Powers (Russia, Prussia, Austria and Britain) to agree, two days before Charlotte's rupture, to hand over the provisional administration of the Belgic provinces to the Prince of Orange. "The Prussian troops are ordered off," he proudly announced to Clancarty one week later and, moreover, there was now a plan for a formal convention on the Netherlands to be drawn up in Vienna. In the meantime the Sovereign Prince would administer the region "in the name of the Allies, so that his Royal Highness may prepare the public mind." So suffering Belgium had a new ruler, Castlereagh's first "barrier state" had been confirmed in a formal protocol, and exuberant Prussia had been forced into retreat: it was a sign that some dramatic moves could be expected at the Congress in Vienna.[124]

But ambitious Russia had also gained a point. Her allies, the Swedes and the Prussians may well have been thrown out of Belgium, but within a year of the rupture with Princess Charlotte Prince William had found a new bride: the Grand Duchess Anne, another sister of the Tsar. Thus Russia had managed to push a toe, if not an army, into an area of vital British interest.

The real losers in this political game of marriage were the Whigs in London. Their whole goal had been, as Castlereagh put it to Clancarty, "to add another complication to the family embarrassments." Instead, the ridicule rebounded on them. They had built their campaign on the moral fiction of love between mother and daughter.

Thomas Creevey was exultant when he heard news that the Dutch marriage had been broken off. Sam Whitbread had shown Creevey a copy of the letter Charlotte had sent Prince William. "By God!" he exclaimed in a letter to his wife, "it is capital." Charlotte had refused to leave the country and, above all, had refused to abandon her mother – whom he thought would also not leave the country as a result. "And now what do you suppose has produced this sudden attachment to her mother?" mused Creevey. "It arises from the profound resources of old Brougham, and is, in truth, one of the most brilliant movements in his campaign."[125]

But Charlotte's "sudden attachment to her mother" was due to her real attachment to another man, Prince Leopold. The Whigs could hardly have known this, but they should have been conscious of how artificial her proclaimed affections for her mother were.[126]

Even more devastating to their cause was their misjudgment of the mother's attachment to her daughter. Just two days after Creevey had been slapping his thighs over news of the rupture, Castlereagh made his famous speech in the Commons in which he offered to increase the Princess of Wales's allowance. To the fury of the Whigs, she accepted.

Whitbread characterised the allowance as "*this insidious offer* made in *so unhandsome a manner.*" Brougham went into "convulsions." St Leger was "thunderstruck and mortified." Sefton, Tierney and Jersey all expressed shock. But Caroline simply shrugged her shoulders, for she had no intention to play the Whigs' game. She informed Whitbread in a curt ungrammatical note that she was ready to accept the offer because "no conditions derogatory to Her as Princess, or to her Honor as a female, have been annexed to the fulfillment of her rights." She was tired of the politics: "The Princess is weary of all the trouble she has endured herself, and been the occasion to her friends, and takes the whole blame upon herself by exhonorating Mr Whitbread for all responsibility. . ." Brougham went into convulsions again. He wrote to Creevey, "I suppose you have heard of Mother P. [Caroline] bungling the thing so compleatly – snapping eagerly at the cash." He said, "She deserves death," but he would not abandon her "in case P. [Prinny] gets a victory after all."

The Whigs' "moral" cause foundered on its own weaknesses. Soon they were fighting among each other. "By God," wrote Brougham, "Sam is incurable." It was a brief victory for "P."; but it was an even greater victory for his friend, Lord Castlereagh, who had routed his opposition at home and could now devote himself to peace in Europe.[127]

Europe? The Whigs would have to make an issue out of that.

The Sovereigns depart

As for the Great Liberator, Tsar Alexander was not one to calculate his visit to London in terms of gains and losses; such politics were beneath him. Alexander had thrown his whole private soul into a great historical enterprise: he had destroyed the Antichrist, he had led his armies into Babylon, he had received his laurels, and now he would turn to his own ideal of Europe, an ideal that he still linked to the "rights of the peoples." In London he appeared to have the support of the peoples. He ignored Oxford, where the Regent had proven to be more popular than he. Nor did he notice the disappointed crowds in the surrounding counties. Alexander, in fact, had hardly noticed anything about England at all; his journey across the Channel had been more a voyage into the interior of his own soul than a visit to a foreign island.

Countess Lieven observed he had a rather lost look in the ballrooms, even when he was dancing. Robert Smirke, the famous architect and a friend of Farington's, found something odd about the Emperor when he attended the review at Hyde Park; "he had a good humoured cheerful look, but [Smirke] thought there was something *Cattish* in his face which caused him to think of Emperor Peter [i.e. Paul], His Father."[128]

Alexander didn't think it hypocritical to eat until midnight, "dance the light fantastic" till dawn, and then pray to God during the three of rest which remained to him. In dining and dancing he thought he could demonstrate both his physical and spiritual superiority to the other Sovereigns. The celebrations at Oxford had been held on 14 and 15 June by order of the Regent because the Regent did not want any of the Sovereigns attending a ball offered in London on the night of the 14th by Lady Jersey, his discarded mistress. Alexander duly attended the Oxford ceremonies and then drove through the night in an open carriage – in thunder and rain – to London. He changed clothes at his hotel and was dancing at Lady Jersey's ball between two and six a.m. The next morning he was up at ten to announce another full day's activity. The Prince Regent couldn't compete with this. He did eventually roll into London late that Wednesday night; Alexander had already attended Lord Castlereagh's dinner, a performance at the Drury Lane Theatre, and a ball at the Marchioness of Hertford's – the Regent's new mistress. The Regent thought Alexander's behaviour insulting. The Whigs considered it heroic. Alexander himself was convinced this showed that the force of God was behind him.[129]

In reverence to God, on Sunday, 19 June he attended a Quaker meeting in Westminster. Quaker thought was closely related to that of the Moravian Brethren, with whom Alexander had been in contact during the German campaign of 1813. They rejected the sacraments, they rejected the formalism of exterior worship, including ecclesiastical hierarchy. For them, Christ within was the only authentic source of faith. "Such are my own sentiments," Alexander told the Quaker leader, William Allen; the Tsar had discovered the meaning of interior faith in the year 1812.

Allen later described Sunday's meeting, attended by Alexander and his sister, as being "very solemn." "The Assembly," he recorded, "remained silent for about a quarter of an hour, during which my spirit was sweetly restored and comforted by the firm conviction that the Supreme Master was accomplishing His work with His own hands."

That evening Alexander received at the Pulteney Hotel ten members of the British and Foreign Bible Society. A Russian branch had been founded in St Petersburg in 1812.

On 21 June, the day before he left London, Alexander received a deputation of three Quakers, William Allen, Stephen Grellet, and John Wilkinson. The meeting lasted over an hour. Allen spoke in English, Grellet in French. Grellet never forgot this meeting: "We exposed to the Emperor our ideas about war, and he said he approved of them. After several other questions, followed by detailed responses, we all remained in silence and my heart was suddenly filled with the love of Christ with regard to the Emperor, whose situation, so full of temptations and perils, touched me; I addressed him a few words. His heart was moved; with his eyes full of tears, he took my hand and held it in his in silence; then he told me, 'The words you have just said are like a balm for my soul and they will rest for a long time engraven in my heart."[130]

It was reported that Alexander left London on 22 June feeling very morose. When he quit the Pulteney Hotel, there were a number of people standing at the entry holding out their hands, but Alexander walked straight past without shaking them. The Russian imperial party, in the company of the other Sovereigns, travelled to Portsmouth to witness a naval review. "The day was certainly more like one in October than in June," said *The Times*, "but it was not forbidding. Gleams of solar glory elicited the green of the ocean."[131]

At the review, a pair of gleaming eyes elicited a response from the Grand Duchess. They belonged to William, Crown Prince of Württemberg, the elder brother of wild Prince Paul. Austrian spies reported back to Vienna that it was love at first sight. So gone were all flirtatious thoughts about Prince William of Orange. Austria's efforts to match the Grand Duchess with Archduke Charles were likewise damned. Grand Duchess Catherine had set her heart on a new royal William.[132]

The Pavilion at Brighton had been prepared to receive the Sovereigns, but Alexander was in a rush. The Regent accompanied the party as far as Petworth House, where they were received by Lord Egremont in the Marble Hall and treated to an early dinner. That was the last the Prince Regent ever saw of the European Sovereigns. The Regent returned to London and the Sovereigns continued on the road through Sussex and Kent to Dover. The towns and villages along the way were decorated with arches and trophies of oak and laurel leaves, flags of all sorts were flying; the golden boot hanging over

Lord Egremont, bowing, receives the Sovereigns at Petworth House on 24 June 1814. Directly to the left of Egremont stand the Prince Regent, Tsar Alexander, the Grand Duchess Catherine and King Frederick William III

Pulborough's High Street was festooned in leaves. But the Emperor never saw this, the Emperor passed in the dark.

Monday, 27 June, was a cold and windy day at Dover. The King of Prussia boarded HMS *Nymphen* and sailed off for Calais at 11.30. Alexander and Catherine remained in the home of J.M. Fector, Esq., all day and emerged only at six to board the *Royal Charlotte*. A despatch to London sent at 6.30 read: "Guns are roaring from every part: the yacht is armoured and will be out of the harbour in half an hour." The Emperor remained on the deck most of the night "being very sick." On leaving the yacht at Calais he called out in English, "Farewell my boys," and the sailors cheered.[133]

The Sunday Monitor noted: "The departure of the Northern *Powers* have [sic] been followed by a departure of the Northern *Weather*, which the common people think kept back the summer in compliment to them."

But summer was on its way, and the people had not finished celebrating.

Equilibrium

The British response to Alexander's mystical vision of Europe had been formulated by Pitt and Castlereagh back in 1805: a Europe of equilibrium. A series of manœuvres, accidents and political blunders had brought this more mechanical, but more practical, vision of Europe to the fore. In 1813 Castlereagh had discovered a kindred spirit in Metternich and Alexander's bizarre behaviour in London did the rest. "The Emperor of Russia every day sinks extraordinarily in the eyes of the Prince Regent, the Ministry and the public," wrote Metternich, delighted, to his Emperor in Vienna. "At the same time, consideration for Austria rises substantially."[134]

But this developing friendship between Britain and Austria needed to be reinforced, the equilibrium of Europe had to be defended, and that would require the help of a third Power. It could hardly be Prussia. Both Metternich and Castlereagh must have seen the transparency on the Bank of England – the "genius of France" clinging to the bust of Louis with the support of proud Britannia. For them it was not just art. Both Metternich and Castlereagh were going to be looking to Bourbon Paris for support.

Fireworks

In one important sense Alexander had been right in his judgment of the Prince Regent: this Sovereign, who wasn't really a Sovereign, had ambitions to build another Babylon in England. In London, an architectural revolution was under way that would soon create Regent Street, would transform old Charing Cross into Trafalgar Square, would change the parks, and modify the whole West End. Thirty years later, Paris would imitate London, building the broad streets, the wide avenues, and the green parks on a scale that London's architects could never have dreamt of; and from Paris the idea would spread to every major city of Europe. The "metropolitan improvements" of London under the Prince Regent started off the whole process.[135]

In 1814, the revolution in urban design had only just begun. Beyond a bank, an art gallery, and a couple of theatres, it was essentially limited to buildings of amusement – constructed out of wood, cardboard, linen, and oiled paper – that appeared in the parks as part of the celebrations of peace.[136]

Work had begun on these strange buildings with the first rumours that the Allied Sovereigns would be visiting London and it continued long after they had gone. The Sovereigns had only stayed two weeks. A Grand National Jubilee was annnounced as if this would compensate for the public disappointment in the visit. Its date was finally set for 1 August, anniversary of the Battle of the Nile and centenary of the accession of the "House of Brunswick," as the House of Hanover was still then known.[137]

General Sir William Congreve, inventor of the military rocket, directed construction of the main building in the parks, a temple set up in Green Park "after the Eastern style." It was designed for a massive fireworks display on the night of the Jubilee, it was over ninety feet high, it had Doric columns of porphyry and Ionic columns of marble supporting Japanese chandeliers and several huge allegorical transparencies; atop was a triumphant statue of the Regent. The whole construction revolved on a circular iron rail, with fifty men required to turn it. On the night of the display it was to be magically transformed from a Castle of Discord – with several hundred square feet of ramparts and images of Strife, Jupiter, and Mars trampling underfoot Truth and Justice (Hope lingering in the background) – into this magnificent Temple of Concord, exhibiting its columns and its various transparencies of Strength, Victory, and Peace (along with the Genius of France being, once more, helped out of an awkward situation by the Allied Powers). Over the canal in St James's Park, within view of Carlton House, was thrown an ornate Chinese bridge, from the centre of which rose a seven-storey pyramidal pagoda, again chiefly designed for fireworks. The principal building material for all these structures was wood – by 1 August, dry wood.

It was to be a Jubilee for everybody. As the official programme put it, "It is his Royal Highness's intention that every possible variety of amusement shall be produced that may be agreeable to every class of society." The show was "to be thrown open to the people" and "accommodate the whole population of the metropolis and its environs."[138]

Not everybody approved. "We really do not see that there is any great wisdom or policy in thus drawing men from their useful occupations, and creating what will be no other than a great riot," commented *The Times* when it published the official programme. The editorialist regarded this sort of celebration as neither manly nor English; "your regattas and carnivals, &c. are things more suited to the licentious manners of the southern nations than to the temperate habits of Englishmen."[139]

It would be wrong to dismiss this as the flat wooden language of reaction; one hears in it the moral tones of London's Radical voice, in praise of *useful* and *valuable* work: "We have rejoiced enough about the peace; we wish men now to pursue their quiet labours." One irate correspondent called on the Corporation of London to stop the celebrations. *The Morning Chronicle, The Examiner,* and *The*

Champion – all Whig papers – followed in denouncing the "Fair Phrenzy," the "Regal Raree Show."

The day of the Grand National Jubilee did begin inauspiciously. On the morning of 1 August angry storm clouds rolled in over London from opposite corners of the sky, clashed, broke and let drop bucketloads of rain. Farington had gone out before breakfast with a friend to inspect the booths in Hyde Park and got a soaking. Yet the rain "was succeeded by a most beautiful day, the air fresh and delightful." At midday the Park and Tower guns roared out to announce to the Metropolis that the fete was on.[140]

Visitors in their gay and ample dresses poured into the three parks. In Green Park, one of Windham Sadler's coloured balloons took off into a cloudless sky with his son aboard (because of a faulty valve he could have been swept out to sea, but was saved by fishermen near Gravesend). On the Serpentine, two mock sea battles, involving over twenty small-scale ships, took place; at sunset, the "French fleet" was burnt by crackling, flashing fireships.

While the sun coated the tips of trees with its last coppery light the crowds pressed into the alleys and lawns of Green Park and Constitution Hill, and by nightfall "the whole ground from Hyde Park Corner to St. James's Palace had become one immobile mass of human beings." The firework display began with a cannonade on the Castle of Discord; cardboard artillery, paper small arms, mortars and maroons belched out red fire and smoke from the gothic wooden ramparts until they were almost hidden in inky billows of burnt saltpetre and sulphur. The building slowly revolved, the fake guns kept blasting, the magic moment was about to happen. Farington said he saw "forming a beautiful structure on the lines composed of lighted lamps and large transparent Paintings." He was one of the few who did see it. According to *The Sunday Monitor*, "the clouds of smoke with which the Temple was enveloped caused the transparencies to be invisible, except to those who were immediately contiguous to the edifice."

Then the long rehearsed, and much proclaimed, transformation scene from "destructive War" to "Glorious Peace" took another bizarre turn before the crowds. It was as if some outside player wanted to demonstrate that they were all being winged along by the hours of fate, unconscious of where they were really going. A brilliant light appeared in neighbouring St James's Park, above the seven-tiered Pagoda. John Murphy, of Parliament Street, was standing on the lawn by the Chinese bridge and was one of the first to notice it. He said a "discharge" took place that "seemed greater than it had appeared at any former part of the evening, and burst from every part of the Pagoda above the second or third circle." A major fireworks display had been going on here too. Immense Catherine wheels spluttered out

dizzying circles of greens and yellows, bombs and pyramids of fire
burst forth, Roman candles and *pots de brin* added gentle touches of
red and violet, while rockets screeched up from the curled blue eaves,
scrawled a signature on a starry sky, then opened up into great webs
of fire, became in a moment a tumbling of green, red and golden
flares, and were gone.

John Murphy got suddenly alarmed. He heard screams. So did M.
Foulkes, a bankrupt hosier from Wood Street in Cheapside. It was
later discovered that he had saved lives in the Custom House fire the
preceding February. As soon as he heard those screams he ran into the
Pagoda and up the wooden ladders. Sparks had fallen on a store of
fireworks on the second floor and set them alight. Tongues of yellow
flame shot out of every window; white, grey and black flinder swirled
and circled upwards like a hundred birds released from a cage. Two
engines, stationed at each end of the bridge and worked by desperate
men, fed streams of water into the hungry flame. Five men escaped
with injuries. But John Taylor, a carpenter, was so badly burnt – several saw him running out of the building his clothes aflame – that he
died the next day. And Foulkes never made it; from one of the top
storeys he made a dive for the waters and fell, head first, into a floating stage. John Murphy was a witness.

Even the waters of the canal seemed "a mass of brilliant living fire,"
its glow picking out the details of the little boats with their high
prows that rode upon it, the arched bridge and its Chinese motifs, the
rows of tents and the flags of the Allies fluttering above them. Fire
flashed in every face. "The reflection of the flames upon the surface of
the water, and over the whole of the Park, was awfully grand," said
The Sunday Monitor – grand like a new growth that had suddenly
filled a vacant space, awful like some unforeseen accident that
hindered intentions and left old plans forgotten.

PARIS
Summer 1814

Previous page: The gardens of the Palais-Royal,
a centre for both leisure and politics

The engine is turned

By the time Castlereagh had scheduled his next trip to the continent, the old plan for the new peace had already been modified. For sure, Europe was going to be governed by monarchies and the peace would be preserved through the "concert of her Sovereigns," as had been decided back in March at Chaumont. The great outstanding problems of disposing of Napoleon's defunct continental empire would be discussed at Vienna, as was agreed in May at Paris.[1] London's newspaper readers had been informed during the Sovereigns' visit that the Congress would be assembling the following month or, at the latest, by mid-August. Castlereagh, for his part, thought it would last six weeks at the most because all it had to do was ratify decisions already made by the Four Powers (Britain, Austria, Prussia, and Russia) who, at Chaumont, claimed to stand for all Europe. "This Peace shall be the Peace of Europe," they had announced as their armies marched on Paris; "my treaty" had been viewed by Castlereagh as a European treaty, a preliminary to the European peace. A "real and permanent balance of power in Europe," the Four Powers had written into the Secret Articles of the Treaty of Paris (where Castlereagh had also played the leading role), "shall be regulated at the Congress upon principles *determined by the Allied Powers amongst themselves.*" It seemed at that time that Pitt's naked machine aimed at France was to be maintained as a tutor of the peace.[2]

But on the day of Charlotte's rupture with Prince William, 16 June, the gulf between Russia and her Allies became dangerously wide. The ministers, meeting in London, had agreed that the Congress should be summoned on 15 August; Alexander, just back from the festivities at Oxford, once more wanted to delay. He claimed that he was being asked to remain idle until the Congress assembled, that he needed to return to Russia first to sound the opinions of his own court. Castlereagh and Metternich became suspicious. Castlereagh, in particular, thought Alexander was responsible for the broken royal engagement, he was poking around too much in the Netherlands, and he had become unbearably secretive and arrogant over Poland. And now this imposed delay. Was all this talk about liberalism, con-stitutionalism and God's rule on earth just a front? Were Alexander and his court in St Petersburg going to resort to arms?[3]

Castlereagh and Metternich tried to get an assurance that the Tsar would at least be in Vienna by 1 September. Alexander retorted by proposing to hold off the Congress until 1 October. But he did agree to having a meeting with the three other Powers in September to settle their affairs and put on a common front. Thus formal discussion of the shape of the new European order was going to be deferred for another three months, if not more. In an attempt to limit the uncer-tainties this caused, Castlereagh and his small team at the Foreign Office rapidly patched together a convention reconfirming the Four Powers' twenty-year commitment to the "repose of Europe," as had been initially agreed at Chaumont. And to give the convention teeth it was decided that each Power would maintain a force of seventy five thousand men, ostensibly to guard against further French aggression but actually proposed by Castlereagh – as must have been clear to all the foreign ministers then present in London – to secure a pledge from Alexander not to attempt to solve his problems with the sword.[4]

As a matter of fact, Alexander was not on the warpath. He spent most of the interval between his London visit and the Congress at Vienna in prayer, meditation, and readings of the Bible. From Calais he headed to the palace of Bruchsal in the Grand Duchy of Baden where his Empress, Elizabeth, had been living for a year with her parents. He arrived in the early hours of the morning, 6 July, in an open droschki, and stayed there for nearly a fortnight. The Baron vom Stein, another man of great plans, was there. So was Alexander's former preceptor, liberal counsellor, and friend, La Harpe.

One witness described the atmosphere at Bruchsal as festive, with tables laid every day for fifty, "a sumptuous family life [in which] the relationship between his wife and he seemed at its very best." As in Paris and London, Alexander paid attention to all those assembled, especially the pretty ladies. "The Emperor was at one moment here, another moment there, lively and chatting with everyone; but it was with Mademoiselle de Stourdza that he talked the longest, her bright conver-sation (with its subtle flatteries) appearing to captivate him most."[5]

Mademoiselle Roxandre Stourdza was slim, pretty, brown-eyed, and a mystic. She was also Empress Elizabeth's Greek lady-in-waiting. Her position in the Russian court had allowed her to develop a correspondence with a Latvian pietist who was becoming quite a cele-brity in 1814, the Baroness Julie von Krüdener – and it just so hap-pened that the baroness was in Baden that week. La Stourdza's sweet form and soul had also attracted the attention of the Grand Duke's Aulic Councillor,[6] Jung Stilling, a theosophist originally from Saxony who had been in his youth a great friend of Goethe's. He was a grey man now in his mid-seventies. One year's residence at Bruchsal had made the relationship flourish; between Stilling and Mademoiselle Stourdza was a concordance of souls, confirmed and sealed by secret compact.

For such were the times. The sort of mysticism Stilling practised had a wide following in Germany in these years. Whole networks had developed, based on rites, oaths, and occult ceremonies. Martinists, theosophists, and chiliasts frequently contracted mystical marriages between men and women that would permit them to commune, close or far from each other, through prayer and through the person of Christ, the Redeemer. Because the ways of the spirit were not those of everyday life, these marriages could include three, four, or even more people. Mademoiselle Stourdza and Jung Stilling had contracted that kind of marriage.

Alexander wanted to join it. On 9 July, Mademoiselle Stourdza introduced the Emperor to her spiritual husband and the following day the two men had a long private conversation. Stilling described it as something akin to a revelation. "The two days I have spent at Bruchsal," Stilling confided to a spiritual son-in-law of his in Bâle a few days later, "are in certain respects the most remarkable of my life." In the course of his interview on 10 July Alexander spoke of "the affairs of Europe, the different religious denominations, the spread of the Kingdom of God, and the near future; and then [he spoke of] the true practice of the Christian religion." Stilling said that Alexander was "a real Christian, in the strictest sense of the term." At one point Alexander had admitted, "I have committed many errors! But for two years, from the moment I began to read the Bible daily," – that was in August 1812 – "I have become another man." He raised his blue eyes to heaven.

The conversation turned to La Stourdza, her spirituality, and her mystical marriage. Stilling, very moved, confided that the two had indeed concluded an "eternal alliance so as to live for the Lord." There followed a long silence, finally interrupted by Alexander. "This alliance," ventured the Sovereign, moving forward in his seat, "we equally are going to perform it" – and he kissed the shaking old man.

That afternoon Alexander visited Mademoiselle Stourdza. "I saw Jung Stilling this morning," he said. "We explained ourselves as best we could in German and in French. I understood however that you have formed with him a bond of love and charity in God. It is indissoluble." Since his father's murder Alexander had always looked for the indissoluble, the rock of permanence; since the invasion of Russia he had found it in God. "I prayed him to receive me as a third member of this alliance, and we have touched hands on that. I wonder, would you also consent to this?" "Your Highness," replied Mademoiselle Stourdza, tears welling up in her eyes, "the bond already exists." She touched his hand.[7]

Roxandre de Stourdza,
the Tsarina's
lady-in-waiting, the
Tsar's mystical adviser
and spiritual wife

By 25 July, Alexander was back in St Petersburg. Those around him found him irritable and morose. He cancelled all festivals celebrating the return from his victory over the "Antichrist," he refused to talk about politics, international affairs, and the reform of his empire, though he appeared very upset over the lack of understanding in his Allies. The Russian Senate and the Holy Synod offered him the title *Blagoslovenitsch* – "Blessed of God." Alexander wrote to the Governor of St Petersburg, had all festivities in his honour stopped, and refused the title. "The events which have put an end to the bloody wars of Europe are the work of the Almighty," he remarked. "It is before Him that we must all prostrate ourselves. Let it be known, this is my unalterable resolution."[8]

That strange "trinitarian pact" of July 1814 – which would turn Jung Stilling, Mademoiselle Stourdza and, eventually, Baroness von Krüdener into a sort of phalanx of angels guarding Alexander's conscience – was to have a major influence on the course of Russian foreign policy over the coming months.

Thus Castlereagh's fears of Alexander's personal belligerence may well have been exaggerated. But, once the common enemy had been beaten, Pitt's old East-West alliance – between Britain, with her parliamentary system and popular press, and the Russian autocracy, tempered by assassination and governed by God – had obviously not the brightest future.

Jung Stilling, Aulic
Councillor to the
Grand Duke of Baden
and another of
Roxandre de Stourdza's
spiritual husbands

There were a lot of troubling signs. Through the spring and summer of 1814 the Foreign Office was flooded with dispatches from Europe, Africa, Asia, from some of the remotest corners on earth, that told of the strange activities of Russian secret agents, spies, and diplomats. The most worrying, for Britain, were the reports of Russia's abiding interest in the Netherlands. "Your lordship," wrote George Jackson, Britain's Minister in Berlin, to Castlereagh, "is doubtless informed of the very marked and studied attention paid by the Emperor Alexander, on his return from England, to the Sovereign Prince of the Netherlands and to the Dutch people at large." There was already talk that the jilted Prince William was to marry a Russian Grand Duchess. The Russians were also hoping to procure, through the Duke of Oldenburg, East Friesland, which neighboured the Netherlands, and to extend their possessions in the Baltic.[9]

It would have been consistent with the Pitt plan to answer these threats by building on the strength of the intermediary Powers that separated Russia from France. During the war, Castlereagh had considered the creation of a strong and independent Poland; Austria would have to be compensated in Italy and the Illyrian provinces, while Prussia would be offered territory in the Rhineland and Saxony. But, during his earlier trip to the continent, Castlereagh came to the conclusion that the project would never work because none of his three Allies would cede enough territory to forge a sufficiently

powerful Poland. A united Germany was another vague option. It
had been written into Pitt's original draft, but even in 1805 it seemed
an unlikely prospect. Well before the peace of 1814 it was clear that
the only intermediary Powers of substantial force were Austria and
Prussia. So Austria and Prussia had, as the expression went, to be
"satisfied."

For generations liberal, fair-minded historians would look back at
the peace settlements of 1814-15 and criticise Castlereagh for cyni-
cally presiding over the carving up of Europe without regard to
national identities. But Castlereagh had no choice. He faced a continent just emerging from over two decades of war. The last thing he
wanted was to encourage, as France had encouraged, nationalist
enthusiasms. Real peace was about power – its balance, and its cur-
tailment. "Europe no longer resembles what she was twenty years
ago," Napoleon's envoy to Châtillon, Caulaincourt, had warned the
Allies back in March. For sure, there could be no turning back. But
there was no question either of allowing a single power, whether
France or Russia, to dominate the continent under some crusading
national banner, for the result would be endless war. So Castlereagh
came back, again and again, to Pitt's policy, the old Whig policy, of
balancing. "The power of Great Britain to do good," he said,
"depends not merely on its resources but upon a sense of its impar-
tiality and the reconciling character of its influence. To be authori-
tative it must be impartial. To be impartial it must not be in exclusive
relations with any particular Court."10

It seemed unlikely that Austria would allow Prussia to have all
Saxony, that Prussia would let Austria lay her hands on Mainz, and
both Austria and Prussia appeared to be suspicious of the other's
intentions in Poland. The demands and counter-demands of the two
Powers tended to cancel each other out, which gave Britain leverage
in her self-appointed role of disinterested arbitrator.

But the rivalry was a destabilising fact in European politics too. In
the past, it had provided revolutionary France with the wedge she
needed to drive eastwards. What now of Holy Russia? Castlereagh's
machinery, as it stood in early August 1814, was clearly inadequate to
withstand a Russian drive westwards: Russia, at this time, occupied all
Poland, all Saxony, and even the Danish province of Holstein.

Of concern too were Prussia's intentions. She had withdrawn her
troops from the Belgic provinces without much grace. King Frederick
William, when in London, had shown an almost obsequious respect
for the conquering hero, the Tsar, and his sons had made fools of
themselves both in public and in the politically sensitive drawing
rooms of Warwick House.

On 8 August, Castlereagh asked the Prussian Chancellor, Prince
Carl von Hardenberg, around to St James's Square for a chat. After

only a few minutes it became clear to Castlereagh that Prussia had her own peculiar understanding of "a real and permanent balance of power in Europe." Hardenberg demanded Mainz and all of Saxony, and he said the left bank of the Rhine outside France should be split between Prussia and Austria with the exception of the Netherlands, which he thought would fit nicely into the as yet unformulated German Confederation by joining a "Burgundian Circle."

Within a week of his encounter with Hardenberg, and only four days prior to his departure to the continent, Castlereagh felt obliged to write a long dispatch to Lord Clancarty, the British Ambassador to the Hague, clarifying the British position on the Netherlands and Prussia's westward extension. He concentrated particularly on the confusion that had arisen over the newly incorporated Belgic provinces in the south. "The Dutch and British troops should occupy Liège, as being on the left of the Meuse," he asserted, "and should not evacuate the ancient Dutch territory on the *right bank*, including Maastricht." He argued that the latter territories had belonged to Holland "as it stood previous to 1792" and thus formed a part of "his Royal Highness's ancient dominions." When the Allies agreed on making the Meuse the frontier of the new Kingdom of the Netherlands they "never meant to derogate from this principle."[11]

Castlereagh was drawing lines, and this time not with the purpose of protecting the Allies from France.

Forced moderation at Paris

Tolstoy, looking back half a century to the international movements of this time, spoke of history as a great ocean seething in its depths: "Coalitions of men came together and separated again; the causes that would bring about the formation and the dissolution of empires and the displacement of peoples were in the course of preparation." The novelist probed the undercurrents: "The fundamental and essential point of European events at the beginning of the present century is the militant mass movement of European peoples from west to east and then from east to west." This was hardly the way Castlereagh would have phrased it, but it was his realisation of that flow and ebb of power across Europe's northern plains which had led him to join with Metternich and impose the moderate Peace of Paris in May. It was a conditioned moderation, born out of necessity, not sympathy for the beaten enemy. It was more pressing, Castlereagh knew, to balance the different interests of the Allies than to crush the enemy and thus satisfy opinion back home.[12]

The tone of the peace had been set the day Alexander led the Allied armies into Paris, on 31 March. A proclamation had been published announcing the Allied Sovereigns' intention no longer to treat with

Napoleon "nor with any of his family," but adding that they would "respect the integrity of ancient France, as it existed under its legitimate Kings." Furthermore, it was stated that the Allies "may even do more" because "they profess it as a principle, that, for the happiness of Europe, France must be great and strong."[13]

This proclamation had been posted all over Paris and its text was published in both French and foreign newspapers. But, though it had been signed by Alexander, its real author was Talleyrand, Napoleon's former Foreign Minister who was now setting himself up at the head of France's Provisional Government. Talleyrand knew how divided the Allies were. Because of years of experience, Talleyrand also knew the issues that separated them; he knew of the problems of Poland, Saxony, and the Netherlands, and, with the ebb and flow of power, he could make a sure bet that some of the Allies would welcome a France "great and strong."[14]

They did. The terms accorded to France in the treaty that May must be among the most generous ever granted to an aggressor state once defeated and occupied. Beyond her "ancient frontiers," as they stood on 1 November 1792, France kept around 450 square kilometres along her eastern frontiers, the most significant addition being Savoy in the south-east. The Saarland, an item of contention a hundred years later, was included in the new French kingdom. So were several strategic points along the Belgian border. Colonies captured since 1792 were returned to their original owners, except Santo Domingo, St Lucia, Tobago, and "the Isle of France [Mauritius] and its dependencies [Rodrigues and the Seychelles]." Incredibly, France was asked to pay no reparations, a fact that caused much protest in Britain. "It will be hard, if France is to pay nothing for the destruction of Europe, and we are to pay all for saving her," snarled one MP at Westminster.[15]

The occupation didn't last long. By the end of July, only two months after the signature of the treaty, the only foreign troops left in France were a few sick Russians who were sent to the hospital at Bicêtre, just outside Paris. Castlereagh's principal concern had been how to evacuate tens of thousands of British troops still camped in the south-west of France without upsetting the sensibilities of the "host country." He asked Earl Bathurst, the Minister of War and of Colonies, to arrange for the removal of all infantry by ship because a long march "might create observation, the protracted presence of foreign troops being a topic amongst the discontented." Major-General Henry Fane, in the months of June and July, led four columns of British cavalry by stages across France from Bordeaux, to Poitiers, Tours, Chartres, Houdan, Mantes, Abbeville, and Boulogne. From there the victorious troops – veterans of the Peninsular campaign – crossed to England to face half-pay, dismissal, unemployment and poverty. "The conduct of the troops during their long march through France has been for the most part remarkably good," Major-General Fane reported to Wellington. "We were so fortunate as not to have occasion to leave a single sick man behind us."[16]

The evening Talleyrand signed the treaty he wrote to his mistress, the duchesse de Courlande, "I have finished my peace with the four great Powers." Talleyrand, like Castlereagh, would always like to add a possessive "my" to these grand international accords. "At four o'clock the peace was signed. It is very good and done on a footing of greatest equality and it is rather noble, though France is still covered with foreigners. My friends, with you at their head, should be happy with me, who loves you with all my soul." Talleyrand and his friends had every reason to be happy.[17]

Castlereagh was quite pleased too – he was adding a new cog to his engine. But problems were developing. Castlereagh already knew he faced some bitter opposition at home. How was he going to explain these lenient terms to his countrymen? The machinery was getting very complicated and Castlereagh's convoluted explanations hardly made good copy in the press. If his defence of the Treaty in Parliament went well that was because, in June, nobody was very interested in the Treaty; the reigning obsession at the time was in the royal comic opera put on by the Prince Regent, his wife, and daughter. But that would not last forever. The temper of the political debate was going to change. And change rapidly.

Castlereagh was perhaps the first major diplomat in history to face "public opinion," as it was now just beginning to be known. None of his colleagues on the continent had to worry about it. Even in Britain, if one takes newspaper readership as a measure, it was nothing like it would be for the next generation. The radical journalism of Cobbett and Wooler had not yet taken off and circulation was small – *The Times* sold about seven thousand copies daily. Nonetheless, more than seven thousand people would have been aware of what was in *The Times*. Many people would read the same copy of a newspaper, or they would hear it in the pubs being read aloud, or even on the streets. The end of the war and the excitement of the royal scandals did a lot to develop British "public opinion;" it was now a part of history's seething undercurrent.[18]

Because it was new, "public opinion" was even less predictable than it is today. No politician could have possibly foreseen how, in a matter of weeks, it would turn like a weathervane, once the problems of the royal family were set aside, to the issue of the Treaty and Britain's place in Europe.

The new campaign in the press started under conditions that would be any journalist's dream. The network for the new cause had already been laid. The issue was a fine, emotive, moral one; its proponents could play as angels and cast their opponents as devils. Moreover, they could say that history was on the side of the angels; no one could argue that the campaign was not for progress and human betterment – even Jane Austen's provincial novels, oblivious of war, revolution, and the rights of citizens, could not ignore this great world scandal. The problem was slavery.

Britain had abolished the slave trade – but not slavery in her colonies – in 1807. The Felony Act of 1811 had made the legislation work by promising slavers long prison sentences and deportation to Botany Bay. A few exemplary cases were brought to court and the trade stopped dead in its tracks as far as Britain were concerned. The United States abolished *the trade* in 1808. Slavery itself had been abolished in France and in her colonies during the Terror of 1794, but, after the rebellion in Haiti and fears of destruction of the sugar economy of the French West Indies, Napoleon restored slavery in the colonies in 1802. For the slave traders of Nantes and Bordeaux, the continental blockade proved, in fact, a more effective obstacle than legal abolition; but with the peace of 1814 they had their hopes – and their friends in the French parliament. The only European country outside Britain to have formally abolished the trade was Denmark.

By terms of the Treaty of Paris, His Most Christian Majesty concurred "without reserve in the sentiments of His Britannic Majesty with respect to a description of traffic *repugnant to the principles of natural justice and of the enlightened age in which we live.*" Natural justice and enlightenment: it was quite a concession to win from Louis, by Grace of God, King of France and of Navarre; it was a most extraordinary formula for the signatories of the treaty, made "in the Name of the Most Holy and undivided Trinity." But there it was for a civilised world to admire. His Most Christian Majesty, Louis, agreed "to unite all his efforts to those of His Britannic Majesty, at the approaching Congress, to induce all the Powers of Christendom to decree the abolition of the Slave Trade, so that the said trade shall cease universally, as it shall cease definitively, under any circumstances, on the part of the French government, in the course of five years."

In other words, France would be free to practise the slave trade for another five years.

This was not enough to satisfy British public opinion. How could Castlereagh explain that the slave trade was going to be re-opened for colonies that his government was willingly returning to France? William Wilberforce, before he had even seen the Treaty's text, set the mood of the campaign by commenting in parliament, "The devil is come upon the earth with great power." Forget Europe, forget the peace, this was a greater moral issue than even the Regent and his wife. The colonies were due to be handed over six months after the signature of the Treaty, in November, the very moment the "season" of slave-trading customarily began.

"This question is become really an embarrassment to us here," Castlereagh wrote to Talleyrand on 16 July; "I must entreat your Highness, cordially and confidentially to lend yourself to the means of reconciling national feelings on both sides." He added for emphasis, "I must earnestly press you to assist in reconciling *me* with my nation in this instance." The conqueror was beseeching the conquered.[19]

Castlereagh had been caught unprepared for the public uproar; he had never seen anything like it. "The nation is bent upon this object," he wrote to the Ambassador at Madrid. "I believe there is hardly a village that has not met and petitioned upon it; both Houses of Parliament are pledged to press it; and the Ministers must make it the basis of their policy." Wellington, who arrived in Britain in July, was astounded at what he discovered. He also wrote a letter to the Ambassador at Madrid – for the Ambassador was his brother – warning him that the country was ready to go to war over the issue. "I was not aware till I had been some time here," he said, "of the degree of frenzy existing here about the slave trade."[20]

It was at this point that Talleyrand made a move toward Britain.

Talleyrand applies for an alliance

Talleyrand was not the slightest bit interested in the slave trade. In the negotiations over the treaty in May he had justified the five-year delay on abolition by telling Castlereagh, "Opinions rooted in long custom do not give way at the first blow. They will give way to reason only if it is supported by experience, and certainly the experience of five years in such a matter must appear very short." In fact, there was no such thing as a public opinion on the slave trade in France; the only people who had any thoughts at all on the matter were the traders themselves, as Wellington would point out: "There is no general knowledge, and therefore no general opinion, in France upon the slave trade."[21]

When, in early August, Talleyrand took up his diplomatic initiative he put the matter of slaves aside and came back to the old issues, the continental issues, that had so absorbed Castlereagh during his last visit: Poland, northern Germany, the Netherlands and Italy, and the position of the Four Powers on these.

The critical matter here was a breach that had recently occurred between Talleyrand and his old friend Emperor Alexander. On his departure from Paris for London in early June, Alexander had refused to receive Talleyrand on the grounds that he had failed to establish a liberal constitution in France and had, instead, lent his support to Bourbon absolutism.

Talleyrand seems to have been genuinely chagrined, for on 13 June he wrote a long letter to the Tsar pouring out praise for the Russian Sovereign's "glory," his "beautiful destiny," his "magnanimous" projects – "if I have followed you in your noble career, do not deprive me of my reward; I demand it from the hero of my imagination and, I dare add, of my heart." He pleaded with the Tsar to have patience ("The Emperor of Russia is a little pressed by time," he remarked to his mistress): "Good Frenchman that I am, let me ask you in the words of the old French expression to allow us to recuperate the ancient *accoutumance* [addiction, habit] of love for our kings; it is not for you to refuse to understand the influence of this sentiment on a great nation." But Talleyrand's *accoutumance* of loving Alexander was broken for good; he discovered that once Napoleon was gone he no longer needed Alexander, just as Alexander recognised Talleyrand was of no more use for his own world projects. Within weeks, love for the liberating Sovereign had turned bitter.[22]

At the beginning of August, as the new abolitionist campaign raged in England, he had a series of conversations with Britain's temporary Minister to Paris, Sir Charles Stuart. He said he was worried about Russia, her influence "through the extension of the territory belonging to the Duke of Oldenburg on the frontiers of Holland," about her "weight in the affairs of the North of Germany," about her plans for "the establishment of a Polish kingdom." On this last crucial point Talleyrand "thought that the question had been lightly considered by the Emperor of Russia, whose mode of viewing Polish affairs was the greatest proof of youth manifested by that Sovereign during his stay in France." Well might Alexander preach the doctrine of liberalism to old Talleyrand; yet, as Stuart was informed, one thing was clear to the French government: "A Russian force of nearly 200,000 men continues in the Duchy of Warsaw."[23]

Talleyrand warned Stuart that Austria was a power to worry about too, and he suggested Britain should not rely so much on her. "Active preparations were continued in the military department at Vienna" – despite the known state of Austria's finances – "which indicated the prospect of new troubles arising out of the negotiation about to commence." Austria had her own plans for Italy, while in Brussels "the Austrian connection had raised a party amongst the clergy which was daily growing more numerous."

Talleyrand made no mention of Prussia. He hardly needed to; he had met Prince von Hardenberg in Paris and knew the kind of territorial demands Prussia was making.

Having demonstrated the inadequacy of Britain's three Allies, Talleyrand drew the obvious conclusion: "He wants Britain to join France at Vienna," reported Stuart. On the issue of Russia's infiltration into the affairs of northern Germany, "it is alike the desire of

France and Great Britain that she should be excluded." On the issue of Poland, France had "formerly laid down" a system "for excluding Russia from all interference in the politics of Europe"; it was a system that should interest Britain as well. Talleyrand expressed deep concern about the delay of the Congress and Alexander's return to St Petersburg where he was sure the Emperor would attempt to convert his court to his own "inexpedient" schemes. As far as Talleyrand was concerned the best solution was to maintain "the old division" – that is, the late eighteenth-century partition of Poland among Prussia, Austria, and Russia – for this formed "an essential part of the politics of Europe." He explained that "the establishment of a Polish kingdom, however inconsiderable, was so dangerous to other States, that he had no hesitation in abiding by the old arrangement, which he considered to be infinitely better calculated for the preservation of general tranquillity." That was the word he kept returning to. "The efforts of both France and England must be equally directed to the maintenance of tranquillity."

They had common interests in Germany, they had common interests in Poland, and apparently they had common interests in Italy as well. Talleyrand wanted to add Sardinia and Genoa to Piedmont, and he didn't want the Austrians in there; that had been exactly Pitt's idea of a "barrier state." And who was that Sovereign down in Naples? King Joachim Napoleon, alias Murat, the son of an innkeeper, Bonaparte's brother-in-law. With Napoleon in Elba? Talleyrand wanted Murat out and the Bourbon candidate, Ferdinand IV, returned. Castlereagh couldn't have agreed more. Talleyrand didn't want to encourage Italian nationalism, nor did Castlereagh.

Talleyrand proposed that France and Britain act as "joint mediators." To arrange this he invited Castlereagh to stop off in Paris before travelling to Vienna; a London-Paris link, he argued, "held out the most favourable prospect of a satisfactory result terminating the most important negotiation which Europe had ever witnessed."

As a further overture, the French government sent the King's younger nephew, the duc de Berry – short, stocky, his head crammed down into his shoulders and, after years of English claret and exile, his face ruddy, but at thirty-six still exuberant and quite likeable – on a mission to enjoy the fireworks in London on the Prince Regent's birthday, 12 August. It was hoped that the Prince Regent would then return with him to enjoy the fireworks in Paris on King Louis' festival day, 25 August.[24]

As Calais awaited Berry's arrival, the Duchess of Devonshire, the Regent's old gambling friend, sailed in aboard a British frigate. British and French cannon sounded out a salute. Three deputies from the United States, on their way to negotiate at Ghent a peace with Britain, also happened to arrive at the same time; they were totally ignored.[25]

Berry reviewed the troops in Calais, spent a night in the largest suite of the Hôtel Desaint, and on the morning of 10 August crossed the Channel to England.[26]

There was absolutely no question of the Regent visiting France; it would have required parliamentary approval, and neither the government nor parliament had, after the row and scandals of June, any desire to let the First Gentleman of Europe out of England.

Berry attended the birthday celebrations at Frogmore – the fireworks display was rather subdued – and on Sunday morning, 14 August, he paid a visit to the Foreign Secretary.

Castlereagh was planning to be on the boat for Holland the following Tuesday and it was a hectic weekend. He spent most of it with his private secretary, Joseph Planta, going over a pile of dispatches, planning his trip, and trying to decide what to do about this new French initiative. That Sunday night, he wrote to his closest associate in matters of foreign policy, the Duke of Wellington, who had just left for the Netherlands prior to taking up his new post as Ambassador to Paris. "I have seen the Duc de Berry this morning," reported Castlereagh. "His visit is intended to remove any impression of alienation, and to second Talleyrand's overture." Berry had appeared disturbed at the idea that the Four Allies were planning on a preliminary meeting prior to the formal opening of the Congress at Vienna. This troubled Castlereagh, because he didn't want the French to feel excluded; "It may render a short visit to Paris possibly the more advisable," he said. Castlereagh asked Wellington what he thought of the idea of a Paris visit.[27]

It was clear that Talleyrand had put a finger on "common interests" in northern Europe and in Italy, but Castlereagh was unwilling to destabilise an alliance system which Britain had been seeking for more than a decade by formalising ties with her old enemy. That same weekend he had written to Stuart to say that Talleyrand "must not expect us to separate from our old connections, in the midst of our concert." In particular, "he must not expect me to depart from any engagement to meet my former colleagues at Vienna about the 10th of September," prior to any intervention by Talleyrand or any other power in Europe.

Castlereagh planned to be in Vienna, then, on 10 September, and he recommended Talleyrand to get there on the 25th; the Emperor of Russia was going to arrive on the 27th, and "we should then have time to discuss the more difficult matters previous to the assembly of the Congress on the 1st of October, having previously methodised the less complicated parts of the arrangement." ("Methodising" was Castlereagh's term for defining diplomatic procedure.) As for the possible earlier encounter with Talleyrand, he wrote to Wellington "forty-eight hours is the utmost I should think it advisable to remain at Paris, under present circumstances."[28]

Thus, despite all the complications that had emerged since the signature of the Paris treaty, Castlereagh, incredibly, thought he could get the Paris meeting done, the "methodising" of the "less complicated parts" between the Four Powers finished, and the whole Vienna settlement completed in two months. But then, no international negotiation had ever been conducted on this scale before, and one can hardly blame Castlereagh for his naivety.

In Brussels Castlereagh would receive from Wellington the recommendation he wanted. "The situation of affairs in the world will naturally constitute England and France as arbitrators at the Congress, if these Powers *understand* each other; and such an understanding may preserve the general peace," wrote the Duke from Mons, where he was inspecting the military defences of the plains in the Belgic provinces. But the situation in Paris was so delicate, argued the Duke, that "nobody can do for you as well as you can do for yourself."[29]

Castlereagh thus decided to make a two-day visit to Paris.

As his frigate sailed down the Thames estuary and out across the German Ocean, Castlereagh, scribbling at a tiny cabin table, might have thought for a moment that the continent to which he was heading was not, in fact, a continent at all. It was a huge peninsula jutting out westwards from the real continent of Asia. It had, vaguely, the figure of a sad old woman bent in prayer, her head bowed in Catholic Spain, a ricked shoulder in Brittany, the line of her aching back tracing the plains from the *bocages* of Normandy, across the Netherlands, onwards through Germany and Poland, to end in the steppes of Alexander's secret, hidden Russia. In the last two decades of war, this odd shaped peninsula had brought the principal foes, Britain and France, into contact in many areas far from their own shores. Britain used the seas to gain access to the interior, the Baltic to the north and the Mediterranean to the south presenting possibilities that would never had been open were Europe a real continent. France responded by pushing her frontiers upwards along the German back and creating those curious sounding departments of the French Empire: Lys, Escaut, Bouches-de-la-Meuse, Bouches-de-l'Yssel, Frise, Ems-Occidental, Ems-Oriental, Ems-Supérieur, Bouches-du-Weser, Bouches-de-l'Elbe. And down through the arm of Italy: Alpes-Maritimes, Montenotte, Gênes, Appenins, Méditerranée, Ombronne, Tibre.

They had all gone now; France was even seeking an alliance with her old enemy. The last time he had been in Paris, Castlereagh, in a letter to Lord William Bentinck in Sicily, had written of "a great moral change coming on in Europe [where] the principles of freedom are in full operation." He warned that "the transition may be too sudden to ripen into anything likely to make the world better or happier." Castlereagh wanted to slow down the continual flow and ebb of power of the last twenty years, and to that end followed his policy of barrier states, the most ambitious of which was the new United Kingdom of the Netherlands.[30]

That is where he landed, in the Netherlands, in the middle of Europe's back.

Wellington inspects the plains

The Duke of Wellington was already on the plains. He had celebrated the Regent's birthday in Brussels where, by August, a large community of the English leisured classes with their trains of servants, cooks, flunkeys, and suitors had come to appreciate the low costs of living on the continent and enjoy life at the new court, that of William, the former Hereditary Prince of Orange, now the Crown Prince of the Netherlands. Charlotte's former fiancé was very happy in his new surroundings because they reminded him so much of those he had left behind in Britain; as Lady Caroline Capel put it, he had everything he wanted, "a little snug *English* Party." Plenty of time in the future, thought William, to worry about what to do with those "Idiots the Belgians."[31]

In fact, as he told both Clancarty and Wellington, he still held out hopes that Charlotte would change her mind, thus giving his court an even more English air. He rigorously denied the rumours that plans were afoot to marry a Russian princess and he repeated several times that he was not going to accept an invitation to visit St Petersburg. Wellington's reports to London were reassuring: the Prince, he said, "was remarkably well received everywhere, and I think the people in general well inclined to the House of Orange."[32]

The ball on 12 August boosted the confidence, already strong, of the English residents in Brussels. Wellington was welcomed as a hero. The dais at the head of the ballroom was draped in damasks of blue and silver, and a white plaster goddess of Peace gazed over it.[33]

The following week, Wellington set out with the Crown Prince to inspect the frontiers south and west of Brussels, for it was Britain's intention to show, prior to the Congress in Vienna, that she was "prepared to defend" the United Netherlands.

Though he had made his name in the mountains and hills of Iberia, Wellington was really a man of the plains. He was born in the same year, the same island, and the same Protestant Ascendancy as Castlereagh, though the exact date of his birth and even its place are matters of some dispute. What is undisputed is that 1769 brought into the world three of the principal players in the events of 1814-15: Wellington entered in March, April, or May (probably 1 May),

Castlereagh on 18 June, and Napoleon on 15 August, Assumption Day. But Wellington had deeper roots than Castlereagh; they dug down six Irish centuries, through a dozen generations of Wellesleys, Wesleys, Colleys, Cooleys and Cowlys, Knights of the Pale, "good Englishe possessioners," faithful retainers to their Sovereign in London, always married into the ruling caste, and forever alienated from the native inhabitants. In the 1720s the family acquired an estate in the "flat country," the bogs of Dangan, County Meath, behind Dublin. Indeed, the country was so flat that Wellington's grandfather, Richard Wesley, decided on a programme of landscaping, building hills, digging dales, cutting out trenches for canals and basins for lakes; he constructed piazzas, arches and obelisks on the hills, and, by the lake, "a regular fort" with forty-eight cannon, which fired salutes on family birthdays. It was all very pretty but did nothing to improve the family's fortune.[34]

Wellington's father, Garret Wesley, was a child prodigy, an extraordinary musician, the composer of madrigals, catches and glees, and, before he was thirty, Professor of Music at Trinity, Dublin. Garret also inherited Richard's obsessions with landscaping, building acre upon acre of ornamental waterways. When the great musician died in 1781, leaving a widow with six children, the financial situation of the Wesleys had become distressing.

All the children developed useful, money-making talents with the exception of the fourth child and third son, Arthur, the future Duke of Wellington. John Armytage, who knew Arthur when he was being tutored at the age of sixteen in that city of impoverished British aristocrats, Brussels, noted in his journal that Arthur was a possessor of exceptional musical skill but he had no other "species of talent" whatever.

Dreamy, idle, shy, "lounging" young Arthur Wesley was withdrawn from Eton after only three years and sent to a tutor in Brighton, then to another tutor in Brussels and finally to the Royal Academy of Equitation at Angers, which was essentially a finishing school for aristocrats whose ambitions were limited to riding, fencing and dancing. His English tutor at Angers remembered Arthur as sickly and alone, spending most of his time on a sofa playing with a white terrier.

His eldest brother, Richard, now the Second Earl of Mornington, found him a place in the army – for the Irish Ascendancy a depository for weaker younger brothers – by buying promotions at suitable moments. With war approaching, it was like speculating in stock; in the year hostilities broke out with France, 1793, Arthur, without any formal military training, advanced from captain in the 18th Light Dragoons, to major and then lieutenant-colonel in the 33rd Foot. He also fell in love with Kitty Pakenham, proposed, and was turned down.

It seems to have been the greatest humiliation of his life. Rejection became one of the leitmotivs of the stark and obscure years that followed. His response to the Pakenham family's rejection was his own rejection of his first twenty years. He rejected his youth, he rejected his "lounging," he rejected his music: that summer he burnt his violin. His language became abrupt, economic, to the point; there is no descriptive prose in Wellington's letters, no poetic turn of the phrase, no hesitation, few qualifications, just the facts and a brief statement of opinion. A former lover of poetry, he expunged poetry from all he wrote and all he said. His orders on the battle field were, as one captain in the Peninsular War described them, "so decided, so manly."

Wellington did, eventually, marry his Kitty. He was by then thirty-seven, she was thirty-four. He proposed to her in a letter, not having seen her for eleven years, and when she was eventually presented to him in Dublin by her maiden aunt he was visibly shaken. "She has grown ugly, by Jove!" he muttered to his brother Gerald, the clergyman, who was there to marry them – unlike the Prince Regent, Wellington would not have asked for a brandy because, since burning his violin, he rejected heavy drinks.

Wellington rejected sentiment, he rejected the domestic comforts of life (which made him so very different from Castlereagh, who hid himself in them). His real "family" was not Kitty and their two sons, whom he left behind in England, but the general's staff where he surrounded himself with the kind of brilliant young aristocrats that he would have liked to have been himself. Among those of his military "family" was a brother-in-law, Ned Pakenham, who seems to have been the first person to describe Wellington as an "Iron man."[35]

Austere, distant, as inflexible in his demands on others as he was on himself, he fulfilled in so many ways the image of an "Iron man." It was what made him so feared and yet so popular with his troops. "Methinks it is something to have seen that wonderful man even do so commonplace a thing as lift his hat to another officer in the battlefield," said Rifleman Harris as he recalled the Battle of Vimiero of 1808. Johnny Kincaid, also of the Rifles, was in the northern army in April 1811 when Wellington entered Spain to give chase to Massena: "We would rather see his long nose in the fight," affirmed Kincaid, "than a reinforcement of ten thousand men any day." In June 1813, young Captain Arthur Kennedy of the 18th Hussars got a glimpse of Wellington in his grey frock coat firing out manly orders at Vitoria "with the sangfroid of an indifferent spectator."

Yet no man is made of iron. After the capture of Badajoz in April 1812, at the cost of near five thousand men, he broke down and wept – "Good God, what is the matter?" exclaimed General Sir Thomas Picton, astonished by his tears. For days after Vitoria, his greatest victory of the Peninsular campaign, he was in a state of deep melancholy.

Son of a composer, himself a talented violinist, Wellington had almost certainly not forgotten all his music. Great operas would move him – and so would great female opera singers. "Wellington with a fiddle, it is hard to imagine!" comments a historian.[36] Yet one must impose oneself on a violin, which has no notes, no frets on its handle; the emotive effect of its music is the product of pure discipline. Wellington possessed a musical culture. If there is one word in Wellington's vocabulary which best summarises the man it is "regularity." Wellington would attempt to run his army, his "family," and his life with the regularity of a metronome. He could introduce pause, trill, and counterpoint in a way that would astonish an enemy. He had a temper that would rise from silence in a startling crescendo, a wit that was expressed in staccato, and melancholy that fell to the lowest tones in the score; all timed to the regular beat of that ticking inner metronome.

Of all the crucial components of his childhood that Wellington tossed out of his adult life, the most wholesale rejection was not his music but his homeland, Ireland. It makes another contrast to Castlereagh. Castlereagh wanted to incorporate, Wellington wanted to reject. As a child he had been dominated by two brilliant elder brothers, as a youth he had been refused marriage, as a young MP to the Dublin parliament he faced failure, humiliation and exclusion. "Because a man is born in a stable," he once famously remarked, "that does not make him a horse." Wellington never, in his adult life, expressed a word of nostalgia for Ireland. He never returned to the country after he resigned his post as Secretary for Ireland in 1809.

Irishmen may have wanted to hang Castlereagh, but Castlereagh never renounced his roots; when he was granted the title of Viscount he adopted the name of the Ulster town at the head of Strangford Lough. When Wellington was named Viscount, following his victory at Talavera in 1809, he left it to his elder brother William – "after ransacking the Peerage and examining the map" – to pick a village in Somerset, neighbouring Welleslie. His wife Kitty did not like it. "Wellington," she reflected in her diary on being given the news of her new name, "I do not like for it recalls nothing."

So much rejection, so much discipline, so much "iron" had created a very complicated man of forty-five. Talleyrand, on meeting Wellington (who had just been named Duke) for the first time in Paris in May 1814, recognised this immediately: "Wellington is the most curious character of our time," he dashed off in a note to the duchesse de Courlande.[37]

Of course the Iron Duke would never have been Iron – the Great Man in History would never have been Great – without the help of others, a lot of others. The distant, classical military hero emerged only late in the war from a cobweb of family and political connections. In particular, three of his brothers, Richard, Henry, and, to a lesser extent, William, by cultivating relationships with the leading British politicians of the day, provided Wellington with the sort of combination of military and political power that no commander, save Napoleon himself, possessed. It was a fantastic system that the family had developed early on in India, where they put an empire together. Richard, the eldest, had been named Governor-General in 1798 (that was when the family changed their name from "Wesley" to the older Somerset form of "Wellesley"); Henry, the youngest, became his secretary. As for Arthur, he not only led the family's campaign of conquest into Mysore and the Maratha lands, but he also developed the diplomacy that brought the subsequent peace. Once again, in Portugal and Spain, the prosecution of the war and the negotiations for the alliances that supported it were very much a family affair – so much so that one historian has called the period 1808-12 the "Wellesley Era."[38] Richard was the Foreign Secretary in London for most of this period, William, the second brother, was Secretary to the Lords of the Admiralty, and Henry was Ambassador to the Spanish government exiled in Cádiz.[39]

Critical support was provided, at the beginning and at the end of the "Wellesley Era," by Viscount Castlereagh. Indeed, for all their personal differences, it is striking how the policies of the Wellesleys and of Castlereagh so neatly complemented one another. The famous Pitt Plan was in tatters by 1809, and Castlereagh knew that the only way to reconstruct the engine was to launch a robust military thrust into the head of Europe, the Iberian peninsula, thus encouraging other former Allies to rise once more against Napoleon. The Wellesleys thought just the same. Arthur drafted a memorandum in March 1809 showing how this could be done. Castlereagh's efforts to get the Cabinet to support the plan turned into a battle; he won the command of the British expeditionary force for Arthur but was thrown out of office that summer following a duel with his rival, George Canning. Arthur waged in Portugal both a political and military campaign. His brother Richard, now Lord Wellesley, became Foreign Secretary and carried on Castlereagh's campaign in London: "It must never be forgotten that in fighting the cause of Spain, we are struggling for the last hope of continental Europe," he wrote. But Brougham, Whitbread, and the Whigs led a powerful parliamentary opposition to Britain's continental involvements, and Spencer Perceval's government was weak and indecisive. The Wellesleys were increasingly isolated and were only able to maintain their policy – Pitt's policy, Castlereagh's policy – through Arthur's successes on the field, Henry's complicated negotiations in Spain, and Richard's lonely efforts in the Foreign Office.

Arthur Wellesley, the Duke of Wellington – a leading diplomat and
politician as well as a soldier

There is something rather tragic about Richard's story. As his star sank and dipped below the horizon, that of his younger brother Arthur's rose. He lost office in 1812, just as the tide of power in Europe began to turn; he would be rejected by his brothers, and has been held in contempt by most historians ever since. He was certainly no saint – "I wish that Wellesley was castrated," Arthur said in a letter to William. "It is lamentable to see Talents & character & advantages such as he possesses thrown away upon Whoring."[40] Richard was arrogant, autocratic, self-indulgent, and an impossible colleague in government (he refused to attend most Cabinet meetings). Yet for thirty years he had been the father figure of his family, and for three crucial years he defended in government a policy that would turn Arthur into the Iron Duke of Wellington. Castlereagh was his successor.

Castlereagh was unable to join Wellington in the Netherlands, for Wellington had to hurry on to prepare for the Foreign Secretary's reception in Paris. That left the Duke just one week to inspect the frontiers.

Castlereagh had borrowed his concept of "barrier states" from Pitt; Wellington had his own ideas about drawing lines to oppose an enemy's flow. He had seen his musical father make hills out of plains; his experience on the field in India and in Portugal and Spain had transformed those childhood instincts for the lie of the land into the fine art of topography. That was the origin of his inevitable comment whenever a problem arose: "I will get upon my Horse and take a look."[41]

This is precisely what he did in the Netherlands. Riding out at dawn and halting at sunset, Wellington, with Colonels Chapman and Pasley of the Engineers, and Colonel Smyth (who reported directly to the commander of the Allied armies in Belgium, Lord Lynedoch), travelled the plains south of Brussels between 14 and 20 August 1814. In a dawning's mist, this tiny group would have been seen from a distance as an inconsequential dot on a land scribbled in the signatures of men and epochs, the straight Belgian roads drawn across the stubbled rye fields, punctuated now and than by houses, hamlets, and high stone farm walls.

"The face of the country is generally open, and affords no feature upon which reliance can be placed to establish any defensive system," Wellington wrote in his report to Bathurst the following month. He emphasised the vital role the United Netherlands played as "a bulwark to Europe" and as a "secure communication with England and the north of Germany." He argued that "strong places are but little useful" in a flat country such as this, and used the example of the outflanking operations of the French in 1792-4 as proof; he should know, for they were his first unhappy experiences in military action. He warned that "in these provinces no position can be taken with an army which is not liable to be turned."

There were, however, some "good positions" for an army to make a stand, such as at La Trinité, or at Renaix, or the several points around Mons, or "the high grounds about Blaton"; there were some hills above Nivelle that deserved consideration, and between Nivelle and Binch "there are many advantageous positions." And finally, immediately south of the little town of Waterloo, "the entrance of the *forêt de* Soignies, by the high road which leads to Brussels from Binch, Charleroi, and Namur, would, if worked upon, afford others."[42]

What Wellington saw in Paris

In Paris, both Wellington and Castlereagh were going to encounter directly the problems statesmen on the continent faced. Continental politics were more open-ended than in Britain, the divisions were not so clear, the choices were not as obvious, the frontiers blurred: compromise always demanded more compromise, old conflicts bred new conflicts. Political description was complex, positions were hard to define. The flow and ebb of power could not be reduced to a simple metaphor – to the restful and detached concept of Castlereagh's mechanical "balance" or Wellington's musical "regularity." Whose side were you on? What did you stand for? Your life was at stake.

British politicians would often complain that their counterparts on the continent were devious and secretive, but that was because the continental politicians could not always see for themselves where the lines of power were next to be drawn. They were obliged to keep their options open, they could not afford the luxury of an island's transparent way of thinking. In France in particular, clarity in politics took second place to the problem of how to hold together a nation so recently defeated in war.

It was an odd spirit, that spirit of defeat in 1814. Wellington and Castlereagh were to arrive in a city in the full swing of a great popular celebration. Thursday, 25 August, was the Fête of Saint-Louis. The celebration lasted right through the weekend, culminating on Monday when the King and his family led a short procession from the Tuileries Palace, down the quays to the Hôtel de Ville – a route lined with the memories of a Christian millennium, and a symbol of royalty's commitment to the people – for a grand banquet in the gilded Salle Saint-Jean. For five days, crowds milled round the central quarters of Paris. They thronged the quays, they wandered down the gravelled alleys among the urns, the statues and the thin taper trees of the Tuileries Gardens which, like the long brown palace at the end, were illuminated after sunset.[43]

Englishmen who were there were astonished at the light-headedness of these crowds of Parisians, their apparent indifference to events. They seemed to lack what John Scott, editor of the weekly *Champion*, called "the violence of public curiosity and interest" which you found back in England. A couple of murders in some dark alley in London could create agitation "all over the United Kingdom"; so just imagine "how our tongues would have run for years relative to the capture of London, the subversion of the government, and what is more interesting still, the bivouacking of thousands of Cossacks in Hyde Park and the adjacent fields."[44]

In truth, there was nothing that successfully gathered together popular attitudes and transformed them into print, as in London. After fifteen years of Bonaparte, nothing resembled a "public opinion"; the press had been stifled and parliament smothered. The political feelings of the population in that wet summer of 1814, whether in Paris or in the provinces, would always be something of a mystery. The only reasonable certainty was that, outside the army (not an insignificant minority), most Frenchmen, and particularly the Parisians, welcomed the peace. Chateaubriand's assessment of popular thought was probably right: "The immense majority of the French were... filled with joy, but this majority was not *legitimist* in the narrow sense of the word, as is applied to the inflexible partisans of the old monarchy... It was the men of the Republic and the Empire who saluted with enthusiasm the Restoration." These republican and imperial men, said Chateaubriand, were, in 1814, more royalist than the King.[45]

The people showed a lot of good will toward their corpulent King. When he set out in his coach on the eve of St-Louis, for a short trip around the new boulevards there was more cheering than during his entry into Paris in May. Later the same day he wobbled out onto the palace terrace and received similar applause from the crowds in the gardens; "one would have said the Parisians were seeing their beloved monarch for the first time."[46]

It *was* almost the first time. Throughout most of July he had been confined to his apartments, taking baths and showers of *eaux de Barrèges* to relieve his arthritic and gouty pains – "a walking sore, a perfect walking sore," Wellington later said of Good Louis. Monsieur, the King's younger brother and formal resident of the north wing of the Tuileries, should have picked up the slack; but he also was sick, and retired to his baths at the Palace of Saint-Cloud. The only truly visible member of French royalty was the duc de Berry, Monsieur's younger son, the envoy to England, a man who regularly hunted deer in the Bois de Boulogne and entertained dozens of court women at suppers in the Pavillon de Bagatelle.[47]

The Bourbons' various physical weaknesses – the most frightening of which, for an hereditary monarchy, was a marked tendency of the male members towards impotence – led to the emphasis on the royal family rather than just the King. It was quite different from the previous regime. Napoleon had lived in the Tuileries alone with his Viennese Empress, Marie-Louise. Louis XVIII lived there with his brother, niece, and nephews, each with their own households and retinue of servants. The Tuileries had never in its entire history been more crowded.[48]

For the Fête Saint-Louis, the family made their first major effort to appear together in public since their arrival in France; Monsieur returned from Saint-Cloud, the duc d'Angoulême and his duchesse (Madame Royale, the "Orphan of the Temple," Louis XVI's only surviving child) returned from the South of France, the duc de Berry came back from England, and the King himself made a number of brave and painful attempts to be seen. That week in August was a *fête de famille*.

Wellington arrived in Paris on Monday, 22 August. Castlereagh arrived on Friday, the 26th, the day after the celebrations began, and he left on Sunday, the 28th, before they were ended. Virtually nothing was said in public on Castlereagh's presence in Paris; everything was said on Wellington's.[49]

The Duke, who once more had left his Duchess behind in England (she eventually crossed the Channel in October), was lionised in Paris. Through the good offices of Sir Charles Stuart he had managed to purchase one of the most beautiful private hotels in the city, a palace that had belonged to Napoleon's sister, Pauline Borghese. It was situated in the heart of Paris's *quartier brillant*, on rue de Faubourg Saint-Honoré, not far from the Elysée-Bourbon, with court and gardens stretching down to the Champs Elysées.[50]

On Tuesday evening he attended an opera, Gaspare Spontini's *Pélage*, where he was "surrounded by several English lords and generals," and the following day, the eve of Saint-Louis, he was received by the King at the Tuileries. He reported all this to Castlereagh with his usual brevity: "I have the honor to inform your Lordship that I arrived here on the 22nd instant, and was yesterday presented and delivered my credentials to the King with the accustomed ceremonies." No ambassador was in fact accustomed to the kind of royal reception he got that eve of Saint-Louis. Though it was spitting with rain a procession of carriages and carosses, pulled by the King's horses and accompanied by dragoons, cavalrymen and a detachment from the Maison du Roi, carried the Ambassador along the muddy rue de Rivoli onto the place de Carrousel. Napoleonic emblems still decorated the cornices and window-frames. Through the guard of honour, Wellington stepped into the Salle des Maréchaux lined with the portraits of marshals and the busts of generals, who would have ordered his murder the year before; down the long Salon Bleu and the Salle de la Paix the Ambassador walked on forbidden carpets and up into the higher echelons of the French Royal State; and onwards into the Salle du Trône, where he would have seen the Grand Officers of the Crown in their robes, the Princes of the Blood on their *tabourets*, and before him the King on his throne, still marked with a laurelled "N".[51]

The Duke of Wellington made a bow.

One of the remarkable traits of the new British Ambassador was that he knew how to make a French reverential bow; he had learnt that at Angers. Most of his countrymen found the gesture embarrassing. The Reverend Burroughs T. Norgate, for example, would attend a rout at Madame du Drée's and comment, "We were much amused by the manner of entrée of the French gentry, who came in bowing and scraping and performing a spiral in their evolutions very like Noodle, Doodle, and Foodle in Tom Thumb." Wellington wouldn't have found this very funny; he had a respect for French royal ways.[52]

On the evening of his reception, as Paris geared up for the celebrations the next day, Wellington attended a "grand dinner" given by the King's Premier Gentilhomme de la Chambre. The whole diplomatic corps was there. Wellington would have known how to behave, and speak – for he spoke and wrote fluent French. And Wellington had his name; Castlereagh himself had admitted, in his initial offer of the ambassadorship, that it was made because of "the authority... your name and services would give, through this Court, to our general politics on the Continent."[53] Good court manners, good French, and a grand name were what Louis XVIII and his entourage looked for in an ambassador. This was more than idle frippery; the issue was a regime's survival in a nation defeated. With the economy in an appalling state, ministers prepared for cuts in every government department with the exception, insisted the King, of the civil list, for: "there must be splendour." Wellington understood that.[54]

Ceremony, manners, and dress provided a means of uniting a divided nation, a principle the Bourbons had always respected, a principle Napoleon had tried to impose on the Revolution. After the defeat of 1814, principle turned into obsession. For the Chamber of Deputies in particular, which had exactly the same membership as Napoleon's Corps législatif of the year before, dress was the civilised way of defining a position in the new regime – one avoided the hypocrisy of opinion by putting on the right clothes and ignoring opinion altogether.[55]

So it was with the King's court. The courtiers, servants and functionaries at the Tuileries were essentially the same as waited on Napoleon; they simply changed their livery. But not even appearances at the palace were much altered. The restored Bourbons had a positive love for Empire furniture and ornamentation; Louis XVIII sat on the same throne as Napoleon (which he eventually threw out in 1822), the apartments were left as they were (save the addition of the King's bath-tub), and no attempt was made to repurchase the furniture of Louis XVI (most of it went to the Prince Regent and other English collectors). The court certainly expanded under Louis XVIII to include personnel from every French regime since 1789, and it was more open than it had ever been under Napoleon; a pamphlet claimed that before 1814 "it was more difficult to approach the humblest official of the palace than it is now to reach the person of the King." Indeed, if you wanted to know, in 1814, what "public opinion" was in France you would go to the Tuileries, where you would find representatives of every political party, nobles of the old regime and nobles of the new regime, the idle and the industrious, bankers, businessmen, poets, and hacks. There was a place for all; everyone felt at home in the King's palace. "The château of the Tuileries, so clean and so military under Napoleon, was filled, in the place of the odour of powder, with the smoke of lunches, which floated into every corner," recollected Chateaubriand, who was living nearby, on the rue de Rivoli, that year; "under Messieurs les Gentilshommes de la Chambre, with Messieurs les Officiers de la Bouche and de la Garde-Robe, everything took on an air of domesticity."[56]

A new domesticity: Chateaubriand was not just talking about the royal family at the Tuileries; every wealthy household in Paris took on the manners of the court because it was again the best guarantee of self-preservation. As the Conseil-Général des Manufactures, which represented French industry, told the duchesse d'Angoulême in May, "You know, Madame, the French people more than any other likes to find its models at the court of its Kings." It was a comforting thought after a generation of revolution. The popular Irish novelist, Lady Morgan, said this obsession with manners made life complicated for foreigners. In the past one would address everybody as "Citoyen" or "Citoyenne," now one had to mention some sort of title, though the meaning of these titles was confusing. "One day I asked a royalist if Monsieur D... was a *gentilhomme*." "Oh no," he replied; "he is of noble birth, but he is not a *gentilhomme*." So she asked what made a *gentilhomme*. He told her it was "the privilege of entering the carriage of the King."[57]

That was the whole difference between England and France: in England, a *gentilhomme* had a seat in the House of Lords; in France, he had a seat in the King's carriage. But despite their misunderstandings, crowds of Englishmen – and not just Wellington – were welcomed, in the summer of 1814, into the new court culture of Paris.

Cross-Channel travellers

Curiosity, along with the winds, drove the passenger vessels across the Channel that year; a forbidden frontier had been opened and hordes of travellers boarded the boats for first admissions to the continent. There were, of course, the famous, who were obliged to travel. Hetman Platov, on his return from London, was spied by a French reporter in Calais on 26 July; he wore his decorations "surrounded by superb diamonds" and was accompanied by three English ladies. There were the rich and the political who had to be noticed, like the Duchess of Devonshire, the prince de Cobay, and a whole team of MP's who had come to inspect the Kingdom of France after Parliament recessed in July. And there was royalty. Princess Caroline, benefitting from the increase in her allowance, drove down to Worthing in the company of her equerry, Captain Charles Hesse, and her young doctor, Henry Holland; dressed in a dark satin pelisse and a huge plumed hat "of the Prussian hussar costume," she set sail on 9 August aboard the *Jason* for the Netherlands, much to the relief of her husband and his ministers; "she kissed her hand to the females who waved their handkerchiefs" and it was reported that she wept.[58]

But most of the English who landed in France, at Calais, Boulogne, and Dieppe, wanted to know what lay on the other side of the waters.

Channel crossings were a haphazard affair, for no bookings could be made in advance. In the hotels at Dover and Brighton, the captains of the private packets would search out their clients by pressing white cards into the hands of the guests; you could haggle over the price of the voyage, and the date of departure was set by the weather, which could mean several days of waiting. The delay, combined with the sight of the dark sea line, its waves tumbling and frothing to the shore, inspired in passengers an excitement, an anticipation, which – without much exaggeration – might be compared to the feelings of the sailors who set out on the voyages of discovery. Benjamin Haydon, the historical painter, temporarily abandoned his great work on "Christ's Entry into Jerusalem' to see France immediately after the fall of Napoleon. Looking back over more than thirty years, Haydon recalled the moment in London when he heard the news of the abdication. "It cannot be comprehended," he wrote; "when I read to a circle of friends that Napoleon, *alias* Nicholas Buonaparte, had ceased to reign, we all stared breathless at each other." Armed with a passport and a French pocket dictionary, he boarded a boat in Brighton with his friend David Wilkie. After eighteen hours at sea, they sighted France: "How many associations crowded in on the imagination," he recorded; "I stood looking at the coast as we neared it, pregnant with anticipation."[59]

Memoirs like those of Haydon's contain elements of Columbus's journal, or of the musings of some eighteenth-century explorer in the South Seas. With the exception of the brief interlude of peace in 1802, the Channel had been closed to English travellers for a generation. John Scott, who made the crossing in the early autumn, spoke of the difficulty of describing the experience; "you seem to be going, as it were, beyond yourself," he remarked in a philosophical strain. But then how surprising it was to discover that the lands on the other side of the Channel looked, in fact, rather like England. "I am not ashamed to confess, that I looked earnestly at the hills which rose before me, to discover something *French* about them," Scott admitted somewhat ruefully on his approach to Dieppe; "they seemed, however, to be round and green, very much like those I had left behind." This startling discovery was confirmed once he had landed: "The rivulet glides as pleasantly through that valley as it does in England; the skies look cheerfully down upon [the traveller in France] with their English faces;" even the common occupations of the country town inhabitants present aspects "with which he is familiar."[60]

Nevertheless the differences were sufficient enough – some of them glaring – to provoke numerous anthropological observations on the natives, particularly the women. Haydon burst into laughter on catching his first glimpse of "two old witch-like Frenchwomen" in "short petticoats and wooden shoes." "For the love of Heaven," cried out an admiral's wife aboard Scott's boat, "look at that creature in the red petticoat!" She was a fishwoman, and Scott admitted she cut "a figure very grotesque to an English eye." The first French figure the Reverend Burroughs T. Norgate described, on sailing into Calais, was "a miserable looking, dirty old woman."[61]

There weren't, in fact, too many men to be seen, apart from the soldiers, "some in long loose great coats, some in jackets, some in cocked hats, some in round ones, some in caps, who darted at us keen looks of a very over-clouded cast...they seemed the fragments of broken-up gangs." Women were doing men's work, dragging the wheelbarrows, pulling the boats, and performing the most laborious duties in the streets. An English reporter found the women's tasks in Calais "quite preposterous," noting that "even the apothecaries' shops are served by women," and cited this as one of the "mournful proofs of the miseries of war." The houses were desolate, the shops scantily furnished. "Calais is a nasty, dirty town," said the Reverend Northgate.[62]

This squalidness, filth, and vulgarity of France's coastal towns had its attractions for a poet or painter, especially somebody like Haydon whose work was not recognised in England (nor would it ever be). England had the wealth and the elegance, but France offered something novel and exciting, a release from an island, a tangle of images, a welcome contrast: "Dieppe dark, old, snuffy, and picturesque, with its brigandlike soldiers, its Sibylline fish-fags, its pretty grisettes, and its screaming and chattering boatmen." Scott too remarked that you could find in France "a bright colouring, so much wanted in England."[63]

The huge dirty old French diligence that you would hire to Paris also had some appealing features, most particularly in the man who drove it. French postilions were a race apart. Most of them wore livery of dark blue and heavy buck's leather breeches, though Norgate was driven to Paris by a village curé in black because the regular man was sick.[64]

If England was a garden, France was a farm, and not a very rich one. By August the rye, the barley and the corn had been cut, and the branches of the crooked trees were now heavy with apples. In June, Frenchmen who had followed the Sovereigns across the Channel were astonished at how little England resembled their own rough rural scenes; the French papers all claimed that the Dover Road had been cleaned up, the houses whitewashed, the fences painted, just for the purpose of the visit. On the roads to Paris, by contrast, the beggars gathered; cripples, paralytics, and "idiots" among them – people who "in England would have been confined in the parochial receptacles for such sufferers" – peasants put on dances for money – *"Quelque chose pour la danse, Madame! quelqu' chose pour la danse!"*[65]

The countryside seemed empty; the larger properties in particular had a look of neglect and abandonment. "Many of the châteaux are in ruins," wrote Scott; "others are inhabited by the poor, whose children were to be seen playing in roofless and windowless summer-houses, standing in desolate gardens." The town houses also had a deserted appearance and, with their shutters closed, seemed far too large for practical inhabitation.[66]

The land was prettier and evidently richer after Chantilly, but the striking thing about the approach to Paris was the small number of vehicles on the long straight main roads. For an Englishman, France appeared an empty, unexploited country. Scarce a wagon or coach was to be seen as the travellers' diligence lumbered past the Basilica of Saint-Denis, now repaired after the plunder of the Year II, round the high hill of Montmartre, the sails of windmills turning to the wind, the slopes freckled with small vineyards. The drowsy talk of economy, peace and politics might have ceased for a moment, for the rural plain they were now crossing had been a battlefield only months before. In Scott's carriage there was a Frenchman who started to point out where the Empire had made its last stand, but "we felt as if it were pleasanter, for a little while at first, to contemplate what we saw, than to hear it described."[67]

The first sight most Englishmen got of Paris was the barrière St-Denis, a rather grim, square, neo-classical structure, about six metres high, with grass sprouting out of the arched cornerstones. Wellington and Castlereagh would have passed by here in late August.

Sixty barrières in all encircled the city, each linked to the other with tall iron fences and walls. They were not popular with Parisians; they were a physical symbol of the intrusion of the state into the affairs of individuals, monuments to the police and the taxmen, *le fisc*. There may have been more delays caused by tolls on the Dover Road than on the roads to Paris, and London was liberally scattered with gates and booths. But London was not fenced in like Paris.[68]

One queued at the barrière with the wine wagons, haycarts, and bullocks, for rural civilisation followed one into the town: chickens clucked and strutted in the alleys; through the old stone arching of the carpenter's abode a goat might be seen tethered in the court; pigs were raised by the barrières. Some travellers, once they had crossed the barrière, would look back up the narrow road to the fencing and suddenly feel locked in – within the girths of a farmyard as much as a city. On the right, the high wall of Saint-Lazare bordered the cobbled rue Faubourg Saint-Denis for several hundred metres; to the left were dark frowning houses, crooked ruins, artisans' cabins, and fields.

Most Englishmen arrived at dusk, after the overhanging oil-lanterns had been lit. Spaced regularly at every sixty metres they would swing on their ropes in the wind, creating a somewhat eerie effect. "Far away their flame burns the eyes, nearby it gives little light, underneath you are in darkness," said a disgruntled Parisian.[69]

Finally one arrived at Paris's old frontier, Louis XIV's frontier, the "new boulevards." There the great king had constructed a great triumphal arch to commemorate his victories over the Palatinate, the Alsatians, and the Dutch. Whoever remembered them? The Emperor had changed the names to Napoleon's glories. Now *gloire* was Bourbon again, and the bronze inscription at the top was clear, *"Ludovico Magno"* – "To Louis the Great." After descending dirty rue Faubourg Saint-Denis, you could forgive a traveller for thinking of Voltaire's remark: that Paris was built like Nebuchadnezzar's statue, of gold and of mud.

Old Paris, new Paris, dirty Paris, Paris

For the paradox was that while Paris was the city of the Enlightenment, the city of the Revolution and of the Rights of Man, the city that had conquered a continent, it was in many, many ways still a city of the Middle Ages. It may have been the second largest city in the world but, with only seven hundred thousand inhabitants, it was not much more than half the size of London. If Voltaire had returned to Paris in 1814 he would have found a city not so very different from the city he died in in 1778, while he would have been astounded at the developments in London.

The Revolution had left no monuments. When Gibbon had called up his muse to write a history of ancient Rome, he sat by moonlight in the Colosseum; when Michelet sought inspiration for his history of the French Revolution, he set out by foot on a summer's day and, at the edge of a field, the Champ de Mars, he sat on an earthen mound. The Revolution's monument is empty space, he wrote, "it is this sand, as flat as Arabia." Nothing physically remained of the Revolution, save that mound of earth, built for the Fête de la Fédération of 1790, and a few inscriptions on old public buildings.[70]

Napoleon had wanted to leave more than monuments in his "first capital of the Universe"; he told the memorialist Las Cases in St Helena, "I wanted Paris to become a town of two, three, four million inhabitants, something fabulous, colossal, unknown until our time." Yet he destroyed more of Paris than he built, and most especially he destroyed some of the most famous locations of the revolutionary events. He destroyed the Salle de Manège, by the Tuileries, where the National Assembly had met; he flattened the convents of the Feuillants, the Capucins and the Jacobins, where the revolutionary clubs once nested, replacing them with one huge market, a "pacific chaffering for poultry and greens"; the Temple in the Marais, where the royal family had lain as prisoners, was turned into another market. Public policy under the Empire, it seemed, was that there should be no monuments to the Revolution, and no places of pilgrimage either.[71]

Napoleon had wanted Parisians to remember Napoleon, not the Revolution, but he did not actually leave much. There was the column in the middle of place Vendôme and a few statues scattered about the town. The Arc de Triomphe on the Etoile was still only a temporary wooden affair and less impressive than the two huge temple barrières behind it. The *ci-devant* rue Napoléon (in 1814, rue de la Paix) and rue Castiglione cut a muddy swath from the boulevards, through place Vendôme, to the Tuileries Gardens; there they made a junction with the new rue de Rivoli and its colonnades that came to a dead end in the place du Carrousel and the slum houses – which half hid the Louvre Palace opposite. Two new bridges crossed the Seine. On the place du Caire, the old Cour de Miracles, you can still see a building that lends an idea of what Napoleon wanted for Paris: pillars, balconies and moorish window frames decorate the façade while, from a second floor, three stone pharaohs give their glazy blessing to the busy tradesmen with their wheelbarrows below. Upon the Revolution's most famous plain of destruction, the place de la Bastille, was supposed to stand a fountain in the form of an elephant. Apart from the circular vault, the damp papier-maché toes, and the high temporary wooden frames, nothing was ever built. With the passing years the abandoned site became a den for robbers and wastrels that Hugo's *Les Misérables* would make famous.[72]

Voltaire's Paris, revolutionary Paris, Napoleonic Paris, Restoration Paris: the stoneware hardly changed. Turgot's eighteenth-century map and Maire's map of 1813 show a topography that is almost identical. Had the people changed?

Oddly, for this capital of the Revolution, one did not speak of the "people"; one spoke instead, in 1814, of the "populace." There was something menacing about that word, like the English word mob. But the populace seemed to have lost its violence. There were no executions on the place de Grève in 1814, no cheerings for blood; artisans did not leave their workshops, the shopkeepers did not abandon their boutiques, the flower girls did not parade before the scaffolding to watch a prisoner die. Lady Morgan took the fact that there were fewer executions in Paris than in London as proof that there was less crime and robbery. How polite the Parisians all seemed to visiting Londoners. It was as if the court culture of the Tuileries had spread not only to the rich, but to every social level in Paris. "Nothing struck us English more in the manners of the French than the sweetness of address in all classes," remarked Haydon after commenting on the women he had found playing battledore and shuttlecock in front of the Morgue. They all appeared to speak the same high language, the same signs of *politesse*: "'Do me the honor to permit me to pass,' says a ragged porter, pulling off his cocked-hat, to a female vendor of roasted chestnuts. A priest, arrayed in his full canonicals, will stop in the street and chatter and laugh for half an hour with a servant girl." So said Scott. He noticed a kind of poor man's pride he had not met in London.[73]

Paris was dirty, Paris stank, Paris was everything Carlyle described it as, "Mud-Town of the Borderers (*Lutetia Parisiorum* or *Barisiorum*)." The Reverend Norgate complained of the smell of "effluvia and fœtish gases" when he put up at the Hôtel de Bourbon on rue de la Paix, and he fled across river to the quartier Saint-Germain. Nothing like London's system of drainage existed in Paris; the city was serviced by an outer-circle sewer called the Grand Canal, much of which remained open. "I have traversed the sewers of Paris several times, very often crouching, my nose in the mud," reported Napoleon's hardy Inspector General of Health, Bruneseau, in 1812; "and even more often I was so choked by the mephitic vapours that I was compelled to have myself pulled out to breathe." There were famous areas in northern and eastern Paris where the soil had dissolved, the tiling had cracked, and the drains had become open cesspools; it was said men could suddenly vanish from sight. Many

English travellers would have passed by the great opening of the Marais drain on rue Saint-Louis and held their noses as they tiptoed round its mouth at rue de la Mortellerie, behind the Hôtel de Ville; it had an iron-pointed grating, which resembled the jaws of a dragon exhaling hell.[74]

Paris's private buildings were less well constructed than in London. The stones, extracted from local quarries, absorbed moisture, giving them a dirty, yellow-white colour. "In rainy seasons," noted a medical report, "one notices water oozing from all the walls."[75]

Paris "with her thousand black domes" had an irregular, chaotic appearance for a Londoner, for there was no law in Paris as rigorously applied as London's Building Act of 1774. One stepped out of the boulevards into narrow medieval streets, past doors and dens, and down cavernous flights of steps that resembled dry waterfalls; a rope, bracketed to the walls, was there for the walker to cling on to. From the bridges on the Seine these clustered houses and towers took on the appearance of "castellated masses."[76]

Yet dirty and chaotic as it was, most visitors seem to have agreed with Haydon that Paris was "the most interesting place on earth." "Dear old Paris!" exclaimed Lady Morgan as she reconnoitred the Marais, "may you live for ever as you are!" Her architecture, she said, was "the printing press of all ages" – "Maison de Voltaire," "Ici demeurait Molière," "Hôtel de Carnavalet." Haydon, on his first evening in Paris, wandered through the narrow streets and then came, suddenly, upon the place du Carrousel: "The arch of Napoleon, the bronze Venetian horses, the gilt chariot, the Tuileries, the Russian guard, and the setting sun casting its glory over all, made up a scene which had the strangeness of a dream, and which affects me now, 31 years after." That colour, that sun made a deep impression on fog-bound Londoners. "The peculiar clearness of the air of Paris," wrote Scott, "gives a glancing brilliancy, an almost startling distinctness to every object."[77]

Paris was a city you could look into; it was an open, not a secret, city. "Compared with the cities of most other countries, it is like a glass beehive ... You see, without trouble, into all its hoards." The riverside line of the Louvre Palace and the Tuileries was striking, but so were the crowds one encountered as one approached the Hôtel de Ville: "cabs, carts, horses, women, boys, girls, soldiers, carriages, all in endless struggle – streets narrow – houses high – no flat pavement – Russians, Poles, Germans, Italians, English, Jews, Turks and Christians, all hot, hurried and in a fidget." It was like a Venetian painting, "such is the floating and swarming vivacity, variety and gaiety ... Bright colouring, so much wanted in England, is here plentifully interspersed: if you look along the streets, the red handker-chiefs, that form the head-dress of the peasant and servant girls, shoot about with much sprightliness." It was "picturesque and becoming," it made one think that the only thing Paris existed for was pleasure and entertainment.[78]

There seemed to be more of that than in London. On the boulevards, along the gravelled alleys beneath the trees, one could always find the street musicians, the conjurors, the dancing dogs, the exhibition prints, books and paintings, the coffee-houses, the baths, and the restaurateurs. It was a fair held 365 days of the year.

Bathing had become a craze in Paris, a gift of the Revolution. One guide tells the story of a Frenchman returning to Paris after several decades – he was not the only one – to discover to his horror that his local church, the Eglise Saint-Sauveur (where St Louis once prayed), had been turned into a public bath; but after an afternoon in the Bains Saint-Sauveur, he came out with a smile, admitting it was *"un établissement magnifique"* and much better than "a useless church." Before attending the English service in a church on rue Saint-Honoré the Reverend Norgate set out for a bath: "I began to bathe at Vigier's Baths on the Seine. These are one hundred and forty in number, and are in a building something like Noah's ark, floating on the Seine, near the banks, with which it communicates by a little bridge."[79]

Public eating was another gift of the Revolution where, once more to the surprise of many Englishmen, the sexes mingled. In Paris one frequently ate outside one's home *chez le restaurateur* – the word *restaurant* had not yet caught on. But what astonished the English were the hours of eating, for the Revolution had invented a new midday meal known as *déjeuner à la fourchette*. The confused visitors insisted on calling it "breakfast." "We went to breakfast with Chevalier Bagarre, one of the old Royalists, an amiable old man of eighty three, of rather singular manners," recorded the Reverend Norgate one Wednesday. What did they eat for "breakfast"? "Hot roast fowls, turkey-and-ham pies, veal-and-oyster patties, green stewed peas, asparagus, trifles, creams, rolls, cakes, sweet puddings, &c, &c, and excellent Burgundy, Claret, and old Malaga." After this "tea and coffee were introduced by way of a second course." A later generation would call it "lunch." This revolutionary meal – Lady Morgan likened it to "the substantial Scottish breakfast" – had won a following among even the most die-hard aristocratic Royalists, like the chevalier Bagarre. Lady Morgan had her first lunch in her life with La Fayette.[80]

The heart of entertaining Paris was of course the Palais-Royal – "Maison Egalité" during the Revolution, when it was a centre for public speaking, a kernel of the sans-culotte revolt. In 1814, it was still a place for politics and reading; in the gardens at an early hour each morning chairs were placed out that could be hired, with a newspaper, for a couple of sous. The Palais-Royal, with its long covered walks, its shops, its cafés, its gambling dens and houses of ill-repute, was a city within a city. At night it was the most brilliantly lit corner in Paris, though shopping meant frequently fumbling in the dark.[81]

The Reverend Norgate – who one imagines was a frequent visitor – called the Palais-Royal "a Microcosm." "It comprises in its character," he said, "almost every scene that can be imagined, every-thing to inform the understanding, and everything to corrupt the heart." The corruption was organised vertically: "The higher you ascend, the more deformed does vice appear." Scott also noticed that to corrupt the heart one needed to climb stairs: "Above the cellars and the shops of the Palais-Royal, there are the elegant Cafés, the com-mon and licensed gambling houses and bagnios, and, still higher, the abodes of the guilty, male and female, of every description." So the wealth was at the bottom while the poverty was on top.[82]

That is what really made the Palais-Royal a microcosm, for working Paris was organised in the same way – vertically. Like most European capitals, wealth lay in the western half of Paris, a pheno-menon that was probably due to prevailing winds and the need to escape from smells. But unlike London there was no fine "line of demarcation" that separated wealth from artisan industry. One of the reasons Londoners found the Parisian crowds so colourful was because these crowds were of mixed social origin. One of the reasons they found even the wealthiest quarters of the city so dirty was because poverty was segregated vertically by apartments, not horizontally by houses as in London. Once in the streets, the people inevitably mixed; this could explain the courtly language of the ragged porter and the chestnut vendor, the pride of the old tailor, and the artistic twirl in the hairdresser's shop sign.[83]

Scott, with his ever acute eye, noticed the mix Paris's apartment system created in the richest quarter in Paris, the place Vendôme. Napoleon's statue had come down from the column and, in the summer of 1814, there flew the white Bourbon flag in its place. Place Vendôme was not like St James's Square: there was "no enclosed shrubbery, opening into lawns," no "pavement for promenaders" and, if "the houses around it are uniform and grand," they all appeared on close inspection to be "neglected and dirty." Why? Because of the social mix. The houses were "let out in portions:" "Those who can afford to pay three hundred and sixty pounds a year for rent, share their stair-cases and entrances with water carriers, duns, and visitors of those who pay but twenty-five."[84]

There was such a mix of peoples in Paris because of the way in which Paris grew. And Paris was growing – much faster, indeed, than London. "If our Revolution has slowed down trade in several towns of France," wrote the author of a guide in 1807, "that of Paris appears to have increased immensely." The Continental Blockade had been a

Visitors to Paris, both
military and civilian,
usually stopped off at
the Palais-Royal

disaster for the Atlantic ports, while industry and agriculture stagnat-
ed in the provinces. It all benefited Paris. State and private capital was
drawn into the city, manufacture converged (despite the lack of
natural resources), and so did people. Between the censuses of 1807
and 1816, the population of Paris grew by nearly twenty-three per
cent, which, on an annual base, was the fastest rate recorded in the
whole of the nineteenth century.[85]

The provincials congregated in Paris by place of origin and by
trade. Napoleon had built his few columns and avenues, but no
housing; so old Paris was crammed. Stone-cutters and masons from
Corrèze packed into lodgings around the place de Grève. Western
France and Lorraine supplied labour to the crowded food and
clothing industries north of the Marais. The water carriers Scott had
noted in the garrets of the place Vendôme probably came from Cantal,
Aveyron, or Puy-de-Dôme. Clusters of the working population
could be found everywhere in the city, including that curious huddle
of buildings in front of the Tuileries Palace itself. "Our grandsons will
refuse to believe that such a piece of barbarism existed for thirty-six

Louis XVIII at Napoleon's desk. Not only furniture but also most of Napoleon's
personnel were retained at the Tuileries by the restored Bourbons

years in the heart of Paris," wrote Balzac when he described the spot
in *Cousine Bette*.[86]

A tramp of soldiery added to the squeeze. Scott noted how the
military formed a regular part of Paris's crowd; troops would mingle
with people rather than force their way through them, "so that their
muskets and uniforms are seen gleaming here and there through the
interstices of passengers and carriages."[87] The Bourbon government
considered these remnants of Napoleon's army as the most dangerous
element of Paris's mixed crowds. While the working population in
central Paris appeared disenchanted with the former regime,[88] the
army was known to regret its Emperor. Well might government
officials and commanders assure the troops that the *gloire* of the
armies had not been diminished, and that the King wished "the
French soldier to be proud under the flag of the lys"; the French
soldier did not feel glorious, proud, or happy.[89]

Another trouble spot for a Bourbon King in Paris was in the

faubourgs, the "false towns," the settlements beyond the boulevards but within the barrières. They had still not been fully incorporated into the city. Carlyle referred to the faubourgs as "that remote Oriental region." Joseph Fouché, the former Minister of Police, remarked one day to the Emperor, "It's all tradition. The Seine flows, the Faubourg plots, demands, consumes and calumnies. It is part of the order of things: to each his prerogative." Faubourg Saint-Antoine knew its prerogatives, and placed them above those of faubourg St-Marcel. But then Saint-Marcel had its own prerogatives and considered them superior to those of Saint-Antoine. The faubourgs were rarely united and, though they might have supplied cohorts to the revolutionary crowds and the revolutionary armies, by 1814 these sweating, toiling, and confused masses had lost their sting. Many of their leaders had been either guillotined or deported (the majority of victims of the national razor were not aristocrats). Others had been conscripted. Strikes were unusual and when they did occur, they focused invariably on the hours of work. The artisans of London had a more violent voice in 1814, and one that was much more political than the men of the faubourgs.[90]

The faubourgs were the real frontiers of Paris. Beyond them lay the barrières once again. But how surprising it was, considering the density of population at the centre, to find so much unbuilt land between them. It was a melancholy land, neither country nor town; a neutral place where paved roads ended in dirt tracks, fenced vineyards, a few windswept elms, and the odd deserted tenement. "Paris suffers from an enlargement of her heart," said Napoleon.[91]

The capitulation of March

In the last weeks of the war, Talleyrand had made several trips out to the barrières to get news, though what he learned was never of great significance. News was a rare commodity back then. "One knew nothing more than what I have just accounted to you," he wrote, frustrated, to the duchesse de Courlande after a visit to the barrières on 1 March.[92] Talleyrand's uncertainties about the future were recorded almost daily in these letters to the Duchess, *petits billets du matin*, so very much in style among French aristocrats of the eighteenth century. The letters show a man fearful and sick that the diplomats would never know. He had just turned sixty in February; the Duchess was fifty-three. It was the most anxious moment of his life. And it was one of the coldest winters in his life. London had celebrated with a frost fair on the Thames; Paris faced the prospect of war at her gates. The city had not been invested by a foreign army since the days of Joan of Arc; she had not experienced war since Condé's entry into Paris during the Fronde of 1652. Talleyrand himself, though for years Napoleon's envoy, had only witnessed war once, and he was in no hurry to repeat the experience.[93] "We are close to a crisis which could be terrible," he wrote on 3 February; "God will protect us." On 10 February: "This uncertainty is in all its horrors, for we are four days from I don't know what." 2 March: "At every hour there has been a cause for worry or a cause for calm." 15 March: "Today they are announcing a victory...One has to rejoice if this opens the road to peace. Without that it will mean again masses killed, and poor humanity destroying itself everyday with a frightful relentlessness." 27 March: "France is in a truly sad situation; we are being pillaged on every side. I see only people ruined."[94]

For eight days in February, Paris had been in a state of total panic. Out at the barrières people had been heard screaming, "The Cossacks are coming! Shut all the shops!" The price of stock at the Bourse fell, there was a run on the banks, the rich started hoarding potatoes, rice, dry vegetables, and salted pork; among the poor, the old cry against *accapareurs* (hoarders) went up. Napoleon responded by marching columns of Russian, Prussian, and Austrian prisoners-of-war, whom he had taken on the field, through the streets of Paris. But the sight of these young men, dressed in rags, their heads bare, their backs weighed down with old baggage, did nothing to inspire Parisians about the glories of war. The official bulletins reported victory upon victory and military parades were held in front of the Tuileries; but there was no enthusiasm in Paris. A slush of snow covered fields and parks until mid-March.[95]

Paris of course never witnessed the horrors of the campaign itself – sixty-five days of forced marching across north-eastern France, the new recruits not knowing how to handle their weapons, the exhausted horses and infantry, the abandoned munitions, the lack of supplies. But Paris did see the deserters. More shocking were the wounded who – refused room in the overcrowded hospitals, or in the barracks that forbade them entry – by March were wandering in the streets begging for bread. It was also in March that the peasant refugees appeared with their barrows filled with furniture, along with their goats, geese, and even cattle.[96]

Nobody knew in the winter what was going to happen come spring, least of all Talleyrand. His letters of February and March speak of a "great trouble," of a "social decomposition," of "*l'incertitude.*" He even seems to have had premonitions of his own death.

Talleyrand's complicated household of women consisted at the time of a shunned wife (the former Madame Grand), an adopted daughter (Charlotte "la Mystérieuse"),[97] and a niece by marriage (the Duchess's daughter, Dorothée). The duchesse de Courlande lived nearby on the corner of boulevard Montmartre and rue Neuve-Grange-Batelière (the Metternichs had owned the house before Talleyrand purchased it for his nephew Edmond). During the panic of February, he sent all four women into refuge at Rosny, outside Paris. To the Duchess he gave a small picture, which she was instructed to place inside her bed and carry with her whenever she travelled as "protection against bad luck." It was shortly after their departure that he spoke of "this uncertainty with all its horrors," adding: "I recommend to you Charlotte. Finish her good education: trace her character on your own."[98]

Following the death of two other women friends in January, Talleyrand had developed a heavy "cold," which persisted right through the freezing month of February. "*Je ne sais que des choses tristes,*" he complained. His women had left him and so, apparently, had his doctor. "In the middle of all these worries of the present time," he wrote at one o'clock in a chilly night, "it is a veritable grief, dear friend, to be fifteen leagues from you... Adieu, angel of goodness and sweetness, I love you with all my soul." He started taking borage, but that only upset his stomach so that, "like the children," he was obliged to eat rhubarb. "I am astonished at drugging myself; this is absolutely beyond my ordinary habits." Doctor Gall (an appropriate name, perhaps) returned on 17 March and the Duchess, along with his three other women, were back in Paris on the 24th. Though the war was reaching its climax, it was decided that they would not leave again. "I am well contented that you have decided not to return to Rosny," he wrote on 26 March as the Allies began their final march on Paris. "In these times of worry one needs to be near the people one loves, and you, dear friend, are the first and sweetest interest in my life."[99] "Dear friend, my wishes are to pass my life with you," Talleyrand would write to the Duchess. "You! you! you! That's who I love most in the world."[100]

So it must have been love; but it was not simple love, for with Talleyrand nothing was ever simple. Talleyrand's private affairs had an odd manner of working their way into his public affairs, and vice versa; in the tradition of the old regime aristocracy, the frontiers between private and public were blurred. "One must always put oneself in the position of being able to chose between two parties" was his wise rule in politics: the duchesse de Courlande, it just so happened, was one of Talleyrand's critical links with the man riding to Paris at the head of the other party, the Russian Tsar.[101]

Talleyrand's double game with Alexander – and his relationship with the duchesse de Courlande – dated back to conversations they had had in 1808 in the Thuringian town of Erfurt. The Erfurt Conference was one of those embryonic developments within Napoleon's Europe that contributed to the formation of the post-Napoleonic order, though nobody could have foreseen it at the time. Talleyrand had acted as Napoleon's official envoy.

For Napoleon, the conference was intended to reinforce his eastern wing, after the initial defeat of his army in Spain, by means of a Russian alliance against Austria. For Talleyrand, who already felt that Napoleon's gigantic edifice was a contradiction of European geography and history, the aim of the conference was the exact opposite: he wanted to bring Austria and Russia together. Talleyrand's actions at Erfurt were pure treason but, being Talleyrand, he got away with it.[102] He had already established a close working relationship with the Austrian Ambassador to Paris, Clemens von Metternich. At Erfurt, he told Tsar Alexander that a most intimate union of Austria and Russia would actually be in France's best interest since it would provide a barrier against Napoleon's insatiable private ambition. Such an opinion, expressed by a dignitary of the Empire, must have been a pleasant discovery for Alexander, who was himself playing a double game with Napoleon.[103]

Talleyrand's intrigue with Alexander aimed not only at reversing Napoleon's alliance system; he also managed, at Erfurt, to destroy Napoleon's early hopes for a second marriage, which could have assured the continuity of the Bonaparte dynasty. Napoleon was, at the time, seeking the hand of the Tsar's sister, the Grand Duchess Catherine. Talleyrand managed to manœuvre Alexander into demanding permission from his most Orthodox German mother – a move Talleyrand knew would stop the project dead. But while speaking of marriage, as they chatted privately in the palace of the princesse de Tour et Taxis,[104] Talleyrand mentioned that he had a young nephew that he wanted married.

Talleyrand's eye had fallen on the unmarried daughter of the duchesse de Courlande, who herself was the richest heiress in Germany. Since the last partition of Poland, the Duchess had been a subject of His Imperial Highness. For eight years, her château at Mittau had hosted the court of the Bourbon pretender, the comte de Provence *dite* "Louis XVIII." Her family was also on most intimate terms with the family of the Tsar. Talleyrand suggested that the proposed marriage could provide a private link between himself and Russia without raising suspicions in Paris.[105]

The marriage between Edmond de Périgord and Dorothée de Courlande was duly arranged by the Tsar and was celebrated in Frankfurt in April 1809 by the Prince-Primate, Karl Teodor von Dalberg, a man of Enlightenment and learning, another close associate of Talleyrand's. His nephew, the duc de Dalberg, would later be a member of Talleyrand's Provisional Government during the Restoration of 1814. "It is sweet to think that on you, Your Highness," wrote Talleyrand, at the time of the marriage, in a letter of appreciation to Alexander, "lie today the destinies of the universe and the progress of civilisation, which are the desire of your noble and sensitive soul." Talleyrand was obviously already aware of the nature of the Tsar's universal and mystical soul.[106]

Talleyrand's extraordinary activities eventually led to his official disgrace. "You are a lump of shit in a silk stocking!" exclaimed Napoleon.[107]

It was a semi-disgrace, indeed a rather glorious disgrace. During the last years of the Empire, he moved from one Parisian palace to another, though he was always pleading poverty. In 1813, by means of a loan he somehow extorted from Napoleon, he purchased a grand dwelling on the corner of rue Saint-Florentin and rue de Rivoli. He was still the prince de Bénévent and he remained Vice Grand Elector – which gave him the crucial power to call the Senate into assembly. Through the marriage of his nephew and with the help of the Russian Ambassador in Paris, he maintained a secret correspondence with Alexander under the pseudonyms "*mon cousin Henry*," "*Ta*," "Anna Ivanovna," "*notre libraire*," "*le beau Léandre*," or "*le jurisconsulte*." And he continued to make friends, lots of influential friends.

Napoleon eventually regretted not having his services. During his last desperate negotiations with the Allies at Châtillon in March 1814 Napoleon admitted, "Ah! if Talleyrand were there he would pull me out of this affair!"[108]

But he did not like the idea of Talleyrand serving, during that winter campaign, on the Regency Council in Paris; it was a nomination Napoleon could scarcely have avoided since Talleyrand, as Vice Grand Elector, was still a dignitary of the Empire. "I repeat to you, don't trust this man," Napoleon warned his brother Joseph, whom he had left in Paris to preside over the Council; "he is certainly the greatest enemy of our house."[109]

And Talleyrand, member of the Regency Council in those last months of the war, seemed to have done everything to make himself look like a conspirator, surrounding himself with people like Jaucourt, the duc de Dalberg, Baron Louis, Montesquiou, and the abbé de Pradt, all known to be hostile to the Emperor. But the same could have been said of much of Paris; the Minister of Police, Savary, had a hopeless task sniffing out sedition, for sedition was everywhere. The princesse de Vaudémont used to hold teas in her *hôtel particulier* to which she would invite all the major figures of the imperial government; but she would also receive the duc de Dalberg, the baron de Vitrolles, and the marquise de Coigny, all three sympathisers with the Bourbon cause. The vicomtesse de Laval's dinners, followed by long sessions at whist, piquet, and craps, were the occasion for many subversive conversations. Similarly, Talleyrand's house was frequented by doubters, dissidents, and fifth columnists every morning, afternoon and evening; the abbé de Pradt (soon to be known as the "pamphleteer prelate") later remembered how

Talleyrand would receive him in the morning in his night-gown and "fourteen bonnets superimposed one on the other."[110]

Talleyrand, however, never saw himself as a conspirator; or rather, as he put it, "I never conspired in my life except when I had the majority of France as an accomplice." Talleyrand always argued that the real conspirator was Napoleon, who "conspired against himself." Napoleon was a man of the Revolution, a man of war, who was quite incapable of defining his own, let alone his nation's, limits. He was caught in a process that had no end. Talleyrand would quote Machiavelli's *Prince*: "The usurper will only have firmly consolidated his power when he has taken the lives of every member of the family that reigned legitimately." That's why, explained Talleyrand, the Revolution wanted the blood of every Bourbon. Napoleon carried that usurping power across frontiers and, quite logically, was incapable of making peace. In his support, Talleyrand would quote Napoleon's message to Caulaincourt in February 1814: "If the nation wants peace on the basis of her old frontiers, I say to her: go and find whoever you can to govern you, for I am too great for you!"

Napoleon *was* too great. Talleyrand would say "gigantic." How could one stop this folly for war? Don't talk of conspiracy, said Talleyrand. No conspiracy could work, however well prepared, however wide the net was cast, because imposed authority was usurped authority, and that could only lead to further challenges, further conspiracies, a continual civil war; in other words, perpetuation of twenty-five years of Revolution. With the Allied armies closing in on Paris, Talleyrand sought not simply the replacement of one regime by another. A real peace required a legitimate authority, a re-establishment of the rule of law and the banishment of fear.[111]

The law: during the long debate in the National Constituent Assembly of August 1789 it had been Talleyrand who defined the law in the famous Article VI of the Declaration of the Rights of Man: "The law is the expression of the general will. All citizens have the right to assist personally, or through their representatives, in its formation."[112]

In March 1814, as Vice Grand Elector, Talleyrand would call on what remained of their representatives – the Senate – to form the new law.

The departure of Empress Marie-Louise for Tours on 29 March caused a minor panic among Parisians, especially among the wealthy, who clambered into their chaises and calèches, and caused a jam on the roads to Rouen, Chartres, and Dreux. But when the battle for Paris actually began, at four o'clock the following morning with a roll of the tambour drums, the city remained surprisingly calm. It was a warm though overcast day. Few vehicles moved on the boulevards, many of the shops were shut, but there was a crowding of pedestrians;

The defence of the porte de Clichy during the Siege of Paris, 30 March 1814.
A typical old oil-lantern hangs above the scene of combat

they would have heard the odd burst of cannon, a faint crackle of musketry. Tortoni's was open, serving ices and punch.[113]

As a member of the Regency Council, Talleyrand should have accompanied the Empress. But Talleyrand, after seeing Her Majesty off at the Tuileries, returned to his home to make his own travelling arrangements; Talleyrand never did things in a rush – *"festina lente"* was his favourite Latin expression, "make haste slowly."

Joseph Bonaparte left Paris after ordering a ceasefire, at midday, 30 March. The abbé de Pradt, his black silk robe thrown over his shoulders, was out with the duc de Dalberg touring the barrières. At the barrière du Trône, they saw Russian troops capture the artillery placed outside the grilled fencing; they thought it was high time to return home. Talleyrand, meanwhile, remained at rue Saint-Florentin – still making his travelling preparations.[114]

Paris had not been prepared for the battle. Apart from a few earthen slopes on the north side of the city, the only defences were the tax barrières. There were only about four thousand regular troops available. In addition, there were two companies of veterans, eight hundred soldiers in the Gendarmerie Impériale, a few hundred firemen, and the famous Garde Nationale, made up of shopkeepers ruined by the economic crisis of the last two years. Yet the the Battle of Paris of 30 March 1814 is said to have been the most murderous of all the battles of that winter campaign. The historian Houssaye estimated that over eight thousand Frenchmen were killed, wounded, and lost, against seven thousand Russians and two thousand Prussians. Even though Joseph had ordered a ceasefire at midday, fighting went on to the north and east of Paris throughout the afternoon.[115]

Preliminary negotiations with the Allies were already under way in a cabaret at the barrière de Saint-Denis when Talleyrand, at five o'clock in the evening of 30 March, decided his "travelling plans" were at last ready and set off to the quai d'Orfèvres in the company of another of his useful young women friends, Madame de Rémusat, to see her cousin, Etienne Pasquier, the Prefect of Police. Madame de Rémusat did all the talking. She said that Talleyrand was the only person in Paris with the weight to negotiate with the foreign Powers, yet he had orders to join the Empress in Tours; could her cousin somehow arrange a revolt at the barrières to prevent him from leaving? Pasquier had a much easier solution: Madame de Rémusat's husband was an officer in the National Guard; why not arrange to have a barrière closed prior to their departure? Within the hour, Talleyrand was again in his carriage, with his secretary riding on horseback beside him, travelling down the right bank of the Seine to the barrière des Bonshommes and the route to Rambouillet. At the barrière the guard politely invited Talleyrand to return home. '*A rue Saint-Florentin!*" Talleyrand cheerfully ordered his driver. They took a back road this time, avoiding the Seine. "I found, dear friend, the barrières closed," he scribbled off to the Duchess; "it was impossible for me to continue on my way."[116]

Talleyrand may well have upheld the principle that one should make haste slowly; but he also knew that when it was a question of re-establishing peace, hesitation "would let burst out the ideas of division and enslavement which silently threatened our unhappy country." Within the next twenty-four hours the restoration of the Bourbons would be decided.[117]

By nine o'clock the same evening, negotiations had moved to the home of the Parisian commander, General Marmont. Many of the high officials of the Empire had gathered there with Marmont, his coat torn and bloodied, along with Count Orlov, the Tsar's representative. Talleyrand turned up just as Marmont was sitting down for a private supper and talk with Orlov in the dining-room. By the end of the meal it had been implicitly agreed that the Empire had come to an end and that the Bourbons would return to Paris.[118]

As they left Talleyrand said to Orlov, the smile on his lips barely detectable, "Monsieur, let me charge you with bearing to the feet of His Majesty the Emperor of Russia an expression of profound respect from the prince de Bénévent."

"Prince, you can be sure of it," replied Orlov, who was as capable a diplomat as Talleyrand, "I will gladly bear such a signed blank document [*je porterai ce blanc-seing*] to the attention of His Majesty." So the message would be passed to the victor: Talleyrand would give Alexander free rein, if Alexander recognised in Talleyrand the authority he wanted in the new Bourbon regime.[119]

At night, in accordance with the terms of the ceasefire, the French forces were withdrawn from the heights around Paris and the Allies moved in. "I will never forget that night," recorded the comtesse de Boigne. "The weather was superb, the full moon magnificent, the town was perfectly calm." The only sound she remembered was of a nearby dog gnawing a bone. The abbé de Pradt was also struck by the calm and the almost fairylike atmosphere of the night as he wandered through empty streets, the windows of the houses all shuttered, the oil lamps extinguished. "Paris had fallen," he recalled, "and it had never been more tranquil." The war was done; a time-frontier with peace had been crossed. And yet, as to the Englishmen travelling the Channel, things seemed so ordinary on the other side of the border: above were the same stars, the same moon, except their light seemed more scattered than before. From the streets he could look out to what were normally the dark shadows of the rural hills north and east of the city; that night they sparkled with little yellow and white dots, the fires of the Allied camps. They were as silent as the heavens. "A foreigner ignorant of what had just happened would not have suspected that a few hours ago, Paris had ceased to belong to herself."[120]

At eleven o'clock, Wednesday morning, 31 March, the Allies entered Paris through the northern barrière de Pantin. They were led by the Red Cossacks of the Imperial Guard, by cavalry, hussars, and squadrons of the Royal Prussian Guard, and by more Russian cavalry in blue and in scarlet, their thick black belts pinching in their waists like wasps; the Emperor Alexander followed on horseback, with Prince Schwarzenberg, the Allied commander, to his right and a timid looking King of Prussia to his left.[121] Then came the rabble of regulars, the ragged-maned horses, the odd shaggy pony, the baggage wagons, field pieces, carts, and a tramp of hooves; and yet more baggage wagons, field pieces, carts, and hooves.

At the barrières and along the road that descended the faubourg Saint-Martin the Parisians who gathered were sullen. Following an incident in February, when an English officer had been wounded by a Cossack, the Allies wore white arm-bands to identify themselves. The Parisians mistakenly took this as a sign of Bourbon loyalty; in the faubourgs, the people wanted peace, but they were not sure they wanted a Bourbon peace. The atmosphere was not nearly as stern in the centre of town; after the Allies passed the triumphal arch of the porte Saint-Denis there were cheers, and several in the crowd waved white handkerchiefs; outside the Tuileries, it was a festival.[122]

The troops set up camp in the Bois de Boulogne and the woodlands of the Champs Elysées. Alexander, it had been planned, was to stay at the Elysée Palace. But he was not one to abide by plans, especially where residence was concerned, and, on the grounds of a vague rumour that the palace had been mined (probably put about by Talleyrand), he headed on horseback for rue Saint-Florentin.

There his proclamation to the people of Paris had already been prepared by a team of five: Talleyrand, Nesselrode, Pradt, Dalberg, and Baron Louis. It sounded like a fresh variation on the Declaration of the Rights of Man. "The Allied Sovereigns welcome the will of the French nation ... They shall no longer treat with Napoleon Bonaparte, nor with any member of his family ... They shall respect the integrity of ancient France, such as existed under her legitimate kings ... They shall recognise and guarantee the constitution that the French nation will grant herself ..."

Nearly six years had passed since their conversations at Erfurt. Alexander had rolled back the armies of Napoleon; Talleyrand was ready to establish a new rule of law. The Tsar, wearing the uniform of his Horse Guards and a cocked green hat with plumes, rode up to the gate, in the company of Schwarzenberg and the Prussian King. Old Talleyrand stood in the courtyard, his hair powdered in the eighteenth-century manner. Alexander dismounted. "Monsieur de Talleyrand," he said, raising to heaven his mild blue eyes, shining with emotion.[123]

Talleyrand's leg

The principle of legitimacy was at the heart of Talleyrand's system. Madame de Staël even claimed that it was he who invented the word. She was wrong; it was Louis XVIII who gave the word currency in a proclamation he made when Napoleon crowned himself Emperor. Louis had demanded, on the day of the coronation, to succeed to the throne of his ancestors by right of "legitimacy." "Never will we compromise the inheritance of our fathers," he announced; "never will we abandon our rights."[124]

Yet a case could be made that Talleyrand had changed the meaning of the word by emphasising not inheritance but the law (which was, after all, more faithful to the etymology of "legitimacy"). For Talleyrand the law was defined by the representative institutions of the nation; at an international level it was the collective expression of the world's Sovereigns. The law was also grounded in time. "A legitimate government," said Talleyrand, "whether it is monarchical or republican, hereditary or elective, aristocratic or democratic, is always the one whose existence, form and mode of action are consolidated and consecrated by a long succession of years, and I would even say by prescription of the centuries."[125]

Legitimate government showed its virtues *à la longue durée*, like civilisation. Indeed, civilisation and legitimacy were, for Talleyrand, part and parcel of the same thing; they demonstrated the deep structure of the universe, the timelessness of being, over and above which the hurly-burly of daily events seemed almost a distraction. "Civilised" people were aware of this eternal, universal harmony; "legitimate" regimes conformed to it.

Talleyrand sought this understanding in others; he made it the criterion by which he judged the people around him, the statesmen he met, the Sovereigns who governed him. "It is up to you to save Europe," he had told Alexander at Erfurt. "The French people are civilised, their Sovereign is not; the Sovereign of Russia is civilised, his people are not; it is then for the Sovereign of Russia to be the ally of the French people."

Alexander should have taken the comment as a warning, for it proved Talleyrand's belief that Western Europe understood the timeless principles of the universe whereas eastern Europe did not. Talleyrand was a western European: Alexander, as a civilised individual trained by westerners, might have had a role to play in overthrowing the usurper, but once the usurper was gone, it would be the western Powers, acting in harmony – in concert – that would defend civilisation.[126]

These were grand French ideas, steeped in the Enlightenment. Yet Talleyrand's principle of legitimacy – and the civilisation it claimed to support – was not a mere product of the mind. It was also a lived experience. Certainly it was an attitude born out of the hubbub of Revolution. But born out of personal turmoils too. The quest for a legitimacy, rooted in time, was not just a part of his own story; it was the single chain that ran right through his story – and link by link one can follow that chain to its source: the conviction, instilled at childhood, that his legitimate place in civilisation had been denied him.

"Without this leg," he once joked, tapping his right knee as he travelled by carriage across Paris with a companion, "I would have probably followed a military career." It was in the last week of the last year of the century, 1799. He was speaking to Hyde de Neuville, an agent of the exiled Louis XVIII. Talleyrand was then Minister of Exterior Relations (as Republicans called Foreign Affairs), and a military coup had just set up Bonaparte as First Consul. Hyde de Neuville was negotiating with Bonaparte – unsuccessfully it turned out – for the return of the King. Talleyrand was in excellent spirits, Hyde de Neuville remembered, talking "almost with love for His Royal Highness, Monsieur [the comte d'Artois]." Obviously he wasn't in a position to serve the Prince, but no one, Talleyrand said, possessed the secret of the future. It was then that he referred to his leg. Without that leg a military career? "Who knows? I would have perhaps been, like you, an *émigré*, or, like you, an envoy of the Bourbons!"[127]

Talleyrand suffered terribly from that leg. In his memoirs he noted how it had influenced his whole life, how his own position as first surviving son in a grand noble family had been refused him, how, unable to be a soldier, his parents directed him into "another profession" (which he did not name – pages later he casually mentioned the date of his "resignation" as an archbishop). Evidently his parents placed the advancement of the family above the interests of their eldest son, "for in the grand houses," Talleyrand explained, "it was the *family* that one loved, much more than individuals, and especially young individuals that one does not know." And he added, "I do not at all like to dwell on this idea . . . I leave it."[128]

Talleyrand believed his lameness was the result of an accident, which is what great noble families, in constant fear of a "taint in the blood," liked to believe. He claimed his wet-nurse had dropped him as an infant; the painter Toulouse-Lautrec was supposed to have suffered from the same fate. There is plenty of room for speculation over what was actually the cause of Talleyrand's limp. Jacob-Nicolas Moreau, who had arranged the marriage of Talleyrand's parents, records that, in the year of his birth, Talleyrand had a fever which almost killed him. What was the fever? There are signs that Talleyrand suffered from a partial paralysis of the right leg: his limp, the shape of his boot (preserved at the family château de Valençay), his need for a lengthy leg iron and walking stick. Paralysis, following a fever, are an obvious hint that what Talleyrand suffered from was the disease of Sir Walter Scott, polio.[129]

Crippled men do not tread a straight path. General Dumouriez called Talleyrand "Père Gambille" ("Father Jigger") because of his limp. What disgusted Rewbell, a Jacobin member of the Directorate in the 1790s, was that Talleyrand was not a complete man. "He is lame, a man lacking a part of his limbs, who can hardly support himself on his two fleshless bones." It made him appear, thought Rewbell, like a "living death."[130] Napoleon's inspired image of dung in a stocking was doubtlessly derived from the fact that, to conceal his fleshless bones, Talleyrand's right silk stocking had to be stuffed. Talleyrand had a foot in each camp, according to a popular satyrical rhyme of the 1790s; he put the good one forward, the crippled one behind.[131] No one ever denied how well he performed those clumsy steps, like a masked courtier in a baroque dance; and with no expression. "I saw him coming into the living room at Malmaison with a cold and nonchalant air, dragging his foot, and supporting himself on the first available chair with hardly a greeting for anyone," remembered

Napoleon's sister-in-law, Queen Hortense of Holland. "He had the face of death, dressed in red velvet," said Madame de Cazenove d'Arlens.

Yet there was something seductive about it all. One of his oldest associates, the comte de Montrond, confessed to Madame Hamelin (who wondered why he was so faithful to this corrupt lame aristocrat), "Eh! mon Dieu, Madame, who couldn't love him? He's so vicious!" The marquise de La Tour du Pin said the attraction was rather like the way a serpent's eye fascinates the victim bird. His winding gait and impassive expression made Aimée de Coigny also think of a snake.[132]

It might be a winding way he followed, it might be one strewn with lies and dishonest traffickings (he perhaps pocketed as much as one third of the sum paid by the United States in the Louisiana Purchase), but Talleyrand always walked with an aim in mind, as though an inner compass guided him. He knew when to take shelter and when to arise again. Above all, he could always give an explanation and a purpose for his turns.

One of the most exquisite passages Talleyrand ever wrote is to be found at the beginning of his memoirs and concerns the eighteen months he spent with his great-grandmother, Madame de Chalais, after he had been withdrawn from his nurse and following the discovery of his "accident." "The first objects that strike the eyes and the heart of childhood," he reflected, "often determine a man's frame of mind, and give his character the trends [*ses dispositions*] that will be his for the rest of his life." He appears to have written these pages in the late summer of 1813, as Napoleon's campaign in Germany approached its disastrous climax.[133] Talleyrand's description of Madame de Chalais and her château is the antithesis of war; it evokes a timeless peace. The old lady was born in 1686 – in the middle of the reign of Louis XIV. Her father was of the high nobility, General of the Galleys, and nephew of Madame de Montespan. Her mother was the third daughter of the King's Finance Minister, Colbert. Her first husband was Michel de Chamillart (Talleyrand's maternal great-grand-father), who was Louis XIV's Minister of War. Thus two of Talleyrand's ancestors were ministers in the court of the Great Louis. Talleyrand presents a childhood vision of that noble grandeur, vested in servants of the Sovereign, now buried within a provincial retreat, within the deeper social strata: "The customs of the nobility in Périgord resembled their old châteaux: there was something in them that was grand and stable; the light penetrated little, but it arrived sweet. One moved forward with a useful slowness towards a more enlightened civilisation."

Everything of Talleyrand is in these phrases; the immobility of time, the stable, unchallengeable nature of his civilisation, a gradual

enlightenment of understanding, even the slow tread of his march –
one can almost hear his footsteps. A little further on in the text he
remarks how the most shattering events could not alter the general
ethos of this grand noble culture; "Even the Revolution did not
succeed in dispelling the charm of these old dwellings, where
sovereignty resided. They remained like those old deserted temples
from where the faithful had withdrawn, but whose traditions still
bore veneration. Chalais was one of the châteaux of that time, revered
and loved."[134]

Talleyrand decorated all the regimes he served with the furnishings
of Madame de Chalais' château, lending them legitimacy, breathing
into them timelessness. One begins to understand what he meant
when he wrote to Alexander, at the moment of their rupture in June
1814, of "the ancient *accoutumance* of love for our kings." "I loved
Napoleon," he wrote, in a similar vein, in his memoirs; but when
Napoleon's ambition pushed beyond reason, Talleyrand could no
longer consider him as "civilised." He had loved the comte d'Artois;
but when Artois decided to abandon France in the crisis of 1789, he
deserted – as Talleyrand told him the day he left – "the interests of the
monarchy." He loved Alexander; but Alexander's blind ideals were
becoming a threat to the harmony of Europe, Talleyrand's Europe,
his civilised Europe. Talleyrand may have been inconstant to those he
loved but, as a masked courtier, he always loved his Sovereign.

The greatest of all the contradictions in Talleyrand's life is that,
though a former minister of Napoleon Bonaparte, he could present
himself as a man of peace. But even here there was a chain of continuity. Throughout Talleyrand's career one finds memoranda and
reports opposing French territorial aggrandisement and warning, as
he put it in a famous notice addressed to the Convention in
November 1792, that "France must remain contained within her
proper limits." As Napoleon's Foreign Minister he had developed a
reputation as a man of moderation, who considered war as a political
instrument only of the last resort. He was, for example, fundamen-
tally opposed to Napoleon's dogged aim to crush Austria and, in late
1805, sent a long memorandum to Napoleon pleading with him not to
humiliate that power. Like the good Parisian he was, he saw European
geography as an extended system of boulevards and perilous outer
faubourgs; Austria, he argued, was a wide and necessary boulevard
that protected Western Europe from the barbarians. Poland, in
Talleyrand's mind, was another of these frontier boulevards, and for
this reason he had always considered France's approval of the first
partition, back in 1772, a disaster for the harmony of Europe. He later
played a major part in the reconstitution of Poland within the
Napoleonic system and the ties this established between his family
and the grateful Poles would outlast his own life.[135]

David's two sketches of Talleyrand, though drawn from memory, show the statesman as he was: wily and wise

In 1807, the year he was dismissed from Napoleon's government, he outlined to Madame de Rémusat his own vision of Europe. It was strikingly similar to the plan which he would propose to the British in early August, 1814 – and it strangely resembled the political map of Europe today. His plan, he said, had been "to restore religion, morality and order to France, to applaud the civilisation of England while containing her policy [this was in the midst of war], to fortify [France's] frontiers by a Confederation of the Rhine, to make Italy a kingdom independent of Austria and of [France], to close the Tsar up within his own territories by creating this natural barrier offered by Poland: that is what ought to be the eternal designs of the Emperor, and where each of my treaties lead him. But ambition, anger, pride, and the few imbeciles he listens to, often blind him."[136]

The most remarkable feature here, of course, was his applause for the "civilisation of England." But then Talleyrand had always felt a certain affinity with England. Talleyrand's enemies at home often accused him of being the instrument of England, even when his projects were directed against that country. There was constant suspicion in Republican circles of the "Anglo-émigré Taleyrand [*sic*]," with some justification, because Talleyrand did have ties with many of England's leading politicians. When William Pitt and Wilberforce came over to France to learn the language, after the peace of 1783, they stayed six weeks in Talleyrand's residence near Reims; they were young men then. Pitt, as Prime Minister, was rather less friendly when Talleyrand arrived in England as an emigrant from Terror in 1792, but the Frenchman did establish important links with the leading Whigs of the day, including Wilberforce, Romilly, Sheridan and Fox. They all came over to France after the peace of 1802 and visited the Minister of Exterior Relations at his château in Neuilly.

Talleyrand's "Anglomania" – as his French critics called it – was not reciprocated on the other side of the Channel; the English really did not like him. A Swiss acquaintance, Etienne Dumont, had noticed this in London where, during the Terror, they had both lived in short exile: Talleyrand was thought to be lacking in "liveliness, intimacy, curiosity and fun"; he had, it appears, a "sententious manner, a cold politeness, an examining air," which were not the sort of qualities that would attract a Sheridan or a Fox. Sir Samuel Romilly attended one of Talleyrand's large dinners at Neuilly in September 1802. Talleyrand was by then foreign minister. "Talleyrand received me coldly enough," Romilly recorded in his diary, "with the air and the manner of a great minister, and not of a man with whom I once was intimate. . . . The dinner was one of the most stately and melancholy banquets I ever was present at." Cobbett called Talleyrand "the lame fiend." Croker said he seemed like "an old fuddled, lame, village schoolmaster, and his voice is deep and hoarse."[137]

But Talleyrand could cut through these English gentilities and dig to the deeper structures again, where he would strike a commercial vein binding the two nations together.

Talleyrand's interest in financial matters went beyond his search for personal gain. In fact, it was probably his obsession with money that convinced him that trade was the sole source and guarantee of peace. "There is no science more avid of facts than political economy," he once told a learned assembly at the Institut de France. "As the proverb says, you cannot dispute the facts. If this proverb one day achieves its truth there will remain very few disputes between men." Britain's Alien Act of 1794 had forced Talleyrand to leave England for America. What struck him there was how close the Americans were to the English, despite the fact they had been at war little more than a decade earlier. The reason was trade; the spirit of war, he would say, had been replaced by the spirit of commerce – "America forgot her resentments and opened up again her old communications." She dug down to the ancient vein. Talleyrand was convinced that it would be the same between the peoples of France and England. He had said as much in his memorandum to the Convention, in 1792, when he outlined the problem of Anglo-French relations: "After a revolution, one must open new roads to industry, one must provide outlets to all the passions." After a revolution, he could have said, one must return to the commercial vein.[138]

In the overture he made to the British government in early August, 1814, Talleyrand knew just how much the two countries had "common interests," even if they saw them in such different ways. Castlereagh was a mechanic, Wellington a musician; Talleyrand took the same ideas and planted them in the old soils of the continent.

August conversations

As soon as Castlereagh reached Brussels, on 22 August, he wrote a cheerful note to his friend Clemens von Metternich, now back in Vienna, to tell him of his planned visit to Paris. "I propose separating from Lady C. here and making an excursion for 48 hours to Paris to see how the land lays there . . . everything here goes well. The Prince gains ground daily and is highly sensible of the loyalty with which General Vincent prepared the way for his reception. I conclude Aberdeen [Britain's guileless Ambassador to Vienna] has apprised you of his change of plans. I don't know whether there is any truth of the newspaper report of *his being in love* . . ."[139] There is no record that he forewarned Alexander, or any of his representatives, of the trip. Given the tensions that had developed in London, it is most unlikely that he would have done so.

Castlereagh's arrival in Paris was announced in the newspapers – one line, between the news that the duc d'Orléans was in town and a list of honours granted to the descendants of old Bourbon war heroes. He does not appear to have attended any of the great festivities that were under way in the last week of August; evil tongues could even have suggested that his arrival on Friday, the 26th, and departure on Sunday had been deliberately planned so as to avoid Thursday's Fête Saint-Louis and the royal reception at the Hôtel de Ville the following Monday.[140]

Talleyrand was now well re-established in his old ministerial offices on rue du Bac. Officially it was the Ministry of Foreign Affairs, but in his private correspondence Talleyrand continued to use the republican term of "Exterior Relations." Liberals and conservatives alike were suspicious of him. Defending the former, Madame de Staël, who at one time had been more than a mere friend, nailed Talleyrand down with a fusillade of abuse: "You have never had any opinions, Monsieur; you have only interests, and the vilest of all. They have been the sole motive of your conduct under every regime. Money and more money, that's all you have ever looked for . . ." "Ah! ah! ah! Madame de Staël, Madame de Staël, please!" stuttered the Prince Minister, "Ah! Madame de Staël!" Most of the royal family thought him too liberal; the comte d'Artois, whom Talleyrand so professedly "loved," actively worked against him. The King himself actually admired him, though he had kept him waiting in an antechamber for three hours at the time of their first encounter at Compiègne because the King did not approve of an "ex-Archbishop" who was still formally married. Talleyrand should have been his prime minister as well as foreign minister, but, largely on account of all these suspicions, Louis kept the ministries of his government apart – an old Bourbon tradition (though not one which had a very good track record). One suspects the King named him Ambassador Extraordinary to the Congress of Vienna "for the definitive arrangement of the affairs of Europe" to keep him out of France for a few months.[141]

Talleyrand was looking for friends.

The exact character of the conversations between Talleyrand and Castlereagh in Paris that August does not appear to have been recorded. Wellington, in a letter to Liverpool on the Sunday of Castlereagh's departure, said they were "perfectly satisfactory." Castlereagh, the same day, described them as "upon the whole favourable." He added in a later note that Talleyrand was so keen to establish a close connection with Britain that he found it necessary "rather to repress the exuberance of this sentiment."[142]

Here were two men of very different temperaments drawn to each other by European "interests." British caution in the face of French "exuberance" was perfectly understandable; as Wellington put it, "only a few months ago it was wished to exclude the interference and influence of France from the Congress entirely."[143]

The extensive diplomatic correspondence available for the months August and September make it easy to imagine what was discussed. Near the top of the British agenda was the problem of the slave trade, just as for the French it was near the bottom. Castlereagh, embarrassed by the uproar at home, was still pressing for immediate French abolition. Short of that he was ready to accept "an early decree" that would prevent a revival of the trade on the African coast north of the equator, where British naval policing had wiped out the traffic in just a few years. He also wanted the ships of war "of both nations" to have the right to inspect all merchant vessels in the northern tropics and urged that France adopt a system of licensing so as to restrict the importation of slaves to their own colonies "to the numbers strictly necessary for the cultivation of the existing plantations." Talleyrand accepted that the slave trade was "repugnant to the principles of natural justice, and of the enlightened age in which we live" – indeed the phrase could very well have been his – and he gave an open ear to the Whigs in town who were urging an exchange of "a Caribbean island" for immediate abolition. But to representatives of the British government Talleyrand kept on repeating that opinion in France needed to be cultivated and that the five-year extension, stipulated in the Treaty, was the only way to allow this. Privately, both Castlereagh and Wellington agreed, believing in their hearts that establishing the authority of the new government in France had more consequence for world peace than the matter of slavery. At any rate, Castlereagh's conversations on this point achieved nothing.[144]

A middle agenda item for both parties was the dismantling of trade barriers between the two countries – in the middle not because it was considered unimportant but, on the contrary, because it was felt that high-handed political action at this point would hinder rather than aid the natural growth of trade, already noted by every traveller in the Channel ports. A generation of war had created national suspicions that would not fade away overnight. Why raise ghosts? "I am of the opinion that fruitless attempts to extend our commercial intercourse with other States generally defeat and retard the object," Castlereagh had written to Wellington on 7 August. Castlereagh wanted to avoid "the manufacturing clamour of France." So did Talleyrand. "Monsieur de Talleyrand's ideas," said Castlereagh, "are very sound and liberal upon these subjects." As in the case of the slave trade, nothing specific was achieved in the conversations of August, but there was clearly an understanding. A cord of "civilisation" was strung.[145]

Finally, and most importantly, the affairs of Europe were discussed. Talleyrand knew he had Castlereagh's ear. The conversation seems to have been limited to what, in diplomatic parlance, one calls "an exchange of views." Castlereagh's letter of 7 August to Wellington expresses particular anxiety to sound out Talleyrand's opinions on Poland and Naples. There was a great question mark over Poland, which none of the international encounters so far had begun to erase. The continuing presence of Russian troops in the area threatened the equilibrium of Europe; Prussia's demand for compensation in Saxony imperilled the balance of power within Germany. Clearly a confrontation with Russia and Prussia was shaping. Castlereagh – mindful of his last conversation in London with the Prussian Chancellor, Prince von Hardenberg – told Talleyrand that he supported the idea of an independent Saxony.

On Naples, there appears to have been some secret accord. Castlereagh had been highly upset over nationalist intrigues between William Bentinck, Britain's Minister to Sicily, and Murat, who remained King despite his known sympathies for Napoleon. Bentinck was eventually recalled from his post and, passing through Paris in mid-August, received applause from certain sections of the population, which did nothing to improve Talleyrand's opinion of Murat. Both he and Castlereagh were concerned about the growth of nationalist enthusiasms in Italy ("a great moral change is coming on in Europe ... ."). Worse, there was worry about a subversive link developing with the Emperor of Elba; one would breathe not a word, but the fear already existed of a return of the eagle. Murat's fate seems to have been sealed in Paris that August. "I have turned over in my mind a good deal the mode of executing our plans against Murat," wrote Wellington on 12 September to Castlereagh, obviously confirming words that had previously passed. "I should think the Austrians will not interfere themselves, and will not like to see the French in Italy; and the operation must be performed by the King of Sicily, the King of Spain, and their Allies, and possibly a few French troops sent by sea into Sicily ... England would be obliged to furnish transports for the whole, and a train of field ordnance of 60 pieces, equipped, and a battering train. With such a force, we ought to be able to effect our object." So Britain was ready to join Bourbon France in a war against Murat's Naples.[146]

Talleyrand gave Castlereagh the authority to quote his views at the preliminary meeting of the Four Powers in Vienna and then began preparations for his own mission to the Austrian capital. A few days after the meeting with Castlereagh, Count Münster, the Regent's principal Minister at Hanover and now his chief private representative on the continent, passed through Paris and made a glowing report on the impressions Castlereagh's visit had left. On 9 September Talleyrand informed the Duchess, "I'm working at my best for the Congress – for I have to arrive with instructions that I'm doing myself."[147]

Talleyrand's *Instructions pour les ambassadeurs du Roi au Congrès* is widely considered, for style and clarity, one of the great classics in the history of diplomacy. It was undoubtedly a joint effort between Talleyrand and his secretary, La Besnardière. The document concludes with a summary of "the points which are the most important for France, classed according to the order of their importance":

1 That Austria be left no opportunity to let fall into the hands of the Princes of her house, that is, into her own hands, the States of the King of Sardinia;
2 That Naples be restituted to Ferdinand IV [the Bourbon pretender];
3 That all Poland does not pass and cannot pass under the sovereignty of Russia;
4 That Prussia acquires neither the Kingdom of Saxony, at least the whole of it, nor Mainz.

Castlereagh would have put priority on the Netherlands, he would have emphasised British maritime rights, he would have included a phrase on the slave trade, and he would have shown less concern about the extension of Prussia into Germany; but as an outline of "European affairs" the intentions of Britain and France were clearly similar.[148]

"I set out this evening for Dijon, where I expect to find Lady C., and proceed on to Geneva," a satisfied Castlereagh informed his Prime Minister on Sunday, 28 August.

Monseigneur at Ferrières

East of Paris, in a château at Ferrières, lived another man of all regimes, now in retirement. He was watched by the police, for he could become a major threat for the newly installed Bourbon regime.

The peasants respectfully addressed him as "Monseigneur," though he had no noble origin and was not, in fact, very respectable. A man of above average height with thinning reddish hair and a thin mouth, dull grey eyes, sallow cheeks, and sober dress; some said he had the appearance of a phantom, others were put in mind of a dead fish. Yet he enjoyed his long walks around the estates, aided by his handsome malacca-cane – for at fifty-five he was beginning to suffer from the rheumatism that, six years later, would kill him. He was a widower, a man who enjoyed the company of his children, a man who decorated his home with simple furnishings, who served a good dinner, who did not drink excessively, and who retired to bed early.

This modest man had been a mass-murderer. When the Republic, in the Year II, decreed that "the city of Lyon shall be destroyed [and] all that was inhabited by the rich shall be destroyed," it was he who carried out the order, who supervised the execution by cannon shot of over fifteen hundred, who mined the great seventeenth-century houses designed by Mansart. "Raised by the Revolution," he said in his memoirs in 1816, "I fell only through a contrary revolution." He must have wondered how a son of a merchant shipper in Nantes, a teacher at a famous Jesuit school, had raised himself on so much blood, although in his memoirs he left not a line on the affair of Lyon.[149]

He was a man of the majority who had a deep fear of being thrown into a minority. That was why, in January 1793, he had called for the death of the King. The Girondins were purged, he sided with the Jacobins; the Jacobins were dispersed, he supported the forces of the Directory; Bonaparte seized power, he rallied to the Consulate and the Empire. Everything he did could be explained in terms of the progress of mankind and of service to the great Revolution. "Wasn't it natural for events so favourable to the interests of the Revolution to turn to the advantage of the men who had founded it and supported it by their enlightenment and energy?" he remarked in connection with the coup d'état of Fructidor (1797). "Patriots had trodden, until then, on brambles, and it was now time for the tree of liberty to bear sweeter fruit; it was time for high positions to be allotted to the men of strength." He was a man of strength because he knew his strength: knowledge, the knowledge of the head of police, the chief of spies. He knew the Jacobins because he had been one of them; he knew the royalists through his agents; he knew the private affairs of every man of state; he knew more about the scandals within Napoleon's family than Napoleon himself. "One must have one's hands in many pies," he once advised Chancellor Pasquier.[150]

Unlike Talleyrand he had no such philosophy as legitimacy, no sense of deeper realities, no touch of "civilisation." Politics was for him simply a double game, and its goal was to win. Balzac thought he was a "singular genius" and used him as a model for one of his leading characters, but when it actually came to defining the great spirit this thinking man of letters had to admit, "the fullness of his genius was purely ministerial, essentially governmental."[151]

So much power he had amassed. But the day would come, as the day did come, of the "contrary revolution." In early March 1814 he was in Italy, by mid-March he was in Lyon, on 8 April his black carriage trotted through one of the barrières into Paris. Too late! Eight days too late! *"Si j'avais été à Paris le 31 mars . . . mais il n'y avait là personne pour déjouer ce coquin de Talleyrand."* He played every card he had, he visited every friend, he wrote to his allies, he visited the ladies of Faubourg Saint-Germain in their salons, he even charmed enemies to recommend him for a place in the new government. He drafted an admiring epistle to the King; he paid a personal visit to Wellington. Everything, he tried everything. But it was too late! The positions had all been filled! "The restoration of the Bourbons destroyed all my projects and threw me into the political wilderness," he wrote. The era of the counter-Revolution had begun; its victim was Joseph Fouché.[152]

VIENNA
Autumn 1814

Isolated diplomats

Lord Castlereagh, unlike his now remarkably friendly French colleague Talleyrand, set out from Paris for Vienna with no formal instructions from his government. It was a situation with which Castlereagh was familiar enough. Foreign policy was not an over-riding concern for the Cabinet in London; its members spent the larger part of their time worrying about problems of trade, the Corn Laws, Ireland, and how to deal with the Radicals. Britain's diplomats, as a result, would often feel quite isolated. "I begin to feel the want of positive instructions," wrote a despairing Robert Liston, Britain's Ambassador in Constantinople, on 26 September. A few lines, he pleaded from Castlereagh, would "remove the ignorance and uncer-tainty, which, in spite of my best efforts, I feel to be attended with embarrassment and disadvantage."[1] Isolation, however, had its advan-tages. British diplomats found they had enormous leeway to act as difficulties presented themselves; they worked day by day, without knowledge of the future, with little guidance from their government, simply addressing the questions and attacking the issues as they arose. Most of them were not policy-makers or inventors of high principle; they were problem-solvers. It was rather ironic: a lack of government interest, which was itself a product of Britain's insular security, and the fact that for the last twenty odd years Britain had had very few embassies open in Europe, had led to a pragmatic style of diplomacy, shed of abstract principles and ideology. Under the continual threat of war and invasion, the continental Powers had been unable to foster such an approach.

Castlereagh himself was a policy-maker, and on the matter of British policy in Europe he stood practically alone. The only other Cabinet member to follow closely events on the continent in the com-ing months would be the Prime Minister, Lord Liverpool, and even he was to show ignorance of the issues at stake. A few letters would also pass between Lord Bathurst, the Secretary of State for War and Colonies, and Castlereagh; but on the single occasion when Bathurst gave official instructions on behalf of the Cabinet, Castlereagh totally

125

ignored him. The one other figure who did take an interest in the progress of Castlereagh's negotiations was the First Gentleman of Europe, the Prince Regent. He got long reports from his own Hanoverian Minister, Count Münster, and was probably one of the best informed inhabitants in the Kingdom. How this bedecked and spangled European Prince longed to be with his fellow Sovereigns in Vienna, how he yearned to lead all Congress in a polonaise, to dance a cotillion with his Austrian hosts, to attend the feasts and put on a royal face for Britain. But government and parliament would never allow him further south than his pavilion on the coast of Sussex.

In general Britain was not a country very interested in what was going on in Europe. "Public opinion" only added to the isolation of the diplomats. There might have been a vague popular sentiment that the eighteenth-century partitions of Poland had been evil continental deeds or that the Kingdom of Saxony should not be wiped off the map by Europe's power brokers,[2] but the most emotional issue, outside the Regent's marital affairs, remained the slave trade, and Castlereagh's correspondence with London that autumn reflected this.

The Foreign Secretary had one crucial associate on the continent, who relieved the burden of his isolation. All his correspondence with London passed, by a special service of "flying dispatch" carriers, through Paris where it was scrutinised by the British Ambassador, the Duke of Wellington. Indeed, Castlereagh's own correspondence with the Duke was almost as voluminous as his official correspondence with London, and it actually revealed a great deal more about his views than, for example, what he wrote to Liverpool. Several important letters were also exchanged between Castlereagh and Wellington's brother, Sir Henry Wellesley, in Madrid.

Thus Castlereagh's correspondence, when considered as a whole, would make three things clear. In the first place, British foreign policy during the critical months of autumn and winter, 1814-15, was moulded not in London but on the continent. Second, it grew out of the old association that had developed between the Wellesleys and Castlereagh, a bond that could be traced back to 1809 and Britain's change in fortune in the Peninsular War. Third, the conceptual roots of that policy, we have already seen, went back still further, to Pitt.

Out of all this a certain British idea of Europe was born – to call it a "vision" would be to make it too romantic. In history it is generally referred to as "the foreign policy of Castlereagh," but it would be more exact to call it the foreign policy of Castlereagh *and* Wellington. Moreover, formed on the continent, amidst the strife of the continent, it was inevitably not impervious to the ideas and influences of the continent.

The German Revolution

At Dijon, just as planned, Castlereagh was joined by "Lady C." She had been honoured in the courts of the Hague and in Paris; in her own apartments at St James's Square she had received the Sovereigns and Ministers of Europe; she had curtseyed at St James's, at Carlton House, and at Windsor; a ship of the line had even been named after her;[3] yet, as her intimates would sadly admit, the faithful consort of the Foreign Secretary was generally a subject of jokes, and not of admiration.

She had once been a startling beauty, the envy of London and of the Irish Protestant Ascendency, the enchanting Lady Emily Ann Hobart, youngest daughter of John, second Earl of Buckinghamshire, a woman of twenty-two who had excited some passion the heart of young Robert Stewart, then soldiering in County Donegal in a regiment under her brother's command. "Tell me *you love me*, on that my existence depends," wrote Stewart during their brief engagement; he married her in April 1794, and the same month took his seat at Westminster.

A very dependent existence it turned out to be; Lord and Lady Castlereagh remained inseparable. It was an age of cynicism, and cynicism led to speculation; and with every subsequent age of cynicism there was more and more speculation; eventually the historians and biographers came in and added, layer upon layer, their own theories. However, as is often the case in these intimate matters, there was little hard evidence to go on. But the theories abounded. It was argued that they clung to one another because they never had children. "They had no children," submits Professor C.K. Webster, the great expert on Castlereagh, "and in such cases a wife must be all or nothing." Yet it seems odd that an inheritor of title and fortune would treat his wife as all, just because she had no children; in that wicked age, a childless wife in an ambitious family was more usually nothing. Unless the husband had the problem . . . But then the comtesse de Boigne, who knew the couple in London, suggests that it was Emily who insisted on their constant companionship, not Castlereagh: "She was following her own desires rather than those of Lord Castlereagh. But he never made the slightest objection." So who was following whom?[4]

Because they were nearly always together there exists practically no written correspondence between them; Castlereagh was not Talleyrand's sort of noble, who would leave us teasing *petits billets du matin*. But on one rare occasion when they were separated – during his first continental visit of 1814 – Castlereagh did write to his wife. They are friendly, bantering letters. "Love to Emma, dearest friend," he wrote from Chaumont in March 1814. "God bless you. We shall soon meet, by hook or by crook." Across Germany, and through Switzerland and France that winter it was always a "God bless you," or a "God preserve you, dearest friend."[5]

Apart from another brief correspondence during a trip Castlereagh made to Ireland seven years later,[6] that is basically all we know of the relations between the Viscount and his wife. Emily somehow seems to have fulfilled a need in solitary Castlereagh; anxious Castlereagh somehow found "repose," a "just equilibrium," in the company of his wife.

She grew fat. Two decades of public dinners and receptions, two decades of turtle soup, sirloin, mutton joints with cranberry jam, turbot, sweetbreads, and Regency jellies gave her a rotund figure which, supported by a pair of spindly legs, delighted English wits and caricaturists. Her grand robes and extravagant headgear added to the effect, from which – unhappily – her conversation failed to provide any distraction. As Lady Bessborough recorded famously, "She talks with equal indifference of bombardment and assemblies, the baby and the furniture, the emptiness of London, Lord Castlereagh's increasing debility and the doubtful success of Mr Greville's new opera – all these succeed each other so quick and with so exactly the same expression of voice and countenance that they probably hold a pretty equal value in her estimation."[7]

Lady Castlereagh's sister, Lady Matilda, also joined the small team of travelling carriages as they rolled south to Geneva. On this occasion her niece, Lady Edgcumbe, remained in England. But faithful Joseph Planta was among the party and Castlereagh probably shared with him his thoughts, his anticipations, though no record survives.

The long diversion south to Geneva was perhaps due to concern over Russian involvement, through Alexander's adviser La Harpe, in the new constitution that was being drafted in Switzerland. Castlereagh was also close to the British Ambassador there, Stratford Canning. From Geneva the train of coaches rumbled onwards and inwards to the heart of Europe. They were in Munich on 9 September. We know that the weather was awful.[8]

Castlereagh had plenty to worry about. He was certainly aware that there were members of the parliamentary opposition who were wondering why Britain even bothered to get involved in Europe and who would have preferred those carriages to turn round home. After all, Britain's own special interests – the colonial questions, maritime rights,[9] and French exclusion from the Low Countries – had been largely satisfied at the Peace of Paris. If the rest of the continent still had to sort out their differences, what business was it of Britain's? The opposition looked with suspicion on the Vienna Congress.

For Castlereagh there was no question of abandonment. For

Castlereagh, it was a matter of war or peace, an issue which, if ignored, could lose for Britain all she had so recently, and painfully, won. He stuck to his own idea, to Pitt's idea, of a "just equilibrium." But time was running short. As he travelled on to Vienna he must have indeed wondered whether he was heading for a peace conference – as history would later record it to be – or a war congress, for there was much talk of war that September.

Russia maintained her demands on Poland. Prussia wanted to annex all Saxony. Austria alone among Britain's three continental Allies appeared to defend the idea of an equilibrium. But to call the latter a "satisfied Power," as it is sometimes said, distorts the reality, because there were many influential men in Vienna, including members of the imperial family, prepared to go to war to impose her "equilibrium." Henry Kissinger speaks of Austria as a "conserving Power"; it is the better term.[10]

Bourbon France also wanted to be treated as a conserving Power, a defender of equilibrium, an opponent of expansionism, and she was making much of her new friendship with Britain to prove it. Wellington in Paris was complaining about "the loose way that people here have of talking upon public affairs."[11]

Castlereagh would have preferred his French conversations to remain confidential, a private matter between himself and Talleyrand. While he himself was open to letting France have some form of representation in the decision-making at Vienna, he knew the "jealousy" of his three other Allies would lead them to oppose direct French participation, and the alliance had to be given priority. Castlereagh's intention was, therefore, to keep France quietly in the background as a passive reserve.

Against Russian expansionism – and without counting on French help – he was obliged to align in the centre of Europe his two German Allies, Austria and Prussia. It was the old Pitt Plan again of assembling an "intermediary system between France and Russia."

Thus Castlereagh actively encouraged the idea of a broad, united Germany. After his conversations with Hardenberg in London he was fully aware of the extent of Prussian ambitions, but he thought these could be used against Russia, despite the ominous fact that these two expansionist Powers were tied together by a commitment that dated back to the campaign of 1813. The engine now had to be turned around if the equilibrium was to be maintained. His fear was that, in the process, the anti-French coalition would break up and be replaced by an alliance system that would pit northern Europe against southern Europe, the expansionist Powers against the conserving Powers, Russia and Prussia against Bourbon France and Austria. What would then happen in the Netherlands? This was where Britain could lose, and lose seriously. Moreover such a conflict would open up again the unending cycle of war, revolution, and nationalist enthusiasms. Would Bourbon France survive it? What would happen to Austria? There was not much choice: the German centre had to hold.

Castlereagh, ever the optimist, was confident that British mediation would do the trick and that his coaches would be returning home by the end of October, in time for the opening of parliament.

The dozen or so metal rimmed wheels rattled and creaked over the wet rough roads of Swabia, Bavaria, and Lower Austria. Castlereagh did not enjoy travelling in Germany. "German dirt is beyond the worst parts of Scotland," he had written to Emily during his previous visit; the roads, he said, were worse than ploughed fields, the inns were dingy and unhygienic, progress was always slow and one's bones were soon "quite sore" – "I only marvel how our English carriages could bear it."[12]

But then, no one took particular pleasure in German travel; it was exhausting, it was always too hot or too cold, and sometimes it was quite monotonous. One thinks of Madame de Staël's first "extremely sad" impressions when she crossed the Rhine into exile ten years earlier. "The deserted countryside, the houses blackened by smoke and the gothic churches all seemed designed for witches' and ghosts' tales," she said. When the painter Sir Thomas Lawrence set off for Vienna to execute portraits of the famous, he was so horrified by his first experience in a German inn that he decided to remain in his carriage day and night until he reached his destination. The Germans themselves complained. Countess Bernstorff, whose husband was named Danish Ambassador to Vienna in 1812, described the extreme discomforts of driving, like Lawrence, day and night because of the awful conditions of the inns; the heat was intolerable, her daughter was having fits and she herself suffered from migraines.[13]

Even across the flat northern plains of Münster, Hanover, and Prussia travel was so difficult that a trip of just a few leagues would be a major expedition that demanded immense physical stamina. It could be very expensive too – the coachman extorting a hefty tip on top of the fare, along with an extra charge for baggage – which is why many preferred to go by foot, if they travelled at all. Most Germans stayed put, shut up in their narrow, hidden, yet at times charming little worlds. The inhabitants one met were frequently silent. "A Frenchman knows how to talk even if he has no ideas," remarked Madame de Staël; "a German always has more in his head than he knows how to express." Germans did not talk to foreigners, and that meant most neighbours. Karl Heinrich von Lang, a southern nobleman who knew the Metternichs, described a move from one Swabian village to another as a transfer to a foreign land with strange customs, manners, and a new dialect that had to be mastered.[14]

Castlereagh's carriages passed through those villages. Did he notice the contrasts? Did he worry when the servants' coach broke down on a practically impassable road? Didn't he have some doubts about the unity of his intermediary system, "Germany"? Or was he too busy discussing the mechanics of diplomacy with Planta?

Castlereagh would have witnessed rural scenes – the fields stripped, the straw stacked, the grains stored – that a sixteenth-century traveller could have recorded. He would have seen forests and hills that hadn't changed since the days of Tacitus. Some German thinkers would now look at that landscape and perceive something grand in it, a confirmation of an older order, evidence that, beyond the immediate agitations of history, all men were children of the universe, part of a vast, eternal, harmonious whole. True, in 1789 the same philosophers proclaimed that heaven was in Paris, not a German forest. But after two decades of war, army requisitions, and taxes paid to the foreigner, most of them were tired of what the French propagandists had called progress and longed for repose and even a return to the nourishing communities of the past. The philosopher Hegel and the poet Hölderlin would speak of a "homecoming." Arndt spoke of tradition, folk, and the Fatherland. The painter and poet Philip Otto Runge sought a community of family, love, and understanding. Clemens Brentano and Heinrich von Kleist returned to the fold of the Catholic Church.

But the old home had changed. The fact was that the French Revolution had been more of a revolution in Germany than it had been in France. France, after all, had survived her Revolution with her territory intact and her society basically what it had been, though there would be plenty of debate. In Germany, by contrast, several dozen sovereign states had been abolished, whole domains had disappeared; almost sixty per cent of the German population had changed rulers. *Das alte Reich*, the Holy Roman Empire, which had ostensibly held the area together for almost a millennium, no longer existed. (On "Germany" and its states see Appendix B.)[15]

That ringing word, the *"Reich,"* meant literally "reach" or "stretch," which conveyed more of a horizontal than vertical image, a sense that you could follow the particular, peculiar ways of your own family, village or your free city-state and yet be included within the "reach"; it had little to do, in origin, with the idea of a centrally administered Empire at the top demanding loyalty from all who lived under it. It was the vestige of an earlier universalist tradition in Europe that had entirely disappeared from the Western nation states but still found its residue in the German centre. Napoleon might have considered himself the new Charlemagne but, strictly speaking, it was Kaiser Franz in Vienna who had a better claim to his mantle. The function of the old Reich was not so much to dominate through a single authority as to balance multiple, fragmented authorities.

Through the eighteenth century, writers and theorists had praised it, not the least of them Jean-Jacques Rousseau, who argued, with phrases that could have been Castlereagh's, that the Reich "holds every other power in check" and it assures that "the European balance cannot be destroyed and no ruler need fear being dethroned by another." But it was an ancient equilibrium Rousseau was defending.[16]

The French Revolution changed all the rules in Germany. Massive armies had to be organised, state resources had to be centralised, huge swathes of territories were annexed by the enemy with compensations made to the larger, richer, most influential losers. Annexation and compensation: it was carried out with a vengeance in Napoleon's Germany. It was a new game of equilibrium based on new principles of national sovereignty, national territory, and national law, along with a new dynamic political goal: consolidation, expansion, and reform. The old Reich just couldn't compete and was abolished, without tears, on 6 August 1806. Germany was being westernised, the national principle imposed on an ancient structure that had not been built for it.

This was the crooked optical box into which Castlereagh had not yet really looked, one with a multitude of scenes and figures, where forgotten pieces came forward while others dropped right out of sight, where the configuration was new but the component parts were as old as the forests and hills. But Castlereagh, still seeking the centre in his own scheme of things, had never in truth had a chance to look. He was an outsider, an islander.

The Minoritenplatz

The road from Munich to Vienna would have taken him through Altötting, Braunau, Lambach, and Sankt Pölten – a distance of 250 English miles which lasted as long for Castlereagh as they had for Mozart more than thirty years earlier: five days. On 14 September, the carriages rode up the Schönbruner Weg to the huge revolving wooden customs gates of Vienna.

Nobody had yet thought how the diplomatic business at Vienna was going to be conducted. From the Rhine to the Vistula, from the Baltic to the Mediterranean, there was barely a frontier in Europe that had yet been fixed. All that had been determined by that September were France's frontiers. Even the shape of the United Netherlands had to be confirmed at the Congress.

The Congress? What was this "Congress"? Article XXXII of the Treaty of Paris spoke of "regulating arrangements" in "general Congress." It sounded like some sort of parliamentary assembly of nations, a very strange and new idea. Nobody had yet decided who would sit in it or even the hall in which it would sit; but sit it was supposed to on 1 October. Castlereagh, like his senior foreign colleagues, seriously thought that a couple of weeks of "methodising" between Ministers of the Four Allies would solve the problem. His hopes would soon be dashed.

A more immediate problem was the tiny quarters the Austrian authorities had put aside for the British. "Zum Auge des Gottes" was a house hidden in the Milchgasse under the shadow of the magnificent Peterskirche.[17] Castlereagh decided the place was not good enough and had everyone moved to a palace which he rented on the west side of the Minoritenplatz, dominated by another great church. Beyond the beauty of the place – Castlereagh reserved for himself the top floor suite, shaded by a great white see-saw pediment crowned with urns, reclining nudes, and cherubs – its main advantage was that it was only a few paces from the imperial court in the Hofburg and Metternich's formal residence on the Ballhausplatz. Castlereagh was positioning himself in the centre.[18]

Just as on his previous visit to the continent, Castlereagh was to take all the main decisions himself. He regarded the fourteen other members of the delegation as subordinates; he told Wellington, "they take no part in transactions between Cabinet and Cabinet." The Earl of Clancarty, who had been serving in the Netherlands, was the most distinguished among them. He had played an important moderating role in Princess Charlotte's affair with the Prince of Orange, had a good grasp of European politics, was liked by Castlereagh, and, most significant, he was very much admired by Talleyrand. Lord Cathcart, the Ambassador to St Petersburg, was generally regarded as some-thing of a dim-wit; his principal asset was his intimacy with the Tsar, but this was to prove no asset at all. Edward Cooke, Castlereagh's chief of staff, was a man who did not easily support strain; he would soon retire to Italy and be replaced by Joseph Planta. As for the Ambassador to Vienna, Sir Charles Stewart – Castlereagh's beloved half-brother – he cheerfully admitted that he lacked the qualities of a diplomat. It appears that no member of the delegation could write in French, despite the fact that this was the language of diplomacy in 1814. It was Friedrich Gentz, Metternich's assistant and later general secretary of the Congress, who translated Britain's formal notes and memoranda for them.[19]

Yet, amateurish as it appears today, this was probably the most efficient delegation in Vienna. It worked in harmony – at least while Castlereagh was present – it produced its memoranda on time, and it had its own courier service; it was the only delegation never to be penetrated by Austria's secret services.[20]

Thus Castlereagh established himself in the ancient capital of Vienna. He could now look out of another window on another square. He could watch the sun play fantastic colours on the strange

Viennese rooftops, hear the street cries from the Herrengasse – "*Keine Asche? Keine Asche?*" – and contemplate the gothic porch of the Minoritenkirche in front of him. After a quarter of a century of war, a quarter of a century of isolation, Britain had a foot in Europe.

Vienna receives Europe's delegates

London was the "metropolis," Paris wanted to be capital of the world, Vienna, Europe's third city, merely described herself as the *Residenzstadt*. Vienna was not interested in more. She was perfectly happy to act as a residence for the Habsburgs – she would provide residence for a quarter of a million other citizens, too – but she had no desire to be a world city, she did not want to send agents and armies out into the five continents or be the centre of a grand international network; her empire was limited to one region of Europe. While London and Paris looked forward to the next century, to the sources of new wealth and expansion, Vienna preferred to look back to the harmonies and balances of the last, an age of pure politics, an age that did not concern itself too much with the fuss of economics, the worry of great social problems, or the tragedies of total war; Vienna did not like to entertain such serious thoughts. Vienna had more a taste for cabinet politics on a human scale and felt quite at odds with the developing grand democratic idiom of the nineteenth-century epic. In Vienna there was always room for the joke, the burlesque; her theatre and her politics complemented each other on that point. More than one sage in town made the contrast with the great western national capitals by noting that their Vienna was a *vegetal* and *organic* city rather than a *structural* and *artificial* city, that she refused to be swept along by great popular outbursts of exultation, that her desire was to grow like the forests around her, at her own time, her own pace, vegetating in her antique splendour, enjoying the decor of past arts and the inheritance of an old, stable civilisation.

Vienna, in other words, wanted to remain small and keep civilisation within manageable bounds. Madame de Staël was about the only person to speak of Vienna as a "capital" – the "capital of Germany" – but she was being ironic. German-speaking Europe had no *grande ville;* Prussia's Berlin was the next largest town with a population of only 170,000.[21]

The choice of Vienna as a site for the peace conference had been decided on the field of battle. It was in Leipzig, on 19 October 1813, with the news just received of Napoleon's retreat after three days of combat, that Tsar Alexander and King Frederick William promised, in a very emotional encounter with Kaiser Franz, to visit their new Austrian ally in Vienna. At the time, the fall of Napoleon's regime seemed imminent. But the war continued and the negotiations got increasingly complicated. It was subsequently Castlereagh who, by incorporating his "system of Conferences" into the Treaty of Chaumont in March 1814, transformed this visit of the Monarchs to Vienna into a European Congress, which was then formally confirmed at Paris in May, though nobody really knew what either "Europe" or "the Congress" meant.[22]

Because no formal system of procedure had been established, the invitation to attend was made in August by a simple announcement in Europe's newspapers that the Congress would be opening on 1 October. As a result, anyone with an interest – or even a curiosity – in Europe's future felt entitled to be present. German princelings and lords, who had lost their properties and privileges after the French invasions, came in the hope of re-establishing the old order; Napoleonic sovereigns and heirs arrived to insist on the new order; nationalists sought one vision; Roman cardinals sought another; mistresses came to enjoy themselves; gamblers came to impoverish themselves; bankers came to enrich themselves; the lawyers arrived to support and oppose them all. An Augsberg newspaper estimated that around sixteen thousand royals, nobles, commoners, travellers, vagrants, and their friends turned up in Vienna that September, but it seems that nobody actually counted them.

The Emperor laid on three hundred free coaches with livery for his guests, which pleased everybody except Signor Castelli from Naples, who described one of them as "a slow-rolling maid's chamber." As for accommodation, the most illustrious Sovereigns had apartments reserved in the imperial palace itself, the Hofburg – the King of Württemberg on the first floor of the Amalienhof, the King of Prussia on the second. The King of Bavaria was housed across the inner courtyard at the Reichkanzlei. Tsar Alexander would actually move into a northern extension of the Austrian Emperor's apartments, his windows overlooking the Ballhausplatz and Metternich's official residence opposite; his two sisters, the Grand Duchess Catherine and the Grand Duchess Elisabeth, had their own apartments on either side of the King of Bavaria's. The Russian delegation, as distinct from the Tsar's suite, had its own luxurious quarters in the Paar Palace on the Wollzeile, the effect somewhat spoilt by the collapse of the main salon's plaster ceiling. The English, we know, had taken care of themselves and were probably almost as comfortably off as the French who, though the losers of the war, had taken over the Kaunitz Palace in the Johannesgasse, just down the street from the cathedral.[23]

But for those of lesser rank and station, housing was the first crisis of the Congress. The bourgeoisie, hungry for rent, opened their homes to large numbers. The crowded inns were dreadful. Many a guest would have agreed with the gentleman from northern Germany who compared his quarters to "a murderer's den" – "no porter, no carpet, no bell-rope, bed so high that you need a stool to clamber into it." Table linen was changed only once a week and the bed pans piled up in corridors. Yet no one could complain that the overworked innkeepers were not friendly; in their green velvet caps and the blue-lined dickeys wrapped around their bellies, they greeted their guests not with today's modest *"Grüss' Gott!"* but with a hearty *"Gelobt sei Jesus Christus!"* [24]

The city of Vienna was itself a greeting. All travellers were struck by the beauty of the place on their first approach, though frequently, after a hot summer's day, a strong wind would stir up clouds of dust from the chalk and gravel of the dry, unpaved roadways; it was like fog, and at times like the worst fogs of London. But in autumn, when the weather was clear, you could look down from the sloping streets of a village like Nussdorf or Döbling at the spire of St Stephan's, at the long bridges that crossed the various branches of the Danube, at the bare meadowed islands, and, to the west, at the hills. In fact, virtually all one saw was fields, prairies, and greenery. Vienna, from the outside, didn't look like a city. Vienna was small, smaller than even the figures of population would suggest because the *Residenzstadt* was surrounded by not just one confining wall, but two. The Bastei, or old fortifications, along with the Glacis, a huge tract of grass and a jumble of tree-aligned alleys, separated the Inner City from the suburbs; the outer Linienwall, soon named the "Linie" (or "Lina" in the local dialect), was also originally a system of fortifications built to protect the suburbs, but had been converted, with the decline of the Turkish menace, into the city's toll barrier.[25]

The Viennese liked their greenery. It was not, like Paris, just a matter of potted geraniums on the balcony or, like London, the odd Sunday stroll in the park; nature in the *Residenzstadt* was a group obsession. The Berlin bookseller Nicolai had noted back in the 1780s how all the gardens of Vienna and its surroundings filled with workers after five o'clock in the afternoon; he had never seen that in Berlin, nor in any of the other cities he had visited in Germany. Madame de Staël, after her 1808 visit, remarked that "one sees whole families of bourgeois and artisans leaving at five in the evening to walk in the Prater." "At the end of the day, inasmuch as the weather permits," wrote the French Ambassador to Vienna in the 1820s, "the artisan of the suburbs takes off his work coat and dons clean clothes; with his wife and his children he then goes out to eat a fried chicken in one of the innumerable inns scattered in the countryside that is watered by the Danube." "One must seek the Viennese in the open air, in charming nature," confirmed a German traveller around 1840.[26]

Walking on the Bastei was one of the ways in which the Viennese escaped civilisation. The area had been cleaned up in the first decade of the century, trees were planted on the Glacis and a "lovely path" was laid for pedestrians, which was "edged with fencing like a woman's skirt and arrayed with a green lawn."[27]

One can recognise that Viennese cult of green nature among the painters and even the musicians of the era; they would seek their inspiration in rural scenes, in the landscapes of the Wienerwald, the regions of Schneeberg or of Salzkammergut, in the sounds of a shepherd's horn, in the clap of thunder, in the "charitable thoughts combined with thanks to the Deity after the storm."[28] Wealthy people would take trips and walks far into Vienna's surroundings. The poor would visit the small inns with their gardens in the hills beyond the Linie. Above all, the cult was a collective affair; it was the conscience of a city. The Viennese were not a people to take lonely Teutonic strolls in the wilderness; they would pile into carriages and wagons, they would walk in masses; nearly every free hour the Viennese had was devoted to greenery.

Pride of place was reserved for the Prater, which lay on the island between the Donaukanal and the principal branch of the Danube, the Kaiserwasser. "Few capitals in the world could have such a thing to show as we have in our Prater," the novelist Adalbert Stifter would explain. "Is it a park? No. Is it a meadow? No. Is it a garden? No. A wood? No. A pleasure place? No. What is it then? All of this named together." The Prater contained so much pasture and woodland that one felt, in some spots, as if one were standing in the midst of a great dairy farm rather than at the outskirts of an imperial city. But then, reflected Stifter, "a huge *Residenz* requires a huge garden." St James's Park, Green Park, and Hyde Park could all have been fitted into the Prater, with plenty or room still left for Kensington Gardens. At the entrance there was in fact a dairy house with a milk bar, and bee hives paralleled the banks of the canal. But there were also taverns, which served roast Styrian capons with sauerkraut and mussels, and cafés, where the women stood at the entrance in tight black bodices and skirts of white fustian; round pavilions offered a "musical conversation," a concert, a dance – "you see men and women, directly opposite one another, gravely executing the steps of a minuet; the crowd often separates the dancing couple and yet the couple will continue as though it were discharging its conscience." Nobles mixed with commoners. Even members of the imperial family wandered about the Prater without guards. Such behaviour would have astonished the King of France and would never even have crossed the mind of the isolated Prince Regent of England.[29]

When, in early September 1814, Matthias Franz Perth, a young accountant working for the Forestry Commission, wanted to know what progress was being made in preparations for the Congress he went to the obvious place for news and gossip, the Prater. As he made his way up the Jägerzeile, leading from the City to the garden, he was surprised to learn that Herr de Bach's "gymnastic circus," which had been running every day since the New Year, had just closed. He asked to know what was happening and was pleased when told that the closure was merely due to rehearsals – "so that the same [show] can be produced with renewed brilliant taste at the imminent arrival of the foreign Monarchs and other persons." Next to the circus he discovered a huge "mechanical optical theatre." "It contains amongst other things," he recorded in his diary that night, "the Fire of Moscow, the Battle of Leipzig, the Crossing of the Rhine by the Allied Army at Schaffhausen, the triumphant entry of the same into Paris, with more than one thousand popular moving figures."[30]

A mass of popular moving figures was exactly what a small Viennese functionary like Perth was looking for in the coming Congress. But it was also a show that forced him to reflect on a world beyond the Linie.

Was Vienna a city? No. Was it a town? No. Then was it a village? No. It was every one of these, mixed with the *grandezza* of a great European court. The Inner City, behind the Bastei, was no larger than a district of London or of Paris, so that palaces were crowded together like so many sheep in a pen, apartment buildings soared to five or six storeys, and the streets were so narrow that no self-respecting bourgeois would rent a place below the second floor because of the smells and lack of sunlight. Poor homes could be found right next to the rich. Just opposite the Coburg Palace lay the Kroatendörfel where vegetable and meat-stalls stood in front of a row a barrack-like houses. There was a crowd of small houses by the Bastei near Duke Albert's palace.[31]

Poverty and wealth also mixed in the suburbs that lay between the Bastei and the Linie. The richest suburbs, Mariahilf, Wieden, and Landstrasse, where many a noble's summer residence could be found, enjoyed a slightly higher altitude than the poorest, like Rossau on the Donaukanal or the stinking tanner's quarters of Weissgerber on the Wien. Industry, as in Paris but unlike London, was a suburban activity. The density of inhabitation in these suburbs would reach a point of crisis after 1830, leading to the nineteenth-century plagues of squalor, high mortality, and violence; but even in 1814 there were areas such as Liechtenthal, Franz Schubert's birthplace, where population densities pinched into poverty and bred a crowd of foulnesses. The life of whole families was played out here at the time of the great Congress.[32]

The social, cultural, and economic distances that could be observed between people in small Vienna were enormous; they didn't even speak the same language (there existed around forty thousand Italian-speakers alone). Yet in 1814 no one was apparently ready to suggest they were a divided people: no one saw any sign of hostile nationalisms in Vienna; no one spoke of social class. Visitors and residents alike would speak of the "respectful" and "colourful crowd," never the "mob," nor even *"der Pöbel"* – the "populace."

Vienna's nobles might speak to each other in French and they would observe the most extraordinarily complex code of etiquette and precedence that some would trace to Vienna's historic ties with Spain. Obviously this created the atmosphere of a "caste" which, as Carl Bertuch, the Weimar bookseller, observed, "thrust itself between the Sovereign and the people." The paradox was that in Vienna this created not division but something quite the opposite – a harmony, an equilibrium. Vienna was still small enough for the system to work.[33]

That sense of harmony, of equilibrium, drove many to portray Vienna as a "happy" town. Johann Pezzl, Freemason and popular chronicler in the late eighteenth century, remarked that "the monarch of Vienna has no need to put his people into a good humour, all he has to do is to preserve it, for the Viennese possess innate good humour, just as sparrows are born to chirp." This is what struck visitors in 1814. Comte Auguste de La Garde-Chambonas, a poet, travel-writer, and wanderer, who arrived in the *Residenzstadt* at the time of the Congress, reflected that "Madame de Staël called Germany the land of thought: Vienna we could call the homeland of happiness." For August Varnhagen von Ense, whose home was in Berlin and the land of thought, Viennese "cheerful good-naturedness" derived from their "half Italian ways of idleness." Gottfried Seume, in a travel book popular at the time, thought it was just the good wine; *Wien und Wein* are so closely related, he asserted, that the Romans named Vienna "Vindabona" or *"Vinum dat bonum,"* "She gives a good wine."[34]

Seume had a point, for the wine was popular. Drinking places in the Inner City were generally underground, in cellars, where the candles burned all day as well as at night. The white and copper-red complexion of the tapsters was said to be due to the fact that they never saw the sun, that their whole lives were passed in Vienna's hidden labyrinths of wine.[35]

The Viennese were also very spectacle-minded. Out on the Glacis there was the odd execution, but these were hushed affairs compared to London. On Thursday, 1 September 1814, Franz Perth walked out in the evening in the hope of witnessing the hanging of an infantry officer for murder, but was disappointed to discover that the body had already been cut down. Theatre had a rather wider following; Perth even had his own play put on in the suburbs, though there is no record of it being well attended. Music was heard in every garden and on every street, in every style imaginable. The *Werkelmänner* or barrel-organ-players, said a visitor, "were drawn in countless numbers from house to house, at the gates of the city, along the walkways, droning out popular melodies from the stage or the opera." Harpists, too, wandered from street to street. There were improvisers who would sing, to accompaniment, songs of topical value, satires on the latest political development or ballads that spread the local gossip about love and money. In 1814, the Tyrolean singers, who worked in Vienna as clockmakers, filled the streets with the mountain harmonies of their *Ländler*. Some of the British delegates were so enchanted that they invited a whole troupe to England; they accepted and eventually gave a performance before the Prince Regent. Less appreciated was the noise of the *Bratelgeiger*, or beggar musicians.[36]

The recent war did not seem to have in any way dampened the Viennese taste for pleasure. While Moscow burned in 1812, they were out on the Prater enjoying a show put on by "our fireworks artist," Kaspar Stuwer. Countess Bernstorff attended the display, following her long trip from Berlin, and was shocked at the crowd's lack of concern for "the distress of our German Fatherland." "Among the Viennese," she complained, "we found only little understanding."[37]

But then great patriotic enthusiasms were something the Viennese would leave to the Prussians. During the war, Vienna had been occupied by the French twice, in 1805 and in 1809. On the first occasion, the enemy inflicted little damage; people remembered the unusual silence of the Inner City that December, abandoned by the Court, the courtiers, and the great landowners – "instead of the usual ceaseless rattle of coaches lumbering through the streets, one rarely heard so much as a simple cart creeping by." On the second, the city was heavily bombarded and the inhabitants stayed in hiding even after the French moved in. But as soon as it was discovered that the soldiers, instead of bayoneting civilians, were intent on bathing half naked in the city fountains, the crowds reappeared; "within a few hours everyone was all over the place and before one could imagine . . . the hot sausage vendors were making their rounds."[38]

The recession in the last years of the war gave the Viennese plenty to complain about. But they didn't complain. The Viennese "public mind is dull and torpid, or rather no public mind exists," remarked an English traveller. Madame de Staël also noted the *"profond repos des esprits"* in Vienna and blamed it all on the censors. No doubt the state censors were a part of the cause, along with the related fact that the Viennese had such little influence in government, even in local affairs – since 1787 the representatives of citizens, the *Äussere Räthe*, was no longer elected but nominated by the central government.[39]

Did the Viennese care? Everybody in Vienna wanted to be like the nobles, or to be *nobel*, as they used to say; to have the right manners, the right dress, the right tastes, the right sentiments, but not necessarily to pass oneself off as rich. The dramatist Franz Grillparzer remembered how his parents, though living in a squalid, decaying old house in the Inner City, maintained this atmosphere of majestic fantasy, joined with a certain resignation. A coachman on the Freyung might take on the air of an emperor; he could be convincing too in a city where the Emperor, out on the Prater, had the allure of a coachman. A surface form of nobility was the essential thing, not your real wealth, nor your class.[40]

And that, visibly, was what Vienna brought you: an upward torrent of movement, a theatre of colour, of detail, of gesture, a mime; an angel's teasing smile, the contorted, ardent body of a saint in venera- tion, the drapes of virgins tumbling in whirls and eddies, a pious siren's inviting little hand; cornices, pilasters, and pediments multi- plying the axes, breaking them, doubling them, changing the centre of the composition; an exquisite view from the shaded side of the street, then a new view in the sun, and the old view seen again; an image, carved in stone, of passing time. In baroque Vienna no distinction was made between the sacred and the profane, all was devoted to sensu- ality, to bringing pleasure to the eyes of the people. The decor inside the Peterskirche was the same as the adornment outside on the Graben and the Kohlmarkt. Every public place in Vienna seemed designed to delight, to seduce and – was that the goal? – to control.

It was a "democracy of style," an aesthetic entertainment for poor and rich alike, an appeal to their senses and their good humour; and quite the opposite to the political democracy developing in the old nation states of England and France, as Hermann Broch, writer and critic, would observe a hundred years later.[41]

Political democracy was a serious business, and revolution was deadly serious. The great paradox was that the democratising world cities of London and Paris sought an immobility in their architecture, they exhorted the classical virtues of rigour, sobriety, and clarity. Small Vienna, which in politics practised the art of harmony and equilibrium, had buildings which exploded with emotion. London detested the baubles and gingerbread houses of their flamboyant European Prince Regent; Parisians could not support the works of the Italian Bernini even for a generation. Londoners and Parisians, with democracy on their doorsteps, were iconoclasts: cut every curve, cut every ornament, cut the "frippery," the "whimsical," the "odd," and the "useless." They sought, as a famous London pattern book put it, "a much neater and more magnificent manner" – or as a Parisian poet said, "I hate the movement which displaces lines."

One didn't hear that in Vienna. The Viennese were the very oppo- site of these western iconoclasts: they decorated every space available, they put statues on every corner and every pinnacle, they sought in curved stones expressions of torment, sorrow, and the burlesque. All that they built was fluid, unstable, inconstant. All that they sought in government was balanced and stable. That was the paradox. As

Castlereagh and his colleagues were about to discover, it was more than an exercise in style.

Kaiser Franz and the Second Reich

For the visiting dignitaries of Europe the centre of the Congress was the jumbled architectural marvel of the Hofburg, city residence of Kaiser Franz, father of his people – and father-in-law of Napoleon. In 1792 he had been crowned Francis II, Holy Roman Emperor, the twentieth Habsburg to take the title. The reorganisation of the imperial electoral college eleven years later, which put Protestants in the majority, made it unlikely that there would ever be a twenty-first because the Habsburgs were Catholic and the crown was not hereditary. For the future of his dynasty Franz had therefore been obliged to found a new hereditary Reich, which he did after much bargaining and bickering in Paris, in 1804; Francis II became Francis I, Emperor of Austria, King of Bohemia, and Apostolic King of Hungary. The old Reich was abolished in 1806. Political pundits of the day did not put much hope in the longevity of Kaiser Franz's new Reich, which they compared unfavourably to Napoleon's dynamic, efficient, centralised modern Empire, also founded in 1804. But history proved them wrong. Franz's Reich lasted over a hundred years; Napoleon's just ten.[42]

Kaiser Franz was forty-six years old when, in 1814, he opened his city to Europe. He was thus one year older than Wellington, Castlereagh, and Napoleon; but nobody would have guessed it. "The Emperor of Austria has conceivably the frailest of all appearances," wrote the banker Jean Gabriel Eynard, who was just then setting up his new offices in Vienna. "He looks quite broken and old; small, thin in figure, with a rounded back, and his knees bent inwards." Throughout the Congress his ceremonial dress would remain the same – a white military uniform with red trousers and black boots. He was no conversationalist. His sister, Princess Marie Therese von Sachsen, complained to her husband that Franz's dinner talk – the guests standing and politely waiting for the imperial chatter to stop – upset her stomach and "always leads me into a sweat." She called him "Venus" because of the vague look that would appear in his eyes as he nattered on. The Emperor spoke in German (in fact, it was a genuine Wiener Dialekt) and he insisted that the members of his court also speak and write to him in German, including his Foreign Minister, Metternich, who would have much preferred, like many of his colleagues, to address His Majesty in the language of Molière. Frequently short phrases would emerge from Franz's Habsburg lips that were quite funny; he possessed a handsome fund of Mother-wit, ruined by this awkwardness.

Kaiser Franz, founder of a new hereditary empire, received Europe's
Sovereigns and Ministers in Vienna in his forty-seventh year

It may have had something to do with his private life, for "Venus" had a problem with his third wife; he had recently confessed to Metternich that poor health prevented her from fulfilling her conjugal duties. The divine Maria Ludovika would occasionally be spotted during the Congress, floating like a pale blonde fairy queen through the crowds and on to her hidden chambers. Poor Kaiser Franz was not the kind of man to seek consolation elsewhere, quite in contrast to the behaviour of his court, his ministers and, indeed, his fellow Sovereigns. As his brother, Archduke Johann, proudly noted in his diary following the Sovereigns' entry into Paris, "The Emperor of Austria visits the museums, the Emperor of Russia the whores." Kaiser Franz was a diligent man, a serious man, an honorable man, *ein Biedermann*, a man, it was said, with the morality of the Viennese petty bourgeois who so loved him.[43]

He had returned to Vienna on 16 June, 1814, like a conquering hero. It was the grandest day in his life. While the other Sovereigns were celebrating victory in London, and with his brothers reigning, sulking, or in exile abroad, Franz was received by the crowds alone. For him, this was the day that confirmed his sovereignty, this was the day the new Reich really began. Suddenly all the problems of the war, the inconsistencies of Viennese politics, the miseries engendered by state bankruptcy, the new bank notes, the shortages of food and work seemed gone. With the fireworks of June the whole city lit up. The Hofburg looked less dreary.[44]

But the total collapse of Napoleon's Empire, if welcomed in the streets of small Vienna, had created complications for Austria. Sometimes an ally, sometimes an enemy, the French Empire had acted as a useful counter-weight to the Russian. The French Empire had also cleared the way to the new hereditary Reich, which was now the sole basis of the Habsburgs' claim to power. Without a French Empire to her west, Austria would find her ability to manœuvre and play a role in European affairs reduced; and that wasn't simply a matter of power politics, it was a question of Austria's survival. The Austrian Empire was not a nation, it was not a people, it was not a culture; it was a power in Central Europe. European politics were the reason for its existence, the unique reason for its existence. Austria had been playing the game for centuries.

For the last half of a century, with the decline of the old Reich and growth of new centralised political sovereignties, that game had developed into a four-way contest involving France, Russia, Prussia, and Austria. France had always been involved in Central Europe. Russian intrusion was a novelty of the eighteenth century: her frontiers had moved west with the first partition of Poland in 1772 and she would push westwards again when Polish civil war broke out six years later. For the next two hundred years Russia's presence would exert an influence of the ebb and flow of power, the march of armies, the exchange of trade, and the movement of peoples across Europe's northern plains. Prussia was also challenging Austria's leadership in the area, pressing the latter south into the mountains and multi-ethnic flatlands beyond. But it was the two flanking powers, Russia and France – the "devouring Powers" as Metternich would call them – that provided the essential momentum.

France had been exceptionally absent from Central Europe at the time that Russia entered the picture; she was, in the 1770s, bent on a war of revenge across the Atlantic against Britain. It took the Revolution to get France moving eastwards again into the Netherlands and beyond the Rhine. Britain, during the long years of war that followed, only saw France, and Pitt built his coalitions against her. Austria, by contrast, was aware of both France and Russia; she started up again her old game of playing the performers off against each other.

With Napoleon annexing great tracts of German territory and Russia bearing down on Poland the stakes were getting high. Yet for Austria this was still the old-style game, a four-way play with France, Russia, and Prussia, even if now it was a game for survival. How significant it was that the site of the Habsburgs' Foreign Ministry should be the family's old tennis court, the Ballhaus, opposite the palace. The chief task of the players in the Ballhaus was, as Metternich would explain it, to reconstitute a German *corps politique* out of the fragments of the old Reich, and reinsert it into the "European concert."[45] It was the game he would play through the war and on into the peace. It was the game of cabinet politics and, in the end, it was what allowed Vienna to be so small, a town of game, of nature, of her meadows and forests, a town whose enthusiasms fed into art, not politics. Cabinet politics was about balance and calculation, not great outbursts of national or revolutionary exaltation.

If Russian involvement was the real novelty in the game, the essential element for Austria was the weakness of Prussia. Metternich would demonstrate this arithmetically. Give the two flanking powers 4, Austria 3, Prussia 2; Metternich ascribed no number to Britain because in the war she had been isolated and, in the first months of the peace, it looked as if she was prepared, in her search for equilibrium, to lend her weight to all sides. In a struggle between France and Russia, it was Austria that held the balance, not Prussia (France + Austria = 7; Russia + Prussia = 6). The nightmare for Austria was a Franco-Russian combination – it had happened at Tilsit in 1807. But what would occur if France disappeared? It was now weak Prussia which held the balance, not Austria (Prussia + Russia = 6, against Austria's 3; Prussia + Austria = 5, against Russia's 4). That was how Metternich understood the challenge facing Austria after the collapse of Napoleon's Empire.[46]

Prussia had never been a Great Power. Even under Frederick the Great, who had died in 1786, she was not considered by the courts of Europe as great, but as possessing the potential to be great. That potential was nearly lost in the wars that followed. After her defeat at Jena in 1806 Prussia suffered a series of bewildering experiences – foreign occupation, physical damage to her towns and villages, harvest failures, spiralling inflation, and numerous social and economic reforms that created division and uncertainty. From 1807 to 1813 she was France's vassal; she then switched sides and became Russia's vassal. After 1806 Prussia was a second-rate power in possession of only a third of her former lands.

In 1814, Prussia, as a major contributor to the Allied victory, demanded compensation for her losses; territorial expansion had to be her principal aim at the Congress if she were to play a role in the future of Europe. But where could she expand? To her east her senior partner, Russia, had her own eyes on Poland. To the south lay an alternative, Saxony. Before the war was concluded Metternich had actually promised Prussia that he would abandon Austria's guarantee of an independent Saxon kingdom. But in recent months he had been having second thoughts. After all, now there was peace why yield Saxony? The kingdom, which had remained in 1813 a loyal ally of Napoleon's, offered Austria rich opportunities for game and manœuvre. To Prussia's west lay other opportunities for expansion. Castlereagh, still concerned in the Pitt tradition with bulwarks against France and the security of the Netherlands, would be ready to encourage Prussia to look in this direction, towards the Rhineland. He called it a policy of "bringing Prussia forward." Karl von Hardenberg, Prussia's Chancellor, would take advantage of the differences between his three allies and push for maximum territorial growth: he had no choice.

In contrast to Prussia, Austria with her new Reich remained a Great Power; expansion was not her first concern. Perhaps she had been pushed back into the mountains and beyond; this was not a problem that really bothered her. Quite the contrary, it was a relief to know that the new Reich would be *stockösterreichisch*, Austrian to the core, and would no longer have to agonise over revolts in the Netherlands, protect imperial knights in the distant principalities, or make the pretence, as had been the case in the 1790s, of fighting a war on the behalf of squabbling German sovereigns. The great German enthusiasms of the north – "aspirations of Teutomania" Metternich called them – were not Austrian. "As far as Austria was concerned," Metternich would later say, "the term 'German spirit' was no more than a myth adopted by the upper classes of the North following the catastrophe suffered by Prussia and other northern countries after

1805."[47] The "German spirit" was not the Austrian spirit. After 1805 Austria concentrated on being Austrian.

Pure Austrian, but not national. The new Reich embraced Germans, Hungarians, Czechs, Slovenes and Slavonians, Rumanians and Ruthenians, Greeks and Croats, Poles and Jews, Russians, Turks, and Italians, not to mention minorities that even Kaiser Franz would never have heard of. But Kaiser Franz's new Reich was not designed to be in the style of the old, diffuse, horizontal "reach" either. The aim was to create a consolidated, centralised, vertically organised state. The ideal was again something drawn from the past, from the blue-prints of the reformers of the eighteenth century. "A well-organised state must be like a machine," wrote the legal theorist Johann Justi, "all the wheels and gears must mesh exactly."[48] So a nice shiny machine, independent of the passions of ordinary people: a mechanical state for the players of politics, not a national state for the masses.

In practice, the new Reich was not actually all that efficient. "You look everywhere for the government and nobody is able to indicate where it is," one rather confused French diplomat would write; he was accustomed to a very different kind of system. He found bureau-crats scurrying all over the place, but "there is here no will, no auth-ority, everyone does just as they want, and it's the subordinates who are the masters." This was Vienna in 1814.[49]

Yet diligent Kaiser Franz did everything in his capacity to act as the master mechanic. He spent hours in his office reading reports and signing decrees; every week he would give audience to large numbers of his subjects. He was a man of detail. He cleaned the cogs, he checked the notches, oiled the pivots, and unclogged the ratchets, but he never stood back and looked at the whole or even wondered what purpose his machinery served.

The most time-consuming mechanical task was his daily review of the activities of the Oberste Polizei und Censur Hofstelle, the secret police (known as the Polizei Hofstelle for short), who maintained their offices next to the Emperor's in the Hofburg. The services had been founded by Franz's uncle, the enlightened despot Joseph II, who, like many a benign father, wanted to know what his children were up to. War and the establishment of the new Reich saw the Polizei Hofstelle transformed into a fantastically elaborate organisa-tion, complete with a Secret Cabinet (charged with deciphering intercepted letters and foreign dispatches) and agencies placed throughout the provinces.

Between 1806 and 1814 there was a fivefold increase in the budget for the recruitment of Austria's secret agents. They worked at the toll gates, in inns, in private homes, at the embassies, and they could even be found nosing about on the Prater. A decree of 1806 had divided them into two broad classes, ordinary agents (like chamber maids, who were instructed to deliver every day the contents of their employer's waste-paper baskets) and "agents of high standing" (*"Vertraute höheren Standes"*).[50]

The Minister of Police in 1814 was Baron Franz Hager, an amiable man, a former cavalry officer, who had been forced into the civil service after a riding accident. On 1 July he sent a letter to Vienna's chief of police, Count Siber, telling him to redouble his efforts because of the approaching arrival of the foreign Sovereigns and their diplomats.

The existence of Hager's Polizei Hofstelle was no secret to anyone in Vienna. Noble ladies noticed a greater inquisitiveness among some of their guests, travellers remarked on the alertness of the guards out on the Linie; how attentive the hotel maids had suddenly become, how friendly the innkeeper as he raised his cap. Huge quantities of material were delivered to Baron Hager's desk. Every day, he would read over them and prepare his own review, including his daily analysis and recommendations, which he would then carry in person to the Emperor.[51]

The most valued of all the informants' reports came from a suave, cosmopolitan aristocrat who signed himself ✱✱. Nobody has ever been able to establish who ✱✱ was, but we know that he came into Baron Hager's service in 1813, that he circulated in the highest circles of Vienna, that he was conversant on all the subjects which mattered – administration, finance, politics, and sex – and that he was consulted on the recruitment of new agents, new officials, and even the nomination of ministers. His letters, submitted almost daily to the Emperor as "the reports of the Eternal Majesty's well-known informer," were written in phrases that would begin in German and end in French, or vice versa, interspersed with sprinklings of Latin. They gave intimate accounts of all that ✱✱ had access to.

Another important "agent of high standing" was "Nota," who was in fact the Italian poet, Carpani. Like ✱✱, Nota pried into various affairs, but his reports proved be especially good on Russian intrigues in ballrooms, *salons*, and bedrooms.

Others were more specialised, such as 1∞, who reported on Hungarian matters; Herr H, who was well connected within the Prussian circle and was on good terms with Hardenberg; or the Chevalier Freddi, who specialised in Italian affairs but had also developed an expertise "on the Bospherus, on the Orontes, and on the Nile." Thus, throughout the Congress, Kaiser Franz was kept well-informed, as was the official resident of the Chancellery (as they now called the Ballhaus), Prince Clemens Lothar Wenzel von Metternich.

Metternich's migration and conversion to Europe

Vienna was not small enough for Metternich.[52] Having made his own triumphant entry into town on 18 July – Count Palffy had organised a concert on the Ballhausplatz that included the cantata, "We salute you, great Prince" – the great Prince immediately set off again for the summer resort of Baden, a favourite retreat for aristocrats and members of the court a few leagues south of the city. There he could enjoy the company of his tolerant wife and their spoilt children, and most especially play to the caprices of his favourite mistress, Wilhelmine, the Duchess von Sagan.

In fact, Metternich would have liked to have conducted the whole business of the European peace in these quiet surroundings; they were so much better suited to his style of diplomacy than the crowded inner city of Vienna. A useful afternoon's chat could be had while strolling down the hidden footpaths of the Helental. The wines of Gumpoldskirchen and Vöslau were very effective at loosening tongues at dinner. And after dinner, there would be cards. Ombre, basset, and quadrille were no longer the fashion in Baden; it was whist and boston now, especially whist because it complemented so well the reserved atmosphere of diplomatic gatherings; silence was a strict rule during the deal and for the Austrian Minister it must have seemed particularly pertinent because it was played, like Central Europe, as a four-way contest.

This tall, blond-haired man of forty-one was apparently equally at ease at the card table as he was in the ballrooms and the boudoirs. His exquisite manners were the talk of the continent; his conversation added lustre to a lady's *salon*; that half-serious smile and the distracted gaze of his bulging blue eyes were proof of a noble pedigree. His career took him onwards and up. His ministry would be one of the longest in history. Never modest, he was the one who compared himself to Cardinals Richelieu and Mazarin. Totally vain, he might just as well have entitled the memoirs he eventually left behind *The History of Me and the World* because, as he never tired of pointing out, the destiny of both marched together.[53]

There was first his birthplace, such a perfect symbol of Europe's destiny. Between Austria and Prussia lay the wreckage of the old German Reich. A later generation – which Metternich would of course encounter – would call it the "third Germany" because, made up of small and middling states, it seemed an alternative to the Austrian and Prussian models of centralised monarchy.[54] In the eighteenth century its western extreme, the Rhineland, was still peppered with principalities, bishoprics, abbeys, and medieval free cities. This was the world into which the future Austrian Foreign

Minister was born in 1773. His father, Franz Georg, was an imperial count, a *Reichsgraf*, which gave him the right to sit in the Reichstag at Regensburg and seek a career beyond the frontiers of the tiny Electorate of Trier. Throughout his life, Franz Georg would remain attached in spirit to the old Reich, its tiny world of crags and castles; he seemed so ideally suited to a life in its rococo courts, as did his son. But that was not to be their destiny.

When France's revolutionary armies pushed eastwards, they destroyed the old Reich: they annexed the whole left bank of the Rhine, which included the Metternich properties, and they built a "confederation" of states on the right.

Destiny pushed the old imperial aristocracies eastwards, in great migratory waves, to Austria, Prussia, and even to Russia in search of jobs and compensation. There were the Stadions, the Steins, Wessenbergs, Windischgrätzes, Schwarzenbergs, and Nesselrodes, all names that would appear in the diplomatic rolls in Vienna in 1814. And there were the Metternichs. They would find jobs because the eastern powers, faced with the Napoleonic threat, had to build up armies and more efficient state administrations. Many of them also gained territorial compensations offered as a reward for their services. Loss and gain, annexation and compensation; it was a useful lesson for the new migrant diplomats.

The Metternichs were among the most fortunate. They found work in Vienna and were well compensated. In land, they actually received more than the territories lost on the Rhine; Franz Georg, moreover, became a prince. The greatest compensation, however, for the Metternichs was the son's marriage to Eleonore, the grand-daughter of the great Kaunitz himself, Austria's former Foreign Minister. No doubt Metternich's mother, the Countess Beatrix, had her role in this for her family had long been affiliated with the Kaunitz circle; but Metternich's charms and talent played a part as well.

It was not a romantic attachment. Metternich would always show respect for Eleonore, or Laure as he called her, but as he admitted in 1818 to another mistress, Princess Lieven[55] – wife of the Russian Ambassador in London – "*j'étais faché de me marier*" ("I was vexed at being married"). Contemporaries made many unkind remarks about Metternich's wife. She was small, she was not apparently a great wit, and she had an absolute horror of social gatherings. When Metternich was Ambassador to Paris, Napoleon managed to get her to smile by slapping her on her shoulders every time she appeared at a reception and saying, "*Alors, comtesse,* we're getting older, thinner, and uglier!" Then after the smile: "You see, you've got more wit than all these idiots around you." That was the year she had crossed the whole of Germany with her children, passing through the lines of battling Prussians and Frenchmen. "If ever you have an army that needs commanding," Metternich wrote to his Foreign Minister, "just call on Madame de Metternich for she is afraid of nothing." It was a useful quality to have with a husband like hers.[56]

So the Metternichs' story was one of extraordinary success won by luck, good looks, intelligence, and adaption to new circumstances. It was not the normal story for the people of their class. The local elites of the "third Germany" were the real losers of the French Revolution.

This capital fact would affect the whole structure of the peace. History remembers the French *émigré* in flight from the guillotine because his story is romantic and has been told many times; but it is strange how history forgets the old Reich's aristocrats in flight from war. The *émigrés* might have passed many years wandering in exile, but most of them in the end returned to their country; they either took repossession of their lands or were compensated, and they won back many of their privileges. The *Reichsgrafen*, the *Reichsritters*, the *Reichsadel* – the *Standesherren* as they were generally known collectively – did not. New centralised states were organised in the "third Germany" which did not want their return.

In the realm of ideas, the exiled German noblemen also differed. While the French *émigrés* really did represent a force of reaction and tried by every means, once back in France, to restore the Old Regime, the *Standesherren* were divided. Some, like Metternich's father, dreamed of return to the homeland and of the re-establishment of the old Reich. But others knew full well that this was now impossible and, instead, committed themselves to the new style of state, or they embraced the new nationalist enthusiasms that had developed as a result of the war, or they spoke of liberalism and constitutions, and even the rise of a people's government. Some committed themselves to the "nation," others to "Europe." It has been said that there was a hypocrisy in all this, that the call for "German liberties" was, like the English Magna Carta, really a hidden call for the rights of barons. But this is simplistic. Many modern ideas of civil liberty, law (both national and international), and of the constitutional state can be traced to the writings, questions, and anxieties of the displaced *Standesherren*.

Metternich himself was not entirely immune to the pull of nationalist enthusiasm, although he omitted this fact from his memoirs. It would have, in fact, been surprising had he not been drawn to it; he had seen his family lands invaded and their properties stolen. At twenty-one, he wrote a pamphlet cursing the "boneheads," the old-style diplomats, "who consider the present war like any other and the Revolution in its commencement mere child's play, and who regard the general conflagration with the true cold-bloodedness of a physician." With the voice of a German nationalist radical, he called for a rising of the people in arms. Later in Paris, when faced with Napoleon's unlimited ambition, he joined the campaign of the nationalist war party in Vienna. He was seeking a war of revenge.[57]

And he lost it. But the remarkable thing about Metternich was that every time he lost his career advanced. The greater the loss, the more he advanced. His family was expelled from their homeland; he emigrated to Vienna and married into the Kaunitz family. His in-laws laid down the rules: that he never leave the Kaunitz household and that he never accept a diplomatic post; Metternich became Ambassador to Dresden, to Berlin, and then on to Paris. In Paris he plotted with Talleyrand, he advocated war, and lost; he was promptly named Foreign Minister in Vienna. He negotiated the marriage between Kaiser Franz's daughter and Napoleon, one of the great mismatches of the century. When Napoleon made his disastrous march into Russia, Metternich was the ally of the loser, France.

It is not enough to say that Metternich knew how to work with slender resources: he built his strength out of weakness and loss. He explained how he did it in a report to Kaiser Franz following the devastating defeat of 1809: to recognise the strength of the winner and, "from the day of the peace, to limit our system exclusively to hedging, evasion, and flattery [*auf ausschliessendes Lavieren, auf Ausweichen, auf Schmeicheln*]," and thus "maybe to spare our existence for the day of general deliverance."[58]

Metternich was not a hero's model. He put aside his own ideologies, he obliterated all nostalgia for his tiny homeland, abandoned all thoughts of return, and became an Austrian and a European; no longer did he speak of the struggle for power in Europe as a contest between the forces of the Revolution and those of the Old Regime, no longer did he dream of a restored Reich. He adopted the traditional "Austrian" view, he became the "bonehead" he had so despised in his youth, he applied to his game of statecraft "the true cold-bloodedness of a physician" that he had once hated. He became a European.

"My heart belongs entirely to me," he admitted shortly after becoming minister, "but not my head, which travels with the traffic of the world."[59]

Among the thousands of travellers who turned up in Vienna in September 1814 were the displaced *Standesherren*, represented by Baron von Gärtner. Most of them had not shared Metternich's good fortune, they did not stand on his high and narrow summit and have a view of the world, they had not mastered the discipline of statecraft, they were not players at his table; they were parochial nostalgic dreamers and not great Europeans.

They spoke of restoring the old Reich. But there were many different opinions on what a revived, wholly German Reich should look like. And there was plenty of room for them: Napoleon's retreat had created a vacuum. One spoke of "Reich," "Reichsbund," "Bund,"

Prince Clemens von Metternich was as restless in his private affairs as he
was tranquil in public

"Confederation"; most of these projects were just dreams, "day-dreams," as Metternich's private secretary Friedrich Gentz put it, "that no one has either the will or the power to realise."[60]

But one dreamer stood a chance of success: Karl Freiherr vom Stein, a rather dour figure by all descriptions, a man who disliked intensely the frivolity of ballrooms and who did not have much of a sense of game. Yet Stein did understand what the ultimate test in the coming Congress would be. He foresaw, in particular, that the Polish question would be linked to Saxony, that the future of Saxony was linked to the German question, and that on all this would stand or fall the "repose of Europe." Like Metternich, he came from a family of dispossessed *Standesherren* (the Metternichs and Steins had been, in fact, virtual neighbours in the Rhineland) and he too had built a career on his losses, except that Stein had joined the Prussian administration, not the Austrian. After Prussia's defeat at Jena, he fled to Russia. "I have only one fatherland," he said in 1812, "and that is Germany."[61] Stein was no European. His single-minded campaign for a restored German Reich in the war that followed earned him the nickname "the German Emperor."

He well deserved it. Stein's programme was bureaucratic and Napoleonic. He placed all his hopes in his ability to direct a grand national uprising, motivated by the promise of social reform and fired by patriotism. In practice this meant a dictatorship in all areas "liberated" by the advancing Allied armies. Unlike Metternich, Stein had no sympathy for Germany's Sovereigns, the "thirty-six petty despots" who had, in their weakness, aligned themselves with the enemy. Not even Prussia was exempt from his contempt. But it was strategic Saxony, staging area of the Grande Armée, the most faithful of Napoleon's allies, which Stein singled out for special treatment. Interests were involved here: the interests of the northern Allies, the expansive Powers, Russia and Prussia; Russia thought Saxony was ideal compensation for Prussia in return for her own free hand in Poland.

What happened in Saxony served as a warning of what might happen when the dream of a unitary German Reich was turned, by consent of powerful allies, into reality. After the great Battle of Leipzig in October 1813, the Russian occupation began. The King of Saxony, Frederick Augustus, was taken prisoner and carted off to the Schloss Friedrichsfelde, outside Berlin. Stein, at the head of a Central Administrative Committee, introduced martial law, extended the power of the police, and doubled the financial requisitions and military levies that had originally been imposed by Napoleon. Then, quite contrary to the Allied convention, he extended his system to the neighbouring states of Thuringia and Anhalt. In response, Austrian troops were moved up to the frontier.

It was a military stand-off and it remained one on into the autumn of 1814, as the delegates gathered in Vienna. Russia occupied all Poland and Saxony. Prussia was demanding immediate annexation of the latter. Stein started appealing to the *Standesherren* to support his plans for a restored German Reich.

Metternich's own position clearly depended on the support he could muster against Russia. At the outset of the Congress he thought this could be achieved through an alliance of the German powers alone. With France excluded from preliminary discussions, Prussia and Austria – according to Metternich's arithmetic – held the balance.

But what would be the price of such an alliance? Late in July, the Saxon envoy, Count Friedrich Albrecht von der Schulenburg, had paid a visit to Baden to make a plea for his King and Kingdom. Metternich admitted that Prussian annexation would constitute "a political crime," but warned that Austria could not "wage war on all Europe." Then, on 1 August, he dispatched a letter to his Ambassador in Berlin, Count Stephan Zichy, informing him that "the acquisition of Prussia in Saxony will encounter no obstacle on our side." It was one of Metternich's typically vague phrases that has kept historians debating for more than a century and a half. What sort of "acquisition" did Metternich have in mind? All of Saxony? Or just a part? The offer to Prussia seems to be a tacit admission of Austrian weakness and her need for an ally; Metternich was once again practising "hedging, evasion, and flattery."[62]

It was based on calculation. If he could persuade Prussia to moderate her territorial demands and to associate herself with Austria in an anti-Russian front, then his vision of Europe – and particularly of Germany – as a society of sovereign states would win the day. But, if Prussia continued to insist on all Saxony and Russia stood firm on Poland, the result, as he told Schulenburg in July, could be war. In that case, Metternich would be looking for other alliances – for he would not wage war on all Europe.[63]

Two old nation states lay to the west, Britain and France. Their Foreign Ministers did not think the same way as the immigrant Minister of Kaiser Franz's Reich.

On first sight, Castlereagh's naked, non-ideological engine might be thought to correspond very nicely to Metternich's naked game. Certainly this is what had struck the two men on their first encounter in Bâle the previous January. They both sought a European equilibrium and a definition of limits; neither of them was intent upon expansion, on the continent at least. "Castlereagh behaves like an angel," said Metternich. He was "the most European and the least insular of all the British Foreign Ministers." Added to this was Metternich's admiration for Castlereagh's master, the Prince Regent, "one of the most beautiful men I have met in my life."

But Metternich's breadth of vision was both narrower and wider than Castlereagh's. Castlereagh was a parliamentarian and he thought as a parliamentarian. While accepting the restrictive secret clauses of the Paris Treaty[64] he in the end believed that the Congress should be an assembly of all the states of Europe, that all should be consulted, and consulted sooner rather than later. Metternich interpreted the Treaty as a sanction for the ministers of the Four Allies to sit around a table in Baden and decide on the future of Europe themselves; the delegates in Vienna were simply to be informed of their decisions. Metternich feared Castlereagh would turn the Congress into a stormy London-style parliament of subjects in revolt against their lawful sovereigns. At the same time Metternich's vision was wider in the sense that he understood that all the pieces involved in the approaching negotiations had a history, an identity, and that they could not be moved around by a simple act of will. Castlereagh might have thought that the bits of "Germany" could be set into a conveniently neutral European hub that would hold the hammers on the perimeter at bay; Metternich knew it would not be so.[65]

Metternich's sense of history should have brought him closer to Talleyrand. It was Talleyrand, after all, who had insisted, in 1806, on having Metternich as ambassador in Paris; even at that time Talleyrand had identified Austria as a counter to Napoleon's ambitions and as a useful instrument in France's own post-revolutionary future. The idea of "legitimising" those states that were to play such an important part in achieving a European balance, whether they owed their origins to the distant past of dynasties or to the Revolution, must certainly have appealed to Metternich; indeed, he had negotiated the Habsburg marriage to Bonaparte to legitimise the French counter-weight to Russia.

But the concept of "legitimacy" was Talleyrand's, not Metternich's, whose writings up to 1815 do not even mention the word. There were, moreover, two important ingredients in Talleyrand's concept of legitimacy that would be forever absent from Metternich's calculations. One was the sovereign people: Louis XVIII was King of France, Talleyrand had insisted, by consent of parliament. The other was economics and trade. For Talleyrand this was the base, the lower stratum, on which to build a European peace. The idea had never even entered Metternich's beautiful head.

Metternich tried in vain to get his three allies to join him in Baden for "private discussion." Castlereagh refused because he was opposed to such secretiveness. Nesselrode, the Russian envoy, refused because he wanted to stay by his pregnant wife. Prince Hardenberg, tardy as usual, had not yet arrived in Vienna. So Metternich had to abandon his idea of doing business in Baden.

On 15 September, just before mounting his carriage for Vienna, he wrote a long, and strange, letter to Wilhelmine von Sagan. "My heart is wrung, *mon amie*, at the thought of the possibility of leaving Baden . . . I had attached great ideas of happiness on staying in Baden – these hopes were based on your promises." It was almost with despair that he added "my hour at Baden has sounded." His head travelled, perhaps, with the traffic of the world, but the Foreign Minister still clung stubbornly to his heart. "My head, *mon amie*, is very full. I am like the general who arranges his army and his terrain for a decisive battle. *Mon amie*, don't abandon me at this moment."[66]

Metternich's women

Metternich was now obliged to set up a working centre for the Congress in his official residence on the Ballhausplatz. The Duchess von Sagan would soon move to her own official residence, the Palm Palace, a few hundred yards up the street on the Schenkenstrasse, overlooking the Löblbastei. Half a century later the palace and its neighbouring battlements would all be torn down to make way for the new city theatre. How symbolic it was that the Palm Palace would one day be replaced by a theatre.

It was, as Viennese palaces go, small but typical in design, with two long wings running parallel to the street and a courtyard in the middle that separated them. The Duchess von Sagan – whose portraits (the small mouth, the large nose, and wide, penetrating eyes) leave only a hint of the dazzling beauty contemporaries like Gentz described – lived in one of the palace wings. The other was inhabited by Her Highness, Princess Katharina Pavlovna Skavronska Bagration, thirty-one-year-old widow of the great Russian hero, Prince Piotr Bagration, who had fallen at Borodino in 1812. In Vienna the Princess, who seemed in no way perturbed by this tragic loss, was known as the "Russian siren" or the *"bel ange nu"* on account of her incredibly scanty ballroom gowns, scandalous even for those days of bare necks and shoulders.

Like sister-enemies, the Duchess and the Princess had a great deal in common. They were almost identical in age. They were both subjects of Emperor Alexander; they were both in fact in his pay. They were both leaders of the Russian party in Vienna; they had, for instance, both vigorously opposed the Austrian compromises with Napoleon. They both were society women who did what society women were meant to do; they held *salons*, they consorted with members of the court, and they gave the most exotic balls. But the most significant thing they had in common was that they were both Metternich's lovers.

Their rivalry was famous. From behind their swagged silken curtains they regularly observed each other's activities across the courtyard, they took note of each other's visitors and gatherings, they paid careful attention to every window that was lit and every one that was not. It was hardly beneath their high rank to put an innocent question to the passing chamber maid, the cook's assistant, or the courier deliverer; after all, at least one of these would also be working for Baron Hager. Life in the Palm Palace was never tranquil. "What a destestable complication your residence is at Vienna!" wrote Metternich to Sagan. "I just do not know how to pull myself out of this awful neighbourhood in Vienna," repeated Sagan to Metternich. She could not pull out, she would not pull out; the Tsar was paying her rent.[67]

Metternich had always been attracted to women and he had no trouble attracting them to him. Women were, as Gentz had observed, his "salt of life," and not just his private life at that; his whole diplomatic career had, in large measure, developed thanks to women. His wife had started him off, while the numerous women he had enchanted in the salons of Dresden, Berlin, and Paris had helped in his advance; the gallant diplomat had even managed to build his own international spy ring out of his relations with different women. Caroline Bonaparte now, as Murat's wife, Queen of Naples, had been his lover. So had Laure Junot, wife of the famous French general and a woman who knew society in Paris as well as the back of her dainty hand. He would soon be the lover of the Princess Lieven, who would open up the secrets of London to him. History and Metternich marched calmly together, hand in hand with his women.[68]

But in 1813 the events of history intensified. That had been the year of the *Befreiungskrieg*, the War of Liberation, in northern Germany, the year Austria had changed sides and fought with the Allies. "This Year about to finish," Metternich had written on 27 December 1813, "will have been the greatest of my life." Eighteen-thirteen, he had proudly claimed, "is a bit *my property* – I ought to know that better than anyone." But at what personal cost! "I dare not think of the days that have passed! I believed myself *alone in the world*."[69]

That was the year a casual affair had turned into a passion, the greatest passion of his life. It had all been triggered by memory. In 1813 he looked back to the first years of his career and became convinced he could see the destiny of the world being traced. He looked to the women he had known. He looked at war-torn Saxony, where he had first met Sagan. As Metternich prepared his mind for the cold diplomatic game that would lead Europe to peace, his affair with Sagan transported him into a state of exaltation. Images, coincidences, places: they seemed to fit together. They were all part of a great human renewal: the war, the promised peace – and Sagan. "*Ten years have passed, mon amie*, since I posed the first foundations of the great edifice," he wrote to Sagan after witnessing the terrible Battle of

Leipzig in October 1813. The great edifice was, of course, his own career – his career and his women: "I have suffered all fates – I have made a martyr of myself and it is this which drenches the soul; my hour has finally sounded; I am triumphant and it is you, *mon amie*, that Providence has destined as the reward!"[70]

But there were other women who had helped in getting him up there, and one other woman in particular. Sagan, in 1813, was certainly as well aware as Metternich that the main object of his attention during those earlier years of "peaceful and sweet pleasure" in Saxony had not been her but the Princess Katharina Bagration.

It was in sweet Saxony's capital, Dresden, the play-pen of Northern Europe, that the rivalry between Sagan and Bagration began. Metternich had been accredited to Frederick Augustus's fantastic court in 1801. It was a place of strategic significance. Just as it would be used as the stepping stone for Napoleon's drive eastwards, so would Russia use it to further her westward ambitions; there were many enticing young Russian women in Dresden.

Metternich met eighteen-year-old Katharina Bagration in the salon of Princess Isabella Czartoryska.[71] Though Latvian in origin, Princess Bagration was described by one contemporary as having the softness of an Oriental and the grace of an Andalusian; being rather small, with dark hair and pale skin, she could also be compared to one of Frederick Augustus's fine pieces of Dresden porcelain. Late in the summer of 1802 she gave birth to a daughter, whom she named after the father, Clementine.[72]

Metternich must have met Wilhelmine von Sagan at about this time. She also came from the Baltic lands, Courland, an eastern duchy of Poland that was annexed by Russia in 1795. At the age of twenty she had been engaged to marry the Hohenzollern Prince Louis Ferdinand, nephew of Frederick the Great; but the wedding was cancelled at the last moment by King Frederick William when he got wind that she was already pregnant by her mother's lover, the Baron Gustav von Armfeld. This led to a rapidly arranged marriage with Prince Louis de Rohan, years older than her, but a man from a family that claimed an older and nobler ancestry than that of the Bourbon crown of France.[73] Rohan, at the end of a great life, made few demands on his wife and his wife, at the beginning of no small story herself, fully reciprocated. But Sagan never forgot that her first proposal had come from genuine royalty; when Louis Ferdinand was killed at Saalfeld in 1806, she went into mourning.[74]

There was only one other man in her life who would ever conform to her sense of high destiny, and that was Metternich. Shortly after Wilhelmine's marriage to Rohan, her mother had organised a salon in Dresden. Saxon liberties were well suited to the needs and fancies of her four beautiful daughters; Sagan's younger sister Jeanne, for example, had already at sixteen eloped with an Italian musician (who was murdered) and had been forced to marry a Neapolitan duke.

Sagan's initial pursuit of Metternich met with disappointment. In 1813 she would refer to "this fondness which drew me towards you, even at a time when you would honour me, if not with your total indifference then at least with a benevolence that strongly resembled it."[75]

In February 1804, Metternich was transferred to Berlin, along with his faithful wife and four children. Princess Bagration did not follow him, but Sagan did; her family possessed a palace on the Unter den Linden which all of a sudden required her attention. Metternich would frequently be seen riding through the Brandenburg Gate with graceful Sagan by his side. But he now developed a serious interest in another princess, Ekaterina Dolgoruka, wife of the Russian military attaché in Berlin. Out of spite, Sagan got married again. She first had to divorce Rohan, which she did at great personal expense in March 1805, and then offered her hand to the Russian Emperor's aide-decamp, Prince Vassili Sergeevich Trubetskoi, who was also years older than her. Troubetskoy, however, wanted to live in Russia while Sagan wanted to frequent the salons of Europe. So she divorced him too. "I am ruining myself with husbands," she exclaimed at the time.[76]

Metternich would be transferred to Paris, where he would plot a war and the downfall of Napoleon with Talleyrand, all the while extending his own ring of female spies. Sagan in the meantime wandered from Prague to Teplitz, from love to disappointment, eventually settling down to a political life in Vienna, next door to Princess Bagration in the Palm Palace. When Metternich returned to Vienna, in 1809, to take up the office of Foreign Minister he renewed his affair with Bagration. "What does Metternich do all day?" wrote angry Archduke Johann in his diary in March 1812. "Around eleven, and often twelve, he gets up, he sleeps through the conferences of right honourable gentlemen, then goes round to Princess Bagration, returning around four. . ."[77]

The Duchess von Sagan, in the opposite wing of the Palm Palace, was not one to pine away. She received visits from several gentlemen of high rank, as Bagration must have spotted through her curtains. John King, the British secret agent, was occasionally seen emerging from the palace at dawn. Then there was that handsome young general, Alfred von Windischgrätz.[78] Sagan's correspondence with Windischgrätz left no ambiguity over what their relationship was about. "With friends one counts the days," she wrote, "with you I count the nights, and I would not want to miss a single one of them."[79]

But Metternich, in the other wing, was still the man of her destiny – even if destiny required, now and then, a little prod. Thus, it was not beyond Sagan's fine sense of politics and of men to set herself up, deliberately, on the family estate of Ratiborzitz in northern Bohemia, equidistant between the French and Allied Headquarters, at the moment (June-August 1813) Austria was changing sides in the war. She had both the Russian Emperor and the Austrian Foreign Minister visiting her. Princess Bagration, who possessed no château in the Sudetan hills, was furious.[80]

Metternich was in the Bohemian capital of Prague when, early that August, Austria finally declared war on France. He delayed his departure for the front in the hope that Sagan would travel the short distance to meet him, because by now he had been caught by her charm. An appointment was set, but she failed to turn up. "Why did you let me down?" he complained in despair. "Why did you say you would come? Why did you put me through one more test of disappointed happiness? Why?" He had premonitions of death – "If I die, let me die far from you" – and became seriously ill.

As Schwarzenberg's Austrian forces joined those of Russia and Prussia, Metternich lay love-sick in bed in Prague. His doctors diagnosed a "nervous malady or flux of the chest." Another seven days passed before he was physically able to join his Emperor and the troops at Teplitz.[81]

The remarkable thing is that Metternich, unlike the Russian Emperor, did, on the whole, manage to keep politics separate from his sentimental affairs, even though they were so evidently linked. His extraordinary self-conceit undoubtedly had something to do with this. "*Be quiet,*" he would typically write (the emphasis his); "I tell you I claim to be at least obeyed *in politics*. Neither you nor anyone will dispute me in that domain." He looked on himself as a kind of ancient colossus standing astride two island massifs, his affair with Sagan under one foot and his great task of peace under the other; he had convinced himself that he could keep them below, underfoot, holding them apart, mastering them both: "*Mon amie et l'Europe, l'Europe et mon amie!* There is hardly any resemblance between these ideas, they are distant from one another, like good and evil, beauty and ugliness, sweetness and bitterness. That does not prevent me from passing from one to the other with the greatest of ease."[82]

It really was an affair of letters, so much so that when the New Year, 1814, arrived they agreed to number their correspondence so that posterity would be able to follow their high destiny. The number of nights they actually spent together could be counted on one hand.

Sagan's letters mimicked those of her lover. They reflected back his own thoughts, they confirmed his self-defined role as conqueror and peacemaker, they framed the colossus, and even added to it a mirror's lustre. "*Your* victory," she wrote from Prague immediately after news of Leipzig (even imitating Metternich's emphasis), "makes me today happier than I have ever been." She mimed his words, she mimed his ideas, though she was always careful, in contrast to Metternich, to use the French formal *vous* or the German *Sie*. On rare occasions she did express her own feelings – in German. "*Mein lieber guter Clemenz, von ganzem Herzen liebe ich Sie . . .*" ("I do not know why I wrote to you in German," she added apologetically in her concluding paragraph, "I hadn't noticed it").

That same German letter also contained a note of doubt – "so few keep what they promise or what we expect of them." But as Metternich travelled ever more distant with the advancing western front, she adopted a tone that echoed the anguished Romanticist call for a homecoming; she called Metternich her *patrie* – "such as I have always sought" – claiming, idealistically, that in him could be found "security, happiness, and hope."[83]

Security, however, was the one thing Metternich did not offer the Duchess. Despite all his boasts of controlling destiny, he had no plans for their future beyond the stipulation that she should continue to love him and blindly support him in his world task. He was generous in his gifts, sending chocolate and caviar, which he forwarded along with his letters through a special line of dispatch riders that he set up between his moving headquarters and Prague. He talked incessantly of Sagan in the presence of the Tsar – a great error. One typical evening, sitting in front of a high silver samovar, Metternich spoke of the last excursion he had made back to Prague and, by implication, a night he had spent with Sagan. Alexander became oddly silent, shut his left eye, and raised the index of his right hand in the form of a pointed pistol. "This man will perhaps kill me if you let me live," Metternich wrote to Sagan later in the night. Nonetheless he went on talking, treating the Russian Emperor as if he were his confidant.[84]

Metternich became increasingly exclusive. At first he was friendly and tolerant towards Alfred von Windischgrätz, who was then serving in the Austrian camp; Metternich even used him as a courier to Prague. But by December the tone had changed; he rejoiced when a meeting between Sagan and Windischgrätz was cancelled and he expressed great satisfaction when the general's regiment got its marching orders. Meanwhile, Metternich continued his own lament of "fever, agony, and death," and he repeatedly professed to Sagan that he loved her "a hundred times more than my life." But he had no plans for their future.

Sagan did. As early as September 1813 she was writing, "Think of what I said about my position," and went on to assert: "There are ties as strong but not as indissoluble as those contracted before the altar. That's the point of view from which we should regard our situation . . ." If Metternich wanted their relationship to last, the implication was clear: they would have to be married. Metternich did not like this at all. He complained of his "sorry privilege" (a reference, perhaps, to his marriage to a Kaunitz) and defined, as he would always define, their relationship as a matter of the heart. There are ties, he said, stronger than the law; "the heart does not need laws because it is stronger than anything; it is above and beyond the law." Then he added, by way of consolation, "I give you what I can; a time will perhaps come when I will be able to give you more." Sagan followed Metternich's advice and kept quiet on the matter – for the duration of the war.[85]

In the second week of December, 1813, Sagan returned to Vienna and the Palm Palace. The war front had now moved so far west that Metternich's special courier service to Prague was becoming a serious drain on Austrian finances. "Go to Vienna," he instructed; "Prague is off all lines." He also sent his secretary Gentz to Vienna, ostensibly "to direct public opinion there," but in fact to spy on Sagan.[86]

Gentz's reports on Sagan were, on the whole, just what Metternich wanted to hear. After several long conversations with her, he concluded that she "only loved him, Metternich, and that he reigned sovereign in her heart." He reviewed her various relationships with men and was pleased to inform His Highness the Prince[87] that she appeared to have broken with her confidant, Windischgrätz. True, she was now often seen in the company of Frederick James Lamb, the young secretary to the English Legation. But then the English were very much in style in Vienna during the Carnival season of February 1814, and it was thought that she was simply trying to make her mark in high English society.[88]

Yet she wasn't seen much in public. Gentz said she spent most of her time alone lost in thought; she had become very restless, even gloomy and upset, a fact which affected her physically. The Duchess herself complained to Metternich of continuing migraines.[89]

Paris fell. Peace was declared. The correspondence between Metternich and Sagan dwindled. "The thing which preoccupies me at the moment," wrote Sagan on 20 April 1814, "is your long silence, dear Clemens. My God, so many days without news from you." With peace, she began to address Metternich with the familiar French *tu*. She begged him for news of her mother and her youngest sister, who were then in Paris. This was no innocent question; it became the ostensible reason for her own trip to the French capital.

She arrived in mid-May, after the Peace had been signed and the celebrations had begun. Metternich's wife stayed behind in Vienna. It was a golden opportunity to raise once again "the ties that are strong"; the time had at last arrived for Sagan to discuss "my position." Sagan had divorced twice, she had in her possession Metternich's declarations that he loved her more than his own life, so surely he could divorce just once?[90]

In June, Sagan was in London. One short letter from Metternich to
Sagan leaves a tiny hint as to what was happening. It is dated
Wednesday, 8 June 1814, the day after the Sovereigns arrived in the
cheering metropolis: "*Bonjour mon amie.* I do not know how or
when I will see you in the day . . ." He reported the long dinner he
had attended at Carlton House the previous night and the various ceremonies he would be participating in that Wednesday. "Share my
happiness, *mon amie*," he concluded, "but don't irritate it."[91]

The first weeks that followed their return to Austria were evidently
as bitter in private as the public praise in the streets of Vienna was
sweet. This may have been one of the reasons why Metternich made
such a quick dash for Baden, though both Sagan and Bagration had
set up their summer residences in the resort.

On a gloomy Sunday, 24 July – it poured with rain all day –
Metternich had to go back to Vienna on urgent business. Gentz, who
was dining almost daily at Princess Bagration's table in Baden, wrote
in his diary: "Ten o'clock, at the Duchess von Sagan's. Drove her to
Madame Cadogan's. From there she returned to town."[92]

So Sagan and Metternich were in Vienna together on 24 July. But
there is no evidence, as has recently been suggested, that Sagan, after
spending the night with the Minister, made some strange pact of
fidelity.[93] Quite the contrary. A letter that Metternich wrote to Sagan
that same week, and possibly that same day, suggests that their relationship was ended: "One relationship, a dream, the most beautiful of
my life, has been lost." He was making a desperate appeal for a
meeting, not for a night, but for a single hour: "*A single hour*," he
emphasised, "that is all I want."[94]

What had happened during that rainy night in Vienna? It is difficult
to tell. As soon as Sagan was back in Baden she wrote to Metternich.
She was clearly not happy. "I do not fear you at all," she said.

> Everything has so completely changed between us that it is not at all
> astonishing that our thoughts and our sentiments no longer agree on any-
> thing. I'm beginning to believe we have never really known each other.
> We were both pursuing a phantom. You saw in me a model of perfection;
> I saw in you all there was of beauty and intellectual grandeur – something
> well above honour. The natural sequel to these illusions is that you have
> [now] pushed me in your imagination as low as I was once high. I, being
> calmer, will make no decision until after our conversation and after I have
> seen its results. But I am strongly inclined to think of you [now] as a man
> one meets almost anywhere. Please excuse my sincerity.

There had certainly been an earlier evening meeting, for she commented, "In opposition to your thinking, it was precisely your heart
this evening that I feared the least." But it seems unlikely that she
spent that night with her lover.[95]

A further indication of the kind of trouble that was brewing comes from Gentz. He wrote to Metternich on 24 July to report that his conversation with the Duchess earlier in the day had totally failed. He accused her of "treachery without equal" and hoped that Metternich would be back in Baden within two days so that he could provide more details. "Wilhelmine has, by the way, begun a War of Separation with *me*." He was taking baths, as he said, "to arm my skin."[96]

That summer Metternich and Gentz could have been seen wandering in the streets of Baden in the early hours of the morning talking, as Gentz recorded, "not (unfortunately) about public affairs but on his relations and my own with Mad. de Sagan." By the second week of August, Gentz was speaking of a reconciliation. By early September, Metternich was writing once more to Sagan of his hopes for renewed happiness. But what he could achieve in Baden would be less easy to maintain in Vienna and that "terrible place," the Palm Palace.[97]

Metternich left Baden on 15 September filled with forebodings of abandonment.

It may seem incredible that Sagan, twice divorced and Protestant, could actually be accepted into the Catholic court of Austria. Yet honest Kaiser Franz not only accepted her; in August he told Metternich that he considered her "one of the most necessary ingredients of the Congress."[98] With this sort of recommendation from the Emperor himself, Sagan must have again wondered why Metternich could not divorce Eleonore. As she had told him in July, she was fearless. Her mistake lay in her misjudgment of Metternich: he was not a man to take risks. "Hedging, evasion, and flattery" could have been as much his motto in private affairs as it had been his proclaimed political guideline when he was named Foreign Minister in that year of disaster, 1809. And he had enemies in the court.

But an even more extraordinary complication for Metternich in the coming Congress was that Sagan's wealthy mother, living in Paris, also happened to be Talleyrand's wealthy mistress, the duchesse de Courlande.

Talleyrand's women

Talleyrand, still in Paris on 15 September, was perfectly delighted about the way things seemed to be developing. He was looking for opportunities that would gain a place for France in the councils of power. The tiniest details interested him: the odd political accident abroad, knowledge of a rival's embarrassment, any sign of weakness, any personal quirk in an Allied statesman that might be ridiculed or in other ways used against him. In August, Talleyrand had managed to take advantage of the sudden turn in British "public opinion" from Princess Caroline to worry over the slave trade; he was sure he had

won Castlereagh to his side. Metternich, responsible to no parliament
and utterly determined to limit discussions to as small a group as possible, would be a tougher nut to crack.

Talleyrand was not the sort of person to have moral quibbles over
applying a little pressure in the private domain. "When one is faced
with matters of importance, one must put the women to work," he
had told a colleague at the outset of his own diplomatic career; it was
a principle Talleyrand never abandoned. It reappears in his memoirs,
expressed in the formal language of the diplomat he was. There he
would explain why he had asked his niece,[99] the comtesse Edmond de
Périgord, daughter of the duchesse de Courlande, sister of
Wilhelmine von Sagan, to accompany him to Vienna. "It seemed to
me," as he exquisitely put it, "necessary to turn high and influential
society in Vienna away from the hostile prejudices imperial France
had created. This required that the Embassy be rendered *agreeable for
them*." Charming young Dorothée would do the job. "With her fine
mind and her tact she knew how to attract and please, and she was
extremely useful for me."[100]

The duchesse de Courlande actually had four useful and agreeable
daughters. Wilhelmine, now thirty-two, seemed to be marking out a
fine career for herself in Vienna. Pauline, a year younger, was the most
retiring of the four. As a child she had been tyrannised by her parents
and, to escape, had married the first man who came along, the Prince
von Hohenzollern-Hechingen – "a great lord no doubt," Dorothée
would later say, "but nothing can be praised in him beyond the
brilliance of his birth." Jeanne, after her adventure with the Italian
musician, had been forced to marry the Neapolitan Prince Francesco
Pignatelli del Belmonte, Duke of Acerenza – who was no match for
Jeanne. But in 1814 they remained married and were living in Vienna.
Dorothée married Edmond de Périgord in April 1809, following
Talleyrand's treasonous discussions with Emperor Alexander at
Erfurt. She was only fifteen at the time.[101]

The Duchess, who was fifty-three in 1814, was still a very attractive
woman. During the celebrations of peace earlier that spring she kept
one of the most frequented *salons* in Paris. Witnesses described her as
being dignified, graceful, with an enchanting touch of the coquette
about her; her dangling diamonds no doubt helped give this impression. Talleyrand would continue to scribble out affectionate *petits
billets* and there is nothing to suggest that his sentiments were not sincere. The fact that she was over fifty could even have been part of her
appeal. As Lady Yarmouth had put it back in 1812, "M de Talleyrand
is tumbled in a very violent love with the D.C. [the Duchess] and
nothing seems to captivate him so much as old age, for all his loves are
really very antiquities."[102]

Talleyrand's relationship with women, in fact, resembled his politics; he never liked, he never bothered, to make an open break with past alliances, so that over time he was surrounded by an ever-growing circle of elderly women. This aging seraglio would gather regularly at his home on rue Saint-Florentin for a game of whist or craps and had become, by 1814, one of the grander monuments of Paris.

But there was one figure missing, his wife. Recently unearthed documents now prove that Talleyrand had set into motion the procedure for a legal separation from his wife the moment Louis XVIII returned to France, in April 1814. It was finalised two years later.[103] The Princess, who was born the daughter of a minor French civil servant in India, had met Talleyrand in 1797 quite by accident while fleeing the police in Paris.[104] She had never been accepted by the diplomatic corps and was despised by high society. Napoleon had been scandalised because this "witless old maid" could bear no children. Barras, the politician, said she had a "grand and robust shape" with a face that put him in mind of Robespierre ("who certainly had no claims to prettiness"). A member of the Académie Française was rather more precise; "she had difficulty in walking, difficulty in digesting, difficulty in everything." But none of this would have been cause enough for Talleyrand to seek a separation. It was, as usual, politics that decided him. The problem was that His Most Christian Majesty, on returning to his Kingdom, could never accept the idea that a man who had made the formal vows of a bishop could ever be married. The Princess had suddenly become an obstacle in Talleyrand's career.[105]

Dorothée, on the other hand, represented a future. At twenty-one she was already one of the most acclaimed young women in Paris and was set to eclipse her eldest sister, Wilhelmine, in both beauty and wit. "Giving happiness is a manner of exercising power that has always had a great charm for me," she confessed in her memoirs, which she wrote at the ripe old age of twenty-nine. This was the quality that her uncle, now sixty, found "extremely useful."[106]

Metternich was perhaps the only man in Europe who thought Dorothée plain, but then his remarks were probably made in consolation for the eldest sister. "Dorothée in my opinion is hardly pretty," he had written to Wilhelmine from Paris in April; "she has too much of what you do not have too little." He was thinking, in particular, of noses.[107]

There was a simple explanation for the physical difference: Dorothée was not the daughter of Duke Peter of Courland but of one of her mother's many lovers, Count Alexander Batowski. Yet she always spoke of the Duke as her father and she regarded his death in 1800, when she was only seven, as one of the great tragedies of her life. "Sad, almost melancholic," she said of her childhood; "I remember perfectly how I wanted to die in order to find my father [for], had he lived, he would have offered me the protection I believe I needed." Surely this was one of the reasons for her attraction to people older than her. "I never had children of my own age around me," she recollected; "their presence bored me, because the greatest pleasure I used to have, and still have, was conversation." Older people were always better at this, she thought. Yet she had little love for her mother. "My relationship with her was never precisely daughterly," she complained, painting her childhood as "a time of oppression."[108]

Her marriage to Talleyrand's nephew, Edmond – arranged at the famous Erfurt Conference between Talleyrand and the Tsar – had not worked out. The couple had had two sons in quick succession and then, in 1812, Edmond set off for war, colonel of the 8th Chasseurs à Cheval. There he made his reputation, not as a warrior but as the biggest dandy of the Grande Armée, with a prodigious love of cards, and an equally prodigious ability to lose his uncle's money. In the German campaign of 1813, he was captured by Cossacks, imprisoned in Berlin, escaped, and in Alsace captured again by Russians, and again escaped, arriving in Paris in January 1814. But it appears that, from that date on, he never actually lived with his wife.[109]

Dorothée was spending more time with her uncle. In 1812, while her mother was in Saxony, taking care of the family estate of Löbichau, Dorothée remained in France. Even in 1814, when her mother was back in Paris, it was Dorothée who resided at rue Saint-Florentin, not the Duchess.

When Dorothée first moved into her uncle's residence there was little warmth between the two. But as the months wore on Talleyrand slowly became aware of his niece's innate intelligence and her beauty, while it gradually dawned on Dorothée that this cynical, indolent, indifferent old uncle of hers actually had "a cool-headed courage, a presence of mind, a bold temperament, an instinctive type of defiance, which rendered danger so seductive..."[110]

Talleyrand set off for Vienna on Friday, 16 September 1814, with his niece, his secretary La Besnardière, and a musician, Sigismond Neukomm, who had for years played soothing airs in the Talleyrand residence while his master worked on his reports and correspondence. In Vienna he would be joined by his three formal assistants, the duc de Dalberg, the marquis de la Tour de Pin, and comte Alexis de Noailles. Talleyrand had picked Dalberg for his knowledge of Germany. The other two gentlemen he had chosen not for their diplomatic expertise but because, as men close to the comte d'Artois, Talleyrand thought they would keep the extreme royalists in Paris happy. "Noailles is a man of the pavillon de Marsan [Artois' residence in the Tuileries]," Talleyrand explained at the time; "it's best to be surveyed by an agent I have chosen myself. La Tour de Pin will serve to sign passports."[111]

Rather like Metternich, Talleyrand was convinced that Providence had selected him to guide the destiny of France and the world. He was sure he was the only person capable of leading France's delegation at Vienna; "I saw no one else who seemed to unite the requirements needed for this mission," as he modestly put it himself. At the same time, being France's man of Providence made him feel uneasy leaving his country at this critical moment of the Restoration. The comte de Jaucourt, a talented man who had followed a career similar to Talleyrand's, would take charge of the Ministry of Foreign Affairs in his master's absence. But the government? A government had really not yet taken shape; Louis XVIII was relying, and relying too much, on inexperienced personal advisers.[112]

On his way through Strasbourg, Talleyrand met another traveller of Europe's highways, Caroline, the Princess of Wales. The Princess had set herself up in Strasbourg in the hope of getting an invitation to Paris. It would have been a disaster for Talleyrand's policy of entente with Britain had she succeeded. The fact that Talleyrand stopped off at the Princess's inn was no coincidence. For the first and last time in his life he was witness to her curious behaviour. "She had accepted a ball at Madame Franck's," he reported in a dispatch to his King. "She danced there all night. In the inn where I was staying she gave a supper to Talma. Her manner of behaving in Strasbourg explains perfectly why the Prince Regent prefers to see her in Italy rather than in England." With Talleyrand in Strasbourg, both the French and British governments were assured that she would not lose her way. The Princess was off for Italy on the same day the Foreign Minister took the road to Vienna.[113]

He was moving at the speed of an express courier. On 20 September he reached Munich, where he made one of those contacts that would be essential in his policy of changing France's fate; he met an old acquaintance, a former courtier to Louis XVI, a former ally of Napoleon's, now King Maximilian Joseph I of Bavaria. Talleyrand assured the King that he would defend the sovereignty and privileges of the German southern states. The "third Germany" had a role to play for France as well as for Austria.

The next day he was hoping he would be in Vienna; he actually arrived at the Kaunitz Palace at midnight, Friday, 23 September.

Practically the first thing he saw there was a diplomatic note lying on a table, addressed "To monsieur le prince de Talleyrand, *hôtel Kaunitz*." The flicker of a smile suddenly coloured his thin pale lips. "Joining these two names seemed to me a good omen," he wrote, savouring the moment years later: the great Kaunitz had masterminded the Franco-Austrian alliance of 1756 against Prussia.[114]

The Big Four

While Talleyrand's coach rolled eastwards under glorious sunshine, Vienna was basking in the first autumn days of festivity. Franz Perth's diary leaves a hint of the excitement that rose suddenly like a breeze in that third week of September and rustled down through the ranks of the *Residenzstadt*. Houses in the Inner City and along the Jägerzeile had been redecorated – the banners unfurled – in preparation for the arrival of Emperor Alexander. Stakes and barriers aligned the streets where troops would be taking up their positions. Cannon were laid out on the lawns before the Bastei; Perth counted forty on the Burggravelin alone. Fat King Frederick of Württemberg arrived amid acclaim on Thursday, 22 September. Every evening crowds assembled in the Burgplatz to hear "Turkish music" blasted out by seven regimental bands.[115] "In general, in the last few days the usual busy life in our city has got visibly more intense with the arrival of the foreign Ministers and their retinues," Perth recorded; "the throngs and waves of the people, the crush of the carriages become more and more of a bustle with each passing day." Victorious Alexander was expected that Sunday. On Saturday evening, Perth joined his friend Herr von Wolf on the Burgplatz to listen to "Turkish music" again, then they supped in "Zum Erzherzog Karl," a nearby inn, and after that they strolled down to the coffee-house next to the Kärnterthortheater, where Perth had "a very good ice-cream." Secret agent ✳✳ was also wandering around the crowd somewhere. "*The Panorama of Europe*," he reported to Hager: "that is what the people call this assembly at Vienna, which will immortalise the Reign of the Emperor and the Ministry of Prince Metternich."[116]

It was a baroque celebration for a baroque city; the mass of Viennese amused themselves in the open air, they revelled in the glow of peace, autumn, and a war gone by, while powerful statesmen conducted the business of politics and territorial division behind closed doors.

Firmly closed doors: not even Hager's agents could get past the gates of Castlereagh's palace. Agent "Nota" bumped into a certain Mr Parr on the Graben. "What are the English up to?" wondered Nota aloud. Mr Parr gave his inquisitor a bland look. "Since they're on holiday they pass most of their time seeing what the city and surroundings have on offer," he finally replied. "In the evenings they visit young Countess Rzewuska, who receives them very well" – the Countess was a popular Polish lady, whose mother had been guillotined in Paris during the Terror – "and then they usually go off with some girl and get drunk on Hungarian wine."[117]

Others enjoyed more select company and drink. Viennese high

society was in a ferment; every important hostess in town was boasting she would soon be receiving emperors and kings. The two rivals in the Palm Palace offered suppers, balls, *salons*, and comfort to the famous. Metternich was seen amid the crowd of guests at Katharina Bagration's nearly every night that week, though he would arrive late and would usually be gone by one. On Wednesday, 21 September, he attended at the Hofburg the formal admission of Kaiser Franz to the Order of the Garter; Sir Isaac Heard, England's Chief Herald had come over from London especially for the occasion. "It's still the most gorgeous weather," noted Gentz in his diary. "Immense movement in the whole city." The next night, Gentz and Metternich were having a long conversation at the Duchess von Sagan's. The *soirée* was, said Gentz, "at first quite dull." But then things picked up, particularly after "a very lively discussion on England." Wednesday's ceremony at the Hofburg was still in people's minds. And a few were perhaps wondering why Castlereagh was not present; he was all of a sudden showing remarkable independence of his Allies. For Gentz, lively political discussion was a pleasant relief after the summer's storms with Sagan. "It was the first time I felt good at the Duchess's," he scribbled into his diary.[118]

The Ballhausplatz was very busy that week. "I found all Europe gathered in my antechamber," Metternich wrote to his wife, still in Baden, on Monday, 19 September. He thought, like Castlereagh, that the whole business of the Congress would be done in less than two months – "four to six weeks of hell," he predicted in the same letter. "We'll finish in six weeks," he had told Sagan in a note written at nine the same morning, "and that is what I am telling you. If we don't it will be the fault of others, and perhaps your fault because you made me lose my path."[119]

With the future of Europe on their agenda, the diplomats, throughout that week and for many weeks that followed, would sit down for an old-fashioned eighteenth-century dinner at about three in the afternoon. It was usually after dinner that the real business of politics began.

A Congress on the future of Europe: it was still only an idea, and a very vague idea at that. There were special state interests at stake, and it was already clear that some of the states were prepared to go to war to defend them. But "Europe"? Was anybody prepared to defend "Europe"? For somebody like Gentz, the words "Europe" and "the world" were interchangeable, were equally abstract notions, and were worth no further thought. For his master Metternich, "Europe" had the historical sense of a game, and he would have preferred the three or four participants who mattered to pack up their bags and move out to Baden for serious, uninterrupted play. In general "Europe" offered, to employ Talleyrand's term, "legitimacy" to the interests of the

Powers; some wanted more of "Europe," some wanted less, some wanted this aspect of "Europe," some preferred that. It was the representatives of the strongest Powers that talked most about "Europe": Castlereagh spoke of "Europe" because the interests of Britain were essentially satisfied and he now sought a general peace on the Continent; Alexander spoke of "Europe" because he was convinced he had conquered it and had thus won the right to fulfil his dreams. For weak Prussia, on the other hand, the only purpose of "Europe" was to sanction and guarantee the territorial gains she expected.

As for the "Congress", the term was just as abstruse as "Europe." Some deliberately avoided mentioning it. Within his first week in Vienna, Metternich, for example, cut out all references to the Congress and, in its place, spoke of the "other Powers," that is, all those outside the decision-making. Castlereagh, on the other hand, constantly talked about the Congress; he was a parliamentarian and wanted all the states of Europe consulted. All the states? Even he wasn't very keen on the idea of having Murat's state in Naples represented. Prussia would never be seen in an assembly that included representatives of Frederick Augustus's Saxony. And who was going to represent Poland?

These were the problems discussed by the representatives of the Four Allies during the sunny, noisy week in Vienna that preceded the entry of Emperor Alexander – and the arrival of Talleyrand. Castlereagh would call it "methodising." Most historians would refer to it less colourfully as the "question of procedure." Whatever one called it, the basic issue debated by the Four, in their first encounters at the Chancellery, was who should be excluded from the decision-making, and how. In the process, Castlereagh and Metternich collided.

The meetings began the day after Metternich's arrival in Vienna, on Friday, 16 September, when Count Nesselrode, representing Russia, and Lord Castlereagh walked into the Chancellery after dinner. Prussia's Chancellor had still not arrived, so it was an informal gathering of three, with Baron Binder, a secretary connected with the Austrian Chancellery, keeping the minutes. The discussions would be conducted in French. And in these early sessions it was Castlereagh who maintained the initiative, despite his poor French accent and grammar.

He aimed at an open Congress diplomacy as opposed to Metternich's closed cabinet diplomacy. He did not disapprove of private talks between the Four, but he insisted that the Congress sanction them. For this purpose, he wanted it be convened immediately.

The reason for this was the 180-degree turn Castlereagh had made with his engine: it was now pointed with full force against Russia. Castlereagh had developed an intense fear of Russian influence, not only on Prussia, but also on Austria. If Austria joined the Russian camp, Europe's "intermediary system" would have no chance of developing; instead, Britain would be faced with another form of imperial Europe with a new Napoleon, this time round, in St Petersburg. Talleyrand had done everything to encourage this view. But Castlereagh had made it clear to Talleyrand that he did not want France to act as a general arbitrator. So he called on the Congress. Castlereagh was a European.

The problem immediately arose of credentials. Nesselrode, supporting Prussia's aims, was not going to sit in a Congress with Count von Schulenberg of Saxony. It was well known that few of the Sovereigns in southern Germany would accept Baron von Gärtner, representing the displaced *Standesherren* – a challenge to their authority. The three Ministers patched together a temporary compromise which would ultimately lead to a distinction between "plenipotentiaries" and "petitioners," the latter designating emissaries of those states or corporations not recognised by "the totality of Europe."[120]

Metternich objected to the whole idea of convening the Congress before the Four had agreed not only on its organisation but also on how the territory of Europe was to be distributed. He referred to the secret articles of the Treaty of Paris. He proposed the creation of a Committee of Six (the Four Allies together with France and Spain) but continued to insist that the two additional members would only be admitted for consultation after the Four had reached agreement. Furthermore, to prevent undue interference even from the Allies in German affairs (the territorial organisation of the states and the complex institutional problems that had arisen since Napoleon's retreat across the Rhine), he proposed that a German Committee be set up, consisting of Austria, Prussia, Bavaria, Württemberg, and Hanover.

This informal meeting ended with no conclusions at all. Baron Binder drafted two accounts of the proceedings and nobody signed either of them. Nobody yet had an answer to the credentials problem or membership of the "Congress." Nobody had defined the role of France and Spain in the Committee of Six. Nobody, including Metternich, saw how German affairs, so critical to the future of Europe, could be limited to a German Committee.

The next day, Saturday, 17 September, Prince Hardenberg's carriage rolled into Vienna.

Hardenberg, The Prince Chancellor of Prussia, was actually a Hanoverian. He had served the courts of Hanover, Brunswick, and Bayreuth before joining the Prussian civil service, had married a former mistress of the Prince Regent of England, and had led, in general, a very full and pleasurable life.[121] But at sixty-four he was nearly stone deaf; he used a horn and required the assistance of a trustworthy interpreter at all meetings he attended. In Vienna, he turned to the services of Prussia's brilliant Ambassador to the Habsburg Court, Baron Wilhelm von Humboldt.

Sunday's agenda for the diplomats was filled with feasts and receptions. This included a huge gathering at the palace of Count Razumovsky, formerly the Russian Ambassador to Vienna but now simply a patron of the arts and of anyone who supported the Russian cause in the *Resdenzstadt*. Princess Bagration also offered a nighttime supper. All the major diplomats attended. Yet, they also managed to fit in, between dinner and supper, a five-hour session in the Chancellery; it was the first meeting of the Big Four in Vienna.[122]

After their initial wrangle, both Castlereagh and Metternich arrived with prepared written statements. Castlereagh remained committed to an open, parliamentary diplomacy, though he recognised the need for a steering committee. He got round the credentials problem by proposing an informal convocation of all envoys present in Vienna who claimed to represent a sovereign state; the invitation, like the original invitation to Vienna, would be announced in the newspapers. Metternich, as representative of the host government, would, after doing a little private prompting of the parties involved, manage to persuade the assembly to approve the creation of the Committee of Six (the Four plus France and Spain). Castlereagh recognised the need for some initial understanding between the Four, but he still insisted on a general approval and on the presence of France and Spain in the steering committee. Castlereagh had the vision of a parliamentarian seeking a centre in Europe. Unfortunately, in Vienna, he found no parliament.

Metternich stuck to the idea of a ruling cabinet. The secret articles of the Treaty of Paris, he argued, clearly placed the responsibility of decision-making in the hands of the Four and relegated the role of the "other Powers" to the end of the negotiating process. He even wanted to reduce the role of the German Committee, which he had only proposed two days earlier. Basically, Metternich's order of procedure now was that the Four decide, France, Spain, and the German Committee then be "consulted," and the other Powers finally "approve." This was the opinion of a migrant Rhinelander who had adopted entirely an Austrian view of Europe.

Hardenberg, who simply wanted Prussian territorial ambitions ratified by the powers that be, must have nodded his head. Nesselrode, who wanted Prussia installed in Saxony to keep her out of Poland, would have been equally satisfied with Metternich's prose. Humboldt, hardly impartial, drafted a protocol[123] to be presented to Talleyrand and the Spanish Minister; it essentially followed Metternich's line. Castlereagh was faced with what he feared most, a combination of Austria, Prussia, and Russia. But Bagration's *soirée* at the Palm Palace was now in full swing, and nobody signed the protocol.

Castlereagh was saved by Nesselrode's announcement the next day that he had news of his Emperor's intentions in Poland: it was what, for over a year, the three other Allies had been waiting for. (On Poland and other European states, see Appendix B.) They put aside the business of Sunday and, on Monday evening, sat in the Chancellery to listen to what Nesselrode had to say. Alexander offered Prussia a narrow stretch of land along the Prosna down to the lower Vistula, and Austria a salt mine; the rest of Napoleon's "Grand Duchy of Warsaw" would go to Russia, including the strategic towns of Thorn and Cracow. Nesselrode defended the claim with an argument familiar to a later generation of Europeans: having liberated the area from tyranny, the Russian people deserved "a military frontier that would preserve them forever from the calamity of a new invasion."[124] Metternich of course answered that Russia had not done this alone. Moreover, he argued that the proposal represented a mortal threat to Austria, territorially because Austria would be outflanked, and morally because a revival of the name Poland could raise the spectre of nationalist enthusiasms. This last point also concerned Hardenberg. Castlereagh must have been pleased. In offering his support to Hardenberg and Metternich, he confirmed the alignment of powers he had been seeking from the outset with his two German Allies turned on Russia. The engine was back on track and the cogs were in mesh.

Or so Castlereagh thought, for the discussion of this specific issue of Poland seemed to confirm his conception of the "intermediary sytem," a united and neutral central German block that would keep the two flanking Powers at bay. With Russia on the defensive, Castlereagh felt less reliant on France. The Foreign Secretary was in a cheerful mood as he watched, that Wednesday, the Chief Herald present the Order of the Garter to Kaiser Franz.

But, on Thursday and Friday, the Four were back discussing the procedural problem, which once again put Castlereagh in the minority and threatened to throw his centre out of gear.

Thursday's meeting began with a paper presented by Humboldt. It pushed Metternich's interpretation of the secret articles to its extreme conclusion. The Congress of Vienna, said Humboldt, was not a peace conference, it was not a deliberative assembly, it was merely the site of individual negotiations undertaken, on the whole, by the Four in occasional consultation with the other Powers whenever the need arose.

Humboldt divided the business of the Congress into three categories: territorial questions, questions of regional interest, and questions of general interest. The territorial questions would be decided by the Four; France and Spain would merely be asked to judge whether the decisions made conformed to the Treaty of Paris. The regional questions (in other words, Prussia's interests) would be decided by an even narrower circle, the Powers immediately concerned: the Four, as defenders of the balance of power, might have something to say about Saxony, the Rhineland, and whether the Netherlands should be included in a German confederation, but everything else should be decided among the German princes themselves. Questions of general interest, like the slave trade, international rivers, and diplomatic precedence (that is, the questions that really didn't concern Prussia), would be left to the "Six Great Powers."

Humboldt's approach was, in short, what would today be called "Europe *à la carte*" – the policy of picking out the bits of "Europe" one wants for immediate use and holding the rest at bay. It was the policy of a weak power, of a power on the defensive. Humboldt made it clear that Europe had nothing to offer Prussia as far as her territorial ambitions were concerned; but Europe, according to this project, did provide "legitimacy" once Prussia's illegitimate act was done.

The meeting was adjourned so that the Ministers could attend Sagan's *soirée*. It was decided that Metternich's original memorandum of Sunday would be presented to the French and the Spanish, but that Humboldt would prepare a separate protocol to be read to the four Ministers the next evening.[125]

Metternich, who, for all his narrowness, did have a European view of things, did wonder if the Prussians were not being a trifle harsh. Nonetheless, after doing one of his arithmetical calculations he decided that support of Humboldt's scheme would provide him with sufficient force to resist Russian ambitions without having to turn to France (Prussia + Austria = 5, against Russia's 4). On Friday, therefore, he signed Humboldt's protocol. Nesselrode signed for an entirely different reason; he didn't want European interference in Poland, so that a scheme like Humboldt's, which kept the number of decision-makers to an absolute minimum (wasn't Poland a "regional question"?), perfectly accorded with Russian interests.

But there was no way Castlereagh could sign. Humboldt's protocol closed the options available for a mediated peace and a general European balance, it deprived him of his French hand, and it even threatened the security of the Netherlands. Castlereagh had not forgotten the way the Prussians had "liberated" the Belgic provinces or Hardenberg's hints in London of a German "Burgundian Circle." He refused to sign the document on the grounds that it insulted the "secondary Powers" by ignoring them; it humiliated them "in the face of Europe."[126]

The Ministers adjourned for yet another evening at Princess Katherina Bagration's. As they strolled into the Palm Palace, Talleyrand's carriage was clattering up the Kärtnerstrasse.

Veni, vidi, vici: Alexander's arrival

Reports were coming into Vienna that Alexander's month's stay in St Petersburg had been really quite lonely. Hager's police intercepted a letter from the Duke of Weimar suggesting that the Tsar had been reduced to no more than a puppet of the Senate. More important was a report from General von Köller, who had been sent on special mission to St Petersburg; it indicated that there was powerful opposition inside Russia to the Tsar's constitutional plans for Poland.[127]

The few foreigners who saw the Russian Emperor at this time found him irritated over his Allies' behaviour, particularly Metternich's. When the Prussian envoy, Colonel Schoeler, dared mention the ticklish matter of frontiers, Alexander went into a violent tirade, threatening to seize both East Prussia and Danzig; the envoy dropped the subject and disappeared as fast as he could. But the Emperor's personal adviser, Prince Alexander Galitsyn, painted a different picture altogether: "He was penetrated by a spirit of humility and self-renouncement," he said on first meeting his Sovereign after near two years' absence; "his usual affability had taken on the character of a sort of detached indifference."[128]

On 12 August (western calendar) Alexander sent his instructions to Nesselrode. It was a noncommittal document, reflecting both his own indecision and the general disarray among his advisers. There was no mention in it of a constitutional "Kingdom of Poland"; it didn't even outline the shape Poland was to take, save the frontier on the Prosna.

Alexander, who hadn't forgotten his father's assassination, was bending to the power of local elites within his own Empire. The displaced German *Standesherren* still at his court might push for liberal reforms but, after Napoleon's expulsion, the conservative and nationalistic "Slavophiles" had increased in number and influence.

The old order in Russia did not want liberal constitutionalists for neighbours; the first thing they sought was a secure military frontier. They, too, could regard Germany as an "intermediary system," a bulwark against further French aggression. The idea that Prussia might annex Saxony was welcome in Russia: this would close the door to France and make Austria and Prussia frontier neighbours, two Powers guarding the gates to the East. All the same, Austria was almost as much a threat to Russian interests as France, so that Russian forces in Poland would have to be built up and the ties with Prussia strengthened.[129]

These were, as things stood in St Petersburg in August, only vague ideas, further complicated by the strange character of Russia's Sovereign.

Nothing, since his departure from Bruchsal in July, had really altered Alexander's vision of the world; it was still coloured by his own peculiar blend of the Apocalypse and the Enlightenment. Alexander remained convinced that the Kingdom of God was at hand and that he, as Russian Emperor, had been chosen to prepare the way. "He related all his actions to the Divine Power," said Galitsyn, "and attributed his victory to God alone."

Alexander also remained essentially alone. His sister Catherine – the one rational if not wholly beneficial influence in his life – had stayed behind in Germany, pursuing the married man she had first met at Portsmouth, the Crown Prince William of Württemberg. Alexander's "spiritual wife," Mademoiselle Roxandre Stourdza, remained in the service of Empress Elizabeth; late in August, they moved to King Maximilian Joseph's Court in Bavaria. If Alexander enjoyed any female company at all it was with Princess Maria Naryshkin, a former mistress, who had already borne him three children. News of a renewed liaison reached Vienna and raised high the expectations among the Poles present, for Naryshkin was a Pole, related to Czartoryski's family.[130]

On 1 September, Alexander set out on his long journey to Vienna, without Princess Naryshkin and without anything that could really be construed as a policy. He was depressed. But as he travelled his old enthusiasms, which had abandoned him since his disappointing visit to London, gradually returned; he saw once more the cheering crowds and the armies that had liberated them; he followed the same narrow roads he had taken when pursuing the Antichrist into Central Europe; the same towns, the same inns, the same fields. At Vilna, Lithuanians lined the streets to welcome their conquering hero.

Even the Poles exulted; they thought this was the sovereign saviour who would create for them a new nation. Alexander undoubtedly believed it, too: what mistake could he possibly make with God and the People as his guides? He entered Pulaway, Prince Adam Czartoryski's home near Lublin. A secret committee, a Polish patriotic gathering, was there to receive him. He promised to add twelve million Poles to the existing Duchy by transferring Russia's former annexations to a new Polish kingdom, and he offered to be their King. "Put together a good constitution," he told the committee members, "organise a strong army, then we shall see." That was Alexander's whole policy: a People's Europe backed up by God's army and secure military frontiers for Holy Russia.[131]

Alexander turned south for Vienna.

There would be no avoiding official receptions this time. Kaiser Franz was not the Prince Regent, and Austrian organisation at the frontiers and at each relay station along the road to Vienna ruled out any attempt to vanish in green carriages. What were His Imperial Highness's desires? His orders? Which route would he care to follow? The bespectacled municipal authorities seemed to be everywhere and, as the official reports put it, their questions were always "most graciously received and answered in the same manner."[132]

In Vienna, Metternich, officially charged with court ceremonies as well as foreign policy, was getting extremely nervous. On Saturday morning, 24 September, the cannon along the Jägerzeile and up the Bohemian post road thundered out the announcement that King Frederick William of Prussia had just arrived in nearby Wolkersdorf. "Don't fret," said Kaiser Franz in his reassuring Wiener Dialekt, "the King of Prussia might keep the guns of Wolkersdorf firing until four this afternoon; those of the Russian Emperor's have not even started."[133] But they did the next day at dawn.

By eleven, cannon were booming all around Vienna. Accompanied by the Archdukes, the generals of his army, the Imperial German and Hungarian Guard, the German Knights, and the court officers, Kaiser Franz rode out of his palace to meet his Illustrious Visitors on the far side of the Taborbrücke, in a green meadowed park by the widest branch of the Danube. The Russian Emperor saluted and got down from his horse. The Austrian Emperor got down. Then Alexander advanced and embraced *"Vater Franz"* in a manner that some witnesses described as most embarrassing. As for the King of Prussia, he simply held out his naked hand to the Austrian. All three Monarchs then mounted the three fine white horses offered by their host. Kaiser Franz rode in the middle with Alexander on his left and Frederick William on his right. "So had we entered Frankfurt and Paris, and so must we enter Vienna," the Emperor of Austria was said to have proclaimed on the Taborbrücke.[134]

Three Sovereigns rode into Vienna, representing Four. The King of Great Britain and Ireland, Defender of the Faith, and so forth was still shut up, mad, in Windsor; the Prince Regent had retired, furious, to his baubles and pavilion in Brighton.

Down along the Jägerzeile trod one of the greatest processions ever witnessed; eight squadrons of Schwarzenberg's Uhlans, six squadrons of Somoriva's Dragoons, followed by Grand Duke Constantin's Dragoons and the Archduke Albert's Dragoons; then marched two infantry regiments with their bands, and ten batallions of Grenadiers; then came the Monarchs; then the Cossacks of Moscow and the Caucasians in their chain mail and high helmets. They crossed the Schlagbrücke, entered the City through the Rotenturmtor, and climbed the streets to the Hofburg. Perth was standing somewhere near the imperial palace. "It was the most beautiful weather and you could say, because it was Sunday, that the whole population of Vienna and her surroundings had streamed in here." Young Countess von Bernstorff, the Danish Ambassador's wife, was seated comfortably on a balcony her friend, Prince von Holstein-Beck, had rented for the occasion. She raised her spy-glass to study the Monarchs. "It seemed

Kaiser Franz (*centre*) greets Tsar Alexander (*right*) and King Frederick William (*left*) at the Tarborbrücke before the three Sovereigns enter Vienna in triumph

to me that [Alexander's] far too friendly mien and his somewhat artificial greetings did not please." She was almost as disparaging of King Frederick William; he "seemed to me too earnest." But she approved of the man in the middle; "my dear Kaiser Franz, with his perfectly natural, smiling disposition and his well intentioned friendliness, pleased me best of all." Talleyrand was also watching. "The Emperor of Russia and the King of Prussia have just arrived," he wrote later that day in his first dispatch to his King. "Their entry was really beautiful."[135]

At one o'clock in the afternoon the three Sovereigns, with their suites, disappeared into the Hofburg for *Frühstück* (or "breakfast" – Perth, outside in the crowd, spoke of it as a "family banquet"). Evidently Alexander, as usual, ate very little, because within the hour he had summoned Metternich to a private audience. By 3.30, Metternich was already back in the Chancellery writing another of his notes to Sagan (he had been hoping to spend a quiet Sunday with her). "I have just got back from the Court," he panted. "Instead of being with *mon amie*, I made my first skirmish with Emp. A." Alexander was reconnoitring the land and testing his opposition, at least according to Metternich, intoxicated by his own magnificence.

"*He knows nothing* of what *I want* and *I am* clear on all that *he wants himself*," he boasted in his normal princely and emphatic way. What a "good captain" he made. "I set up my outposts, my main guard is in place, and I can sleep tranquilly – the army corps will not be surprised." But like many a good captain he was utterly wrong; Alexander delivered the first wave of his offensive unexpectedly the next day.[136]

While Metternich scribbled away to Sagan, the cannon boomed out again, festive horns, trumpets, drums, and cymbals erupted and the crowds beyond his window sent up another roar: the Grand Duchess Catherine, the Tsar's beloved sister, had just entered Vienna through the Burgthor.

The Grand Duchess very quickly won the hearts of the Viennese. She was regarded by everyone, except Metternich (who had fallen under the influence of the Prince Regent whilst in London), as beautiful, graceful and, despite her mother's veto, still a candidate for marriage to the Kaiser's brother, Archduke Charles. Even Sagan, who was hardly Lady Bountiful when it came to other women, took Metternich to task for his harsh judgment of Catherine; "I find her really pretty," she said, "but really pretty."[137]

If the Grand Duchess would marry the Archduke, Austria could hope to have some moderating influence on Russia. If, on the other hand, she married the Crown Prince of Württemberg, Russia would have made another advance into Germany. September's sun kept alive the hope of a Viennese marriage.[138]

Princess Bagration gave a reception at the Palm Palace later that Sunday afternoon. Only ladies – "distinguished in beauty or youth," said the Countess Bernstorff – were invited into the marquee that lined the great ballroom; they were sitting on benches along the sides when the Tsar stepped in and made a deep and reverential bow to the Princess. Female sanctuaries of this kind were often organised as the opening ceremony for a ball or a banquet when an honoured Sovereign was present. With the presentations done the gentlemen entered, the orchestra struck up a polonaise, and a long train was formed that began to wind its way into the dining hall. Alexander led, offering his arm to Princess Bagration. Countess Bernstorff joined the dance behind her, after accepting an invitation, which everyone must have noticed, from the second man in the train: William, the Crown Prince of Württemberg. Russia had made a step into Germany.[139]

In the evening there was a première performance of the ballet *Zephir und Flora* at the Kärntnerthortheater. Rotating cylinders gave the effect of waves, a mechanical peacock opened its tail, ballerinas flew in through the cardboard clouds; the dancers were the best from London and Paris. When the Sovereigns entered their loges, "there began an indescribable jubilation." Alexander was accompanied by his sister. "A great, festive, and forever memorable day for Vienna," recorded Perth late at night in his diary.[140]

The first offensive

Baron Hager's dossiers were gradually filling up with reports of troop movements in Poland and along the frontiers of Saxony. Prussians were said to be manœuvring in the Electorate of Hesse-Cassel, thus threatening not only Saxony but also the Rhineland to the west. Assessments of Russian intentions were contradictory. The fact that Alexander's brother had been ordered to Vienna rather than take charge of his army in Warsaw was interpreted as a sign that Russia was ready to relax her pressure on Poland. But there was also evidence of a build up in the forces of occupation. "The Russians and Prussians," read an alarming report received by Hager on 29 September, "have in Silesia and Warsaw 230,000 men prepared to march on Vienna, where they will be in seventeen days if the Congress does not give them satisfaction."[141]

On Tuesday, 27 September, Empress Elizabeth arrived in Vienna from Munich. There was the usual din of cannon, after which the crowds pressed into the Mariahilfestrasse and up the neighbouring alleys just for a glimpse of the marching Grenadiers, the Dragoons, the Uhlans. One witness recorded a brief sighting of the six-drawn open landau carrying the Austrian Emperor and the Russian imperial couple; "they wriggled so much we could hardly see them."[142]

But it was not the crowds that made the Emperor of Russia wriggle, or the troops, or the bands, or the presence of his Empress. What excited Alexander that Tuesday was the reappearance of the Empress's lady-in-waiting, Mademoiselle Roxandre de Stourdza. A small chamber on the fourth floor of the Hofburg had been set aside for her. "How I was moved when, in the middle of the most brilliant festivals, I would see him approach me," she later recalled. "He would also sometimes dedicate several hours to me in the evening, and we would talk in my little apartment just like at Bruchsal. In these moments he would forget his importance and would open up his soul, so hungry for trust and freedom."[143]

Yet neither the soft drone of La Stourdza's voice, nor meditations on the word of Christ, nor long conversations into the night on the laws of the universe and of Europe were going to protect Alexander from the fury his actions on the diplomatic front were causing.

On Monday he had told Castlereagh what he had previously promised the secret Polish committee in Pulaway – that he was going to create a new constitutional Poland, which would include Russia's earlier annexations. Castlereagh, horrified, wrote to Liverpool that this would add ten million Poles loyal to Russia and leave Austria and Prussia with five million disaffected ones and no military frontier to defend themselves.

On Wednesday, Alexander repeated the same message in a three-hour audience with Metternich. It was the worst of all possible scenarios. Even faithful Prussia started complaining about "the arrogance of Alexander's entourage" and a strategy session was organised by Humboldt and the Prussian General Knesebeck to discuss the military ways of holding Russia back. It was surely no coincidence that Russia, that same night, offered to transfer the administration of Saxony from Russia to Prussia.[144]

Metternich was no longer boasting of tranquil nights. Castlereagh was wondering what was happening to his German centre.

Talleyrand inserts a wedge

Talleyrand, clad in wig, white frockcoat, rings, seals, and brooches, limped past the scrutinising gaze of the porter at the door and the footmen moving tables in the antechamber of Metternich's summer palace on the Rennweg. He was accompanied by the Spanish Minister, Don Pedro Gomez Labrador, who followed like a poodle as they entered the conference chamber. The Ministers of the Four Allied Powers were there ready and waiting. It was Friday, 30 September.

The Congress, according to the public announcement in August, was supposed to be formally opened the next day. Vienna was teeming with Emperors, Kings, Princes, and Sovereigns, balls were being held in every palace, there had been a great fireworks display on Thursday out on the Prater, the theatres were filled and stinking, as were all the inns, but nobody had yet heard a word about the Congress. "Nothing has yet been determined on how to go about the business of the Congress," complained Talleyrand in his first dispatch to Louis XVIII. "Even the English, whom I thought more methodical than the others, have done no preparatory work on this matter."[145]

Talleyrand had occupied his week with more than just the fleas in his palace (all the mattresses had to be replaced). Dorothée had already established contact with her two sisters in Vienna, Wilhelmine and Jeanne, and was seen practically every evening in the company of her uncle at the Palm Palace. "I am very happy with her," the kind uncle wrote to his mistress in Paris.[146]

Hager's police were wondering how on earth the Prince de Talleyrand (he had tactfully dropped his Napoleonic title "Bénévent" a few weeks before leaving Paris) managed to be so well informed about the affairs of state in Vienna. Some gossip attributed it to Prince Louis de Rohan, Wilhelmine's former husband, who prowled the corridors and salons of high society. Others thought it was Count Sickingen, trusted friend and Chamberlain of Kaiser Franz. There were even those who thought that Gentz had entered into some sort of pact with the French Minister: Talleyrand was known to have a liberal purse; Gentz, like many in the Kaiser's service, was recognised as a man with expensive tastes. The most surveyed member of the Talleyrand's own household was the musician, Sigismond Neukomm; he remained Hager's principal suspect for months. Incredibly, nobody posed any questions about Dorothée.[147]

The *soirées* at the Palm Palace and his official visits during the day to the various members of the Austrian imperial family had given Talleyrand ample opportunity to meet and talk with the Ministers of the Four Allied Powers. Talleyrand was fully aware of the developments over Poland since Alexander's arrival; Castlereagh, looking for allies, had gone straight round to the Kaunitz Palace to report immediately after his interview with the Tsar on Monday. As a result, where the Congress was concerned, Talleyrand would be pushing the English "idea of Parliament" for the next few weeks.[148]

In addition to the Allied Ministers, Talleyrand had also had the occasion to talk with many of the plenipotentiaries of the Secondary Powers, and most particularly his old friend Count von Schulenberg of Saxony, who was beginning to wonder whether he had a kingdom to represent at all. "The King will make no act of transfer, of abdication, or of exchange which could destroy the existance of Saxony and injure the rights of his House," Schulenburg had bravely stated to Talleyrand on his first day in Vienna. But Frederick Augustus was not a free Sovereign; he was still locked up in Berlin. Talleyrand passed on to Schulenberg the message he had picked up in Munich, that King Maximilian Joseph of Bavaria was prepared to use his troops to defend his northern neighbour.[149]

Support of the Secondary Powers, a little friendship shown to the unhappy Sovereigns of southern Germany, the crucial British connection, and "a few divergences of opinion" among the Four would help Talleyrand drive in his wedge and gain France a place within the councils of power.[150]

As for the Four Allied Powers sitting at the conference table on that last day of September, they were perfectly aware that the only legal basis to their claim to represent Europe lay in the Treaty of Chaumont, signed in the last month of the war, while their avowed right to decide on territorial matters relied on a *secret* provision in the Treaty of Paris. The Committee of Six and the German Committee – the only institutions of the Congress the Allies had so far agreed on – had no legal basis whatsoever; the Treaty of Paris had been signed by eight Powers (the Four, plus France, Spain, Portugal, and Sweden), not six; and "Germany" had no legal existence at all.

Not even Castlereagh, however, was going to deny the need for some sort of steering committee; it was Castlereagh himself who had pleaded for a "limited body" to be constituted from "among those who have borne the principal share in the councils and conduct of the war" and those who framed the several treaties which ended it – in other words, a committee made up of those states possessing the power both to prosecute and to stop European war.

The problem that Castlereagh faced was that every time the Four had met to discuss procedure, he had found himself in a minority of one. Alarm at Russia's actions in Poland would, on the other hand, always improve his position, for it gave him the opportunity to play the role of mediator that he had sought at the outset. First, he thought he could reason with Alexander; second, he thought he could pull together a German coalition within the established anti-French alliance if needs be; but, third, he was certainly comforted by the contact he had established in Paris that August. His mistake was to imagine that Bourbon France was simply a passive, inanimate card in his own hand. It was the great weakness in the mechanical way in which he regarded Europe.[151]

So it was that Talleyrand and Labrador entered the Austrian Minister's suburban summer palace to find six men at a long table in a room so large that their voices echoed. Castlereagh was at one end, apparently presiding. Friedrich Gentz was at the other, with his large sheets of paper and a feather quill; he had been named Secretary of the Congress the week before. On either side sat Metternich (*"le blafard"* or "pale one," as Talleyrand called him), Nesselrode, and Prince Hardenberg with hearing horn and Humboldt. Talleyrand took the empty embroidered chair between Castlereagh and Metternich; Labrador sat down opposite.[152]

This was the Committee of Six Powers that Metternich had demanded two weeks earlier. But Metternich had also demanded that the Four Allies reach agreement before presenting their general plan to France and Spain. They had neither agreed nor planned. Castlereagh initiated the proceedings by reading a letter of protest from the Portuguese envoy, Don Pedro Count Palmella – thereby virtually dissolving the Committee of Six on the spot. Talleyrand and Labrador, of course, immediately expressed solidarity with their excluded Portuguese colleague (the Swedish envoy was still in Sweden). Metternich remained pale.

But he presented the next item on the agenda, the Allies' protocol.

"Allies?" asked Talleyrand. "Allies against whom? Not against Napoleon; he's in Elba. Not against France; peace has been made. Surely not against the King of France; he guarantees the durability of this peace. *Messieurs, parlons franchement.* If there are still Allied Powers, then I don't belong here."[153]

Gentz appeared to be very moved. Metternich remained pale. It was Gentz's turn to present a report he had been working on for over a week, which followed again Metternich's principle that the Four decide, the Six consult, and that the Congress would finally approve.

Talleyrand, in his dispatch to Louis XVIII, said that "a general conversation ensued." Gentz, in his diary, recorded that Talleyrand and Labrador "berated us for two hours; it was a scene I shall never forget."[154]

"When is the general Congress going to open?" demanded Talleyrand, playing the parliamentary role Castlereagh had begun. He tossed the Treaty of Paris back into the Allied court by quoting it: "*All the Powers* which were engaged on one side or the other in the present war will send Plenipotentiaries to Vienna to settle, in *a general Congress*, the arrangement which shall complete the terms of the Treaty of Paris." "When are the conferences going to begin?" he continued. He refused to accept a dictatorship of the "privileged Powers." It was a matter of principle, sacred principle. "The presence of a Minister of Louis XVIII engages us to the principle on which rests the whole social order. The first need of Europe is to banish forever the idea that one can acquire rights simply by conquest, it is to revive the sacred principle of legitimacy from which follows order and stability." Castlereagh knew that. And so did Metternich.[155]

Both Metternich's protocol and Gentz's report were abandoned and the meeting adjourned.

Metternich and Gentz went for a walk in the garden. The Minister's summer villa, opposite the Belvedere Palace, lay in a part of the suburbs that was virtually open country in those days; its vast gardens, stretching eastward towards one of the minor branches of the Danube, ended in fields and meadows. Great works, however, were under way for the celebrations of the first anniversary of Leipzig. Strolling with his master between the Temple of the Arts and the Temple of Peace, with the large open-air amphitheatre before them, Gentz got into a fume about the way "these two characters had savagely messed up and torn up our plans." Like in London, the Temple of Peace was being designed to double with a Temple of Discord. Metternich looked around; he was pensive. Gentz recorded, "The Prince did not feel like me the embarrassment and the awfulness of our position!" The Prince was marking time and showed no sign of distress.[156]

Talleyrand in the meantime had boarded his carriage and had headed back into town for the Hofburg, where he had an appointment with His Imperial Majesty Alexander. Talleyrand had not seen him since their breach in June. Alexander might have clasped Talleyrand's hand on receiving him, but the affection shown was strained, artificial. His words were brief, his air solemn.[157]

"In the first place," Alexander asked, getting straight down to business, "what is the situation like in your country?"

"As good as Your Majesty could possibly desire and better than anyone would have dared hope," answered Talleyrand, expressionless.

"The public spirit?"

"It improves every day."

"The liberal ideas?"

"There is no place more liberal than France."

"And the freedom of the press?"

"It has been re-established, with the exception of a few restrictions that circumstances dictate; and these will be lifted in two years."

"And the army?"

These were the issues that had caused the initial breach – Alexander's disappointment in the terms of the French Royal Charter. It didn't worry him that Russia had no Charter, no liberal laws, no free press, and that her armies were occupying the eastern third of Europe. He was convinced that the cause of Russia's recent woes was misguided western despotism and he was personally going to stamp it out; he had the means, he had his armies.

"Let's speak of our affairs. We must conclude them here," the Tsar continued.

"That depends on Your Majesty. They will finish promptly and happily if Your Majesty brings to them the same nobility and the same grandeur of spirit as he has to those of France."

"But each one has his interests."[158]

"And each his rights."

"I keep what I occupy."

"Your Majesty will not wish to keep what is not legitimately his."

"I am acting in agreement with the Great Powers."

"I do not know whether Your Majesty counts France within the rank of these Powers."

"Oh certainly. But if you do not want each to satisfy his interests, then what are you driving at?"

"I put the law first and the interests second."

"The interests of Europe *are* the law."

"This language, Your Highness, is not yours. It is foreign to you and your heart disavows it."

"Oh no!" said Alexander, with the conviction of a Russian welling up from his inner soul; "I repeat it: the interests of Europe are the law."

Talleyrand turned to the white and gilded panelling that lined the apartment's walls; he leaned his head against it and tapped his knuckles on the wood. "Europe, Europe, unhappy Europe," he repeated and then, turning back to Alexander, he asked, "Is it going to be said that you have lost Europe?"

"Better war than renounce what I occupy," answered Alexander coldly. Talleyrand was absolutely sure he meant it; or at least he adopted the grim posture appropriate for such a dramatic occasion. "Yes, rather war," repeated Alexander after a moment's silence. The tinny sound of the Hofburg's clock rang out. "Ah! It's time for the show," his blue eyes lit up; "I must go, I promised the Emperor I'd be there."

Talleyrand limped out, leaving the door ajar. Alexander rushed after him and flung both arms around the wobbling French envoy in an extravagant embrace. "Adieu, adieu, we shall surely meet again," he exclaimed, almost as if parting from a mistress of yore; the ancient *accoutumance* of love for the Sovereign seemed to have reversed itself.

Not once had the words "Poland" and "Saxony" cropped up in the conversation, but the Emperor had made an allusion to an accord among the "Allies." Talleyrand took note. In the evening he attended with his niece a reception given by the Duchess von Sagan. "A huge crowd," reported Gentz; Dalberg was there, Humboldt was there, and the Crown Prince of Württemberg twirled on the ballroom floor to the sounds of a waltz.[159]

Castlereagh finds his centre

Alexander was the one who had originally picked 1 October for the opening of the Congress. Yet the only person who did anything that day was Talleyrand. He composed a formal memorandum (in fact, it was probably La Besnardière who wrote it) and addressed it not, as etiquette demanded, to his host in Vienna, Metternich, but to the man he regarded as his ally, the British Foreign Secretary. Within hours, every diplomat in town was talking about it.

Talleyrand claimed that the Congress not only had the right to sanction but also the right to initiate and so it should be called forthwith. As for the steering committee, legally, argued Talleyrand, it would have to be composed of all eight signatories of the Treaty of Paris and its only role was to propose to the Congress what working committees were to be set up and who was to sit on them. And even on this question of committees the final decision would again rest in the Congress. In other words, Talleyrand was presenting a plan that would make the Congress a sovereign parliamentary assembly for the whole of Europe. It was a radical idea. Too radical.

Castlereagh, good parliamentarian that he was, got as furious as he could ever get. Hadn't he told Talleyrand in August that he had no intention of separating Britain from her Allies? His first concern was to build up his German combination of Austria and Prussia against Russia and he feared this brash kind of initiative from France could upset the whole delicate process. Why couldn't Talleyrand wait? Just a little patience! Talleyrand's whole stength within the Allied deliberations relied on the goodwill of Castlereagh. Why hadn't Talleyrand consulted him in private first? Why a formal memorandum? As for Talleyrand's extraordinary parliamentary views, Castlereagh knew perfectly well that no government in Britain would ever be willing to share sovereignty with a Congress in Vienna.

Early Sunday morning, Castlereagh went round to the Kaunitz Palace to block any further moves from Talleyrand. This memorandum served no purpose, the British Minister explained in his usual awkward and embarrassed manner; it had "rather excited apprehension in both the Austrian and Prussian Ministers than inspired them with any confidence in his views."[160]

Without Castlereagh's support, Talleyrand was once more on his own. Castlereagh, on the other hand, had actually positioned himself well; by taking advantage of the Russian threat and by presenting the possibility of a French counter-threat, he had broken out of his own isolation and made himself the principal mediator in Vienna. It was the job he always wanted; Castlereagh was at last in the centre of things.

As if to demonstrate the ineffectiveness of Talleyrand's demands, a meeting of the Four was immediately called in the Chancellery. Gentz was ordered to prepare another protocol, which tossed the Treaty of Paris once more back into the French court. Fine, they argued, the steering committee should consist of the Treaty's eight signatories; let the Committee of Six became the Committee of Eight. It really made no difference because the secret provisions of the Treaty limited initiative to the Four, and until they had come to some agreement there would be no convocation of the Congress. Talleyrand was left right out in the cold.

Or not exactly the cold. The Four met again the following afternoon to approve of Gentz's document. They all signed. Then they went over to the Palm Palace for another evening with the Duchess von Sagan. Metternich wanted to be absolutely sure Talleyrand attended. "Here is my frank reply," he confirmed in a short note to Sagan outlining the personalities he thought should be present: "Dorothée is to be invited once and for all, and I want to leave her no doubt that Mr Talleyrand is also invited. I'll write to him myself."

That evening at the Palm Palace, it was not Castlereagh who delivered the Allies' answer to Talleyrand's memorandum, it was Metternich, who took great pleasure in placing Gentz's protocol in the Frenchman's hands to the throb of the Viennese band: it was all a matter of etiquette.[161]

A paper dispute, turning and turning; a threat of war, the promise of peace. "These festivals are exhausting me," Talleyrand confessed in a letter to the duchesse de Courlande. Yet the great Viennese festival had hardly begun; Talleyrand was simply frustrated: "We haven't yet started talking seriously of business." Well, the Four had, but France was not included. "Metternich is in love," continued Talleyrand in his letter, "he paints himself up, he writes notes, his Chancellery muddles along. Dorothée is well, though she has difficulty keeping up with the activity of her sister. *Cher ange, je vous embrasse et aime de tout mon âme.*"[162]

Ballroom manners, bedroom discord

Agent Schmidt reported at about this time that the Kaunitz Palace was beginning to look like a "locked up castle." At the door stood an old porter who had worked for three previous French Ambassadors in Vienna; one could bribe him to purloin "a few bits of torn up paper in Talleyrand's hand" – there was half of an old scribbled note to Sagan, a list of invitations to dinner, the odd scrap of a letter draft – but they didn't reveal a great deal. The guests to Talleyrand's table were not much of an aid to the hapless agent either; "they are either foreign diplomats who work for their own interests or local ones who are already won over by another important side."[163]

The one man who was getting information on the French was Castlereagh, and quite surprising information it was. His source was the British Ambassador in Paris, who was communicating with Vienna through special flying dispatch. On 27 September, Wellington wrote to say he had learnt of a letter from La Besnardière, Talleyrand's secretary, stating that Bourbon France was preparing for war.[164] The comte de Blacas, a leading government figure, came close to confirming this in an interview with Wellington the following week.[165]

Talleyrand's whole campaign in Vienna had been designed to assure the Four that French militarism had finished with Napoleon – and Talleyrand undoubtedly meant it. But France's deteriorating domestic situation, coupled with her diplomatic isolation, could lead the most pacific minded Frenchmen to rattle a sabre.[166]

There were several signs of war in Vienna. Some of the public demonstrations must have made one wonder. On Thursday, 6 October, an enormous *Volksfest* was held in the Augarten, next to the Prater. "We considered it prudent to maintain our distance," Countess Bernstorff later recorded. "Many of the most distinguished ladies returned with their dresses in tatters. Countess Colloredo, a pretty strong woman, had both her skirt and one of her sleeves torn away at the waist." Crowds had been swarming into the park and garden alleys since morning. War trophies decorated the imperial stands, in front of which were laid sixteen long tables for a feast Hoftraiteur Jahn had prepared for four hundred disabled Austrian veterans. At around five in the evening, the Illustrious Sovereigns arrived to a mob of waving caps and flags. As they approached the lawn where the veterans were assembled, Gunner Vanderasdorg, one of the wounded heroes of Leipzig, staggered to his feet and proposed the first of several toasts. *"Es lebe unser Kaiser Franz! Der Vater und Beglücker seiner Volk!"* four hundred male voices repeated and fifty round of cannon thundered. *"Es lebe unsere Kaiserin..."*; the cannon thundered again. After the Russian Emperor was toasted, Alexander astonished everybody by raising his own glass and shouting in German, "The Emperor of Russia drinks to the health of you, old men! Let you all live!" – then he smashed his glass against one of the great garden urns. The cannon thundered. The toasts continued, with the crowds joining in; rockets and catherine wheels whined and whizzed. *"Es leben die Anführer..."* boomed out the voices, "Long live the Leaders of our Allied Armies! They led us to Victory!" "Long live the Allied Warriors, our Brothers!"[167]

Nobody there that evening would have quite grasped the subtlety of Tallyrand's arguments, the idea that "Allies" had no place in a peace conference. Nobody was about to disband the Four Allies. For twenty thousand Viennese in the Augarten that night, the Four Allies existed all right; they had fought, they had suffered, they had led their armies to victory, and they would lead the Congress and Europe into Peace, their Peace, their imposed Peace.

Two days later, on 8 October, Metternich organised a series of meetings that ended with a formal agreement to postpone the opening of the Congress to 1 November. He also managed to lay the groundwork for the kind of Congress he wanted. He did this in his typical fashion: private encounters were arranged, step by step, with the main actors involved until he got what he wanted.

First, what was at the heart of his system? The German centre. At ten o'clock in the morning, Metternich went round to Hardenberg's rooms in the Hofburg. Hardenberg was as delighted with this sudden preferential treatment as he was with the news. The Congress delayed for three weeks! Three more weeks available to grab Saxony without the interference of all Europe!

Second, who was going to decide on the shape of this Europe? Metternich had not yielded an inch, and the *Volk* of Vienna apparently agreed with him: it would be the glorious Four. So, at three o'clock that afternoon, Metternich arranged a council of ministers – Castlereagh, Hardenberg, Nesselrode, and himself – at his Chancellery. After an hour and a half's deliberation, Gentz's formal draft for the postponement of the Congress was approved. The four Ministers then adjourned for dinner.

Third, on what basis could the decisions of the Four be considered legal? Here Talleyrand had won a point; it would have to be a Committee of Eight. But that presented no problem for the Four. The Swedish envoy, Gustavus von Löwenhjelm, had just arrived in town; he was the Russians' puppet, and that would assure that Talleyrand would always be easily outvoted. After dinner, the representatives of the Four proceeded to Metternich's summer villa, where the Ministers of Sweden, Portugal, Spain, and France awaited them. The first meeting of the Committee of Eight – formal steering committee of Vienna's Congress – then began.

Gentz described the meeting as "extremely lively and infinitely curious." Just before entering the conference chamber Talleyrand warned Metternich that he had let the Russians surround Austria "like a belt." Was he also going to let go of Saxony? Metternich simply shrugged his lovely shoulders.

The meeting dragged on until eleven at night. Metternich got his votes, Talleyrand kept his principles. Metternich read Gentz's project for the postponement and immediately called for the vote. Most of the debate centred on an amendment Talleyrand wanted to add: the Congress would be adjourned only "in accordance with the principles of public law."

"Public law!" interjected the deaf old Prussian Chancellor; he scrambled to his feet, banged on the table, and – as Talleyrand put it the next day – shouted "like many who are inflicted with his infirmity." "Public law!" screamed Hardenberg once more, "it serves no purpose! Why say we are acting according to public law? All that goes without saying." And Hardenberg would have preferred it not to be said – at least for the three crucial weeks between now and the opening of the Congress.

"What is public law doing here?" asked Humboldt calmly from his seat.

But Metternich thought it had a purpose. And so did Castlereagh. So the amendment was adopted. It was a face-saving device for Talleyrand. It was a small victory for a slowly forming Europe. "This evening, gentlemen, belongs to the history of the Congress," declared Gentz as the Ministers got up from their chairs.[168]

It was an exceptionally warm October. The *Residenzstadt* started to take on the air of a great European capital; life hummed around her embassies and foreign missions.

The eighty-odd Englishmen in town developed a rather poor reputation for drunkenness and philandering. Hager's dossiers were filling up with ignominious tales, like that of the feast out in Baden, where the English were so tipsy that "they could not get into their carriages." Among the worst behaved at the Minoritenplatz was His Excellency the Ambassador, Charles Lord Stewart, Castlereagh's half-brother. He had made his name as a fighter on the battle fields of Germany – and maintained it on the streets of Vienna.[169]

Castlereagh himself showed a certain dignity. He was often seen in the Herrengasse taking his daily stroll as if he were in Pall Mall; he was always in black English costume, he was always in the company of his lady. "Lord and Lady Castlereagh step out into the bright sunlight dressed as if they were going to a masked ball, never noticing how they are being noticed," chuckled Varnhagen von Ense of the Prussian Legation. Carl von Nostitz, a Prussian in the service of the Russians, found Lady Castlereagh the most extraordinary sight to behold; she "is colossal and plump, and her get-up, through its ridiculous variety of tasteless ostentation, is a cause of never ending surprise." But her Tuesday suppers, at the Minoritenplatz, did not make everyone smile. "They are extremely irksome," complained ✳✳, a frequent guest; "you can't get in there until after ten o'clock at night." Once supper was consumed, dancing would begin, not with the customary polonaise, but with an Irish gig performed by Lord Castlereagh himself. Most foreigners considered it decidedly offtaste. Not, however, Countess Bernstorff, who became attached to this exotic stranger. "I liked to dance with the cheerful statesman," she recorded, "because it was such a pleasure to discover in him the oppposite of that dullness and weariness of life, which is so often the stamp of fashionable people." He was, she added, more urbane than his brother; he was also frank, generous, and he possessed what her own countrymen called *Biederkeit*, a good-natured honesty. Was he ever false? Under pressure he was at times too pliable, and this "might often give his politics an air of falsity."[170]

In fact, once he had manœuvred into the centre of European politics Castlereagh found it virtually impossible not to give off "airs of falsity." It was quite obvious now that his coaches would not be returning home in time for parliament's autumn session. Liverpool and his Cabinet, by waving a few magic wands, did manage to reduce the session to a three-week sitting. If the slave trade was still the burning issue in Britain, the Radicals had started to show an interest in the rights of Poles and Saxons. Nobody in Britain was aware of the menace Russia presented. Consequently Castlereagh, who was by now thoroughly absorbed in the Russian problem, found himself pursuing a policy that was at odds with British public opinion, parliament, and indeed his own government.

In September he had thought, like the Austrians, that Alexander was wavering over Poland. But his interview with the Russian Emperor on 26 September, as well as another on 13 October, proved that the Russian position was implacable. From then on it was clear that only some show of force would break the deadlock. Castlereagh began assembling his forces.

French behaviour had limited his choice. Talleyrand's memorandum of 1 October, by exacerbating his Allies, had forced Castlereagh to distance himself from the French; the news of their sabre rattling didn't make him feel any closer. Throughout October, Talleyrand would continue to warn Castlereagh that he was making a grave error in yielding to Prussian demands in Saxony and the Rhineland. Castlereagh would admit there was some danger. "I was, from the outset, aware of the extreme difficulty of making Prussia a useful ally," he said in a letter to Wellington. But then, "it ought not be despaired;" introducing Prussia into his formula of balance was a better prospect for Britain than having a French army on the wrong side of the Rhine, even if it did march under the fleur-de-lys. Castlereagh dismissed Talleyrand's warnings as signs of French "jealousy" and "particularism." "France need never dread a German league," he told Wellington, setting a policy line for one school in the British Foreign Office for over a century: "it is in its nature inoffensive, and there is no reason to fear that the union between Austria and Prussia will be such as to endanger the liberties of other States."[171]

Not far from the Minoritenplatz, on the Graben, in the apartments of the widowed Princess Elisabeth von Fürstenberg, there gathered a group of counts, dukes, and princes who had no states: the dispossessed *Standesherren*. Their exclusion from power went on unabated. They had no seat on the Committtee of Eight, the German Committee, or any of the other committees being devised in Metternich's Chancellery. Word had got round by now of Hardenberg's plan for Germany – the creation of seven Circles or *Kreise*, a federal court, and a Directory run jointly by Prussia and Austria – and they did not like it one bit. They wanted their "third

Germany" returned to the Reich, with their rights protected by Austria, and not torn up by greedy Prussia.

The clause relative to Germany in the Treaty of Paris –*"Les Etats de l'Allemagne seront indépendants et unis par un lien fédératif"* – was both their hope and despair. Despair because it opened the way to Prussian hegemony; hope because the phrasing contained the important idea that a "federal tie" was designed to protect rather than destroy the independence of states. Moreover, the clause broadened the perspective of that independence: the French word *état* could be translated into German either as *Staat* (the modern "state") or *Stand* (the old "estate").

Such subtleties lay quite outside Castlereagh's mechanical vision of Europe.[172] They did not escape Metternich, who, with his keen historical sense, realised that, if negotiations stalled on territorial questions, he could always retreat into the constitutional issues of "Germany." The existence of the *Standesherren* – a social group he knew only too well – gave Metternich a freedom of movement that Castlereagh lacked because he did not understand them, and Hardenberg lacked because he had alienated them.

Virtually next door to von Fürstenberg's apartments lay a palace on the Bräunerstrasse. Baron vom Stein, the most ardent proponent of a restored German Reich, lived on the third floor while the floor below was taken up by Baron Hans Christoph von Gagern, acting as plenipotentiary for both Duke Frederick William of Nassau and Prince William of Orange-Nassau; these two positions had made Gagern spokesman of the dissatisfied smaller states of Germany. The United Netherlands paid for the grand wines that flowed at his table, around which were regularly gathered the unhappy plenipotentiaries. There was much talk of "sovereignty" and "federation" in the residences of the Bräunerstrasse. Like the members of Princess von Furstenberg's *salon*, the guests here would prefer an Austrian imperium with equal rights for all states to the narrow, centralised plans of Prussia. Stein himself, a centraliser, was an isolated exception.[173]

The presence of all these dissatisfied German nobles was Metternich's trump card. Castlereagh, considering the internal affairs of Germany none of his business, remained indifferent. For Hardenberg, their presence represented a serious challenge and another reason for pressing his claims before the opening of the Congress. For Alexander, it promised rich opportunities to stir up Prussians against Austrians, Germans against Germans.

For Talleyrand, it was viewed as an ominous sign of instability in Europe. "Revolutionary ferment is spread all over Germany," he reported to Louis XVIII. "Jacobinism reigns there, not like in France twenty-five years ago, in the middle and lower classes, but among the wealthiest and highest placed nobles." So displaced aristocrats were the revolutionaries in Germany: "The union of the German Fatherland is their cry, their dogma, their religion, exalted to the point of fanaticism." Talleyrand feared that this German aristocratic Jacobinism might one day threaten the whole European order.[174]

During that same month of October, another ostracised group turned up in Vienna in large numbers: the Poles. They arrived like Arcadian youth, innocent, wide-eyed, expecting "the total regeneration of their Fatherland" and utterly convinced that Alexander's promises were genuine.

But their spirit soon changed. Their heroes, Prince Eugène de Beauharnais and Prince Adam Czartoryski, refused them audience. Beauharnais never saw them; Czartoryski accorded them one brief rendezvous at the great fancy dress ball held in the Spanish Riding School on 9 October. There he told them – one tries to imagine what they were all wearing – that Emperor Alexander, "unable to resist the firm and combined intentions of the Courts of Vienna and Berlin, had decided to acquiesce to the partition of Poland." Moreover, the Russian sector would continue to be called the "Duchy of Warsaw" and "there would no longer be any question of a 'Kingdom of Poland.'" The Prince, in his feathered cap, promptly disappeared into the crowd of four thousand.

"Treason!" cried one Bavorovski at Count Skarbek's dinner in Nussdorf the next afternoon; "the Emperor has lavished pretty words on the Poles to lull them and paralyse them, and make the enslavement of the country easier." Another Pole added that he was glad his properties were not in the Russian sector.[175]

The Grand Duke Constantine, commander of Russia's army in Warsaw, was getting worried for different reasons. A revolutionary spirit was developing, he warned. "The Poles," he said, "especially the soldiers who have spent a lot of time in France, have returned with so many philanthropic principles that they often say to me, 'You'll see, it will be us Poles who will create the order of things in Northern Germany in a few years from now.'"[176]

At the Hofburg itself, Kaiser Franz and his Court Festivals Committee worked a ceaseless round of parades, banquets, concerts, theatrical events, fancy dress balls, masked balls, and chamber balls. It had become an essential part of the Congress since all the main political business was being done by a few gentlemen behind closed doors; most of the visitors to Vienna found they had nothing to do.

Not many Sovereigns actually danced at Vienna. On one rare occasion, at a chamber ball, Kaiser Franz made a few turns with the Empress of Russia; "an extraordinary event," noted Perth in his diary, "since this Monarch otherwise never dances." That night even old Duke Albert of Sachsen-Teschen, along with the Archduchess Beatrix, the Austrian Empress's mother, "romped themselves around

A view of the Redountensaal in the Hofburg, where many of the greatest
festivals of the Congress were held

the rows." Prince Leopold of the Two Sicilies had a "bear style dance
that was the terror of the ladies."[177]

Nonetheless, the star of the ballroom floor, in his green uniform
sporting the Russian Order of the Sword, was Emperor Alexander, a
little plumper and a little balder now. "A wild man," said Count
Sapur, one of his attendants. At the grand fancy dress ball in the
Riding School on 9 October it was said that Alexander danced with
over fifty women. Countess Bernstorff was one of them. She remembered that ball as one of the greatest spectacles in Vienna: the high
staircase, the galleries running around the upper part of the hall, the
orchestras, the huge windows converted into mirrors that reflected a
thousand lights. "Dazzled, almost dizzied, I stopped for a few
moments at the top of that staircase to gaze in amazement at the
glittering train beneath, as large numbers from the Viennese Court
united with the members of the foreign Courts and approached the
bottom of the stairs." The Countess described the Tsar's style of
dancing as a *tempête* (the same *tempête* features in Mozart's *Figaro*):
he would strut out in a wide circle before his partner and, on coming
round to face her, make a ceremonial bow that struck Bernstorff as
quite old-fashioned. "I had to respond at least twenty times to his
unusual deep and reverential bows." Alexander's affectations, his
excessive politeness, did not make him popular in Vienna.[178]

It became evident in some circles that Alexander was taking
seriously Talleyrand's grim warning that he was losing his reputation

as the "liberator of Europe." On the very evening following his dramatic interview with the French Minister it was being reported in Hager's offices that the Tsar had become more accommodating. He spent a week listening to the complaints of the *Standesherren*, the small German Sovereigns, and the Poles.

In the second week of October, Nota had a two-hour conversation with Capo d'Istria, the Russian Emperor's influential secretary, who had been complaining about the lack of great statesmen in Vienna. The Ministers were wasting time, said Capo d'Istria; "they make quick fixes one way or another, but they achieve nothing beautiful or solid"; they had let the moment pass when the basis for a general European system could be laid and they had allowed old passions, forgotten pretentions, to come forward once more. "One has forgotten that this last war was not fought by Sovereigns, but by Nations," Capo d'Istria pointedly remarked.

And what a lot of destruction they caused, interjected Nota; at least the Ministers today understood the principle of equilibrium.

Capo d'Istria laughed. "Yes, but how can you establish that when only one Power is master of the seas? Is there any other Maritime Power than England? Can one be formed? No, then good-bye to equilibrium!"[179]

For all the signs of accommodation, Russia's engine still pointed westward.

To the guardians of Europe's equilibrium Alexander seemed to have no consistent policy. One hour he would be talking of peace, the next it would be war. Part of the problem was the Tsar's strange private advisers. As if hunts in the Prater, balls at the Hofburg, dancing the *tempête* fifty times, and long sessions with his Ministers were not enough, Alexander still found time to mount the spiralling stairs to the fourth floor of the imperial palace to imbibe the spiritual milk of La Stourdza. Roxandre de Stourdza – the lady-in-waiting he had first met at Bruchsal – maintained a long correspondence with her spiritual husband in Baden, Jung Stilling; but then they were all spiritual spouses now. "Our dear Alexander always displays to me so much kindness and progresses along the narrow path," she piously told Stilling. "Let us redouble our prayers that Heaven may strengthen him in his noble intentions and accord him the Crown, which he merits."

Stourdza would read aloud to Alexander the letters she was receiving from Baroness Julie von Krüdener, leader of the cult. They were filled with dire prophecies and omens. She warned "how terrible the year 1815 will be!" She wondered, "Do you really think the plans of the Congress will succeed?" The Baroness, now in Strasbourg, damned the tinsel show in Vienna: "What! these audacious festivals will they never strike fear in us? What! will we never shudder at the idea of offending a God so great, so tender?" And she made the most calamitous prediction: "Emperor Napoleon will leave his isle!"[180]

Opposite the Hofburg, in the Chancellery, the Austrian Foreign Minister worried most about how to build up his front against Russia. "We must keep the French out of the game," he told Baron Linden, Württemberg's key representative. The *lien fédératif* of Germany would have to be strengthened. On that, he stood on common ground with Castlereagh. But, understanding the institutional issues involved, Metternich could see further. Castlereagh regarded the questions of Saxony and Poland as inextricably linked; it was why he was willing, against the inclination of Parliament and British public opinion, to cede Saxony to Prussia. Metternich was determined to unlink the the two questions: to separate Saxony's future from Poland's and thereby break Prussia's dependence on Russia. He had, furthermore, the time to do it: the opening of the Congress had been adjourned and Prussia, unlike Russia, was not in possession of its prize. This is what had made him appear so calm when had walked with Gentz in the gardens of his summer villa after the meeting of 30 September. "I barricade myself behind time and make patience my weapon," he told Schulenberg. He went back to his old policy of *Lavieren, Ausweichen und Schmeicheln*. He hedged on Saxony, telling Hardenberg that while he was personally willing to let Prussia occupy the kingdom he would need his Emperor's approval. He evaded any specific federal plan for Germany, knowing full well that there was a host of lesser German princes who would attack Prussia's project for him. Then he flattered the princes, the small sovereigns, the dispossessed nobles, Hardenberg, Münster, Wessenberg, Wrede; he flattered them all.[181]

It was not a policy that made him popular. Stein accused him of "shallow frivolity," Castlereagh said he had no fixed plan, Dalberg thought he was timid and uncertain. Metternich's enemies within the imperial family and the Court joined in the chorus, some of them even claiming that, if Metternich was not replaced, Austria would soon find herself at war with Russia. Old dowager countesses and duchesses carped about his "many stories with women." Agent ✶✶ warned that even the people in the Chancellery were complaining. "I wonder," he remarked, "if our Prince Metternich realises how bad things are among the personnel of the State Chancellery, as observed by the secret services, and how little they are attached to his person?" It would have been astonishing if the harshest taunt had not come from the Prussian Humboldt: the Austrian Minister was, he said, "mad with love, pride, and selfishness, wasting all his mornings by getting up only at ten and then running off to sup with Sagan..."[182]

Those who were closest to Metternich were beginning to wonder if the Ambassador had a point. Sagan was becoming a political problem.

As before, the intensity of diplomatic activity and the intensity of the Prince's private passions showed a positive correlation. Just prior to the important meeting of 30 September he had written to Sagan: "Tomorrow night will be, after the nights you have let me pass, the most terrible of my life! It will be the night of Altenburg!" – Metternich had been in Altenburg when the Battle of Leipzig began – "The fate of the world is going to be decided tomorrow on the caste of a die." Then the Great Man of History made an appeal: "If the friend of my heart will accord me another night it would make up for all the sufferings of my life!"[183]

He had to wait. It was only on 8 October – the day the Eight formally postponed the opening of Congress – that Sagan accorded her favours; it was probably the first night Metternich had spent with her since his return to Vienna in September.

The next day, an important meeting with the Prussians and the representative of neighbouring Hanover took place in the Chancellery. The mood was tense. The Prussians were pushing their claims. Humboldt worked himself into a fury over the right of German states to wage independent wars. Metternich, typically, let the Hanoverian take the brunt of the attack while he composed a letter to his beloved. "*Mon amie*, my colleagues are arguing in a corner of the room," he explained; "I want to let them bang away at each other before I get involved." It was an opportune moment to recite a little romantic poetry!

Metternich described in his letter how he had returned from the Palm Palace in the glow of dawn and taken to his own bed to rest prior to the meeting. He told how he had picked up a book on his bedside table – "my praiseworthy custom" – and read: "*Man geht aus Nacht in Sonne ein . . .* One emerges from Night into Sun,/ One emerges from Gloom into Joy,/ One emerges from Death into Life." Humboldt was still bellowing away about the rights of war. Metternich went on writing: "*Mon amie*, I started crying like a child – but these were, after 25 July [the day that followed that gloomy Viennese evening of "treachery without equal"] and 1 October [the mysterious "night of Altenburg"], tears of happiness; and I owe *you this happiness, the greatest of my life!*"

In return for a night of happiness, he sent her two tickets for the great fancy dress ball in the Spanish Riding School, which was to take place that evening, 9 October.[184]

Over at the Palm Palace, relations between the two residents were getting very tense; Emperor Alexander had discovered a new front in his diplomatic offensive. On the evening of 30 September – the same day as his famous first interview with Talleyrand – he had gone round to the Palm Palace to have a Russian tea with Princess Bagration. Their meeting lasted until well after midnight. "People are talking only about this," reported Nota, who was getting inside information from Mr Fontbrune, a member of the British delegation currently in the Princess's favour. Nota concluded that a Russian party was being set up in Bagration's wing of the palace to counter the Austrian party, supported by Talleyrand and Dorothée, which was forming in Sagan's: "The bets are on," wrote Nota, "the armies lined up, and firing has already begun."[185]

The Princess had been enthusiastically advancing Russia's interests in Germany; she had had love affairs in swift succession with a Prussian diplomat, with the Saxon envoy (Schulenberg), and most recently with Prince Charles of Bavaria. But Alexander's night-time visits to the Palm Palace involved politics of a higher order. Hager's agents had noticed, on many an evening at around nine, how one of those free coaches, which Kaiser Franz had laid on for his guests, would pull up outside the palace. It would depart again after midnight.

Nota managed to get a report on the kind of conversations Bagration and Alexander were having. The Russian Emperor showed immense curiosity in Metternich's love life; he wanted to know all the details of Bagration's previous liaison. The friendship had cooled, the Princess would sigh, for he had become so "totally devoted to La Sagan." "Metternich has never loved you," reassured the Emperor, "neither you nor La Sagan. He's a cold man, believe me; he loves neither one nor the other. He's a cold-blooded creature. Don't you see it in that plaster face of his? He loves no one."[186]

The Duchess von Sagan was reportedly wounded by her rival's success with the Tsar. Had His Gracious Imperial Majesty forgotten her hospitality at Ratiborzitz? Sagan wanted recognition in Viennese society and she knew now that she could hardly rely on Metternich's self-serving exaltations to get it. Two tickets to a ball in return for a night's favour were not enough for Sagan. Was the man going to divorce, or would 1814 be the same comedy as the year before? The Duchess had more than patience as a weapon.

Her balls and suppers in the Palm Palace brought many a handsome young prince, duke, and count to her table; she had a particular attachment to Englishmen, and even Irish lords. More worrying for jealous Metternich was the fact that, since the turbulent "days of repose" in Baden, she had been seeing General Alfred von Windischgrätz again. Just what was that "night of Altenburg"? All Europe was now begging at the Austrian Minister's door; a good time to inflict a little humility on the man. At the very moment Uncle Talleyrand began to insert his wedge and upset the Allied plans, Sagan probably spent a night with Windischgrätz.

Talleyrand was another weapon at her disposal. Among the beggars at Metternich's door were the French, so isolated, so eager to find a chink in the Allies' armour...What a source of strength is family life. Such a pleasure their reunion. What a joy it was for Sagan to be in the company once more of her lovely younger sister; they had been separated for many, many years. And it was Metternich who said it: Uncle Talleyrand could come along too.

Friedrich Gentz records in his diary that on Wednesday evening, 12 October, a supper took place at Sagan's: "At 10.30 at the Duchess von Sagan's, supped with her sister Périgord, Windischgrätz, etc...At midnight at Princess Bagration's, where I found Grand Duke Constantine, Prince Charles of Bavaria, Count Stadion." In other words, it was an evening of family, lovers, and diplomats. Talleyrand had accompanied his niece, Metternich had accompanied his secretary. At one point in the supper, Talleyrand drew Metternich and Gentz aside and pleaded for firmness on Saxony. Austria with her German allies, he assured, had a superior military force to Russians and Prussians combined; moreover, France would be willing to join Austria in a war to liberate Saxony. That would have been no news to the British. Was it for Metternich? The Prince apparently said nothing.

But other things were said that night. "Prince Metternich now seeks to disperse the abuse inflicted on him by the Duchess von Sagan yesterday evening," read Hager's official report to Kaiser Franz the next day. On Friday, with international tensions over Saxony straining to breaking point, Gentz was summoned to the Chancellery, where he had a long conversation with Metternich – "alas! on the unfortunate liaison with Windischgrätz, which seems to interest him much more than the affairs of the world."[187]

Hardenberg moves, Castlereagh responds

The Prince Chancellor Hardenberg had not attended the fancy dress ball of 9 October. Unlike the Austrian Prince Minister, he was at that moment very interested in the affairs of the world, his Prussian world. Prussia had just been given three weeks to lay her hands on Saxony. So while the others danced, Hardenberg composed a formal diplomatic note.

He assumed he had Castlereagh's support. Talleyrand's initiatives had, so far, only further isolated France. The *Standesherren* and the smaller German states he knew were against him. Metternich had only been making half promises, all pledged with the condition that they needed Kaiser Franz's approval. Hardenberg, counting the days, decided to offer a *quid pro quo*: a strong stand against Russian plans in Poland in return for Saxony.

This pleased the Prussians in Vienna, especially the military, who had no love for Russia. It pleased most of Prussia's population;

Russian troops marching home across their lands had become the new scourge; eastern Prussia, in particular, was being treated as conquered territory.[188]

Hardenberg, in his note, demanded the whole of Saxony along with the fortress of Mainz. King Frederick Augustus and his family could be transferred to Italy if they wished, but there was no question of making any territorial concessions here. The concessions he did make were at the expense of others; specifically he proposed to add to the Kingdom of Bavaria slices of territory taken from the smaller neighbouring states of the south. This was meant as an offer to Metternich in return for Kaiser Franz's approval of the Prussian annexations.[189]

It was Castlereagh, so centrally placed and now generally accepted as a mediator, who responded to Hardenberg on Tuesday, 11 October. Castlereagh's only concern was to make Prussia a "useful ally" while keeping French troops at bay. All he saw was the need to construct his concert between the two German Powers against Russian encroachment – it was a builder's job of erecting barriers and cementing alliances. For Castlereagh, Saxony was to be Prussia's reward for standing up to Russia. Balance on one side of the barrier required balance on the other: Castlereagh saw a direct link, like Hardenberg, between Saxony and Poland. So Castlereagh agreed to the Prussian annexation of Saxony.[190]

Metternich said nothing on either territory or annexations. His great public concern, for the moment, was Saxony's place within the developing debate on the constitution of "Germany." This was the week the German Committee, consisting of Austria, Prussia, Hanover, Bavaria, and Württemberg, met for the first time. Throughout the month of October, Metternich would focus attention on Austro-Prussian cooperation in matters of federation, curial votes, precedence, rights of war, the *Präsidium*, the *Direktorium*, the *Kaisertum*, and many other complicated issues besides.

One was of particular interest for Lord Castlereagh and his countrymen: Hanover. That northern German state, where King George III of England ruled, was still an electorate, the only member of the German Committee that was not of royal rank. Hardenberg and Metternich had been urging Count Münster, Hanover's envoy in Vienna, to change its status. Münster agreed but, following a riding accident, was confined to his bed. Hardenberg and Metternich came round to consult with him and a circular was immediately issued from Münster's obscure rooms declaring Hanover a kingdom.

So it was that, on the other side of Europe, the sovereign mad resident of the North Terrace at Windsor added another title to his name, the "King of Hanover." But the German Committee strangely never found time to discuss the question of who would govern Saxony.

A battle remembered

Vienna still bathed in the glow of autumn; there had not been a single day of rain since the arrival of the Allied Sovereigns. Diaries and memoirs describe festivals, theatre, walks in the gardens, quiet visits to museums. None of them give the impression that anyone in Vienna worked; the struggle for existence went on unseen, unheard. Crowds filled the paths of the Glacis and the long alleys of the Prater, the coffee-shops served afternoon drinks, and at night the dance halls were all open; the rich mingled with the poor, the famous with the unknown. One could hardly tell the difference between them because the emphasis in dress, in autumn 1814, was on restraint, simplicity – with the exception of Prince Esterházy, who wore pearls on his boots and jewels on his "Kucsma."

Somebody like Franz Perth, the small functionary, seemed to spend his whole time wandering from one great festival to another, sitting in the Wilde Mann to take his *Jause* (or afternoon coffee), or joining his friends at the Weintraube. Because of the imperial hunts, he had some of the best meals in his life; on 11 October, every agent in the Forestry Commission had received half a boar from the Emperor.

But the grandest feast of them all was on 18 October, the day Vienna remembered Leipzig. It was, perhaps, the first mass commemoration of war in history, though to say it was "modern" would be to underestimate the part tradition played in every act of that sunny day. It was not a national festival because Kaiser Franz's Reich was not a nation. The goal, rather, was to provide an "opportunity to see once more how strong the bond was between the people and the Sovereign;" Leipzig's day was a celebration of Sovereignty.[191]

A whole army lined up on the Jägerzeil in front of the Panorama and Herr de Bach's Circus to hear Vienna's aged Archbishop pronounce a blessing from a high, red damask covered altar. At the signal of a hundred guns, the Princes, Kings, Emperors, the Generals, and their soldiers fell to their knees and prayed in silence. The crowd behind them took off their hats and knelt in the dust. For one long minute all that could be heard was the sound of a thousand-and-one pennants flapping in the breeze.

A roll of drums, the clink of arms, and three orchestras struck up the theme of a Hymn of Peace sung by the tens of thousands present and joined by the ringing of every church bell in Vienna. "This blending of war and religion," wrote comte La Garde-Chambonas, apparently not thinking of peace, "formed a unique kind of picture that perhaps will never be seen again, that no brush could ever reproduce, a sublime and poetic scene beyond all description."[192]

The troops gradually filed down the wide, tree-lined Hauptallee of the Prater to the Lusthaus, a two-storey pleasure dome that stood on another winding branch of the Danube. Three pontoon bridges had been thrown across the river, all of them with hand-railing made up of French muskets seized on the field of battle, now prettily tied together with trusses of willow and interspersed with small Austrian flags. In the middle of the main square of the Lusthaus, a tall pyramid had been erected out of fir branches; a captured French tricolour flew at its summit, while at its foot a man clad in armour stood guard. The Lusthaus itself was decorated from bottom to top in muskets, pistols, small cannon, and other war trophies linked together by laurel wreaths. From the first-floor balconies, the Sovereigns and Princes could look out to the tables laid out, in the form of a star, for an army of eighteen thousand. Finally the troops arrived. The Musketeers downed their muskets, stacking them upright in rows of little pyramids, the cuirassiers downed their cuirasses, the uhlans downed their pikes; and they all sat, under a glittering sun, to the greatest dinner Vienna had ever seen.

Each man received from his sergeant and his sergeant major a bowl of soup with noodles, a pound of pork, three quarters of a pound of roast beef, three fritters, rolls, and a quart of wine. The Emperor of Austria called out the toasts to "my high guests and friends," to "my own brave army," and the "valiant Allied Armies." Alexander drank to "the health of all the People." And twenty-five thousand people cheered.

"I attended this beautiful festival," Perth proudly recorded in his diary, 'I was a participant and witness to the general joy, the abandoned rapture of this place. We will all, in a Germany liberated from the foreign yoke, remember it."[193]

At nightfall, the ballroom at Metternich's summer villa on the Rennweg, which had been under construction all summer, was finally inaugurated. It was larger than the villa itself, though it was built entirely out of wood. Surrounding the whole hall was a lobby under the cover of Turkish tents where the ladies could retire to cool themselves – for despite the warm weather, Metternich had insisted that the ballroom be heated by a system installed under the carpeted staircases that were "as high as a house." The hanging candalabra made night seem like day. For the few firemen on duty, dreams seemed like nightmares.

A manned balloon took off to a fanfare of trumpets the moment the Sovereigns arrived. They were immediately conducted on a formal tour of the illuminated gardens. Into their pathway wafted soft music from the chamber orchestras hidden behind strategically situated bushes. Before their eyes Discord was transformed into Concord in a grand splutter and belch of fire. Supper was followed by a ball, during which Alexander was heard to complain that too many diplomats were present; Count Razumovsky promised to invite to his own next ball a company of Russian Hussars.

Dancing continued right through the night. The scene along the Rennweg in the early hours of the morning resembled the Haymarket in London as the coachmen jostled in a rude queue to pick up their lords and ladies. Among the ladies, waiting under the red Turkish tents as a new day dawned, was young Countess Bernstorff feeling quietly romantic. Like Perth at the Prater, she thought she was witnessing something unique and wonderful; and yet, aware of the tensions present, she said "there reigned real thunder in the air."[194]

Rupture

Though Gentz had gone to bed well after three, he got up before ten the next morning and walked over to the Chancellery for a breakfast with Metternich and his wife. "What a sad day after a festival! The constellation is looking very bleak!" he exclaimed in his diary. After breakfast he had a long conversation with a government official and then went round to the Kaunitz Palace for dinner with Talleyrand. Both Prince and Princess Metternich were there. So was the Duchess von Sagan.[195]

Talleyrand also thought Wednesday a gloomy day. "The festivals are going well, *chère amie*, but business goes badly," he complained in a note written that night to Sagan's mother. All the Allies, he remarked, were under the influence of the "principles of Prussia" and were absolutely determined to destroy Saxony "as if conquest alone was the source of sovereignty."[196]

Castlereagh appeared to be more cheerful; he was on the verge of taking his great initiative. That very day, 19 October, Metternich at last received his Emperor's assent to abandon Saxony to Prussia. It might have been bad news for Gentz and Talleyrand, but it was good news for Castlereagh. At last he could concentrate on his German concert against Russia. He had, however, no time to lose because it had just been announced that the three Allied Sovereigns were going to spend the whole of the next week together, far from their Ministers, in Hungary; Alexander, through his influence on Frederick William, could wreak havoc on his plans.

For Metternich, this was not a very good day. Some have argued that the third week of October marked one of the crowning achievements of his career, and it is true that he had, by now, met some of his goals. He had, for example, separated the German constitutional issue from the general affairs of Europe, thereby giving himself a field of manœuvre that others did not have. He had also loosened the link between the Saxon issue and the Polish issue: Saxony was virtually his to grant or refuse once Hardenberg had written his pleaful note of 9

October. More importantly, with the written promise from Hardenberg to support Austria against Russia, Metternich could claim some responsibility in breaking up the dangerous, expansive Russo-Prussian coalition.

But these were not the first things on Metternich's mind after the festivities of 18 October. Gentz recorded in his diary what did pre-occupy his master: "Affairs of the Duchess von Sagan – Conversations with Metternich on relations with her."[197]

Private passions and public tensions were always, in Metternich's life, closely connected. The dinner at the Kaunitz Palace, that Wednesday afternoon, 19 October, appears to have marked a new critical phase in both.

Metternich, like Castlereagh, was in a hurry to get an Allied commitment on Poland and Saxony before the Sovereigns left for Hungary the following Monday. Talleyrand thought this a fine occasion to win some influence for France. It does seem that he decided to apply his old principle of "putting the women to work," though we unfortunately have no detailed record of what happened at his dinner.

We do know that both Dorothée and Sagan attended. Metternich turned up with his wife, perhaps out of revenge; Sagan had never replied to his imploring notes and she had had the audacity to invite Windischgrätz to her supper of the 12th. That preceding week, Metternich had been seen courting the beautiful Julie Zichy, daughter of the Austrian Ambassador to Berlin.[198]

This was just the kind of complication that Talleyrand revelled in. For two weeks, he had been pouring derision on Metternich's love life. Why? Because the Austrian Minister had been the principal obstacle to France's inclusion in the Allied conferences. So Talleyrand would now attempt to isolate Metternich – and Talleyrand could do this through his women. Dorothée was spending her days with Sagan. Sagan was spending many evenings at the Kaunitz Palace.

What actually happened at Talleyrand's dinner will probably never be known. But it surely is significant that, two days later, Metternich announced the rupture of his relationship with Sagan.

On Friday, 21 October, the weather finally broke. Water streamed down the central gutters of Herrengasse and the Kärntnerstrasse, the open stores on the Graben were packed up in a hurry, and people rushed for cover in the café cellars.

At eleven that morning Gentz had a meeting with the Duchess von Sagan ("for the most remarkable negotiations!" he noted in his diary). In the afternoon an important conference between the representatives from Austria, Prussia, and Hanover took place in the Chancellery; Metternich, for the first time, hinted at his own alternative, decentralised plans for Germany. There were the usual receptions in the evening. Metternich did not get back to his own chambers until the early hours of the morning. At four am. he was writing to Sagan.

It was a rambling, incoherent letter. He complained that their relationship had become solely one-sided, that he had made all the sacrifices and – worse for Metternich – that he had abandoned his own heart. "You have broken all the springs of my soul," he said; "you have compromised my existence just when my life is tied down by questions that will decide the fate of generations." No lover in history had ever made such sacrifices, he claimed. "I only asked for a faint glow of happiness – I thought I had acquired the right to be your friend! But you have refused me everything."

Metternich complained Sagan never answered his letters. For the Prince this demonstrated a weak feminine will. "It tears my soul to pieces." he concluded. "But then what does it matter after everything you have said? I shall pronounce my own sentence: our relationship is ended!"199

Sagan, who received this note the next morning, responded by inviting the Emperor of All the Russias around for breakfast. Alexander was at the Palm Palace by eleven. Sagan, thereby, got the social recognition she sought. For Russia, too, it was a small gain. For Austria it supplied one more reason for strengthening other alliances, and not only with Prussia; perhaps it was time to start considering France.200

Gentz's comments in his diary for that day focused on the obsessions of the moment: "Metternich told me of his definitive rupture with the Duchess; this is, for today, an event of the first order!"

It is amazing that he did not mention Metternich's memorandum delivered to Hardenberg's apartments the same day – a really capital document in the history of the Congress. As the Congess's secretary, Gentz must have been aware of it. The memorandum conveyed the Austrian Emperor's approval of Prussia's annexation of Saxony in return for "absolute uniformity of policy between the two Courts in the Polish question" – a condition that would prove, within days, absolutely crucial.

But, while Gentz did not mention the memorandum, he did jot down that he had had a meeting with the French Foreign Minister.201

Talleyrand was becoming increasingly active in the affairs of Europe. On Sunday, 23 October, as Metternich, Hardenberg, and Castlereagh sat down under the see-saw pediment in the Minoritenplatz to discuss how to deal with Russian intransigence over Poland, Talleyrand was already arguing with the Tsar. It is impossible to imagine that this was not by design of the Allies: they were warning Russia of their French card.

Talleyrand, in his dispatch to Louis XVIII, reported that Alexander was awkward. Without giving as much as a handshake, he began by saying, "I've got two hundred thousand men in the Duchy of Warsaw. Try and chase me out! I've given Saxony to Prussia. Austria has consented to this." He spoke very fast and left nothing open for discussion. If Frederick Augustus refused to abdicate his Saxon throne, Alexander promised that he would be carried off to Russia where he would probably die; King Frederick Augustus, he claimed, was a traitor.[202]

The three Allied Sovereigns were to leave for Hungary the following afternoon. Castlereagh and his colleagues at the Minoritenplatz patched together a "memorial" (or memorandum), which, if not binding, did demonstrate that a common front against Russia existed. If Alexander, it stated, showed no willingness to negotiate on the Polish question on his return to Vienna then the entire case would be laid before the Congress. Metternich was appointed to carry the message to Alexander.

On Monday morning, before presenting Russia with the Allies' ultimatum, Metternich found time for a long conversation with Gentz; he talked, according to Gentz, "principally about the affair with Wilhelmine."[203]

Metternich then crossed the square to the Hofburg. Alexander's mood was icy, his words brief, his attitude unyielding. He told Metternich that the proposals he was making were inconceivable, indecent, and, worse than that, insubordinate. He said the Allied Monarchs were united in their policy, were supported by the people, and that the only source of tension in all Vienna was this pretentious Austrian Foreign Minister in front of him.

Metternich was so shaken by the remarks – and the way in which they were said – that, when the Tsar finally dismissed him, he could not find the door. People observing him cross the square back to the Chancellery said they had never seen the Minister in such a state.[204]

On Tuesday morning it poured with rain.[205]

VIENNA
Winter 1814-1815

Previous page: A generation of war had made settlement between the Powers of Europe no simple game and the outcome, as this cartoon suggests, would not inevitably be peace

Prussia defects

The ebb and flow of power over the northern plains were what had driven war in Europe for quarter of a century. To stop this, an engine of peace had been designed that was aimed at raising a dyke across Poland, or, as Castlereagh had put it, "opposing a barrier to Russia." But nobody had yet defined the course this engine should take if Russia successfully resisted it. After Metternich's disastrous interview of 24 October, some sort of plan was needed.

The shape of the plan was determined by Prussia's actions. Prussia was the most exposed of the Allied Powers because Prussia had nowhere to retreat but the Baltic; so Prussia was forced to take action. If Prussia could resist the flood of Russian power and stand by her two western Allies then one could contemplate pushing the Russian forces back and erecting the barrier somewhere across Poland. But, if Prussia gave way, the barrier would have to be moved west, to Saxony.

Whole populations were involved in constructing that barrier, national identities were forming, early popular enthusiasms had been thwarted, new ones were being created. In Vienna there were pressure groups, minor delegations, arcane petitioners, wily lawyers and potentates who didn't always let the leaders act as they wanted. Alexander's uncompromising stand on Poland was certainly in-fluenced by members of the Russian delegation – particularly the Germans among them, such as vom Stein, who wanted the link main-tained with Prussia. Metternich had been pushed by his Allies; one can't help but think that Castlereagh would have made a better choice as representative of the western Powers.

At any rate, Austria and Britain, even after the interview of the 24th, were still determined to erect their barrier in Poland and they demanded that Hardenberg of Prussia support them – for this was Metternich's main condition for ceding Saxony.

But Metternich, following the interview, first had to assure himself that he still had his job. As soon as he got back to the Chancellery, he wrote to his own Emperor, who was just about to set off for Hungary, and pleaded for his support.[1]

Fortunately for Metternich, Alexander's behaviour at Buda, Hungary's capital, shocked most people who were present. "Emperor Alexander occupied himself only with pretty women," confided a police report; "the men, especially the the older ones, he ignored – so much so that they did not speak very well of His Russian Majesty and much abused him." Alexander, in his turn, abused the Kaiser. The Austrian Emperor, defending Metternich, had quietly suggested that political affairs were the business of Ministers, not of Sovereigns. Alexander angrily protested.

Count Palmella, one of Hager's agents, was creeping around the imperial apartments of Buda when the row occurred. There was a slamming of doors, the King of Prussia then appeared in a corridor, flushed and nonplussed, shortly followed by the Emperor of All the Russias; they both vanished into Alexander's apartments. After a moment's solitary meditation, Kaiser Franz sent for an aide and instructed him to make peace with the two offended Sovereigns, which he ostensibly did.[2]

The immediate upshot of this was that Alexander showed a great deal more tolerance of Metternich when he returned. Metternich wrote a few bold words to his Emperor: "I am fully convinced that Your Majesty's forceful stand in Buda not only completely reinforced my last vehement declaration [!], but I am certain that we are nearing a development in Polish affairs that we could hardly have contemplated." They were, however, only words. It was now up to old Hardenberg to extract concessions from the Tsar and thus prove to Austria his "unity of policy" in the Polish question.

Hardenberg came up with a very timid plan for action; it included a frontier for Russia's Poland along the Rivers Warta and Nida, far west from what most of Metternich's Austrian colleagues were demanding – they wanted their barrier on the Vistula.

But Hardenberg's plan was too much for Alexander. On 5 November, Hardenberg was summoned to appear before his King and the Russian Emperor to explain himself. Since the scene in Buda, Frederick William had become utterly beholden to His Russian Imperial Highness, promising total commitment to the glorious task of re-establishing the Kingdom of Poland. "That is not enough," retorted Alexander, "your Ministers must conform." The problem was that the Prussian Chancellor's plan did not conform.

Hardenberg turned up in the Tsar's apartments with neither Humboldt nor his ear trumpet; he hardly needed them. Alexander went into another of his imperial rages, while the King of Prussia silently watched from a corner. Hardenberg managed to stammer out a few phrases. "Will you not obey the orders of your King?" screamed Alexander. "These orders are absolute!"

Hardenberg returned to his rooms and opened his diary: "Russia,"

King Frederick William
III, King of a Prussia
much diminished in size
and influence since the
reign of his grand-uncle,
Frederick the Great

he wrote, "Russia, supported by the King on all points, is wrong. But what to do?" Prussia was defecting from her western Allies and Poland was lost. The barrier would have to be built in Saxony.[3]

Castlereagh loses his centre

Castlereagh had just lost his German centre. Lines were now being drawn right across the old Reich. Prussia and Austria were separating. "Germany" was dividing.

It was not a prospect that pleased most Prussians. They feared their country would become a province of Russia, like Poland. Humboldt suddenly started talking about "the cause of Europe" in the hope of avoiding the worst; Hardenberg thought of calling on Austrian assistance, even at the price of giving up a bit of Saxony; the General Staff, on the contrary, wanted to march on Dresden and take the whole Saxon Kingdom before the Congress assembled in November. King Frederick William, on the other hand, remained obstinately loyal to his "divine friend," the Tsar.

The Austrians, in their turn, got frightened and began to insist on territory: no way would they yield all Poland *and* all Saxony. Metternich's political enemies in Vienna made it clear that they were getting very tired of the Foreign Minister's procrastination, philandering, and his obsession with abstract German constitutions; they wanted land and safe frontiers for Austria. Castlereagh warned London that Austria, "rather than have the Russians at Cracovie and the Prussians at Dresden," might well risk war.[4]

And there was little Lord Castlereagh could do about it. With Alexander directly intervening into political affairs, Castlereagh's role as mediator was effectively ended. He wrote to Liverpool to say he was "unwilling to abuse the indulgence of a direct intercourse with a Sovereign." Alexander agreed. "A mediator is only useful in a discussion if he tries to conciliate," the Tsar informed the Foreign Secretary; "otherwise he had better leave the parties concerned alone." So Castlereagh washed his hands of Poland; he told Liverpool that he was going to leave the Polish negotiations "with the Powers more locally interested than Great Britain."[5]

In other words, Castlereagh's European policy was in pieces, the hub of his engine had been shattered. Unfortunately, he had pushed himself so far into the centre of the fray that he knew neither how nor where to retreat.

All this pleased Talleyrand, who had been watching from afar. He had been calling Castlereagh's doomed programme *"une politique d'écoliers et de coalisés"* – "this policy which sees only blocks and doesn't bother about the elements that make them up." Indeed, Castlereagh began to develop the vague look of a lost schoolboy while Talleyrand, fifteen years his senior, took on airs of the gentleman master. They were often together at the Kaunitz Palace. The French Prince Minister would present his lessons assisted by the faithful duc de Dalberg (his arm bandaged because of a duel with a dining companion) along with a pile of maps: a geography of Central Europe, a history of Prussia in the eighteenth century, even a little economics. England, expounded the Frenchman, could not always be sure of peace with Prussia; why would a commercial nation want to let Leipzig, which had one of the largest fairs in Europe, fall into the hands of King Frederick William? Castlereagh "was struck by a sort of astonishment and fear." But he was a bright enough pupil to see where Talleyrand's Parisian vision of Europe was leading – the civilised West, the boulevards of Central Europe, the menacing faubourgs beyond.[6]

One sunny Thursday morning, Castlereagh came round to the Kaunitz Palace; "I thought he was going to let me into some secret or make some important overture," Talleyrand wrote to his King as soon as the meeting was ended, "but all he wanted to talk about was the embarrassment he was in." Castlereagh confessed he had put rather too much hope in Prussia and, as a result, his whole system had turned over at its base. "His mood was sort of despondent," reported

Talleyrand. What could be done to get the business of the Congress moving again? wondered Castlereagh. Talleyrand said the whole problem was that the Allies insisted on making the Saxon question subordinate to Poland. Separate them, he advised. Get Austria to work out as best a deal she can on Poland and then let us all get together and concentrate on Saxony. With the support of France and Spain, Austria will feel secure and England will have her peace. Talleyrand's thinking was almost identical to Metternich's – except that Talleyrand had introduced a role for France.[7]

Castlereagh's failure over Poland was, in large measure, due to in-experience, which was itself a product of Britain's long wartime iso-lation. There were other tell-tale signs of this. Lady Castlereagh, for instance, astonished everybody at Metternich's masked ball on 8 November when she entered the grand hall to a fanfare of trumpets with her husband's Order of the Garter in her hair. Castlereagh's brother, Lord Stewart, was embarrassing Salon society by getting all his facts wrong; he bragged to Prince Eugène de Beauharnais, who had never as much as laid eyes on the Pyrenees, that he had beaten him in battle in Spain. And the Ambassador would have been killed in a night brawl with coachmen had not the police arrived in time.[8]

Nevertheless, the explanations Castlereagh made to his government of his political predicament were highly dignified and even today command admiration. Great Britain, he said, had "to contend for an European question of great magnitude" during this critical transition to peace. Britain's own particular interests in the Low Countries, he pointed out, were inextricably tied to the general security of Europe; Castlereagh had been impressed by Talleyrand's maps of the northern plains. If Austria gave up on Poland then "the contest of negotiation" would turn on Saxony, Mainz, and "other German points." A divid-ed Germany, in its turn, would open wide the plains – which included the Netherlands – to the free flow of armies once more. Unless the Emperor of Russia could be brought "to a more moderate and sound course of conduct," Castlereagh warned, "the peace, which we have so dearly purchased, will be but of short duration."[9]

But Lord Liverpool, in London, had problems of his own. In the first place, nobody in his Cabinet had thought about a long-term policy for Europe; if they had visions they were the visions of mirrors reflecting back into centuries gone by. Liverpool spoke for all his col-leagues when he told Castlereagh that Poland was a distant local problem that should have been quietly settled between the Powers concerned. Britain had never worried about Poland in the eighteenth century; why worry now? "We have done enough on this question of Poland," Liverpool wrote to Castlereagh. The Cabinet concurred.[10]

The war with America dragged on with little hope of peace foreseen by the negotiators at Ghent. Liverpool offered Wellington the command, but the Duke refused. "No material success is likely in America," said the Duke. So the government sent his brother-in-law, Ned Pakenham, who was not a very good choice. But then Wellington had a sense of Europe and was better suited for Europe, for France was in a "combustible state."

That was what really haunted the British government. Never mind if the Russian Emperor could at some distant date cause war; the situation required peace now, even if it were a transitory peace. All one needed was a little time, time to allow Good King Louis to settle down in the Tuileries, time for the Prince of Orange to establish himself in Belgium. The rest was a matter of local detail. "A war now may be a revolutionary war," advised Lord Liverpool, gazing into his rear-view mirrors; "a war some time hence need not be different in its character and in its effects from any of those wars which occurred in the seventeenth and eighteenth centuries."

Bathurst, the Secretary of State for War and Colonies, sent formal instructions on behalf of the Prince Regent, away in Brighton. They were the only instructions Castlereagh ever received. The Minister was informed of the "impossibility of His Royal Highness consenting to involve this country in hostilities at this time for any of the objects which have been hitherto under discussion at Vienna."

But if the members of His Majesty's government remained isolationist and defeatist, the opposition had suddenly discovered they were Europeans. Samuel Whitbread and his friends – with little more to say on the slave trade and with Princess Caroline in Italy – started cultivating an interest in Poles and Saxons. The independence of Poland became an issue in the press. So did the pending annihilation of the Kingdom of Saxony under the evil auspices of the British Tory government.

Once articles started appearing in the press, issues like Poland and Saxony could no longer be ignored. "I ought to apprise you," Liverpool informed Castlereagh, "that there is a strong feeling in this country respecting Saxony... It would be very desirable that a *noyau* of it at least should be preserved." How could such a kernel be preserved? Liverpool seems not to have realised that he was contradicting Bathurst's recent instructions. But then, Liverpool's comments had little to do with British foreign policy; they had everything to do with British domestic policy. "The Opposition are particularly rancorous," Liverpool warned, "and evidently mean to find us good employment."[11]

It was at this point that the Duke of Wellington started to play a more active diplomatic role. With all the correspondence between Vienna and London passing through his offices and with his connections (particularly with Castlereagh) dating back to the days of Pitt, Wellington undoubtedly had a better grasp of European affairs than anyone in the Cabinet. But, being in Paris rather than Vienna, he was also more aware of British affairs than Castlereagh; every day, cross-Channel travellers reported to him and the London newspapers he received were only three days old – Castlereagh had to wait two weeks. He was thus in a position to perform two vital tasks: first, to ease the retreat Castlereagh was going to have to make on Poland and, second, to bridge the serious differences that had developed between Castlereagh and his own government.

Castlereagh himself gave Wellington the occasion. In line with his original policy, Castlereagh had written at the end of October to ask Wellington to stop France threatening war over Saxony – "a collateral point" – and concentrate on opposing Russia in Poland; Castlereagh made it clear that if France did not cooperate he was ready to negotiate a peace with the Bonapartist King in Naples, Murat, to free Austrian troops for Poland. Early in November, Wellington proudly reported success back to Castlereagh. After two interviews with the comte de Blacas, instructions were being sent to Talleyrand to lay aside the "small points" (Saxony) and concentrate on opposing the aggrandisement of Russia (in Poland); "they are quite convinced M de Talleyrand has acted foolishly," said Wellington of the French government. It was just what Castlereagh wanted.

But Blacas and the French King had got a very different impression of the interviews. "The Duke of Wellington will be a good weapon in your hands," Louis XVIII wrote in a most unusually enthusiastic letter to Talleyrand. Have no fear of an Anglo-Austrian plot to abandon Saxony, wrote Blacas in an accompanying letter; Wellington had assured the French that British policy was to oppose the designs of Emperor Alexander in Poland "*and, therefore, in Saxony.*"[12]

That was the key; that was what would allow Castlereagh to save face, retreat and, at the same time, meet British "public opinion" halfway: with French support, he could make his stand and build his barrier in Saxony.

For the time being Castlereagh either deliberately overlooked or simply misunderstood Wellington's creative interpretation of British foreign policy. Reporting on a meeting with Talleyrand on 20 November, Castlereagh thanked Wellington for making the French so much more accommodating. Talleyrand, he was pleased to report, was now "most obliging and conciliatory" (this was the same meeting that inspired Talleyrand to speak of Castlereagh as "sort of despondent"). Nothing in French policy had actually changed, as Castlereagh quietly admitted himself: Talleyrand "spoke, apparently with openness, his mind, always returning to the old notion of urging Austria to finish the Polish question as well she could, and then to turn the whole combination upon Saxony."[13]

Talleyrand also misunderstood, or overlooked, what Wellington had been saying. He told Louis XVIII that Wellington's link between Saxony and Poland went in precisely the opposite direction from the one supposed by Castlereagh, and he cited the note the British Foreign Secretary had sent to Hardenberg back on 11 October as proof. Talleyrand even described Wellington as an obstacle to a French *entente* with Castlereagh.[14]

The problem was that both Talleyrand and Castlereagh were look-ing backwards to their stand-off in October. Prussia's defection had changed the situation entirely. Within two weeks of their meeting, the Polish question had become the Saxon question. Wellington, in Paris, had laid the groundwork for an Anglo-French accord on a new European barrier.

Metternich turns

Outside Berlin, from his surveyed residence of the Schloss Friedrichsfeld, King Frederick Augustus of Saxony addressed a note, dated 4 November 1814, to the Delegates of the Congress of Vienna. "We have just learnt with great sorrow that our Kingdom of Saxony is to be temporarily occupied by the troops of His Prussian Majesty," announced the King; he demanded "prompt reinstatement" by "the Congress of Vienna, before all Europe." Would the Congress allow Saxony to be occupied by Prussians?[15]

No Austrian, including Metternich, was going to welcome even a temporary transfer of Saxony to the Tsar's *"valet de chambre,"* as Prussia's King was now dubbed in Vienna. Resentment in political circles was mounting against the way Metternich had handled the affair. Prince Starhemberg, Austria's former Ambassador to Paris, thought Austria was in a worse position than after her defeat in 1809. "What a singular spectacle we have today!" he exclaimed to Agent ⁂, "the Government holds fast to the Princedoms of Isenburg-Birstein and Neuwied, and then it goes and dethrones the King of Saxony!" In the *salons* it was the women who complained, thereby setting the tone of the closest thing Vienna ever came to a "public opinion." The star of the *salons* was no longer Metternich; it was the Prince de Talleyrand, always in the company of his pretty young niece. "This Talleyrand asks nothing for France," said one *habitué* of the ladies' drawing rooms, "he seeks only justice, balance, moderation on the holy grounds of law and reason." "Even if the Gospel is preached by the Devil," chimed in an old duchess, "that makes it no less the Gospel."[16]

Metternich could not remain totally insensible to what was being said about him; nor could he ignore the fact that Russia remained obstinate while Prussia was obviously defecting. If he couldn't de-liver the territories demanded in Poland then he was absolutely obliged to turn on Saxony.

Just as he had done every other time he had reversed his policy, he waited for others to take the initiative. He still refused to give France a role in the great issues. When Castlereagh abandoned his role as mediator, explaining that Poland should now be left to the "locally interested Powers," he had recommended the services of Prince Hardenberg, a suggestion Metternich took up like a shot. It was the perfect opportunity to separate the Saxon question from the Polish question, that is, first to negotiate as good a deal he could get on Poland and then focus all the force he could muster on Saxony; Metternich was setting a trap for Prussia.

Hardenberg promptly accepted the offer, promising to make every effort he could with the Tsar on Poland. But he clearly did not have the support of his King and he had nothing further to offer Alexander; for a whole fortnight he remained totally silent.

This provided Metternich with his next critical opportunity: with Hardenberg concentrating on Poland, Metternich could now start withdrawing his offer on Saxony. On 12 November he wrote to Hardenberg, "His Majesty sees with much regret that the point of view of the Prussian Cabinet differs in several ways with his own." In other words, Prussia was not fulfilling the crucial condition of "unity of policy" with Austria.[17]

Metternich took no pleasure in any of this. Almost every day, Gentz would have long, anguished conversations with the Minister in the Chancellery; on sunny days they would wander together along the Bastei. They agreed that the current arrangements with Prussia were impossible, but "the point of crisis had not yet arrived." Perhaps by some miracle Prussia might manage to negotiate a favourable deal on Poland, in which case Austria could still avoid calling on France for help – truly a last resort in Metternich's mind.[18]

A very troubled mind it was too. Politics were not the only subject Gentz and Metternich discussed. One can guess what the main topic was: "Dinner with Prince Metternich," Gentz recorded on Sunday, 6 November; "big interview with him on his affairs of the heart." Friday, 11 November: "Long conversation with Metternich, still more on that damned woman than about business." Sunday, 13 November: "Between three and four this afternoon, a very curious conversation with the Duchess von Sagan about her fatal story with Metternich..." Metternich could not kick the Duchess out of his mind.[19]

The story that had been going around the *salons* was that Alexander had made a deal with Sagan: break with Metternich and Russian funds, which had been temporarily blocked, would be made available again.

It was noticed that Sagan was now defending Alexander in public.

When, for example, Charles Stewart came round to the Palm Palace and started, in his unique ambassadorial style, insulting the Tsar before a dozen people – "What do you think of Alexander? As far I'm concerned, I believe him to be a madman, a coveter, and an imposter; that's what I think. And you, eh? how do you find him? what do you say, eh?" – Sagan would have none of it: "I find, my lord, that you've got a horse's bit stuck between your teeth, just like that horse that you lent my sister Dorothée this morning; and it nearly broke her neck in the Prater." Sagan then abruptly stood up and joined another of her guests.[20]

Count Hochbert of Baden chatted with Count Schenk of Württemberg; Count Senfft-Pilsach from Saxony passed the news on to Baron Ried of Bavaria. "Perhaps Metternich will now pick up courage," whispered Hochbert into a receptive Württemberger ear, "and out of hatred against the Russian Sovereign will oppose his pernicious designs." That was the hope of many representatives of the smaller German states.[21]

Metternich was not going to move so fast. He clung to his older alliances just as he clung to Sagan. Sagan! He could not let her go. All through November he continued to write to her, sometimes in French, sometimes in German, pleading for just a short private meeting, or simply a line, or anything. The rumour was that she was leaving at the end of the month. "I am completely ill, my body is attacked, my soul will not be able to defend it for long," wailed the crumbling colossus. "I will have to hold on for a few more weeks; they will end the most painful year of my life, and if they actually end my life the world will only lose the sad remains of an existence I deserve to lose myself." Yet he would only now see her in dining-rooms and ballrooms, with dozens of others; it was worse than no meeting at all. "Everybody bores me and you, I cannot have in *petit comité.*"

On 16 November, she did actually accord him a private meeting in the Palm Palace – "the good hour that you grudged me." Metternich again stood before her "as God had created me, neither better, nor worse, nor stronger, nor weaker." There is no record of what Sagan said of this sight, if she said anything at all. But Metternich did receive a line; in fact, more than one line: "Nothing, nothing will ever get me back into the situation I rightly abandoned. No more complications, no more divisions, no more what degrades, what kills the most noble part of our being. I have shattered a liaison that was criminal for me and criminal for you."[22]

The police were demanding that, for the sake of official decorum and the maintenance of order in the city, Princess Bagration and the Duchess von Sagan be expelled from Austria, so vicious were the rumours that they spread about Metternich. Bagration often received her fellow schemers and confidants in her bed chamber. Most of them were either members of, or were linked with the Russian Legation, for the Princess was more than a simple loyal subject. "I do not love Alexander, I *adore* him – ah! ah! ah!" she would exclaim with the asthmatic voice she adopted whenever the name "Alexander" was mentioned. Sagan was now openly backing the Russian side, competing with her neighbour for the Tsar's favours. The French were actually encouraging her. For who were her guests? Her sister, Talleyrand, and Dalberg. Talleyrand always had something malicious to say about Metternich.[23] But the source of the worst rumours was neither Talleyrand, Sagan, nor Bagration; it was Alexander himself. "Alexander detests Metternich," said Bagration, "he knows him, and doesn't fear him at all; he says he will get out of him all that he wants."[24]

A few hours before a great masked ball was held in the Hofburg, Metternich wrote to Sagan pleading with her not to talk with the Russian Emperor and to ignore all proposals he made hostile to him. "Never forget that our relationship, so pure and simple on my side, has never lent itself to the kind of ridicule some people would like to suggest." On the night of the great masked ball, Sagan was all ears.

"Europe without distances"

One of the first casualties of the conflict over Poland and Saxony was the idea of the Congress itself. Russia and Prussia had no intention of presenting their claims before a European assembly, Castlereagh was backing away from the idea because of hostility at home, and Metternich had never accepted the idea in the first place. The only major Power which still championed it was France, but France remained isolated.

By early November, the Four were promoting a new idea, a "Europe without distances." As a semi-official article at the time explained it, "The presence of so many Monarchs, Ministers and Plenipotentiaries of Courts of the first and second order removes the obstacles that distance and the loss of time have so often stood in the way of success for complicated negotiations." The great European courts were negotiating directly with one another, the major German Powers were deliberating on a constitution, the Swiss and the Italians were trying to settle their own particular problems. The essential feature of the Congress of Vienna was that "the European Powers had been brought together in the same theatre," distance had been abolished.[25]

The article, probably written by Metternich himself, was the most positive way of admitting that the Great Powers had so far failed to resolve the great problems of Europe and had no intention of explaining their failure before any kind of European parliament.

Hardenberg had wanted to confine the Congress to general issues, but Metternich knew that not even this would work, for it was obvious that once a deliberative assembly sat there would be no way of limiting what it discussed. So he hung on stubbornly to his original proposal that the general assembly should only be called after the Great Powers – and he meant the Allied Powers excluding France – had decided on the shape of Europe among themselves. For Metternich, the first session of the Congress should be the last session.

How could he assure this? At the end of October, only days before the Congress was once more due to be convened, Gentz and Metternich came up with a plan. The same obstacle that had stood in Castlereagh's way, when he had been advocating an immediate convocation of the Congress back in September, could be used again to hold up the Congress in November: the credentials problem. Metternich was sure he had the majority vote on the Committee of Eight, the signatories of the Treaty of Paris. So he came up with a proposal that all plenipotentiaries wanting to attend the Congress would have to come to the Chancellery and present their credentials to a committee named by the Eight. It was the perfect delaying action.

Gentz made a long speech in front of the Four (who pretended to control the Eight) on 29 October, two days before the new deadline. He got home at three o'clock in the morning full of himself; "I have killed the idea of the Congress," he wrote in his diary.[26]

He had, but it involved a fight. Castlereagh had mellowed since his earlier stand on a more parliamentary Europe; his first concern was to keep his Allies together. But Talleyrand was as committed to the idea of convening the Congress as he ever had been. Why not assemble all those with credentials? asked Talleyrand when the question was brought before the Eight the next day, 30 October. Talleyrand won surprising sympathy from the Swedish envoy, Löwenhjelm, who thought that the new Allied idea of a "Europe without distances" contradicted both the Treaty of Paris and the declaration of 8 October promising the opening of the Congress on 1 November. He wrote to his Minister in Stockholm that it would be impossible for the Allies to escape this dilemma "with the honours of ordinary logic."

Metternich tried. In a long-winded speech before the Eight – "abundant of words and empty of substance," said Talleyrand – he explained, that the Congress was not a "corporate entity" and that the committees were really not committees at all since they had to be delegated powers by a deliberative assembly, which had no legal existance; one would have to invent new words.

It was Castlereagh who came up with the solution, a practical

British solution. Put aside all theory, he said, don't worry about defining the Congress or committees; while credentials were being checked the committees could get on with their work, for there already existed, in effect, two committees, a German Committee and a Polish Committee – and it wouldn't take long to set up an Italian Committee and a Swiss Committee. No protocol was ever drawn up of this meeting, so there was nothing official about their discussion.[27]

But the committees that were not really committees did get down to work, in closed cabinets, *salons,* ballrooms, in walks along the Bastei, chance encounters on the Graben, in a King's apartments, in theatres, and boudoirs. For months, that would be the real Congress of Vienna. A Credentials Committee was named by the Eight, its members, the delegates of Russia, Prussia, and Britain, being selected by lottery. The plenipotentiaries were invited to present their credentials to the Committee in the Chancellery.

On Sunday, 13 November, the Eight met again to discuss what to do about the ancient Republic of Genoa. After three hours of drawn-out legal Italian argument, Metternich, at around eleven o'clock that night, popped his question to the exhausted Ministers: given all the current difficulties, should a general meeting of plenipotentiaries be called after their credentials had been checked? "It was decided," read the last line of Gentz's protocol, "that, considering the current state of private negotiations, this general meeting would be of no utility and that it would be better to postpone it to a later date." The Congress had been postponed indefinitely. The Congress, in effect, had been killed.[28]

The next day the only major committee of substance, the German Committee, had its last meeting. Tension had been building up over the last few weeks. Stein had been wanting to bring in the Russians, while the smaller German states objected to Prussia's plans of "Circles." But what paralysed all discussion was was when Württemberg's Minister that Monday demanded a comprehensive plan for all "Germany." Clearly a comprehensive plan on "Germany" required a comprehensive plan on "Europe" The committee adjourned and its members did not sit down together again. It was the death knell of Castlereagh's German centre.[29]

For the tens of thousands, who had gathered in Vienna to witness Europe deliberate in open assembly, the new scheme of limiting business to multilateral negotiations between the *parties intéressés* came as a bitter disappointment. The opinion grew that the Congress was merely an armistice, "a theatrical pause in the great tragedy of our world's history," something to be compared with the short-lived Treaty of Amiens of 1802 – "they will separate as friends with an intention of war in mind." War, everyone was talking of war.[30]

The hunt

Or, to be more exact, everyone with an access to politics talked of war; in the *Residenzstadt* this still only represented a minority. For the month of November, one finds no talk of war in Franz Perth's diary. There was a brief note of concern when, in the middle of the month, he received a letter from his friend, a priest living in Zwettl, northern Austria, who had heard through local gossip that there was trouble in Paris, that the French were demanding the return of Napoleon. "It would be the greatest evil if this monster were to return again to the throne," wrote the priest. Perth dismissed this as a lot of rural humbug. "Where are the country folk who do not know everything?" he wondered. "In Vienna nothing has been said about this, and even if the rumour were true the Allies would have taken such measures that we would have nothing to fear from Napoleon for a long time." Having seen demonstrations like the great Leipzig commemoration, Perth's faith in the strength and unity of the Allies was unshakable.[31]

Early in the morning of Thursday, 10 November, in "exceptionally beautiful weather," he mounted a wagon with many of his colleagues of the Forestry Commission and drove through Shönbrunn to Lainz, where – like ancient citizens on a Roman holiday – they all sat and watched an imperial hunt.

Twenty stands had been arranged in the form of an amphitheatre overlooking a wide meadow, a lake, and the high hills beyond. Eight thousand voices roared when the Kaiser and his wife entered the "hunting arena" in a coloured coach, followed by the Foreign Sovereigns, the Princes, and the Archdukes accompanied by thundering "Turkish music" – enough noise, one would have thought, to scare most game out of Lower Austria. Yet, after a wail of forest horns, Archduke Charles took up his musket, the Tsar sat bolt upright on his horse, the rotund King Frederick of Württemberg brandished a barrel, and the whole host of the *sämtliche hohe Herrschaften* took aim.

The imperial gamekeepers had prepared their quarry. Out from the forest's edge sprang wild boars, hares, foxes, roe deers, and badgers; over two hundred boars alone were slaughtered in less than an hour by Kaiser Franz and the visiting Sovereigns.

The Emperor and his guests then returned to Schönbrunn for dinner, while Perth and his colleagues in the Forestry Commission were treated to a meal at Lainz. "Our society was, after the savoury wine, very cheerful and merry," recorded Perth, "and at 6.30 we returned to Vienna where we arrived at around eight." Like all functionaries he received from the Kaiser a share of the kill – a hare, half a boar, along with two month's salary.

Perth was "cheerful and merry" all through that weekend. He

attended a great drinking carouse in one of his favourite inns to celebrate the "peace achieved." Toasts broke out, songs were sung; Perth
himself composed a drinking song. The Allies! The Allies! The Peace!
The Peace! Perth and his friends were still drinking at dawn on
Sunday morning.[32]

It was on the same day as the Lainz hunt, 10 November, that
Prussian troops marched into Dresden. The Russian Governor
General, Prince Repnin, announced, on leaving his post, that "His
Majesty the Emperor, my august Master, will never cease to play a
role in Saxony's fate." Saxony did not doubt it.

Baron von Reck and Baron von Gaudi of the new Prussian
Government General had notices distributed throughout the occupied Kingdom. They appealed to the local authorities and inhabitants
to "execute rigorously their decrees" and to continue to observe "the
same behaviour that has, up to now, so honourably distinguished the
Saxon nation." The Saxon nation had had no choice.[33]

Saxon souls

During the three critical weeks that followed the Prussian occupation
of Saxony, most of the principal actors at the Congress fell ill; some
virulent form of influenza was spreading through town. A huge
Carousel and masked ball in the Redoutensaal had to be postponed
for a week because Kaiser Franz was unable to attend. Metternich disappeared from public view in the last days of November. "They say
he is suffering from an *ébullition*," said Talleyrand, referring to a disease of hot sweats currently in mode;[34] "if all his duplicity could be
eliminated that way it would be a mighty *ébullition*." Chancellor
Hardenberg coughed and dribbled till mid-December. Castlereagh
seems not to have suffered, though many reported him to be in low
spirits. Dorothée de Périgord retired to her rooms in the last week of
November. Surprisingly the uncle – who dreaded winter – remained
in fit form. But the athletic Emperor of All the Russias became very
ill. Stomping out the *tempête* one night with an anonymous lady in
the popular dance-hall, the Mehlgrube, he fell in a swoon and had to
be carried out. He was confined to bed for almost two weeks.
Castlereagh wrote to Liverpool on 25 November that the illness
could cause the the Tsar to "moderate his pretensions." That was also
the hope of his Allies, indeed, the hope of most of Europe.[35]

According to Prince Repnin, the Prussian occupation of Saxony
would be followed by a permanent union of the two states – an act
that had already won the consent of Austria and Britain. Both
Metternich and Castlereagh immediately denied this, but, as
Talleyrand pointed out, not without hypocrisy; Castlereagh's note of
11 October read very much like an approval of the annexation and

Metternich, throughout November, privately held out hopes for Hardenberg.[36] Metternich did this because Hardenberg – though blissfully unaware of it – provided the Austrians useful time to nego- tiate a separate accord with Russia on Poland: Metternich had already decided to concede the lion's share of Poland while seeking an even- tual partition of Saxony. In other words, the "barrier" of Europe, in Metternich's mind, had already shifted westwards.[37]

In 1814, the whole game of equilibrium was based not – as in a later age – on material resources, the division of markets, and economics; it revolved, rather, around a calculation of the number of "souls" each Power possessed. Since 1805, Prussia had lost "souls" to Hanover, to southern Germany, and to Poland (the "Duchy of Warsaw"). As one of the key Allies involved in the defeat of France, Britain and Austria both agreed that Prussia merited compensation.

Metternich's task now was to prove that Prussia did not need the entire Kingdom of Saxony in order to be compensated in souls. Unlike Prussia, Austria was not seeking territorial expansion; but, having failed in Poland, Metternich did have to impose a plan for Saxony's partition. Early in November, Talleyrand saw just such an Austrian plan that would grant five hundred thousand Saxon souls to Prussia – "which might be regarded as necessary for covering Berlin" – while maintaining 1.5 to 1.6 million souls within an independent Kingdom of Saxony. But how could this be achieved while Prussian troops occupied Dresden?[38]

Austria's first step was to make menacing signs to Prussia's chief ally, Russia. The link between Prussia and Russia somehow had to be broken. A Bavarian army of seventy-five thousand poor souls was mobilised. Schwarzenberg and General Josef Radetzky drew up a scheme to advance the bulk of Austria's army, some 370,000 men, into Hungary and Galicia in preparation for a strike at Russian forces across the Vistula. Count Münster wrote a number of panicky letters to the Prince Regent warning him that Great Britain could not stand idly by if it did come to a war on the plains: George III's new Kingdom of Hanover would be threatened as would, ultimately, the Netherlands. "It is most important," he pointed out, "that the troops in Hanover not be cut off from those in Belgium."[39]

Austria, however, looked weak. "Currently you cannot make war on us," Baron Johann von Anstett told **. "Your armies are not con- centrated, while we have 500,000 men ready on our first line, not far from your frontiers; our cavalry is concentrated and better equipped than yours; our artillery is twice as numerous . . . With the first word of 'war' you will have lost your Galicia."

The Russian adviser was speaking frankly. He was worried about war; he had been heard saying at one of Bagration's Russian dinners that a "rage of empires" endangered a peaceful outcome of the

Congress. He had even offered the Tsar his resignation. Like almost everyone else in Vienna that November, Anstett was sick. "Now I am a dead man and you should regard what I tell you as prophecies from another world," he declared. Don't talk of war, he advised, wait.[40]

Waiting was Metternich's game.

There were signs, in fact, that the sick bed was having a moderating influence on Alexander. Gentz first heard the rumours that he was backing down at another *grande soirée* held in Metternich's summer villa on 21 November. Reports filtered in through Hager's services that the Tsar was "rather more disposed to make concessions," that he "appeared ready to limit his claims on the Duchy of Warsaw." It was even stated that a letter had been delivered to the Tsar from the Prince Regent pleading him to renounce his projects on Poland and Saxony, and that "Alexander has yielded."

The problem was that Alexander was so prone to the influence of his personal advisers, some of whom had very extreme ideas. Baron vom Stein, for example, was appalled at the idea that Hardenberg was prepared to cede a part of Saxony and implored the Tsar to maintain the link between the Saxon question and the Polish question, and to stand firm on both. That was also the opinion of Humboldt and Czartoryski.[41]

They could argue that Russia, from both a military and political point of view, was in a strong position. As Anstett had pointed out, her armies were already concentrated. Russia could also appeal to nationalist opinion, to the discontented; she could fly the colours of the "liberator" again. She could turn to the minorities of Poland, she could treat with dissidents of Hungary; support for an independent "Kingdom of Hungary" had been expressed within Alexander's circle. An even greater nightmare for Austria was what Russian agents could get up to in Italy. It was fertile territory for nationalist propaganda and, just off the coast of Italy, lay a prince only to ready to stir it all up: Bonaparte, or "Robinson Crusoe" as they called him in Vienna.[42]

"We could strike in Italy where fire is hidden under the ashes," warned Anstett. Austria could not afford to move too many troops out of Italy. And a treacherous Russian accord with Napoleon? It would be the horror of Tilsit again.[43]

A further complication for Austria was the situation in France. Letters intercepted by the Polizei Hofstelle, along with torn bits of wastepaper and agents' chatter, indicated that the French were getting very concerned about the situation at home and sought Napoleon's removal from Elba. They also wanted Murat out of Naples. Ironically, the Austrians seemed to be their own worst enemy; Talleyrand told Louis XVIII that Austrians were the main arms suppliers to Murat's army and that Metternich's whole policy in the region was determined by *"une femme de sa connaissance"* – Metternich's former lover, Napoleon's sister, Murat's Queen. As for

the political atmosphere in Paris, Talleyrand advised Louis that stories of "conspiracies, secret discontents, and muffled whispers" were
not helping his cause in Vienna; he blamed it all on leaks from
Wellington's correspondence with Castlereagh.[44]

Louis and his Ministers in Paris, who were perfectly aware of
Russian projects in Italy, were pushing for an open alliance with
Britain and Austria. They had a friend in Count Münster. He was
sending the most alarming reports to the Prince Regent over what
could happen if prying Russians and "crowned Jacobins" were left in
Naples. "It is of the utmost necessity to come to an agreement with
France," he said.

The moment had arrived for Louis XVIII to take one of his rare
political initiatives. Such occasions always called for an appropriate
quotation from Horace, Virgil, or Cicero. "I believe in the intentions
attributed to Emperor Alexander with regards to Italy," he wrote to
Talleyrand; "it is in this case of the highest importance that Austria
and England grasp the meaning of the old adage, trivial if you will,
but full of sense, and eminently applicable to the circumstance,
Sublata causa, tollitur effectus." "Suppress the cause and the effect is
also suppressed": make an alliance with England and Austria, and
Murat will disappear.[45]

Officially, Hardenberg remained Metternich's main mediator with
Russia. Formally, the deal was still on over Saxony: the Kingdom was
his if he could prove "unity" with Austria. Secretly, Metternich knew
this was impossible.

Days went by and Hardenberg kept his silence. The Russian
Emperor remained in bed. Would Alexander swing in the direction of
moderation (and abandon expansionist Prussia), or would he listen to
the extremists around him (and support Prussia's annexation of
Saxony)? Informed opinion in Vienna was that he was moderating. It
was time to strike.

On Sunday, 20 November, Metternich wrote to Hardenberg: "I
pray you, my dear Chancellor, go as soon as possible to the Tsar."[46]

Beethoven and horses

With temperatures plummeting in continental Vienna, the entertainment for idlers and procrastinators had to be moved into heated halls.
Life inside the city of two walls became more cramped, the tensions
created by the presence of so many state representatives intensified.

"What a variety of costumes and languages!" exclaimed La Garde-
Chambonas, the wandering poet. "It is like a bazaar of all the nations
of the world." Talleyrand, recalling no doubt the magnificence of the
ceremonies devoted to Louis XVIII in Paris the previous August,
thought that royalty in Vienna was losing its dignity. "To find four

Kings and even more Princes at balls or taking tea in the houses of simple Viennese citizens appears to me quite unseemly," he told King Louis. In this new "Europe without distances" a Sovereign risked the loss of dignity and glory. Their Ministers risked war.[47]

Controversy permeated every level of polite society; the entertainments themselves became subjects of dispute. One of the most disputed was a grand concert, directed by Herr Ludwig van Beethoven, which was due to be performed in the Hofburg's grand Redoutensaal on Sunday, 20 November.

Beethoven was a familiar, now famous, figure in the *Residenzstadt*. He was regularly seen walking along the Bastei, in rain and shine, the crown of his felt hat knocked out of shape, the unfastened lapels of his blue frockcoat flying out in the wind, even though the pockets were weighed down with music notebooks, an ear trumpet, and thick gauge carpenters' pencils. He lived in a small apartment on the Mölkerbastei where the street urchins could watch him through the window pacing about in his flowered cloth dressing gown. The Viennese thought of him as one of their own and so he should have been; he had first visited the town at the age of seventeen and had set himself up as a permanent resident at twenty-two. But deafness had made him restless and he was constantly threatening to leave. Like his fellow Rhinelander, Metternich, he referred to Vienna as "the enemy." "From the Emperor down to the last shoe polisher, the Viennese are all a worthless lot," he said, adding that the worst of them all was his pupil, Kaiser Franz's younger brother, the Archduke Rudolph.[48]

Yet Beethoven would remember, for the rest of his life, the year of the Congress. If he derided the Archduke Rudolph, he was all the same proud when he was invited round to his apartments in the Hofburg to be introduced to the visiting Sovereigns. They all expressed their regard in the most flattering terms; the Russian Empress Elizabeth, in particular, was carried away in her praise.

However, Beethoven's favourite in Vienna's "bazaar of nations" was England. He was always talking about following in Haydn's footsteps and visiting, even living, in England. One of his great ambitions was to visit the House of Commons. Whenever the House was in session, he would have newspapers delivered to his apartments so that he could follow the parliamentary debates; Beethoven was a man of the English opposition – his favourite speaker was old Brougham.

Beethoven faced his own opposition at home. As one of Hager's agents explained in November, Vienna was divided into two factions, pro- and contra-Beethoven. Count Razumovsky, the enormously rich former Russian Ambassador, who lived out in the Landstrasse, led the Beethoven clique; but against them stood the "substantial majority of knowledgeable people who want to hear no music whatsoever by Herr Beethoven."

The main reproach of the contras was that Beethoven's music was "not clean." Their criticisms might be compared to the strictures of the neo-classicist architects of London and Paris who so hated the curves and curlicues of Vienna. Similarly, Beethoven's music was faulted for being too ornamental. Ignaz Moscheles, the great Viennese pianist, called it "a Baroque music in conflict with all the rules." Most of Beethoven's critics complained that the works were too long, too "drawn out," that they lacked "organic connection and a gradual development of ideas." "The symphony would gain immensely," thought the anonymous reviewer for the *Allgemeine Musikalische Zeitung* after listening to the *Eroica*, "if Beethoven would decide to shorten it and introduce into the whole more light, clarity, and unity." His words could have been lifted out of a London pattern book.[49]

Beethoven aimed over the tiny heads of his critics to the *Volk* of Vienna, to their love of play and their love of greenery. Something melancholy, something joyful, something passionate, something that grew: that was Vienna's style. For many years Kaiser Franz refused to attend a Beethoven concert for this very reason; "There is something revolutionary in that music!" he exclaimed. But the people came. His concerts in the Burgtheater, out in the open air of the Augarten, or in the suburban Theater an der Wien were always crowded and always extremely noisy.

For his grand concert, Beethoven had proposed a new Seventh Symphony, followed by two pieces written in honour of the European peace and the Congress. The powerful contra-Beethoven faction, of course, campaigned to stop it. But what finally led to its postponement was the attitude of the countrymen he admired most, the English. The concert fell on a Sunday and – as a representative of the Legation on the Minoritenplatz explained it – the English, being a religious people, did not listen to music on a Sunday.[50]

That was the Sunday evening Prince Hardenberg received Metternich's invitation to go to the Tsar. For more than two weeks, Hardenberg, the mediator, had done no mediating at all; following his disastrous interview with Alexander on 5 November, he was in no hurry to do so either. Hardenberg put off his visit for another couple of days.

Perhaps he had been waiting for some great festival, like Beethoven's concert, to divert the attention of Europe's leading diplomats while he conducted the delicate task of negotiating with Alexander. Beethoven was postponed. But on 23 November, the occasion arose; that Wednesday was the night of the great Carousel.

The manœuvring of the previous month had made foreign ministers – with the exception of deaf Hardenberg – more mindful of the French. Were they going to tilt the balance? Should the initial plan, as expressed in the Paris treaty, to exclude them be revised? In the diplomatic field, Talleyrand had won a few points. But every activity in Vienna was, that autumn and winter, steeped in meaning, including entertainment. Beethoven's concert would have been a strictly German affair. The Carousel – a spectacular series of horse trials – shifted attention to the French, even though it would be held in the Hofburg's Spanish Riding School.

Preparations for the event had been under way for months; old records and prints of the famous carousels held by Louis XIV were dug up; dress designs of Valois, Medici, and Papal Courts were studied; manuals on medieval chivalry were scanned for enticing motifs, useful hints, images, sounds, colours, and shadows that would excite a crowd of thousands. Twenty-four "paladins" were selected from noble families, who had served in the last war, to charge at suspended rings and Turks' heads, and to perform other impressive feats of horsemanship and gallantry before their twenty-four *"belles d'amour."* Among the latter was Dorothée, comtesse de Périgord, Talleyrand's niece: she had been very active in the preparations.[51]

There was a black market for tickets. The audience were seated by rank, the Sovereigns in a separate tribune, the galleries reserved on one side for the diplomats (Lady Castlereagh a landmark for England with the Order of the Garter once more tangled into her hair), the other side for Austrian, Hungarian, and Polish nobility. What was performed in that hall, the size of a cathedral, was an early nineteenth-century medieval pageant that would have been more familiar to the ear of Louis XIV than to that of a Romantic.

When the horse trials were over a supper was served in the neighbouring hall, which one approached through a corridor lined with orange trees and garlands of flowers. Minstrels strolled around the tables and when the meal was done a grand ball was held. It was all enough to forget the fate of the excellent King of Saxony and the fact that armies were, at that very moment, on the march.[52]

On their way to supper, Talleyrand had bumped into a very grim-faced Prussian Ambassador, Baron Wilhelm von Humboldt. "Does Your Excellency prefer horse-riding to statistics?" asked Talleyrand (hinting at the recent count-up of Saxon souls); everybody laughed except Humboldt. Metternich and Castlereagh were observed, at supper, having a serious conversation. But Hardenberg was nowhere to be seen: the Prince Chancellor was spending his evening at the bedside of the sick Russian Tsar.[53]

The interview went well. Hardenberg presented a moderate plan in which Austria and Prussia would agree to a Polish frontier along the Warta and Nida rivers; Austria would also be ready to accept a Polish constitution. All references to Saxony and to Prussia's other demands for German territory were, however, excluded; the implication was that the linkage between Poland and Saxony had been broken. Reports from Alexander's own envoys later in the week indicated that Alexander himself was quite relieved at the thought of dropping his earlier obligations to Prussia. At any rate, Alexander promised to give an answer within days and Hardenberg left the imperial apartments apparently feeling relieved, happy that his role as mediator still had a future. Alexander then called for Metternich, who left the Carousel for the encounter. Metternich also found Alexander conciliatory but did not discuss details for fear of undermining Hardenberg's mission; he reported back to Castlereagh, who was enjoying the ball, that the Tsar was now prepared to enter into "regular negotiation."[54]

That was not counting on his advisers. Stein, Czartoryski, and Humboldt were naturally furious at the implication that Russian support for the Prussian demands was being withdrawn.

Later that week, Stein drafted a declaration stating that the whole of Saxony would be annexed to Prussia, that Bavaria would be excluded from Mainz, and that the strategic Polish garrison towns of Thorn and Cracow would be neutralised as "free cities" under the aegis of the Allied Powers. Alexander, reminded of his promises and persuaded that Russia needed a strong Prussia united with Saxony, signed it. Hardenberg's mission was doomed.

He was shown the declaration on 27 November and the next day, a Monday, he went round to the Chancellery to break the news to Metternich. Hardenberg made as good a case he could, arguing that it would be impossible to expect more concessions from Russia. He still had to lay down the Russian response in writing, but Metternich was already aware that Hardenberg was demanding the impossible: Austrian cession of both Poland and Saxony.

It is incredible to what lengths Metternich was prepared to go to keep France excluded. He would rely on Bavaria and Denmark joining Austrian troops in a stand against the Prusso-Russian combination, but there was no question yet of appealing to France. He evidently felt that there was still room for a diplomatic manœuvre which would separate Russia from Prussia. "I have passed the most wearisome day and tomorow will be no lighter burden," he wrote on Monday night to Sagan (he was sending pleaful notes to her almost every day).

After his conversation with Hardenberg, Metternich had himself gone round to see Alexander, but the interview did not provide much ground for optimism. "I spent several hours this evening with Emperor Alexander," Metternich said in his letter to Sagan, emphasising once more the great role he played in the fate of the world. "Few, so few moments have decided such great questions. So much weighs down on my soul; I bear a huge burden like a wanderer in the desert. Not a handshake, not a generous look, not a word of sympathy will be shared with me. 1814 is truly an awful year."[55]

The next morning, Tuesday, 29 November, a meeting between Alexander and Kaiser Franz was arranged. Alexander told the Austrian Emperor that, where Saxony was concerned, he should consult the King of Prussia. That was no help, replied the Kaiser, because the King was getting all his advice from the agents of the Emperor of Russia.[56]

On Tuesday at noon – an hour when the breach between the Allies appeared inevitable – Beethoven at last gave his huge concert in the Redoutensaal.

Emperor Alexander attended with his Empress and the Grand Duchesses. So did the King of Prussia, although he walked out in the middle of the performance. The only other member of royalty present was the Crown Prince of Sicily.

But the hall was full and noisy. Public concerts in 1814 were not the polite affairs of a later age. On the floor there were no seats. Those who disapproved jeered, those who loved the music applauded, the indifferent continued their indifferent chatter, a mistake in the programme commanded laughter, while a piece that pleased demanded an immediate encore. The musicians were rarely prepared. At a concert like this anybody who could play a string, blow in a pipe, or sing a song expected to be invited to perform. "I and my orchestra naturally consented to take part," recollected the composer Louis Spohr on that Tuesday's performance "and *for the first time I saw Beethoven conduct.*" Many other illustrious musicians with their orchestras were invited along too. There is no actual record of how many actually took part in the concert but, judging from other occasions, it probably involved well over a hundred unprepared, unrehearsed musicians.[57]

Beethoven lunged towards the conductor's podium, his pockmarked face redder than usual, his hair bristling, his eyes intense. The concert began with the first spiralling chords of the Seventh Symphony. In the *forte* parts, Beethoven stretched to heaven; in the *piano* parts, he sank to his knees. He was a figure so small that many of the musicians could not see him. And he could not hear them. In the second part of the *Allegretto*, Beethoven overlooked the repetition of the *pianissimo* and jumped to his feet beating out another *forte* – while the musicians lingered in his measures of peace. Surreptitiously *Kappelmeister* Umlauf crept up behind Beethoven as he banged about and indicated to the assembled players that they should follow him, not the maestro. It could have been a disaster.

But that second movement, a haunting funeral march, so excited the audience that they kicked on the floor and screamed for a repetition. The players obliged. Every movement was followed by wild applause.

After the symphony, a chorale was performed, *Die glorreiche Augenblick*. "All that it [the text] really contains is the fact that there are now many Sovereigns in Vienna," recorded the bookseller Carl Bertuch in his diary, "but the music is excellent." This was followed by another grand orchestral piece, *Wellington's Victory at the Battle of Vitoria*, that included drums, the fanfare sound of "Rule Britannia," shots of cannon, roars of brass, and Beethoven's own peculiar version of "God Save the King."

At its end, the deaf composer from Bonn turned to face the applause, his applause. Awkward Castlereagh in the Minoritenplatz may not have heard it; but the sound was so forceful and divine that Wellington, the musician in Paris, could have stood up and clapped.[58]

Advent

It was Advent in Vienna. As Metternich explained in another un-answered letter to Sagan, there would be no more dancing done in Catholic houses; all the Catholics would have to go to the houses which did not pay allegiance to the Pope – the Stackelbergs, the Razumovskies, and the Bagrations. Alexander held, in the first week of December, a great "Muscovite festival" in honour of Grand Duchess Catherine's name day at Razumovsky's palace in the Landstrasse. His riding school was converted into a ballroom and the climax of the evening came when "this ravishing, beautiful" Catherine plucked a flower from her bosom and threw it to the feet of the Crown Prince of Württemberg; there was no doubt now for whom her pearly hand was intended. Though this was a serious setback for Austria, Gentz admitted the ball was "the most beautiful of all the festivites I have attended since the foreign Sovereigns arrived here."[59]

Generally, however, the Viennese were getting tired of the "fes-tivals, *fêtes* and *coucheries*"; they wanted to see more progress in the business of the Congress. The women, who were both the guides and gauge of opinion in Vienna, were complaining of the expenses involved. The feeling spread that the whole idea of an international gathering in the *Residenzstadt* had been a mistake: foreigners could spy on Austrian homes and Austrian government, while Austria's own defences remained weak. The Empress herself complained that "the Congress has cost me ten years of my life" (she, in fact, died one year later). Vienna wanted to close her gates.[60]

Political opinion filtered down through the ranks. This was one of the lasting effects of the Congress. People who had never had a political opinion – the same people whose frivolous indifference had so annoyed visitors like Madame de Staël or Countess Bernstorff – started to have one.

One finds this development in the diary of Franz Perth, the civil servant. No longer did he describe the daily foreign arrivals, the receptions, nor the stories of personalities and Sovereigns. On 1 December, Perth took note of a "generally spread rumour": "Prussia wants to seize Saxony for herself." It was the first time he had noticed it and he was outraged. "Shouldn't Prussia be shown as false to the world if she persists in this demand?" he wondered. The Allied Sovereigns had "promised Europe that they had no intention of engaging in any old or new expansionist projects." Perth placed his faith in God, justice, and Austria. "Our Court," he had no doubt, "will press with might and ensure that the old [Saxon] King's family is returned to its throne in accordance to the will and hope of all Saxony."[61]

Metternich's offensive

Hardenberg now had to make sure it would not. But once more he delayed. He only sent his formal written report on his negotiations with the Tsar to the Austrian Chancellery on Friday, 2 December. It was worse than what he had told Metternich in their conversation the previous Monday: Prussia would keep the whole of Saxony, Mainz and Luxemburg were to be occupied by Austrian and Prussian troops (the Bavarians could join in if they wanted to), and the King of Saxony would be transferred to the tiny Rhineland territory of Münster and Paderborn. The whole plan, the report pretended, was based on Britain and Austria's consent given in October.

The two men actually had a meeting that Friday evening, both of them sniffling with colds. Poor Hardenberg was so pained by the encounter that, the next day, he sent Metternich a poem, one of his own compositions ending with the line, "There blooms but one Reich so mighty and so fair."[62]

The old Reich, in fact, was now hopelessly divided. With the failure of Hardenberg's mission, Castlereagh began to play a more active role again, less this time as a mediator than as an Austrian ally in the creation of an entirely new European combination.

The following Tuesday, Castlereagh paid a visit to Hardenberg and showed him the letter he had received from Liverpool in November expressing Britain's "strong feeling" over Saxony and the need to preserve a "*noyau*" of the Kingdom. The situation had changed, he explained, "the concert on the affairs of Poland, which was the basis of [our previous] understanding, had avowedly failed"; all earlier promises on Saxony should therefore be considered null and void. Later in the day Castlereagh told Metternich that he had "prepared Prussia for a negative from Austria."

Castlereagh was taking an aggressive new view of the situation. The day before he had written two dispatches to Liverpool warning him of "actual or impending war" and, particularly, of the apparent willingness of Russia and Prussia to provoke it. Such a war, he said, would quickly become "general in Germany." Castlereagh recommended that Britain step in as "armed mediators" for she could hardly avoid involvement. Moreover, she should operate "in conjunction with France."

"Armed mediation" was hardly the word for peace; the phrase had been used, famously, by Metternich when going to war in 1813.[63]

With Castlereagh covering him and France standing ready on the side, Metternich launched his own diplomatic offensive on Saturday, 10 December, in the name of "Germany" and of "Europe." A vast propaganda campaign was orchestrated with the aim of isolating Prussia. The most important issue Europe faced at Vienna, he said in a memorandum dispatched to Hardenberg that evening, had been the question of Poland. But this was no longer the case. Because Hardenberg's mediation had failed, Austria had decided to enter into direct negotiations with Russia and the whole problem had suddenly been "reduced to a simple assessment of a few frontier points" – or, as Gentz put it privately, Poland "was tacitly regarded as lost." With the Polish question thus "solved," Saxony had become the pivotal issue for all Europe.

Metternich did admit that previous treaties guaranteed Prussia compensation for all territories lost since 1805, but that did not demand the destruction of the Kingdom of Saxony; Prussia could be compensated elsewhere. He enclosed a statistical table of "souls" to prove it. The table showed that Prussia could be compensated through concessions from Russia, various territories in western Germany, and *only one fifth of Saxony*, or 432,000 Saxon souls.[64]

"Betrayal! Treachery!" cried Hardenberg. Never had Metternich expressed an interest in maintaining more than a *noyau* of the Saxon Kingdom; now he was demanding almost full restitution. Either out of exasperation or some misled idea to draw Russia closer to the Prussian cause, Hardenberg decided on the spot to show all his correspondence with Metternich to the Tsar. "A very incorrect act," commented Castlereagh.

Alexander flew into another of his imperial rages. On 13 December, he had an audience with Metternich – another "stormy interview" according to Castlereagh – which ended with Metternich striding out of the imperial apartments all in a flush; the two men would not again address a word to each other for months.

A calmer encounter between the two Emperors took place the next day. But Hardenberg continued to insist that the whole of Saxony be incorporated into Prussia and that King Frederick Augustus be transported to the west bank of the Rhine. What Hardenberg failed to understand was that, since he had not even managed to establish the River Warta as Prussia's own frontier with Russian Poland, Saxony had become the main defence line for not only Austria but the entire west.[65]

Prussian intransigence played into Austrian hands. "All the Prussians I know," reported one of Hager's agents working in the confidence of Crown Prince William, "no longer doubt that war shall be declared." And the Prussians were sure that they could win it: they were convinced Russia would stand solidly behind them; they did not doubt the support of the smaller German states because they, the Prussians, were the ones proposing a liberal federal German constitution; and with the nationalistic league, the *Tugendbund*, active in Saxony, they thought even the Saxon people would rise in their favour. It would be – they sincerely believed – "a struggle between democracy and aristocracy."

But, unlike in 1813, there would be no British subsidies. And what attraction could there possibly be in the centralised plans Prussia had for "Germany" even if, on paper, they were liberal? In the propaganda war that developed over the next few weeks, Austria won hands down. "In 1813, Prussia raised the flag of German nationalism so as to gain support," one old baron explained to **; "in 1814, they demonstrated on every side the nature of Prussian greed." "Prussia is a traitor to the interests of Europe and to the interests of equilibrium in Europe," said another; "against Prussia and against Russia the tocsin of Europe and of Germany must be sounded."[66]

After publicly censuring Prussia and having, for a second time in less than two months, been humiliated in front of the Tsar, Metternich, on 16 December, paid a visit to the Kaunitz Palace. The French reports would lead one to believe that Talleyrand was standing at the door waiting for him. Metternich's popularity in Vienna suddenly soared, for he seemed to have restored the old eighteenth-century combination of power, the formula of his grandfather-in-law, Count Kaunitz: an opposition to Prussia in collaboration with France.[67]

Once this new alignment had been confirmed, Talleyrand published, on 19 December, a note that he formally addressed to Metternich. In it, he outlined his vision of "Europe" and "Germany." Even historians partial to Metternich admit that it was the most eloquent document to emerge from the Congress of Vienna.[68]

The first striking thing about it was its use of metaphor, its allusion to the tides. France had returned, claimed Talleyrand, to her "ancient limits" like "the sea that bursts beyond its beaches only when storms are stirring"; she had rediscovered calm in her legitimate princes. Without accepting such an "order of things," no state could feel secure in the future. The spirit of revolution must cease everywhere and forever so that legitimacy be re-established, the "public law of Europe" be recognised, and a "civil society," rooted in custom, be encouraged to flourish. Without that, the nations of Europe would lose the moral tie between them; they would be like the "islands of the South Seas," linked only by the water and the tides – and thus reduced to the wild laws of nature. Water and earth: Talleyrand was asking Europe that she stop the flood, withstand the storms, by digging into her ancient soils.[69]

Upon such a base could be built a second principle – one dear to Castlereagh and Metternich – that had been defined in the Treaty of Paris as the "real and permanent balance of power in Europe."

Both principles (the "legitimacy" of the Powers and the "equilibrium" of Europe) could be undermined by what was happening in Saxony. The Prussian annexation of this Kingdom could set legal precedents for an ugly nineteenth century: that Kings could be judged by those who wanted to seize their territories; that their condemnation would include their families and their peoples; that the robbery of a Kingdom was in some way more acceptable than the theft of a simple cottage; that people could be shifted like beasts on a farm. It was Talleyrand's peculiar way of combining his two principles – neither of which were, when considered separately, of any great originality – that explained why he was the only diplomat in Vienna to speak out against the counting of "souls," why he alone refused to reduce the notion of "equilibrium" to a simple arithmetical calculation. Equilibrium had to be based on moral force, on justice, and on economics; the embezzling old French Minister had a unique interest in what the soils produced.

Castlereagh found himself drawn into the propaganda war even if in private he would still go on about the Kingdom of Saxony not being "paramount to the interests of Europe." The problem was, as he had commented to Hardenberg, that "sentiment" in Germany and in Great Britain would no longer support annexation.[70]

It was Metternich who had invited Castlereagh to step up his diplomatic activity again and join the Austrian effort to win European approval. It was Castlereagh's close association with Metternich that allowed France to enter the newly developing combination of Powers. Once more, Castlereagh was acting sublimely independent of his government in London. Liverpool couldn't trust Metternich whose whole policy, he said, consisted "in *finesse* and trick"; he ruled out an alliance with France because it would be so unpopular in both countries; and a war was still going on in America so "it would be quite impossible to embark this country in a war at present." Castlereagh, on the other hand, was perfectly aware that his new policy could very well lead Britain into war, though he would do everything in his power to prevent it.[71]

As for Russia's role, nothing much could be expected from "direct negotiations"; their principal purpose, from the Austrian point of view, was to render Hardenberg's services meaningless and thus break the link between the Polish question and the Saxon question. Alexander, probably worrying about the development of a Franco-Austrian alliance, underwent another of his shifts in mood and became most conciliatory. In a series of audiences with Kaiser Franz, he offered the region of Tarnopol along with the salt mine of Wiélitchka. But these were consolation prizes. Alexander refused to talk to Metternich and the Tsar's advisers had not changed. Stein, in particular, was still emphasising the pernicious effect a partition of Saxony would have.[72]

Hardenberg himself went on insisting on the promises both Castlereagh and Metternich had made back in October. But, two days after Talleyrand had published his important note, Hardenberg did approach Castlereagh and ask him to act as a mediator. Castlereagh warned Hardenberg that there would be no question of removing the King of Saxony to the left bank of the Rhine. There followed more calculation and counter-calculation of "souls." Finally Castlereagh recommended the creation of a Statistical Committee. It sat for the first time on Christmas Eve, 1814. The capital fact was that France had a seat on it.[73]

A Christmas crisis

A curious object attracted the attention of Agent ✳✳, who had somehow got himself invited to the Prussian festivities that night. In the middle of the main hall stood a fir tree decorated with presents and souvenirs that were distributed to the guests in the course of the evening. The Prussians called it, "according to a Berlin custom," a *"Weihbaum"* or a *"Christbaum"* – a "Christmas tree." Quite obviously ✳✳, though knowledgeable of the languages and traditions of Central Europe, had never seen anything like it before.

It was odd that the tree should first be seen in Vienna at the home of a Jewish banker, Nathan Baron von Arnstein. The guests, principally Prussians, gathered around the tree and comic songs were sung; Frau von Münch bellowed out the musical poetry of Kasperle; Prince von Hardenberg was overcome by fits of laughter. Then the presents were handed out; the guests formed a queue, which stretched through every room in the house, and the colourful packets were passed along it.[74]

Baron von Humboldt was notably absent. He was at that moment agonising over gifts of a larger nature; he had been excluded from the negotiations that had led to the creation of the Statistical Committee and he was very angry. Baron vom Stein – who usually attended Prussian events – was not present either. He was spending his Christmas with Grand Duchess Catherine, for whom, being Russian,

Christmas was not Christmas at all.

The Italians, like the English, celebrated Christmas on Christmas Day. A dinner was given by the prelates of Rome for representatives of the northern states. There was much discussion at the table about the recent arrests, on Austrian orders, of three nationalists in Milan. It was a great mistake, said one of the ladies (it was the ladies who dominated the conversation). "Listen to me, my dear Countess," hailed the Countess of Bellegarde to the Countess of Crennevilla, "they're sending off Germans, and recently Hungarians, to govern Italians." Now, Napoleon would never have done that; though he had ruled with an iron hand, the French Emperor had assured that all his functionaries in Italy would be Italian. The Austrians were inviting trouble.[75]

On the Minoritenplatz, Christmas was celebrated with a supper event. Castlereagh had spent most of the day writing dispatches, although he was – as he always would be at Christmas – in a cheerful mood. He told Liverpool that he was highly pleased with the way negotiations had recently developed and felt that an "amicable arrangement" was probably within days of settlement. He was happy Humboldt had been excluded and that the French were at last playing an active and constructive role.

A large number of people gathered in Britain's palace that evening. Stratford-Canning had arrived from Switzerland; the two Bernstorffs were there, as was Cardinal Consalvi from Rome, along with many of his Italian colleagues.

The prize for beauty went to Prince Eugène de Beauharnais, Napoleon's stepson, whose "sense, knowledge, and youthful qualities" won him the hearts of the princes, ministers, and the women. The prize for ridicule went to the Crown Prince of Bavaria; he outdid both Lady Castlereagh and the British Ambassador that Christmas night by insisting on speaking in Greek which, he assured the company, was his fourth language, after German, Italian, and English.[76]

What were the Russians up to? Castlereagh had been happy to announce, in his Christmas dispatch to Liverpool, that Count Razumovsky was taking over negotiations from Nesselrode. Castlereagh took this as a signal that the talks between the Austrian and Russian Emperors had had a positive effect.

Count Razumovsky was known in Vienna as the "King of the suburbs" because of the huge palace he owned in the Landstrasse. He was a great patron of painting, books, horses, and music; he established, with life-long contracts, a famous string quartet that performed some of Beethoven's grandest and most revolutionary works. He was an extravagant entertainer, he was a proud man with a proud demeanour – some said even haughty – and in politics he was utterly unpredictable.

On the day after Christmas, Metternich invited him to start direct negotiations with Austria on Poland. The Count promptly responded that the questions of Poland and Saxony could not be separated; it was exactly the opposite of what Metternich intended.

Metternich had no alternative but to call on France. This he did through Castlereagh's mediation. Castlereagh met with both Razumovsky and Hardenberg to propose that France be introduced into into the Allies' Committee of Four; they refused, but said they would be willing to discuss the matter at the next Four Power conference.[77]

In the meantime a Prussian army was mobilised in Saxony; there were rumours that Dresden was being fortified. The Dutch were complaining that Prussian activities in the Rhineland had become a threat to peace in Belgium. The propaganda war for Germany was stepped up. Within the Prussian delegation itself, a vicious power struggle developed between Humboldt, who was dogmatic about Saxony, and Hardenberg, more ready to compromise. Once more, the women were pulled into combat: Stein worked on the Grand Duchess Catherine, while Humboldt sought Russian assistance through Princess Bagration. The line of battle over Saxony, in fact, ran straight down the middle of the Palm Palace courtyard, for Sagan had joined her sisters in the "French party."[78]

Even Lord Castlereagh had lost the Christmas spirit by the time the Four Powers convened in the Chancellery on Thursday, 29 December.

Metternich asked Razumovsky to open the proceedings, which he did with a statement that made Alexander sound like the Tsar of Europe. Then Hardenberg presented a plan to remove the Saxon King to a castle in Luxemburg; he pointedly added that it would be futile to offer France a seat on the Committee of Four. Metternich countered by demanding France's inclusion – a complete reversal of his policy in September.

The next day the Four sat round their green table once again. As on Thursday, Count Razumovsky opened the proceedings. He startled both the British and Austrians by linking Russia's threadbare offers on Poland to all the Prussian demands made during the previous session – thus proving that Russia intended to support Prussia on Saxony. Count Razumovsky said he had a vision of Europe, one of "Sovereigns united in brotherhood" and a "Christian religion common to all."

Castlereagh promptly demanded that Talleyrand be offered a seat, not out of any sacred principle but for the sake of equilibrium. Metternich seconded him, adding that not only France should be consulted on Saxony but also the King of Saxony himself.

Hardenberg dropped his ear trumpet and started banging on the

Count Rasumovsky's Palace in the Landstrasse had become a cultural centre
for music, painting and rare books

table. He would rather see the Congress break up than grant the King
such a right, he bawled out. And, if the expenses of occupation
demanded permanent annexation, then Russia and Prussia together
would regard its refusal by the other Powers as "tantamount to a declaration of war."

Tempers eventually calmed. But Castlereagh, for one, left fully
impressed that Prussia was preparing "some bold and desperate
coup."[79]

Like many ordinary residents of Vienna – unaware of diplomatic
brawls and green tables – Franz Perth had been getting bored in these
last few weeks of December. He was looking forward to the opening
of Carnival season on 1 January. At six o'clock in the morning,
Saturday, 31 December, he was dozing in his bed when the bells of St
Stephan's started ringing out. Prelude to the festival? He turned over
and snored. "Fire! fire!" came a distant cry; there was a patter of feet
on the street below. Perth sat up. "Fire! fire!" rose a louder clamour
of voices. "It's burning on the Landstrasse!" Perth quickly got
dressed and rushed to the walls near the Stubenthor that overlooked
the southern suburb.

A crowd had already gathered to watch as, in the first light of dawn,
flames shot out of Count Razumovsky's palace. It seemed to be
exploding at every corner.

The few thin hoses and hand-driven pumps disposable to the city's fire squads were in action. Civilians formed into lines to hand along useless little buckets and pots of water; five to six thousand troops were brought in to combat the flames. At 9.30 they seemed to be partially doused, but half an hour later they exploded again and spread to a neighbouring slaughterhouse.

There was a rumour that the fire had started in the stables, in a bakery, in the kitchens. Surely, argued others, if it had broken out in so many places at once it must have been a criminal act. The truth was known the next day, 1 January 1815. It was the heating system or, as Perth emphasised in his diary, the *French* heating system.

Kaiser Franz had come out in the early morning to give courage to the firefighters. Emperor Alexander was seen standing in a stare for several hours. Not only was a Russian treasure lost. A library was gone, paintings were gone; part of Europe's heritage disappeared on the last day of 1814. The Russians were in a subdued mood when they met with the Prussians to discuss their common plan.[80]

Gift-giving

Carnival, which stretched from New Year's Day to Mardi Gras, was the most important festival season in Catholic Vienna. People would come in from the countryside to participate. Pretty calendars and coloured notebooks, filled with poems and old sayings, would be published months in advance so that one could plan on what events to attend. Carnival would set dress styles for the year. The simple lines and narrow forms, inspired from antiquity, were gone. 1815 would be the year of the "old German" mode of puffed out sleeves and floating robes; bright scarves and draperies added buoyancy to volume; huge round hats, decorated in lace and feathers, could save a delicate young face from being totally overwhelmed by the dress which lay beneath it.[81]

Carnival always opened with the gala of 1 January, when a great masked ball would be held in the Redoutensal. The custom in Vienna was to give gifts on New Year's Eve and, on New Year's Day, to pay visits to friends and acquaintances. Gentz, for example, was very busy on 1 January 1815. After first receiving the compliments of his house servants, he paid a visit to Prince and Princess Metternich, then a visit to the King of Denmark (where he met Talleyrand and Madame Dorothée de Périgord), a visit to Baron von Wessenberg (the Austrian plenipotentiary), and a dinner with the Duchess von Sagan and her sisters; Windischgrätz was there, as was most of the French Delegation. Gentz was in high form. "The end of this last year was brilliant," he wrote in his diary. According to his calculations he had earned in the course of the year seventeen thousand golden ducats or the equivalent of about seventy-seven thousand guilders. On top of this, he received a nice little New Year's gift from Talleyrand: twenty-four thousand guilders "on behalf of the King of France." Henceforth Gentz was French to the core.[82]

His master, Metternich, was not as cheerful, and certainly not as French. He spent his New Year's Eve alone, overcome by waves of melancholy. But he had one gift to give, a fabulous "Gothic" bracelet with diamonds, emeralds, and amethysts. The clock was approaching midnight as he scribbled a note in German to Sagan.

He described again his wandering "destiny" and his suffering; "all my claims to love are, with the year that leaves us, gone to the grave." He made an elaborate analysis of the symbolism behind each of the precious stones in the bracelet (the emerald was his birth stone – "it would have been just as well if I had never been born"). Yet the Prince felt generous enough to give Sagan the traditional New Year salute – *"Gott gebe Gnade, Glück, Gedeihen!"* ["May God grant you favour, happiness, and prosperity!"] – and wished that 1815 would be for her the first in a long series of happy, tranquil years. "And now good night," he signed off, "and sleep better than I will ever be able to."[83]

Sagan was not sleeping that night. She saw the New Year in at the Palm Palace with her sisters Dorothée and Jeanne, with some of the younger members of the French delegation, Friedrich Gentz, and her lover, Windischgrätz. As a matter of fact, Gentz spent more time, over the next week, with Sagan and Uncle Talleyrand than he did with Metternich; he had, it seems, declared himself for Sagan's side, the Courland side, the French side.[84]

Sagan had actually written to Metternich on New Year's Eve, though it was not, from what one gathers from Metternich's reply, a very polite note. "I put this letter aside for the first days of the year," he answered on 3 January, "with the intention of not starting the year off with this grief on top of the others."

Did she return the bracelet? Metternich's correspondence indicates that he was selling jewelry on behalf of Sagan at the end of March. So, not only was he being "thrown away"; Sagan had actually managed to badger him into helping in the process.[85]

Castlereagh also received a New Year's gift, the greatest gift of them all: peace. On the first morning of 1815, news was received in Vienna that the negotiators in Ghent had signed a peace treaty with the United States.

"It is difficult to describe to your Lordship the impression produced here by our pacification with America," Castlereagh reported to Liverpool. Difficult indeed. But France understood, Austria understood, Prussia understood, and Russia understood that Castlereagh's hands were now freed for a new military engagement.[86]

1815: a new year, a new treaty

On 1 January 1815, Castlereagh submitted to the French and Austrian plenipotentiaries the draft for a Treaty of Defensive Alliance. Its signatories pledged mutual assistance in case any one of them came under attack – but only an attack, Castlereagh insisted, resulting from their joint efforts to enforce and complete the Treaty of Paris.

The treaty was designed as an answer to Hardenberg's threat of war made two days earlier. But, in a profounder way, it undermined the alliance Castlereagh had worked so hard to create one year before by making Britain, Austria, and France the guarantors of the Treaty of Paris. "Without some such bond," Castlereagh explained to Liverpool, "I feel that our deliberations here are at an end." Castlereagh's centre of equilibrium had shifted.[87]

The close association between Britain and Austria was what had made France's entry into Europe's club of Powers possible. Prussia's threat and Russia's reticence demanded it. But it is difficult to imagine that someone with Talleyrand's immense mercenary talents remained idle. "Prince Talleyrand's conduct throughout all our late transactions," said Castlereagh, "has done the utmost honour to his Court" – at a cost of twenty-four thousand guilders to his court, if not more.

What was the purpose behind bribing Gentz? Metternich's secretary was wined and dined by Talleyrand and his allies in the Palm Palace every night during this week most critical to France. How odd it also was that, during the days of the most bitter exchanges between Sagan and Metternich, Talleyrand had always been there, standing on the side-lines. He had attended Sagan's dinner of 12 October, he had offered his own dinner on 19 October and, at the New Year's festivities in the Palm Palace, he was one of the centres of attraction in the Palm Palace. Talleyrand's presence was never innocent; Napoleon had appreciated that in the last years of the war, as had his niece Dorothée when she spoke of her uncle's "bold temperament, an instinctive type of defiance, which rendered danger so seductive." Talleyrand had been isolating Metternich by "putting the women to work."

The "secret" treaty between Britain, France, and Austria – which everybody was talking about within twenty-four hours – was signed on Tuesday, 3 January, just before the Four sat down for another formal conference in the Chancellery.

The mood at the conference was quite different from that of the previous Friday. Razumovsky was most obliging after Metternich requested a few minor changes to the Count's project on Poland. That meant the Polish question was settled. There were some topics, Metternich then pointed out, which required the presence of France.

Hardenberg and Razumovsky reluctantly agreed, but Hardenberg made one last desperate effort to have the Saxon question discussed before France took her seat. It didn't work. Razumovsky backed down, probably on the instructions from the Tsar, who had received hints of the new Triple Alliance from Castlereagh himself. Razumovsky, in front of Metternich and Castlereagh, told Hardenberg he would have to be satisfied with "a part of Saxony." Which part had still not been defined when France was formally admitted, on 9 January, to their councils and the Four became Five.

By then the crisis had passed. "The alarm of war is over," Castlereagh told Liverpool on the 5th. "Sire, the coalition is dissolved," Talleyrand triumphantly announced to his King, "and France is no longer isolated from Europe." What were the causes of this happy event? The principal ones on Talleyrand's list, "after God," were "my letters to M. de Metternich and to Lord Castlereagh and the impression that they made . . .." "I have never been stronger, more careful, more reasonable than in this affair," he wrote to the duchesse de Courlande[88]

The news that Prussia had renounced Saxony spread well beyond the salons and palaces. "General rumour has it that the Congress will now, after much discord, take a turn for the better," Perth recorded on the 7th. Perth's hero was Talleyrand, who "notified the Prussian cabinet" that "France was ready to defend Saxony with the sword, in alliance with Austria, Germany [*sic*], and England against Prussia and also against Russia" – so much for the "secrecy" of the Triple Alliance. As for Bourbon France, she had never looked stronger to the ordinary man in Vienna than during that January of 1815.[89]

Castlereagh's departure

That same month, the minor branches of the Danube froze over and the Wien was transformed into a popular skating rink. The Graben became the main meeting point for crowds still drawn to the open air now that the cold had closed the alleys of the Prater; some described the Graben as an outdoors club where people would receive and pay visits like in a regular *salon*. The Kaiser's Festivals Committee laid on sixteen grand fêtes, a great sleigh-riding party, and a pheasant shoot for the Illustrious Sovereigns. Zacharias Werner, a northern German poet who had converted to Catholicism and had become a priest, provided entertainment for the bored. He preached in the same way Beethoven conducted, reaching to the roof and sinking to his knees. The freezing churches were crammed solid whenever Father Werner spoke. "My Graceful and – well – perhaps Not-so-graceful Ladies," he might begin (Werner disapproved of their morals), "you really believe that our Kings and the nobles have established peace?" he pounded out from his pulpit; "*Dummheiten!* (What silliness!) Amen!" Werner did not have much faith in the Peace.[90]

Yet no one now talked of armies marching, no one whispered of war. And a peace of sorts settled on the Palm Palace where, Hager's agents began to report, there were signs of conciliation. The Russian wing invited members of the French wing to participate in their plays. Vienna's best "living pictures" (elaborate forms of mime) were displayed in Princess Bagration's apartments: the Princess was praised for her role as a virgin; Sagan and Madame de Périgord were praised for their beauty.

When Lent eventually arrived, the feasting went on. "Dorothée's fête, the Duchess von Sagan's fête, Wellington's arrival, the end of the Saxon affair: all this means dining, and no ending of dining in Vienna," Talleyrand wrote to the duchesse de Courlande on Ash Wednesday.

That day was, in fact, Sagan's birthday. She spent it in the company of her uncle and her sister. She received some porcelain and another sorrowful letter from Metternich. "This life is finished," he whined; "believe me, take all that you want; I am no longer good for anything." It was a matter of total indifference to Sagan. With Lent, she took on a new lease of life and found another lover – somebody with a different temperament, the man they called "Lord Pumpernickel" or "the Golden Pheasant" (his high leather boots were bright yellow): His Excellency the Ambassador, Lord Castlereagh's rude brother, Sir Charles Stewart.[91]

The resolution of the Saxon crisis had made the British popular in Vienna. They were seen as friends of Austria. Castlereagh wanted to set that link within a durable framework. So, despite urgings from his colleagues in London to return and help fend off the opposition, he decided to stay on until the "territorial settlement of Europe" was tied up. As he put it to Bathurst, "You might as well expect me to have run away from Leipzig (if I had been there) last year to fight Creevey and Whitbread, as to withdraw from hence till the existing contest is brought to a point."

It was brought to a point in Lent. On 11 February, a final agreement on Poland was reached. Prussia kept the province of Posen, Austria the province of Galicia; the remainder would form a constitutional "Kingdom of Poland" under the Tsar of Russia. Prussia, thanks to Castlereagh's intervention, came off better than she deserved; she obtained the northern two-fifths of Saxony, several fortresses on the Elbe, Swedish Pomerania, the Duchy of Westphalia, and a large portion of the left bank of the Rhine. Austria was assured compensation in northern Italy, along with the Illyrian provinces on the Adriatic. Thus Castlereagh, while he had lost on Poland, did manage to re-establish a European equilibrium. Its key was a division

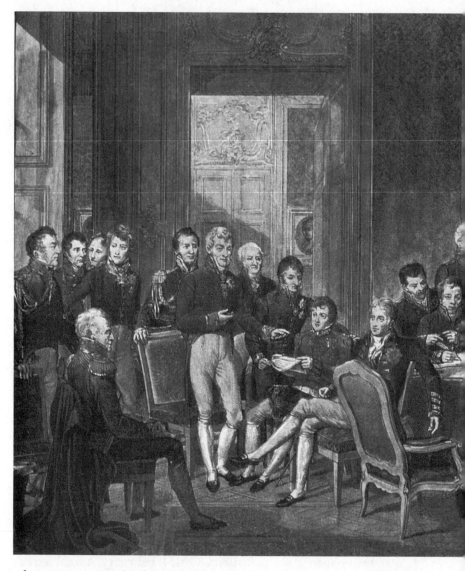

of Germany; its chief feature was a great, though as yet disjointed, Prussian arc stretching across the northern plains into the hills of the Rhineland.[92]

The Duke of Wellington arrived from Paris on 1 February with the famous opera singer Giuseppina Grassini in his calèche. Princess Bagration prepared the same elaborate reception for the Iron Duke as she had for the Tsar on his arrival in September. The ladies once more gathered in the great marquee, where no man was permitted to enter until the Duke had been presented like a Sovereign. "Is it true," wondered Countess Bernstorff some time after the event, "that when the

A print of Jean-Baptiste Isabey's
official portrait of the Congress of
Vienna. Isabey chose the occasion
of the Duke of Wellington's
introduction to the Congress as his
theme. Wellington, in profile, stands
at the extreme left. Hardenberg is
seen seated, isolated, to the left.
Metternich stands. Castlereagh is
seated in the centre, with his legs
crossed. Talleyrand sits to the right
of the table, ignoring the articulating
Russian plenipotentiary,
Count Stackelberg

women thronged around him for presentation each were offered a
kiss by him?" It seems most unlike the Duke of Wellington. Countess
Bernstorff and the Prussians, at any rate, boycotted the reception;
they were still bitter over the arrangement in Saxony and blamed the
British, particularly Wellington, for the alliance that had been made
with France. "The Prussians," reported Nota, "do not appear to be
the partisans of Wellington."[93]

Two weeks later, Castlereagh left Vienna. What was on his mind
when his carriages at last returned down the snow-swept roads of
Sankt Pölten, Braunau, and Altötting?

Europe looked different now. He realised that no simple mechanical device would hold together the German centre but he was as aware, as ever, that the break up of that centre meant war, a European-wide war that would touch on Britain's vital interests in the Low Countries. He had left Russia more powerful than he had wanted, Germany more divided. But he could be proud that a settlement had been achieved on a more realistic assessment of the Powers in the region than ever he or his colleagues in London had imagined. And a European war had been avoided.

The weakest point in his system was in Italy. The problem of Murat had not been resolved. The old Republic of Genoa was to be ruthlessly incorporated into the Kingdom of Piedmont. Nationalist aspirations were flouted. Because of the crisis in Germany, Castlereagh had ignored Italy. Metternich had refused to create an Italian Committee on the grounds that "there is no Italian problem." Castlereagh simply followed Metternich, regarding Italy as a region for territorial compensation for Austria. Undoubtedly he was wrong and his mistake sowed the seeds of later troubles. But it was better to make the mistake in Italy than in Germany; a war in Italy could be contained.

The concept of a Congress had also changed. The idea of a great European parliamentary assembly had been abandoned. When Castlereagh left Vienna, the Congress had become a club of the Great Powers.

How strong was Britain's commitment to this club? Lord Castlereagh wanted it to be total. Yet he might have taken as an ill omen that, on his return, he found London to be in a state of riot, not over Poland, not over Saxony, not over any of the issues that had engrossed him, but over his government's bill to restict the importation of corn. England was still an island and had not yet developed an interest in the arcane politics of Europe.

Whither Bonaparte?

The work of the Congress was far from over. Several problems, such as the future of Swiss Confederation, the rights of the Jews, the disposal of the Dutch colonies, and navigation on the Rhine and the Danube, had hardly been touched on. Castlereagh had got the major Powers to agree to a general condemnation of the slave trade, but how this was to be executed was another matter altogether. The committees took over, the experts moved in.

As for the territorial settlement in Germany, it was not a brilliant success for Metternich, and he was much criticised at the time for accepting it; Saxony was too small to act as an effective ally and the new "Kingdom of Poland," even if Austria had managed to retain the province of Galicia, could become a centre for dangerous nationalist enthusiasms. Austria would have to establish her strength in the institutional organisation of Germany and it was on this issue, temporarily set aside in November, that Metternich now concentrated most of his attention. The membership of a new German Committee was expanded. Prussia came up with a novel scheme which, typically, mixed constitutional rights for every state with a centralised judiciary and a bicameral legislature. Metternich responded, typically, by appealing to the smaller states and proposing a system of countervailing powers that would effectively deprive the central institutions of authority. As before, the arguments involved became immensely complicated and the Committee's sessions often lasted until the early hours of the morning.

By 6 March, the work of the diplomats had made so much progress that the Committee of Five (the Four plus France) decided to hold a meeting to discuss the question of whether to draft a single comprehensive treaty covering all the separate agreements made in Vienna over the preceding months. The meeting was held in the Chancellery and went on until about three in the morning. By that time, the concept of a comprehensive treaty had been accepted: so the moment of a great European-wide peace settlement, recognised and signed by the major Powers involved, was at last approaching.[94]

Metternich, exhausted, retired to his chamber and ordered his valet not to awake him, whatever courier arrived while he slept. But at six o'clock the valet banged at his door and delivered the Minister a dispatch marked "Urgent." Metternich noticed from the envelope that it came from the Imperial Consulate General in Genoa. He had hardly been in bed two hours, so he put it on his side table and tried to sleep. But he couldn't. He kept staring at the great envelope from Genoa marked "Urgent."

Unable to resist it any more, at 7.30 he decided to open it. "The British Commissioner Campbell," read the short note enclosed, "has just sailed into harbour to ask if anyone had sighted Napoleon at Genoa since he has disappeared from the Isle of Elba. Because the response was negative the British frigate has, without delay, set sail once more."

Metternich was out of his bed like a shot: Bonaparte was on the loose.[95]

ELBA and PARIS
Winter 1814-1815

A GRAND Manœuvre! or. The Rogues march to the Island of Elba —

Napoleon's choice

When Napoleon, the previous May, formally notified General Dalesme, the Governor of Elba, that he was about to set foot on the island he emphasised three important things: first, that Elba had been his own choice ("I have sacrificed my rights for the interests of the *Patrie* and have reserved for myself the sovereignty of the Isle of Elba"); second, that the choice had been approved by "all the Allied Powers;" and third, that the inhabitants should be immediately informed that his choice had been made "in consideration of the gentleness of their customs and their climate." As was often the case with Napoleon, each of these three statements contained a grain of truth and a bushel of distortion.[1]

History itself has implicitly endorsed Napoleon's claim that he chose his residence by calling the treaty that granted him Elba the "Treaty of Fontainebleau." The Château of Fontainebleau was where Napoleon had set up temporary quarters following his military defeat. But the treaty was not signed in Fontainebleau, it was signed on 12 April 1814 (backdated 11 April) in Talleyrand's home in Paris. And it was not called the "Treaty of Fontainebleau", it was referred to at the time as the "Treaty of Abdication."

Napoleon's plenipotentiaries who were present at the signing certainly did not have the impression that they had much choice in the matter. Armand de Caulaincourt, at the head of the team, described in his memoirs the total sense of despair they felt; his account puts one in mind of sentiments expressed by a German delegation at Versailles a century later. "We were no longer plenipotentiaries," Caulaincourt complained; "our role was limited to what force imposed on us." In a letter he sent to Napoleon at the time he reported that they were "handed over to the mercy of your enemies." No choice there. The treaty's articles were read aloud to Napoleon's representatives and then signed. "One would have to go to one's own execution to have an exact idea of what it was like," said Caulaincourt; *"quelle journée!"* But Caulaincourt's team differed from the German delegation at Versailles in an important way: they represented a fallen Emperor and not a people. That was the great strength of monarchy; you could blame all the misfortunes of Europe on a Sovereign.[2]

The peacemaking of 1814-15 was built on pretences like this. And Napoleon knew how to take advantage of them. The language of peace was ambiguous, complex; it provided room for different interpretations; it allowed Napoleon to talk of "choice."

It was actually Emperor Alexander who chose the Isle of Elba for Napoleon. He had plenty of reasons to do so. On Elba Napoleon provided a useful threat to Austria, holding down her troops and thus giving Alexander more freedom for manœuvre in Poland. Besides, Alexander did not want to banish Napoleon to some far-flung colony; he still had an uncanny attraction for this fallen emperor. "I am more his friend than he thinks," he told Caulaincourt only three days after entering Paris. Alexander even wept when he informed Caulaincourt that Talleyrand's Provisional Government in Paris was going to opt for a Bourbon restoration. In place of France, he offered Elba and guaranteed Napoleon full sovereignty on it.[3]

Castlereagh and Metternich were not in Paris at the time. They had been keeping a low profile in Dijon because they did not want to give the impression that the Allies were imposing a new regime on conquered France; they considered it vital that the Bourbon restoration be seen as the nation's choice. But they didn't want Napoleon anywhere near Europe and they were astonished to learn of Alexander's choice.

Metternich did eventually sign the Treaty of Abdication so as not to delay negotiations for the peace with the Bourbons. But he did not yield with grace. "I will put my name at the bottom of an act that in less than two years will return us to the field of battle," he said when he arrived in Paris. Castlereagh, on the other hand, did not sign. He argued that the treaty with Napoleon was none of Britain's business. Instead, he attached an "act of accession" to the formal protocol of the April meeting in Paris where the treaty was finally discussed; the act limited Britain's commitments to the territorial clauses.[4]

"Public opinion" in Britain lay behind Castlereagh's decision not to sign. The treaty, in addition to granting Elba to Napoleon and the Italian Duchies of Parma, Placentia, and Guastalla to the Empress Marie-Louise, had permitted the couple to keep their imperial titles; it also provided Napoleon with an annual revenue of two million francs to be paid out of French funds. If Castlereagh had signed this there would have been an uproar in the British press. As it was, the territorial commitment alone was enough to cause a frenzy; over the next months, there would be cries that "Beelzebub" had been treated too leniently.[5]

But the British guarantee of the territorial arrangements was necessary; Napoleon refused leave Fontainebleau without it. In the first place, a treaty pledged to the sovereignty of Elba was quite meaning-less, argued Napoleon, without the involvement of the world's only maritime Power; "England possesses all the islands," he continually repeated. Second, Napoleon had developed an intense fear of being assassinated or – an even worse fate for the Corsican that he was – of being publicly insulted. He knew that the journey south down the Rhone valley to the Mediterranean coast would take him through towns and villages that demanded his murder. If he made it to Elba he would still have to protect himself against the States of Barbary, against Maltese and Sicilian pirates and, not least, against the Allies that had so reluctantly signed the treaty.

This last menace was the reason why Napoleon also insisted that a British commissioner reside in his realm of fifty thousand acres. He would take it as proof of the British pledge. Neither an Austrian nor a Russian commissioner, explained Napoleon, would really commit their Sovereigns to the full independence of Elba, whereas a British commissioner would commit his "because national honour would be engaged." Or, as Napoleon put it more bluntly, "the English nation would not tolerate an assassination."[6]

Napoleon's suspicions had been aroused by Austria's treatment of his wife and son. Marie-Louise had been escorted to Rambouillet where she was to meet her father, Kaiser Franz, for the first time in four years. "Orders have been given to prevent me from joining you, and even to resort to force if necessary," she scribbled, while en route, in a desperate note to her husband. "Be on your guard, my darling, we are being duped. I am in deadly anxiety on your behalf, but I shall take a firm line with my father." Some sinister plot, thought Napoleon, was being hatched; he asked Caulaincourt to investigate the possibilities of asylum in England.[7]

Castlereagh was absolutely astonished at this last request – even embarrassed, according to Caulaincourt. But he did recognise that that there was a problem of security involved and he promised Caulaincourt that a British Commissioner would accompany him to Elba and remain with him for as long as Napoleon requested. He also promised that he would lay on frigates for the sea voyage.[8]

Castlereagh's choice of Commissioner was Colonel Sir Neil Campbell, a Highland gentleman, born into a family of ancient lineage. He had fought in the West Indies, in the Peninsular War under Wellington, and in the German and French campaigns of 1813-14. He made his first distant sight of Napoleon during the Battle of Bautzen in May 1813. At Fère-Champenoise, on 26 March 1814 (only four days before the fall of Paris), a party of Cossacks – "these wild sons of the desert" – took him for a French officer and one of them "forced his pike through his back."

Campbell was in a very doddery state when he eventually arrived in Paris on 9 April, three days after Napoleon's abdication and three days before the signing of the "Treaty of Fontainebleau." He was totally unprepared for the message he received from Castlereagh on the 14th asking him to accompany the Emperor from Fontainebleau to Elba, but he accepted, though "still very unfit for travel."

Castlereagh's instructions for Campbell were deliberately vague because he was in the awkward position of guaranteeing the independence of a Sovereign whose formal title he had refused to recognise. It was an ambiguity Napoleon would be quick to exploit. "You will acquaint Napoleon," Castlereagh wrote in a classic piece of diplomatic evasiveness, "that you are directed to reside in the island till further orders, if he [Napoleon] should consider that the presence of a British officer can be of use in protecting the island and his person against insult or attack." When, a couple of months later, Campbell wrote to Castlereagh asking him what it was he was actually supposed to be doing, Castlereagh came up with another magnificent formula: Why, of course, Campbell should act as a "British resident in Elba without assuming any further official character."9

Britain's guarantee to Napoleon's security, Colonel Campbell, arrived in Fontainebleau on 16 April, his head in bandages and his arm in a sling. He had his first audience with Napoleon the next morning. It must have been a strange sight. Three nights earlier His Imperial Highness had swallowed a powerful concoction of opium, hellebore, and belladonna ("more than enough to kill two troopers"). "I saw before me a short active-looking man, who was rapidly pacing the length of his apartment, like some wild animal in his cell," Campbell recorded of his first encounter. Napoleon was unshaven, uncombed, and particles of snuff were scattered profusely upon his upper lip and breast. His knowledge of Scotland, which he had always regarded as a part of England, was essentially limited to Ossian's epic poems; "I like them a lot," he told Campbell, "because there is something in them that is very warlike." He paid many compliments to the English and concluded that they were much better united than the French. "*Votre nation est la plus grande de toutes*," he exclaimed. "*Eh bien!* I'm at your disposition! I am your subject. I depend entirely on you." And then, though still formally unrecognised by England's Foreign Minister, he made a graceful bow to the wounded Campbell and dismissed him.10

On 20 April, a convoy of fourteen carriages with an escort of sixty-two Polish Lancers set off from Fontainebleau for the new island realm. In the coach marked with the insignia of eagles rode not a banished man but a Sovereign, the free Sovereign of Elba. It was sovereignty approved by the Allied Powers and guaranteed by Britain. This had been Napoleon's choice.

Elbans and Englishmen

Part of the choice, Napoleon claimed, had been made in consideration
of Elba's "gentleness." Yet there was nothing gentle about Elba in
1814. Perhaps the scent of juniper and myrtle in the heath, the close
humidity of the valleys, the sight of vineyards layed in terraces and
the villages perched on hills offered a moment's illusion. But the soils
were red or yellow or pale brown, never black and never very productive; little wheat was grown in the fields, and there was not much
oats for the horses. Elba's chief produce was stone. The Romans had
fashioned the columns of the Pantheon from the granite dug out of
Elba's quarries; the walls of Pisa's cathedral and the Medici chapel in
Florence had been carved out of the same pit. Elba's hills also contained quartz, beryl, garnet, magnetite, and limonite that were sold at
a pittance to travellers and souvenir hunters. And there was iron. It
was the iron that made the cliffs red and made the shoreline look, in
an evening, like a row of glowing coals. The iron ore mines of Rio
Marina were the principal source of income for Elba in 1814.[11]

Elba had had rulers as varied as her stones and minerals. The
Genoese had sold the island to the Luccans, the Luccans to the Pisans,
the Pisans abandoned it to Turkish pirates, the pirates abandoned it to
Medicis, Borgias, and Florentines. Later it would belong to
Neapolitans, Spaniards, Frenchmen; even Germans took possession
of the island in the early eighteenth century. Not surprisingly, Elba's
twelve thousand inhabitants were of all origins. Portoferraio (the
"port of iron") and its surroundings were populated mainly by
Tuscans. Porto Longone was still largely Spanish-speaking, though its
tunny fishers were Neapolitan. Nature, politics, and demography had
created a small island, but not a united island.

What Elba experienced during the revolutionary wars was the history of Europe in miniature. The island was invaded by Hudson
Lowe (later Napoleon's governor in St Helena) and his Corsican
Rangers in 1799, after the British had helped the Corsicans rise against
their French rulers. Because it was a strategic point in the control of
Italy, the island was the site of many a clash and skirmish; it changed
hands between the British and the French almost annually. The
Tuscans of Portoferraio tended to support the French; the Hispanics
of Porto Longone and Marciana were more British in their tastes. But
the British eventually recognised the island as French by the Treaty of
Amiens in 1802. It was incorporated into the French Empire, its territory was divided into six communes, and the island sent six representatives to sit in the Corps Législatif in Paris. Napoleon, as
Emperor, ordered the strengthening of Elba's fortifications and sent
in a reinforcement of troops – the worst of the worst. According to

the French Commander, General Duval, they consisted of "Italians, Corsicans, Tuscans, along with deserters and robbers picked out of a colonial depot."[12]

Napoleon's Continental System, which closed all ports to British trade, was as much a disaster for Elba as it was for the rest of Europe. The island returned to its ancient trade, smuggling. The French repressed it. The British, with a foothold in the Tuscan port of Leghorn, responded with a naval blockade of the island. They encouraged the garrisons to mutiny.

By December 1813, the island was completely cut off from the continent and its inhabitants were facing starvation. Nobody, including Governor Dalesme, was aware that Allied forces had crossed the Rhine, not a word was heard of the winter campaign in France, no news was received of the fall of Paris. In Elba, it was war as usual. Governor Dalesme and General Duval continued to defend a French Empire that no longer existed. In mid-April 1814, the island, wholly ignorant of the peace negotiated in Paris, rose in insurrection against Napoleon's regime. It began with a mutiny in the garrison of Porto Longone; the French local commander was shot dead and hacked to pieces. Crowds of hungry peasants, led by their mayors, joined the soldiers. Tricolour flags were torn up, the imperial cockades trampled underfoot; in Marciana, to much song and dance, an effigy of Napoleon was burnt on the village square. The real Napoleon in flesh and blood was, at that very moment, heading for his new realm.

The insurrection was put down with brutal efficiency. "I shot down the rebels with my four hundred Frenchmen, who had remained loyal to honour," boasted Duval in a later report. "I armed the good inhabitants of the country with arms seized from the rebels. These I deported to the continent." But the western quarter of the island never surrendered.[13]

As if Elba were not isolated enough, the island's tiny navy managed to capture that same month two merchant vessels, only to discover that they came from Malta where plague – the Black Death – had broken out. Elba was placed under complete quarantine by every neighbouring state.[14]

Then, on 27 April, a British captain arrived in Portoferraio with news of the fall of Paris and of Napoleon's abdication; he demanded that full powers of administration be transferred to the British. The next day it was the turn of an officer of France's Provisional Government to disembark with a message for the Governor; it demanded an oath of loyalty to the Bourbons. But the French officer had forgotten the name of the new French King, so Dalesme delayed, not knowing what to do. For nearly a week, nobody in Elba knew whether the island was British or Bourbon.

It would be neither. On 2 May, a British frigate, flying a white flag, sailed into Portoferraio. Dalesme had the guns of Forts Stella and Falcone trained upon it. Another envoy of the French Provisional Government stepped ashore bearing the most incredible news: Napoleon himself was on his way, sailing in a second British frigate. Moreover, he was not a prisoner, but an independent Sovereign. Word spread quickly among the inhabitants; the hated Napoleon was to be their King, the King of the Isle of Elba.

Napoleon's presence could electrify a crowd. When he first appeared in his green Chasseur uniform on the deck of HMS *Undaunted* as it manœuvred into the harbour of Portoferraio, the crowds ashore let out a deafening roar, accompanied by guitars, flutes, and tambourines. On the water floated wreaths and bouquets of flowers. The twenty-four rowers of the ship's tender had difficulty finding their way through a mass of sail boats, Mediterranean tartanes, and dinghies to deliver Napoleon to the makeshift wooden landing station. It was neither the devil nor a fallen emperor that the crowds saw that 4 May; it was a hero. Napoleon had conquered the hearts of the Elbans in less than an hour.[15]

There was never any question of him being anything other than "the Emperor." Commissioner Campbell was the only man on the island who refused to use the term. Napoleon lived up to his title. Within a fortnight of his arrival, the Emperor was annexing territory. *"Eh! mon île est bien petite,"* he had exclaimed to Campbell after he had first clambered up the heights behind Portoferraio and gazed out to the sea in all four directions. While touring St-Pierre-de-Campo he noticed an island twelve miles offshore. Pianosa, he was told, had been abandoned in 1809 as a result of the British blockade, but its soils were fertile. Napoleon ordered out a boat, fired cannon, and raised his flag (a band of orange and three bees on a white background). One hundred families were sent out and ordered to cultivate wheat. It was too late to plant for the harvest of 1814, and in 1815 Napoleon would be otherwise occupied. But he laid down the rules, a reprint of his Continental System: no grain was to be exported from Elba and all prices were fixed by the government.[16]

From his palace of I Mulini ("The Mills," a rather modest house that the Medicis had built in the eighteenth century for the Governor's gardener) rained down the decrees: *"Napoléon empereur et souverain de l'Ile d'Elbe, avons décrété et décrétons . . ."* The plain of Lacona would be irrigated, the valleys reforested, olive trees and mulberries grown in the south, chestnuts pushing up in the north, potato plots dug in every commune, roads were to be constructed linking all villages to the capital (which he wanted to rename Cosmopoli), urban renewal was to be undertaken in Marciana, health measures were planned everywhere, and designs for a new hospital and military cadet school were made. Again, as in Paris and most of his former Empire, the decrees were passed but the works were not finished. And for the very same reason: there was not enough money. "The island would have to have produced not iron but gold," commented Pons, the director of the iron ore mines; "yet his own pension was not even being paid." The Emperor's decrees laid down the number of workers to be furnished by each commune for the building of roads; one half of the expenses would be covered by his own account, the other half by the communes. Already, in early June, there were heard rumours that the inhabitants would not be commandeered into work and that they were not prepared to pay Napoleon's taxes.[17]

In his first months on the island, Napoleon would often be seen riding in his carriage, accompanied by his two chamberlains, the officers of ordnance, a captain of the gendarmes, the intendant general, and his secretary, General Bertrand. "I have never seen a man in any situation of life with so much personal activity and restless perseverence," wrote Campbell. On his tours Napoleon would be received in each of the villages with a firing of musketry and cannon, the priests would lead a procession, and young girls and children would strew the way with flowers. But, on 5 June, Campbell was noting in his journal, "The cries of 'Vive l'Empereur!' are no longer heard." The popularity won in an hour was lost in less than a month.[18]

By autumn 1814, the Emperor had become more retiring. There were days when he never emerged from his two-storey palace. Yet his presence continued to exert an attraction. Corsicans arrived on the island in search of jobs, foreign spies sought information. There were also adventurers and plenty of sightseers, among whom figured, in no small number, the cross-Channel travellers, the English.

Many Englishmen had made it as far as Italy; some boarded vessels for Elba. Altogether sixty-one of King George's subjects visited Elba during Napoleon's residence. Chevalier Mariotti, the French consul at Leghorn who doubled as one of Talleyrand's spies, was worried that more than idle curiosity was involved. "The English," he warned Talleyrand in August, "have an intense admiration for Napoleon. They have bought up all his alabaster busts in Florence. All the English captains have his portrait in their cabins."[19]

Mariotti was right: the visits were not so innocent. Many Whigs – not wholly unlike later English admirers of Lenin and Stalin – regarded Napoleon as the man of the future, the man who had saved the Revolution, the man who would establish in Europe a new social order with justice. They did not have to pay Napoleon's taxes; as landowners, they did have to pay the taxes that had kept the wars against him going. One of the keenest supporters of Napoleon in London had been Henry Fox, the third Lord Holland, and his wife. During the war they had given dinner parties for their literary and political friends in a dilapidated Jacobean mansion outside London,

Elba, impressive at first sight, was a poor and divided island. Napoleon
attempted to forge some old-fashioned imperial unity out of it

just down the turnpike from Kensington Palace. "Our guests are
foreigners, fashionables and courtiers," Holland had boasted to his
mother in 1813.

They all loved Napoleon; they all heartily disapproved of the new
Bourbon restoration. The third Lord Holland was well-known to
Napoleon; they had met when Holland visited France with his uncle,
Charles James Fox, in 1802 after the Treaty of Amiens. In autumn
1814, Lord Holland could be found with many of his English poli-
tical allies in Florence – less than a hundred miles from Elba.[20]

Napoleon knew he could rely on some support from England's
opposition and might well have imagined it strong enough to stop a
further war against him, should he ever decide to return to France.
Even aboard HMS *Undaunted*, on his way out to Elba, he was
expressing satisfaction with the English opposition. Sir Neil
Campbell said he did not belong to it; Captain Ussher, the boat's
commander, admitted he did. Three weeks later, Ussher received from
Napoleon a thousand bottles of wine, a thousand Spanish dollars, and
the Emperor's portrait set in diamonds.[21]

Napoleon had many flattering things to say about the English.
Campbell got tired of hearing "how much regard he had for me! how
much he esteemed the British nation! etc., etc." But his visitors
enjoyed it. "England is at its height of power and glory," he told
Colonel Douglas, a young Whig sympathiser. "I believe you thought,
in England, that I was the devil," he said to Viscount Ebrington,

another Whig, "but now that you have seen France, and seen me, you will probably allow that you have in some respects been deceived." Ebrington found no devil in Napoleon. "His manner put me quite at my ease," he recorded on their first of two meetings in December 1814.[22]

To every one of his visitors Napoleon would emphasise that he had no ambitions beyond Elba, that he considered his political life in Europe as ended. "I am a dead man," he told Douglas. "I am a dead man," he repeated to Campbell. "I was born a soldier, I mounted a throne, and then I descended."[23]

A simple man, an imperial man

It was not only the English Whigs who had this passion for Napoleon. Almost everybody who met him fell under his spell, including some of his worst enemies. Alexander wept for Napoleon after taking Paris in 1814 and continued to call him a "friend." When Talleyrand speaks in his memoirs of his former "love for Napoleon" one gets a distinct impression it was a love he never quite relinquished. One feels, on reading Metternich's sketches of the French Emperor, that the great disappointment in the Prince's life was not to have been born Napoleon. And what an astonishing thing it is to find Chateaubriand say, "My admiration for Bonaparte has always been great and sincere." An *émigré* and staunch supporter of the Bourbons, he devoted a whole volume of his memoirs to Napoleon, filled with complaint. Yet Chateaubriand claimed that Napoleon possessed "the most powerful breath of life that ever animated human clay."[24]

Napoleon's energy bewitched people. His conversation, even if it went only in one direction, delighted because it was witty; it was a stream of fundamental truths – or, at least, that was the impression it gave. Napoleon's style was direct, his judgment quick, his analysis usually very simple. Speaking and dictating were his style. He was not a writer for he could not spell. He criticised his younger brother, Lucien, who was the orator in the family, for making his speeches too flamboyant: "Too many words and not enough ideas. You can't speak like that to the ordinary man in the street. He has more common sense and tact than you think." When he read, Napoleon would enjoy scratching out with a pencil all the words and phrases he considered useless. In St Helena he proposed to the memorialist Las Cases what he thought would be "a most valuable task": a review of all the major works of French literature with a view of cutting out the "parasitic" passages. "Montesquieu is practically the only one who could escape such a reduction," he commented. Napoleon's tastes in architecture were equally reductionist: straight lines and a few arches. He had had a number of playful nymphs outside the Tuileries removed because they disturbed the geometric order of the place du Carrousel. The Napoleonic style was the very opposite of baroque.[25]

Behind Napoleon's uncomplicated vision of the universe were the simple values he had inherited from his Mediterranean ancestors: honour, loyalty, and friendship, the greatest of these being friendship. Physical attraction, Napoleon believed, was at the root of all friendship; its first waves, he said, gave him "a sort of painful tingling . . . the squeaking of a saw sometimes gives me the same sensation." Napoleon's friendships with men were very manly, with women they were feminine, and never for a moment would he confuse the first with the second. The frontier that separated them was drawn in black. "Women should be kept at home away from politics"; politics and history were the affairs of men.

Indeed, for Napoleon, politics and history were made up of the stories of male friendships and what went wrong with them: friendships that worked created the alliance of powers, friendships that were betrayed turned into vendetta. Napoleon invaded Russia because he believed that Alexander had broken the sacred bond of their friendship. Caulaincourt reported that the thing which upset Napoleon most in April 1814 was not the loss of his throne – he referred to it as "a mere piece of wood" – but the betrayal by his father-in-law; the Austrian Emperor had refused to allow Napoleon to reunite with his wife and son. "This indifference and this contempt for their own blood," he said, "dishonours them [the Austrians] in the eyes of all peoples *and all men*" (my emphasis). Napoleon's attempted suicide at that date was due, again according to Caulaincourt, to the humiliation inflicted; his own honour had been questioned, his life had become insupportable.

The simplicity of his style, the liveliness of his mind, and his male passions were what made Napoleon so attractive to soldiers. Napoleon did not find it easy to speak in parliamentary assemblies; every time he tried he had been a dismal failure and in nearly every case had to resort to the threat of force, to soldiers. But before his troops Napoleon's effect was magical and cannot be explained with words. The words were trite; they read today like lines taken from a second-rate comic opera: "Soldiers! I led you to victory! Can I count on you?" "Soldiers! Over there is the enemy! Will you swear to die rather than allow France to be insulted?" "Soldiers! The enemy has stolen a march on us and become master of Paris! They must be chased out! The cowards!" "Soldiers of the Old Guard! I bid you farewell!"

Napoleon explained to Campbell how he did it. "With soldiers," he said, gradually raising himself on his toes as he spoke, "it is not so much the speech itself as the mode of delivering it." He then glanced up to the ceiling, stretched out one of his arms as high as he could, and exclaimed, "Unfurl the eagles! Unfurl the eagles!" Campbell was struck by "something wild in his air." Lord Ebrington was also treated to a Napoleonic commentary on his rapport with the troops. He said they regarded him as their comrade and they knew that they would be well rewarded; "but now," added Napoleon poignantly, "they feel they are nothing."[26]

In fact, whenever Napoleon was talking with Englishmen he always somehow managed to mention how popular he was with the soldiers. France still had plenty of them on her soil. What was she going to do with them all?

Napoleon's purity of style was more a virtue of the eighteenth than of the nineteenth century. Napoleon often claimed to be the guarantee of the "ideas of the century," meaning of course the nineteenth century. But the century was not his. The ornate nineteenth century belonged to Talleyrand, whose capacity to adapt to different regimes would set a model for Frenchmen for the next hundred years; to Metternich, whose policy of patience and survival would be the policy of Austria through most of the same period; to Castlereagh, whose mechanical balance of power was frequently imitated; to the Congress of Vienna, which outlined the labyrinthine frontiers of Europe's states. The German philosopher Hegel might have dismissed the Congress statesmen as "ant, flea, and bug personalities" as compared to the great Napoleon; but the nineteenth century was filled with ant, flea, and bug personalities. It was the twentieth century that attempted to return to simplicity again, a century of lines, squares, and blocks; a century that tried to impose great leaders on the world; a reductionist century; the century of war.

If Napoleon's thoughts were those of the eighteenth century, it was not in the sense of the harmony, equilibrium, and game found in baroque Vienna, but rather in the Parisian *philosophes'* humanitarian dictatorship of reason. Early in 1791[27] Napoleon, a second lieutenant billeted in Auxonne, wrote an essay on a subject which much preoccupied these philosophers, human happiness. Its principal themes were conventional for the time and were close to Napoleon's own outlook on life. "Man," he wrote, "is born to be happy. Nature, an enlightened mother, has endowed him with all the organs necessary for the achievement of her creation. Happiness is thus simply the enjoyment of life that conforms best to her [Nature's] organisation." He went on to explain the need to guide feeling with reason.

Not surprisingly, the lasting achievement of Napoleon's Empire was a law code, for it was in the chapters, articles, and clauses of law that the ambition to conform to Nature's reason was most easily realised. Napoleon bequeathed France a system. It would make quite a contrast to the achievements of Metternich's German Committee, which had to cater to so many special interest groups. Napoleon's system was an attempt to assimilate the perfect work of Nature; Metternich's system was an attempt to adapt to the imperfect work of History. Behind Napoleon lay the rationalising projects of a revolution. Behind Metternich lay the Viennese system of political compromise and territorial balance. That was not the Revolution's system. The old French provinces had been divided up into *"departements";* Napoleon had placed a prefect at the head of each of them. Space, volume, and weight were measured metrically. Old time had been divided up into equal months, decimal weeks, and there had even been an attempt to impose decimal hours and decimal seconds. Yet, when all Europe lay under the rule of Napoleon and the eagles were unfurled in Russia, the earth still circled the sun in 365¼ days and the moon never quite managed to prolong its trip around our planet to a neat thirty-day month. Nature was imperfect, and so were the men born under her.

Napoleon claimed that the power of his throne lay in the consent of the people. "I did not usurp the Crown," he once told his Council of State, "I picked it out of a ditch and the people placed it on my head." Yet, in Napoleon's French it was always "the people *is . . .* " and never "the people *are . . .* " The people was a single undivided entity, like Nature.[28]

Napoleon would frequently refer to the struggle of the people against "divine right" and "feudal law", or other variations on this. When he marched his troops into Austria he was standing up to the Viennese "oligarchy." When he turned Switzerland, by force, into a satellite state, he was striking at "aristocracy" and he informed the "people" that "it will be content with nothing but a republic formed after the example of France." The English "oceonocrats," of course, he never managed to overthrow.

The struggle against aristocrats and oligarchs was all part of Napoleon's single-minded vision of history. "Religion, the feudal system, and monarchy have in turn governed Europe for twenty centuries," he reported to the Directors in Paris in 1797 after imposing one of his treaties on Vienna, "but from the peace just concluded dates the era of representative government." He declared that Frenchmen could henceforth "behold with joyful expectation the Spirit of Liberty rise from the graves of their ancestors."[29]

It is now estimated that, between 1789 and 1815, two million Frenchmen violently went to their graves with the rise of this "Spirit of Liberty" – no small figure for a country with a population of twenty-seven million at its first census in 1801. Napoleon should not be blamed for all the losses; the Napoleonic wars killed approximately one million Frenchmen. In eight years of war in the Iberian peninsula two hundred thousand Frenchmen alone were killed or died in hospitals. Nobody really knows how many died during the Russian campaign of 1812. Napoleon himself estimated that he had lost around four hundred thousand. Later historians have placed the number at over six hundred thousand. One striking report comes from the Russian Ministry of Police, based on the special teams that had been organised to follow Napoleon and bury the dead he left behind. They buried 430,707 men; yet they were not the only ones to undertake that task. No contemporary "aristocratic" government – oligarchic, oppressive, feudalist, or reactionary – could ever be accused of destruction at this scale.[30]

After he had lost his throne in 1814, Napoleon would frequently claim that he was not a man of war, that he was no Don Quixote, that if the English had let him he would have ruled in peace, that he was at heart a European, that his sole aim was to blend all peoples into one "great European family." "Don't speak to me any more of war!" he said to his director of fortifications shortly after he had stepped ashore at Elba; "we have made war all our lives, and the future will perhaps force us to make more wars, but war will one day be an anachronism." It was the sort of forecast that would stand well with his admirers and with those who shared his one-dimensional history of the world. But, as Talleyrand would repeatedly point out, the Europe Napoleon actually created had no history and it had no geography. He had set up a totally unmanageable "France", with 141 departments and a population of eighty-five million, which stretched from Hamburg to Rome; he had created a "Kingdom of Italy"; and further afield lay his "vassal states." Very little modernisation was undertaken in the states he controlled, beyond his law codes. The Dutch continued to pay tithes, the Bavarians still built their roads with unpaid peasant labour, Württemberg maintained a system of serfdom, Napoleon's Poland remained under the rule of the large landed families.

It was not only in human lives that Europe paid for Napoleon's single-minded visions of Honour, Liberty, and Fraternity. There was a steep economic price attached, too. Adolphe Thiers, historian of the Empire and Head of State after France's military defeat in 1870, never forgot the sight, in the Marseille of his childhood, of three hundred merchant ships moored to the quays, "rotting there without ever changing place." The children of Bordeaux, La Rochelle, Nantes, Brest, Saint-Malo, Cherbourg, Dieppe, Le Havre, and Dunkirk would have had the same memory. Along the whole coast of Europe it was a similar story. That was what struck English travellers in 1814: the people of the ports were so poor. Commercial traffic declined, in the port of Amsterdam, from 2,400 ships in 1805, to 1,300 in 1806, 400 in 1808, and 300 in 1809; Holland became a part of France in 1810.

The internal commerce of Europe also suffered. In October 1810, two French infantry regiments were sent into Frankfurt and all "contraband" was collected and burnt in a big public bonfire. As a result, the banking system of Germany collapsed, there was panic in the major financial markets across the continent, and this was followed by the worst food crisis ever recorded in the nineteenth century. Peasants in Normandy, in central, and in southern France were reduced to eating roots and grass; as was indeed the case throughout many parts of Europe.

Some historians point out that Napoleon succeeded in altering the routes of commerce. It is true, but the new routes were bizarre to an extreme. Europe, which is in reality a maritime peninsula, was turned into a continent without sea ports. One of the most important new continental routes began in Salonika, Greece, which was held by the British, wound along the mule tracks and humped bridges of Serbia, crossed the plains of Hungary, and joined the Danube at Vienna. It made life in Vienna more comfortable than Berlin, but this route did not conform to geography – or history. "When I think," exclaimed the Emperor in his final exile at St Helena, "that for a cup of coffee with more or less sugar in it, they checked the hand that would set free the world!" Europe preferred sugared coffee and had had enough of Napoleon's freedoms.[31]

One region in Europe that Napoleon did indirectly help advance – though he was not the instigator, for the origins of its strength lay buried in the centuries – was Belgium; or more particularly the long, narrow, intensely populated zone stretching from Aachen in Germany down the Sambre and the Meuse westwards to the Scheldt in France. Here there was running water, coal, and, because the French Revolution did not destroy its aristocrats, also capital. Isolation from competing Britain gave this region a boost. The mines were extended, the iron works grew, steam engines were built, textile factories were developed, and an export market extended into France, Germany, and beyond. Belgium, during the Napoleonic wars, experienced industrial take-off. In Elba, Napoleon would insist that Belgium was a part of France. In economic terms, what would actually happen would be precisely the reverse: exhausted France would become part of the Belgian system, as would eventually most of Europe.[32]

The Emperor was not a cold-hearted man; he was a man of passion, he enjoyed friendship, and he sincerely believed that his cause was good. Napoleon was not driven by unbridled ambition either: his acts were measured; he disciplined himself with reason, absolute reason. The people, he said, had put him in his position, and so in a sense they had: there was an angry, vengeful crowd behind Napoleon.

That perhaps was the problem. What Napoleon lacked most was a sense of what Europeans in the twentieth century – after two world wars – would call "collective responsibility." Napoleon either moved with the crowd or he repressed it; but he never thought for a moment that he and the crowd that moved with him were collectively responsible for the appalling acts they committed. The idea was foreign to his culture. He boasted to Lord Ebrington that he had never put a single man to death without a trial; but he also told Metternich that he could look a million corpses in the face. The idea that a nation, a society, or the movers of a revolution should accept responsibility for mass slaughter and economic catastrophe never crossed his mind. The idea did not exist.

On St Helena, Napoleon would meet a slave called Toby. He told his captors that he would buy Toby and give him back his freedom. But he did not: Napoleon, typically, yielded to his own reason. He could damn an individual for the enslavement of another man, but he would not be the judge of a whole society. As he explained to Las Cases, if the captain of a British ship had personally taken Toby from his family by force, then the captain would be guilty of a crime and would be the object of the suffering family's revenge. But, if the whole crew were involved in the capture, there could be no vendetta because one would be unable to identify the criminal. "Perversity," said Napoleon, "is always individual and almost never collective." The triumph of civilisation, he went on, was that the great majority of men could not be criminal, society was "born of its own nature."[33]

Nature, the single-file march of civilisation, the responsibility of the individual and not the group: all of Napoleon is in that story.

Winter in Elba

By November 1814, Napoleon was facing serious money problems. The salt marshes failed to produce salt and the iron mines failed to sell iron. This last problem was due to Napoleon's own wars, which had created a glut in the iron market; the British, well established in nearby Leghorn, were selling huge quantities of scrapped cannon at cut prices. Even more distressing for Napoleon was the failure of the Bourbons to pay the annuity promised in the third article of the "Treaty of Fontainebleau." Campbell got so concerned about the poor state of Napoleon's finances that, in November, he wrote a warning to Castlereagh: "If pecuniary difficulties press upon him much longer, so as to prevent his vanity from being satisfied by the ridiculous establishment of a Court which he has hitherto supported in Elba, and if his doubts are not removed, I think he is capable of crossing over to Piombino with his troops, or of any other eccentricity." He sent another warning in early December, pointing out that Napoleon could even attempt a return to France. But Castlereagh still had Saxony on his mind. It was only in February – after the Saxon question had been settled through the French alliance – that he made a formal representation to Talleyrand, in which he demanded payment of the allowance. By that time, Napoleon was on the point of embarkation.[34]

Talleyrand was perfectly aware of the danger. As early as November, Chevalier Mariotti had established a whole network of spies stretching out to Corsica and the department of the Var in the south of France and which included a highly competent agent planted on Elba itself, known as the Oil Merchant. He was probably a man by the name of Alessandro Forli, an Italian from Lucca, who had once served in Napoleon's Army of Italy. Within a week of his arrival he was selling bottles of his prized olive oil to members of the imperial household, gathering information, and sending regular reports back to Mariotti at Leghorn. He took great care not to exaggerate his reports and he handled rumour with caution, but by mid-December he was getting repeated signals that Napoleon was seriously considering a move to the mainland, and he wasn't apparently thinking of Italy.[35]

But one hardly needed spies to discover the kind of mood Napoleon was in. The taxes he had imposed on the inhabitants by decree were not being paid. The people of Capoliveri, in the southern part of the island, even managed to force the withdrawal of his troops. Napoleon blamed the troubles on the priests and "bad subjects"; he had his Grande Vicaire in Portferraio declare the priests' functions suspended and sent in a corps of four hundred Corsicans backed up with the faithful Polish Lancers. By the end of November, there were more troops in Capoliveri than there were inhabitants. Two priests and three laymen were thrown into the dungeons of Fort Falcone. Capoliveri eventually paid up, the troops were withdrawn, and the prisoners released. But out of the tax received, the bonus promised to the Poles and Corsicans had to be settled; that was the classic cycle of Napoleonic economics.[36]

In the meantime, Napoleon was making menacing remarks about France and Europe. The Bourbons, he kept repeating, were ill-equipped to rule the French, who were a martial people that had been mortified by a shameful peace and then further humiliated by the appointment of the Duke of Wellington as British Ambassador. Napoleon told Ebrington that it would have been much better if the British had partitioned France than to leave her intact and in a state of irritation "which, if not employed in foreign contests, must break out into revolution or civil war." He thought the weak Bourbons might get a chance to prove their mettle with the renewed threat of war over Saxony. "The Bourbons should make war as soon as possible, in order to establish themselves upon the throne," he told Campbell in January 1815. "With such an army as they could assemble, it would not be difficult to recover Belgium." Belgium, always Belgium;

Napoleon was obsessed with Belgium and those northern plains.[37]

A correspondent in Leghorn reported to the Parisian *Journal des Débats* on 26 November 1814 that Napoleon was "very sick" as a result of a *"fluxion de poitrine"* and that the famous Doctor Vaccari was being sent out to attend to him. "Buonaparte has been constantly sad and pensive," the correspondent noted.[38]

Bonaparte was no longer receiving letters from Marie-Louise. He had prepared apartments for her at I Mulini and, for their summer residence in San Martino, he had ordered his Florentine decorators to paint, on one of the ceilings, two doves linked by pale ribbons in a knot that tightened as they fluttered off in their separate ways. As the artists were preparing their paint pots, Marie-Louise was actually making her way to Elba. But she was not alone and she was not in a hurry. The Austrian authorities had decided – it was said that Metternich had personally intervened – that Marie-Louise needed a companion for the voyage. The man selected for this task was Count Alfred von Neipperg, an Austrian Hussar, who had been introduced into Napoleon's court at the same time as Marie-Louise's marriage in 1810. Despite the loss of an eye, shot out by musket-fire, the Count strangely resembled the Austrian Foreign Minister; he was tall, his hair dangled in golden curls, the eye that remained was blue, and he was an expert seducer of women. Marie-Louise's innocence remained intact just as far as Aix-en-Provence, where the travelling party stopped off for repose; they remained there for most of the month of August. In September their carriage was finally rolling again, but not in the direction of Elba. On 24 October, they turned up in Vienna. Agent ** reported to Hager that day that Neipperg had not been a very good choice (** had obviously not grasped the finer subtleties of Austrian foreign policy). All contact between Marie-Louise and Napoleon was henceforth cut off.[39]

Napoleon became totally silent on the matter of Marie-Louise; no interlocutor dared even bring it up. But a portrait of the Empress remained on his desk and the two doves still tightened the knot on the ceiling of San Martino. The apartments were eventually occupied by Napoleon's pretty sister, Pauline.

On 15 February 1815, Napoleon received a visit from an Italian sailor calling himself Pietro Saint-Ernest. But he was not an Italian, he was not a sailor, and Pietro was not his name. He was Fleury de Chaboulon, a former sub-prefect of Reims, who had come with a message from Napoleon's old Minister of Foreign Affairs, Hugues Maret. France was ready, said this cautious man, for Napoleon's return.

The discontented French

Was she? The censored press in Paris would never for a moment have admitted that life under Napoleon, the warmonger, could be better than the "repose" offered by the Bourbons. The *Journal des Débats* – which, with a circulation of twenty-three thousand, was the widest read paper in the country – filled its columns with articles on the *félicité publique* and the gratitude most Frenchmen felt at having peace. "Could we have reasonably expected such profound calm after so long a tempest?" the editors would keep asking their readers. To this the answer was always an uncomfortable silence: everyone by now knew that the transition from war to peace was not going to be easy.

Some were not so bound by silence. Foreign diplomats, for example, sent home worrying reports about French discontent; some of them even hinted that the country might soon be devouring her neighbours again. Among the most concerned was the Duke of Wellington who, with the onset of winter, felt a distinct chill developing in the French capital.

Outwardly, Wellington remained just as glamorous an ambassador as he had been in August; he would always appear in public in his scarlet field-marshal's uniform decorated with the Orders of the Fleece, the Bath, and the Garter; nearly always the great operatic singer, Giuseppina Grassini, stood at the receptions arm in arm by his side. The little Duchess of Wellington only arrived in October and was barely noticed. "I am afraid he is behaving very ill to that poor little woman," wrote a scornful Lady Bessborough, but then she was a Whig and not the greatest family friend. The balls continued at the Tuileries, royal hunts at Bagatelle, and gracious visits to the *salons* of Germaine de Staël and Juliette Récamier. But Wellington was no idle player in Paris. He scored some great diplomatic successes while there: he eventually persuaded the French to sign the general condemnation of the slave trade, which would be published in Vienna in February; it was Wellington who laid the foundations of the Anglo-French agreement on Saxony. He was not so successful in the efforts he made on behalf of British creditors in Paris. But then that was not what mattered most.[40] What haunted the Duke throughout the winter of 1814-15 was what secretly haunted the newspaper editors: Was France – her society, her economy, her army – really capable of completing the transition from war to peace?

During his five months in Paris, Wellington sent a number of reports on the state of France to Vienna and to London. They were all written in the Duke's straightforward style and demonstrated a conscious effort not to exaggerate. "All is new here," he wrote, for example, to old General Dumouriez, who had defected from the French and was now living in England; "and you know that new things, especially when they are complicated, never go well." There was general discontent and widespread poverty. "This wretched Revolution and what followed it have ruined the country from tip to tail," explained Wellington. "Everybody is poor and, what is worse, their institutions prevent any family from becoming rich and powerful. Everybody therefore has to set their sights on getting public employment, not, as formerly, for the honour, but simply to find the means to live."

That was what struck Wellington most: the huge state bureaucracy spawned by the Revolution at the expense of a mercantile class. Bonaparte, he said, had left behind an army of a million and a French administration that had directly governed one half of Europe and indirectly controlled the other. Now they were all looking for jobs. Worse, there was a competing group of returning émigrés who were also looking for government jobs.[41]

Wellington was not optimistic. From November onwards, he was writing letters and reports to both London and the Prince of Orange in the Hague warning of the need to improve the frontier defences of Belgium. The French, he confided to his brother Henry in Madrid, were so accustomed to revolution and war that they could not go on without it.[42]

Joseph Fouché, as Napoleon's former Minister of Police, was the archetype of the unemployed revolutionary civil servant. Like Wellington, he spent his time warning ambassadors, ministers, and courtiers of the dangers inherent in France's transition to peace. Having been refused an audience with Talleyrand, he wrote a letter to the Minister the week he left for Vienna. "I would have liked to have talked about the interior of France and of Paris, and especially about the Frenchmen who have been excluded from positions." He gave a list of former colleagues who had been obliged to leave the country. "The Government reassures itself," he went on, "but an unforeseen event could happen that could change everything." He hinted at troubles in Naples, at discontent in Belgium; he warned the duc d'Artois, the King's brother, that Napoleon on Elba was for France and Europe what Vesuvius was for Naples. To the comte de Blacas, the King's closest adviser, he remarked that "a nation, whose spirits and souls for twenty-five years have been shaking the universe, cannot, without long drawn-out steps, be returned to a smooth, peaceable state; one should not try to stop her activity." France, he said, was a devouring nation that needed to be fed (Metternich would have agreed with him on that). The best way to do this was to divert her activities into commerce and industry (an admission that this had not been an overwhelming concern when Fouché was Minister): "The nineteenth century has hardly begun," he said; "it will have to carry the name of Louis XVIII just as the seventeenth carried the name of Louis XIV."[43]

Another lost servant of the state was a man called Benjamin Constant. He was actually a Swiss Protestant who had been educated in England, Scotland, Belgium, and Germany. He settled briefly in Paris during the Revolution when he got one of the only jobs he ever held in his life: Napoleon named him to his Tribunate. But a stormy affair with Madame de Staël led him into the liberal opposition and eventually to a life of drifting in Germany. Madame de Staël had convinced him that he was destined for "high office," though one would hardly have guessed it in 1814 when, at the age of forty-seven, he returned, almost by accident, to Paris with virtually nothing published and no career in sight. In Germany he had been exposed to the same school of mysticism that was to have such an influence on the Russian Tsar, he had joined a drinking and dining club for academics in Göttingen (though no academic himself), and he had written a long poem against Napoleon. In his studies he concentrated on theology and religion, which he described as "the purpose of my whole life and its consolation." He frequently recorded in his *Journal intime* that he was going mad and became quite obsessed with the idea of suicide. "Miserable morning," he wrote when back in Paris in July 1814. "I shall never be anything in this country if I do not succeed by way of its government, and that is no easy matter. I must devote my whole mind to it" – like tens of thousands of others.[44]

Yet he had an edge on many of them. The previous January, while still in Germany, he had published a pamphlet, *De l'esprit de conquête et de l'usurpation dans leurs rapports avec la civilisation européenne*, which was probably the profoundest study of war and peace made in that age of transition; some have regarded it as a prophecy of the totalitarian regimes of the twentieth century. The pamphlet leaned on his unpublished religious works of the preceding decade. Constant made a distinction between two worlds: a modern world devoted to commerce and the production of goods, which required peace among nations and guaranteed the rights of the individual to self-expression, property, and privacy; and an ancient world dominated by a priestly caste with rigidly imposed dogmas, held up by a strong military wing in control of civil life and perpetuating itself through expansionist wars and the suppression of all opposition. He quoted the *philosophe* Condillac who had said that there were two forms of barbarism, the one that preceded the enlightened centuries, and the one that came after it. Twenty years ago, claimed Constant, such barbarism could not be found in Europe, but it could today, in France, in the regime presided over by Napoleon. Constant placed Napoleon squarely in the camp of the ancients. But he did not say that the nineteenth century did not belong to Napoleon; he simply hoped it would not.[45]

Constant never found work under the Bourbons. He led a campaign for the freedom of the press, he had a chaotic affair with Juliette Récamier ("Oh God, I give up. She has put me through another appalling day. She is a linnet, a cloud, without memory, discernment or preferences"), and he became increasingly bitter.

What exactly the French people as a whole thought of the Bourbons – the commercial sector virtually destroyed and a multitude in search of work – has never really been determined. It was the British parliament, after Napoleon's return, that talked most about "what the French people wanted," in the same way as they would speak of "British public opinion." But all this was misleading. In truth, there was no "French people" to speak of because, despite two decades of Terror, centralisation, imperial bureaucracy, and Napoleon, France remained a deeply divided, fragmented culture of regions. Beyond the *barrières* of Paris lay the vast seas of a peasant economy made up of families that wore no silks, ate no meat, watered their wines, sent their sons into the army, paid their taxes in coin, their rent in wheat, and struggled to survive on two or three hectares of dirt. They were sublimely indifferent as to whether it was a Bourbon or Napoleon who sat on the throne in the Tuileries; most of them had forgotten who the Bourbons were. There were a few regions that might be described as having a political orientation. In the west, for instance, peasants supported the Bourbons because the Republican armies had massacred their families and destroyed their villages. Much of Provence and Languedoc was Bourbon because Paris was identified with Napoleon and, since the days of the Crusades, anything to do with Paris was hated. But that was not true of the Protestants of the Cevennes; they hated the Catholics, so they supported Napoleon to a man. Eastern France hated foreigners, particularly after the war and occupation of 1814; there was widespread support for Napoleon in Lorraine, Champagne, and Burgundy. Furthermore, there were regions in central France that had been totally dechristianised – a drawn-out process not wholly due to the Revolution; the Bourbon attempt in 1814 to impose religious processions and to close the shops on Sundays incited resentment. Worse, when the duc d'Artois first visited the Burgundian capital of Dijon he promised to revoke Napoleon's hated *droits réunis*, a series of commodity taxes; but the government needed the revenue, so the taxes were never abolished. In Dijon a trade developed in plates, cups, pots, spades, hammers, fire pokers and candle-holders all decorated with the image of Napoleon; it was still a thriving trade in the 1830s. "Tremble, royalists," read a placard posted in July 1814 on the door of the hôtel-de-ville in nearby Auxerre, "Napoleon is a republican: he does not want slaves and is about to stir himself to come and crush you."[46]

If the "French people" did not exist, nor did national political parties. Vague terms like "Royalist and Republican" may have been scribbled on placards, but few in 1814 spoke of "ultra-royalists," "liberals," and "Bonapartists." The divisions were blurred, the loyalties uncertain. Fouché, the best political organiser in France, wrote of "affiliations [of] influential men who contracted political commitments between themselves"; this was a narrow, private, secret world of salons and cafés. Wellington noted how weak were the ties in these affiliations; everybody, he said, was suspicious of each other, "including those of the constitutional party, who wish well to the King." The most dangerous groups, he thought, were not the "Republicans and Imperialists" but rather the "Party of Royalists and Chouans" or, as he sometimes called it, "the Emigrant Party." Even those closest to the King were causing problems; so many people were trying to protect him that they were creating their own suspicions. As Jaucourt reported to Talleyrand, the *petites polices* were denouncing the *grandes*, while the *grandes* were denouncing each other. There poured downwards from the court of the Tuileries a cascade of contempt and suspicion, and there was no force to counter it. Jaucourt summed up the situation for Talleyrand when he wrote on 8 October, "only the strongest, the most constitutional union, can resist, and that kind of force we are far from possessing."[47]

France had no effective government. There were ministers, but no ministry; there were four councils – a Council on High, a Council of Parties, a Council of Ministers, and a Private Council – where the King sat and the Princes attended, but there was no cabinet; the King had his favourite, the comte de Blacas, who had run the King's Court at Hartwell House in England and was now Grand Master of the King's Wardrobe, but there was no Prime Minister. None of the Ministers had either the will or the means to dominate their colleagues. The only one who could have done this was Talleyrand, and he had been packed off to Vienna. His colleagues in Paris soon divided into clans and merely used the councils as a means of obtaining the King's signature. "What is the good of making reports to him?" complained baron Louis, the tough little Minister of Finance. "You might as well make them to a saint in a niche. I just give him the ordinances to sign, and he signs them."[48]

The Bourbons lacked the experience of government. Napoleon kept on reminding his English Whig friends in Elba that Bourbons surrounded themselves with people who had been buried in attics in London for twenty years. In England, Napoleon said, it was all right for a Sovereign to have a private life; he could even be a little mad. But in France "the Sovereign is the source of everything" – which was a pretty just comment from the former Emperor.[49]

As usual, there was a grain of truth in what Napoleon said, but it was not the whole truth. No Bourbon had ever exercised the kind of power Napoleon had held; they might have returned with a few of their friends from the London attics, but they also listened to high placed administrators in Paris, who advised that the Napoleonic state be left intact. King Louis XVIII sincerely sought a reconciliation. There were no purges made in the civil service or the army – functionaries were fired, just as army officers were put on half pay, not out of vengeance but because the state was facing bankruptcy. The two houses of the legislature were maintained, only their names were changed; almost all the members of the Chamber of Peers and all the members of the Chamber of Deputies had been sitting in Napoleon's two houses in 1813. The curious executive system of Royal Councils had been directly inherited from Napoleon.

The problem was that Napoleon's state was designed for a dictatorship, whereas the Bourbons were to introduce a degree of real representation. It is true, the Charter of June 1814, a compromise between constitutionalists and extremists, would not satisfy the tastes of a twentieth-century democrat; it did not satisfy the liberal ideals of Tsar Alexander, who rode off to London in a huff. But it did grant more power to the legislature than had ever been permitted under Napoleon, it did guarantee more representation than any rotten borough of England, and it cautiously opened the door for a free press to a country which, under Napoleon, had only had one newspaper. All this in a country that was regionally divided, had such little tradition of parliament, and for quarter of a century had been perpetually at war. It was not unreasonable to fear that the Charter was opening the way to anarchy; wits of the day called it a "paternal anarchy," an expression that went back to the rule of Louis XVIII's late brother.

The greatest threat to the security of the new state and to a successful transition to peace was Napoleon's huge unemployed army. Again, the whole emphasis of Bourbon policy in 1814 was on reconciliation. "Soldiers! The King has just brought peace to France," declared the duc d'Albufera to the Army of the Midi at the end of June 1814. "He openly declares that the glory of the armies have suffered no prejudice in the great struggle that has just come to an end." Maybe. But two weeks later the Army of the Midi was disbanded. The government would explain that it had no choice, for it had no money; baron Louis' devastating report on the state of French finances had been revealed in mid-June. But no officer put on half pay, no private returning to fields that had such meagre crops, to artisan shops that offered no work, to the recently installed soup kitchens of Paris and Lyon, no disabled veteran whose pension had been reduced was going to believe that it was simply a question of money. The glory of their army did not belong to King Louis, the shame of the peace did. When the war scare over Saxony spread through France in January 1815, the King called up sixty thousand former deserters from the class of 1814, "those who had returned to their homes without permission." By February, only thirty-five thousand had responded. They might have accepted King Louis and peace but, if it was to be war, they preferred to march with Napoleon.[50]

Wellington's first reports on the discontent in France arose, not surprisingly, from troubles in the army; and, none too surprising either, it was noted that the discontent was aimed at the English. In the first week of October a handful of printers were arrested and their presses seized for publishing a pamphlet that warned of the dangers of "English influence" and especially of the British occupation of that northern neighbour that obsessed all soldiers, Belgium. But, according to Wellington, the damage was done; the pamphlet was "circulated in all the coffee houses and public places" of Paris and, moreover, had been "industriously circulated throughout the country, and particularly in the army."[51]

As the discontent grew, so did the unpopularity of the English. It began with a relatively mild underswell of resentment over such issues as the way the English dressed.[52] But the mood became ever more vicious. One of Joseph Farington's colleagues in the Royal Academy, William Westall, returned to London in October 1814 with gloomy reports on how the English were being treated. "He told me," noted Farington, "that several persons who lately returned from France remarked how strong the hatred of the French People is towards the People of England, whom they impute all the discomfitude that has fallen upon them."[53]

Wellington deemed such reports exaggerated. "I am quite convinced," he wrote to Liverpool in December, "there is nothing to apprehend but extreme discontent and talk." Yet Wellington himself was the object of much abuse. Was it true, as reported in London, that at one military review a bullet whistled past his head? After October he certainly attempted to keep a low public profile; his meetings with Blacas and with the King would not be covered in the press. He stopped his hunting parties with the Bourbons after his hounds overran peasant properties just sown in winter wheat. The peasants demanded indemnity; Wellington responded by handing all his hounds over to the duc de Berry (for which act he was amply recompensed by a magnificent royal gift of Sèvres porcelain, now on display at Apsley House).[54]

Lord Liverpool, in London, became in the meantime absolutely convinced that his valuable Ambassador in Paris was about to be assassinated and he determined to remove him to the safer climes of America. "I confess," Wellington answered on 16 November, "that I don't see the necessity for being in a hurry." A couple of days later rumours of his removal were published. "We must not disgrace ourselves," Wellington, quite incensed, wrote to London. "We must not act with precipitation. There is really no evidence of danger, excepting general discontent." So Wellington remained, holding on to his rich fort at rue Saint-Honoré. When he finally left at the end of January for Vienna, it was not a retreat; Liverpool knew, just as every man in London's Cabinet knew, Wellington was the only diplomat capable of replacing Lord Castlereagh.[55]

King Louis the Desired remained unperturbed by the reports of trouble in his kingdom. Unlike the Sovereign of Elba, he was not shy of public appearances. On many an afternoon he could be seen waddling around the Jardin du Roi behind the Tuileries Palace. He took outings to the woods of Vincennes to the east of Paris and to the Château Saint-Cloud to the west; he stood outside the Louvre to admire the new colonnade and his carriage followed the whole length of the recently opened canal de l'Ourcq because he was proud of the building works accomplished; he went to Saint-Maur, he sat in his box at the Théâtre Français, his coach often rolled along the exterior boulevards to the barrière du Trône and around to the faubourg Saint-Antoine. Wasn't that the crowd that shouted "Vive le Roi"? It was true. But they shouted other things besides. On the last day of November Marshal Marmont, who directed royal security, warned the King not to attend the Odéon that night. "Messieurs," said the King to Marmont and his attendants, "your duty is to protect me, mine is to go and enjoy the show." Wellington reported to London that it had been a false alarm, another case of French bureaucracy tripping over itself. Four thousand men were put on guard when Louis went out to enjoy himself.[56]

Shortly after the incident, the King wrote to Talleyrand to say, "My sleep is as peaceful as it was in my youth." Committed to the constitution of the land, confirmed by his legitimate authority, resolved never to stray, he claimed he merited that description in Horace's poem, "justum et tenacem propositi virum" – a man just and firm in his designs.[57]

New Year in Paris

As in Vienna, it snowed in Paris with the New Year – the winters at the end of Napoleon's wars were extraordinarily cold. And, again as in Vienna, the Carnival season of 1815 began amid widespread fears of war over the Saxon crisis. King Frederick Augustus's protestation at the Prussian occupation of his country had appeared in all the French papers, there were editorials on the unfortunate and oppressed Saxon people, appeals not to let the "right of conquest" triumph in the heart of Germany, and concerns expressed that Russia and Prussia were just a little too friendly for the health of France. Several of the diplomatic notes exchanged during the crisis were reproduced verbatim in the *Journal de Paris*, the *Journal des Débats*, and the *Moniteur*. "Some of the clouds that seem to have obscured the political horizon," anxiously remarked the opposition paper, *Le Nain Jaune* (the Yellow Dwarf), on 5 January, "far from having vanished, have darkened, and several of the conferences between the Ministers of the Great Powers have involved the most alarming arguments." The call-up of sixty-thousand troops did not allay these worries.[58]

If it was Carnival season, it was a poor and confused Carnival in Paris. The city was unaccustomed to snow. The lake of La Villette froze over and so did the canal de l'Ourcq; the ice floes in the Seine allowed a few rash persons to venture across on foot. Posters went up in every street ordering residents to sweep the snow and break the ice that coated the cobbles in front of them. The papers of the day reported fogs and low cloud – webs of vapour held in suspense, muffling the tramp of horses and wagons; rootless sounds for Paris. "I must think carefully and lead a sensible life," wrote the forever doubting Benjamin Constant in his diary on New Year's Eve; he was still wondering what to do with himself. "I am so tired and so unhappy because of all my follies. I must get a grip on myself, it is high time I did." Joseph Fouché, having passed several months at Ferrières, had returned to Paris to make the most of the Carnival's receptions. He was also wondering what the future held for him; the government had offered him nothing. He had a long talk with another of the King's favourites, the duc d'Havré, but he recognised that the chances of a job were hopeless. "Never," he said, "had I felt in my life such a sense of abandon."[59]

Parliament had been prorogued on 30 December. Ill-intentioned people spread the rumour that the King intended to rule without it, and many historians have repeated this. But no parliament sits for twelve months a year. The Mother of Parliaments itself had only sat in Westminster for three weeks since its adjournment in July. Just before the King's Ministers arrived to complete the ceremonies the President of the Chamber of Deputies, Joseph Lainé,[60] summed up what he felt had been achieved to date. The law on the freedom of the press did not satisfy all temperaments, he said, but it had laid the way to greater liberties while providing needed reassurance to the government. One would have liked to have lessened the public charge, he went on, but the public debt proved immense; "your hearts were broken, Messieurs, by the need to re-establish taxes against which a large part of France has revolted." Not enough had yet been done for industry, not enough for commerce. But an enormous effort had been made to reconcile "representative government" with some of its greatest adversaries, the "brave warriors" who had been separated from their homes.[61]

On New Year's Day, the King received the members of both Chambers in his Salle du Trône. He told them how enchanted he was to meet "the representatives of my children," pleaded with them to remain united, and dismissed them saying, "go then into your departments and say to all my subjects that you have seen their true father." The deputies left. One fifth of them were to face elections and the new parliament was due to reconvene on 1 May 1815.[62]

In the second week of January a serious revolt broke out in the Breton capital of Rennes. An old administrative city of grey granite and stinking drains, Rennes had seriously suffered in the last two decades from the forced emigration of its nobles, the closure of its old institutions, the disruption of its textile industry and, most particularly, a civil war which pitted a Republican city against a Royalist countryside. When the Bourbon government decided to send in a commission to honour the "officers and soldiers of the royal armies of the West, wounded in defence of the throne," the city was, for three days, put to the sack by law students, dismissed army officers, and apparently not a few local administrators. Several people were killed, yet neither the police nor the city authorities intervened.[63]

That same week a popular actress of the Théâtre Français, Mademoiselle Raucourt, died in Paris. Actors and actresses had, by some ancient papal bull ("I imagine in the reign of Louix XV," remarked Wellington in his report to Castlereagh), been excommunicated by the Church. Mademoiselle Raucourt, however, had in the last years of her life become a devout member of the congregation of the Eglise Saint-Roche, so her followers were understandably outraged when the church's curé refused to perform a funeral. On 17 January, five or six thousand of them marched down the rue Saint-Honoré, bearing the coffin, and shouting out the old revolutionary slogan, *"Les prêtres à la lanterne!"* They smashed open the church doors and dragged the curé to the coffin. Just at that moment, one of the King's chaplains arrived, accompanied by the royal guard, and it was he – whether by order of the King or by order of his Chancellor has never been determined – who actually performed the ceremony. When it was done, a few cries of *"Vive le Roi!"* were heard. But priests remained unpopular and for several days thereafter were assailed by snowballs on their way to mass.[64]

It was not an auspicious debut for the solemn transfer of Louis XVI's remains from his unmarked grave at the Madeleine to the Basilica of Saint-Denis, due to take place on 21 January, the anniversary of his execution. There were a few unfortunate incidents that day. On her way to the ceremony, the Grand Dowager Duchess of Orléans, widow of the regicide Philippe-Egalité, slipped on a flight of icy stairs and broke a leg; after four doctors had practically bled her to death, it was announced that she was in a "tranquil state" by evening. Her son, Louis-Philippe, the duc d'Orléans and future King, popped his head out the carriage while accompanying the cortège up the boulevard des Italiens and was booed by a group of ardent Royalists standing nearby. After the procession turned into rue du Faubourg Saint-Denis, it was greeted in turn by the Republican cries of *"A la lanterne!"*[65]

The thermometer recorded one degree of frost at two o'clock that afternoon; the Basilica was not heated. A row of pews had been set aside for the diplomatic corps. One seat was notably empty, that of the Duke of Wellington, who found an excuse not to be there.[66] Three days later he left for Vienna in a snow storm with Giuseppina Grassini by his side. The Duchess of Wellington was abandoned once more; she remained at the Embassy in the company of young Lord Fitzroy Somerset, who was Wellington's secretary, nephew by marriage, and temporary replacement during the Ambassador's absence. As Wellington explained to Jaucourt, he hoped to be back by spring.

The spirit of Carnival picked up in February, despite the continuing freeze. With the approach of Mardi Gras the crowds on the boulevards grew bigger and merrier, though there was not the same number wearing grotesque masks as had been the case in former times. On the Sunday before the great festival, the butchers of Paris led, as was the tradition, a fatted ox up the rue de Rivoli to the Tuileries, where the King and the duchesse d'Angoulême saluted them; then on into the courtyard of the Palais-Royal to receive the greetings, from a balcony, of the duc d'Orléans, his wife, and their infant son; they crossed the narrow streets to the Prefecture of Police, and the procession ended in front of the Hôtel de Ville. That night there was a masked ball held at the Odéon and on Tuesday afternoon, after a downpour, the sun was seen for the first time in a month. Down rue Saint-Honoré and the boulevards marched huge floats, the most remarkable being a wagon carrying caricatures of the Paris press – the grenadier of the *Journal de Paris*, the Cassandra of the *Débats*, the knave of the *Journal Royal*, and at the summit the nodding head of *Le Nain Jaune* – all accompanied by a cat's concert of fiddles, pipes, and drums. The King, although suffering from a fit of the gout, preceded them with his Swiss Guard.[67]

The news gradually filtered in that the Saxon crisis had been concluded peacefully. "It is a beautiful success for French diplomacy," rejoiced the *Journal de Paris*, "and a happy event for all Europe." Even *Le Nain Jaune* was impressed by the apparent tranquillity. True, there was concern about Italy with rumours that Murat's armies were on the move. But France was quiet. Britain had opened her parliament. And most important was the settlement of the Saxon problem: the Eastern menace had been checked. British officers in Belgium were granted extended leave; Hanoverian troops were sent home. Perhaps this really was a European peace.[68]

A telegraph

Freezing February gave way to wet March, fit weather for arthritis and gout. The King was so stricken he was unable to attend Sunday mass in the palace chapel and, instead, had a private service performed in his apartments. An iron framed four-poster bed with green silk curtains had been rigged up next to his study because His Majesty could not even make it to his bedroom. Most days he spent on a couch, his feet wrapped in sheepskins. As more than one royal attendant would observe during the three dramatic weeks that followed, the King would not – and he could not – leave his couch in the Tuileries.[69]

It was on a Sunday, 5 March, shortly after the morning mass, that Monsieur Chappe, the rotund Director of Telegraphs, was seen making a dash down one of the Tuileries corridors in the direction of the offices of the baron de Vitrolles, secretary to the King's councils. He was quite out of breath when he got there; all he could do was brandish the message he held in his hand and beg Vitrolles to take it straight round to the King. It was not normal procedure, but Vitrolles, impressed by the state Chappe was in, did as he was asked.

King Louis was, of course, on his couch. With his crippled fingers he painfully slit open the envelope, extracted a short note, read it in total silence, and then sank his head in his hands. Vitrolles was standing, perplexed, nearby. "Do you know what this telegraph contains?" the King eventually inquired. "No, Sire, I do not," admitted Vitrolles. "Well, I will tell you" the King continued. "It is Revolution once more. Bonaparte has landed on the coast of Provence. Have this letter taken instantly to the Minister of War."[70]

The Minister of War at that time was Marshal Soult, who had been one of Napoleon's ablest commanders, had defended the Pyrenees and the south of France the previous year but, on accepting the ministry from the Bourbons, had made himself unpopular with the army. That was the problem Soult faced in March. All the military leaders repeated the same point: the decisive moment would be the first contact between Napoleon and the army; if the forces held out, Bourbon France could hold out; if they defected, it was feared there would be a snowball effect. The duc d'Orléans' proposal of sending out a small loyal corps instead of relying on troops of the line was probably the best solution, but time was of the essence, and the government in Paris did not have time; Napoleon had been in France for five days.[71]

It was reported that Napoleon, with a thousand men, was crossing the Maritime Alps and heading for Grenoble. Theoretically, Soult had ample troops available in the garrisons of Valence and Grenoble, along with a sizable force in Lyon. But they were not trustworthy. Soult thought the best solution was to devise a vast plan, a plan of royal dimensions, mobilising practically all the forces in southern France against the Elban invader. He sent the King's younger brother, the duc d'Artois, down to Lyon to act as commander-in-chief. The duc d'Angoulême, Artois' eldest son, then on a state visit in Bordeaux, was directed on to Nîmes to hold out the right wing, while the duc de Berry, Artois' younger son, was given command of the Franche Comté in eastern France to strengthen the left. All three princes were assigned marshals, who had earned their batons in the service of Napoleon, to act as advisers – Gouvion Saint-Cyr for Artois, Macdonald for Angoulême, and Ney for Berry. Artois and Berry left Paris within twenty-four hours.[72]

It was only on the 7th that the news of Napoleon's landing was published in *Le Moniteur*, but by that time every citizen of Paris was aware of the fact. Prices on the stock market tumbled. "Nobody wants to buy anything," said one police report. "One can see how far we are from the habits of the Revolution," said another. "In the past, thousands of groups would have formed and there would have been motions and violent proposals made from all sides. Today people meet, they anxiously question, and they accuse Bonaparte of wanting to trouble the peace, of bringing us back civil war and foreign war." Even those overtly in sympathy with Napoleon wondered if Napoleon had not chosen a poor moment and was going to compromise the good cause forever. The old revolutionary, Joseph Fouché, continued to manœuvre into a position that would give him the advantage, whichever way events went. On Monday he was organising a military coup that would set up a provisional government in Paris; on Friday his troops, from the northern garrisons, failed to turn up; on Saturday he was an ardent royalist again. Benjamin Constant was still in love and despair. On Saturday, 4 March, he was writing in his diary, "It's decided," – in the case of Constant, a sure sign that nothing was decided at all – "I'm leaving." On Sunday he wrote a letter to Juliette and then spent the evening with Juliette; and on both occasions he told her he was leaving. On Monday he began to arrange his departure. But all of a sudden: "Unexpected news. Could it be possible that Bonaparte is in France? My departure has been delayed." And he spent one more evening with Juliette.[73]

Children would remember for the rest of their lives what it was like to be in Paris after the announcement that Napoleon had landed. Hippolyte Carnot, son of the great Carnot who had saved the Republic in 1793, was at Lycée Louis-le-Grand at the time. The streets and boulevards, he recalled, were crowded with sombre and dejected people, the news hawkers lost their voices, the shopkeepers kept silent. "Paris," he said, "had the characteristic air of a great city on the eve of a catastrophe." The future historian Jules Michelet was attending the Lycée Charlemagne. His mother had died just after the Carnival, on Ash Wednesday. What Michelet remembered especially was his family's poverty: the lack of light in their one-room apartment on rue de Périgueux, the shortage of food, and the cold. The news of Napoleon's approach pulled him out of mourning; "it exploded like a clap of thunder." Paris was in a state of agitation and on everybody's lips was the question, "What is *he* going to do?" "My poor Greek and Latin authors suffered," recollected Michelet; no exams were set, no prizes were given in the winter and spring of 1815.[74]

Hortense de Beauharnais, Napoleon's stepdaughter, had an apartment overlooking one of the boulevards. She could see the Royalist volunteer corps being recruited, "young enthusiasts and old servants, some proud and threatening, others out of breath, already exhausted by the weight of their weapons." A cavalry regiment might pass, soldiers of the "old army," always maintaining a scornful, preoccupied look. And the people? They simply watched, as if they were attending a spectacle, and "waited for the outcome in silence." The former Queen of Holland was expecting civil war.[75]

Flight of the Eagle

Napoleon had no master plan when he stepped ashore at Golfe Juan with 1,026 men, forty horses, two cannon, and a coach. There had been no conspiracy, no concerted effort among French officers, no organised party in Paris calling upon him. All he knew was that he had to get out of hostile Provence as fast as possible and cross the mountains to Dauphiné, where he could expect somewhat more sympathy. Napoleon had no idea what path he would take, what resistance he would meet, what the reception of the population would be. He had prophesied at sea that "I shall reach Paris without firing a shot"; but he knew just as well as the administrators in Paris that the real test would come in his first confrontation with regular troops. In the first four days of his march – after Grasse, single-file up a winding, icy track, where two mules and one tenth of his treasure had disappeared down a precipice – he had added only four recruits to his band: two soldiers had been picked up from the garrison at Antibes, a tanner from Grasse, and a policeman.

The test came at Laffrey, a tiny village forty kilometres south of Grenoble where the road was hemmed in by a lake on one side and a chain of high hills on the other. It was the classical military trap. The garrison of Grenoble was the home of five regiments, including the 4th Artillery in which Napoleon had begun his military career. Its commander was General Jean Marchand, a native son of the city. His hasty conversion to the Bourbon cause in April 1814 had made him unpopular not only with the troops, but also the townsmen and the peasants of surrounding Dauphiné, who remained attached to the former Emperor. When Marchand's order of the day – with the observation that Napoleon was advancing with only a thousand men – was read out to the troops they shouted back, "And us! Don't we count?" "*Bougre d'imbécile!*" came an anonymous cry from the ramparts, "it's not in his direction we're going to shoot, it's in the other." The general decided to shut the city gates and ordered the garrison to be placed "in a state of defence." To gain time, he sent out a small company of engineers with a battalion from the 5th Infantry Regiment to blow up a bridge. These were the troops, about a thousand in all, that confronted Napoleon at Laffrey.

They were under the orders of Commandant Delessart. He never made it to the bridge. Peasants and tradesmen had already heard of the approach of Napoleon and lined the road exclaiming, "*Vive l'Empereur!*" Several of the soldiers joined in their cries. When Delessart learned that he was about to make contact with Napoleon's advance guard he beat a swift retreat to what all French military schools at the time termed a "*belle position,*" a narrow pass where he could deploy his men, the defile of Laffrey. All next morning, 7 March, the two forces faced each other just beyond the range of musket shot, Delessart placing a company of light infantry on his first line, Napoleon deploying his Polish Lancers. A large number of peasants had accompanied Napoleon's forces in the last leg of their march, and they now crossed the line and started fraternising with Delessart's troops. Delessart would later describe the soldiers as trembling in every limb and "pale as death." Napoleon had spent part of his morning inspecting a high position that had been seized the previous night. He then took a carriage to the rear of his troops, descended, mounted a horse, and galloped through the ranks, to his own tense front line. Delessart's infantry saw the Lancers approach and were immediately ordered to retreat – for Delessart calculated that, if they could not fight, he could at least avoid their defection. But the Lancers were now so close he was obliged to make a stand. He commanded his troops to halt and turn. At that moment the Lancers peeled off to the left and the right, revealing behind them the Old Guard in their blue greatcoats, red epaulettes, and their tall bearskin busbies: and Napoleon, within the range of pistol shot. "Soldiers of the 5th Regiment!" he cried to the troops opposite, their guns trained on him, "I am your Emperor! Recognise me." He opened his grey coat. "If there is a single soldier who wants to kill his Emperor, here I am!"[76]

Bourbon France was lost. Wellington had said it the previous autumn: no Sovereign is sovereign without an army. Columns of

LES PORTES DE GRENOBLE APPORTÉES AUX PIEDS DE L'EMPEREUR PAR LES HABITANTS.

Artisans and peasants bring the gates of Grenoble
to the feet of Napoleon

peasants would follow Napoleon to Grenoble – the same ragged columns, with drums, pennants, and a song, that had been seen at the time of the Revolution (they would reappear, like phantoms, in 1850 in defence of the Second Republic). When, a week later, Napoleon left Lyon for Autun and Auxerre, he was accompanied by columns of workers and artisans from the suburbs and the country. Benjamin Constant was right: it was an ancient rural and corporate world, not the modern world of commerce, which supported Napoleon.

But it was the army that brought Napoleon to Paris, and especially the older veterans of war. Colonel Louis Fantin des Odoards, who had served for fourteen years in Napoleon's armies, described in his memoirs the temptation he had felt at Gap to rejoin his old regiment as the Emperor passed. "Concealed in an obscure back room I felt my heart throbbing violently," wrote Fantin, recalling the painful moment, "and at each pulse beat I was on the point of emerging from my hiding-place and throwing myself into the arms of old comrades of the Guard whose voices I recognised, and of saying to them: 'Take me to Napoleon.'" Fantin was actually one of the few who did remain faithful to his Bourbon oath; he left by a back door with a young companion who had not the slightest interest in Napoleon.[77]

Napoleon himself claimed that he returned from Elba a new man, committed to the humane principles of the Revolution, a "Messiah of peace and of the people's rights." At Lyon he declared himself to be less "the Sovereign of France than the first of its citizens" and issued a series of decrees that, among other things, abolished the two parliamentary Chambers (for they had "carried arms against France" and had lost the confidence of the nation "by adhering to the re-establishment of the nobility"), proscribed the white Bourbon flag, suppressed "feudal titles," dismissed the King's Swiss Guard and the Royal House Guard, expelled the returned *émigrés* from France and sequestered their properties. Then, in a measure steeped in revolutionary nostalgia, he called for the assembly in May of a great national congress on Paris's Champ de Mars to decide on a new constitution. "I am," he declared, "returning to protect and defend the interests that our Revolution has given us. I wish to grant you an inviolable constitution, prepared by the people and me together." The next day, the "people and me" were marching on Paris.[78]

Flight of the King

A successful defence of Paris would have required a fast, efficient, and experienced government. Louis XVIII's government was none of these. Vitrolles described its chief spokesman, comte Blacas, Grand Master of the King's Wardrobe, as "the model of beatitude; he had not a thought for the next day and I kept forcing myself to shake him from his impassive attitude." Soult, the Minister of War, was accused of conspiring with the Bonapartists because he had placed the least trustworthy troops on the front line at Grenoble, and was fired on 11 March. He was replaced by another of Napoleon's former generals, Henri Clarke, the duc de Feltre, chosen not because of his competence but because of the Royalist friends he had cultivated in the Chamber of Peers.

Countless plans were spawned, each one as extraordinary as the other. Vitrolles wanted the King to retreat to La Rochelle and lead an army of Chouans and Vendéens on to Paris. Blacas proposed that the King get into an open calèche surrounded by members of the two Chambers and that they all ride out, like medieval knights, to meet Napoleon and ask him what he proposed to do; Blacas was convinced that Napoleon, on the sight of them, would immediately retire. Marshal Marmont was keen to prepare the Tuileries and Louvre for a seventeenth-century style siege defended by the Household Guard. The Household Guard, countered the duc d'Orléans (who had just returned to Paris after the loss of Lyon), was "a vicious and gothic organisation" – and that was the opinion of most.

The duc de Berry, who had also made a humiliating return to Paris, replaced his father as commander-in-chief and had the idea of concentrating what forces he could at Melun, some fifty kilometres south of the capital. But Melun was a town with no defences. He then, like a good cadet, thought of taking a *belle position*, reinforced with trenches and parapets, somewhat closer to Paris. The duc d'Orléan countered again: the problem of a *belle position* was that Napoleon could simply outflank it. In the meantime, troops were being ordered north, south, east, and west; up to Melun, down to Roanne, up again to Vincennes. Marching, marching. Yet, during the twenty days of Napoleon's advance, not a bridge was blown and not a tree cut down that might have hindered his progress.[79]

King Louis himself added to the confusion by issuing, right at the outset of the crisis, a proclamation to the National Guards calling them to defend the Charter, "which is our free and *personal* work." In other words, Louis was suggesting that the Charter was a product of the King's will; a constitutional monarch, responsible to parliament, was not supposed to talk like that. Every liberal, in and out of parliament, became frightened. So, as Napoleon marched north, Paris became absorbed in a great political debate that pitted "Constitutionalists," like Lainé, Lally-Tollendal, and La Fayette, against what Benjamin Constant called the *"royalistes exagérés,"* who seemed to be gaining an upper hand in the court and government. The Constitutionalists scored some important successes; there was no extension of illegal executive powers (one is tempted to say, because there was no Executive) and the two Chambers were convoked for an emergency session that began on 11 March.

"We have carried off an immense victory in obtaining from the King the convocation of the Chambers," wrote Jaucourt to Talleyrand on the 8th, as if this were the most important item in the news. Though fervent supporters of the Bourbons, these Constitutionalists seemed quite unconcerned about the outcome of the military effort against Napoleon. The great battle for them was the battle of ideas, the need to establish a line of continuity – similar in concept to Talleyrand's notion of legitimacy – that led from the liberal constitutions of 1789 and 1791 to the Charter of 1814. By mid-March, they were convinced they had won. Just one day before the King fled Paris, the Chamber of Deputies victoriously passed a motion that confirmed "the natural and inalienable rights of all peoples."[80]

The political success of the Constitutionalists put the *royalistes exagérés* on the defensive. Several had already left the country by 15 March. Others attempted to forge the devil's alliance with old Jacobins and former supporters of Napoleon, people who had little regard for the rights of parliament.

One of the main objects of their attention was the jobless Joseph Fouché. A meeting between Fouché and and no less than the King's brother himself, Monsieur, the duc d'Artois, was arranged on the night of 14 March in the apartments of the princess de Vaudémont. Artois offered Fouché, on behalf of the King, the Ministry of the

Police. How touched the old Terrorist was! But how sorry he was to declare that the offer came too late! Too late! Too late! "Save the King," Fouché advised Monsieur, "and I will take care of saving the monarchy."

The next day the government ordered Fouché's arrest – because a man like Fouché, who was not a committed ally, had to be considered an enemy. Fouché went into hiding.[81]

King Louis, meanwhile, had to demonstrate his loyalty to the Charter and to Parliament, so he called a joint session of the two Chambers to be held in the Luxembourg Palace on Thursday, 16 March. News had already been announced that the second city of France, Lyon, had fallen to Napoleon, but nobody in Paris was yet aware that the returning Emperor intended to abolish the Chambers.

It was pouring with rain when the royal procession set out from the Tuileries for the joint session. King Louis was too busy rehearsing his speech in front of the duc d'Orléans to observe the reaction of the soaked crowds lining the streets. But the Duke had a look. Only a few of the troops called out "*Vive le roi!*" But the people behind them cheered. Captain Edmund Walcot, who had been sent over from England to observe the "French Royal Army," was in that crowd; he described the procession as "very fine."

"I have seen again my country, I have reconciled it with the foreign Powers," declared the King from his throne in the Luxembourg Palace; "I have worked for the happiness of my people: I reap every day the most touching signs of their love. Could I, sixty years old, better terminate my career than to die in their defence?" When the old King finished the duc d'Artois jumped to his feet, flamboyantly raised a hand high, and sweeping it round the whole assembly, regally announced, "We swear on our honour to live and die faithful to our King and the constitutional Charter, that assures the happiness of Frenchmen!"

Le Moniteur reported the next day that the response was "electric." Chateaubriand said the sight was "pathetic." The King was aged and crippled, and Monsieur's public oath had come too late, too late. During the session, the Chamber was plunged into darkness as black storm clouds swept by outside.[82]

Later that same day Joseph Lainé told the Chamber of Deputies in their house on the Seine that this was not the time to look for faults in the regime: it had, after all, brought peace to France. Many families, he said, were still suffering from the war. There was no hope of liberty from "*him*" – Lainé could not even mention the former Emperor's name. "No more justice, no more property," he exclaimed; "industry would become the object of snubs." With the unnamable "*him*" in power, foreign war was inevitable because "the blood of war is his element; he would waste no time before swooping down on neighbouring states, carrying our children with *him*." Lainé had faith in the French army and, more specifically, its leaders to save the country.[83]

Two days after this speech was pronounced the great Marshal Ney, who had been sent out to command the army of the Franche Comté, was in Auxerre kneeling before Napoleon. He had received no orders from Paris; Berry had never turned up at headquarters; the news of defections to his south was bad; and many of the towns and villages around him were in a state of insurrection – eastern France, which had suffered a quite brutal occupation the preceding year, was not favourable to the Bourbons. Ney faced the prospect of French civil war, and the marshal decided against it. "I am your prisoner rather than your supporter if you continue to govern tyranically," he sub-mitted to Napoleon. "Good Ney is mad!" replied the Emperor.[84]

There was complete confusion in Paris. The duc d'Orléans was astounded when he discovered that no provisions at all had been made for the King's departure. He recommended that the government and the two Chambers set up a provisional capital at Lille, close to the Belgian border and in an area that was staunchly Bourbon. The new Minister of War said it would be too expensive and the roads could never handle the traffic. When the Duke suggested to the King that Napoleon might soon enter Paris, Louis gave him an astonished look and said, "One should not even make such a supposition." But the Duke insisted, adding that Berry's small army at Melun did not inspire much confidence. "I know, I know," said the King. "From the very beginning you have always seen everything in black. Well, if he comes, he comes. I'm sixty years old. At my age, you make up your mind and then wait." The King would wait on his couch in the Tuileries.[85]

On several nights, as fresh news of Napoleon's advance arrived, Vitrolles would run to the King. His Majesty would be lying in his iron-framed bed. "The enormous corpulence of the King," recalled Vitrolles, "not only seemed to fill the width of the bed, but appeared to extend beyond it." He wore a white night cap that gave him the appearance of "a colossal child." Vitrolles would read him the latest dispatches, one more despairing than the other. But the King never panicked. Vitrolles believed that it was the King's own impassivity that prevented any discussion in the court of plans for departure.[86]

Perhaps another Napoleon could have created a more defiant mood in the Tuileries which might have carried into the streets of Paris, but this was not in the character of Louis. The crowds that gathered out-side the palace in the rain received no news. The Guard at the gates was doubled. It would seem that it was the King himself who made a last-minute decision to leave for Lille, as the duc d'Orléans had recommended. The King left Paris on 19 March, Palm Sunday – a par-ticularly sad moment to commemorate Christ's entry into Jerusalem.

According to this artist, Napoleon was carried on the
shoulders of troops into the Tuileries

The crowds outside were as numerous as they had been on Saturday,
the rains just as torrential. The King inspected the Household Guard
on the Champ de Mars and returned to his palace at four. At nine
o'clock, the Guard were informed the King would be leaving. At midnight, a procession of coaches rolled up at the pavillon de Flore, the
King painfully descended the staircase, guardsmen and courtiers
falling to his feet with every step he took. The coaches then left in
silence.[87]

The whole Government left Paris that night. So did many of its
supporters. Chateaubriand remembered his wife pushing him into a
carriage at four in the morning. "I was in such a state of rage," he
recollected, "that I did not know where I was going or what I was
doing."[88]

The same motley crowds were still milling around the Tuileries on
Monday morning. The main streets and boulevards were lined with
people who collected around the jugglers, singing dogs, and the news
vendors; "the city at this time had, as it had the day before, the
appearance of a fair with not the slightest alteration in the occupations
of the people, except that it seemed a general holiday," said Captain
Walcot.[89]

Only the soldiers, veterans, and officers on half-pay actually
cheered Napoleon when he entered Paris. A troop of half-pay officers
had been waiting out at the porte Saint-Denis for news that the King

had gone. They immediately directed themselves on to the Tuileries with a small company of horsemen, making much of a din as they entered the place du Carrousel. After prolonged negotiations with the Royalist National Guard it was decided that they should share the duty of guarding the palace: that afternoon one had the singular spectacle of guardsmen in both white cockades and tricolours standing at the gates.

Night had already fallen when an unmarked black berlin stopped outside the pavillon de Flore, at the same spot where the King had departed only twenty-four hours before. Few civilians would have witnessed a man get out in his grey greatcoat; he was surrounded by soldiers. Alexandre de Laborde, grenadier of the National Guard, claimed Napoleon was carried on the shoulders of officers into the Tuileries. But comte Lavelette, one of Napoleon's former aides-de-camp, distinctly saw the Emperor mount the staircase by foot. Lavelette even stated that he preceded Napoleon, one step in front, walking backwards, eyes bathed in tears as he repeated to himself, "It's *you!* It's *you!* It's finally *you!*"[90]

Vienna and *la vindicte publique*

Legend has it that Napoleon, on landing in France, declared the Congress of Vienna dissolved. Unhappily for the Emperor this was hardly the case. He would repeat many times on St Helena that the greatest mistake he had made in his bid for power in 1815 was to start too early, before Europe's Ministers and Sovereigns had left Vienna. "Isn't it lucky this has happened now while we are all still assembled here," exclaimed Kaiser Franz on learning of Napoleon's escape from Elba. If Napoleon had waited just three more weeks they would have all dispersed and the history of Europe might have been very different.[91]

In his memoirs, Metternich gives a dramatic account of the events in Vienna that immediately followed news of Napoleon's escape. He tells how, on the morning of the 7th, he rushed from his rooms in the Chancellery across to the Hofburg and was in front of Kaiser Franz before eight. "Go immediately to the Emperor of Russia and the King of Prussia," instructed the Austrian Emperor; "tell them I'm ready to give the order to my army to take up again the road to France." At 8.15 he was in the Tsar's apartments. Because of the tensions over Poland and Saxony the two men had not spoken to each other for three months. It didn't take a moment to discuss the measures to be adopted; the decision was prompt and categoric. But Alexander would not let Metternich go without, first, laying bare his great Russian soul. "We have still to settle a personal difference," he said. "We are both Christians. Our sacred law commands us to pardon offences. Let us embrace so that all be forgotten." They embraced, and Metternich dashed off to the King of Prussia's apartments, where he was received at 8.30. At nine o'clock he was in conference with the Austrian commander, Schwarzenberg, and at ten "the Ministers of the Four (*sic*) Powers" were in his office deliberating. Couriers were already on their way to the various army corps with their dispatches. "It was thus that the war was decided," recorded Metternich, "in less than an hour."[92]

Other witnesses do not accord with this. Gentz recorded that, before he took his morning bath, he had a meeting with Metternich. No mention was made of Napoleon at all; he got the news much later in the day from Humboldt. Wellington first got the news in a dispatch he received that morning from Lord Burghesh, the British Consul in Genoa. Talleyrand received two notes, one from Metternich, the other from Wellington with a copy of Burghesh's dispatch. By midday couriers were indeed riding out to the armies, but only to alert the commanders; they carried no orders because nobody at that time knew where Napoleon was heading. Talleyrand was sure he was going to land in northern Italy. "I cannot believe that he would dare attempt our southern provinces," he wrote to Louis XVIII that night.[93]

The Committee of Five was called in the afternoon as scheduled, not to discuss Napoleon, but to finalise the accord on Saxony – the barrier against Russia. King Frederick Augustus had been released from the Schloss Friedrichsfeld and had spent the weekend in the Schönbrunn, outside Vienna, before taking a leisurely ride to Pressburg.[94] The King had to be persuaded to accept what the Five (Austria, Russia, Prussia, Britain, and France) had decided: the kernel of Saxony had been preserved, but two-fifths of the Kingdom were to be transferred to Prussia. At the conference it was decided that Metternich, Wellington, and Talleyrand would together inform the King, a very clear confirmation that it had been the three-power alliance – Austria, Britain, and Bourbon France – of 3 January 1815 that had resolved the problem of Saxony.[95]

Before the three set out for Pressburg the following day there was a theatrical performance to attend in the Redoutensaal, which, as it turned out, was the last great festival of the Congress. It was there, in the Redoutensaal, that the news of Napoleon's escape began to spread through Vienna. Countess Bernstorff described the evening as "unforgettable." She remembered standing at the head of the staircase, the same stairs where she had stood on so many occasions before, watching people as the rumour fanned out. "Even if the politicians were in the habit of controlling themselves," she said, "at that terrible hour one could clearly read the meaning in their faces." La Garde-Chambonas recorded, in his typical romantic fashion, that "a thousand candles seemed snuffed out in a second." "It was not difficult to perceive that fear was predominant in all the Imperial and Royal personages there assembled," remarked Lord Clancarty of the British Legation in a letter written to Castlereagh four days after the event. Gentz, in his diary, noted that the evening was "quite boring," but he did stay to watch the Sovereigns as they left "with applause from everyone."[96]

Talleyrand returned to the Kaunitz Palace in the early hours of the morning and penned a letter to the duchesse de Courlande, still in Paris. "Chère amie," he began, "I am writing just after a performance, in which Dorothée was a prodigious success. She acted in two plays, as admirably in one as in the other. She was beautifully dressed and very pretty." He said he had to return to Pressburg the next day – he had been there only the previous week to visit one of his ancient lady friends – and was determined to take young Dorothée along with him. And, oh yes, there was Bonaparte. Almost by way of a postscript he casually noted, "Buonaparte's departure from his Isle of Elba at the head of two hundred men makes him a brigand wherever he goes." It didn't seem to be the most important item on his agenda. "Our business has been proceeding quite well in the last few days," he concluded. "A month like this and all will be finished."[97]

The meeting between the three Foreign Ministers and the King of Saxony did not actually go very well. Frederick Augustus did not want to cede a square foot of soil to Frederick William. On their first encounter he chucked the Ministers' prepared statement aside and limited conversation to courtesies. "Did you have a good trip?" It was only on the fourth day of the Ministers' visit, Saturday, 11 March, that diplomatic notes were exchanged: the Saxon King informed the Ministers that he would not consent to the division of his kingdom; the Ministers informed the King that he had no choice. The Ministers were preparing their horses for Vienna when a courier arrived with news that Napoleon had landed, ten days earlier, in the south of France.

Metternich, Wellington, and Talleyrand were confident they had built their dyke across Saxony against the menacing flood from the east. The whole dispute had been a play of force, and the three had force on their side. As their carriages trundled back down the post road to Vienna they began to reflect on the new threat of flood from the west.[98]

Vienna was not deeply troubled by the news, for it had never been the tradition of Vienna to be deeply troubled – even when an enemy banged at her gates. A brief official announcement of Napoleon's escape was made in the *Österreichischer Beobachter* on the 9th; a short paragraph on his landing in France appeared on the 12th. Some in the secret police thought this was being a little too sparing and several agents warned of "agitation" if information was not provided more freely and promptly. By the 15th the initial anxieties had given way to "perfect calm and hope, now that the public papers are providing details." In the *salons* bets were placed – fifty ducats against five hundred – that Bonaparte would be dead or captured within a fortnight. The crowds were enjoying the first spring weather for, unlike in western Europe, Vienna in March was sunny and warm. The vendors at their makeshift stalls did brisk business on the Graben; the Eipeldauer's cousin could watch pretty girls in their fine silk pelisses saunter along the Bastei; Perth spoke of dining outside in the Augarten. Spring sap rose in the Palace of the Palm: Sagan began in earnest her affair with the British Ambassador, Sir Charles Stewart; Bagration developed new schemes on behalf of the Russians; ** made fresh demands for the expulsion of both ladies.[99]

The only genuine excitement in Vienna, it seemed, was among the Poles, the desperate Poles. For them, Napoleon's arrival in France represented a hope of liberation from Russian subjugation. Agents reported that Napoleon was the sole subject of conversation among them.

As for the Big Five, no decisive action could be taken until it was known where Napoleon was heading. Once it was confirmed he was in France, the armies could be regrouped and a policy statement made.

Concerning the first point, a general military plan was established by Schwarzenberg in a meeting with the Prussian and Russian commanders on 11 March, the day before Wellington, Metternich, and Talleyrand had got back to Vienna. Necessarily, it depended to a great extent on where forces at that moment could be found. Three "large corps" were consequently defined, in Italy, in the Upper Rhine, and in Belgium. Schwarzenberg gave himself the Upper Rhine; Wellington, because of the presence of British troops, would be offered Belgium (thus Wellington initially received his command from Vienna, not London); nobody at that time was designated for the general command in Italy. Two important reserve corps were also identified, the first in northern Germany under Blücher, and the second drawn from the Russian forces, still in Poland, that would be commanded by Barclay de Tolley, one of the heroes of the 1812 campaign.

Austria, having sent most of her troops into Italy in response to menacing manœuvres by Murat, was virtually excluded from playing a major role in northern Europe. Nor could Russia be expected to do much, at least in the initial military operations, because, in the first place, her forces were a long way from the Rhine, and, secondly, because her Allies were determined not to undo the main accomplishment of the Congress – the dyke across Saxony. "The corps of the Russian army, which advances on the request of the Emperor of

Austria, will not be crossing Saxony," Alexander's sister, the Grand
Duchess Maria, announced to the relief of her husband, the Grand
Archduke of Saxe-Weimar. A narrow corridor across Bohemia in the
direction of Württemberg was eventually traced out for them; it made
a very long march. With Austria and Russia absent, the main task of
defending Europe's northern plains from the new threat in the west
therefore fell on Britain and Prussia. It would not be a happy part-
nership.[100]

The second early task of the Five was the drafting of a policy statement. Like so much else in Vienna, it would be the product of compromise. The original draft was drawn up by the French. One gets its
tone from a letter Talleyrand wrote to Louis XVIII the day he heard
of Napoleon's escape: "Any undertaking of his [Napoleon's] in
France would be that of a bandit. That is how he would have to be
treated; and any measure permitted against bandits could be
employed against him." Wellington denounced Talleyrand's ideas,
which the French Minister argued in front of the Five on the 13th, as
the right to murder for private sport. The British attitude was much
more cautious; while they regarded the re-establishment of Napoleon
in France as incompatible with the peace and security of Europe they
did not want "too dictatorial a pledge." Specifically, they did not want
to be seen as imposing the Bourbons on the French. That was also the
Austrian attitude.[101]

Gentz drew up a more moderate statement that was adopted, with
amendments, by the eight signatory Powers of the Treaty of Paris at
midnight, 13 March, everybody apparently talking at the same time.

For all that, the text hardly lacked force. Since Napoleon had
broken the terms of the Treaty of Abdication, the Powers declared
that he had "destroyed the only legal title on which his Existence
depended" and, on returning to France, he had "deprived himself of
the Protection of laws." They therefore declared Napoleon "outside
civil and social Relations and, as Enemy and disturber of the peace of
the World, has delivered himself to public condemnation" – la vindicte publique.

As the author of this text, Gentz pointed out in an article he published in the Österreichischer Beobachter two days later, the
Declaration was not intended as an attack on the person Napoleon.[102]
Rather, it was a challenge to the "appalling System" that Napoleon
wanted to re-impose with his "former army" against the nation of
France. The term "Existence" – as must have been clear to anybody
with a legal training at the time – meant Napoleon's legal existence as
a Sovereign, an "Existence" that had never up to now been denied.
Gentz also pointed out that there was a political principle in the
Declaration in that it paid homage to the "founders and associates of
the European alliance" to which "Europe owed its deliverance."

France herself, he noted, had joined this "grand league." Napoleon's invasion of France was not a matter to which Europe could remain indifferent: Napoleon in Paris called into question the Alliance, the Congress, the whole peace settlement.[103]

The problem with news in Vienna was not so much censorship as a genuine lack of sources. The secret police obviously had no idea what was going on in France. Nor did the French Minister, who, next to Baron von Hager, was probably the most informed man in town. "Bad news is being spread," Talleyrand wrote on 16 March to his substitute, the comte de Jaucourt, in Paris, "and we have to destroy this." He pleaded for the tiniest details. "For heaven's sake inform me. We have no reason to fear; we are sure of our cause. But we need news to destroy news." Jaucourt's answer did not arrive until three weeks later: it was a dispatch from the seaport of Ostend. "If you can't write to me everyday, at least write to me when something happens," he urged the duchesse de Courlande on that same 16 March: she was on his doorstep in Vienna the following week.[104]

Gentz won five hundred guilders at whist the day (17 March) it was confirmed that two regiments at Grenoble had defected to Napoleon. He was in no gay mood. "The dinner was somewhat troubled by the bad news from France," he remarked. After dinner he went over to the Palm Palace for a *soirée* at Sagan's: "General consternation – Metternich, Talleyrand, Humboldt, etc."[105]

That was the day the Big Five decided to renew the Treaty of Chaumont – the legal base of the Alliance in the last month of the 1814 campaign – and to set up a military council to work out the details on the plan already outlined by Schwarzenberg on the 11th. Neither of these would prove simple tasks. The Tsar wanted to sit in the council and had even insisted on being named Generalissimo (the urge of being Liberator of Europe was once more returning). Wellington eventually persuaded him to sit in the council as a member, along with the four military commanders, Schwarzenberg for Austria, Wellington for Britain, Knesebeck for Prussia, and Wolkonski for Russia. It was an arrangement similar to that of the year before.[106]

The Treaty of Chaumont had to be amended. Initially it had been a closed treaty between four Allies. The Congress had changed entirely the nature of alliances and an effort was made to make the new treaty a truly European league. Accession clauses were therefore added. France would be one of the Allies, for the treaty was not against France, it was against the false Sovereign, Napoleon. Talleyrand added his signature to the treaty just one day before news arrived that his King had fled Paris. With Talleyrand's signature, the secret treaty of 3 January between France, Britain, and Austria was rendered null and void.

But the new treaty made no guarantee that, after the overthrow of Napoleon, France would be Bourbon. Article VIII invited the co-operation of Louis XVIII. However, a British declaration expressly stated that this was "not to be understood as binding His Britannic Majesty to prosecute the war, with a view to imposing on France any particular Government." There was a vague hint of national self-determination in this. Talleyrand proved sensitive to it. When he eventually learned of the King's flight from Paris he recommended that the King leave with the two Chambers, that the King not appear isolated, and that those around him be drawn from groups sufficiently varied to give their cause at least some national complexion.[107]

But what really delayed the signing of the new treaty (it was signed on the 25th and the accessions were drawn out for weeks thereafter) was the same German problem that had haunted much of the Congress.

In the first place, the creation of an army corps on the Upper Rhine, in which Austria would for long remain a minority force, gave the southern states significant leverage in the initial stages of the war. To the north there developed an even more complicated situation, where Britain and Prussia openly competed for recruits from among the smaller states. Wellington's basic idea was an old British idea of building up a continental army with paid mercenaries, though the terms of payment had evolved since the eighteenth century; Britain now offered "subsidies" to "sovereign states" rather than paying directly for the delivery of troops. Prussia, the loser in the Congress, claimed that every "sovereign state" in northern Germany, except Hanover, should come under Prussian command; for example, Hardenberg, quoting the accession treaties, argued that German states did not have the freedom to run off to the highest bidder, the mercantile British. Wellington countered that the states were perfectly free to do what they liked since no German Federation yet existed. The centraliser, vom Stein, sulking because he was not present at these debates, started campaigning for the immediate convocation of a German federal legislature, a *Bundestag*. "A Federation gives us strength," he wrote to Mecklenberg's Minister, "and those who will not enter it will remain outside, branded with ineptitude, stupidity, and childish arrogance."[108]

Castlereagh, in London, created problems for Wellington by stalling on the subsidies to the German states. Parliament and members of his own government were becoming hostile to the mercenary idea because Britain was facing a major problem with her national debt. Castlereagh wanted France to pay the expense of her own liberation. Wellington pushed for subsidies. "Nothing can be done with a small or inefficient force" he said; "the war will linger on, and will end to our disadvantage. Motives of economy, then, should induce the British Government to take measures to bring the largest possible force into action at the earliest and the same period of time."[109]

The accession treaties allowed for some compromise between Britain and Prussia. Instead of fighting for the British army as mercenaries, the states would join the coalition as allies. Britain would supply the subsidies, but the distribution of the troops would be decided jointly by Britain, Austria, Prussia, and Russia.

The result, as one can imagine, was a chaotic European army in Belgium.

Three days after the treaty was signed, on 28 March, the news arrived in Vienna that Napoleon was in the Tuileries. A great *soirée* had been organised at the Palm Palace by Sagan and her mother, the duchesse de Courlande, who had just arrived from Paris. Talleyrand would of course turn up, his face that night expressionless. Metternich made an appearance, pale as ever; he was still writing lonely, doom-ridden letters to Sagan, but she was by now fully occupied with the jovial British Ambassador. Wellington was described by Gentz as being "tender." At the close of the evening he bid farewell to all, and the following morning he mounted his carriage for the Low Countries. The weather was summerlike.

Castlereagh, in London, had received news of Napoleon's entry into Paris several days earlier. "If we are to undertake the job, we must leave nothing to chance; it must be done upon the largest scale," Castlereagh wrote at once to the Duke. "You must inundate France with force in all directions."[110]

London's "Week of Wonders"

Lord and Lady Castlereagh, with their suite, had landed at Dover under the salute of guns and the acclamations of a small crowd that had gathered at the pier on Friday afternoon, 3 March, two days after Napoleon had set foot in France. According to Robert Fagel, the Dutch Ambassador who had seen him in Paris, Castlereagh appeared in no hurry to get back to London. He was dreading the parliamentary debate over the Congress. He spent Friday night in Sittingbourne and was not back at his home in St James's Square until late on Saturday. He was due to appear in the Commons on Monday afternoon. He knew nothing, as yet, of Napoleon's venture.[111]

As was his custom, Castlereagh set out for the Commons on foot. Descending Great George Street he ran into a "tumultuous mob, using insolent and threatening language." All the other usual avenues to the House were also blocked; New Palace Yard and Old Palace Yard were filled with people "hallooing and hooting." Castlereagh eventually found his way into the Commons by taking the portico passage opposite the Abbey and making his way through the Speaker's apartments.

He was not the only member of parliament to have difficulties getting to work that day. John Croker reported that his carriage had been surrounded, he had been dragged out by the collar, and he had received several blows; he eventually made it to the Commons through the coffee-room of the House of Lords. Sir Robert Heron stated that he had been "shoved about by the mob just like a shuttle-cock between two battledores"; one of the skirts of his coat was torn off in the tumult. Sir Frederick Flood declared that he had been "carried above one hundred yards on the shoulders of the mob, just like a mackerel from Billingsgate Market, and that he thought they meant to quarter him." There was not enough of the constabulary to re-establish order, so the Horse Guards were called in. "No Corn Bill!" screamed the mob, "No Corn Bill!"[112]

Castlereagh had arrived in England the week the Corn Laws were pushed through parliament. Even if there had been no news from the continent, this would have been one of the most momentous weeks in British political history.

In France, the transition from war to peace had created a crisis in her redundant army and bloated bureaucracy. In the area that was once the German Reich it had led to a new crisis of identity, and to constitutional questions concerning the *Stände* and the States. In Britain, its most immediate result was the Corn Laws.

The Corn[113] Laws – or the Corn Importation Bill as they were officially known – were introduced by one of Castlereagh's close associates, Frederick Robinson, later the Earl of Ripon. He had accompanied Castlereagh on his mission to the continent in the winter of 1814. After the Treaty of Paris had been negotiated, Robinson returned to Britain to worry about the future of his estate – just as many British landlords began to worry about their estates. The Corn Bill, which he presented to parliament on 16 February 1815, prohibited the importation of foreign wheat at less than eighty shillings a quarter; minimum prices were also set for other grains. Robinson's Bill began a debate on free trade and protection that would last for thirty years and would change the political landscape of Britain. Battle lines were drawn up in February and March, 1815, and the first shots fired in what would become one of the most furious political struggles of the century.

The landowners, seated in parliament, developed the most ingenious arguments in favour of their Bill. Most of them repeated ideas first propounded by the Reverend Thomas Malthus, economist, demographer, founder of the "dismal science." Eighty shillings, they claimed was a fair price for a quarter of wheat. If the farmers could not pay their way, then labourers would have their wages cut and manufacturers would suffer from the decline of purchasing-power within the agricultural sector. Besides, one could become dangerously dependent on foreign imports. As Mr Henry Grattan argued in his thin sharp voice, the question before parliament "was no less than whether the people of these United Kingdoms should be fed or starved by foreigners. It is a horrible conjuncture, in which I am sure Parliament will never consent to place the people of the country."[114]

Mr Samuel Whitbread, who spoke fluently on every subject under the sun, argued that governments and legislatures might as well try and control the air as control the flow of trade. Not even the mighty Bonaparte, he reminded the House, could prevent the French from exporting corn. The war had given Britain certain advantages. To listen to some of these country gentlemen in parliament complain about not selling their wheat made one think, said Whitbread, that "it would be better to set Boney up again." Yet, having said this and won a laugh, Whitbread – a landowner as well as a brewer – would not oppose Robinson's Bill. A superabundant supply of corn to the country would produce an increased population, reasoned Whitbread, and this was in nobody's interest.[115]

The response of the towns, under-represented in the Mother of Parliaments, was ferocious. Petitions against the Bill poured in from practically every urban centre in the country. A quarter of a million signatures were gathered in less than a fortnight.

In the face of unrepresented opposition, the Bill was rushed through the two Houses at a speed hitherto unknown in the annals of parliament. "Panic has seized the country Gentlemen," exclaimed Mr George Philips, the "Cotton King" of Manchester. Within the third week of Robinson's introduction of his Bill – the week Castlereagh returned to parliament – the Commons was already considering the third reading. Wouldn't it be better, asked Mr Edward Protheroe on presenting a petition from Bristol signed by forty thousand, to wait and see the effects of peace on British commerce and manufactures?[116]

The commerce and manufactures of Britain were already suffering from a sharp decline in demand. Labourers were thrown out of work. Demobilised soldiers and sailors found no jobs. The petition from the City of London spoke of "unexampled distress and privation." Sir James Shaw, who presented it to the Commons, suggested that the House examine the relationship between the price of wheat and the bills of mortality. Several of those opposed to the Bill argued that, with the peace, people had a right to expect a diminution in the price of bread. Iron was cheaper, labour was cheaper, why not bread? Young Sir Robert Peel stood up in the Commons and asked, "What is it that constitutes the wealth of the nation?" It was the labour of the manufacturers, he said. Don't penalise them by raising the price of bread.[117]

Samuel Whitbread now weighed nearly twenty stone and was looking more and more like the beer barrel that appeared in the popular cartoons: "Whitbread's Intire." On Monday afternoon, 6 March, he spied for the first time in eight months, on the Treasury bench in front of him, Viscount Castlereagh: "the Noble Lord in the blue ribbon." Whitbread got to his feet and asked the Noble Lord to make a statement on his recent mission to Vienna. Nobody, in fact, was the slightest bit interested in Europe that day, not even Mr Whitbread. Outside could be heard the chant of the mob, "No Corn Bill! No Corn Bill!" Castlereagh promised to deliver a full statement on the Congress at a later date. The attention of the House turned, with relief, away from Europe to Mr Robinson's Corn Importation Bill.[118]

But the debate had not got very far when Mr Lambton interrupted the proceedings to announce that the House was surrounded by a military force. He demanded an immediate adjournment because, he claimed, the independence of the House was challenged. Castlereagh replied that the House was being protected and would not allow itself to be dictated to or controlled by a mob. Mr Whitbread supported Lord Castlereagh.

The debate on the Corn Bill was resumed. Castlereagh made a short address in support of the Bill, arguing that the eighty shilling minimum was in the interest of the poor because it would give wheat a fixed rather than fluctuating price; he added that he wanted to see agriculture and commerce equally protected. Mr Alexander Baring, the banker, said he had never before in his life heard such a prolix, "declamatory" speech and the House then adjourned.[119]

The crowd outside parliament had been dispersed without violence; but after nightfall smaller groups of about fifty to sixty people began attacking houses in the West End. The homes of supporters of the Bill were their principal targets. Castlereagh on his third night in London could hear the rabble huzzaing; the Foot Guards managed to keep them at a distance. Frederick Robinson was not so lucky. The railing outside his house in Burlington Street was torn up and used to split the front door in two; his paintings were ripped up, settees and tables were smashed, and the smaller pieces of furniture thrown out the windows.

On Tuesday afternoon, the City of Westminster held a meeting outside parliament to collect signatures for a petition. New Palace Yard was crammed with people. Sir Francis Burdett, the Radical MP, gave an address which focused on parliament's "system of corruption." When he was finished he was carried off like Blücher, the conquering hero of the preceding year – the crowds unhitched the horses from his hackney-coach and dragged it by hand up Parliament Street and then down Pall Mall and St James's Street. Opposite

Carlton House the triumphant procession stopped and cried out, "No Corn Bill!" The windows of White's, the Tory Club, were smashed. Then along Piccadilly they marched, breaking more windows. By evening they were on the rampage again. Troops guarding what remained of Robinson's property opened fire, killing one man – a demobilised sailor – and wounding another.[120]

On Wednesday and Thursday nights the rioting was repeated. Castlereagh's house was stoned. Sir Joseph Banks, the famous naturalist now seventy-two years old, lost many of his papers and saw his furniture destroyed. "If the Legislators of Great Britain cannot debate on these measures without being threatened in their persons and injured in their property, the liberties of Englishmen are gone," asserted Castlereagh in the Commons. Further attempts were made to delay the Bill, but they were not successful. Passage of the Corn Bill through the Commons was set for Friday, 10 March.[121]

The situation on Thursday evening was explosive. The military were increased in number, particularly the cavalry. Foot soldiers were stationed outside the homes of supporters of the Bill. The West End began to take on the look of an occupied city and many of its residents prepared for the worst.

But on Friday morning the news hit London: Boney the Ogre was back in France.

"We have often heard of the Year of Wonders," wrote the anonymous columnist of the *Examiner*; "this has been the week of them." All one needed now, he said, was a visit from the Man in the Moon or the announcement of the invasion from some undiscovered people who would be for the British what the Spaniards had been for the Mexicans.

"Can the Noble Lord state whether it is true that Bonaparte had landed with troops in France?" asked Mr Whitbread in the Commons. "His Majesty's Government has received official information of that event," confirmed Lord Castlereagh.

The Corn Laws were passed, as scheduled, through the Commons that same Friday, 10 March 1815, 245 votes against 75. And not a stone in London was thrown.[122]

Whitbread's ail

The Times hoped that the Viper of Corsica would soon be murdered. *The Morning Post* reported that "the whole of French soldiery" was attached to the Tyrant. *The Morning Herald* thought the "French people" would treat him as "a common traitor or felon." Nearly every paper in London called for renewed war if the Ogre did reach Paris.

There were two major exceptions. *The Morning Chronicle*, an Opposition newspaper, claimed that the wise British people "will hardly be induced to enter into new confederacies, or waste their remaining means on new subsidies." And Leigh Hunt's weekly *Examiner* pulled out the old Whig argument. The last war, they said, had not been the responsibility of Bonaparte, it had been the fault of the Allied Monarchs. It was their hostility that forced Napoleon to go to war, expand his territory, increase his strength, push it to the limit, and then fall. Worse, after his fall the Allied Monarchs had attempted to imitate him, "copying" – as the *Examiner* put it on 12 March – "his vices without his talents, and shewing a taste for the worst part of his appetites without redeeming it even by the resolution to be bold." The Princes' Congress in Vienna had threatened Poland with re-division, torn away a slice of Saxony, and usurped the rights of Italians. It was the bad politics of the Congress that was responsible for the return of Napoleon, not Napoleon himself, nor his army.[123]

For those who opposed the war in the spring of 1815, Napoleon never represented a menace, just as the year before Russia had not been seen as menace. The threat to peace from the flanking Powers was simply not a reality for them. It was as if the people of each state in Europe could live for themselves as on an island, could enjoy the luxury of electing their own parliaments, and behave like civilised freeborn Englishmen. Why did the Congress have to interfere? Why should Europe be "organised"? And above all, why did Britain have to get involved?[124]

There were scarcely any countries worth talking about nowadays, complained the *Examiner*, other than Austria, Russia, and Prussia. But there was one other vital force in Europe: "public opinion," noted the the paper's leading columnist. He meant, of course, British public opinion. The British, he reflected, would take much more interest in the affairs of the continent "if it were generally known with what intense anxiety foreigners look towards us for our opinion and voice." Public opinion was made up of those who spoke for the sufferers of oppression abroad and the downtrodden at home: the press, the "independent part of Parliament," and one private English gentleman, Mr Whitbread – for Mr Whitbread had a voice, "and a strong one too."

Mr Whitbread had the qualities of a moulder – or as Admiral Sir Sidney Smith would say, a "fermentator" – of public opinion. His voice and energy were the equivalent of a crowd of ordinary men. A more frequent speaker has never been recorded in the history of parliament. Since 1806, when Lord Grey had excluded him from a Whig Cabinet on account of his brewery, Whitbread had always been heard from the bench, totally ignoring the official Whig leader in the House. In the winter and spring of 1815 his speaking became obsessive. Napoleon's rule was going to last One Hundred Days; Mr Whitbread would manage to make over one hundred speeches, many of them two to three hours long. In debate he was athletic: he drew circles around poor Castlereagh.

Like many in the opposition, Whitbread came from a family of Nonconformists. Academic success had taken him from Eton, to Oxford, to Cambridge, and on to a brilliant, aristocratic marriage with Charles Grey's daughter, Lady Elizabeth. But Whitbread was not an aristocrat, and the Whig grandees never let him forget it. That was Whitbread's ail, one that troubled him enough to seek the help of Sir Henry Halford, a medical counsellor to the mad Sovereign at Windsor. Whitbread was the friend of castaways, refugees, slaves, and debtors, because Whitbread was an outcast himself. When Princess Caroline set up her "rival Court" in Kensington, Whitbread was there. Liberty, equality, and reform were as much of his person as his folding jowls and his bright red hair. And, as H.G. Bennett told Thomas Creevey, Whitbread was "all for Boney."[125]

Castlereagh wrote to Wellington in Vienna on Tuesday, 14 March, to tell him that the corn riots in London appeared to have ceased; "I hope this embarrassment will pass away," he said. In the meantime, he reported, Lord Grey and Mr Whitbread were attempting in parliament to prevent British interference "in what is passing in France." "I was not myself present, being confined by a cold," he went on; "but I understand this sentiment was very coldly received, and I am sure will not be re-echoed by the nation."[126]

Castlereagh's "cold" on this occasion, as during the Sovereigns' visit to London, was probably of diplomatic origin. He had spent Sunday writing formal instructions for Wellington and he passed the rest of the week preparing his formal statement to parliament on the business of the Congress.[127]

He did make a brief appearance in the Commons on Thursday. Whitbread demanded that Britain not interfere in the "internal affairs or Government of France." Castlereagh responded that the policy of his government had never been to dictate to France but, if the peace of Europe was likely to be disturbed, he trusted the House would not call in question whatever action the government, in conjunction with its Allies, deemed necessary. The theory persisted that foreign policy was part of the royal prerogative and was not subject to the questions of parliament. Nor, as in a later age, were leaders of the opposition kept confidentially informed. Whitbread accepted this. "I am not trying to give advice to the Government," he said, "I am merely protesting, as a Member of Parliament, against any interference of this country in the internal affairs of France."[128]

The one noun Whitbread repeated more than any other – more

than "Bonaparte," "corn," and "slaves" – was "Vienna." Whitbread
hated Vienna. Hadn't Whitbread married into a family of aristocrats
that had later politically rejected him? Vienna had done the same to
Bonaparte. It was an exclusive club of princes. When Whitbread
spoke of the "unholy Congress of Vienna," the "league for the extermination of Bonaparte," he was righting a personal wrong.

Before Castlereagh made his policy statement on Monday, 20
March – the day Napoleon entered the Tuileries – Whitbread delivered the longest speech he had made to date on Europe, France, and
the Congress. It was almost as long as Castlereagh's statement. He
returned to the old theme of Bonaparte's untalented imitators. The
Peace of Paris, he said, had been a model of moderation in victory, but
by the time the Sovereign Princes met in Vienna they had "forgotten
all the lessons" and instead pursued "the same paltry, pilfering, bartering
system, which had led heretofore to the destruction of so many States."[129]

Castlereagh, in his answer, revealed the whole engine that lay
behind his policy. His speech was a classic defence of Pitt's old plan,
readjusted in the light of the experience of the Congress – "the great
machine of the Congress," as he called it that day. On the slave trade,
he announced the public pledge for its abolition made in Vienna the
previous February; Whitbread was painfully unaware of the fact.
Regarding Europe, he said it would not have been possible to revive
all the governments that had been overturned in the last twenty years
for "this would be to recreate the dangers from which Europe had so
recently escaped." The great object had been to strengthen the centre,
Austria and Prussia. He underlined the absurdity of Whitbread's
charge that the Allies were "motivated by the same love of conquest
which they themselves had so loudly condemned." They were in no
way the imitators of Bonaparte, but they did not want an enfeebled –
Castlereagh's term was "stultified" – Europe either. With Bonaparte
back in France, he said Whitbread's attack on the Sovereigns of
Europe was "indecent as well as dangerous." This won prolonged
cheers in the House. The Allies had made war, he said, repeating the
main principle of his policy, "not for the sake of subjugating any
power, but for the sake of perserving the whole of Europe from subjugation." Castlereagh said, with some pride, that at Vienna they had
succeeded in giving "to the different Powers of the European
Commonwealth a protection from that danger," the threat of a single
Power's hegemony. It was not so much a question of whether this
little state survived or that little state was incorporated with another;
it was the whole balance that mattered. And that was an issue of vital
British interest.[130]

Castlereagh was right. Whitbread's problem was that he had no
general view of Europe. His was the insular view: he saw a Europe
made up, as it were, of totally independent little islands, like those of

Talleyrand's South Seas. Whitbread and his allies had been campaigning for an undivided Kingdom of Poland. Basically, they got what they had been asking for: a Kingdom, but one dominated by Russia. They were as furious as King Frederick Augustus at the slicing up of Saxony; they did not see that here lay the barrier against Russia.

During the Easter recess, a poorly translated version of the Allies' Declaration of 13 March appeared in the British press. The version that Mr Whitbread read was much more violent than Gentz had ever intended. *"La vindicte publique"* was translated as "public vengeance," not "condemnation"; *"Napoléon Buonaparte s'est placé hors des Relations civiles et sociales"* became "Napoleon Buonaparte has placed himself without the pale of civil and social relations." For every English columnist, the announcement that Napoleon had *"détruit le seul titre légal auquel Son Existence se trouvoit attachée"* was interpreted as a condemnation of his physical existence, not his legal existence as a Sovereign. In other words, the Declaration was a call for murder.

Members of the Cabinet at first doubted the authenticity of the document. But Castlereagh would vouch that it was genuine. He was also well aware of all the legal arguments behind it – in his private papers one finds, attached to the original French text of the Declaration, a French translation of Gentz's article in the *Beobachter*.[131]

In an effort to repair the damage done by the press, a Message from the Prince Regent was presented to the two Houses of Parliament for their approval on Friday, 7 April. Though identical in principle to the Declaration, the Message was considerably milder in form.[132]

In the Commons debate that Friday, Castlereagh argued that Bonaparte had displayed contempt for all treaties and that he had abdicated the previous year with a deliberate intention to deceive. Bonaparte was not supported by the people of France, he was supported by the military, and that military force threatened the whole peace of Europe. But Sir Francis Burdett of Westminster saw no threat in France at all, neither this year, nor in any preceding year. "The country was tricked into the war of 1793," he claimed. "At first it was for one pretence, and then for another, but it was always a war of Monarchs against the people." He hoped the House would vote against the Message. So, of course, did Mr Whitbread, who contradicted Castlereagh by pointing out that Bonaparte had walked from the south of France to Paris "without a single arm being lifted against him"; you could have no better proof that the people were behind him. Neither Whitbread nor Burdett, however, had the majority of the House, which voted 220 against 37 in favour of the Message.

It was not a declaration of war, but by the second week of April it was clear that, if Napoleon did not remove himself from Paris, Great Britain and her "concert" would do the job for him.[133]

Imperial chaos

Benjamin Constant, French liberal and defender of the people's freedoms, wrote an article on Napoleon, likening him to Attila the Hun and Genghis Khan. It was published in the *Journal des Débats* on Sunday, 19 March, the day King Louis fled Paris. The following Tuesday, Constant himself tried to flee Paris, but he found no horses, so he went into hiding with Mr Crawford, the American Ambassador: "Sadness, fears," he wrote in his diary. On the Thursday, he did get out of town and "galloped post haste all night." By Saturday he reached the Vendée, royalist territory; but there he changed his mind and decided his home, after all, was Paris. So he "galloped post haste" all Easter Sunday and at five o'clock, Monday morning, arrived in the village of Sèvres, outside the gates of the capital. Once again he hesitated. Did he really want to enter Napoleon's Paris? He spent the day in the village, trying to make up his mind. That night he took the plunge. "My return has astonished people," he wrote in his diary the next day.

On Thursday, 30 March, he had an interview with Joseph Bonaparte, Napoleon's eldest brother, who himself had only just arrived in Paris. "The intentions of Joseph are liberal," thought Constant, "the practice will be despotic." For two weeks, Benjamin Constant hovered between "intentions" and "practice," between exile and remaining in Paris. Fouché, the Minister of Police, personally advised him to stay put.

Constant started a major theoretical work on government constitutions, had an argument with his mistress, Juliette Récamier, and decided it really would be better to quit Paris. But then again, perhaps he shouldn't. His hesitations eventually paid off: on 14 April he was invited to the Tuileries Palace to meet Emperor Napoleon. "He's an astonishing man," recorded Constant. "Tomorrow, I bring him my project for a constitution. Will I finally make it?"

On 20 April, Constant was named member of Napoleon's Council of State. So at the age of forty-eight he had made it. On the 22nd, his amended project was published as the constitution of France.[134]

True, not every Frenchman would have an interview with Napoleon or have the chance of drawing up the nation's constitution. But Constant's story does illustrate, in a most graphic manner, the kind of confusion that was developing in France in March and April, 1815. None of the formulae designed to bring France peace appeared, so far, to have worked. Talleyrand's notion of "legitimacy" had been conceived as a way of restoring stability by combining tradition with reform; it had not yet succeeded. Parliamentary liberalism did not look very strong either. There had been those who had put their faith in "style": court dress and manners had been adopted by the upper and middle classes of Paris; by looking peaceful and civilised – to parody the old French moralist La Bruyère – they hoped they would become peaceful and civilised. But now everyone was complaining. Since the defeat of 1814, French government and administration had gradually fallen apart. That process of decomposition was to continue right through Napoleon's second short reign.

Napoleon's own formula for success stood on wobbly foundations. His followers had been shocked by the cool reception they had received in Paris – "We had been so spoilt *en route*," sighed Fleury de Chaboulon.[135] Paris broke the illusion. Napoleon's whole claim to the throne in 1815 was based on the "enthusiasm of the people," the "love of my people," which had carried him 220 leagues, from the Golfe Juan to the capital, without a gun being fired. But the crowds of Grenoble did not represent the nation. Napoleon's decrees abolishing the two parliamentary chambers and his promises to expel the *émigrés*, sequester their properties and generally to stamp out "feudalism" might have impressed the people of Lyon, but this did not make good news in Paris. The artisans of Lyon might have been looking for a Liberator to defend "our Revolution"; most people in Paris wanted to forget it.

One promise, made in Lyon, that was soon heaped with ridicule in Paris was Napoleon's alternative to parliament, the Champ-de-Mai, or the grand assembly on the Champ de Mars of all the electoral colleges in France. It would have been an unmanageable body, involving more than eighty thousand deliberating members. Leaders of "public opinion" in Paris – former deputies, intellectuals of the *salons,* and the pamphleteers – called it a piece of imperial charlatanry.[136]

Once in office, Napoleon faced more than ridicule. Within days of his arrival in Paris, he had to confront the threat of civil war in the west and civil war in the south. The first petered out because of the incompetence of the Royalists' leader, the powdered and puffed duc de Bourbon, who belonged to the Condé branch of the family, one of the very worst elements of reaction. The second was more dangerous. It was the only point of Soult's original three-pronged plan against Napoleon that had stood a chance of success. The duc d'Angoulême, as soon as he had received the order from Paris, had left Bordeaux for Nîmes where he arrived on 12 March, the day Napoleon entered Lyon with the regiments of Grenoble trailing behind him: Napoleon had left the south undefended. Most of the troops in Lyon followed Napoleon on his march to Paris: the Rhône and central France were undefended. Angoulême organised an army of Languedoc and Provence and developed a plan to march on Lyon. His troops were no regulars. They were mostly peasants and workers, fired by old southern religious quarrels and an abiding hatred of Paris. Locally they were known as the "*miquelets.*" They had no uniforms, save the insignia of the fleur de lys that they stuck to their jackets; they armed themselves with pitchforks, cudgels, and hunting guns; they were not gentle. In response, Napoleon sent Lieutenant-General Grouchy, who had seen service in Spain, Russia, and Germany, down to Lyon. There he pieced together an army of volunteers and marched south. Angoulême's rag-tag army proved no match against Grouchy's volunteers. At La Pallud, near Marseille, the royal prince capitulated and, after delays, was allowed to set sail for Spain on 16 April. But the civil war did not end neatly. Throughout the Hundred Days there continued, in the south, armed raids on villages, vendettas, thuggery, revenge murders, and other acts of abomination.[137]

In the meantime, a struggle for influence and power was developing in the capital. Every political faction, besides the excluded Royalist extremists, attempted to manœuvre into positions that would give them an advantage under the new regime. Constitutional Republicans saw new hope as did former Terrorists. Monarchists pretended they had always been Imperialists. There were revolutionary plans, vague plans, and complicated plans. There was much intrigue and conspiracy. As for more ordinary people, Constant was probably right to say that they were indifferent to the form political organisation took – whether it was republican, monarchist, feudalist, or imperialist: what they wanted to avoid was inquisition and persecution. What nearly every class wanted to avoid was another war.[138]

Within the first week, all the major public institutions in Paris had declared themselves for Napoleon. But their pronouncements were left-handed compliments. "You have been called," announced the Council of State to Napoleon, "to guarantee again through our institutions all liberal principles: individual liberty and equality before the law; freedom of the press and the abolition of censure; ... national properties of whatever origin." This had not been Napoleon's plan. "You are going," proclaimed the Institut de France, "to assure us the equality of citizens' rights, the honour of the brave, the security of all properties, the freedom to think and to write, and finally a representative constitution." That was not quite what Napoleon had said either. It was almost with insolence that these institutions called on Napoleon and did not wait for His Imperial Highness to call on them. This is not the way it had been under the Empire.[139]

Joseph Fouché, good functionary that he was, had sworn complete loyalty to Napoleon on the day he accepted his post at the Police, a loyalty that he said was guaranteed by the fact that a warrant for his arrest had been issued by the Bourbons. He would have preferred to have Foreign Affairs , where he would have had a hold on his old rival in Vienna, Talleyrand. "No," said Napoleon, "Police is your affair." Fouché "was as deep as he was spiritual," said Fleury de Chaboulon, "as provident as he was able; he embraced the past, the present, and the future all at once." Fouché also accommodated every side all at once. While he was being loyal to Napoleon he never forgot his old friend and former co-conspirator Metternich; they were in correspondence throughout this period. And, of course, there were services he had provided to the Wellesley family back in his second Ministry under the Empire, services that had made the Duke of Wellington an everlasting friend; they maintained a correspondence, too. He received Wellington's agents in his offices, gave them information on the state of the French army, and even hinted at the date of opening hostilities. At the same time, he received useful information from them on the position of the Allied armies that he passed on to his Emperor.[140]

If Napoleon had a secret desire to re-establish a dictatorship in France, he no longer possessed the means. He might have promised the crowds in Lyon that he would return France to the principles of the Revolution; there were too many factions in Paris for him ever to achieve this. None of these parties were dominant. Not even Fouché was master of the international network into which he was gradually drawn. The wits had said that Louis XVIII had established a "paternal anarchy"; the joke now was that Napoleon presided over imperial chaos.

According to Fouché, Napoleon was prepared to march on Belgium almost as soon as he had appeared in Paris.[141] But weakness at home demanded peace abroad. So Napoleon overcame his disdain for the Sovereigns and feudal oligarchies of Europe and he tried to obtain an international understanding.

He aimed his first efforts at the diplomatic corps still residing in Paris at the moment of his arrival. There was widespread fear, at the time, that Napoleon would attempt to hold them hostage; Napoleon dealt his first card by issuing them passports. Lord Fitzroy Somerset and the officials of the Borghese Palace left as soon as they could; and so did most English residents in Paris, save a few hardy Napoleonist Whigs.[142] The Austrian and Russian diplomats, on the other hand, did delay their departures and talk. But the message from both was the same. As the Russian Ambassador put it in a letter to Queen Hortense, Napoleon's stepdaughter and chief mediator: "Neither peace nor truce; no more reconciliation with this man [Napoleon] . . . All Europe has the same sentiment. Outside this man, everything that you want."[143]

Napoleon then tried a direct appeal to the Sovereigns. His letter, which had the look and style of a circular to his prefects, was no diplomatic masterpiece. It was addressed to *"Monsieur mon frère,"* and outlined ideas abhorrent to most of the Monarchs of Europe. Written on 4 April and published in the *Moniteur* four days later, it must have been designed for internal consumption rather than as a sincere appeal to the Powers. Napoleon claimed he had returned in response to "the national will" and that France had called for a Liberator. Caulaincourt, in a letter to the Foreign Ministers of Europe, also evoked the idea of a Liberator; "it was on the arms of his peoples that His Majesty crossed France."[144]

None of these letters was received. To please the English, Napoleon abolished the slave trade and made use of Fouché's good offices to get his letter delivered to the Prince Regent. Castlereagh, confronted by Fouché's agent, refused even to open the envelope and had the letters returned to the sender. On the continent, all outward bound diplomatic mail was stopped on the frontier – all with the exception of Fouché's private couriers, who could gallop on to wherever to whomever they wanted.[145]

The Allies' Declaration of 13 March was only officially published in France on 13 April, the same day as full reports on the British parliamentary debates over the Prince Regent's Message appeared in French papers. But the Declaration had been reproduced in the Paris broadsheets long before that. Copies were being distributed on the frontiers and in Alsace-Lorraine in the second half of March.

In the Council of Ministers on 29 March, Fouché declared that the document was a forgery because he couldn't imagine the Austrians or the British – and most especially Lord Wellington – putting their signatures to a statement that appeared to call for assassination. Fouché said it was the evil work of Talleyrand. Napoleon himself made extensive comments that were reproduced in a report made to the Council of Ministers on 2 April. The report repeated Fouché's theme: the language of the Declaration was "so unusual" and "so strange" that it must be a forgery created by the treasonous French delegation in Vienna. Napoleon remained convinced that the Allies themselves were obliged to recognise their "Brother" as an independent Sovereign. The "Convention of Fontainebleau," he explained had been a treaty between Sovereigns. If it had been violated, then the worst that could happen would be "an ordinary war" and the Sovereign would become conqueror or conquered, an imposer of the peace or a prisoner of war – that was the Napoleonic view of honourable warfare. If, on the other hand, the Declaration were proven genuine, then the ensuing war would be "extraordinary" and the combatants would no longer be bound by honour.[146]

The British parliamentary debates eradicated all doubt. The Declaration was no forgery. So France geared up for an extraordinary war. All the frontier forts, from Dunkirk to Charlemont, were put on alert, locks and dykes were prepared for flooding, in the Argonne trenches and earthen mounds were built, the forts of Lorraine were armed and provisioned, the defences of the five passes in the Vosges were improved, the ammunition wagons rolled once more onto the forts of Alsace, and the passes of the Jura and the Alps were armed. In Paris, reviews of new recruits were held every week. They would wave their hats at the tip of their guns or their swords and cry, *"Vive l'Empereur! vive l'Empereur!"* The soldiers were back at work.[147]

It was on the day after the publication of the Allies' Declaration – just as the arms build-up began in earnest – that Benjamin Constant received his invitation to meet the Emperor. Fouché appears to have been the most instrumental in this move, but, judging from comments in Constant's *Journal intime*, Hugues Maret and Michel Regnault, both members of the government, could also have played a role. At any rate, somebody had convinced Napoleon that he needed him. "He is a man of great talent," Napoleon told his stepdaughter, Queen Hortense, just a few days before the interview. "I liked his work on press freedoms; he has a strong sense of reason."[148]

Napoleon was pushing war on a country with a government made up of ministers whose loyalties were at best divided, with an administration that had no loyalties at all, and with nothing resembling a parliament beyond the unworkable "Champ-de-Mai." The situation in France was even more chaotic than under Louis XVIII. Clearly some constitutional arrangement had to patched together, and quickly at that. This was why Constant had been called in.

At the Tuileries, Constant found Napoleon alone, striding back and forth in his office overlooking the Seine. As usual, the Emperor did nearly all the talking. He first wanted to answer Castlereagh's charge in the Commons, repeated in the French press, that he only had the support of the army. "You didn't see that multitude pressing on me as I marched, people rushing down from the mountains, calling on me, searching me out, saluting me," he said. "I am not only Emperor of the soldiers, as they've claimed, I am also the Emperor of the peasants, of the plebeians of France." Nobles might serve him; Montmorencies, Noailles, and Rohans might bow to him. But with the people it was something else. "The popular fibre responds to my own," and he banged his chest. "I came from the ranks of the people: my voice acts on it. Look, here are the conscripts, the sons of peasants: I don't flatter them: I treat them rudely. They won't crowd round me any less, they won't cry out any less, 'Vive l'Empereur!'" Napoleon claimed all he had to do was to ask them to massacre every noble in every province and they would do it. Then he made one of his dramatic pauses, turned, and added: "But I don't want to be the King of a *jacquerie*."[149]

A constitution could help one avoid this. "Public discussions, free

elections, responsible ministers, freedom of the press; I want all that."
Constant, listening, got a distinct impression that Napoleon in fact
did not know what he wanted. As trenchant as his language might
have been, there was something indecisive in his manner, in his
pauses, and in the deliberate way in which he contradicted himself; a
debate appeared to be going on inside him.

What he *had* wanted was a world empire and unlimited powers in
order to govern it. "Who wouldn't have wanted that in my place?"
asked Napoleon rhetorically. "The world invited me to govern.
Sovereigns and subjects alike rushed to the glitter of my sceptre." But
now? Now it was a question of restoring France, and only a question
of restoring France and giving her the government that suited her
best. "I am no longer a conqueror," he said. "To govern France alone
it's quite probable that a constitution would be the best thing." He
said this as if he had a choice. But then Napoleon always gave himself
a choice even – indeed, especially – when it was not evident to anybody else. Others might regard Napoleon as caught in a jam; the
Emperor never saw this: there was always some choice in his mind,
some alternative was forever tracing itself out. Just as he had *chosen*
the Isle of Elba the year before, so Napoleon, in April 1815, *chose* a
constitution for France, along with the man who would write it. "I'm
getting old," he said. "One is no longer at forty-five what one was at
thirty. The repose of a constitutional king could suit me."

So it would be peace, a contained France, and a constitution? Not
quite. There was still one more battle ahead. "I foresee a difficult
struggle, a long war." That was always the way it was with Napoleon:
peace just the other side of the horizon, just over the hill: one more
great chain of mountains for the nation to clamber over. But who
would then be left to enjoy this golden peace?[150]

Constant had dinner that evening with Juliette and Marshal
Marmont's sullen wife. "The future is bleak. L.v.D.s.f. [*La volonté de
Dieu soit faite* – God's will be done]," he wrote in his diary. The next
day he was back again in Napoleon's office. The Emperor handed him
a great packet of constitutional projects made up by various
Republicans and Imperialists. "One has wanted to attribute the whole
Acte additionnel [as the Constitution would be known] to me,"
Constant later complained in his memoirs, but "I was not alone to
receive this invitation [to make a contribution]." The constitution
that was finally pieced together and published on 22 April – only a
week after Constant's first interview – was a compilation of the works
of many men, the most important being Napoleon himself.[151]

Constant had wanted to make a complete break with the previous
constitutions of France, but Napoleon would not let him. "I want to
keep my past," he said. Napoleon demanded that the document be
regarded as a complement to the last two imperial constitutions,

hence the title "The Additional Act to the Constitutions of the Empire." In the long preamble – probably dictated by Napoleon – one finds the same distinction between the needs of an international Empire and a constrained France that Napoleon had made during his first interview with Constant. Thus the goal in the previous constitutions had been "to organise a great European federative system" that the political imperatives of the day would not allow to be liberal. Because the Emperor now regarded himself as a Frenchman rather than a European, the purpose of the constitution was more limited; it was merely designed "to increase the prosperity of France by the strengthening of public liberty."

In practical terms this meant that an enlarged Chamber of Representatives would be balanced by a Chamber of hereditary peers. The Chamber of Representatives would be elected by universal manhood suffrage – but in two degrees. The "people" would vote for electoral colleges and the colleges would vote for the representatives. In practice, the whole process of replacement was so drawn out that this was essentially a return to Napoleon's old system. The Act also included articles guaranteeing freedom of religion, freedom of the press, and the rights of property.

As in the case of the previous two imperial constitutions, the Act was to be approved by a national plebiscite, the results of which would be announced before the electoral colleges assembled at the Champ-de-Mai – that was about the only political function left to the Champ-de-Mai.

But the Act was not popular. John Cam Hobhouse, a Napoleonist Whig living in a house on rue Saint-Honoré with fellow revolutionaries and English dissidents, said he had never experienced in his life such a rage in "public opinion" – "that is, the opinion of those amongst whom a man lives and moves, and the voice of ephemeral publications." Thousands of pamphlets appeared on the streets. "Never was blame so bitter, never was censure so unanimous," wrote Constant in his memoirs. "Each article seemed a trap, each arrangement a snare to impose unlimited power." The very title of the Act was considered offensive; the political classes in Paris did not want a return to the Empire. Republicans and Jacobins balked at the idea of hereditary peers. Liberals complained that there were not enough guarantees for individual liberty. The Royalists simply refused Napoleon the right to reign. Most would have preferred a constituent assembly – which at least the Champ-de-Mai was originally designed to be – to a declaration from the throne followed by a plebiscite.

Constant felt particularly singled out for criticism and began to lose faith in his rising star. "I think I bring bad luck to whatever party I embrace," he recorded in his diary; these were days of "sadness and anonymous letters." His article on Napoleon the Hun was republished by an anonymous enemy. He felt an outsider on the Council of State and most uncomfortable in the presence of Fouché, who had become viciously critical.

Almost as soon as the Act was published Napoleon realised that something had gone wrong. "*Eh bien*! The new Constitution is not working," he complained to Constant on 24 April. "That's because one hardly believes in it," replied Constant. "Make people believe in it by executing it." Constant, a confirmed mystic, had unbridled faith in the hidden truth of texts: let the people see and judge for themselves; put the Constitution immediately into action; the truth would emerge and Parisian factionalism would disappear.

Napoleon was ready to try anything. One week after publication of the Act, he convoked the new Chamber of Representatives to meet in Paris immediately after the assembly of the Champ-de-Mai. Since the Act was not yet operational, the Chamber would have to be elected by the electoral colleges already existing. Thus, in the month of May, as France prepared for war and while the battle of pamphlets continued in Paris, two national elections were to be held, one a plebiscite on the Act, the other a vote for the Chamber. The long-promised Champ-de-Mai, now due to meet on 1 June, had lost all its original significance. Moreover, many saw in the Chamber the constituent assembly they wanted, so the Act had lost much of its value. And Napoleon had been Emperor for just fifty days.[152]

The country was sinking steadily into chaos. Members of the government were writing pamphlets against each other, betraying each other, even duelling with each other. Napoleon in his constitution might have wanted to counter individual liberties with a centralised system. But the central administration, impressive as it was, was receiving no direction. Napoleon's own acts were inconsistent.

If Napoleon thought that the French people were going to manifest their liberty by taking part in a plebiscite, he was wrong; participation was low. If Constant imagined the people would in some way reveal the liberal secret behind an imperfect text, his illusion was soon broken; few understood the Act. Since the administration had not been prepared, the plebiscite disintegrated into a series of local elections with local officials taking the initiative. The mode of voting differed from village to village, with each mayor and each *notaire* having his own concept of how the election should be run. Officially, the voting was to be done in ten days, but it went on throughout May. One department never declared a result: Corsica. Registers were made up according to whim and often had nothing to do with the formal purpose of the plebiscite, approval of the Act. "*Siganatures pour Napoleon Empereur des François*" was inscribed in large letters on one register prepared in the Landes by an "*encien notaire âgé de soixante-six ans*" (*sic*). Not much thought was given to the Constitution there.

A *notaire* in the Vendée drew up four columns in his register: "this column was not necessary"; "this column was useless"; "this column was more than useless"; "this column was of no use at all." Nobody voted in that village. In the village of Treffiagat, near Quimper, in the department of Finistère, the mayor recorded two weeks of voting activity. "No votes," he noted for 6 May. "Rang the bell, nobody came," he wrote on the 7th. "Idem," he recorded for the next eight days. "Rang the bell and nobody came," he repeated on the 16th, and he followed this with two more "idems." The register for Treffiagat was closed on the 19th.[153]

The results were a pure disaster for Napoleon. Whole regions, which had given him a vote of confidance in the plebiscites of 1802 and 1804, remained silent during the consultation of May 1815: the north, the Massif Central, the south-west. Even the Dauphiné, through which Napoleon had marched in triumph, showed no eagerness to vote. The final tally was something slightly over 1,500,000 for the *yeses* and slightly under 5,000 for the *noes*, which made a poor comparison with the 3.7 million Napoleon had received in 1802 and the 3.6 in 1804 – even allowing for territorial adjustments. In 1815, barely one fifth of the French electorate voted. Among the worst results was the city of Paris where only thirteen per cent voted. As one historian who has studied the details put it, "the city of Paris was the centre of an isle of abstentionism."[154]

In the legislative elections, Napoleon fared no better. Only about a hundred out of the 629 representatives elected could be described as fully committed to the new regime. There were around thirty or forty Jacobins and old revolutionaries. Otherwise, the assembly, though larger, had much the same composition as the former Chamber of Deputies that Napoleon had abolished on the grounds of its support of "feudalism."

Paris was not a cheerful place in May. Spring never did seem to come. The *Journal de Paris*, which appeared every day including Sundays, used to give the three daily recordings of the weather – dawn, midday, and late afternoon – made at the Observatoire near the Luxembourg Palace. They show that, during Napoleon's Hundred Days, there were only three days of sun. White frosts lasted until the end of April. The fogs continued well into May.

The three exceptionally sunny days were 18 April, and the weekend of 27-8 May. These were happy days for Napoleon. It was on 18 April that Paris received news of Angoulême's capitulation at Le Pallud. "Sire, I have the honour to announce to Your Majesty that the city of Marseille raised the national cockade yesterday morning," wrote Grouchy from his headquarters in Avignon, "and thus the tricolour flag floats throughout the territory of the Empire." Grouchy was named Marshal of France for his pains. That same day Napoleon took up residence at the Elysée Palace. Queen Hortense pretended that he made the move on account of the "beauty of the weather," but one cannot help feel that it might also have been because the Emperor was rather better hidden at the Elysée from the sullen Parisian crowds. His government, however, continued to function – in its peculiar way – at the Tuileries and after hearing mass, Napoleon always attended the Sunday military parades on the place du Carrousel.

The greatest of these was held on 28 May, the only sunny Sunday of his reign. Twenty-five thousand men lined up in front of him to shout *"Vive l'Empereur!"* – five regiments of the line, four of the Young Guard, plus a body of recruits that had not yet received its uniforms. As a battalion of the Guard marched by, Napoleon stepped out into the sun and joined them. A grenadier approached him with a petition and the Emperor tweaked him on the nose; next a colonel ran up, apparently carrying some news, and received "a sound box on the ear." Hobhouse, who was watching, thought it "gross and vulgar" but was assured by a general officer standing by that such "friendly flaps" were not unusual with the Emperor. *"Les soufflets,"* Fleury de Chaboulon called them, "they were Napoleon's favourite caress" – and sometimes they hit pretty hard. They were Napoleon's way of responding to the "popular fibre."[155]

On grey days Paris was also massed with troops, troops, and more troops. Free corps, fusiliers, *conscrits-grenadiers*, sharp-shooters, light battalions, partisans, and volunteers passed through the capital every day, singing the "Marseillaise" and other patriotic songs. Drums beat and fifes whistled. The Old Guard, the *vieux des vieux*, gave picnics to the mobile national guards on the Champ de Mars, the crowds gathering on the sloping sides of the plain. "On to the column!" they'd shout and, with a discharge of artillery, everybody – guests and spectators – would march off to the place Vendôme under the billowing sails of reds, whites, and blues on a windy April or a chilly May day. The girls of the Palais-Royal only walked with uniformed men now. No wonder Hobhouse (like his hero Napoleon) thought that the army was the French people; soldiery was practically all one saw, days on end, marching by: the dominant sound in Paris.

Did Napoleon have any support outside the army? Some of the workers in Paris, like the carpenters and stone-cutters of the galérie Napoléon in the Louvre, who voted to a man for the *Acte*, were very Napoleonist. And there were the *Fédérés*. The movement began in late April, just after the publication of the *Acte*, in Rennes, Britanny, where there had been the rioting the previous January. Lawyers, functionaries, *les jeunes gens des écoles*, and unemployed soldiers united behind a "federative pact" to defend, above all, the principles of the Revolution. The movement developed in Burgundy and Lyon, under the encouragement of the departmental prefects, and spread among the rural populations: these were people who had seen foreign invasion. So had the people of Alsace-Lorraine. "Terror advances us, death follows us: conquer or die," declared the *Fédérés* of the Meurthe.

The movement germinated in the suburbs of Paris in the second week of May and, within a few days, multiplied to some tens of thousands. "We need to strike terror in the traitors who might once again seek the perversion of their *patrie*," proclaimed the purists of Saint-Antoine and Saint-Marceau. It has recently been estimated that, at its height, near the end of the Hundred Days, the federative movement "numbered in the hundreds of thousands" – but even nine hundred thousand would be no more than a mere fragment in a nation of thirty million. Did Napoleon really represent the national will?[156]

The federation of Saint-Antoine and Saint-Marceau demanded that they march past Napoleon at the Tuileries, which they did on Sunday, 14 May, just before the regular weekly military parade. They wanted arms. Twelve thousand men participated. "They made no preparation for appearing before their Emperor, the greater part being in their labouring dresses and in their dustman's hats," reported Hobhouse.[157]

Napoleon, in a brief address, promised the *Fédérés* arms. But his Ministers were divided; it took another month – 10 June, one week before Waterloo – before muskets appeared, and then only for training, with a stipulation that they be returned to the town hall at the end of each exercise.

The *Fédérés* proved much more useful as the builders of earth forts and the diggers of trenches beyond the barrières. Plans for the defence of Paris were decided in an afternoon by Napoleon and his architect, Pierre Fontaine, with the aid of hunting maps. Napoleon would ride out nearly every morning to inspect the works and encourage the men. From Montmartre to the heights of Belleville and down as far as Vincennes stretched out great flanks of sodden mud: another temporary Napoleonic monument.

The Field of May

The sound of builders banging away at the wooden scaffolding on the Champ de Mars had been heard since early April. A vast pentagonal amphitheatre, facing the Ecole Militaire, gradually took shape. Opposite, steps of painted wood led down from a first floor balcony of the school to a platform, a bare throne, and seats placed on the oblong wings that jutted out from each side of the structure. A few hundred yards behind the amphitheatre another strange-looking platform, pyramidical in form, with a throne atop – perhaps inspired by the Egyptian campaigns of the Year VII, or copied from a

Initially proclaimed as a
great national congress,
the "Champ-de-Mai"
was eventually held on a
cloudy day in June as a
celebration of Napoleon

Freemason's primer – sprouted out of the plains. The whole mighty complex of wood, canvas, and coloured cardboard was the work of Monsieur Fontaine.

But would there ever be a Champ-de-Mai? It was precisely in May that people began to have their doubts. The plan had already been changed four times in April, from a great national congress, to a deliberation of constitutions, to a ceremonial acceptance of a decreed constitution, to an announcement of the election results. The sudden convocation of the Chamber of Representatives on 30 April seemed a nail in the coffin of the Champ-de-Mai. Yet the builders went on tapping, canvases were spread out, and gaudy wooden eagles were stood on poles around the amphitheatre.

A programme was finally announced for 1 June. It would be a combined civic, military, and religious affair. There would be a mass, a proclamation of the election results by the Arch-Chancellor of the Empire, a declaration by the imperial heralds of the *Acte additionnel*, signatures, promulgations, speeches, responses, a Te Deum, and a distribution of the eagles to the National Guards and the army.

Two hundred thousand people witnessed the Champ-de-Mai. It was a grey, cold day.[158] The dignitaries of the Empire – the court of cassation, the court of accounts, the council of the university, the imperial court, and the magistracy of Paris, all dressed in robes, Spanish mantles, and feathered bonnets – descended the wooden steps from the Ecole Militaire, but nobody in the Champ de Mars could see them because the amphitheatre hid their view. When Arch-Chancellor Cambacérés tottered down to his platform in his blue cloak spotted with golden bees the assembled electors all burst into laughter.

In fact, few of the honourable members of the departmental electoral colleges had managed to get to Paris in time, and their seats – fifteen thousand of them – had, instead, been filled up by a last-minute hand-out of tickets. "A profusion of tickets were distributed by the court," explained Hobhouse, "and my companion had five or six sent to himself. Nor was there much choice in the selection, for the audience drank brandy, and gave into other plebeian amusements, which by no means recommended their neighbourhood."

Tedious hours passed by before the Emperor appeared at the balcony in a Spanish black bonnet, shaded with ostrich plumes and looped with a large diamond in front. He had difficulty coming down the stairs because his purple mantle was obviously too tight and too short. After flinging himself onto his purple throne the Mass eventually began. The Emperor, looking "very ungainly and squat," took out a spy-glass to observe the scene about him.

"My will is that of the people," he said in a prepared speech after Arch-Chancellor Cambacérés had read out the two election results.

The signing was done and the *Acte additionnel* was proclaimed the constitution of France. The steps were then cleared and the dignitaries, led by their Emperor, proceeded round the amphitheatre and out of sight of the electors to the pyramid and the crowds on the Champ de Mars. Young Jules Michelet was there with his widowed father. "I do not know how to describe my astonishment when I saw Bonaparte appear in his Roman Emperor's robe," he recalled years later. "It suited neither his age, nor his Moorish complexion, nor the circumstances, for he had not come to give us peace." War hung, like the clouds that day, over the Field of Mars.

Napoleon, still crowned with white feathers, mounted his open throne on the pyramid, now transformed into a mass of eagles, waving sabres, and military uniforms. "Soldiers of the National Guard of the Empire!" he exclaimed in a speech that probably few could hear. "Soldiers of the troops of the land and of the sea! I place in your hands the imperial eagle with the national colours. You swear to defend it at the price of your blood against the enemies of the *patrie* and of this throne." He repeated, with a piercing scream, "You swear it!" And those gathered round the pyramid shouted: "We swear it!" There followed, said Hobhouse, the loudest acclamations of the whole ceremony; "but," he added, "neither then, nor at any other period, were the cries very animated." They were generated by the troops and particularly, he noted, by one individual soldier, who was the object of some mockery.

"What a beautiful moment to abdicate in favour of our son!" wrote Napoleon's younger brother, Lucien, in a note written shortly after the event – apparently in perfect accord with the sentiments of the Minister of Police, Fouché. "Solemnity, eagles, speeches." – was all Benjamin Constant managed to fit in his diary on the Champ-de-Mai. He was much more excited about the "success of my book" (a piece, published that day, which he had cobbled together from old manuscripts), for Constant had a reputation to re-establish.

The crowds left no record at all. But we do know that they stood so dense on the plain that they seemed like "a carpet of heads." Here were the people, glum and silent.[159]

WATERLOO
Spring 1815

Previous page: A detail of Denis Dighton's imaginative portrayal of a British cavalry charge during the Battle of Waterloo

Golgotha

The mariners of Flanders used to say that London was nothing but an old suburb of Bruges which had been lost out at sea. Look, they would tell you, wasn't it the wind and the sea that smashed the dykes and flooded the peasants' fields? So it was when the wind and sea cracked the soils and separated England from Europe. Flanders was the place where it happened. Earth and water, sea and air had no fixed frontiers in Flanders. You even crossed the prairies by boat: from town to town the canal barges floated, graceful horse-drawn vessels that looked from a distance as though they were gliding through the grass. Vast prairies: they stretched westwards to Artois, Picardy, and on into the hills of the Perche and "Norman Switzerland;" northwards to Friesland, Pomerania, Courland, and the steppes of Russia: European prairies that the winds could transform in a moment into mud and cold water.

At dawn, on Monday, 20 March 1815, Louis XVIII's coach and four appeared on the prairies. None of the King's men knew where they were heading; no town had been prepared to receive him, no royal bed had been made up for him. Louis did not want to repeat the error of his late brother, captured by peasants on the frontier at Varennes in 1791. Six identical carriages, with their curtains drawn, had set out from the Tuileries the previous night; they had separated on place de la Concorde. Louis, in one of them, wrote on a small square of paper the name of his first destination, Saint-Denis, and then handed it to Marshal Marmont; thus he continued on to every relay post, lurching northwards in the direction of the sea.

Behind him, his nephew, the duc de Berry, organised the Household Guard – or the *Maison militaire du Roi* as it was officially known – along with a troop of volunteers, Swiss mercenaries, and students from the Ecole de Droit. The vicomte de Reiset, who commanded a company, said that several of them were "virtually children." Shortly before midnight, in drenching rains, they had collected into formation on the Champ de Mars and then crossed the bridge, marched up the Champs Elysées, rounded the wooden Arc de

331

Triomphe, and turned northwards; not even their commanders knew their ultimate destination. Marshal Macdonald, galloping north in search of his King after his own troops had defected to Napoleon, ran into the tail end of the *Maison* at Beaumont at around one o'clock in the morning. The men had dismounted, some leading their horses by their reins, others lain out on wagons, others wandering alone on foot with suitcases under their arms. It was the same scene all along the road as far as Nouailles. The *Maison militaire* already had the look of a routed army.[1]

Macdonald, the next night, finally tracked down his King to the sub-prefecture of Abbeville, in western Picardy, though there was nothing there that indicated his presence: no guard at the gates, no movement in the streets, no flags, no troops, no crowds. As Macdonald groped his way through the dark narrow streets towards an inn, he stumbled upon the comte de Jaucourt, who had run Foreign Affairs since Talleyrand's departure for Vienna in August. Yes, confirmed Jaucourt, His Majesty was in Abbeville. Macdonald found him seated in an easy chair in the town hall, just as calm and royal as he had been on his couch in the Tuileries. In fact, everyone who saw Louis over the next hundred days made the same remark: the King remained, by the Grace of God, King of France in spirit.

But he had made no preparations for the material defence of his title. He had left the Tuileries in such a hurry that nobody had thought of stopping Monsieur Chappe's mechanical telegraph system, so messages continued to pour into the palace from all over Europe for the benefit of Napoleon and his minions. Practically all government papers lay abandoned in their drawers, including a copy of the Secret Treaty between France, Britain, and Austria signed in Vienna the previous January. Virtually no financial preparations had been made for the flight. The King did remember to take his crown and diamonds, but he left most of his personal effects behind. He had packed a few clothes in a trunk – six shirts, a dressing gown, and his slippers – but the trunk was stolen. "They've taken my shirts, and I was already short of them," he wailed to Macdonald. "But it's my slippers that I regret most; you'll know one day, my dear Marshal, what it means to lose slippers that have taken on the mould of one's foot!" No couriers accompanied the King, so no dispatches could be sent and none were received. The King was completely isolated. He did not even know what had happened to the *Maison militaire*.[2]

The duc d'Orléans, head of the younger branch of the Bourbons, stuck to his plan of building a rump kingdom in the north of France, where he had been stationed. For the rest of his life he argued it would have worked if only preparations had been made. He wanted to canton troops along the line of the Somme, thus protecting Picardy, Artois, and Flanders. But he only found seven thousand men, so he concentrated on holding the forts on the frontier with Belgium. While he was out inspecting them, a telegraph came into his headquarters at Lille from the Tuileries. It was the King, attempting to report that he was leaving for the north. But only the first few syllables got through and the message remained a pure mystery. Later in the day another telegraph arrived: orders from Emperor Napoleon to obey the new government in Paris. Where was the King?[3]

Macdonald, like the duc d'Orléans, wanted the King to remain in France. When he discovered that Louis was in Abbeville, he was concerned because Abbeville lay on the road to England, not Lille. Macdonald persuaded the King to head directly for Lille. The hour of dinner was advanced and that same night, 20-21 March, the small royal party took to the road again, across flat and soggy Artois.[4]

Every town, every hamlet, every crossroads that bore a name had been the site of some battle, some treaty, some temporary accord between enemies, some dreadful slaughter. Picardy, Artois, and Flanders? They should have called it Golgotha, the plain of skulls. Yet the people who inhabited it had a reputation of friendliness. They were also Catholics, who literally worshipped their King. Their towns sprung up like coloured tulips out of the field; fortified places, whose ramparts and outworks formed the petals: little Viennas on the plain.

At one o'clock in the morning Louis stopped to change horses at the village of Saint-Pol. He entered the the house of a poor woman for a moment's respite from his journey. The woman tore down a curtain to place at the feet of her King. But even before he had reached the doorstep he was surrounded by inhabitants, kneeling prostrate: some kissed his knees, some touched his coat tails, others simply called out his name. The prince de Neuchâtel, a captain in the Guards, made a way through and, with the comte de Blacas, Keeper of the King's Wardrobe, they stood to attention at the door, swords drawn, while the King slept.

They were in Béthune by five in the morning. The people ran out in their night dresses; the sub-prefect arrived at the door of the King's carriage with one leg naked, his feet in slippers, a coat under his arm, his shirt unbuttoned, and a hat cocked on his head. It still poured with rain.

Progress was slow along the last ten leagues of mud track that led to Lille. They sighted the spires and walls through the mists early on Wednesday morning, 22 March. Macdonald was sent ahead. The gates were closed, the draw-bridge raised. Macdonald scribbled a note on a scrap of paper announcing the King's arrival, wrapped it around a stone, and lobbed it into the battlements, where it was picked up by a sentry and rushed round to the duc d'Orléans' residence. The Duke was just sitting down to a republican-style lunch with Marshal

Mortier; the last person he was expecting to meet that day was the King of France. He had actually closed the gates, save one, for security reasons; he remembered how Napoleon had taken Grenoble by infiltrating agents. It took him no time to organise his troops in double rank down the main street. Then he rode out to greet his cousin, who was sitting in his sodden, mud-spattered carriage in a suburb, wondering where to go next.[5]

Wednesday was market day in Lille, and this was the week of Easter. Rural folk had already crammed into the city before the news spread of the King's arrival. When his carriage creaked through the porte de Béthune, its wheels wobbling, the crowd broke into hosannas; handkerchiefs, undergarments, every piece of white linen one could lay hold of was waved from the streets to the chimney pots in hasty improvisation of the Bourbons' royal flag. And the troops stood silent, their eyes fixed to the ground, without as much as a glance to the carriage which passed. "Is there any immediate danger?" the King anxiously inquired at the first conference held that afternoon in the town hall. "No, Sire, the danger is not immediate," answered Marshal Mortier, "but it could become so at any moment; I cannot speak for the troops." Blacas wanted all the troops removed from Lille and then await the arrival of the *Maison militaire*. Quite impossible, retorted the duc d'Orléans; first, the troops would not leave, second, the *Maison militaire* was incapable of defending the city and, third, it was too late now to consider a siege – no preparations had been made, no food had been stored for Lille's sixty thousand inhabitants. In the evening the Duke proposed Dunkirk, in French Flanders, as a seat for the King's government. It was a small port, but strong, explained the Duke, and because of its advanced position Napoleon would have difficulty taking it without first conquering Belgium. The King agreed to leave that night. But he must have already noticed that between Dunkirk and Lille lay twenty-five more leagues of mud. Was it worth the effort? The rump Kingdom had been reduced to a pimple.

At midnight Louis changed his mind. "I didn't want to leave Lille like a robber in the night," he told the surprised Duke the next morning. He would set the government up in Lille. Three hours later he changed his mind again: "I'm going to cross the frontier," he announced, "I see I cannot remain in Lille; it is better to decide one's course once and for all." The previous night, copies of Vienna's Declaration of 13 March had arrived in Lille; Louis had decided to retreat into the arms of his European Allies.

That afternoon the King's carriage descended the same cobbled street he had climbed only twenty-four hours earlier. The crowds were there and so were the silent soldiers. The carriage broke down twice and the wheel treads had to be mended; Louis and his attendants pretended not to hear the anxious pleas of those who wanted to know where he was heading.

Many times would the King describe in later years the extraordinary sight of peasants – that Thursday afternoon of Easter 1815 – kneeling in the mud on either side of the road which led to Menin, Belgium. The frontier was unmarked; Macdonald had to call out a French customs officer to stand at the point in the empty plain where France became Belgium, for, while Macdonald swore loyalty to his King, he would not leave his country. King Louis XVIII was escorted into Menin by a red-coated English officer. The Duke handed over the command of Lille to his marshals and left for London the next morning.[6]

As for the *Maison militaire*, it struggled on in the mud for another three days. The artillery was abandoned, the baggage-wagons and ammunition-wagons too, so also the horses, sinking to their girths in swamps of dark mire; coaches, single and double, were left floating in the small lakes that strewed the plain after Béthune; the elegant carriages of the princes were last seen by their owners lopsided in ponds. Some of the men reached Estaires, only to learn, late on Saturday, 25 March, that the King had crossed into Belgium. They returned to Béthune where the *Maison*, on 26 March, was formally disbanded. The day before – it was Easter Sunday – they had watched the two royal princes, the comte d'Artois and the duc de Berry, with a small company of musketeers, fade into the rains as they rode off on the road to Ypres.[7]

Royal Ghent

King Louis spent Easter in Ostend. After hearing mass he wrote a letter to Talleyrand explaining why he had abandoned his kingdom. "The total defection of the troops," he said, "left me no choice." If he had remained only a few more hours in Lille, his position would have been compromised. "Buonaparte thus has all the armed force, but all the hearts are for me," smiled Louis, who never lost his composure. A few days later he told one of Lord Liverpool's special envoys to Belgium, "I could have got myself killed, it's true; that mattered little to me," to which he added another of his Latin phrases, *"uno avulso non deficit alter"* – one cut does not undo the other. "I feared I was going to be made prisoner," he went on; "perhaps they would have let me live, and my situation as a prisoner would have complicated affairs."[8]

But Louis' second exile did not simplify matters either. As long as he remained in France it was clear he was still King. None of the major Allies doubted that Napoleon would eventually be defeated but, once Louis had crossed into Belgium, there was nothing less certain than that his exile would be followed by a second Restoration. Emperor Alexander hated the Bourbons, the British attitude was equivocal, and even among those who followed Louis across the border many, especially of a liberal persuasion, were not sure they wanted to return to France under his leadership. The politics of the new French exiles in Belgium and their relationship with the Allied Powers would affect not only the future of France but also the shape of the European post-war settlement.

The first critical decision to be made was where to lodge the King next. Ostend itself stood on one of those wavering Flemish frontiers between Belgium and France, between land and sea, as well as between languages. An English officer arriving in April described the port as a dismal place with "narrow dirty streets, gloomy, old-fashioned, low, mean houses, the whole surrounded by marsh, sand-hills or sea." Where was poor Louis to go? The comte de Jaucourt reported to Talleyrand on Easter Monday that "the philosophy of the King goes straight to Hartwell" (his former residence in England). That was the fear of all the Constitutionalists: Louis in England would never again be Louis in France. Talleyrand wanted the King to move to Liège, in eastern Belgium, near Aachen, Prussian headquarters: Talleyrand's ideal of Europe had always been based on a link between France and civilised Germany. Louis himself told Harrowby that his intention had been to execute the Dunkirk project as proposed in Lille; but without his *Maison militaire*, that prospect soon faded.[9]

Back in 1792 Louis, in an earlier exile, had been invited by Count Hane Steenhuyse to join him in his magnificent hotel on the Veldstraat in Ghent, but the Republic's armies had got ahead of him so Louis had to look elsewhere. Now he had a fresh opportunity and he decided to accept. Louis XVIII entered the Flemish capital on Thursday afternoon, 30 March 1815, in a coach and six, the crowds cheering; the French were popular in Ghent. Louis told Harrowby that the people of Ghent, like the Belgians in general, would have preferred to have been French to Dutch.[10]

Ghent was a little under fifty miles west of Brussels, which was where Wellington set up his headquarters. The French in exile thus found themselves "near the scene of action," as the British press liked to point out. There was considerable correspondence between Ghent and Brussels, and Wellington himself visited the King on several occasions. Indeed, Ghent was his main source of intelligence on what was going on in France; for example, most of his assessments on the strength of Napoleon's forces came from the duc de Feltre, the King's Minister of War, who was getting reports from the other side of the border.

Nevertheless, the French did feel isolated in Ghent, a sentiment that was hardly helped by their own internal bickering. "The King has called me to his Council and charged me to make reports on the *interior*," the poet and memorialist Chateaubriand wrote to tell Talleyrand, "but, my Prince, one first has to have an *interior*." A strange Lilliputian kingdom grew up within the walls of the city, complete with court, ministers, and foreign ambassadors; a kingdom with no territory. At first it was hoped that an umbrella organisation would develop that would "admit without distinction of condition all who were religious, honest, and devoted to France and to the King." That was an idle dream. Jean-Claude Beugnot, who came to Ghent as Minister of the Marine (like Chateaubriand, he found his duties limited) made a distinction between the "party of Government" and the "party of the Court." One side defended the Charter of 1814, the other side condemned it; one side was committed to an evolving constitutional, parliamentary regime, the other was dead set against it. Most of the Ministers belonged to the former, along with a number of young people, like François Guizot, the future Prime Minister, who had come to Ghent on the gamble that the future of France was being moulded here. This group often referred to themselves as the "men of business." In the party of the court one found the Gentlemen of the Chamber, the Captains of the Guard, the Princes, and officers of the *Maison militaire* who had drifted into Ghent after their disbandment at Béthune. In Ghent, said Beugnot, all the naive attitudes these people had had during their first exile returned. It was as if their year in France had been only a masked ball; once they were out of the country again, they could throw off their masks and return to their backward ideas and obstinate dogmas. "It is in the leisure of misfortune," said Guizot, "that men deliver themselves to all their dreams." The leisure of misfortune was the father of French Royalist fanaticism.[11]

The two parties lived separately at Ghent. True, as individuals they would frequently meet each other at the King's house, at the theatre, or on a walk along the battlements – and they were exquisitely polite to one another on all these occasions. But they never dined together, they would never sit at the same card table, they would never even have a conversation together. Two distinct visions of the state developed in Ghent that would influence the pattern of French politics for well over a century.

Ghent would be unfairly compared to the *émigré* community that had grown up in Coblenz in 1792. It was the reformist party of government which had all the real power in Ghent, though its attitude was frequently defensive. Jaucourt, for example, might well write letters to Talleyrand despairing of a new "air of Coblenz" that was developing in town and complaining that the King had fallen under the influence of the Princes and their allies. But it was actually Jaucourt's party of government which controlled all the networks with the foreign courts, which corresponded with ambassadors and ministers, which ran the official newspaper, the *Journal universel*, wrote the bulletins and composed the reports. These were the people Wellington supported, for Wellington had as much contempt for the "violent *émigrés*" when in Brussels as he had had in Paris. It was the party of government, not the *émigrés*, that Talleyrand really represented in Vienna – in fact, they were all writing to him and pleading with him to join them. And it was these "men of business" in Ghent who maintained the link with Paris, their principal man being, of course, Napoleon's disloyal Minister of Police, Joseph Fouché.[12]

One of the chief targets of the party of government was the comte de Blacas, Keeper of the King's Wardrobe and, as Guizot described him, the discreet and constant ally of the comte d'Artois, the King's brother. It was indispensable, Jaucourt told Talleyrand, to take whatever measure was necessary "to make M de Blacas disappear from the line of the men of business": Blacas stood in the way of the Ministers and their King. With his long drawn-out face crowned with a white powdered wig, the Count cut a very sorry figure in Ghent; Blacas knew his days of influence and power were numbered.[13]

The party of the court did have the support of what remained of the King's armed forces – *la petite armée* as it came to be known – but it was not a very convincing force. It was made up of the debris of the *Maison militaire*, a small number of officers and soldiers who had deserted Napoleon's army, and the always enthusiastic students of the Paris Law School. One of the main reasons the duc d'Orléans emigrated to England was that, as a military man, he did not want to be seen among them. Wellington would have nothing to do with them either. King William I of the United Netherlands was horrified by their presence. Above all, the "men of business" in Ghent, supported by Talleyrand, wanted to keep their distance and urged the Allies not to accept any military assistance from these curious regiments. All the barracks and army facilities in Ghent were taken up by British and Hanoverian troops, so the *petite armée* was parked out in the Camp of Alost or Aulst, as the Flemish called it – a canal harbour that was several hours' ride from Ghent. Every day the duc de Berry, the commander of the troops, would set out from Ghent accompanied by his travelling equipage, with "their glazed hats stuck on one side, queues, each with side-hair neatly plaited in, short, very short jackets, and, above all, enormous jack-boots." If the handling of their whips made music, they were hardly equipped to make war.[14]

The intrigue and pettiness of politics in Ghent created an atmosphere that was not unlike, said Chateaubriand, that of those great enclosed nunneries which could be found in the north of France. Ghent was famously silent. An English visitor described a solitary individual walking down one of the town's long and narrow streets listening to his own feet reverberate as "a sexton stepping down the echoing aisle of a cathedral."[15]

There was certainly something very holy about the place, whether one compared it to a nunnery or a cathedral. King Louis' presence contributed to this, for, as Chateaubriand again remarked, the "King was King everywhere, like God was God everywhere, in a crib or in a temple, on an altar of gold or of clay." Nothing could diminish Louis' proud sense of his ancient race, even if he had no kingdom. Every day, he would follow the same regime as at the Tuileries: the *lever du roi* at six in the morning, a *déjeuner* at 10.30, council, audiences, an afternoon dinner (when he would carve the roast himself with a twinkle in his eye), and then his daily promenade through the town or along the Brussels road in a carriage and six. Just as in Paris, the Ministers complained of being isolated from their King, only now their lodgings were a good deal poorer.[16]

Yet life in Ghent was not sad. The quality of the plays put on by the French Theatre was awful, but they were usually very funny. Dinners could be had at a *table d'hôte* for three francs. They were animated and gay. Beugnot, like Chateaubriand, remembered in particular the great platters of white fish and potatoes, served up "in the English fashion" and washed down with "the good beer of Louvain."[17]

The army of Belgium

Thus one King was unmade. But another was made. Two days before Louis XVIII fled Paris, the Congress of Vienna proclaimed that the Sovereign Prince William of Orange was King of the United Netherlands. Britain, as a result, obtained the "barrier state" she had been seeking on the plains of Brabant and Flanders; Prussia found herself faced with a new kingdom to the west that could not be easily incorporated into a system of German Circles; while Austria was perfectly happy to forget the whole busines and turn her attentions southwards, away from her old provinces in the west, and concentrate on Italy.

The House of Orange itself was not very pleased with the way the accord had been drawn up. It felt it was being cheated of its ancient hereditary possessions east of Maastricht and it strongly objected to the new Prussian presence on its frontiers. Disgruntled Dutch diplomats had dampened the spirits of the Christmas parties in Vienna in 1814. All through the New Year, and on into the spring, the dispatch boxes in London and Vienna were filled with their letters of complaint.

The residents of the Belgic provinces were none too happy either. After being "liberated" by Prussian armies, having had their barns emptied of produce, their livestock killed, their wagons, their horses, and their equipment requisitioned, they were now annexed by their hated Protestant neighbours and rivals, the Dutch. Lord Castlereagh might have viewed this as a necessary part of Europe's balance; the Belgians did not.

In April the garlands, which had been strung from window to window along the main streets of Brussels for the Dutch King's entry, were still green. The town hall and some of the buildings in the park were still hung with strips of orange bunting. There was a wooden triumphal arch standing by the edge of the canal leading to the Palace of Laeken recording Belgium's initial reception of "Gulielmus Primus." But when King William appeared at the city's theatre for a second time in April, only thirty people stood up in the pit as he entered and everybody moved off without ceremony at the end of the play without waiting for His Majesty's exit.[18]

The Duke of Wellington arrived on the night of 4 April. It was raining. "The reports on the location, number, and intentions of the enemy are still excessively vague," he wrote the next morning to General Count Gneisenau in his Prussian headquarters in Aachen; "but it seems to me we have to be prepared for a *coup de main* that could be attempted at any moment." He established his own headquarters in a four-storey hotel on rue Montagne du Parc that overlooked, to the south, the Park of Brussels. Beyond the city ramparts, on the horizon, was the Forest of Soignes. Travellers coming in from Ghent would notice the same woodland on their approach to Brussels; a slight undulation in the land developed so that one could actually look down into the city and then across to the black outline of the forest on a ridge in the distance.[19]

During the Easter weekend, the English community had been in a panic because it had been rumoured that Napoleon was in Lille with an army. "The English were flying off in all directions, whilst others were arriving from Paris," reported the Whig Thomas Creevey, who, following his disappointing campaign on behalf of Caroline, the Princess of Wales, had come to Brussels with his invalid wife for what he had imagined would be a little repose.[20]

It was the jilted fiancé of Caroline's daughter, the twenty-three-year-old Prince of Orange – son of King William – who was now Commander-in-Chief of the Allied armed forces in Belgium. Wellington's arrival, along with the official papers from London (received in Brussels at the same time) that named the Duke "Commander of His Majesty's Forces on the Continent," caused serious tension between British headquarters and the Dutch court. "Slender Billy" withdrew his claim to the supreme command within days; but weeks passed before King William appointed Wellington commander of the Dutch army.[21]

In theory the Allies could "inundate France with force in all directions." The renewed Treaty of Chaumont, signed in Vienna, was designed to bring over a quarter of a million men onto the French frontiers by the end of April. They included the combined British, Dutch, and Hanoverian forces in Belgium, the Prussians between the Meuse and the Rhine, and an Austro-Bavarian "corps" on the Upper Rhine; an additional Russian reserve was due to arrive in early May. But things looked very different in Brussels. Reports gradually came through that the Austrians were hopelessly entangled with Murat in Italy and that the Russians were encountering delays in their march down the narrow corridor in Bohemia traced out for them by the distrusting Austrians.

What, however, worried Wellington most was the situation within Belgium. There remained the remnants of Sir Thomas Graham's British force – which had failed to take Bergen during the last campaign of the previous year. It now consisted of about fourteen thousand poorly armed and badly disciplined troops. These, all the same, were a treasure compared to the Dutch-Belgians, most of whom were veterans of Napoleon's armies, including their officers. Wellington, while conscious that he could not afford to ignore a force of thirty thousand men, refused to recruit more of them. "They would desert us," Wellington warned his Quartermaster General. Wellington did not even want to employ Belgians as drivers of army wagons and used dismounted British dragoons instead. Many an angry Belgian veteran of Napoleon's armies was left to find civilian employment as a carter, a road-sweeper, or the hotel porter who would refuse to polish the boots and carry hot water to the British tourists of Brussels.[22]

Unlike in Spain, it was a European army that Wellington commanded on the plains of Belgium. Wellington solved the problem of divided loyalties by completely reorganising the force, combining the good with the bad, and mixing the nationalities in nearly every one of his army divisions. For the first time in his military career he cut his force into three permanent corps, the First centred on Braine-le-Comte, south of Brussels, under the Prince of Orange, the Second to the west at Ath under Lord Hill, the Third in Brussels itself under his own command; different national units were blended into each one of them.

Wellington made every effort to increase the strength of the British infantry, which had been the main arm of his force in Spain. "There," said Wellington to Thomas Creevey as they stood in the Park of Brussels watching a red-coated private wander among the statues, "it all depends on that article whether we do the business or not. Give me enough of it, and I am sure." But Wellington did not have enough of it and, like many a British commander before him, he had to go shopping elsewhere.[23]

After a quarter of a century of European war, the number of shops remaining open to Britain were limited. Britain's main recruiting ground had always been "Germany." But the "Germany" of 1815 was not the "Germany" that had filled out Marlborough's armies at Blenheim and Oudenarde, or that had carried the flag in America, in Ireland, or in Jacobite Scotland. The old Reich was gone and, along with it, the German mercenary tradition. Clancarty had been left in Vienna to haggle out an arrangement with Austria and jealous Prussia: they formally granted Wellington command of troops from Hanover, Bavaria, Nassau, Oldenburg, the Hanseatic towns, and what remained of Royal Saxony after partition. But an agreement in Vienna was no guarantee that Wellington would have his troops. The Duke of Cambridge made sure Hanover's regiments were marching to Belgium in the first week of April. The Duke of Brunswick's contingent of ten thousand men arrived in Brussels on the 10th. The Nassauers only arrived on 2 May. The troops of the Hansa towns did not start walking until 19 May. For lack of Austrians (still engaged in Italy), the Bavarians were tied down for good with the corps of the Upper Rhine. And the Prussians never did let go of the Saxon troops.[24]

British subsidies handed over to sovereign states were no assurance of troops either. Nor did subsidies safeguard Belgium from plunder by Allied forces, though by design they were supposed to. Wellington complained of overt robbery. The worst offenders were, once more, the Prussians, who, since their visit in 1814, had perfected a system for ransacking Belgians by dividing up the host country, on their return, into *rayons* (a French word meaning "shopping departments") and then emptying the contents. The system was invented in Vienna by the champion for a new German Reich, Baron vom Stein.[25]

But Wellington's hard diplomatic efforts, his constant pressure on London, and military reorganisation did raise the number in his Anglo-Dutch force from forty thousand at his arrival to over sixty thousand by the end of April. And as the number increased, so did morale.

Napoleon's expected *coup de main* of early April did not materialise, so Wellington, in his second week in Belgium, made a four-day tour of the southern forts and borders of the province. He covered, in fact, much the same terrain as he had inspected the previous August. Ostend, Nieuport, Ypres, and the citadel of Tournai were now pretty much able to withstand siege, but improvements were needed at the strategic points of Ghent and Ath if Brussels were to be properly defended.[26]

While in Ghent, Wellington received a number of reports from the French exiles that things were not going too well for Napoleon in Paris; by the time he returned to Brussels he was beginning to think that the war could be avoided and that Napoleon might fall on his own account. This opinion was reinforced by reports coming in from his own agents – Correspondents B and C (the latter placed in Paris)[27] – along with those of English travellers returning home from France. "The opinion of several people I know in the present French Council is that Buonaparte cannot remain six months Emperor," wrote, for example, J. Frissel after landing in Brighton. "The greater part of his ministry, which his present weakness has obliged him to compose against his will, is against him." On 22 April Thomas Creevey met Wellington at a ball given by Lady Charlotte Greville. Creevey was so astonished by what Wellington had to say that he made a special note of their conversation in his diary: "He maintained that a Republick was about to be got up in Paris by Carnot, Lucien Bonaparte, &c., &c., &c. I asked if it was the concert of the *Manager*, and what the name of the piece was to be. He said he had no doubt it would be *tragedy* by Buonaparte, and that they would be at him by stiletto or otherwise in a few days." Wellington repeated the same idea in a letter to Blücher the next day.[28]

As his campaigns in both India and the Peninsula showed, Wellington never really made a clear distinction between defensive and offensive strategies. His chief concern was always not to be cut off from his supplies and, above all, not to be defeated. Moreover, Wellington was well aware of Napoleon's fondness of attacking Allies at the point where they joined, "on the hinge" as Wellington said; the whole campaign of France in 1814 had demonstrated this. Wellington had to assure that the hinge, this time, was forged of iron.

Wellington positioned his armies in a way that would allow him not only to defend Brussels (joining his Anglo-Dutch force with the Prussians along a line south of the town) but also, at short notice, to march on France: in the light of the information he was getting, he considered this a real option in April. Wellington sought "the freedom to act without waiting for all the forces [of the Allies] to be united," a delighted Louis XVIII informed Talleyrand after meeting Wellington in Ghent on 8 April; "I do not need to tell you that this demand should have your keenest support." On 10 April, Wellington was recommending his Allies in Vienna that operations begin in France on 1 May rather than await the arrival of the Russians later that month "and thus give Buonaparte the advantages which he will certainly derive from *l'Assemblée du Champ de Mai.*" Throughout most of April, Wellington considered the Champ-de-Mai – which he naturally thought would take place in May – the decisive moment when Napoleon would either succeed in concentrating his troops for the invasion of Belgium or would be swept out of office by enemies in his own government. By that time he hoped the Allies would already be *en route* for Paris.[29]

The signals being received from Paris suggested that France was heading for a Republic, not a Restoration of the Bourbons. At the very least it was believed that, after Napoleon's forced departure, France would opt for a monarchy that would be much more liberal in complexion than the regime of 1814. London did nothing to discourage this. Nor did Wellington in Brussels. An urgent three-way correspondence developed between London, Brussels, and Vienna on the kind of regime that would be installed once the Allies entered Paris.

In this, the link Wellington forged with the "men of business" in Ghent played a critical role. King Louis and the court party wanted the Allies to enter France as soon as possible. As the King explained to Talleyrand, early in April, he was quite convinced Napoleon would be defeated but he feared, not unjustifiably, that a delayed entry would bring the worst elements into France, particularly the "furious Prussians," who were regarded in Ghent as equally destructive as the followers of Bonaparte. Wellington remained very cool to the idea and not just because he thought such advice misplaced; the "men of business" were urging him not to listen. They argued that Frenchmen in exile could only act as a guiding "moral force," they regarded involvement in "physical force" as the mistake of the *émigrés* in the 1790s, and they did not want to bear the taint of the *émigrés*: the "men of business" wanted to govern France.[30]

A key figure in the discussions on the future of France at this moment, and also a leading spokesman for the idea of "moral force," was the King's cousin, the duc d'Orléans. The day after the King crossed the frontier into Belgium, the duc d'Orléans left Lille for England – to join his wife and children, as he explained in his *Journal*, written and published years later. But when he wrote to Talleyrand that April he explained he was on a diplomatic mission. Letters were exchanged between Orléans, the King, and Wellington, and several of these found their way into Castlereagh's private papers, now deposited in Belfast: the Duke and the British Foreign Secretary appear to have been closely collaborating during the Hundred Days over possible alternatives to a second Bourbon Restoration.[31]

Orléans himself showed no ambition for returning to Paris as "King Louis-Philippe," but he had a strong following among the "men of business" in Ghent and he was supported by Talleyrand in Vienna. He did advise the King not to allow the royal Princes to participate in any foreign armies or allow the *petite armée* to move out of its isolated camp at Alost. He also expressed hostility to the former *Maison militaire* and hoped that it would never be reconstituted.

Castlereagh went much further than Orléans in his demands on King Louis. He wanted the court party purged and all the King's personal advisers, including Blacas, replaced. Like Wellington,

Castlereagh was seeking an "acceptable middle term," a royal government that would include former Jacobin leaders, the most prominent being Napoleon's current Minister of Police, Joseph Fouché. Castlereagh criticised Blacas for his narrow-mindedness and venality, and went so far as to propose that the King employ Talleyrand, unofficial leader of the "men of business," as his chief minister. If the King did not at once adopt such measures, Castlereagh said he could in no way guarantee the Restoration of the Bourbons. This message was passed on to Vienna and was constantly rumoured in Ghent: it would be surprising if it did not reach some ears in Paris. Castlereagh was thus not only laying the framework for a more liberal French parliamentary regime but was also, by holding out a carrot to the Jacobins, encouraging discord within Napoleon's own government: as Wellington kept on repeating, perhaps the war against Napoleon could be avoided.[32]

But in early May there was fresh panic in Brussels. The French press reported that the Imperial Guard had already marched as far as Beauvais and was about to be joined by Napoleon, who wanted "to inspect the frontier fortresses." Unlike most Englishmen – rushing backwards and forwards in wagons – Wellington's first impression was that the French were going to attack the Bavarians on the Rhine; he had received a report that the enemy were reinforcing their fort at Bouillon, near Sedan. But further evidence suggested that the French were about to attack between the Lys and the Sambre, either on Wellington's right flank, where Hill's Second Corps was located, or towards his centre, in an area held by the Prince of Orange's First. In either case, with Brussels threatened, it was essential to move up the Prussians, who were still far out on the left.[33]

Fortunately for Wellington, the Marshal Prince Blücher had just arrived in Belgium to set up his headquarters in Liège. There were problems of language to be overcome, for Blücher spoke no English and little French ("Hint to Blücher that I have as yet nobody about me who can read the German character," Wellington asked his liaison officer); but Blücher belonged to the old practical school of soldiering, untainted by the ideology and dogma that had made young Gneisenau and his colleagues so difficult to deal with. A meeting was quickly arranged between the two commanders to take place at Tirlemont on 3 May. In the meantime, to protect his right flank, Wellington ordered that preparations be made for flooding at Mons, Ghent, Ypres, Nieuport, and Ostend; at Oudenarde the sluices were actually opened.

Blücher nearly didn't make it to the meeting – not because of the French threat (which turned out to be a false alarm) but because of a Saxon mutiny.

King Frederick Augustus's troops had been transferred by the

Prussians, after the occupation of Saxony in November, to the Lower Rhine where they had been marched back and forth between Marburg and Coblenz. The command structure had already broken down; several Saxon officers indicated that they would be willing to serve the King of Prussia. No blending of military units, as Wellington had successfully carried out in his army, was attempted by the Prussians. Instead, when they entered Belgium after Napoleon's return, they posted the entire Saxon force in Liège, the Prussian head-quarters, "without a single Prussian soldier nearby." Because Frederick Augustus had refused to consent to the partition of his kingdom, the Prussians refused to divide the Saxon forces as was agreed in Vienna – the Royal Saxons were supposed to come under Wellington's command. But with the approach of war their position became untenable. On the eve of the scheduled meeting between Blücher and Wellington, the Prussians finally decided on partition of the force: each Saxon regiment was to be divided into two battalions, one to be Prussian, the other to remain Saxon. But before this was carried out – by unwilling Saxon officers – news spread amongst the ranks that Frederick Augustus had still not given his consent.[34]

"Long live the King of Saxony!" cried a party of Saxon soldiers that gathered outside Blücher's house. They were unarmed and so they were easily dispersed by officers. But, between eight and nine that night, a disorganised band of troops arrived uttering "wild cries" and armed with sabres. They stoned the house, taking special aim at the room where Blücher was known be. "Long live the King of Saxony!" yelled some. "Long live Napoleon!" shouted others. Blücher and his staff escaped out a back door where horses were standing; they spent the night in a nearby village.

It was a tired and worried Blücher that Wellington met at Tirlemont the following afternoon. "The Saxons mutinied last night at Liège," wrote Wellington, drily, to Clancarty in Vienna, "and obliged poor old Blücher to quit the town." Blücher, General Gneisenau, and General Grolman wanted the three Saxon battalions involved deci-mated (one man in ten shot). Wellington recommended, instead, that they they be sent as prisoners into the Prussian provinces. Baron von Müffling, who at that moment was still Gneisenau's chief of staff but would be named, days later, liaison officer to Wellington, also argued against decimation. He had, he said, a list of seven "ringleaders."[35]

Eventually, the three Saxon battalions were lined up, their flags were burnt and they were ordered to turn over six of the "ring-leaders" to the Prussian authorities, or else face decimation. Six men were turned over; neither their names nor their fate are recorded. Blücher then had the three battalions marched up to Antwerp where he demanded Wellington supply transport to the Prussian ports. Wellington refused, arguing that British ships had other things to do.

So the battalions were turned round, marched across Belgium, into the new Prussian provinces – and out of history.[36]

The conference at Tirlemont of 3 May was the most important military summit prior to the Battle of Waterloo. Minutes were kept, but nobody in 180 years has ever found them. Nonetheless, the two main decisions seem to have been made at that time. In the first place, it was agreed that Wellington and Blücher would work in close personal cooperation, supported by liaison officers and staff. Second, the two armies would weaken their outer flanks and bulk their forces in the central zone in front of Ghent and Brussels. The line that separated them was an old Roman road, still then in use, which ran from Cambrai in France, through Bavay, and on to Maastricht. Blücher moved his headquarters westwards to Namur. "I met Blücher at Tirlemont this day," Wellington reported to Charles Stewart in Vienna, "and received from him the most satisfactory assurances of support." But then added, "I am not satisfied with our delay."[37]

Originally, Wellington had planned to be in France by 3 May. But few Austrians had yet collected on the Upper Rhine and the Russians were still winding their way through Bohemia. At Tirlemont, Wellington and Blücher agreed that when their two armies did advance into France, Wellington would go by way of Mons and Cambrai while Blücher would pass through Charleroi and Maubeuge. But when would they advance? Summer? Autumn? It was estimated that Napoleon would have over eight hundred thousand men on foot by September, an army of the size that had invaded Russia.

Britain, meanwhile, had not yet even called out the militia. As Wellington confessed to the Prince of Orange, their armies were in an uncomfortable situation, "neither at peace nor at war;" they were unable to patrol up to the enemy, unable to act offensively, unable to combine in an operation. He was franker still with Charles Stewart: "I have got an infamous army, very weak and ill-equipped and a very inexperienced staff. In my opinion they were doing nothing in England."[38]

Brussels was in a state of uneasiness. It rained nearly every day. English, Scots, Irish, and Hanoverians – citizens and military – thronged in the streets. Batteries of artillery lay in rows in the park, the horses picketed in a long line behind them. There was still a bustle of commerce and the foreigners were amused by the sight of so many dogs hauling small carriages.

Eventually, in the last week of May, news arrived that the House of Commons had voted for the war against Napoleon. "By God!" exclaimed Wellington, "I think Blücher and myself can do the thing."

London declares war

The main reason why Britain so long delayed making a formal decla-ration of war was that the government was hoping to avoid it. The Ministers were not at all sure the country would be able to afford another European war. The economy showed no signs of improve-ment. Nor was the government too confident of its own survival; opposition in and out of parliament was getting vicious. In particular, the Radicals, with their small but noisy following in the City and in some of the towns of the Midlands and the North, were getting increasingly interested in European politics and were opposed to war of any kind. Anyway, why go to war if the French themselves were about to throw out Napoleon? Castlereagh, in London, was receiving the same information as Wellington.

Optimism on that count faded as April dripped into stormy May. The French civil wars appeared settled in Napoleon's favour (the duc d'Angoulême was now in Ghent and the royalist Vendée was for the moment silent) while Napoleon's own military force grew without a pause. British papers reproduced verbatim the enthusiastic reports on French troop levies published in the *Moniteur*. Londoners did not have to read newspapers to know what direction their own country was taking: troops were seen marching off to Deptford and to Harwich to board the boats for Belgium; a million and a half ball car-tridges were shipped out from the Ordnance Wharf at Chatham; six thousand horses were purchased and transferred to every port on the Thames. In southern England, "neither at peace nor at war," the military encampments once more sprung up in the fields of Kent and artillery wagons rolled down the roads again.

It was, however, a phoney war. The concerns of the people remained those of an island nation. The freak weather dominated the talk of most farmers and tradesmen. For the poor, the main worry was the price of bread. In London, it was the season of the great painting exhibitions. The King was still absent; every month the med-ical bulletins appeared in the press – "The King's health has been uninterruptedly good, though His Majesty's disorder continues with-out any sensible alteration."

Madness indeed, remained a popular topic. "Insanity," warned a newspaper correspondent, "is a calamity to which we are all liable, and of that most awful of visitations no man can tell the hour!" Within months this would be proven to be the most terrible augury.[39]

But the greatest concern in England in the spring of 1815 was money, where it came from, where it went. The government wanted to extend the time limit on the new Income Tax. Britain was the first country in Europe to be subjected to the Income Tax (or the Property

Tax as it was often misleadingly called at the time). It had been introduced by Pitt in the 1790s as a temporary war measure designed to help the government pay its military bills. The Whigs abolished it in 1803, during the brief period of peace. The return of the Tories and war also brought about a return of the Income Tax, "the most grievous and most insulting of all our taxes," as the Radical party's *Examiner* put it. With the peace of 1814 the Ministers had promised that they would abolish it, but they had second thoughts after the news of Napoleon's return. A Bill was introduced in April to extend the tax for another year and on 12 May this Bill became law; like the Corn Laws, it was another piece of rushed legislation.

The Income Tax became an obsession that spring. There were public demonstrations and petitions to parliament. People with a liberal temperament opposed it, while conservatives supported it. Earl Stanhope, a Whig in the Lords, complained "on the ground of its tending to bear hard on the poorer class of farmers." Liverpool said, on the contrary, that it lightened the burden on the poor.[40]

Parliamentary discussion of the Prince Regent's expenses did not help matters for the government. Having been excluded from the festivities at Vienna, His Royal Highness, it seemed, had found compensation in the splendour of his own palaces. A new gothic dining-room, divided into five compartments, was added to the east end of Carlton House, while a second gothic library was installed in the west; new Corinthian rooms, complete with a golden drawing room, were also constructed. As Kings and Emperors danced in Austria's baroque capital, John Nash, the Regent's new architect, designed for Windsor Great Park an ornate Royal Lodge (Whitbread called it the "Thatched Palace"). While Viennese skated on the frozen Wien, Nash received a commission to refurbish the Marine Pavilion in Brighton. It was the sort of European show of glitter and grandeur that was hated by the dictators of taste in England.

"Was there equal profusion displayed even in the expenditure of the continental Princes?" asked the Whig George Tierney after estimating some of the costs in plate, upholstery, and jewelry. Tierney mourned the passing of the "chastened and dignified splendour" of old King George's court, a true "British Court."[41]

Ambassadors were paid out of the Royal Household purse. One unfortunate consequence of this was that criticism of royal expenditures could very quickly lead to criticism of Britain's diplomatic missions abroad and, indeed, of the whole structure of British diplomacy: Britain's ties with the continent were thereby called into question. The same people, who attacked the Regent for his continental-style improvidence, inveighed against the "Gothic Regenerators" of Vienna, the foreign envoys *"ensnared* in the labyrinth of diplomacy."[42]

Tierney's Whigs scorned, in particular, the head of the diplomatic corps, Lord Castlereagh, while Napoleon got every benefit of the doubt. It was not Napoleon, they argued, but the noble Lord Castlereagh and his Congress of Vienna – dominated by the continental Powers of Russia, Prussia, and Austria – that were responsible for the overthrow of the Bourbons. "The war with which we are menaced will be a war against the independence of nations," they said, repeating the lines of the independent-loving Emperor of the French. Castlereagh defended the principle of the Congress, the eternal principle of European diplomacy: "The Congress," he replied, "had not assembled to discuss moral principles, but to effect great practical objects for the general security of Europe."[43]

Leading the attack on the government was the tireless Samuel Whitbread. In speech after speech he denounced Castlereagh's display of "diplomatic treachery" and the "league of extermination," which appeared ready to plunge the continent into blood "in order to put down one man." Whitbread always came back to two documents, the Allied Declaration of 13 March and the Allied Treaty of 25 March. One complemented the other, he claimed – a point that none of the Allied Ministers would have denied. But none of them would have agreed that they were based, as Whitbread argued, on a "doctrine of assassination."[44]

On 28 April, Whitbread tabled a motion "to prevent this country from being involved in war on the ground that the executive power of France was vested in the hands of any particular man." Again he insisted on the cruel Allied "doctrine of assassination," adding that Napoleon had the support of the French people and was disposed to peace. Castlereagh answered that Napoleon's peaceful intent would become clear once he had assembled four hundred thousand troops, that the so-called Constitution would then mean nothing, and that Ministers such as Fouché and Lucien Bonaparte would be liquidated. Whitbread's motion was rejected by 273 votes to 72.[45]

Whitbread did have some support in the streets, but he would have probably been happier without it, for the tone of the small crowds that protested against the war was distinctly anti-parliamentarian. The largest assemblies took place in Palace Yard, opposite the old House of Commons – Palace Yard was, in politics, the equivalent of Trafalgar Square today.

Two personalities were always present, Sir Francis Burdett, the darling of the London "mob," and "the veteran Patriot" (as he was invariably introduced) Major Cartwright. "The people of England have now no constitutional organ left but public meetings," announced Sir Francis. They protested against the Corn Laws, the "oppressive Tax upon Income," the slave trade, the Regent, the partition of Saxony, the annexation of Genoa, and, almost parenthetically, the war – "the only object of which is to set up despotism wherever it is put down, or put down freedom wherever it is set up."[46]

Until the third week of May, neither the Allied Declaration nor the Allied Treaty of 25 March had been formally laid before parliament, although the full texts had been published in all the national newspapers in April.[47] The Declaration did not require parliamentary approval; it had anyway been amply debated and the Regent's Message of 7 April served as a valid substitute. The Treaty was another matter. Because it established a military alliance against Napoleon its ratification by parliament would in effect be a declaration of war.

By May, it was clear that Napoleon was not about to fall from his throne. The Treaty was presented to the two Houses in the week of 22-26 May, along with a second Message from the Prince Regent asking for support. Referring to the latter, Lord Liverpool declared in the Lords that "it was certainly to be regarded as a war message." It was approved by 156 votes to 44. The Commons approved by 331 to 92.

There was a curious delay in the Commons debate. It had been set for Tuesday, 23 May, but the sitting was cancelled because there was not a sufficient number of Members present. The next day some minor business of corruption within the East India Company was discussed. It was only on Thursday, 25 May, that the debate on the war took place.

The major event within the House was the support the government received from Henry Grattan, the Irish parliamentary leader and a Whig. Members of the opposition, no less than the Ministers on the Treasury Bench, were stunned. His speech was "as luminous as a Chinese Feast of Lanterns" and, after it was finished, the applause lasted so long that the Speaker thought the debate finished and was ready to put the question to the vote. But Burdett spoke against war, and so did Tierney. Mr Ponsonby, House Leader of the Whigs, also mumbled a few words for peace.[48]

But where was Mr Whitbread? One heard from him the next day, when he made a few comments about subsidies. The only other major intervention he made between the declaration of war and the announcement of victory at Waterloo was during a debate on Ordnance Survey Maps on 9 June. Admittedly, the parliamentary debates during this period were not of immense interest; Stamp Duties were discussed, as were public beggars, the Elgin Marbles, and nude bathing in the Thames – a question that particularly preoccupied Mr William Wilberforce, whose house overlooked the river.

But there was more involved in the silence of the great Whig orator. Whitbread had financial problems. On 3 May, he had announced his intention to relinquish his management of the Drury

Lane Theatre, into which he had invested a considerable sum of money. "The responsibility and anxiety arising from the fluctuations of so important a concern," he explained to the theatre's sub-committee assembled in the Crown and Anchor Tavern, "are more than I can continue to endure." During the next three weeks there was, within the committee, heated debate, most of it not very complimentary of Whitbread. Sir Francis Burdett took over the chair. On the eve of the Commons war debate, 24 May, Kean, the actor, gave a benefit performance in the theatre, but it did little to lift Whitbread out of his strange and worried silence.[49]

For Radicals, Burdett was the rising star. He and Cartwright continued to hold their public meetings in Palace Yard. They were joined, on Thursday, 15 June, by Henry "Orator" Hunt, who told the gathering that the duc d'Enghien deserved to be shot in 1804.[50] Burdett concluded the meeting by saying that the current war was a "war against liberty."

Shortly after these words were pronounced there appeared, astride his steed and accompanied by a single groom, none other than the Noble Lord in the Blue Ribbon, the Foreign Secretary himself. Castlereagh proceeded across the square at a "gentle pace" and up Parliament Street. He was followed by several screaming "desperate looking fellows," but he remained unperturbed. On he trotted through the Horse Guards, across the Parade, eventually disappearing into St James's Park.

Later that afternoon he returned, on his way to Downing Street. The same scene was then repeated in reverse. The newspaper correspondent who told this story commented, "He laughs and he rides away." But the noble lord was not laughing; his thoughts that Thursday afternoon, 15 June, were concentrated on the European centre.[51]

Vienna's Final Act

About a month earlier – it was one fine day in May – Baron von Hager's trusty agent, **, spied Castlereagh's half-brother riding across the Graben. Sir Charles Stewart, the British Ambassador, took a left turn down the Kohlmarkt in the direction of the Minoritenplatz. "The horse he was riding," reported **, "had its head all covered with lilies-of-the-valley; he held an enormous bouquet of the same flowers in his hand, was roaring with laughter, and looked as if he had drunk one glass too much. The whole crowd in the streets stopped to look at him and to poke fun at him."[52]

Hager's agents had their hands full with stories about "Stewart and Co.," as the British Embassy had come to be known. Stewart's affair with Sagan was the talk of the town. Off he would go, every night, to the Palm Palace and return to the Embassy at dawn, exhausted. Morning visitors were turned away because the Ambassador remained in bed. Cardinal Consalvi, the Vatican envoy, never took a refusal as an answer and would stand at the Embassy door shouting. This led to "some very curious scenes." The Genevan doctor, Jean de Carro – famous in Vienna for introducing the smallpox vaccine – wrote to one of his Swiss friends to say that, in addition to the Embassy, Stewart and his companions had taken over an inn in Laxenberg, "which they have converted into a *foutoir*." Both Embassy and inn served the same purpose: "Masters, valets, chamber maids, suburban actresses, all are in constant movement. They don't even bother to close the doors. Thus it is that the two main houses of the English Mission, ordinary and extraordinary, have been transformed into brothel and gaming parlour." Gambling, he said, was carried out in Lord Clancarty's very offices.[53]

Relations between Stewart and the Earl of Clancarty – who had replaced Wellington as leader of the British delegation at the Congress – understandably became strained. Castlereagh had to intervene at one point.[54] But the real problem was that Clancarty, zealous and upright though he was, exerted nothing like the authority of either Castlereagh or Wellington. Nor did he have his predecessors' understanding of policy. Clancarty simply executed instructions, instructions that took up to two weeks to make their way from the Foreign Office in London.

The British were therefore not in as strong a position as they should have been during the last two months of the Congress. They had neither a Sovereign nor a Foreign Minister present. Two decades of war and isolation had deprived them of diplomatic experience. Moreover, news of opposition to the war in Britain got considerable coverage in Vienna and it did them no favour. Clancarty's task of representing Britain, both in the European settlement and in the French war, was further complicated by the decision that the envoys of the Allies would follow their armies, as they had done in the campaigns of 1813 and 1814. So the business of the Congress had to be settled fast.

On the question of Europe, there were two major items still on the agenda, Germany and Italy. Resolution of the Saxon crisis had settled the most difficult of the territorial problems in Germany, but what "Germany" was and how she was to be constituted remained as vague in April as it had been in November, when the German Committee had been adjourned. As far as Britain was concerned, the constitution of Germany was an internal matter. But the war, and especially the subsidies, meant that Britain, despite herself, was going to exert an influence on the shape of Germany – one that would give a major advantage to Metternich in his dealings with the other German powers. In Italy, too, the pendulum swung in Austria's favour. Italy was the weakest point in British policy. It might have been improved had either Castlereagh or Wellington remained in town. But what actually happened immediately after Wellington's departure for the Netherlands did not help matters at all.

On 30 March, Napoleon's brother-in-law, Joachim Murat, the King of Naples, proclaimed at Rimini the independence of Italy "from the Alps to the straits of Scilla" and marched with a band of Neapolitan volunteers northwards into the Papal States. Austria responded by declaring war on Naples and, for good measure, formally assumed the responsibility of administering Lombardy, Venetia, as well the small, contested duchies of Parma, Piacenza, and Guastalla that nominally belonged to the Emperor's daughter, Marie-Louise. The campaign was over in a month. In a two-day bloody battle (2-3 May) at Tolentino, on the eastern slopes of the Appenines, Murat's army was routed. The Austrians entered Naples on 23 May and a British naval squadron accepted the city's surrender – but not that of Murat, who, disguised as a sailor, fled for France where he hoped to show his valour at the head of one of Napoleon's divisions. Napoleon, however, refused to see him, on the grounds that he had sent strict instructions not to attack the Austrians. After an unhappy sojourn in Cannes, Murat finally took refuge in Corsica. In October he would launch another desperate expedition into southern Italy, where he was captured and shot on the orders of Ferdinand IV, the new Bourbon King of Naples.[55]

The result of all this was that the whole of Italy west of the Kingdom of Piedmont-Sardinia and south of the Alps was effectively placed at Austria's disposal; debate in the Congress on the future of the peninsula was thus silenced.

News of the Italian venture filtered only slowly into Vienna. "The news of Murat and his retreat would have had more effect here," wrote a Milanese envoy to a politician in Bologna, "if one was not so preoccupied with the great struggle that is being prepared."[56]

There was some urgency in the air but, because this was Vienna, that urgency was self-contained. A freak meteorological condition undoubtedly explained why, while all of Western Europe was being drenched in rain, Vienna basked in sunshine. Gentz thought it was the prettiest spring he had ever seen in his life. "Are you going to the Prater?" asked Talleyrand in a *petit billet* to the duchesse de Courlande. Aristocrats, like artisans, drove out to the gardens in the evenings. Kings and dukes wandered in the hedged alleys. English barouches and two-wheeled chaises had become the mode; Gentz was manifestly more excited about his new English rig than anything going on in Italy. The Zichy family moved to their summer residence on the Jägerzeile. Rasumovsky rebuilt his palace in the Landstrasse.

Metternich gave garden parties at his home on the Rennweg.

The talk was of "Germany." The balance of power had changed within this Central European zone because the military situation had changed. All forces were now directed westwards. The demand for troops had given the smaller states a bargaining power they had not known since Napoleon had played with them, one off against the other. Every state demanded a separate treaty of accession to the alliance. "From the very beginning I have never ceased to regret the turn these acts of accession have taken," Clancarty complained to Humboldt on 29 April, after the Kingdom of Württemberg demanded for the umpteenth time the drafting of a separate treaty. Clancarty called it blackmail. Grand dukes and princes from Nassau, Mecklenburg-Strelitz, Schwarzburg-Rudolstadt, Reuss, Anhalt-Dessau, Anhalt-Bernberg, Saxe-Hildburghausen, Saxe-Gotha, and Saxe-Weimar were all lined up, but they were in no hurry to sign. It was estimated that Baron von Gagern's powerful new Association of Princes and Free Cities could provide a force of between thirty-five and a hundred thousand men – depending on the effort they made. None of the Great Powers could ignore such numbers.[57]

What Clancarty refused to see (his instructions, after all, ordered him to keep a distance) was the role this haggling over treaties played in the developing German debate over federation and "sovereignty."

The small German states wanted their sovereignty written on paper and recognised by Europe; the accession treaties provided them with the occasion. In contrast, Stein and most of the Prussian Delegation (Humboldt was somewhat of an exception) wanted all Germany united, with a single government, a law court, a parliament, and German-wide laws; but if all Germany could not go along with this, they would aim, as a second option, for a *Nationalbund*, a concentrated northern German state directed from Berlin. Metternich, understandably, was totally out of sympathy with such a view. He warned that this kind of little Germany, dominated by Prussia, would be as dangerous a neighbour as France. So he would turn to the *Standesherren*, the dispossessed princes, and the smaller states for support. The war against Napoleon gave him the opportunity. He would force a decision before hostilities on the French border began. The choice had become clear: between a narrow, deep Germany, and a broad, shallow Germany. Projects were even afoot for a two-speed Germany. The word "federation" was used for all these conflicting ideas.

Metternich's hand was strengthened by the slowness of Russia's advance, which increased the reliance on the small German states. "They say the Russians will not arrive on the Rhine until 25 May," complained Talleyrand in a note to the duchesse de Courlande in late April; "that is very late." Like his colleagues in Ghent, Talleyrand wanted action before Napoleon's *Champ de Mai*, and he actually wrote to Clancarty to tell him so. But Clancarty had no more control over the march of Russian troops than Talleyrand. Nor, in fact, did the Emperor of Russia himself, though he kept the matter a closely guarded secret. The reason was that there was trouble in Poland.[58]

Alexander formally assumed the title of "King of Poland" on 30 April. "The Kingdom of Poland will be united with Russia by the bond of its own constitution," Alexander wrote that day to the President of the Polish Senate. Thus was born "Congress Poland." Prince Czartoryski described the treaty that led to this grand announcement as "very miserable and very mean"; it spoke of the "extinction of the Duchy" and it did not even dare mention the "Poles." Many Poles, both in Vienna and back in their homeland, saw Napoleon as their only hope. Parts of the army deserted in mass and crossed Germany to join the French Emperor's army; it was Poles, not Frenchmen, that Commandant Delessart first encountered in the defile of Laffrey. Constantine, Alexander's brother and commander-in-chief of Russian forces in Poland, decided to take a hard line, which led to yet greater disaffection.[59]

So, though Russian forces marched westwards, they kept on casting a glance to the rear. Barclay de Tolley, the hero of 1812, stayed on in Warsaw, along with many of his troops.[60]

Meanwhile, in Vienna, Alexander continued to play the gallant soldier. Perth would catch sight of him reviewing troops out on the Glacis or on the Jägerzeile, often in the company of his two sisters, the Grand Duchesses Catherine and Maria. He still enjoyed wandering out on the streets alone, chatting with the vendors, or handing to the poor the odd round Kreuzer. "If I were not Emperor of Russia," he told his valet while preparing for bed one night, "I would like nothing better than being a general in the Austrian army." He also found time to read, in Italian, *The Spiritual Combat* that Father Lorenzo Scupoli had published in 1600. Roxandre de Stourdza had left Vienna in the last days of March to accompany her Empress to Munich, but she continued to correspond with Alexander, with Julie von Krüdener in Schluchtern (Hesse), and her spiritual husband, Jung Stillung, in Switzerland. This had an appreciable influence on Alexander. He told his brother Constantine, in Warsaw, that he now knew he had the assistance of divine Providence in his new struggle with the Genius of Evil and Perturbor of Public Repose.[61]

Alexander also found time to begin a passionate affair with Princess Gabrielle Auersperg. "I love Gabrielle Auersperg so much," he admitted one night in the Zichy household, "that if I were not already married, I would certainly marry her." This was not such an innocent idea. Auersperg was a great friend of Princess Elisabeth von Fürstenburg, whose salon on the Graben was the centre of intrigue for the displaced *Standesherren*. With his sister engaged to the eldest son of the King of Württemberg and this new liaison with a friend of the *Standesherren*, Alexander had a role to play in the middle of Germany and a platform on which to build his "grand European family."[62]

"I have known Alexander ever since he came into the world," Serra Capriola, the Spanish envoy, said one evening at dinner to Agent ⁂. "He has no character, but an extremely ardent imagination." Talleyrand, as usual, pushed the analysis one step further. He thought Alexander's whole project was to create confusion so as to seize control of Europe. Britain, Austria, and Talleyrand's Embassy in Vienna – the signatories of the "Secret" Treaty of 3 January – wanted the opposite: order and balance. The aim of the war was not to chastise France (Talleyrand wrote to Louis XVIII expressing the hope that the main action would take place outside French borders) but simply to topple Napoleon. Letters from representatives of the three courts show that their main concern was France's continuing descent into chaos, a trend that all agreed had begun with the country's defeat in 1814. Once the Powers were committed to war, there naturally arose the question of what would be best for France and Europe after Napoleon had gone. Talleyrand was brought into the debates. So, of course, was Alexander.[63]

Talleyrand wanted a second Declaration that would clarify Allied war aims. In the Committee of Five he was enthusiastically seconded by the Russian plenipotentiaries. This led the British, and specifically Clancarty, to accuse Talleyrand of falling under the influence of Alexander. Talleyrand hotly denied it.

Because of the tensions in Poland, Alexander was looking for friends. Napoleon, idol of the Polish nationalists, was obviously not one of them; Alexander totally ignored the French Emperor's correspondence, which included a copy of the Secret Treaty. Instead, he embraced Metternich, professing Christian charity. The British also found him "good humoured," while Talleyrand reported to Louis XVIII that the Tsar "had never been so amiable."

Talleyrand could, perhaps, have said more on his happy new relationship with the Tsar. Was it a mere coincidence that Alexander's new analysis of the situation in France was the same as that of Talleyrand? Even their phrasing was identical. Clancarty must have been aware of this.[64]

Alexander, like Talleyrand, argued that there were three political parties in France, the army, the Jacobins, and the King's party. The first were generally attached to Bonaparte, though even here there were a considerable number who actually sympathised with the Jacobins. The second had been unhappy under the Bourbon Restoration but saw no future under Bonaparte and could easily be gained by the Allies, were they offered certain guarantees. The third consisted, as Alexander put it, of "*Compagnards* and husbandmen," men who had nothing to offer a progressive France; Talleyrand's tone differed on this point only when he was writing formal letters to Louis XVIII. It was a gross oversimplification of a situation in a regionally diversified country like France where, in fact, no political parties, in the proper sense, existed. But it was an analysis that caught the imagination of the men in Vienna. It also bore strong resemblance to Wellington's assessment of France, which had so astonished Creevey. Talleyrand himself wanted it incorporated into the second Allied Declaration.[65]

What was the origin of this extraordinary similarity in the analysis? It was unquestionably Talleyrand's idea, built upon three sources.

The "men of business" in Ghent had been flooding the Embassy in Vienna with their criticisms of the court party and pleas to open negotiations with the Jacobins. There was, secondly, Talleyrand's faithful old friend, the comte de Montrond, who came to stay at the Kaunitz Palace during the month of April.[66] Hager's agents generally dismissed him as one of Napoleon's men, whose approaches, they thought, would have no influence on the proceedings of the Congress.[67] But, in all likelihood, Montrond was working in the interests of Joseph Fouché, and not those of the French Emperor. Thirdly, Talleyrand was getting information from his cousin, comte Auguste de Talleyrand, who had set up what amounted to a press office in Zurich, Switzerland, with correspondents (the so-called *Philadelphes*) spread along lines that stretched down to Provence and up into Paris.[68]

Montrond left Vienna on 24 April, but not before having long consultations with Metternich and the Russian envoy, Nesselrode. Metternich, in the meantime, had opened up negotiations with another of Fouché's agents in the Inn of the Three Kings, in Bâle, Switzerland. Napoleon got wind of this and replaced Fouché's agent with his own man, Fleury de Chaboulon. Fleury ruined the whole proceedings by making loud professions of loyalty to the French Emperor and claiming that his army represented the entire nation. Herr Werner (in fact, the Baron von Offenfels, Metternich's agent) noticed the change in tone and broke the discussions off in May.[69]

That month, Alexander started making the wildest proposals for a successor to Napoleon. He thought the King of Sweden, Charles Bernadotte, another of Napoleon's brothers-in-law, would make a good candidate. "I beseech Your Royal Highness not to accord Sweden the means of sending any more troops onto the Continent," wrote Count Münster to the Prince Regent after it became clear that Alexander was being serious; "they will only foment troubles." Alexander even suggested the Archduke Charles, Kaiser Franz's brother, on the grounds that he was a descendent of the ancient House of Lorraine, which "could please the French and induce the Bourbons to abdicate in favour of this hero."[70]

Alexander's extravagances, combined with the failure of the negotiations at Bâle, made it impossible for the Allies to agree on a new Declaration. Instead, on 12 May, the Committee of Eight issued a report confirming their original Declaration of 13 March. The Allies did not want to impose a government on France, the report repeated, but Frenchmen had no right to choose as their head of state Napoleon Bonaparte: he was a proven threat to the security of Europe.[71]

The mass of documents on this period of the Congress of Vienna seem to suggest that in the spring of 1815 a number of Europe's leading statesmen – including Metternich, Talleyrand, Wellington, and even Castlereagh – were prepared to consider the establishment of a Second French Republic in the place of the Bourbons. If it did not happen, this was not due to ill-will or hostility to the idea, but rather to a combination of events: the difficulty of communicating with the right people in Paris, the breakdown of the negotiations in Bâle, the complexity of politics in Ghent, the strange personality of the Tsar, and, above all, to the kind of stubborn polarisation that war inevitably produces. That the openness of statesmen at this time has been so often overlooked is due to the *fait accompli* and a certain determination of later generations, particularly that of the revolutions of 1848, to regard the Congress as reactionary and monarchist. It was not due to the "principle of legitimacy," which was originally an idea of Talleyrand's that embodied both durability and a sense of cultural compatibility, but not necessarily monarchy.

The second Declaration of the Allies never came to anything. But the groundwork for a post-war France had been laid; and it would include the Jacobins.

An even grander project than the second Declaration was, however, eventually committed to paper and signed, the Congress's Final Act. At the time, it was known variously as the "Grand European Treaty," the "New Charter of Europe," or simply the "Treaty;" Gentz would always refer to it as the "great treaty," while most Austrian officials called it the "Recess," as if it were just another Habsburg edict. Its most enthusiastic advocate was Talleyrand, who argued that it would add moral force to the coalition; he refused to leave Vienna without signing it, despite instructions from his King, in April, to join him immediately in Ghent. The Russians opposed the project, confirming the suspicion of others that their goal was to divide and rule. Metternich maintained his policy of "hedging, evading, and flattery"; on this occasion he made a masterpiece of it. The British do not appear to have had any policy at all.

The last great piece to be fitted into the European jigsaw was "Germany"; it was no simple task. It had not yet been decided whether "Germany" was a territorial entity, an administrative unit, or a legal concept. Through Metternich's skilful negotiation, it was to remain all of these. Besides some of the older *Standesherren*, like Metternich's father, Franz Georg (who was very active in these last weeks of the Congress), everybody realised that there would be no turning back to the old German Reich. Most German envoys also recognised that Napoleon's new order, with its kernel in the Confederation of the Rhine, was finished. But the territorial prince-doms that Napoleon had created were still there. These were what Metternich successfully managed to organise into a new Germany; the essential aim of his efforts was to legitimise what was, in effect, a creation of the Revolution, the German Revolution.

The Saxon crisis had been resolved on the basis of revolutionary principles: annexation and compensation. The new crisis in France had brought bargaining power to the smaller German states, most of which were Napoleon's creations. Metternich, unlike Prussia, sought a whole German solution, but, being an Austrian, not a national solu-tion. Metternich wanted a whole German solution because he want-ed Germany integrated into Europe; Prussia's plans for a truncated northern *Nationalbund* would have excluded Germany from Europe. The national principle conflicted with the European principle – the perennial German dilemma.

Metternich gave himself the time to achieve his solution. He lived as a family man now. His wife, Eleonore, was five months pregnant;[72] his closest confidante was his eldest daughter, Marie. On 15 May, he invited a few acquaintances around to his garden on the Rennweg to celebrate his forty-second birthday, but the dinner had to be called off because of a downpour of rain. From that date on, the dark clouds of Western Europe rolled into Vienna. "Rain pouring all day," wrote Gentz on the 19th. "The air has been really cold for several days now," he wrote again on the 28th. But he was unable to keep up the daily entries to his diary, because the Secretary of the Congress sud-denly found himself very busy.[73]

On Tuesday morning, 23 May, the proceedings of the new German Committee opened in Metternich's conference chamber. In recogni-tion of the new power of the smaller states, the membership of the committee had been expanded from the original five, in November, to well over a dozen, including five deputies from Baron von Gagern's Association of Princes and Free Cities. Count von der Schulenburg and a colleague were there, representing Saxony, for the old King had finally relented and abandoned to Prussia the northern part of his kingdom. Metternich announced that the new German Confederation, anticipated in the Treaty of Paris, would have to be created before the French war began, when he and his colleagues would have to join Allied headquarters. That evening, the Committee of Five was summoned to his green table. He told them much the same thing: if there were to be a Final Act, it would have to be drafted and signed before hostilities began.[74]

Three days later Kaiser Franz, Tsar Alexander, and King Frederick William left Vienna for Allied headquarters in Heidelberg. King Frederick William departed in the middle of the night "crying like a child," for his infatuation with Julie Zichy had not ended; he lavished gifts on her entire family. Kaiser Franz set off in the afternoon, passing by the Schönbrunn Palace to bid farewell to Marie-Louise and her son. *"Cher grand papa, n'est-ce pas, tu ne fera pas de mal à papa!"* the little Napoleon was reported by ✶✶ to have squealed as the Kaiser boarded his coach.

Alexander was in the bleakest of moods. He left in the dark morning hours of Saturday. He changed his horses at Kleinmünchen without saying a word, sat through a silent dinner at Lambach, and then headed straight on for Munich, where apparently it was the same story: he refused to see anyone, save Prince Eugène de Beauharnais. Perhaps his bad humour was due to the Prince's failure, in spite of Alexander's pleas, to win any position of authority in Austria's new Italy. Perhaps it was due to the fact that the Grand Duchess Catherine (who decided to make a brief tour of Hungary before joining her fiancé in Württemberg) did not accompany him. Perhaps it was his parting from Gabrielle Auersperg. One could never know with Alexander.[75]

In any case, his departure gave a new lease of life to Metternich. "The Ministers and representatives of the German Princes continue sing praises of Prince Metternich," reported ✶✶. "They say that if one had worked since November as they now work, the Congress would have been over in March." Conference followed conference, dinner followed dinner; Gentz was having two dinners a day.

Back in the autumn of 1814, Hardenberg had been offering Metternich a centralised plan which would have given Austria and Prussia joint hegemony of Germany. But Hardenberg's mission had, in October, dismally failed. On Saturday, 3 June, in front of the reconstituted German Committee, Metternich abandoned Prussia to its own devices by recognising the full "sovereignty" of the German princes and the lesser states. During the weekend it looked as if there would be no agreement. But after many more meetings, on Thursday, 8 June, Bavaria made a critical offer, changing the balance; on Friday, the *Bundesakte* was signed.[76]

The new Confederation of Germany had no federal court, no bicameral representative institutions, no executive; gone were the Prussian plans for "Circles," gone too was the shared presidency. All that was left of the federal institutions that had been hammered out in cabinets and committees since the previous summer was a Diet, which was to meet in Frankfurt and was presided over by Austria. Talleyrand called the Confederation a "formless germ."[77] The romantic patriots in Berlin were furious. The *lien fédératif* in Metternich's Confederation was a federal tie of the weakest kind: a German defence community made up of independent sovereign states.

Metternich had succeeded in maintaining a Germany that was whole, stretching from the Baltic to the plains of Hungary, a Germany that was acceptable to Europe because it posed no threat, a Germany that consolidated and legitimised the states created over the preceding decade. But the achievement had a heavy price. The princes who had territories might have been happy, but those who did not – the dispossessed *Standesherren* – were not. "I doubt very much that the future will be rosy, even after the war is over," wrote their representative, Baron von Gärtner, on the day the *Bundesakte* was signed. Gärtner and his allies would keep alive the idea of a national Reich.[78]

Prussia was bitter. She had been pushed into a European mission despite herself. No one, including the Prussians themselves, realised at the time that the strange shaped northern arc of territories she had won at the Congress as compensation for lost Saxony and Poland included some of the richest iron and coal resources in Europe; one only counted "souls" in 1815. Moreover, Metternich might have imagined that Austria would be presiding over a balance of states, an association of equals. This would prove to be an illusion. Austria would have to turn constantly to Prussia to acquire the votes necessary for any action. Fifty years later, the combination of votes in the Diet and the industrial power of Prussia would be fatal to Austria.

The greatest irony of the time was that, though the main articles of the *Bundesakte* were incorporated into the Final Act, no European guarantee of the Confederation was acquired. Within two years, most European governments would bypass the Diet.

A draft of the Final Act, "in the name of the very holy and indivisible Trinity," was signed that same night, 9 June, in the Chancellery by the Eight, excluding Spain (who objected to the clauses on Italy) and Sweden (who protested at the recognition of the Bourbon crown in Sicily). It had been prepared by Gentz, Clancarty, and Humboldt; but it was Metternich who received all the glory. Even **, who had been running a campaign against Metternich throughout the Congress, commented that "the Congress will immortalise the name of Kaiser Franz," and that the one man responsible for this was "the Minister of Foreign Affairs, who has the right to be proud of his work."[79]

For all their incompleteness – the injustice to Italy, the vagueness over Germany, the omissions, the unresolved paragraphs – the one hundred and twenty-one articles of Vienna's Final Act constituted a most remarkable document. One could understand why some people wanted to call it the "Charter of Europe." It traced out a Europe made up of territorial states based on the concept of equilibrium; it brought into being a political map that did not exist in the summer of 1814. When else has a working model of Europe, the main features of which would outlast the century, been created in a period of nine months?[80]

Only days before its signature it looked as if the project would not be realised. Clancarty recommended that four or five of the major powers simply draw up a treaty between themselves – a position that contrasted strongly with Castlereagh's initial parliamentary vision of the Congress. It would, in effect, be an agreement between the major powers. After the initial signing on 9 June, twenty-six secretaries presided over by Gentz, prepared hand-written copies of the treaty that were then distributed to the smaller powers. They all gathered in the Chancellery on Monday, 19 June. But officially, this was simply another meeting of the Committee of Eight, and, of the Eight, only Six signed that night. Sweden signed a few days later. Spain ratified in 1817. Thus, one could very well argue that the Congress of Vienna – a parliamentary assembly of the states of Europe – never actually took place.[81]

All the Kings, Princes, and most of the Ambassadors and Ministers had left Vienna by 19 June. "I remain alone in this huge house," wrote Talleyrand to the duchesse de Courlande on 4 June; "it is going to be totally deserted." Dorothée left to spend some time in the Courland properties of Bohemia. Talleyrand complained of headaches, of *ébullition*. He was overcome by the same kind of melancholy that he had felt in the last weeks of the siege of Paris. "If this affair is not finished well and soon, we will have revolutions for the rest of our lives;" he hated the war, he hated the uncertainty. "Never has a separation been so painful, *chère amie*"; in times like this, the duchesse de Courlande was his anchor. "You go one way, I go another, and neither you nor I know where we will meet again." Talleyrand's train of carriages rolled out of Vienna on Saturday, 10 June, at half past six in the evening.[82]

The Palm Palace emptied under a cloud of scandal. Though his departure was announced on 1 June, the British Ambassador always found enough cause for staying on for just one more day: one more promenade around the town with Sagan, a trip out to Reichenau with Sagan, another night with Sagan. He eventually took leave in the last week of June, long after his principal colleagues had gone. The Duchess von Sagan left at the end of July – for Switzerland, so it was rumoured.[83]

The Princess Bagration, in the meantime, had gone into hiding with her "loyal friend," the comtesse Aurore de Marassé. All her effects in the Palm Palace would have been seized by Austrian bailiffs had not Serra Capriola, the Spanish envoy, paid off her bills in a last minute act of human kindness. Hager's agents pleaded that she be transported by force to the Russian frontier. Instead, she set off at the end of June for Allied headquarters, thus posing – so ** claimed – a threat to the security of all Europe.[84]

Metternich slipped out of town on Tuesday, 13 June, at one o'clock in the morning after a small family gathering in his summer palace on the Rennweg.[85]

The bad weather continued. Gentz recorded days on end of storm and rain. With the Final Act signed, he retired to his new country retreat at Weinhaus, a fine eighteenth-century manor that he had purchased on the proceeds of gifts from his princely admirers. On Sunday, 25 June (another day of slashing rains), he was working alone on a report to one of his patrons in Bucharest when a courier arrived with news that a great battle had been fought on the plains of Belgium.[86]

The Duchess's ball

Neither Thackeray nor Lord Byron attended the Duchess of Richmond's ball – and they were the two writers who made this the most famous ball in history. Thackeray was an infant of four in Calcutta, India. Lord Byron was just getting over his disastrous marriage to Miss Annabella Millbanke; he was commissioning the odd script for Mr Whitbread's bankrupt theatre, facing the bailiffs in his home at Piccadilly Terrace, and drinking for escape.

"There was a sound of revelry by night . . ." – what Victorian child could not quote a few Spenserian lines from Byron's verse? The poem was as much a part of nineteenth-century British lore on the great battle as Hugo's *Les Châtiments* was for the French. The contrast between the evening's ball and the morning's battle provided a theme for one of the masterpieces of English literature: Belgium's capital gathering her Beauty, her Chivalry; the bright lamps shining over fair women and brave men, all as merry as a marriage-bell. Then the note of doom, as in a romantic symphony: "But hush! hark! a deep sound strikes like a rising knell!" Is it the wind? or a cart rattling over a stony street? Careless, happy youth continues to dance. But the heavy sound breaks out again, louder and clearer this time; "Arm! Arm! and out – it is – the cannon's opening roar!" There is the march to war at sunrise: a hurrying to and fro, the sudden partings, the choking sighs, "While throng'd the citizens with terror dumb,/ Or whispering, with white lips – 'The foe! They come! they come!'"

Thackeray's chapter on the Duchess's ball turned around the same kind of dramatic sequence: the fated George Osborne is caught up in a spiral of glitter, he flirts with Becky Sharp, ignores his wife, learns of the French invasion over a bumper of wine, and, amidst the sound of bugles and bagpipes, sets off for his death at dawn.[87]

What, in fact, happened? Contemporary witnesses of the ball are so contradictory that it is impossible to give a precise account of that Thursday night, 15 June. Wellington – to take one example – is reported to have visited the house of his Prussian liaison officer, Baron von Müffling, at midnight, when he announced his intention to attend the ball. Yet at two o'clock in the morning, his Quartermaster General, Sir William De Lancey, claimed the Duke was sound asleep in his bed. Even for the efficient Duke of Wellington, to get to three different places in under two hours – including dance, supper, and a snooze – was quite an achievement.[88]

There was certainly a lot of talk about the ball in Brussels at the time. Where both Byron and Thackeray went wrong was that, by sundown Thursday, most people in Brussels were already aware of Napoleon's presence in Belgium; news of his invasion that morning reached town during the afternoon dinner. Von Müffling records that people were out on the ramparts the same evening listening to the distant boom of cannon. All through the following night there was a clatter of troops collecting in Place Royale and this surely would have been heard in the Duchess's ballroom – a converted coach-house on rue de la Blanchisserie – from the very beginning of her reception. Music may well have risen, as Byron put it, with a "voluptuous swell," but there were other sounds less voluptuous than that rattling in through the window panes. Captain Verner of the 7th Hussars came in from Grammont (a two-hour ride) with an invitation to the ball; he poked his nose through a door and saw a room "in the greatest of confusion," it "had the appearance of anything but a ballroom."[89]

It was only a few days earlier that the Duchess, before sending out her invitations, had asked the Duke of Wellington whether the ball should be held or not. "Duchess," reassured the commander, "you may give your ball with the greatest safety, without fear of interruption." Indeed, Wellington had only just announced that he would be giving his own ball on the 21st to celebrate the second anniversary of his Spanish victory at Vitoria.[90]

This was the same calm *chef d'orchestre* that had so inspired his troops in the Iberian peninsula. Wellington, it would appear, was using the Duchess of Richmond's ball to maintain morale in Brussels. By chance, that Thursday evening it also became a cover for a staff meeting.

The British community in Brussels was, by now, huge. A walk in some of the streets must have, at moments, resembled a wander in the roads of Brighton. Lady De Lancey was in Brussels for a week and never met any Belgians. Her compatriots had flocked in from Paris, while wives, children, aunts, uncles, and unwanted in-laws had crossed over from England to join the troops. War was still a family affair in 1815. That did not make the European army, which Wellington commanded, any more trustworthy. A panic of the kind that had occurred in late March or early May would have been a disaster had it fanned out the moment he was concentrating his troops. The face of "gay Brussels" therefore had to be maintained; it was a matter of military security. During the weeks that preceded Waterloo, there were military reviews in the Park, theatre, balls at the Concert Noble, cricket in Enghein, even foxhunting (although this had to be confined to the Forest of Soignes after numerous peasants had complained about Englishmen charging across their fields). The Duke himself could put on a cheerful mien, winning a reputation for "humbugging" the ladies – Kitty had been sent straight home to London after Napoleon had entered Paris.[91]

Most of the high ranking officers of Wellington's army were present at the Duchess of Richmond's ball. What an opportunity it presented! The three Anglo-Dutch corps, with Uxbridge's cavalry included, covered a front of almost sixty miles: ninety-two thousand men – only twenty-eight thousand of whom were British – were cantoned out westward from Brussels in villages situated as far as the Scheldt and beyond. By contrast, Blücher's Prussian four corps of a hundred and twenty-one thousand men, located in the eastern corner of Belgium, were much more concentrated. Inevitably, military theorists (Karl von Clausewitz was one of the first) would, in hindsight, take Wellington to task for spreading his army too thin; Wellington has even been accused, unjustly, of anticipating an illogical French enveloping movement to the west (which would have driven the Anglo-Dutch and Prussian armies together – an overwhelming force for the French). Yet Wellington could hardly be blamed for keeping an eye over his right shoulder towards the sea; unlike Napoleon, he had never in his career risked cutting off his source of supplies and, as a result, he had avoided Napoleon's kind of epic disasters (Egypt, Moscow): Wellington saved lives. Wellington could watch his right flank and, at the same time, stick to the original plan of protecting the "hinge" as had been elaborated at Tirlement in May.

But where exactly was the "hinge"? Charleroi or Mons? The roads to Charleroi had been torn up by the French in April. The Prince of Orange's unreliable Dutch-Belgians were behind Mons. A slight miscalculation of where the enemy would attack could have enormous consequences for a defender. Like the hand of a mis-timed clock, the effect of the error would increase the further one moved from its point of origin – and Wellington knew that Napoleon could race up that hand with the speed of lightning, striking out in jagged deviations to left and to right. No responsible defending commander could concentrate his forces until he knew where the attacker was heading.

For two weeks, Allied forces had been expecting Napoleon to attack. Wellington boasted that he was able, through his staff, to write out and transmit his orders to every command post in his army in less

The news of the Battle of Ligny is announced in this romantic
rendering of the Duchess of Richmond's ball. The ball was actually
held in a converted coach house

than six hours. He could concentrate his forces on either flank in
under forty-eight hours. When, after three pm on 15 June, he received
the message that Napoleon had crossed the frontiers, he gave orders
for the troops to collect at their stations and "stand to arms"; this was
what had caused all the noise in Brussels that evening. But Wellington
would not give the order to march until he knew precisely where
Napoleon's main attack was focused.[92]

The news arrived, with most of his commanding officers present,
during the "confusion" of the Duchess of Richmond's ball. Napoleon
had picked Charleroi, not Mons.[93]

Thomas Creevey, Wellington's Whig acquaintance, stayed at home
that night with his invalid wife, waiting for his two step-daughters to
return from the ball. He was living on the rue du Musée, next to the
Place Royale, where he could hear "a great knocking at houses." At
half past two, Friday morning, 16 June, he wrote in his diary, presumably with no small sense of relief: "the girls just returned." "Our
troops are all moving from this place at present," he went on. "Lord
Wellington was at the ball tonight as composed as ever."[94]

Roads to Waterloo

It does appear to be true that among the dead, found the next day at Quatre-Bras, were men dressed in their ballroom stockings.[95]

Quatre-Bras was a hamlet situated on a strategic crossroads about twenty-five miles south of Brussels. There were, on either side of the main *chaussée* leading to Charleroi, wet rye fields partly flattened during a brief skirmish on 15 June; there were a few copses, a woodland, a couple of enclosed farmyards, several ditches, and a very hesitant Marshal Ney. Many of the Dutch-Belgian troops ran away during the fight of the 16th. They all returned to Brussels, screaming French victory.

If Ney had moved on the 15th rather than the 16th, it very well could have been. Napoleon had planned one of his classical offensives, hitting at the juncture of the two enemy armies and driving through a path with lightning forks to his left and right. Marshal Grouchy commanded the right, Ney had the left, while Napoleon, of course, intended to guide his centre. Napoleon had left Paris at dawn on the 12th and, within forty-eight hours, had concentrated an army of a hundred and twenty-two thousand in and around the small town of Beaumont, equidistant from Mons and Charleroi. The four-day battle for the plains of Belgium had begun at dawn on the 15th when his troops crossed the frontier at Leers, Cour-sur-Heure, and Thy; they had secured Charleroi by noon. From there, Napoleon's main objective was to inflict a devastating defeat on the Prussian army, already concentrated to his right. Ney's role was to contain the Anglo-Dutch army while this job was being done. That is probably why Ney moved so cautiously.[96]

Ney – who, two weeks prior to his defection in March, had promised Louis XVIII to deliver Napoleon to the King in a cage – only received his command on the morning operations began, the 15th. He had spent May living in retirement on his estates of Les Coudreaux. Napoleon had every reason to distrust his marshals and yet, because of the way French army command was structured, depended on them more than either Wellington or Blücher depended on their generals. Of the twenty marshals of France, four had joined Louis XVIII in Ghent, three had defected to the Allies (another one joined Blücher on the day the French crossed into Belgium), and two had gone into hiding. Doubts also ran rife among other high-ranking officers about the future of the new Napoleonic regime, but they marched into Belgium because of the enthusiasm of the old regulars, who adored their Emperor. As for Napoleon himself, he had been forced into an offensive not only to impose his will on an indifferent nation, on a hostile parliament, and on a government that did not

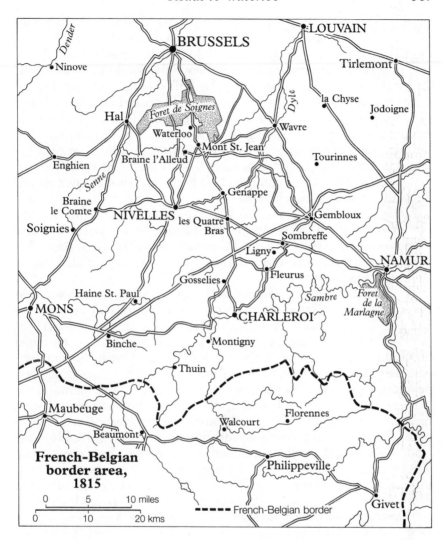

Dender

•Ninove

BRUSSELS

•LOUVAIN

Tirlemont•

Dyle

•la Chyse

Foret de Soignes

Jodoigne
•

Hal•

Waterloo•

•Wavre

•Mont St. Jean

Enghien
•

Braine l'Alleud•

Tourinnes
•

Senne

•Genappe

Braine
le Comte •

NIVELLES

les Quatre•
Bras

•Gembloux

Soignies•

•Ligny

Sombreffe
•

NAMUR

•Fleurus

Gosselies•

Sambre

*Foret
de la
Marlagne*

Haine St. Paul•

•**MONS**

•**CHARLEROI**

•Binche

•Montigny

•Thuin

•Maubeuge

Walcourt
•

Florennes
•

Beaumont•

**French-Belgian
border area,
1815**

•Philippeville

0   5   10 miles

•Givet

0   10   20 kms

- - - - - French-Belgian border

support him, but also, most importantly, to win the respect of his own army.[97]

Instead of seizing Quatre-Bras on the first day of the battle for Belgium, Ney settled most of his forty-two thousand troops in Gosselies, eight miles to the south. Late in the afternoon, a small detachment of Polish Lancers was sent up the road to investigate, but they were pushed back by four thousand Nassauers who had, fortunately for the Allies, taken up position at Quatre-Bras on their own initiative. Had Ney marched, at that moment, he could have advanced virtually unopposed to the gates of Brussels.

Napoleon, in the meantime, was channelling the remaining two thirds of his army into the rightward swing against the Prussians. Unlike Wellington, Blücher did not have to worry about his supplying flank. When he heard, on the 14th, that Napoleon was concentrating at Beaumont it was clear the enemy was not going to storm the Ardennes; so he started moving the bulk of his army up behind Charleroi. A few skirmishes on the 15th determined both Napoleon's and Blücher's positions. The great contest began the next afternoon around the village of Ligny, eleven miles north-east of Charleroi and only six miles east of Quatre-Bras. It was fought in fields of ripening wheat in suffocating, stormy weather. Old Blücher personally led two cavalry charges; in the second one, his horse was shot under him and he was left for dead in a pool of mud.

No sun set that evening. As the Prussians retreated in disarray, black clouds rolled in and soaked the plains – where eight thousand Frenchmen and twelve thousand Germans lay wounded or dead. But the Prussian forces had not been destroyed and the Marshal Prince Blücher was still alive.

The previous night, immediately on hearing the news that Napoleon had occupied Charleroi, Wellington had moved his Reserve Corps from Brussels to Mont Saint-Jean, just south of Waterloo village and the Forest of Soignes. He himself had continued down the Charleroi road to Quatre-Bras. A full Dutch-Belgian division had by now gathered around the hamlet. After inspecting their positions he ordered his Reserve Corps forward to join them.

Ney's troops remained posted several miles further south. It was only after midday that they finally advanced to Quatre-Bras. A force of ten thousand and growing – hidden in ditches, in slight folds in the land, or behind the still standing crops – was there to receive them. The first phase of the battle did not go well for Wellington; it was at this moment that many of the Dutch-Belgian units began to retreat in disorder. But by evening Wellington was able to push back the French so that the contending forces were in roughly the same positions as they had been that morning – only now four thousand Frenchmen and five thousand of the Anglo-Dutch lay strewn across the flat soggy ground.

Nine thousand Rhinelanders deserted the Prussian army after Ligny. Rhinelanders were not really German, Müffling would later explain in his memoirs.[98] They fled eastwards, along the route to Namur. From a distance, in the dawn, they looked like a routed army with their broken wagons, their convoys of ambulances, and exhausted men crouching on the sides of the road; French scouts thought they were an army, the Prussian army.

But the Prussian army had made an orderly retreat north in the night. Wellington received news the next morning. So his army made an orderly retreat north in the day to a site he had already noted in his reports nearly one year before: the plateau of Mont Saint-Jean, before Waterloo.

Napoleon had been ill during the night and he arose late in the morning of Saturday, 17 June. He thought Ney had pushed Wellington's army back towards Brussels and that the Prussians were fleeing eastwards – for separation of the two armies had been his plan and, when Napoleon had a plan, it was the equivalent, in his mind, of a historical fact. Witnesses described Napoleon as visibly shocked when he learned by letter from Ney that at six in the morning Wellington still had ten regiments and two thousand horses deployed around Quatre-Bras: this appeared to be his front line. Shortly after midday, the Emperor, with the idea of attacking the flank of what he took to be Wellington's army, swung his main force towards the west but not without first detaching nearly thirty-thousand men, who, under the command of Marshal Grouchy, went wandering off in search of supposedly fleeing Prussians.

At around two, scouts brought before the Emperor an English canteen woman they had just captured. She revealed that all there remained at Quatre-Bras was Lord Uxbridge's cavalry. The scouts had seen no sign of Ney's French forces. They were eventually discovered further south, sitting around their fires calmly munching at their Republican lunch.

Shortly after Napoleon launched his pursuit of Wellington's army a violent, slapping rainstorm burst upon the plains. One officer remembered Napoleon, astride his white charger, the cocks of his hat in a droop, shouting, "Shoot! shoot! *Ce sont les Anglais!*"[99] The last of *les Anglais* had, in fact, just managed to get across the single-lane stone bridge over the River Dyle. Gradually, the French also filed their way across. In a grim twilight, Napoleon began to position his seventy-five thousand exhausted troops on a ridge where there stood an inn – La Belle Alliance – overlooking a shallow damp valley and the Anglo-Dutch army opposite.

The wind of panic

Not everyone in Belgium that weekend had the composure of the Duke of Wellington. This was something which apparently worried the Duke himself; so much so that, at three o'clock Sunday morning, he rose from his bed to write four letters. Outside his whitewashed brick inn the first glimmer of dawn made a grey silhouette of the church's dome on the opposite side of Waterloo's village square. Rain still pelted on the rooftops. Water rushed down the gutters.

"We had a very bloody battle on Friday," he wrote first to the duc de Berry, who remained commander of the *petite armée royale* at Alost. Wellington wanted to warn Berry that the enemy might outflank the Anglo-Dutch army to the west through Hal and from there enter Brussels. If that were to happen, he recommended that Louis and his *petite armée* retreat along the left bank of the Scheldt as far as Antwerp. But he pleaded that the King and his court remain calm and not make any precipitous decisions; the King should leave "not on false rumours, but on the definite news that the enemy has entered Brussels."[100]

He then warned the Governor of Antwerp, who had not been very cooperative in the past, to prepare to receive refugees. He should allow the King of France to enter the city, permit the King's troops to be cantoned nearby, and, furthermore, he should open the port to all families – "English or of any other nation" – that had been obliged to leave Brussels.[101]

What worried Wellington most was Brussels. He composed a note for Sir Charles Stuart, the British Ambassador in Brussels (not to be confused with Sir Charles Stewart in Vienna): "Pray keep the English quiet if you can" and "let them all prepare to move, but neither be in a hurry or a fright, as all will yet turn out well." He ordered that all the post horses in Brussels be embargoed in the name of the Allied Armed Forces "to prevent people from running away with them."[102]

His fourth and final letter was addressed to a twenty-one-year-old female acquaintance of his in Brussels, Lady Frances Wedderburn-Webster. He asked her to make preparations to remove herself from Brussels to Antwerp, "in case such a measure should be necessary." But he didn't believe that such a case would arise. "I will give you the earliest intimation of any danger that may come to my knowledge," he concluded: "at present I know of none."[103]

Wellington donned his blue frockcoat, a cloak, his Hessian boots, and low cocked hat, and between five and six was out on the inn's balcony to watch his troops marching down to Mont Saint-Jean. At the moment of his greatest trial, what Wellington wanted to avoid most was the spread of a wind of panic behind him. But on this point he had no hope of being satisfied, because the wind was already howling.

Lady Caroline Capel, whose brother, Lord Uxbridge, commanded the Cavalry Corps, spent that night in an isolated sixteenth-century château three miles north of Brussels. "The Horrors of that night are not to be forgot," she later wrote to her mother. "The very Elements conspired to make it gloomy; for the rain and darkness and wind were frightfull and our court yard was filled during the night with poor wounded drenched soldiers and horses . . ." The wounded had come in from Quatre-Bras. Mr Capel set off early the next morning to seek horses, only to return two hours later to say that all horses had been requisitioned by the military. Rather than remain alone in their empty château, Lady Caroline and her husband set off for Brussels on foot.[104]

It was the sight of the wounded and reports from deserters and stragglers which set in motion rumours that the Allies had been beaten. The weather kept spirits low; the sound of cannon frightened. Together, they forged a strange combination: the low clouds acted like the vellum of a drum, sending the sound of cannon over huge distances. Lady De Lancey and the poet Richard Southey reported hearing the cannon of Quatre-Bras in Antwerp that Friday. On Sunday, Chateaubriand sat in a hop field beyond Ghent and listened to the dull rolling of distant artillery. And, incredibly, the *Kentish Gazette* reported to its readers on 20 June, before any courier could have arrived in England, "A heavy and incessant firing was heard from the coast on Sunday evening in the direction of Dunkirk."[105]

On Friday evening the ramparts of Brussels had been crowded again with people listening to the rumble of cannon. But the atmosphere was calm on Saturday morning. It was only in late afternoon, with the first reports that Wellington's army was retreating from Quatre-Bras, that the English community began to panic. At around five, the baggage of the army was seen coming down the rue de Namur; horses were picketed all around the Park. Wagonloads of men, wounded during the previous day's action, started rolling in. The Belgian deserters appeared. The rain storm began.

No hospitals had been prepared in Brussels. Not even temporary shelters had been erected. Several Belgian families opened their homes to the troops – a family on place de Louvain reportedly took in fifty wounded Englishmen. More than one Engishwoman's drawing room was exposed to the sight of blood.

The English wanted to get out. Within hours, a black market had developed in horses. The price varied: ten guineas for a pair, twenty-five guineas for one, a hundred Napoleons for two. Within minutes, the streets, roads, and canals were covered with carriages, wagons, horses, boats – the wounded carried in, the fit flying out, and French-speaking plunderers and marauders picking up everything they could find. Miss Charlotte Waldie recorded how her friends, the Honourable Mr and Mrs H., made their way up to Malines, halfway between Brussels and Antwerp, and – a terrifying prospect in those days – had to sleep in "a room filled with people of all sexes, ages, countries, and ranks."

Miss Waldie, a lady with foresight, had made an early escape to Antwerp in the company of her two brothers. "The morning – the eventful morning of Sunday, the 18th of June – rose, darkened by clouds and mists and driving rain," she remembered. She remembered, too, the crowds of refugees. On this one extraordinary day, the idea of social class and of nationality disappeared; strangers talked to one another as if they were friends. From morning till night the central Place Meir made a single compact mass of coloured umbrellas that covered the people, people in conversation, people waiting for news.[106]

There was one national group, however, that was beginning to feel very obscure – the French in Ghent. They kept to themselves; there were no dinners or theatrical performances that weekend. Chateaubriand likened the French in Ghent to the native ladies of that town, who were said to sit in their rooms and spy on the streets through the mirrors on their dressing-room tables. Louis XVIII never moved from his couch on the first floor of Count Hane Steenhuyse's hotel. Monsieur had left for Brussels. The Keeper of the King's Wardrobe was a little paler than he had been in May, but as uncommunicative as ever. None of the Ministers knew what was going on. There was some hope that Talleyrand would shortly arrive in town, but nobody had heard from him in more than a fortnight. The whole atmosphere was strangely reminiscent of a weekend in March at the Tuileries.

"Let those who are afraid depart," said the King from his couch. "For myself I shall not leave here unless forced to do so by the march of events." Louis had not changed.

On Friday, notice was received that Bonaparte had passed the frontiers. There were rumours that the Prussians had been crushed and that the Anglo-Dutch forces were no more to be relied on than the King's army in March. Frenchmen in Ghent, anyway, felt very uncomfortable about having to rely on them. They faced an awful dilemma. If the Allies won, what would happen to France? If Napoleon won, what would happen to freedom? When one heard in Ghent the distant roll of cannon, one knew that Frenchmen were dying. The vicomte de Reiset, who served with Berry's *petite armée*, described it as a kind of "immobile anxiety." Chateaubriand admitted that, although Napoleon's victory would have meant for him permanent exile, he was at that moment *pour la patrie*.

The panic of Brussels spread to Ghent on Saturday evening after a confused report that Napoleon had scored considerable success just north of Charleroi at a place called Quatre-Bras. The Anglo-Dutch army was said to be retreating. The gates of Ghent were shut, the post horses requisitioned, the sluices prepared for flooding; the King held Council. The King himself said he would be moving nowhere until he had more definitive news, but many of the French set out on the rain-swept roads for Nijmegen and Germany. The King's treasure had already been removed to Antwerp.

On a grey Sunday, the King rose from his couch like Lazarus suddenly finding life in his legs: he was anxious, agitated, his moods switched from joy to fear, he waddled to the windows and back, he examined the tapestries, he played with the curtains; he seemed at last decided to leave Ghent. But brave King Louis XVIII, in the twentieth year of his reign, was determined to wait for just one more courier.[107]

Central Brussels was by now a scene of turmoil. Carts and carriages of all description choked the streets. Rumours spread at every corner that the battle was lost, the campaign done. Not an hour passed by when it was not reported that some famous officer had been wounded or some popular general had been killed. In mid-afternoon, the Duke of Cumberland's Hussars (a volunteer regiment of inexperienced wealthy young Hanoverians) rode into town, overturning the baggage and wagons in their way; the French cavalry, they shouted, was on their heels. What they had perhaps seen behind them was a detachment of the Royal Horse Guards escorting scores of French prisoners, but not many in the panic and the plunder that ensued would have paid much attention.

At around three p.m., the intrepid Mr Creevey decided to take a walk through the Porte Namur and snoop around the suburbs neighbouring the Forest of Soignes. What a contrast this made to the scene within the gates. There in front of him were Belgian workers tranquilly sitting at the café tables, drinking their beer, smoking their pipes, and "making merry as if races or other sports were going on instead of the great pitched battle." So the panic was not universal.

Nothing, it seems, would have prevented a man from going even further down the white cobbled Charleroi road, across the forest and into the battlefield itself. Several sources speak of civilians actually running messages during the battle. Lieutenant-Colonel Basil Jackson, one of Wellington's staff officers, made the trip across the forest on Sunday afternoon. The paved road was so encumbered with carts and carriages hastening to the rear that he, and the other officers accompanying him, were forced to thread their way through the trees. Their horses sank to their fetlocks in the mire. But neither mud, thicket, nor the late spring's foliage could muffle the continuous, infernal pounding of the cannon.[108]

Eye of the storm

Jackson would have to push his way through a crush of wounded men, ambulances, empty caissons, and no small number of deserters to get to the front lines. The ground would stink of effluent where men had relieved themselves. There was fear in the faces of the people he met; many shouted out that all was lost. In the two miles that separated Waterloo village from the farm buildings at Mont Saint-Jean lay a noisy, squalid zone of concentrated anarchy. It would have required a trained eye to discern order even on the front lines, deployed along four thousand yards of the Ohain road (an unpaved track) where it crossed the main route to Charleroi. No general view was possible because of the thick smoke spat out from burnt powder;

it hung low in the moist air. The Charleroi road disappeared south-wards into a whitish-grey fog: no view of the La Haye-Sainte farm one hundred yards distant, no sight of French front lines on the opposite ridge barely two-thirds of a mile further on. Jackson did catch sight of some of Wellington's famous red square formations and he actually witnessed a cavalry "charge." It was no great dash. "Seeing the steady firmness of our men, [the French Cuirassiers] invariably edged away and retired," recorded Jackson; "sometimes they would halt and gaze at the triple row of bayonets." One is tempted to dismiss this as ridiculous. But several others reported the same phenomenon: French horsemen and English infantry gazing at one another over as small a distance as three or four yards.[109]

"I was an eye-witness to the beginning of the battle to the ending of it," Private John Lewis of the 95th Regiment wrote to friends in England three weeks later; "but my pen cannot explain to you, nor twenty sheets of paper would not contain, what I could say about it." Would a hundred or a thousand sheets have sufficed? Replying to an inquiry from an author in April 1816, Wellington commented, "The Battle of Waterloo is undoubtedly one of the most interesting events of modern times, but the Duke entertains no hopes of ever seeing an account of all its details which shall be true." Many, however, would make the attempt. The Battle of Waterloo only began in earnest at 1.30 in the afternoon and was over by 7.30; they are probably the six most prolifically described hours in the history of the world.[110]

The Battle of Waterloo was in fact two battles, one between the French and the Anglo-Dutch, the other between the French and the Prussians, together covering two-and-a-half square miles of plain. It was quite a squeeze for over a hundred and fifty thousand combatants and it did not leave much room for manœuvre. English historians speak of mysterious pauses and lulls in the fighting that miraculously allowed Wellington the time to strengthen his line; but these were inevitably moments when Napoleon decided to concentrate on the Prussians to his right.

Both Wellington and Napoleon were aware of the Prussian presence before the main French offensive began at 1.30 with a vio-lent canonnade and d'Erlon's massive infantry assault on Wellington's centre left.[111] There is some disagreement as to when exactly Wellington received the crucial message from Blücher that troops were arriving, but by ten o'clock in the morning he could see them on the fringe of the Bois de Paris, immediately to the east of Napoleon's right flank. Napoleon saw them just before the cannonade clouded up his field of vision. The fact that these were Prussian troops, and not Marshal Grouchy's forever wandering corps, was immediately con-firmed by a Silesian courier that a French cavalry detachment had just taken prisoner. Napoleon was still, at that time, seated at a table in front of the Rossomme Farm, which was almost a mile behind his front lines. From there he could not have had a very good view of the Brussels-Charleroi to his north, but he could see far beyond his eastern flank: he must have been expecting something here. Napoleon ordered the cannonade and moved his headquarters *forward* a thousand yards to the Belle Alliance Inn. Eighty-four of the Emperor's twelve- and nine-pounders roared out in the direction of the north, the gunners, however, unable to see exactly where they were firing. Wellington pulled *back* his line one hundred yards to the relative protection of the rear slopes at Mont Saint-Jean.

The comte d'Erlon marched sixteen thousand infantry into the vale of smoke and powder. They were nicely packed together, two hundred files wide and twenty-four deep, as if they were setting off for a parade across the Champ de Mars. "Load! Make Ready! Level! Fire!" came the order from the hidden banks and hollows of the Ohain road; one didn't aim in those days – at thirty yards one didn't need to. Two thousand heavy leaden musket balls flew out at d'Erlon's columns every minute. Within half an hour, Napoleon's first offensive was over. The positions of the two armies had barely changed, except that the valley between them was now littered with over ten thousand dead and screaming wounded; horses lay writhing, for among the casualties of that initial outburst lay one third of Britain's cavalry, which had foolishly overextended itself after the French retreat. General Sir Thomas Picton was on the ground with a bullet in his head. Sir William Ponsonby, the brigade commander, was horribly killed by lancers who had captured him.

At three o'clock Napoleon learned that Marshal Grouchy continued to march thirty thousand troops away from the battlefield in an obstinate search for his Prussians. Napoleon's immediate reaction was to make another forward movement: he ordered the seizure of the farm of La Haye-Sainte. This would lead, through a series of accidents, to the most disastrous action of the day. Marshal Ney, as he pulled back from the farm and a pile of his own dead, caught a glimpse of the zone of chaos behind the Anglo-Dutch lines and read this as a sign that Wellington was retreating. He was tragically wrong. Ney ordered wave after wave of unsupported cavalry into the waiting muzzles of British Brown Besses.

Meanwhile, the Prussians slowly encroached on Napoleon's right. Blücher had already joined forces with Bülow's IVth Corps by one o'clock. Gradually they moved down a dirt track, west of the Bois de Paris, in the direction of Plancenoit, a village that was actually behind Napoleon's lines. One cause of their slow progress was that the old Prince Marshal, typically, wanted personally to lead the attack, despite having been knocked unconscious during his evening charge at Ligny. Blücher, furthermore, insisted on ordering his columns, with

Wellington hails his troops.
The Duke, who had developed
his tactics on the plains of
Spain, combined a defensive
approach with offensives

Napoleon hails his troops.
The Emperor believed that the
secret of military success on
the plain lay in the offensive

his freshest troops at their head, in a manner that slowed them down. Finally, Blücher's younger commanding officers had a distinct distrust of the British; they thought that Wellington was going to withdraw and that, as at Ligny, they would be left alone to face Napoleon. But advance they did. In a mounting rage of violence, Plancenoit passed from the French to the Prussians and back to the French again during the course of the afternoon.

Yet, when the situation was totally hopeless, with the sound of the Prussian struggle echoing in every French soldier's ears, with d'Erlon's infantry virtually destroyed, the cavalry lost, Napoleon once again ordered an offensive – an order he made with the lie that the noise everyone heard to the east was the sound of Grouchy marching to save them. *"Vive l'empereur!"* cried out fifteen thousand "Immortals" – the Old Guard, Napoleon's elite foot-soldiers – along with Grenadiers and Chasseurs and what remained of d'Erlon's mauled troops. *"En avant! En avant! Vive l'Empereur!"*

Why didn't Napoleon ever consider a strategic withdrawal? To take on both Allied armies was pure folly; the final assault by the Imperial Guard was pre-meditated suicide. The answer surely lay not in military science but in politics. Napoleon had been following the straight and simple line forward ever since he had stepped ashore at Golfe Juan. Onward! and onward! The moment he withdrew, the second he halted, his whole fragile edifice crumbled. Behind him he had left a nation sinking further and further into chaos. He marched with an army commanded by men he could not trust. Their insubordination was extraordinary. Grouchy ignored him. D'Erlon on two occasions found himself caught between conflicting orders. Ney had only received his commission on the eve of the campaign; at Waterloo he ordered the cavalry charges without consulting his master. Even Napoleon's younger brother, Jerome, turned the "diversion" on Hougoumont into his own private battle.

Thus the imperial anarchy of Paris was transformed, during the march of his army north, into the military anarchy of Waterloo. This was the relentless logic of Napoleon; he could only follow that straight line forward in a desperate effort to impose his own will, his own order. His plans at Waterloo were perfectly consistent with the Napoleonic logic. He would smash straight through Wellington's central position, "cutting the Brussels road and the entire right flank of the English army." "If my orders are properly executed, we will sleep in Brussels this evening." But his orders were not executed; nor could they be. "Buonaparte did not manœuvre at all," remarked Wellington a few days after the event. "He just moved forward in the old style, in columns, and was driven off in the old style."

The desperate Emperor, seated on his charger, personally accompanied the columns of the Guard to within two hundred yards of the

Anglo-Dutch lines and there handed them over to Marshal Ney. At
that moment a French cuirassier deserted and galloped up the road to
the Allies, shouting *"Vive le Roi!"* He warned Sir John Colborne,
who commanded the 52nd Foot, that the Imperial Guard were
preparing to advance. General Maitland's Guard Brigade was lying
concealed behind the banks of the Ohain road. They could soon hear
drums of the *pas de charge* but they would not have been able to see
the two broad columns of French infantry scambling over the dead of
a previous charge along a shallow fold in the land, just west of the
Brussels-Charleroi road. "Now, Maitland, now's your time!" shouted Wellington, who at this critical moment was seen everywhere. The
French advanced another twenty yards. "Stand up, Guards!" A long
red line suddenly rose out of the ground. "Ready! Fire!" To
Lieutenant Edward Macready of the 30th Foot the French Imperial
Guard appeared gigantic in their red epaulets, their blue great-coats,
their high bearskin hats – but in an instant he was looking at their
backs: "In no part of the field did I see carcases so heaped upon each
other," he went on. An officer in Picton's division, located on the
other side of the Charleroi road, also observed something that was
gigantic. "The slanting rays of the setting sun," he recollected,
"reached us through the medium of the smoke of the guns [and] rendered the atmosphere a *camera obscura* on a giant scale."

Colborne's 52nd descended the slopes and fired into the French
flanks. "Go on, Colborne!" screamed Wellington in his high pitched
voice. "Go on! Go on. Don't give them time to rally. They won't
stand." Napoleon's straight line forward had been broken. His army
was in a rout.

"We burst from the darkness of a London fog into a bright sunshine," said a commanding officer as he recollected the hour
Wellington ordered the Allied advance. That was one of the curious
facts of Waterloo: through the smoke of cannon and musket shot, the
sun on the evening of the 18th made its first appearance in days.

Every semblance of soldierly order and virtue disappeared under
those final slanting rays of the day as one mob of fugitives attempted
to escape from a pursuing crowd of marauders. Men huddled in
groups. In the gathering darkness an English ranker-officer, Duperier
of the 18th Hussars, came across "a regiment of infantry of the
franch," who were all shouting out *Vive le Roi!* "Our men do not
understined franch," he later explained, "so they cut a way all through
till we came to the body of reserve when we was saluted with a voly
at the length of two sords. We tacked about and had the same fun
coming back." The Prussians sytematically bayoneted any wounded
they found. The British fired on their own men. Every nationality
joined in the search for loot, rifling the pockets of the dead and
slaughtering those that moved.[112]

It was almost dark when Wellington met Blücher by the Belle-Alliance Inn. *"Mein lieber Kamerad!"* exclaimed the exhausted old man, *"Quelle affaire!"* Wellington claimed it was all the French he knew. The British bivouacked on the plain of the dead. The Prussians went in pursuit of the French. Wellington, on horseback, returned to Waterloo.

The moon was in its second quarter on 18 June. On either side of the Charleroi road, lay forty to fifty thousand dead or wounded, trembling horses, and abandoned weapons, amid a twinkling constellation of torches, for the robbers were already at work.

Napoleon abandoned his famous *berline* carriage at Genappes, near the same narrow stone bridge he had crossed in a storm the evening before. With his Guard, he continued by horse on to Quatre-Bras. "We thought we saw ghosts calling for their graves," remembered one grenadier; the men killed on the 16th had not been buried. Three to four thousand bodies, which had been stripped naked by soldiers and peasants, lay in heaps by the road, around the copses, and in the trampled rye fields. Under the the light of the moon, their flesh was as pale as ashes, their blood as black as burnt timber.[113]

False cheer

The British pursuit of the French exhausted itself – understandably – on the Waterloo battlefield. The Prussians halted before dawn at Frasnes, ten miles further south, in front of an old inn that was named, ironically, "A l'Empereur." The French scrambled on and on. At Charleroi, the wooden parapets of the humpback bridge, which crossed the Sambre, collapsed and many brave cavaliers were drowned. By nine o'clock, Monday morning, the Emperor was in Philippeville, a strongly fortified town in the north of France, not far from where he had crossed the border four days earlier. "All is not lost," he wrote to his brother Joseph in Paris. "I suppose that, when I reassemble my forces, I shall have 150,000 men" – more men than he had led into Belgium.[114]

From a strictly military point of view, he probably could have reassembled a respectable force, because there remained Rapp's army of the Rhine, Grouchy's corps would presumably turn up one day, and there were the *fédérés* in Paris. But Napoleon's problem was not military; it was political. There were ministers in his government just waiting for a chance to overthrow him and, as in 1814, members of a parliament only too willing to cooperate with them. His only hope now was to get to Paris to prevent this.

Napoleon took an indirect route to avoid Prussian scouts. At Laon he stopped at a post house where, as was often done to quieten the rattle of coaches, straw had been laid thick on the cobbled driveway.

Napoleon paced upon it, backwards and forwards, looking utterly dejected. "It's Job on his dung heap!" commented one witness. He was in Paris at eight a.m., 21 June. He was breathing heavily – "I'm suffocating here!" he said, banging his chest – and his attendants found him pale and overwhelmed; he ordered a hot bath. When Napoleon, in his tub, saw his Minister of War enter he lifted his arms in the air and let them drop with all their weight. "*Eh bien! Davout!*" he sighed to the minister, who stood silent in his uniform, soaking wet, "*Eh bien!*"[115]

He told his Council of Ministers that he could put an army together by the first days of July, that he could meet the Allies behind the Somme and the Oise, and that Paris would be defended by men in trenches. "This devil of a man!" exclaimed Fouché the same afternoon to one of his friends, "I thought he was going to start all over again. Fortunately, we are not going to start all over again!"[116]

Lucien, who had played a major role in the *coup d'état* of 1799, explained to his brother that he had a choice between dissolving the new parliament or abdicating. Napoleon toyed with the idea of a dictatorship. But this was not 1799. Within twenty-four hours he signed his abdication.

He spent a few days at his old palace of Malmaison, which had not been inhabited since Josephine's death the year before. There he dreamed of a quiet retirement in the United States of America. To prepare himself, he read Alexander von Humboldt's *Voyages aux contrées équinoxales du Nouveau Continent* and he asked his librarian Barbier to collect together "some works on America" that would constitute his travelling library. With the Prussians bearing down on the western side of Paris, he boarded a carriage for Rochefort, where two fast frigates were waiting to take the Emperor to America. But Captain Maitland of the HMS *Bellerophon* was lying under the cover of an offshore island with orders to blockade the port. Various plans of escape were put forward, such as raising an army in the south-west of France that would come to the Emperor's rescue, or sailing out of the port in a small boat at night and then hijacking a merchant vessel to make the Atlantic crossing, or simply hiding the Emperor in a barrel. The idea of an English officer lifting the lid to discover the Emperor of the French did not appeal to Napoleon.

Dressed in his green Chasseur uniform, Napoleon boarded the HMS *Bellerophon* – "Billy Ruffian" as her sailors called her – on the evening of 15 July 1815. "Sir," he said on being presented to the captain, "I am come on board, and I claim the protection of your Prince and of your laws." He raised his hat and bowed as low as he had when he had first met Sir Neil Campbell in April 1814. The next morning, Napoleon was sailing for England. The *Bellerophon* anchored in Torbay on 24 July and, three days later, sailed round Start Point to Plymouth.[117]

When it was announced in the British press that Napoleon was on board a warship off the coast of Devon, huge numbers flocked to Plymouth just to catch sight of him. Napoleon fascinated the English. During the Hundred Days, an exhibition of Jacques-Louis David's paintings, which had included two famous portraits of Napoleon, had been the most popular of all London's exhibitions that season. The newspapers frequently advertised the sale of medals of Napoleon's exploits, small portraits, or busts. But actually to see the "Extraordinary Man" in person was something nobody had expected, even after the news of Waterloo. *The Times*, which wanted him

HMS *Bellerophon*, near the centre of this picture, lies at anchor outside Plymouth harbour. Napoleon is standing by the main mast, surrounded by English sightseers

hanged outside the gates of Paris, was incensed at this interest. "It is remarkable," commented an editor on 8 August, "that while British blockheads are crowding around Buonaparte and viewing him as an object of wonder, the Parisian wits have been treating his person with ridicule."[118]

On the Plymouth breakwater a healthy trade developed in biscuits, fruit, porter, tea, and coffee with cream. It was estimated that over a thousand small boats sailed out every day to circle the *Bellerophon*. Two ladies were drowned on the day the fallen Emperor was transferred to the *Northumberland*, which would take him to St Helena.

Evenings were the most popular time for a cruise because it was known that Napoleon would usually appear on deck just before his dinner at six. Even if, as *The Times* reported, "his face was remakarbly plump, and his head rather bald upon the top," (on most occasions he actually wore his hat) Napoleon was able, by his physical presence, to have that same extraordinary effect on the crowds at Plymouth as he had had on his arrival in Elba or at Laffrey, outside Grenoble. "On Sunday [6 August]," one read in the *Morning Post*, quoting the *Plymouth Telegraph*, "we regret to say a large portion of the spectators not only took off their hats, but cheered him."[119]

PARIS
Summer 1815

Previous page: One notes, in this anonymous British cartoon, that a stern
John Bull, following Napoleon's second defeat does not stand beside his Allies

Mrs Boehm's dinner

Every capital in Europe felt the effects of June's events in Belgium. But it took time for the news to travel: St Petersburg ten days, Vienna seven, Berlin in around four or five. London got its news from Brussels in three to four days, depending on whether the reports came in by horse or through the mechanically operated vanes of the telegraph; occasionally, they were delivered by pigeon.

In Carlton House, the Prince Regent kept court. The information he managed to piece together was so detailed that there were moments he fancied he was out on the Belgian plains himself. At eleven o'clock every morning he would rise, don one of a variety of marshal's uniforms – the cocked hat and cock's feathers balanced on his head – and brace himself for whatever cruel contest his couriers might announce. Evenings he spent over a decanter of marischino wine endeavouring to forecast the next day's deployment of the Allied forces, the next move of the enemy French.

The Regent was convinced he was Britain's most popular hero. "No prince was ever idolised by the people of this country as myself," he remarked confidently to an astounded Lord Moira. There had, it is true, been sadder times for the royal prince. Caroline at least had left, trumbling across Italy in her comic caravan of lovers, lackeys, and courtisans. Charlotte was now reconciled to her father and she even confessed that she did not miss her mother at all. Her father reciprocated. He at long last agreed that Prince William of Orange was not the right husband for Charlotte and let himself be persuaded of the charms and talents of Prince Leopold of Saxe-Coburg, who, when plied with tea and cake, had taken a liking for the resident of Warwick House during the Sovereigns' visit in 1814. So the way to Charlotte's marriage was opened, although the engagement was not actually announced until January 1816.

In the meantime, another royal marriage served to divert the poisoned arrows of the press. In the spring of 1815 the Regent's younger brother, Ernest, the Duke of Cumberland, announced his engagement to Princess Frederica of Solms-Braunfels, despite the opposition of both his mother, Queen Charlotte, and the Whigs in parliament: Frederica was twice married, once divorced, and had even managed to turn down the hand of another of Britain's royal princes, the the young and infinitely more popular Duke of Cambridge. Cumberland had no following in the country, in parliament, or in the royal family (Princess Charlotte, who hated him, would only refer to him as "Whiskerandos," while the Duke of Kent spoke of him scornfully as "the *Black Sheep*"). Though he lived in Hanover (where he would one day be crowned King Ernest I), the British government had decided in 1813 to name his jilted brother, the Duke of Cambridge, Governor – an act for which the Duke of Wellington was eternally grateful.[1]

The day Cumberland arrived in England to arrange his marriage, Wednesday, 21 June 1815, Mr and Mrs Boehm, a wealthy Russian merchant couple, held a magnificent dinner in honour of the Prince Regent at their home in St James's Square,[2] just three doors down from Lord Castlereagh's residence. The Foreign Secretary and his wife were present, but their niece, Emma, Lady Edgcumbe, stayed at home.

She was sitting quietly alone when all of a sudden a great hubbub and scream came up from the square. Thinking, no doubt, it was the Corn Law mob that had turned up again, she ran over to the window just in time to notice a dusty post-chaise and four dash across the cobbles, first in the direction of Castlereagh's door and then, making a quick turn, towards Mrs Boehm's. Out of its windows hung three torn French eagles. A cheering crowd followed.

At Mrs Boehm's, dinner had just ended and the brave Prince Regent was mounting the royal dais to observe the first quadrille of the ball that followed. But the music fell suddenly silent. Instead of a courtly dance being performed, into the room strutted Major Henry Percy, one of Wellington's dispatch officers, with the three French eagles in his arms. He walked straight up to the Regent, sank on one knee, placed the flags at His Highness's feet, and, looking up, cried: "Victory, Sir! Victory!"

It is told that Percy was still in the blood-stained uniform he had worn at Mont Saint-Jean and had had to row to Kent because his ship was becalmed. Mrs Boehm was not very happy. "I always shall think," she remarked many years later, "it would have been far better if Henry Percy had waited quietly till the morning, instead of bursting in upon us, as he did, in such indecent haste." Lady Edgcumbe records that the ladies were not present; they had retired to another room following the dinner. Mrs Boehm, in contrast, remembered that the ladies were ordered out of the ballroom so that Wellington's dispatch, dated "Waterloo, 19 June 1815," could be read aloud. Mrs Melesina Trench, writing to her husband on 23 June, claimed that the "Ministers and all wept in triumph *among the bottles and glasses"* and that the "Regent fell into a sort of womanish hysteric." As in the case of many such great occasions of this great romantic age, the contemporary accounts and memoirs of Mrs Boehm's dinner party are not consistent.[3]

The dispatch – wrapped, it was said, in a purple handkerchief that Major Percy had received from a pretty partner at the Duchess of Richmond's ball – described in Wellington's plain words the battles of 16-18 June. "Such a desperate action could not be fought," related the Duke, "without great loss; and I am sorry to add that ours has been immense." All the accounts of the evening note that the Prince Regent was moved to tears. "It is a glorious victory, and we must rejoice at it," he is supposed to have remarked on reporting the dispatch to the ladies, who had been waiting patiently in the adjoining room, "but the loss of life has been fearful, and *I* have lost many friends."[4]

So, of course, had many in Britain. The Regent left the party, fantasising that it was he, under the name of General Brock, who had led a mighty charge of the King's German Legion at Waterloo. The royal brothers also filed out. Ladies, who had ordered their carriages for a departure at dawn, rushed away "like maniacs" in their satin shoes across the square. The chairs of the orchestra were all left empty; the midnight's supper lay on a table untouched: twenty minutes after the Regent had gone, Mr and Mrs Boehm stood alone in their ballroom, staring at one another in silence.

Outside the nightwatchman continued, every half hour, to call out the time and the state of the weather. In the dark hours of the morning, the mail coaches left, decorated in oak leaves, to deliver news of the victory to the four corners of the kingdom. At the crack of dawn the dustman could be heard with his bell; then the porterhouse boy arrived for the pewter pots that had been laid out in rows the night before.

And thus, gradually, the city awoke on a sultry Thursday, 22 June, to a succession of jingles and cries. As the traffic began to rumble up and down Fleet Street so ordinary Londoners began their ordinary worry, not about the fate of the King's German Legion, or the Prince Regent's next plan for battle, or the remains of Mrs Boehm's dinner, but rather – as had their fathers and forefathers – about the continuing rise in the price of bread.

Parliament spent little time discussing the Battle of Waterloo. That Thursday, Castlereagh read to the Commons a message from the Regent on the "signal and splendid victory" of the 18th that had "contributed largely to the independence of Europe." The next day he delivered a long speech based on the text of the Waterloo dispatch. Cheers were heard from all parts of the House; the members immediately voted their thanks to the army along with a handsome grant of £200,000 for the Duke of Wellington, a sum that went into the purchase and refurbishment of Apsley House at Hyde Park Corner. The only serious voice of dissent was that of Sir Francis Burdett.[5]

Sam Whitbread, on the other hand, was almost apologetic. He rose slowly from his bench; his legs and ankles were swollen; his general countenance was described as "retired." He began by remarking that he "most cordially agreed" with the grant for Wellington, who "had done more than had been achieved by any other human being than himself." If, he went on, one were to read about such acts being performed ten centuries ago, one would discredit the story: the achievement of the British army was unsurpassed.

Five days later the House voted war credits amounting to £6,900,000 – an extraordinary sum for that age. Once more Whitbread gave his approval, while expressing the hope that "the Duke of Wellington would interpose his protecting arm to diminish the horrors of war in those countries whither he might judge it necessary to carry his arms."[6]

The press in London was more triumphant – and more violent – than anything said in Parliament. If one were to believe *The Times* and *The Courier*, the French government, after Napoleon's defeat, had been taken over by desperate Jacobins and Terrorists, and Paris had sunk into a state of outlawry. Articles and letters from the public called for Napoleon's immediate execution and for the partition of France by the Allied armies.

This inevitably had an effect on policy. In April and May, Castlereagh and Wellington might have been dropping secret hints on the dawning of a new French Republic, but that was before the war broke out and the press went wild. Even Castlereagh, in the last fortnight of June, was infected by the victory – it had been fought on his forty-sixth birthday. Waterloo, he told the Commons, was "an event so truly glorious in itself and so highly advantageous to the best interests, not only of this country, but of all Europe." He shared some of the popular spirit for revenge: the battle had shown the "restless and ambitious" French that "their mischievous and wicked career was at an end." Castlereagh was especially pleased with Wellington. "No man on earth," he said, "could have expected such extraordinary results to have proceeded from a battle begun and ended in one day as had been produced by the memorable victory obtained by the Duke of Wellington."[7]

But all this merely confirmed the old political alliance between the Foreign Secretary and the Duke. In private, Castlereagh was as cautious as he always had been, for the war was not yet finished and there remained serious doubts about the future of the great peace project they had both laboured over in the preceding twelve months.

"Grant, O merciful God," asked a thanksgiving prayer repeated throughout England, "that this mighty battle may put an end to the

miseries of Europe and staunch the blood of Nations." It concluded
by beseeching the Almighty to control the Allied armies: "Let not the
step of their progress be stained by ambition, nor sullied by revenge."
That, too, had always been Castlereagh's policy, as it had been
Wellington's strategy. But war had its own terrible logic.[8]

News of Napoleon's abdication arrived in London on the night of
25 June. "Your Grace will proceed in your military operations," the
Secretary of State for War and Colonies wrote to Wellington the next
day. Forty-eight hours later a letter was received from Count Otto in
Calais; he claimed to represent the French "Provisional Government"
and asked that the British proclaim an immediate "Armistice" while
guaranteeing safe conduct for the former Emperor to the United
States of America. "We have refused to receive Otto," Bathurst wrote
again to Wellington. "There is a very strong feeling in this country of
the necessity of having security against a recurrence of this attempt to
disturb Europe, especially if Buonaparte survives." He asked the
Duke to disregard "the propositions for a suspension of arms."[9]

On 30 June, the government drew up a memorandum outlining
"the course of policy which it may be expedient for the Allies to
adopt." It was drafted in the form of instructions from Lord
Liverpool to Lord Castlereagh. Castlereagh was, in fact, still in
London and several of the memorandum's long and awkward sentences bear the unmistakable mark of the Foreign Secretary. It was, in
all likelihood, a collective work. Underlying the whole document was
this worry, typical in times of war, about security.

Would the demands of security demand revising the whole
European peace settlement? Certainly not. The terms of Vienna's
Final Act, Europe's "Charter" – ratified the day after Waterloo –
would not be called into question. But the Treaty of Paris of May
1814 was looking very fragile. The "Treaty of Fontainebleau" had, of
course, been thrown to the winds.

The memorandum sketched three scenarios, ranging from the most
secure kind of French settlement, from an Allied point of view, to the
least secure.

The Treaty of Paris had the best chance of being maintained, it was
thought, if Louis XVIII were restored and Bonaparte were either
dead or in the hands of the Allies, although "it does not appear possible to give any precise or positive instructions until we are more
particularly informed of the sentiments of the Allies." If, on the other
hand, Louis XVIII were restored while Bonaparte had "escaped to
America or elsewhere," then the Allies would have a right to demand
of France additional securities, and most particularly her frontier
fortresses, including Lille. The least secure scenario outlined in the
memorandum was the case where Louis XVIII would not be restored
and where the Allies would have to treat with "some other govern-

ment as representing the French nation." Since no guarantee of peace could arise out of such a situation, it was argued, the Allies would be fully justified in reducing "the power and territory of the enemy;" in other words, France would have to be partitioned.

The government's demand for security did not stop there. Even in the first case, the memorandum noted, it was quite indispensable that "a severe example should be made of those commanding officers" who had deserted King Louis for Bonaparte; an example should also be made, it went on, of the "most dangerous" civilians.[10]

Castlereagh's correspondence with his brother in Vienna shows that, since the month of May, he had had the intention of joining the Big Four at Allied Headquarters, just as he had done in the winter and spring of 1814. With Wellington playing the role of soldier, Britain's diplomatic corps on the continent was looking extremely weak. "I hope our progress towards Paris," pleaded an overworked Lord Cathcart on 21 June from Heidelberg, "will induce your lordship to make arrangements to come to us as speedily as possible."[11]

First, however, Castlereagh had the unenviable task of defending the Duke of Cumberland in parliament. This he did throughout most of the last week of June. Cumberland eventually celebrated his marriage, but he never won the marriage grant demanded of parliament.

In the first weekend of July, Castlereagh boarded a boat and sailed off across the German Ocean to Ostend, once more in search of a European centre.[12]

Whitbread's devils

Honest Sam Whitbread would never find it. "The devils are after me!" he exclaimed to his old friend Launcelot Holland. Around him all he felt was distrust, scorn, and revenge; he became convinced that serious charges were to be made against him by the "public voice." One evening, after dinner, in front of his guests, he called out to his secretary to bring in the documents to prove it – which the secretary could not do because they did not exist. That was the same week he took a walk with his wife in the pleasure gardens of Vauxhall. On their return, he happened to notice the footmen at the gates were slightly agitated. "They are hissing me," he said; "I am become an object of universal abhorrence."

In Whitbread's eyes, this was confirmed by everyone, everywhere. People seemed to sneer and stare; he felt uncomfortable in his own body. He became obsessed with trifling matters – like the replacement of wooden columns in his theatre or the tracing of the garden boundary on his estate at Southill – and would go on arguing about them as though they were great national concerns. There were his

Samuel Whitbread, brewer, politician and leading critic of Castlereagh's foreign policy

enormous expenditures. Drury Lane Theatre had taken a heavy toll on Samuel Whitbread; for the first time in his life he realised his vast inherited fortune was limited. Friends and dependents were involved, including his own butler. Poets, playwrights, and political reformers bickered over the way the theatre had been run.

Whitbread was worth over £600,000 in the summer of 1815 – a multi-millionaire in our day. Yet the state of his finances tormented him. Since 1812 he had made eleven codicils to his will, the final one signed and dated in his own hand, "22 June 1815!"

That was the day he learned of the Battle of Waterloo.[13]

Lady Elizabeth became alarmed about her husband's depressed state. She invited one of Whitbread's oldest friends, William Willshiere, to come and stay in their home in Dover Street, Piccadilly. Willshiere found Whitbread "bereft of reason." It was not possible to have any serious discussion with him; "he was not in possession of his mind," Willshiere later explained.

Launcelot Holland, a magistrate for the county of Surrey, was equally shocked on discovering this. Whitbread himself admitted he did not have "the command of his intellect." Holland thought it would be a good idea to invite Lady Elizabeth and her invalid husband down to his country estate at Epsom. They arrived in the first weekend of July. After their first night, Whitbread complained he had not had half an hour's sleep. The next morning Holland heard such a noise proceeding from the bedroom that he went to have a look at what was going on; there he found Whitbread lying on his bed alone, stark naked, thumping on his chest and muttering incoherently about his "devils." The following day he insisted on returning to London and the Commons.[14]

"Would to the gracious God I had [not] brought such a burden upon you," he wrote to his wife from the Commons, "but in vain are wishes now and I will support myself as well as I can."

The Commons were at that time considering a motion of thanks to the Duke of York, Captain General and Commander in Chief of British Forces. No man in Britain had been more obstructive to the building of Wellington's army in the Netherlands. Even Vansittart, on the Treasury Bench, thought it would have been wiser to wait until the war was over. Mr Charles Western for Essex – friends and enemies called him "Squire Western" – considered the motion unconstitutional. And, inevitably, one of the friends of the court, Mr Serjeant Best, claimed that, if thanks were voted for the Duke of York, so were they due to "another Illustrious Personage," His Royal Highness, the Prince Regent.

But Mr Whitbread did not oppose the motion. While recognising the importance of Western's argument and resisting the idea of a grant to the Duke, he supported a vote of thanks because of "the enthusiasm at present existing in the minds of all classes." It was pretty abject reasoning for the man who, for more than ten years, had opposed the government's position on the war in Europe. Yet his friends present were impressed by the speech and said it was "more in his usual style than of late." The motion carried.[15]

The next day, Wednesday, 5 July, Whitbread attended another meeting of the Drury Lane Committee, but sat silent, with a vacant stare on his face while playing with his fingers. Returning home with Launcelot Holland he remarked gloomily that the world was scoffing at him. At dinner that evening, with his wife and Willshiere, he seemed tolerably cheerful, but he did not talk much. He retired to bed at midnight.

Whitbread usually got up at seven when his butler would shave him in his dressing-room; the room connected with a study on the ground floor. Noticing his master had not left the bedroom, the butler went upstairs at eight o'clock and called out from the door. "Very well," responded Whitbread; at 9.30 he was heard descending the staircase to the dressing-room. His secretary knocked at the door. There was no answer. Ten minutes later, the butler knocked. There was still no answer. Both secretary and butler knocked, they shouted; they discovered the door had been bolted from the inside. They raced round to an outside window and, on breaking it open, found Samuel

Whitbread sprawled on the floor in his yellow striped morning gown, his arms and legs extended, his head bathed in blood, his throat cut from ear to ear by two self-inflicted blows with his razor.[16]

Wellington's web

It did not require much assistance from the grand old Duke of York for the Anglo-Dutch and Prussian armies to begin their march into France. None of the troops bivouacked at Mont Saint-Jean thought for a moment they had seen the last of the fighting. In his Waterloo dispatch, Wellington proposed to move upon Nivelles and then press the pursuit across the frontier. "I have not allowed the grass to grow under my feet," he boasted once the invasion got under way.[17]

Behind them, the armies left fields of indescribable desolation. A heatwave had followed on the rainstorms of 17 and 18 June so that thirst was added to the torments of the wounded. Forty thousand men and ten thousand horses lay strewn on the plain, while all around, in the grass, fluttered scraps of white paper – memoranda, muster rolls, letters home, love-letters shed by soldiers in flight or tossed out by robbers hunting for valuables. Collection of the wounded only began on the 19th and continued for three days thereafter. The stench of decay made the cart-horses scream as they tramped up the road from Brussels. Civilians, many of them women, drove out in carriages in search of a husband or a loved one. The dead horses were so swollen that the men could hardly drag them to the bonfires; dead soldiers were stripped by the peasants – handkerchiefs on their nostrils – and pitchforked into pits. Within a week, the battlefield had become a grim tourist sight.

Brussels was not equipped to receive the wounded, who were carried into town on open wagons. Many had to wrap themselves in blankets or carters' smocks to hide their nakedness; the robbers had not discriminated between the living and the dead. Since there was only one small hospital, they had to lie in the streets, which had been lined with straw for this purpose.

Wellington was in Brussels on the 19th. Next to a battle lost, he often said, the greatest misery is a battle gained; and Wellington had never lost a battle. Reflecting on what he had seen in twenty-four hours, he wrote, "The glory resulting from such actions, so dearly bought, is no consolation to me." "It is quite impossible to think of glory," he repeated to Lady Shelley the following month; "every feeling in your breast is deadened."[18]

Five thousand French prisoners were marched to Ostend and, from there, transported to England. At Nivelles, on 20 June, Wellington issued his General Order, which was designed to inject a little discipline into his exhausted international army. Lists of the wounded and lists of those attending the hospital were demanded; officers had to provide lists of deserters. There was nothing that could be remotely described as a military police in 1815; Wellington had to appoint special guards with instructions to flog every man found loitering behind his regiment without a pass. The baggage trains, following the armies into France, proved a particularly delicate problem. In another of his General Orders, Wellington noted with regret that "private baggage and women are put upon the carts destined to carry tents and hospital stores"; he ordered that the private baggage be burnt, that the officers to whom it belonged be court-martialed, and – in a commanding separate article – that "the women must not be allowed to get upon the public carts."[19]

With that off his chest, Wellington sent a letter straight off to Bathurst (he had a habit of by-passing the Duke of York): "I really believe that, with the exception of my old Spanish infantry, I have got not only the worst troops, but the worst equipped army, with the worst staff, that was ever brought together." To make sure London got the point, he added, "I never was so disgusted with any concern as I am with this."[20]

There were a hundred and fifty thousand men in the two armies that descended on France. They took the ancient route reserved for invaders. Wellington's Anglo-Dutch forces followed the right bank of the River Sambre, in the direction of Le Cateau and Cambrai, while Blücher's Prussians lunged down the left. "To the French I announce that I enter their country at the head of an already victorious army" – the Duke proclaimed on 22 June at Malplaquet, where Marlborough had once smashed Louis XIV's army – "not as an enemy but to help them shake off the iron yoke which has oppressed them."[21]

A chaotic and tired, if victorious, army it was. The next day, from Le Cateau, Lieutenant Boldero of the 14th Foot wrote to assure his mother that he and his brother were alive, that they had entered France on the 21st "dressed out with Laurels," and that whatever remained of Bony's army was "flying in all directions." Bony himself was thought to have "concealed himself in the woods." Boldero had been hungry. In the weekend of the battle all he had had was "a Bit of old Cow about as big as my thumb," a "handful of Pear," and a smoke – a "Segar."[22]

For many like Boldero, Le Cateau was the first real halt they had made in a week – a week that had included Waterloo. It was here at Le Cateau that the full extent of the French defeat first sank in. "I may be wrong," Wellington wrote on the 23rd to Lord Uxbridge, who was lying in Brussels after losing a leg, "but my opinion is that we have given Napoleon his death blow; from all I hear his army is totally destroyed, the men are deserting in parties, even the Generals are withdrawing from him."[23]

United in peace? The principal commanders of the Allied armies are looking
in different directions and Wellington's name is misspelt

That was the truth. Although Marshal Soult had managed to pull together about fifty thousand troops in Laon, well south-east of the Sambre, they were demoralised men and they hardly constituted an army. Nearly half of them came from Marshal Grouchy's surviving corps, which after wandering around the plains of Brabant had finally encountered and defeated a Prussian force at Wavre; on learning of Napoleon's defeat, Grouchy had beaten a hasty retreat south down the Meuse to the French border, crossing it the same day Wellington entered the country. Wellington was right: the generals were withdrawing, as were most of the other officers. They sat in Laon waiting for the inevitable news, the abdication of Napoleon. When it arrived, on 23 June, they showed a little too much delight. Treason! cried the troops and they threatened to put their officers to death; common soldiers then abandoned their army and, to save their Emperor, marched on Paris in disordered groups; others simply walked home. Soult himself left for Paris, leaving his command to the unfortunate Grouchy.[24]

On learning that the enemy's army was "diminishing by the hour,"[25] Wellington and Blücher decided to skirt Laon and follow the route south via the River Oise. Many of the frontier forts – such as Maubeuge, Mézières, Rocroi, Bouillon, Montmédy, Charlemont, and Sarrelouis – remained in the hands of Napoleon's "national" guards. But Paris was Wellington's goal, not forts on the border.

Victory had made Wellington a key figure in diplomatic affairs as well as military. Yet it would be a mistake to regard the important decisions he made in the early summer of 1815 as the isolated acts of a commander imposing his will on the conquered. Wellington was part of a great diplomatic web that had, since Napoleon's first fall in 1814, been spun across the whole continent of Europe. It was Napoleon's acts which were isolated, and it was he who paid the consequence.

Though a simplification, it is useful to think of Wellington's web in terms of a few leading personalities. There was, first, the old tie between the Wellesleys and Castlereagh that provided, by the end of the war, the basis of British foreign policy; if the policy was characterised by a rather mechanical view of how power was distributed, it at least favoured a balance that allowed threads to be joined with other statesmen of Europe. One of them was Metternich. Metternich also argued for balance; his contribution was essential because it was derived from historical experience, not an abstract mechanics, and it came from a "Germany" that straddled the divide of the Revolution, a "Germany" that opposed the national option, a "Germany" committed to Europe. But Metternich was a game-player, a committee man; it was not Metternich who provided principle, and principle was another critical filament in the web. Talleyrand brought the principle; he recognised the permanences behind the movement, the pattern of continental relationships, the networks of exchange, the slow march of the centuries. Talleyrand also had his links, links that he shared with the victor of Waterloo. The "men of business" sat in Ghent; they were the party of government, Talleyrand's allies, who, when forced to make a choice between Napoleon and Louis, had opted for Louis. Then there were their colleagues who had stayed behind in Paris – politicians, writers, members of the King's old parliament and Napoleon's new parliament, professional men – people who had accepted the Emperor, though not with much enthusiasm.

This was the background – an enlaced, complex net, woven by many statesmen – to Wellington's decision on 20 June, while still in Belgium, to invite King Louis to move closer to the French frontier. Two days later, marching on to Le Cateau, he heard that Talleyrand had arrived in Brussels. Once installed at Le Cateau, Wellington again wrote to Ghent, emphasising the need for the King's presence in France. Then he wrote directly to Talleyrand to explain why he was inviting the King: first, he said, because he had become aware of "the extent of our success in the battle of the 18th"; second, because he wanted to use "the influence of His Majesty's name" to take advantage of that success; and, third, because he realised that Napoleon's defeat would occasion a "a crisis in the King's affairs, particularly at Paris." For Wellington, the only alternative to Louis now was anarchy, which was hardly the aim of the Allies and their Europe of equilibrium.[26]

When inviting the King, Wellington had his own international army in mind as much as the fate of France. "The Field Marshal desires it may be understood by the troops of the several nations composing [this] army," he announced in his General Order of 20 June, "that their Sovereigns are *in alliance with the King of France*, and that France therefore must be considered as a friendly country." His Proclamation to the French contained the same message: they were viewed by the Commander as friends, not enemies. Fortified towns would be summoned to yield with the understanding that "the in-habitants are considered allies." Opponents, of course, would only see the Duke's iron fist inside the velvet glove and Wellington deliberately left them no doubt that he still meant business.[27] But, for waverers, allies, and disorderly troops, the French King's name could be used as a moderating force.[28]

That was essential. Atrocities were committed by soldiers of every nationality. Hanoverian hussars and English infantry (including a regiment commanded by Sir Neil Campbell, the former resident of Elba) went on the rampage the day Cambrai's city gates were opened to them; an English colonel, trying to protect a village outside St-Quentin from the raging Dutch, was challenged to a duel by their commander.[29]

Nothing, however, equalled the campaign of horror waged by the Prussians. The spirit of revenge for Jena and the devastation of their land ran deep among them. Moreover, they felt they had not been sufficiently "compensated" for their losses by the diplomats in Vienna; the fact that so many of the troops of the smaller German states now served in Wellington's army caused still more resentment.

The Prussians took "compensation" into their own hands as Blücher's army raced ahead of Wellington's. After the sub-prefecture of Avesnes, where Napoleon had slept the week before, was blown up by Prussian artillery, the town was put to the sack: carts, horses, mules, clothing, linen, rugs, and mattresses were seized – and what could not be seized was smashed and slaughtered. Avesnes set the pattern for every town that followed. Not that the countryside was spared: whole orchards were cut down, crops were destroyed, the livestock was butchered. Those in Wellington's army who crossed Blücher's desolate path were appalled by what they saw. "The work of devastation I have no language to describe," wrote Private George Farmer of the 11th Light Dragoons after his column had marched past a large château and village visited upon by Prussians; "in the château there was not one article of furniture, from the costly pierglass down to the common coffee-cup, which they had not smashed to atoms. The flour-mill, likewise, was all gutted . . . And as to living things, there was none – not so much as a half-starved pigeon." Long after the Prussian invasion of 1815, rabid dogs in the north of France were known as "Blüchers."[30]

At one of the forward Prussian outposts – near Laon, but neither the exact time nor place appears to have been recorded – a request for an "Armistice" was received from six French Commissioners, who said they represented the "Provisional Government" in Paris. Among them was a stout, middle-aged marquis de Lafayette, inventor of the French tricolour, and the peripatetic Benjamin Constant. Napoleon had abdicated, they argued, and therefore there was no more reason for war. Lafayette asked that the fallen Emperor be granted safe conduct to the United States of America – a real gift to the New World from the defender of American freedoms.[31]

Blücher treated the affair as a "trick." He wanted Napoleon killed at the first opportunity as a "service to mankind." He was, furthermore, worried that Wellington might make a deal with the Commissioners behind his back.

Wellington, it is true, was not so keen on Napoleon's death ("I will have nothing to do with so foul a transaction," he told Charles Stuart), but he was just as sceptical about the Commissioners' intentions as Blücher. He received their message at Anglo-Dutch Headquarters in Joncourt on 26 June and responded the very same night: "The Field Marshal cannot consent to any suspension of hostilities," he informed them, because he did not consider the "abdication of Napoleon Buonaparte of his usurped authority" as being the Allied aim: as long as Napoleon was at liberty, he was to be regarded as a threat to the peace of Europe. Wellington was, however, willing to meet the Commissioners, though he warned them that it would probably be "an useless waste of their time." The interview took place in Orvillé and it did prove a waste of time. Immediately after it, the Commissioners set out off in search of Allied General Headquarters that they reckoned were still east of the Rhine.[32]

In the meantime Grouchy, the French commander, did not stand idle. With the forces remaining, he made a rapid march on Paris, which he reached after a series of minor skirmishes on 29 June. Blücher had already occupied Compiègne on the 28th and the next day swung the larger part of his army westwards in the direction of Rueil, Malmaison, and Saint-Germain-en-Laye; that was the day Napoleon escaped a sure Prussian fate by fleeing to Rochefort. Wellington headed for a town called Roye: the second siege of Paris in fifteen months was just about to begin.

The Court of France

After his departure from Vienna on 10 June, Talleyrand had not been at all sure where to direct his carriages. France was closed to him; he had even been warned of assassination if he approached the border. At Ghent, the King had been demanding his presence for over a month, but, by the third week of June, military operations blocked the way. *"Festina lente"* remained Talleyrand's motto – "Make haste slowly." The previous September he had travelled from Paris to Vienna in seven days; that June it took him nine days simply to cross Germany to Aachen, on the Belgian frontier, where he first heard the rumours of Waterloo. He was in Brussels two days later, searching out the Duke of Wellington, not the King of France.

During the journey, he had prepared a long report on the Congress of Vienna because he thought it might be useful to remind Louis of his services to the legitimate Crown of France. He recommended Louis not to repeat the "errors" of 1814, not to exclude whole parties from political life, and not to cater to the Royalist zeal of the Princes.[33]

Talleyrand spent more than two days (21-23 June) in Brussels, so he could have probably caught up with his King, who left Ghent on the morning of the 22nd. Talleyrand, however, apparently preferred the company of the Austrian Ambassador, the baron de Vincent, and some of the other minor German officials who had gathered in Brussels: a fine opportunity to discuss adjustments to the northern Prussian frontier with Denmark and Pomerania! Never mind the battle! Let us not worry about Louis! The future of France will be determined on another day! Only when Talleyrand knew that the King was on the move did he order his carriages out again.[34]

The scale of the violence of the battle fought five days earlier was obvious to anyone in Brussels at the time. "The Battle of Leipzig was nothing compared with that of the 18th," he wrote to the duchesse de Courlande just before leaving; "the battlefield is covered with dead. I am well. The trip was painful."[35] Talleyrand's brief brush with battle in December 1805 had been enough to disgust him for a lifetime, so he bypassed Waterloo by taking a road through Hals. On 23 June, at six o'clock in the evening, he finally rode into Mons on the French border.

Panicky coachmen and postboys had been standing ready in the courtyard at Ghent to take the King north to Antwerp when, in the early hours of 19 June, the news of Napoleon's defeat arrived. The French community at first showed a certain bewilderment, coupled with sadness, for it was after all an army of their own countrymen that had perished. But by midday sleepy Ghent was awake, the church bells rang out, and crowds, which had never been seen before, gathered in the streets, cheering and chanting. Strangers hugged each other and shouted *"Vive le Roy!"* His Majesty appeared in a blue carriage at two. The town was illuminated that night.[36]

Wellington recommended the path to France which the King should pursue: Grammont on the 21st, Ath on the 22nd, Mons on the 23rd. He also asked that the duc de Berry not accompany the King into the towns with his *Maison militaire*, the "little army" initially stationed at Alost. Wellington wanted to keep the "Emigrants" at a distance.[37]

So, of course, did the "men of business." During their last days at Ghent they had received a visit from Joseph Lainé, President of the Chamber of Deputies that had been dismissed by Napoleon in March. In a series of interviews with the King, he warned that the "Regicides," under Joseph Fouché, were manœuvring in Paris to bring forward the duc d'Orléans as Napoleon's replacement. He recommended immediate "convocation of the Chambers" (i.e. the old Chambers) and "the establishment of an executive government guided by a responsible administration." Such a government would require a prime minister, and the only conceivable prime minister at the time was the prince de Talleyrand.

While Lainé was in Ghent, King Louis received a message from Jean-Denis Lanjuinais, a longtime enemy of Napoleon's, who had, as a result of the disastrous elections of May, been named president of Napoleon's Chamber of Representatives. It was known in Ghent that Lanjuinais was collaborating with Joseph Fouché. In his message,

Lanjuinais declared his intention "to omit no opportunity of advancing the King's interests." The King, in his answer, promised Lanjuinais that he would be rewarded for his services and advised him to contact six delegates who had been named to represent his interests in Paris.[38]

The threads linking the King to Paris – to Fouché and the Chamber – were thus already tied before Louis and his court bid a ceremonial farewell to Count Hane (who received a diamond-studded snuffbox for his hospitality). Louis then took the road for Grammont and Mons. As the King moved, so the balance of forces within his court shifted: in moments of isolation, in favour of the court party, or the "Emigrant Party" as both Wellington and Talleyrand were wont to call it; in moments of exposure, in favour of the liberals, the party of government, the "men of business."

In Belgium, the King was exposed. The party of government was in a position to force the resignation of Louis' favourite, the comte de Blacas, an event which took place at Mons just prior to Talleyrand's arrival. The King was in a dreadful mood.

Talleyrand, in his memoirs, explains his subsequent rift with Louis was a result of a disagreement over where the court should be heading. Talleyrand wanted the King to go to Lyon, where he could convoke the Chambers and set up a "unified government" that would be entirely independent of the Allies. The King wanted to go directly to Paris. Given the situation in Lyon (one of the most active, even violent, Bonapartist centres in France), one has to conclude that the King was right. But Talleyrand could not accept this. "I offered my resignation and retired," the prince diplomat coolly recounts, "after handing in a report on our work at the Congress."[39]

Beugnot, Chateaubriand, and Sir Charles Stuart – all of whom were present – report an encounter that was far from cool. As a matter of etiquette, Talleyrand should have presented himself to the King on his arrival at Mons. But Talleyrand refused. "I am never in a hurry," he remarked somewhat familiarly to Chateaubriand, grasping him with both arms; "there will always be time tomorrow." King Louis was furious. "Monsieur de Talleyrand is only tired, Your Majesty," explained Chateaubriand, who found himself mediating between King and Minister. He returned to Talleyrand's inn with the warning that the King intended to cross the French frontier without him. Talleyrand thought this mere bluff and went to bed; but, sure enough, at three o'clock the next morning, the King's coaches started to roll. Talleyrand, for whom dressing was normally an affair that would last at least an hour and a half, never got up as quickly in his life.

With the first glimmer of dawn, there were sounds of screaming across the town square: "Sire! It is Monsieur de Talleyrand!"

"He is sleeping," answered the King in his coach.

But the unmistakable profile, leaning on an arm of one of the royal postilions, could be made out in the obscure light: "There he is, Sire!"

The coaches ground to a halt, the King descended, and walked slowly back to his apartments, Talleyrand limping behind him. Their interview was brief. When Louis had returned to his carriage Talleyrand inquired through the window: "I have a favour to request of the King, that is, the permission to take the waters in Carlsbad, which are necessary for my health."

"By all means," replied Louis, "I grant it. Those waters are excellent. Good bye, Monsieur de Talleyrand."[40]

The Ministers remained in Mons and, for the next two days, it looked as though France's "unified government" was going to retire to a watering spot in Bohemia, without a King; that the King was going to advance on Paris without a government. The Burgermeister of Mons gave, in the Flemish manner, a sumptuous dinner at his home, which had been designed to receive the great and the famous; comte Beugnot had never seen so many bottles of the world's finest wines arranged in battle formation. Talleyrand appeared in high spirits, bursting out in an endless flow of anecdotes and witticisms.[41]

On the other side of the frontier, King Louis installed himself at Le Cateau, or Cateau-Cambrésis as he preferred to call it – for it was here that England, in 1559, had signed a royal treaty under that name which ceded Calais to France. The peasants and inhabitants of the tulip fortresses of northern France showed the same devotion to the King as they had in March. At Le Cateau, the mayor and his officers as well as the curé with his clergy stood in tight formation at the gates to welcome him; thirty youths, dressed in white, unhitched the royal coach and hauled it up the main street; thirty maidens performed a living tableau on a stage hastily erected in the square. The Princes and the court party were triumphant. After hearing mass in the parish church and dining in the open before the crowd, the King ordered his "Proclamation of Cateau-Cambrésis" read aloud. "Now that the mighty exertion of our Allies have scattered the satellites of the tyrant," it announced, "we return to our Estates to re-establish the constitution we gave to France." The good would be rewarded, the guilty would face the law.[42]

The Duke of Wellington was still in town, and he did not like this at all: the whole purpose of inviting the King was to provide an authority that was not directly linked to the "mighty exertion" of the invaders, would not re-establish the weak regime of 1814, and did not seek revenge. News had just arrived in Le Cateau that Napoleon had abdicated. Wellington requested an interview with the King. The Duke would claim that they did not discuss French politics; but he did immediately afterwards write a letter to Talleyrand to say that the King "had been received with the utmost demonstrations of joy by all his subjects, and I only regret that your Highness did not accompany His Majesty." The next day a royal courier also crossed the frontier to Mons to announce that the King would shortly be holding Council, which *all* Ministers were expected to attend, including Monsieur de Talleyrand.[43]

On that day the citadel of Cambrai fell to Allied forces. Wellington thought this would be an ideal temporary residence for the King until operations were ended: the inhabitants had never made any secret of their Royalist sympathies and, unlike Avesnes or Saint-Quentin, they had not been exposed to the fury of Prussians. The King agreed. Peasants lined the road between the two towns, crowds gathered on the glacis at Cambrai, cannon thundered from the ramparts as the royal train entered, *jeunes demoiselles* – "chosen from among the prettiest and the most respectable" – threw flowers upon King's way and chanted to the honour of the Bourbons. Eighteen nearby villages came to render homage to their Sovereign; they filed past with white banners and held fronds of oak in their hands. A great public banquet took place on the square. After a *Te Deum* was sung in the cathedral a second Proclamation was read from the town hall balcony; it was countersigned by the prince de Talleyrand.[44]

Several of the Ministers in Mons had tried to dissuade him from leaving, but in the end they all made the great sacrifice, as Talleyrand explained in his memoirs, in order to prevent foreigners, such as Wellington, from abusing their influential position: "I followed the King to Cambrai to put myself, like him, in the baggage of the English army." Before he set off, he found the time to write once more to the duchesse de Courlande. He had not been happy with his first interview with the King, he told her: "Those around him are intoxicated by the success of our great, admirable Duke. They have gone quite mad. If I am to be of any use, they have to sober up a bit."[45]

Talleyrand already had, apparently, a rough draft of his Proclamation prepared.[46] But comte Beugnot, Minister of the Navy (he was not overburdened by his responsibilities), worked with him on a new version for the Council.

As in Vienna, Talleyrand was not master of the situation. What he had was an understanding, which he could present – and even find others to present for him – in simple, precise language. His Proclamation of 28 June ought to be compared to his Note in Vienna of 19 December. Neither document radically altered the course of events, but they both provided a clear indication of where those events were going. Just as the Note had articulated the two principles upon which post-war Europe was founded – legitimacy and equilibrium – so the Proclamation described the most acceptable constitution for post-war France. It could easily be fitted, for example, to the memorandum Castlereagh and his colleagues drafted in London two days later.

The Proclamation noted, first, that all members of the royal family had kept their distance from the foreign armies and, second, that the King's government had perhaps committed "errors" in 1814. The principle of legitimacy was confirmed and a united government (something that hadn't existed in 1814) was promised. Napoleon's attacks on Bourbon "feudalism" were dismissed as calumnies and lies; "all classes," stated the document, would be included in the constitution of the new regime – a pardon would even be granted.

But Talleyrand recognised that war and its victims would always exact some form of justice. The Proclamation promised to condemn the "instigators and authors of this horrible plot," those who had committed treason and "had brought foreigners into the heart of France." They would be tried before the "two Chambers" – that is, the two Chambers dismissed by Napoleon in March.[47]

Writing his memoirs in 1816, Talleyrand said, "I still believe today that it was the best one could do in such circumstances."[48]

The Ministers were amiably received by the King; it was as if Mons had simply been a bad dream. But the Council proved turbulent. The comte d'Artois strongly objected to the Proclamation's reference to "errors"; such language, he said, debased the authority of the King. Talleyrand replied that the phrasing was necessary because the King had made errors; his affections had been led astray.

"Is that me, who is being implied?" asked Artois, furiously.

"If Monsieur wants to put it that way, yes," responded Talleyrand; "Monsieur has done a lot of harm."

"The prince de Talleyrand is forgetting himself!"

"That I fear. But then truth prevails on me."

The duc de Berry could support it no more: "Nothing but the King's presence would let me tolerate such treatment of my father. I would like to know…"

King Louis waved his hand. "Enough, my nephew," he mumbled. He asked that a few editorial touches be made to the document with a view to maintaining propriety. Berry continued to interrupt. The King demanded that he stop. "Messieurs," he said, "I have listened to this discussion with much regret. Let us pass to another subject."[49]

Talleyrand now had open royal enemies. But he could count on his friends, he could pull on the threads of the web. Charles Stuart dashed off a dispatch to Wellington that reported Talleyrand carrying the day. The Ministers, he said, had been so irritated with the Princes that they had published their Proclamation on the spot. He believed this would have a positive effect "by laying the foundation of an Administration upon the principle which Lord Castlereagh has so frequently recommended."[50]

Stuart also reported the fall of the neighbouring citadel of La

Quesnoy. But with many of the frontier forts still holding out, it was thought wise that the King's court and government should be moved further to the interior, to a town called Roye.

Talleyrand set off alone, well ahead of the King's procession. Baron Louis, the Finance Minister, who had always been an observant man, leaned over to comte Beugnot, his travelling companion in the procession, to express a concern that the Foreign Minister might be getting up to mischief – which, of course, he was.[51]

The Elect of God

Another thread in Europe's peace was being strung. Alexander, Emperor of All the Russias, was now defender of all the religions. This new role arose from doubts he had developed, on travelling westward, about the justice of the war against Napoleon. His reputation as "Liberator" had been undermined at the Congress. Furthermore, he knew his army would not be the first in the field. Allied Headquarters had been first set up in Heidelberg, in the Kingdom of Württemberg, certainly one of Russia's closest allies (Grand Duchess Catherine was engaged to be married to the Crown Prince). But it would be Austrians and Bavarians that would first cross into France, not the forces of Russia. In early June 1815, Alexander was a thwarted man – he said Napoleon's return was God's way of punishing Sovereigns, who had "spent five months arguing about trinkets"[52] – and he appeared emotionally withdrawn.

It is possible that women were at the root of this.[53] Just as in the weeks that preceded the campaign of 1812 so again, with the approach of another war, he was writing despairing letters to his sister Catherine; she would soon receive instructions to join him before the invasion of France began. In one of these letters he spoke of a mysterious "Virginie": "put me at her feet, tell her my affection for her is eternal, that she is so pure, so much a tribute for admiration." He was probably referring to Gabrielle Auersperg, whom he had left in Vienna. Hager's agents reported that he was still dreaming about her in late October. Nor had the Tsar seen Roxandre de Stourdza since Vienna, and he missed those long spiritual conversations on the fourth floor of the Hofburg.[54]

More generally, Alexander was uncertain about the future of the world and himself; he was haunted by feelings of emptiness. If he could not be the Liberator of Europe, then why was he riding to Heidelberg?

During the voyage, he received from his influential religious adviser in St Petersburg, Rodion Kochelev, a copy of a Russian translation of Eckartshausen's *Cloud over the Shrine*, a book that had had much influence in romantic, religious Germany; its idea of returning to an early Christian style of ecumenical Church was particularly appealing to the mystical sects. The book brought him back to his own conversations with La Stourdza, to the letters she had read from Julie von Krüdener, to the prophecies of Napoleon's return, and the warning that 1815 would be a year of hunger and massacre.

As his horses drew into Heilbronn – the name meant "holy spring" in old German – he wondered where Baroness von Krüdener could be found. Was she in Baden? Was she in Strasbourg? Could she even be in this tiny Kingdom of Württemberg? How could he meet her and talk with her? Faced with a new trial of war, he needed a spiritual friend, a sign from God. He was frustrated, sad, tired; "my ideas were confused, my heart oppressed," he later told Roxandre de Stourdza.[55]

Everything that happened, in the few hours that followed, would convince him that the hand of Providence was at work.

Baroness Julie von Krüdener had also been thinking about Alexander. The baroness was, like the four sisters of Courlande, another daughter of the Baltic, another Russian subject born to a German landowner; the estates lay just outside the port of Riga. Krüdener's private life, turbulent and extravagant, also bore a certain resemblance to the Courlandes'. In 1782, at the age of eighteen, she had married an elderly Russian diplomat, whom she abandoned ten years later for travel, love, and adventure – all meticulously recorded in her bestselling autobiographical novel, *Valérie*. But there the Courlande parallel ended. On turning forty she fell under the spell of the religious revival then sweeping war-torn Germany, a movement one of Hegel's biographers would appropriately call "the apocalyptic consciousness of the present."[56] Krüdener's apocalypse was just that: it lay right around the corner; it was set for the next season. But her vision was not that of Dante's descent into the inferno, or Milton's ruin upon ruin, and rout on rout; rather, the world ended for Krüdener with a great explosion of love. She quoted the Psalms and the Epistles of Saint Paul. She rejected the rationalist excess of the Enlightenment in favour of prayer, meditation, and an intuitive, sentimental understanding of the world, the body, and the spirit. Indeed, all was one with Julie von Krüdener – a high truth, she went as far as to claim, that could be discovered in the physical union of equally inspired persons. Through spiritual husbands and kin, a network that extended from the Quietists and Pietists in northern Germany to members of the "Awaken" sect in Switzerland, she sought a return of the many to one, a unity born out of diversity: one Christian church: one Europe.[57]

For there was this political side to the baroness's philosophy. "I preach to crowned heads as I do to ploughmen the love of Christ," she once professed; but she quite obviously preferred the crowned heads.

For more than a year she had kept an eye on Alexander. Many in her circle had met the Tsar and had reported that, though a sinner, his heart was ready for their "great work," the founding of a single European religion. In particular, Baron Franz von Berckheim, who lived in Baden and was engaged to Krüdener's daughter Juliette, persuaded the two women to seek out Alexander before the hostilities against Napoleon began. Krüdener herself harboured no doubts about the justice of the war or its outcome. Before setting out from Baden for Heilbronn, where she was sure Alexander was heading, she composed a prayer: "We implore Thee, King of Kings, to grant divine protecton to our beloved Emperor Alexander of Russia, to sanctify his actions, to invigorate his heart with the all-powerful rays of Thy love, in order that he may realise his great mission as a Christian and a Sovereign." Thus prepared and confident of success she headed for Heilbronn and the Emperor of Russia like Joan of Arc – with a stray daughter – riding off to Chinon to meet the King of France.[58]

Alexander was reading in Eckartshausen's book a passage about the divine grace of God when Prince Volkonsky, his aide-de-camp, knocked at the door. He entered to report that for several hours two women had been outside insisting on seeing him. They had finally gone, but they had left a letter; Volkonsky handed it to Alexander. The Tsar opened the envelope and then rose, stupefied. "Madame de Krüdener! Madame de Krüdener! Madame de Krüdener!" he repeated in a kind of daze. "Her! Is it possible?" The whole town was searched; Krüdener and her daughter were finally discovered in a poor suburban inn. Juliette had already undressed for bed when Prince Volkonsky stepped into their room. He accompanied them to the Tsar's residence. The interview lasted until the early hours of the morning and was recorded in Juliette's journal.[59]

Alexander was humble and awkward. He said he was struck by the fact that he had just been thinking about the baroness and reading Eckartshausen. The baroness responded that she had come, by order of Heaven, to announce the grace of the God and victory. Alexander remarked he was not entirely convinced of his own grace and election, but he was certain that everyone who sought God would eventually find Him. The discussion then turned to prayer and the Bible; Alexander admitted that it was the pain of his past which had driven him to daily worship and reading.

He had been planning the next morning, 5 June, to leave for the Heidelberg headquarters, where he would be joining the Austrian Emperor. But he delayed his departure until late afternoon in order to talk further with Krüdener.

It was an emotional encounter. He repeated once more that he was not sure he was one of God's elect and he mentioned, in this context, the proposals Napoleon had addressed him while he was still in

Vienna; Alexander had profound doubts about the purpose of the war. On hearing this, Krüdener became vehement. "No, Sire," she exclaimed, "you have not yet approached the Man-God" – she spoke frequently of Christ as the Man-God (flesh and spirit) just as she referred to the human heart as the work and wage of His blood – "you have not approached the Man-God as a criminal requesting grace." She told him he was still immersed in his sins, had still not humbled himself before Jesus: "And that's why you don't have peace. Listen to the voice of a woman who was also a great sinner." That was also why he remained confused in his goals; a man who humbled himself before God was a combatant. She quoted Judges: "Go direct thyself to Mount Thabor and take with thee ten thousand men."

Alexander stuttered a few words, leaned forward, put his head in his hands, and burst into a torrent of tears. Krüdener was so shocked by the effect she had on the Emperor of All the Russias that she demanded an immediate pardon; "I only speak with the sincerity of my heart," she said. Alexander shook his head to reassure her, confessed that he had just discovered things he had never understood in his life before, and finally pleaded: "I do need talks like this and I pray you not to distance yourself from me."[60]

And off he rode to his Mount Thabor. There followed an exchange of passionate letters, Krüdener declaring Alexander a "great man," Alexander professing to owe her "a million thanks" and to hold for her "the purest and truest sentiment I have ever cultivated in my heart."

Outside Heidelberg he found a peasant's cabin on the banks of the Neckar with a cross in its garden. He took this to be another divine sign and invited Krüdener to join him there. She arrived on Thursday, 8 June. Juliette recorded in her journal that Alexander followed her like a child; nearly every night he came to the cabin to review his life and discuss the "regeneration" of Europe. Often he was accompanied by his advisers. When the first news of fighting in Belgium was received in Heidelberg, Alexander told the devout baroness that this war was driven by "the positive will of the Lord." At last the Tsar had found his new vocation: no more did he think of himself as the Liberator; in this campaign he would trace out a path for Europe as the Elect of God.

Heidelberg

A more practical problem for the Allies at Heidelberg was the trouble they were having in collecting their forces. Back in Vienna, a three-pronged attack had been planned that would send Prince Schwarzenberg with his Austrians and Bavarians over the Rhine at Mannheim, Archduke Ferdinand across the Rhine from Bâle (where most of Napoleon's weak Army of the Jura under Marshal Lecourbe was awaiting him), while a corps of Austrians and Sardinians was to clamber over the Alps from Italy in the direction of Geneva and eventually Lyon. When Alexander arrived in Heidelberg, the famous Russian reserve of six corps was still strung along a road of over forty leagues between northern Bavaria and the Rhine.

Arrangements had been made to accommodate not only the staff of many armies but also all the diplomats at the Allied Headquarters;[61] several familiar faces could be seen in Heidelberg, though the most important were still missing. Kaiser Franz had set up court in the centre of town, but he kept out of the politics of the war. The King of Prussia was away on business and his Ambassador Prince Hardenberg was, as always, late. Castlereagh had been invited, but he remained in England to deal with the furore over the Duke of Cumberland's marriage; Clancarty was still in Vienna, working with Gentz on the last draft of the Final Act. Britain was therefore represented at Heidelberg by Sir Charles Stewart, who arrived suffering from "Blue Angels," as he called his bouts with depression.

Metternich reached Heidelberg on 17 June. Thus, at the moment of Waterloo, the chief political protagonists at Allied Headquarters numbered only two: Emperor Alexander and Prince Metternich. This was yet another thread in the web.

News of the battle was received in snatches all through Wednesday, the 21st. Many of the officers must have felt like Charles Stewart, who wrote a long letter to his mother, Lady Londonderry, that night. "I confess to You my beloved Mother," he bemoaned, "that I can not but feel deeply mortified that My Lot did not lead me to share a part in the splendid triumph that has added new Lustre to the British Name." He complained of how slow progress was at Headquarters and hoped "these last Triumphs in the Low countries have given us a Spur." Yet there was the appalling thought that they might have nothing left to do: "Perhaps we may see a Shot or Two fired; but I confess I don't expect it." Sir Charles was tormented by the loss of so many of his friends and he was convinced Napoleon's machine would "tumble down like a pack of cards" before he and the forces in Germany had even crossed the Rhine. Sitting in the Headquarters of the whole Allied effort, he felt isolated. "I am so thoroughly alone in the world now," he concluded, "that I am often very gloomy and feel I should be only well at Mt Stewart."[62]

Alexander did write to congratulate Wellington and actually sent him a sword decorated with laurels; he promised that the armies "arriving on the Rhine" would soon be following. Metternich, in the meantime, sent a letter off to his favourite daughter, Marie, to report "the most violent, most murderous battle of all times." He assured her that half a million additional men were now ready "to pay a visit to Napoleon"; like Stewart, Metternich thought they might do this without firing a shot.[63]

The celebrating at Headquarters, however, was muffled. Alexander and Kaiser Franz would raise their glasses to Wellington, but the church bells did not ring out in Heidelberg as they had in Ghent. On Friday, the 23rd, Metternich received news from Marie that an iron bridge had collapsed at Baden, outside Vienna; there were "two dead, a hundred and twenty wounded, and thirty broken feet"; three of Metternich's children, including Marie, had fallen into the waters and had been miraculously saved. "You have no idea what in impression your letter made on the whole Headquarters," Metternich wrote back. "People are talking here more of Baden's bridge and the thirty broken feet than they are of the thirty thousand dead and mutilated of the victory of the 18th."[64]

The first troops to enter France from Germany were Field Marshal Wrede's IVth Bavarian Corps. Ironically they took a route, on 23 June, almost identical to the one Helmuth von Moltke would follow in the Franco-Prussian War of 1870, across the Sarre at Saarbruck and Sarreguemines. The Crown Prince of Württemberg pushed on with the IIIrd Corps to Wissemburg in Alsace.[65]

With troops on the march and the prospect of chaos in France, Alexander and Metternich were now bound, like Wellington, to regard Louis XVIII as the only viable head of state. Metternich, in particular, feared a Jacobin takeover in Paris. But eastern France was not as enthusiastic for the Bourbons as the Catholic north. The Allied Proclamation to the French, prepared by Metternich and published on 23 June, was therefore vaguer on the issue of Restoration than Wellington's Proclamation of the 22nd. There would be no peace or ceasefire with Napoleon, it boldly declared: "Frenchmen! it is for you to decide whether it will be peace or war." But it equally asserted that "Europe does not wish to encroach upon the rights of a great nation."

Metternich wanted French politics and Allied armies kept separate. "We cannot make ourselves loved in France," he advised Wellington the next day on hearing the news of Napoleon's abdication. He hoped resentment over the invasion would be directed towards foreigners, not Frenchmen, and for this reason opposed the idea of having French royal commissioners administer Allied requisitions. He also recommended dividing the country into an occupied zone and a royal zone, going so far as to support Talleyrand in his efforts to move the King to Lyon rather than Paris.[66]

Rachevski's Russian IVth Corps had by now collected at Mannheim and was ready to cross the Rhine; Allied Headquarters – the Sovereigns, the decorated officers, the crowd of diplomats, and the courtisans – moved to join them. Julie von Krüdener, her daughter, along with the Grand Duchess Catherine saw Alexander

Prince Metternich rides ahead of Kaiser Franz as the Austrian army
crosses the Vosges in early July 1815

off. Metternich sent a short letter to his wife: "Here we are at a beginning that furiously resembles an end."[67]

An important meeting was held in Mannheim, in which Metternich
managed to get Alexander to agree to take a firm stand after General
Rapp had proposed a ceasefire with Crown Prince Württemberg's
forces at Wissemburg; indeed Metternich was astonished at how
malleable Alexander had become.

A joint Austro-Russian note was sent to Wellington stating that all
requests for a ceasefire would be turned down on two grounds: one
could not recognise Bonaparte's "abdication" since he had usurped
his power in the first place, and one could not recognise delegates

from Napoleon's "Chambers" that had only sat in Paris for a fortnight. The Allies would let the "run of events" decide; they were not going to halt the march of their armies.

Charles Stewart wrote to London pleading with Castlereagh to hurry over because he had fears that an Austro-Russian combination might decide the peace.[68]

On 1 July, at Haguenau in Alsace, the six French Commissioners who had set off from Joncourt on the 26th in search of an Armistice, finally caught up with Allied Headquarters. They were told there would be no separate negotiations and they "left immediately on their route to Paris by the way they came."[69]

Meanwhile, the three Sovereigns (King Frederick William had eventually joined them) followed their troops up the narrow path that led into the Vosges. "When you are on horseback for seven or eight hours under a scorching sun, on a totally white road, among twenty-five thousand men and six thousand chariots, canon, etc," Metternich wrote to his daughter, Marie, from Sarrebourg on 2 July, "you get a foretaste of the pleasures awaiting you in one of Lucifer's *salons.*"[70]

There had been fighting between Bâle and Belfort, Strasbourg was under siege; but, with both Lucifer and the Elect of God among them, there was nothing to stop the march of the Allied armies on Paris.

The Siege

Sixteen dramatic days in the French capital began early on Sunday morning, 18 June, when a hundred cannon at the Invalides roared out to announce Napoleon's victory at Ligny. E. Labretonnière, who studied mathematics at Lycée Louis-le-Grand, woke up from a doze in his small hotel and, like many students in the Latin Quarter, rushed to the nearest café to find out what was going on. There he read the brief bulletin, dated 16 June: "The Emperor has just won a complete victory over the combined Prussian and English armies." The English traveller, John Cam Hobhouse, who arrived in Paris a week later, reported that there had been "extravagant rejoicings."

But, on 19 and 20 June, there were no bulletins; the newspapers simply repeated accounts of the glorious victory at Ligny. On Wednesday, the 21st, people became visibly agitated. It was said that Empress Marie-Louise had entered town. Wicked Royalists put about the rumour that it was the Emperor himself who had returned, like after the disasters of Egypt, Moscow, and Leipzig; at midday, this was no longer an ugly rumour. Crowds gathered around the Chamber of Representatives, opposite the place de la Concorde, or went directly to the Elysée to pick up news. Labretonnière first heard of the disaster of the 18th from an old stuttering deputy on the steps of the Chamber. *Le Moniteur universel,* the official government paper, published a special supplement that afternoon.[71]

It was a masterpiece of obfuscation and distortion, which fully justified the fears of liberals in Paris and Allies on the frontier that Napoleon was prepared to set up a dictatorship. After eight hours of fighting, wrote its anonymous author, "the battle was won...and the battlefield was within our power." Then right at the last moment *la moyenne garde* (a corps of pure invention) was thrown into disorder "by a charge made on their flank of a few English squadrons" (i.e. Colborne's 52nd Light Infantry followed by the entire British cavalry). The *moyenne garde* were taken by the near victorious French troops to be the Old Guard (not surprisingly, for that is what they were) and the cry went up, *"Tout est perdu, la garde est repoussée."* All turned into confusion. "Thus a battle finished, a day of errors corrected, the greatest success assured for the next day; all this was lost in a moment of terrified panic." Nonetheless, by the following morning, Prince Jerome and General Morand were already said to be rallying the troops at Philippeville and Avesnes. As Lucien Bonaparte explained that night to a horrified Chamber, Napoleon was back in Paris with new plans to unify France.[72]

Marshal Ney, in the Chamber of Peers the next day, demonstrated the lie. "The enemy is the victor on every point," he told the stunned assembly. "I saw the disorder since I was commanding under the Emperor. They dare tell us that there are 60,000 men on the frontier! This is false. The most one can expect is that Marshal Grouchy has been able to rally 10 to 15,000 men." Ney predicted – accurately it turned out – that the enemy would be before the walls of Paris in six or seven days. "This incredible declaration," remarked one general, "has spread more ill than the loss of a battle." It was the truth, but it did not save Ney, now hated by the supporters of Napoleon as well as of Louis; he was executed for treason the following December.[73]

But it was not Marshal Ney who sealed the fate of Napoleon; it was the marquis de Lafayette. He was one of the many liberal opponents to the Empire who had been elected to the new Chamber of Representatives that May. He was certainly the most eloquent. On the very afternoon of Napoleon's return, with crowds massed outside the Chamber – National Guards, *Fédérés*, citizens waving branches of greenery, tricolour pennants, and other more threatening things – the Marquis, mindful of the fact that Napoleon had never shown himself to be a great friend of parliament after his military disasters, mounted the tribune and moved that "the independence of the nation is threatened" and that "the Chamber declares itself undissolvable."

His speech had the same electric effect as that of Sieyès at the time of the Tennis Court Oath in June 1789 (when the National Assembly swore not to be removed). There was loud applause and the motion was carried: parliament would not be removed.

Napoleon was paralysed and was obliged to abdicate the next morning, though he took care to address his Act directly to "Frenchmen" and avoided all mention of the Chambers. Moreover, he abdicated in favour of his son, which he, his advisors, and many in parliament interpreted as a condition. As General de La Bédoyère, one of Napoleon's staunchest supporters, ominously warned the Chamber that same day, "The abdication of Napoleon is indivisible; if you refuse to proclaim the Imperial Prince Emperor, Napoleon must draw his sword."

The Chamber eventually came up with a legal formula that committed them to nothing. But the Allies were perfectly right to be sceptical about Napoleon's "abdication"; there was nothing absolute about it at all.[74]

Paris was more radical in June 1815 than it had been fifteen months earlier, during the first siege; something of the spirit of '89 was present. The Waterloo campaign had a lot to do with this. The drawn-out winter campaign of 1814, fought on the plains of Champagne and Burgundy, had pulled the French armies away from the capital; in fact, Napoleon had lost because he had been, at the crucial moment, cut off from Paris. The rapid march of the Allied armies after Waterloo had exactly the opposite effect. They had declared they were the friends of the French and enemies only of the supporters of Napoleon. So where did the supporters of Napoleon go? Most of them ended up in Paris. The *Fédérés*, created during the Hundred Days, became more aggressive, generals were vying for leadership, while extreme young Royalists hoped for nothing better than an open battle in the streets.

A camaraderie developed between troops and certain sections of the population, particularly students. Labretonnière claimed that most youth were, like him, in sympathy with Napoleon and that during the Hundred Days they had developed ties with the army; a year and a half of press freedoms (a gift of the Restoration) had revitalised, among the young, patriotic sentiment. Napoleonic enthusiasts, like him, would regularly attend the huge Café Montansier at the Palais-Royal.

The Napoleonic Legend was not invented on the isle of St Helena; it was born in the centre of Paris, during the Hundred Days, in this café. In May and June, it had become a temple to the God Napoleon. Queues would form down the open arcades of the Palais-Royal to gain entry. It was a place of mirrors and bright lights; on the stage stood a large bust of the Napoleonic god, decorated in flowers and tricolour pennants; *orateurs chantants* (whose talents could be compared to the singing improvisers in Vienna) stomped out vaudeville tunes like *Les Lanciers Polonais*, *Le Retour de l'Aigle*, or – to the melody of "Julie":

Napoléon, gloire et patrie:
Ah! répétons ces mots si chers:
Napoléon, gloire et patrie!

Soldiers and students whooped it out together. Officers in uniforms of every colour thronged the floor and the balconies. Women examined the magnificent decor with spy glasses. "The club was purged of garlic and red bonnets." Good old middle-class love and glory were what one found here; union and force![75]

Some of the most violent of the demonstrations that followed Napoleon's abdication took place in the neighbourhood of this café. Shops of the Palais-Royal and of the rue Vivienne were obliged to shut; for a moment, the armaments depot in the nearby Bibliothèque Impériale seemed threatened; patrols of the National Guard were brought in; rues Richelieu and Saint-Honoré took on a military look; sentries stood in the arcades. At nine o'clock, Friday evening, 23 June, the Café Montansier was closed for good.[76]

Given the neighbourhood and the kind of clientèle to whom the café catered, one suspects that it was not just workers from the suburbs who had been throwing stones that Friday. Paris crowds were as complex as its social geography. *"L'Empereur ou la mort!"* was the cry of the most fanatical among them. The sexes were as mixed as the classes. "One has noticed for some days," wrote a contributor to the *Journal de Paris* on Sunday, 25 June, "in the streets and public squares, in the cabarets, and even in the *guinguettes* [open-air cafés] outside the town, agitators, among whom are to be found women of easy virtue." Paris was a good deal noisier than it had been at the first siege.[77]

It was also more populated. Grouchy turned up, not with ten thousand men as Ney had predicted, but with forty thousand; his cavalry and artillery were paraded up and down the northern boulevards on 30 June to the sounds of fife and drum. Marshal Masséna held a military review nearly every day on the place Vendôme. In addition to fighting men, there were the wounded; the first casualties of the Belgian campaign arrived in Paris on the day Napoleon abdicated, 22 June, and from then on it was a continual stream. Some of the Old Guard were seen in the city on cart and horseback on Saturday, the 24th. Posters, appealing for mattresses, bolsters, sheets, men's shirts, bandages, and rags, were stuck up on walls and reproduced in the newspapers. "The greatest need is for shredded linen," it was announced; a corner of the place Vendôme served as a hospital for a week. Peasants poured in from neighbouring villages with livestock, furniture, and wives; "where they find asylum I know not," recorded John Cam Hobhouse, who had just returned from a trip to the Swiss frontier.[78]

Some people, however, were pretty festive. The owners of government stock (*rente*) saw their holdings rise at a rate that had rarely been experienced before. Every time a major disaster was announced the price went up: Waterloo, the abdication, the approach of the Allied armies, the possibility of foreign occupation. On the Thursday Napoleon abdicated, men on the floor of the stock exchange applauded as the criers announced the new price of *rente*. There was a slight dip on Saturday, because of the rioting, but, with the National Guard in control of the streets and the certainty that the Allies would soon be in town, prices soared again that Sunday – a day of work for French stockbrokers in those revolutionary times.[79]

That same Sunday, Labretonnière noticed Paris taking on an "aristocratic look"; joy had returned to the heart of the faubourg Saint Germain, the wealthiest neighbourhood of Paris, and the Tuileries Gardens was filled with "brilliant society." Labretonnière thought he was the only gloomy person walking in the crowd. Hobhouse had a similar experience: he was asked why he had such a melancholy face and if anything had happened to him. He thought it strange that the only man with a melancholy face in the Tuileries should be a foreigner "when you consider that the Square Vendôme, close by, is covered at one corner with wounded men, laying on straw." On rue de Rivoli could be seen the soldiers marching in the direction of an invisible war.[80]

The riots, the presence of so many troops and refugees, along with the activities of the orderless *Fédérés* created a situation so much more explosive than that of March 1814, when the Restoration of the Bourbons had been accomplished basically through intrigues in Talleyrand's drawing room. Napoleon had gone off to war in 1814 with a Regency governing Paris. When he set off for Belgium in 1815 he left nothing of the kind, only a "Council of Ministers," who were united on no issue save the vague, unpronounceable feeling that they did not want to serve under the Emperor.

News of the disaster of the 18th arrived in the Tuileries on Tuesday, the 20th, in the form of a dispatch to Joseph, the Emperor's brother. He immediately informed the Ministers, who immediately got in touch with their friends in the parliamentary Chambers. The members of the two Chambers regarded an abdication as inevitable. While Napoleon was taking his bath in the Tuileries, they devised a plan whereby ten parliamentary delegates – five from each Chamber – would join the Ministers in a meeting and decide what to do next.

The ten delegates were elected that afternoon (the 21st) and the meeting lasted all through the night. That session in the Tuileries decided the course Paris would attempt to follow in the next ten days: first, they had to be assured of Napoleon's abdication; second, they would, in the name of the Chambers, open negotiations with the

Allies. Nothing was certain about either. Napoleon abdicated the next morning, but he continued to make noises about "saving France" and nullifying his Act if his son (still Austria's prisoner of the Schonbrunn) was not recognised Emperor. The Chambers were divided into bickering factions and their very existence was threatened by street gangs calling for Napoleon; the National Guard provided a thin envelope of protection. As for negotiating peace in the name of the Chambers, these were Chambers created by Napoleon and they had not been recognised by the Allies.

The most urgent matter, of course, was to set up a provisional government. A "Commission of Government," with three members chosen by the Chamber of Representatives and two from the Peers, was voted into office immediately after Napoleon's abdication, though the parliamentary debate ran late into the night. The Peers nominated Caulaincourt (Napoleon's able Minister of Foreign Affairs) and Quinette (a baron of the Empire). The Chamber of Representatives chose the Revolution's military hero, General Lazare Carnot; another soldier, who had served in Italy, Germany, and Russia, but had been given no command during the Hundred Days, General Grénier; and, on a narrow margin at the second ballot, Napoleon's Minister of Police, Joseph Fouché. Undoubtedly, the Chambers expected the Commission to elect the Great Carnot their president; the *Journal de Paris* announced the next day that this was so. But Carnot – not for the first time in his life – was outmanœuvred by the professionals. The new president of France was Joseph Fouché.

On the day Waterloo was fought, Fouché had published a report on the state of the French Empire. Civil war once again threatened the west, rumours of trouble had been heard in the south, the north had made open overtures to the King, and the east was menaced by invaders. It all recalled the dangerous, revolutionary period of the 1790s. But Fouché appealed, on this occasion, for a "system of moderation" guided by the Chambers. "The times have changed," he stated. No longer was it possible to pursue outdated practices like "seizing property, pursuing the families of the guilty, striking *en masse*, proscribing whole classes defined in terms of imaginary categories" (all state crimes Joseph Fouché understood because he had committed every one of them in person). No more could one return to a former age when policy was "not so wise and not so enlightened." After twenty-five years of turmoil, the idea of "the people" [*"le peuple"*] had changed; no longer was it simply a numeric majority, but more a quality that revolved around something that Fouché called "public opinion": "the opinion, [on which] the universality of citizens is derived, is based upon that of *the calm and enlightened people* [*"gens"*] of France and of Europe."

This was, in other words, an argument for representative rather than direct democracy, an argument for the "legislative power." "It is urgent, Sire," he concluded, addressing the Emperor and executive incarnate, "that the Chambers put their mind to the laws that current circumstances demand of them."[81]

Ninety years later, the patriotic historian, Henry Houssaye, would call the events that put Fouché in power a "parliamentary *coup d'état*."[82] They certainly did not conform to Napoleon's way of defining the law. But they were not a strictly parliamentary affair either. Parliament had buried itself in a constitutional debate – in the same way the former Chamber of Deputies had, a hundred days beforehand, pondered the issue of the "natural and inalienable rights of peoples" as Napoleon marched on Paris.

In addition to a parliament, France required the stern hand of government. This she got in the form of Joseph Fouché, regicide, Jacobin proconsul, slaughterer and revolutionary, minister of Barras and Bonaparte, a man totally lacking in principles. *"C'est l'homme nécessaire,"* said General Grénier as he cast the decisive vote at the Commission's first meeting that Friday morning. Carnot had nothing like the links that Fouché, at his police ministry, had been developing throughout Europe in the last few months.[83]

Fouché's method of government was by subterfuge. France had to assure that Napoleon's abdication was final? He played on everyone's fears. He assured liberals that parliament would be dissolved if Napoleon returned. He warned the supporters of Bonaparte that the Emperor's life was threatened if he remained in Paris. Thus he succeeded in removing Napoleon, first to Malmaison, and then to Rochefort.[84]

France was to seek an Armistice? "Plenipotentiaries have left in the name of the nation to negotiate with the Powers of Europe," he announced in his first public proclamation on 24 June. He didn't for a moment believe in their success. Their essential purpose was to assure that Lafayette would not present himself as a rival in government: Lafayette headed the delegation and disappeared, with Benjamin Constant, behind enemy lines. Fouché was also testing the web, the European web. Lafayette and his colleagues focused on the problem of Napoleon. On the same day they left Paris, Fouché sent an old friend of his, Monsieur Gaillard, in the direction of Ghent to discover if the "men of business" were interested in pushing the duc d'Orléans' candidature ("No," replied Talleyrand, but a slot might be found in King Louis' ministry for the duc d'Otrante – Fouché's official title, granted by Napoleon). The arch-Royalist the baron de Vitrolles was released from his prison in Paris on the day Fouché was elected president and told by Fouché in person that the secret goal of the Commission of Government was the restoration of King Louis:

"We are working in his service."[85]

Fouché was a master practitioner of secret diplomacy, as opposed to the open – and one might say ingenuous – method of Marshal Davout, commander of the forces at Paris. Davout would have sent a clear message to Louis' travelling court that their goal was Restoration. "There is no other way of saving the *patrie*," he explained rather desperately to Fouché on the 27th, before the first of the Allied troops had even been sighted. Fouché agreed; "but we have to know what the enemy wants," he cautiously added. He aimed at squeezing the maximum of favours out of the Allies for himself and his government – but most especially the former. He wanted to keep the fighting beyond the *barrières*, to quieten the militants, to calm the parliament, and to keep the shops of Paris open. He sought to square a circle. The situation demanded a man without principle: Talleyrand could not have accomplished the task that lay before Fouché in June 1815.[86]

The Muncipal Council, sitting "in permanence" in the gothic splendours of the Hôtel de Ville since the 28th, supported the policies of Fouché. In its first session, it elected a delegation to expose before him the *"effroyables malheurs"* that a defence of Paris would involve – "an eminently sage and paternal measure," commented the editorialist of the *Journal de l'Empire*, which was now sounding curiously Royalist. The following day, these calm and enlightened *gens* issued a proclamation to their fellow citizens. "Parisians!" one read on the posters placarded throughout the city, "It is not you who are called to pronounce on the great interests of the nation: free yourselves from all those who would counsel you to take a part...Your duty commands you not to be divided." Everyone knew who these divisive counsellors of the streets were.

That same day the Commission of Government declared Paris to be in a "state of siege" and posted its own declaration of what was to be done: only the *approaches* to the capital were to be defended, a task that was assigned to "troops of the line"; the *garde nationale ordinaire* (the regular and respectable National Guard) would police the city; federal sharpshooters (the *Fédérés-tirailleurs*, or the citizen volunteers who had managed to get into neither the regular army nor the regular National Guard) were to serve "as auxiliaries with the troops of the line."

The intent was obvious: the bad elements, Napoleon's most devoted supporters, were to be thrown out of town under the pressure of their own exuberance, their own pledges to defend *la patrie*. It is interesting to note the role the Commission of Government accorded to the poor peasants of the surrounding villages: "the inhabitants of the countryside will hasten to bring to the fortresses the largest possible quantity of food supplies and will dig the trenches that will protect the troops."[87]

The defence of the "approaches to the capital" was a very doubtful business. The *barrières* had been built for the purposes of taxation, not war. Lines of wooden stakes were placed along the front of the Butte Montmartre, the walls of the old abbey were crenelated, the windows of farm houses were bricked up, and, in whatever walls did exist on the north side of Paris, holes were pierced for shooting. And the peasants did suffer. E. Labretonnière walked out beyond the *barrières* on a hot summer's evening to discover a "long line of little shacks put up in haste by a cavalry regiment"; horses were peacefully grazing in the green wheat, while the soldiers had "harvested whole fields" for the purpose of thatch.[88]

Already on the 27th, there were complaints about the conduct of the *Fédérés-tirailleurs*; very few turned up for work and those that did removed their uniforms and insulted the passers-by. The defenders of Paris squabbled among themselves as well as with the local residents. The artillery parks had to be guarded because some of the inhabitants would sneak out at night and spike the cannon.[89]

On 29 June, the day Napoleon left Malmaison for Rochefort, rumours were rife that the Emperor was on his way to "save France." Napoleon's supporters in the Chamber had managed to publish a patriotic proclamation to the army and, that afternoon, were seen out on the defence lines between Belleville and Saint-Denis. Wrapped in their tricolour scarves, they set off a tumult among the troops and *Fédérés-tirailleurs*. Some chanted, *"Vive les représentants"* But for most of them it was *"Vive Napoléon! Pas de Bourbons!"*

In the meantime, the generals at Marshal Davout's headquarters became incensed, partly under the influence of the revolt in their army, partly because, most undiplomatically, Vitrolles, the Royalist, had accompanied government officials to one of the strategy sessions at La Villette. The generals planned a *coup d'état*: they would surround the Tuileries with troops, seize Fouché, and shoot him on the spot. Davout thought this was not a very good idea. But he did sign a proclamation to the Chamber protesting against the eventual return of the King. Many military men were worried about their futures.[90]

It is not difficult to understand why the Allied armies insisted on driving on to Paris without signing an armistice; if they failed to hold a strong upper hand, they could end up drafting their treaty with Napoleon or with a new military dictator of France.

One of the peculiar features of the defence of the "approaches" to Paris was that it was almost wholly concentrated on the north. The pont de Neuilly, to the west, was barricaded with a few carts, pots, and pans, but you could easily walk round them. Entry and exit at the northern *barrières* proved difficult; in the south you would have no trouble.[91] So all the Allies had to do, to assure themselves of success, was to attack Paris from the south. Fouché must have been aware of the situation, as must Davout, with his headquarters at the northern *abattoir* of La Villette. One is tempted to think they had done this deliberately: they emptied the city of soldiers and then opened the gates of welcome.

Like on 18 June, Paris awoke at dawn, on Friday, 30 June, to the bellow of cannon; only this time it came not from the Invalides, but was carried by a north-easterly breeze from the plain of Saint-Denis; and this was not to announce a new victory but was the beginning of a genuine battle. Hobhouse, who was now living near the place Vendôme, recorded that the cannonading was at times loud, at other moments faint; by five a.m. it had fallen silent. There then could be heard the distinct crackle of musketry; by eight o'clock, this too had faded. Was the battle already done? Had Paris capitulated? Hobhouse noted that that the people in Paris were ignorant of events occurring less than two miles away. Outside he noticed that many of the shops had been shut, but he did see soldiers loitering about and he presumed that they would hardly do this if they had just lost a battle.[92]

The sounds Paris heard were the raid launched by one of General Bülow von Dennewitz's divisions of the IVth Prussian Corps on Aubervilliers and Vertus. They met stiff resistance and pulled back after two hours, for those were their orders – it was simply a reconnaissance attack. Vertus was taken later in the day by an Anglo-Hanoverian force; the untrained *Fédérés-tirailleurs* suffered a number of casualties here. The Prussians in the meantime moved west, in search of a crossing of the Seine. Most of the bridges had been burnt down by the French the previous night, but the bridge at Le Pecq was still standing; by afternoon Tielemann's IIIrd Corps was in possession of the heights of Saint-Germain-en-Laye, from where he sent a brigade of Brandenburger and Pomeranian hussars on to Versailles – the eager Prussians were, not for the first time, overstretching themselves.[93]

The Commission of Government met early the next morning in the Tuileries. Everyone in the room wanted to sign a capitulation; nobody wanted to be seen doing it. At La Villette, Davout organised an offensive – rather like General Trochu during another siege, fifty-five years later – not to defeat the enemy, but to satisfy the enthusiasts in his own army. Like Trochu, he sent his forces towards Versailles. Unlike Trochu, he met with success. The Brandenburgers and Pomeranians proved no match for Exelmans' cavalry, part of former Grouchy's corps, which had wandered in the wrong direction in Belgium on the 18th and was filled with a kind of fury.[94]

It was a warm Sunday in Paris. The horses of the Prussians were paraded in place de la Concorde and a French squadron galloped down one of the dusty paths of the Tuileries with two of the standards taken in the previous day's action. There was a brief notice on the wounded, but the place Vendôme had been cleared and what struck Hobhouse, Labretonnière, and even the newspaper reporters was the cheerful look of the crowds; women, strolling in the alleys, stopping for a chat, showed off their finest silks and puffery; the men sat in staggered rows upon the benches, reading their gazettes "almost as tranquilly as if the main subject were England's parliamentary debates and the affairs of India"; the reading cabinets – "between the boulevard Montmartre and the Chinese Baths there are no less than twenty" – were crammed with young and old debaters, who supported their arguments with the "numerous maps of the seat of war" that were stuck upon the walls; all, save the two state theatres, remained open. No one knew what the Commission of Government and the Command were up to.[95]

Desperate efforts in fact were being made by both to conclude an Armistice, "pure and simple." As soon as Wellington heard that Napoleon had left the region of Paris he urged that this be accorded. Blücher was at first unwilling, but the Versailles affair had made him more cautious. Versailles was retaken that Sunday (Gneisenau reported to Wellington that "a lot of people came out of Paris to watch the combat and the Parisians witnessed the defeat of their troops").

At dawn on Monday, 3 July, the Prussians stormed Issy, south of Paris and by seven o'clock Zieten's Ist Corps, which had been so badly mauled during Napoleon's first offensive at Charleroi two and a half weeks earlier, was facing the remains of France's IIIrd and IVth Corps on the plain of Grenelle. Zieten sent a note to Davout. "If the deputies of the Government," it read, "declare to my aide-de-camp that they wish to surrender the town this day and that the French army also wishes to surrender, I will accept a suspension of arms."

The capitulation was signed at Saint-Cloud five hours later. For Paris, the war was done.[96]

The King's entry

The King's Council met that same day in Roye, a small town in southern Picardy on the frontiers of the Ile de France, a place almost equidistant between Paris and the Belgian border; it was about as isolated a spot as one could find on the map. Wellington had recommended it because, having contacted some of Fouché's negotiators, he realised that he had to have the King ready to make his move into Paris.[97] With the exception of Fouché, who had his own sources of information, most people in Paris, including members of the Commission of Government, thought the King was still in Ghent. At Roye, the web, woven by the "men of business" in Ghent and in

Paris, was drawn several notches tighter.

The inhabitants gave the King a warm welcome. Madame de Chateaubriand was mistaken for the King's daughter and carried in triumph into the royal dining-room, where there was a roaring fire (although it was summer) and a table laid for thirty. The landlady refused payment, explaining that for over two decades she had risked the guillotine for her King.[98]

It was in Roye that Talleyrand, the first to arrive, had been introduced to Monsieur Gaillard, Fouché's old friend. At last Talleyrand had a first-hand account of what was going on in Paris. He realised that Fouché was now the key man and could not be excluded from the King's government, despite the promise of vengeance against plotters in the Proclamation of Cambrai. But, then, the same document had declared as a principle the "unity of the Ministry" and a regime open to "all classes." Talleyrand prepared a new memorandum.[99]

On the morning of the Council's meeting he attached two extra horses to his coach and drove over to the King's inn; his team filled the courtyard, which had actually been reserved for the King. Majestically, he limped into the chamber, sat down and, for perhaps the only time in his life, read his own memorandum aloud. He described the kind of political "party" they could expect to be in control of Paris on their arrival and he spoke of the need to open the King's first government to everyone – including, he added, men who had judged and condemned King Louis XVI. King Louis XVIII went bright red in the face, banged his fists on the table, and screamed, "Never!"[100]

As Chateaubriand, who was present, put it, it was a "never" that lasted twenty-four hours.

News arrived of the capitulation just after the meeting. Talleyrand immediately sent a letter off to the duchesse de Courlande, who was then taking waters in Carlsbad. He expected to be in the capital within two days. "Your trip to Switzerland is now useless," he told her. "I advise you to come to Paris: it is the best way of passing one's summer." True, it could be a trifle difficult at first, what with the Allies occupying the town. But Wellington was doing an admirable job; indeed, "all alone, he conducts the affairs of everyone." Talleyrand had already informed the Allied commander of his intention to bring Fouché into the government – an idea London had been urging since spring.[101]

Within an hour of receiving the news, the King and his court were on the road again, only this time the scenery about them was less cheerful: no more the applauding crowds, the innkeepers were not as hospitable, there was a lack of food, and there were troublesome signs of violence. Somewhere between the village of Cavilly and the village of Gournay the royal procession passed a house in flames; a poor old widow stood on the porch.

The subject was mentioned just before the King sat for his dinner at Lihus. "What can I say, Messieurs?" he remarked. "It's not our fault. We shall manage like last year; time and patience will do the rest." That afternoon he ate in private. "You will have to manage as best as you can," he said in dismissing the dismayed Ministers; "but I do recommend you rabbit." The rabbits of Lihus were said to be the best in France.[102]

In the evening they rolled on in the direction of Paris, passing the bivouacs of the Prussians, the English, and the Hanoverians; eventually they came to a halt at the château d'Arnouville, on the north side of the capital. One looked out on the spires of Saint-Denis from its rooms. Both Chateaubriand and Beugnot speak in their memoirs of the emptiness of the place, but then they were among the Ministers being eliminated – as was the whole court party.

King Louis was by now surrounded by Fouché's men. There were people like H. Macirone, Esq., Italian by birth, British subject, former aide-de-camp to Joachim Murat, and now aide-de-camp to lord knows whom. But there were also teams of aging aristocrats, who urged the King to take Fouché into his government. The whole faubourg Saint-Germain seemed to be present – all petitioners of a single cause: "It's Fouché who protected us after the flight of the King," explained the bailli de Crussol, not a man to go demonstrating in favour of Jacobins; "we are old in the faubourg Saint-Germain, we have suffered too much, and we need repose."[103]

The movements of the Prussian and Anglo-Dutch armies during the last days of the campaign had led to the establishment of military command posts to the west of Paris. Blücher set up his headquarters at the château de Saint-Cloud on the left bank of the Seine. Wellington could be found at Neuilly, on the right bank, in another property belonging to Pauline Borghese, Napoleon's favourite sister; it was her former summer palace. Ambassadors gathered here, as did representatives of the King, representatives of Paris, and, of course, the disciples of Joseph Fouché. For three days, Neuilly was the capital of France.[104]

Wellington had laid down the conditions for the capitulation on 1 July, the moment he had confirmation of Napoleon's departure for Rochefort and before he had even got an accord from Blücher. It would be a strictly military convention, he told the plenipotentiaries from Paris that day: the Allies would advance no further; the French army would retire beyond the Loire; and the National Guard would police Paris until the King of France should order otherwise. There was no disagreement. These were exactly the terms signed at the château de Saint-Cloud the following Monday.[105]

Before Marshal Davout, in Paris, had even had time to ratify the agreement, Fouché had asked for an interview with Wellington. "I would be happy to meet Your Excellency," the Duke immediately responded, "wherever you wish and at whatever hour you name." On Wednesday afternoon, 5 July, Fouché was in Neuilly bowing before Wellington and his old ministerial colleague, the prince de Talleyrand.[106]

Was it there that a list of Ministers for King Louis' first formal government since exile was drawn up? Louis had a list in his hand by Thursday morning. But one name was still missing, that of Joseph Fouché.[107]

Most of Paris, on Monday, the 3rd, still imagined the war was going on. During the previous night crowds had gathered on the heights of Chaillot to hear and watch the flashes of the cannon as the Prussians advanced on Issy. At around eleven a.m. a French cavalry regiment, which had been stationed on the Champ de Mars, rode along the left bank of the Seine, presumably to take up positions in the line of battle. A whole infantry corps crossed the town in the early afternoon. Heavy patrols of the National Guard, without music, created a sombre, grim mood in the streets; groups of people collected around and trailed three straggling dragoons leading their wounded horses to place Vendôme for orders; the doors of the houses and courts were shut; occasionally an upper window would be thrown open as a gendarme clattered by on horseback. But there was no news.[108]

People were still expecting to hear the sounds of a great battle when, between four and five, the first rumours spread that Paris had capitulated.

The poorer quarters and the troops and *Fédérés-tirailleurs*, stationed to the north of Paris, did not hear the news until the following morning. "The *faubourgs* contain a terrible horde," commented the broadsheet *Patriote de '89*. "From the heights of Montmartre to the *barrières* of Saint-Antoine," reported the *Journal de l'Empire*, "gunshots, fired in the streets, on the bridges, in the boulevards, have been heard; cries of rage, threatening gestures, clamours, the galloping of horses, the discharge of arms have been repeated." The commotion was worst in "the most populous parts of town." Fouché's Restoration, in contrast to that of Talleyrand's in the previous year, did not pass tranquilly.[109]

Wellington had told the French plenipotentiaries on 1 July that "I would not consent to suspend hostilities as long as a soldier remained in Paris." With troops in Paris, he explained, there would be no Restoration and therefore there would be no peace.[110]

Carnot was brought in to organise the officers, for Carnot was still the Great Carnot. The National Guard of Paris was reinforced. *"Nous sommes trahis!"* cried the soldiers; "we have been sold off like beasts of the field." They spread through Paris in small groups, creating terror. Hobhouse saw them in the place Vendôme on their knees, weeping before the column of their sacrificed God. But evacuated they were. "The last of the troops of the French army," read the official bulletin of 6 July, "left the capital this morning to take up their stations behind the Loire."[111]

All the *barrières* were occupied that day by the Anglo-Dutch. "It is true we shall not have the vain triumph of entering Paris at the head of our victorious troops," admitted Wellington on urging Blücher to sign the Armistice on 1 July; but the following Friday, 7 July, fifty thousand Allied troops entered Paris and marched in parade down the Champs Elysées. The Prussians were, of course, the first to enter. Zieten's corps crossed the barrière de La Canette at eight o'clock in the morning and were standing in formation on the place du Carrousel, outside the Tuileries, as Fouché dismissed the final session of the Commission of Government. Napoleon's two Chambers were adjourned, with no objection, the night before and they would never meet again; the steps of the Palais Bourbon that Friday morning were packed with the National Guard. The gardens and all the gates of the Tuileries were shut and doubly guarded. Everywhere, however, the tricolour flag flew. Allied soldiers were given strict orders not to carry white. Poor old Monsieur Viosménil made the error of sporting a white cockade and was quietly conveyed to a guardhouse; a lady walking past the Tuileries with a bouquet of lilies in her bosom was ordered to remove the emblem and, on her refusal, had it taken from her "with as little rudeness as possible by one of the national guards." It was only that afternoon that Parisians learnt that the King of France was not in Ghent but on the other side of the barrière de Saint-Denis. Hobhouse was persuaded he would *never* enter.[112]

With the Commission of Government dissolved, Fouché left immediately for his palatial home at rue Cerutti, on the corner of the boulevard des Italiens, where he was spied standing in front of a mirror in a court costume, emblazoned with badges and heraldry: Fouché had an appointment with the King. In Saint-Denis he was greeted by crowds of admirers as France's new saviour.[113]

The King, in the meantime, had been forced to bow to the *homme nécessaire*. Fouché's nomination as Minister of Police demanded a decree because, unlike others appointed to the King's government, he had not, during the first Restoration, received a royal pardon – nobody at the time had quite felt the compulsion. Talleyrand asked Beugnot, who acted as secretary, to present the decree among other official papers that needed the royal signature. Beugnot put it at the bottom of the pile. The King cheerfully signed every piece, chatting about the weather and rabbits – until he came to the last slip of paper: "The King threw it a glance and let it drop on his desk; his plume fell from his hands; blood ran to his face; his eyes turned sombre and he sunk into an expression as if overwhelmed by the thought of death." There was a long silence. Then he sighed, "Well it has to be done! Let's get on with it." There were tears in his eyes as he accorded his pardon to one of his brother's murderers.[114]

Friday must have been a busy afternoon for Louis. Not only Wellington was at court. Britain's chief diplomat, Lord Castlereagh, had also just arrived.[115]

But Chateaubriand found time to wander in the gothic nave of Saint-Denis' grand abbey. Parts of it were still to be repaired. He bent a knee and said a prayer at the tomb where Louis XVI's remains had, five months earlier, been buried. Somebody was having difficulty persuading the girls' choir not to cry *"Vive Napoléon!"* After nightfall, with the noises of the Royalist supporters outside, he proceeded to the King's quarters. He was sitting in an antechamber – Beugnot claims to have been in his company – when a door opened and in hobbled the prince de Talleyrand with the help of a resplendent Joseph Fouché. It was "vice supported on the arm of crime," in Chateaubriand's brilliant eyes. They crossed the room slowly and entered the King's Cabinet.[116]

Fouché had ordered that all the gates of Paris be closed that Friday night. He had difficulty himself returning to rue Cerutti. The crowds that had swarmed to Saint-Denis were thus locked out and were forced to spend the night in the fields neighbouring the abbey. The night came to be known as *la campagne sentimentale de Saint-Denis*, a kind of rural bachanal held by city folk in celebration of the war's end; there was much dancing and fireworks exploded in the night sky.

But just as Fouché had succeeded in emptying Paris of Napoleon's enthusiasts at the time of the siege, so had he managed to exclude the larger part of King Louis' enthusiasts at the moment of peace. The gates were opened only minutes before the King made his entry on Saturday afternoon, 8 July 1815.[117]

At the barrière de Saint-Denis the whole Municipal Council was lined up to greet His Majesty, a battalion of the National Guard stood at attention, an orderly group of citizens gave a cheer, and Monsieur de Chabrol – who had been destituted by Napoleon and had just taken up again his functions as Prefect of the Seine – gave a little speech.

"Sire," he uttered, a white cockade trembling upon his cap. "One hundred days have passed since Your Majesty was forced to tear himself away from the affections of those most dear to him . . ." It was not a very good speech and Prefect Chabrol could not count. But the phrase, "One Hundred Days," was never forgotten.[118]

Louis entered Paris as he had left it, in a shut coach, and, since there were three or four carriages that looked exactly the same, it was difficult to know which one he was sitting in. He was accompanied by the National Guard, a detachment of the Swiss Guard, body-guards, foot and horse, old coaches and new coaches, diligences, and military wagons. Around the Tuileries awaited a crowd in exultation.

Captain Mercer of England's Royal Horse Guards thought how strange it was that the French should be so happy in their defeat. Labretonnière sulked in a café at the Palais-Royal. Hobhouse thought it all a show put on for "the degraded and numerous classes of municipal functionaries." Talleyrand sneaked in through the barrière de l'Etoile and drew up in the courtyard of his home on rue Saint-Florentin in a borrowed calèche still marked "Garde Impériale"; it was his first sight of Paris since the Congress of Vienna. But this was Fouché's Restoration, not Talleyrand's.[119]

For the great historian of the Revolution, Consulate, and Empire, Louis Madelin, 8 July 1815 marked "the end of principle" for both the Revolution and the Counter-Revolution, for both Jacobins and Royalists. It was certainly the end of an era. It was the day peace began in Europe.[120]

There was a thunderstorm that Sunday.[121]

EUROPE, EUROPE

Previous page: St Helena, south of the equator and lost in the seas, was a place where one might dream of a united Europe

Napoleon's Europe

Napoleon applied a little chalk to the tip of his billiard cue and remarked to his companion, General Gourgaud, "What leads me to believe that there is no avenging or rewarding God is that honest people are always miserable and the scoundrels happy." He took a glance at the sun beyond his northern window. "You will see, somebody like Talleyrand is going die in his bed."[1]

Talleyrand did, in fact, die in his bed, in 1838 in Paris, at the age of eighty-four, surrounded by members of his family, his friends, and old lovers. Just as the young abbé Dupanloup prepared anointment for the sacrament of extreme unction, Talleyrand closed his fists and muttered, "Don't forget, Monsieur l'abbé, that I am a bishop" – and he received the anointment on his palm, as a bishop should. Napoleon, however, might have been satisfied to learn that Joseph Fouché died in agony, disgraced, and in exile, on Christmas Day 1820. His body was so bent with rheumatism that a special box had to be designed as a coffin and he was buried in a sitting position, like the diligent functionary that he had, in effect, been for so many years at the Police Ministry.[2]

It was not the Kingdom of God that Talleyrand and Fouché restored to Paris in July 1815. Talleyrand set up a government at the Tuileries on the day after the King's entry; but it only lasted three months. Fouché was outmanœuvred by Talleyrand and Talleyrand was ousted by his King.

Nonetheless, these three months finalised the shape of post-war Europe, and both Talleyrand and Fouché left their mark. In the first place, Talleyrand did succeed in creating his "unified Ministry." The "men of business" were brought in, Talleyrand was named "Président du Conseil," and the Council of Ministers met on a regular basis to discuss matters of policy. This set the pattern of cabinet government in France for more than a century, it created a new, more healthy equilibrium between the executive and the legislative branches, and, not least significant, its leaders maintained their bond with other Europeans who no longer needed to regard France with fear.

Secondly, Talleyrand did not hesitate to carry out Allied demands for the liquidation of Napoleon's army. After their evacuation from Paris, the troops began a slow and disordered march southwards to Orléans. Infantry, dragoons, hussars, and artillerymen deserted in hordes "because the Emperor is no longer with us." They crossed the Loire on 11 July and were organised in camps on the left bank of the river; there were perhaps as many as a hundred thousand men among them, still angry, still ready to fight, and still armed. But within a fortnight, the corps were broken up, the commanders dismissed, and the troops scattered into small detachments of three to four hundred men relocated between the mountains of Auvergne and the Atlantic Ocean. Napoleon's army ceased to exist.[3]

As an extra precaution, a royal decree of 24 July proscribed fifty-seven individuals (of which nineteen were from the army) for "a conspiracy without precedent" (*"un attentat sans exemple"*). The Proclamation of Cambrai had called for the "vengeance of the laws," but a vengeance implemented by the King's two Chambers, which had not yet been called. Talleyrand thus opposed the measure. But the Allies were in no mood to wait, and they had their own man in the King's Ministry, Joseph Fouché. Fouché was only too willing to oblige. He came up with an enormous list, secretly hoping that they would all eventually receive amnesty. "In all fairness to the duc d'Otrante," quipped Talleyrand, "he hasn't omitted from his list a single one of his friends."[4] The list was eventually whittled down and the Minister of Police provided all those proscribed with a means of escape; coaches and carriages left for the frontiers carrying men with shaven moustaches. General La Bédoyère made the mistake of returning to Paris to say farewell to his wife; he was recognised, court-martialled, and on 19 August shot in front of a firing squad.

Fouché, ally of the Allies, was also the protector of liberals and old revolutionaries. He thought this is what would save him. Early in August he read to the Council of Ministers two memoranda, in which he warned of a possible national uprising over Allied exactions (Wellington, in fact, made an identical warning to London) and the excesses of Royalist factions in the south of France; then he promptly published them. Foreseeing the return of a liberal Chamber of Deputies, like that of 1814, Fouché thought these documents would turn himself into the hero of parliament.

If Wellington had not intervened, Fouché would have been dismissed on the spot. But nobody had imagined the kind of reactionary assembly that was returned by the elections of 14 and 22 August. It came to be known as the *"Chambre introuvable,"* an unhoped gift for the old court party. The British were dismayed. Castlereagh wrote to Liverpool to say that the new assembly represented the party of the comte d'Artois and the duchesse d'Angoulême (Louis XVI's surviving daughter): "it is a mere rope of sand without leaders, without any fixed system, but with an inordinate infusion of passion, resentment and spirit of inversion."⁵ Fouché could not be tolerated by this new Chamber. He was dismissed on 15 September. Talleyrand resigned less than two weeks later.

But their legacy to the nineteenth century could not be erased: a non-military France, a parliamentary France, and – despite the ephemeral *Chambre introuvable* (it would be dissolved the following year) – a liberal France.

The greatest loser was not Fouché, nor Talleyrand, but their former master on St Helena. Events did not follow Napoleon's simple line forward; in Longwood, the fallen Emperor had a few moments of uncertainty about the direction of the world and he wondered aloud about the meaning of life: where did it all come from ? where did it all go? "The drive in us was immense," he said, reflecting on his own short half century of existence. "There was prosperity and progress growing at unprecedented rates . . .The advance of Enlightenment in France was gigantic, ideas were everywhere, rectifying errors and spreading out." He predicted that public morality would eventually improve because it complemented natural law; once the great revolutionary forces of our time were released, nothing could withstand *le juste, le honnête, et le beau*. Yet over billiards he had to admit that scoundrels died in their beds.⁶

Napoleon dismissed the post-war age as a reaction. It couldn't be anything else. They were turning the clocks back. It was the revenge of old ruling classes, no longer capable of responding to the new destinies of Europe. Poland was occupied, Saxony had been partitioned, Austria was back in northern Italy, the Bourbons were in Paris and Naples. Napoleon, however, would insist that time in the end would catch up with his own grand schemes. "The first fury passed, people of intelligence and judgment will come back to me," he told the memorialist Las Cases one evening in confidence; "I will only have as enemies idiots and bad men."⁷

He kept on returning to his maps of Europe, for Napoleon was not only a soldier; he was also a scientist and geographer. That determined his whole view of Europe. He thought it essential to know how many cubic metres flowed in the rivers of Europe and wanted tables drawn up indicating the portion in each valley; he had proposed this project to the Institut in Paris. Those maps! He could gaze from one end of Europe to the other, he could estimate the distance from Cape St Vincent to the Kola Peninsula, he could put a finger on the Alps, and trace the plains of Germany. Poland, he said, thumping on Cracow and Warsaw, was "the veritable key to the whole vault." He would have set up a strong monarch in Poland. In destroying his empire, Napoleon argued, the Allies had created a disequilibrium in Europe: they had opened the way to Russia.⁸

Russia was going to inundate Europe, he repeated; Russia could dictate the future of Europe. Europe would belong to Russia if she had a real emperor – *un czar qui ait de la barbe au menton*. Napoleon boasted that, given the current situation and especially such a weak Poland, "I could be in Calais in a few days and I would be master and arbiter of Europe." "But, Sire, what would be the point?" one of his dining companions innocently inquired. "To found a new society," answered the Emperor. "Europe awaits, it solicits this service. The old system is at an end and the new one is not yet established, and will not be without yet further upheavals."[9]

Exactly what sort of Europe Napoleon envisaged after his soldier's peace is a matter of some controversy. Las Cases's *Mémorial* reports a number of fanciful schemes, but no other witnesses of Napoleon at St Helena gave the slightest hint of them. This was perhaps because Bertrand, Gourgaud, and Montholon were *only* soldiers; O'Meara and Antommarchi were not very accomplished doctors; whereas Las Cases was a writer and, moreover, the author of a famous *Atlas*.[10]

Again, it was Russia that represented for Napoleon the end and the beginning of Europe. A peace in Moscow (which he only missed, he maintained, by accident) "would have terminated my expeditions of war"; it would have been "the end of risks and the onset of security"; the Revolution would have been accomplished; the great work could begin and "the European system would be founded." Europe would have had one legal code, there would have been a single European currency (though "under different coins"), there would be uniform weights and measures. More important, Europe would have become a "single people," all belonging to the same *patrie*: they would travel from one end of Europe to the other and still find themselves in the same country; the rivers, flowing in cubic metres, would be open to all. There would be one, single European *Institut*, distributing European prizes for European-minded scholars; one, single "university." It would have been the most efficient empire the world had ever seen, with a uniformity of action felt across the entire territory – Napoleon likened it to the movement of the heart to the extremities.

Napoleon did recognise that there would be a certain local variety in this Europe of his, but even here he saw progress in uniformity. "One of my greatest thoughts," he told Las Cases, "was the idea of agglomeration, the geographical concentration of the same peoples." He wanted each of Europe's peoples to belong to one and the same national corps. "No doubt, if heaven had let me be born a German prince, I would have, with the various crises of our time, inevitably ended up governing thirty million united Germans." Italy, he predicted, would soon be a single nation. Europe would be a grand agglomeration, a "confederation of great peoples."[11]

One subject, corroborated by several witnesses, that suggests this dream of one Europe was not entirely a figment of Las Cases's imagination is what Napoleon reports he would have done if, instead of enjoying British hospitality on St Helena, he had emigrated to the United States. With the help of his brother Joseph – who now lived in Trenton, New Jersey, and had an extensive property in upstate New York – he would have founded his own state. He had total contempt for "elected presidents." He would have created a great *rassemblement national*, a *patrie nouvelle*, that would have particularly profited from Franco-Canadian discontents with the British. Moreover, in America he would have been able to exploit the dynamic force created by the French Revolution; "the current French Revolution," he told General Gourgaud, "is going to people America as Florence's Revolution peopled Corsica." Napoleon spoke of gathering around himself as many as a hundred and sixty million people, angry with Europe, but talented and educated.[12]

But Napoleon was ill. He became increasingly bitter over what he considered an unjust imprisonment by England's backward ruling classes. His greatest hope was that there would be a change in London's government. In April 1821, the last month of his life, he followed as closely as he could the Queen Caroline affair in the expectation that this would eventually bring down Lord Liverpool and his ministers. The last news he received came in, ironically, through the HMS *Wellington*: the government was still standing. "I die prematurely," he wrote in his last will, "assassinated by the English oligarchy." He left £500 to Wellington's would-be assassin and muttered to General Bertrand, "I would like to learn that *they* have lost Lord Castlereagh."[13]

Alexander's Europe

The Allied armies of Austria, Russia, and the various German princes were still struggling across the Vosges, in eastern France, when news arrived that Paris had capitulated; Napoleon's prediction that the country would be overrun by the Cossack and Tartar hordes could not occur overnight, even if this had been the Tsar's goal. But the Tsar, anyway, was thinking of God: "That He be a thousand times blessed for His countless good works," he wrote to the Grand Duchess Catherine on learning of the capitulation, "and let us remain deserving of His guidance."[14] The three Sovereigns and their Ministers called a conference and it was decided to make a rapid march on Paris "in light convoy;" they made their solemn entry into the capital on Monday, 10 July 1815, only two days after King Louis had established himself at the Tuileries. This time, Alexander decided to refuse Talleyrand's invitation to rue Saint-Florentin and, instead, set himself up at the Elysée Palace.

Like Napoleon, Alexander had a grand, unifying plan for Europe; he sought a Europe living in peace under one law. But whereas for Napoleon this law was the accomplishment of universal mankind, for Alexander its source lay in Christ. Both Alexander and Napoleon, however, paid homage to "the people."

Alexander's guardian angel would be, for this peace conference, the Baroness von Krüdener. She arrived in Paris on 14 July and installed herself with her daughter and a dozen members of her spiritual family in the Hôtel Montchenu, next door to the Elysée. A hole was knocked in the garden wall and nearly every night, during the following two months, Alexander would attend the baroness's prayer meetings.

Alexander missed the simplicity of the peasant's cottage outside Heidelberg and he frequently complained about the way in which the meetings were conducted, but he was convinced that they would provide the basis for a "pact of love" which would save France and all Europe. One of the leading figures at the meetings was "Papa" Bergasse, an elderly Mesmerist from Lyon, who expounded on the "high science" of the earth's regeneration with the aid of a spherical magnet, or "melon," that he hung from the ceiling. Maria Kummer was another major figure. During the meetings she frequently had visions of "our Angel," the "second Abraham" (i.e. Alexander), who would bring the mysteries of the cross to France, the "second Egypt."[15]

When not at meetings, Julie von Krüdener would write long missives to Alexander on the need to build a new Church that would unite all Christians of Europe, although, she warned, this was not something the Tsar could do alone: "You, who are so great and yet so much a child, I tell you without fear, you cannot advance without me." Alexander, in fact, did not show much interest in Krüdener's new Church and he made no commitment to its construction. But her idea of heading a mystical pilgrimage to save the *malheureuse patrie* of France led him to oppose all talk of the "right of conquest" among the Allies and to pursue, in conjunction with the British, a policy of moderation.[16]

Under pressure from the French members of Krüdener's circle – including Bergasse, Chateaubriand, and Madame de la Saumaye (a pious friend of the royal princes who had been excluded from Talleyrand's government) – Alexander agreed to performing a "public act," a grand prayer meeting that would signal the dawning of Europe's new peace and order. The idea was to enact it before the entire Russian army, which by August was gathering on the plains of Champagne. The chief Russian engineer, the Baron de Sarth, selected as a site Mont-Aimé, near Vertus, in the bleak, open lands south of Reims; he requisitioned peasants from thirteen villages to flatten the top of the hill, erect balustrades, and construct platforms that could contain not only an army of a hundred and fifty thousand men but also the huge crowds that were expected from Paris. The works were completed in a month.

A military review was finally held on this landscaped mount on Sunday, 10 September, in front of the three Allied Sovereigns, the diplomatic corps, a multitude of princes, and the Allied general staff. Wellington said, "I would never have believed it possible to bring an army to such perfection"; Emma, Lady Edgcumbe wrote to her father that "there never was a more magnificent sight"; Baroness von Krüdener admitted to her daughter that it was just "a lot of dust."

But she was impressed with the mass held the next morning. So, again, was Lady Edgcumbe. "I shall never forget," she wrote, "the moment when, having turned the point of the hill, [the army] burst suddenly upon our view, formed into seven open squares of 25,000 men each, placed at short distances one from another, and each with one side of the square formed by a green tent in which the service was to be performed." Eight altars were employed, the whole army knelt in silence, the perfume of incense drifted across the fields, the music was entirely vocal: "it seemed more like a tale in the Arabian nights than an occurrence of real life."[17]

On their return to Paris, the Russians were in a state of exaltation. Even Count Nesselrode, one of the most sober-minded diplomats at the Congress of Vienna, spoke of Vertus as "the most beautiful thing of the world!" Pastor Louis Empaytaz from Geneva was in the Hôtel Montchenu when Alexander paid a call on the Baroness von Krüdener. The Tsar and his entourage, he later reported, were in a state of "psychological shock." "This has been the most beautiful day in my life," exclaimed the Alexander. "Never will I forget it. My heart is filled with love for my enemies." He went on ecstatically talking about the experience into the early hours of the morning: old humiliations were overcome, old sufferings gone. He spoke of "interior voices" and how God had supported him throughout the terrible course of the war. "Whilst weeping at the foot of the cross," he explained feverishly, "I asked for the salvation of France."[18]

This was Alexander's mood over the next couple of days as he drafted, in pencil, his famous "Holy Alliance." Though it was formally addressed to the three Allied Sovereigns (the Tsar, the Austrian Emperor, and the King of Prussia), it was not initially designed as a personal association of monarchs. It was, instead, a treaty that concerned people and nations. Alexander's source of inspiration was probably an article Julie von Krüdener had published immediately after the mass at Vertus. In it, she demanded, in her usual extravagant way ("all breathing people implored, from the seven altars, the blood of the Man-God"), a new union of nations based on the Gospel.

Metternich described Alexander's treaty as "a mixture of religious ideas and liberal political ideas . . . The Holy Alliance was not founded to restrain the rights of peoples, nor to favour absolutism and tyranny."[19] This was certainly true before Metternich started tampering with the text. It was liberal and somewhat disdainful of monarchy. One can find early hints of Woodrow Wilson's "Covenant" of 1919 in Alexander's draft of the Holy Alliance.

The original version, consisting of a preamble and three articles, called for a completely new style of diplomacy "founded on the sublime truths that the eternal religion of God the Saviour teaches us." This religion was no longer to be uniquely applicable to private life "as has been thought up to this day," but was to provide the base for "consolidating human institutions and remedying their imperfections." The first article concerned fraternity: the Scriptures "order all men to regard themselves as brothers, the subjects of the three contracting parties." The second concerned nationality: participating governments and their subjects should "consider themselves as members of the same nation under the denomination of the Christian nation"; the three Allied princes were delegated by Providence to "govern the three provinces of this same nation, that is, Austria, Prussia, and Russia." The third article provided the possibility of extending the treaty to "all states willing solemnly to avow these sacred principles."[20]

If the text anticipated ideals of the twentieth century, it also bore a strong resemblance to the plan Novosiltsev had presented to William Pitt in the autumn of 1804; the old notions of the rights of the peoples, the league of the nations, an international law, and the determination to abolish war were still in there, now clad in the wrapping of the Holy Scriptures.

Alexander was in a hurry. He wanted the three Sovereigns to sign his treaty and the Ministers to approve it, so that he could leave Paris – "this damned Paris" – the following weekend. He presented the scheme in person to Kaiser Franz and King Frederick William. Juliette von Krüdener recorded in her diary that they received it "with joy and warmth." That was not the impression of the diplomats. Metternich said the two Sovereigns were highly embarrassed. Castlereagh noted that the Austrian Emperor "felt great repugnance to be a party to such an act" and that the King of Prussia "felt in the same manner."

If so, this didn't inhibit Alexander in any way. Having called on the two Sovereigns, he went round to the British Embassy to invite the Prince Regent to sign up too. Wellington and Castlereagh (who was on crutches as a result of an accident with a horse) were barely able to keep their faces straight as the Tsar elaborated on his strange views. "Foreseeing the awkwardness of this piece of sublime mysticism and nonsense, especially to a British Sovereign, I examined with Prince

Metternich every practical expedient to stop it," Castlereagh reported almost immediately to Liverpool.[21]

But Metternich could not stop it because his Emperor did not want to thwart Alexander, "however wild." Instead, he rewrote the treaty. In the first article, on "fraternity," he barred the reference to "subjects" and replaced the phrase "the three contracting parties" with "the three Monarchs": Metternich's Holy Alliance *was* a personal accord between Sovereigns and a celebration, not a condemnation, of the old cabinet diplomacy of Vienna. The reference to "provinces" was erased from the second article, as was the notion of "the same nation," while the relationship between Austria, Prussia, and Russia was redefined in patriarchal terms as "three branches of the same family," governed by *pères de famille*. Even the third article invited other "Powers," rather than "states," to accede to the treaty. If there remained in the text an idea of fraternity and of an ecumenical Christianity, it was left to the Sovereigns to decide what this meant.[22]

Metternich's version of the Holy Alliance was signed by the three Allied Sovereigns in Paris on Tuesday, 26 September 1815.

Two days later Alexander left, though he was not very happy. "I have nothing good to tell you about Paris," he wrote to the Grand Duchess Catherine from Brussels on 1 October; "basically all I saw about me was a desire to profit from this situation in France and the wish to indulge in this passion for vengeance." He, nevertheless, was convinced he had advanced the work of the Lord and, as he wrote to Roxandre de Stourdza from Bâle, he was proud to "belong to this nation unknown to the world, but whose eventual triumph advances with great strides." In Warsaw he promised a constitutional charter for his new Polish Kingdom, and then returned to old Russia, where he began to work on the problem of reform.[23]

Poland never got its constitutional charter. Russia was never reformed. Alexander's vision of a united Christian Europe had as dim a future as Napoleon's Europe of one law.

Alexander died unexpectedly in 1825 while staying in a winter retreat on the shores of the Sea of Azov. Some say he had caught malaria; others have argued it was typhus; there are those who think he was suffering from syphilis and those who prefer the theory that he was poisoned. But the most persistent story of them all is that Alexander faked his death and then retired to the Urals to become a saintly monk, known locally as Fyodor Kuzmich. Tolstoy intended to write a novel about this strange Tsar, his apocalyptic visions, and his mysterious death. It is said that when the Bolsheviks opened Alexander's coffin, one hundred years after his funeral, they were astonished to discover that there was nothing in it.[24]

Metternich's Europe

It was not just spite that led Metternich to empty the "Holy Alliance" of meaning; Austria could not live with the concept of "one nation." Nor was it a dogmatic archaism that had made him insist on the dynastic bond of the Sovereigns. Under Kaiser Franz, Austria had had her own revolution: she was a territorial hereditary Empire now. The peace of 1815 was not an end for Metternich's Austria, but a beginning. If Austria was to survive in a century of state centralisation and nationalism, then she would have to prove to Europe that she was politically useful, that she represented a bulwark of power in the centre, that she was independent, that the revolutionary days of French and Russian collaboration in the division of Europe were over, that the great tides of power that had swept across the continent had been stabilised. She also had to demonstrate, because of the way in which Central Europe was settled, that a central authority was compatible with cultural diversity. Brave pledges to "the people" for parliament and sovereignty could not achieve this because every "people" would demand their own parliament; but the dynastic bond could do it.

The remarkable thing is that Metternich also claimed his policy was based on universal truths, like Napoleon and Alexander. He was as much a son of the eighteenth century as they. He had an eighteenth-century man's high regard for nature and for science. But he came to conclusions that were the absolute antithesis of those of Napoleon and of Alexander. When Metternich said that policy was based not on novels but on history, he meant that a true statesman worked in accord, and not against, the laws of nature, that his actions had to be built upon the world as it existed, not on empty dreams. "It is not given to man," he once remarked, "to create out of nothingness."[25] Revolutions were dangerous because they were unnatural; they obstructed the physical harmony and equilibrium of the universe. Despotism, likewise, did not stand on solid ground; despotism was a symptom of weakness, not strength, and it somehow always managed, over time, to condemn itself. A real statesman was obliged to observe the given order of nature and let the universe develop at its own pace. This was why Metternich would accuse Napoleon of being a usurper and why he regarded Alexander as a "man with no science."

Metternich's constant effort to make history conform to nature's ways conditioned his view of Austria's – and Germany's – place in Europe. He wanted to maintain Germany as a whole historic entity that had a role to play in Europe. He resisted the idea of a narrow German federation, as advocated by Stein and his followers, first, because the plan was incomplete and denied Austria a part to play, and second, because, founded on a nationalist principle, it would turn

Germany into itself rather than open up the historical route into Europe. He had also opposed, for the same reason, the demands of the *Standesherren* for a return to the old Reich. Metternich pursued, and got in June 1815, a confederation of independent German states that he hoped Austria would lead into Europe. "For a long time," he wrote in 1824, "Europe has taken on for me the sense of a *patrie*."26

Throughout his life he would deny that what he created was, as his enemies called it, the "Metternich System." For him, it was nature's system, based on the eternal laws of the universe.

From the window of his house on rue Faubourg-Saint-Honoré, where he stayed through the summer and autumn of 1815, Metternich could look out on the Champs-Elysées, "transformed into an English military camp"; on two occasions he watched the Russian troops file by on place de la Concorde (renamed "place Louis XVI"); in July he visited Prussian headquarters at the Palace of Saint-Cloud – the soldiers were fishing out of the windows for carp and goldfish in the moat. These reminders of the commanding position of the British in Paris, of the presence of the Russians, and of the destructive Prussians out in the suburbs did help Metternich grasp nature's ways and define Austria's position in post-war Europe.27

Metternich's policy in Paris was to develop as close a tie as possible with the British while keeping his distance from the Russians. He did not, in particular, want the Russians to become the sole defenders of defeated France. At the same time, he wanted Austria to be the champion of German interests. An association of Britain, France, and Austria against Prussia and Russia – along the lines of the secret treaty of January 1815 – would have suited nicely Metternich's vision of Europe. He would have made a tacit Anglo-Austrian alliance key to the system: the flanking powers on the continent would have been checked, Prussia would have been marginalised, while Austria would have maintained her privileged position in Central European affairs.

Prussia in the end was successfully marginalised. But the British, and particularly Wellington and Castlereagh, became suspicious that Austria was trying to create Anglo-Russian tensions for her own purpose. This was the point where the troubled history of the Austrian Empire began: without British support, Austria would be forced to fall back on the association with her powerful neighbours, Prussia and Russia. At first ridiculed by Metternich as "an empty resonating monument," the Holy Alliance became, with the years, one of the main instruments of Austrian foreign policy.

At Paris, however, Metternich was characteristically proud of his achievements. Until Gentz arrived in mid-August, it was he who acted as secretary and who drafted all the protocols. If the atmosphere in Paris was similar to to that of Vienna during the Congress – nearly all the main personalities were there, including the Courlande sisters and Princess Bagration – Metternich this time successfully imposed his own style of cabinet diplomacy: discussion of the terms for the new Treaty of Paris would be limited to a Conference of the Four Allies; the Secondary Powers would be informed of their decision; with France there would be no negotiation – she would simply be presented with a declaration of the Allies' will.

In early August, Metternich wrote triumphantly to Joseph Hudelist, who was standing in for the Foreign Minister in Vienna, that "the union of the cabinets is complete" and, what was more, "from the very beginning it was I who organised the conduct of affairs." Whether it was peace or war, whether he was in Prague, Leipzig, Vienna, or Paris, Metternich always seemed to find himself at the centre of nature's universe. In November, shortly before the Second Treaty of Paris was signed, he wrote to his wife, "Certainly, if I am not the greatest minister in the world, I am at least the most active negotiator of Modern Times." Nature and Metternich never changed.[28]

He probably had Hager's spies in mind when he wrote to his wife to summarise his achievements since becoming Austria's Foreign Minister in 1809. Austria, he said, comes out of this war "stronger by 2,500,000 souls and with more territory than she had at the height of her splendour (Charles V excepted) and with a return of more than double the funds she paid to France in all the earlier wars." While Austria had made no territorial demands at Paris (she had, after all, won all she wanted at Vienna) she had been pushing for a steep reparations bill to fill the empty Habsburg coffers.[29]

But it had taken the Allies five months to negotiate the second Treaty, whereas the first had been done in a month. Castlereagh blamed the delay on the demands of the Austrians and Prussians – the longer it took, the more they were paid. But a more fundamental reason was that the cohesion of the Alliance had begun to crack. They had been close to war with one another in January 1815. The Hundred Days was merely an interlude.

The development after 1815 that most damaged Metternich's alliance system, which was reliant on its association with the Western Powers, was Britain's gradual abandonment of Europe. As a result, Germany eventually did turn into itself.

"For *Europe*," George Canning told a cheering House of Commons in 1822, "I shall be desirous now and then to read *England*." When, that year, Canning succeeded Castlereagh at the Foreign Office he gave England his priority and laid the ground for a generation of empire-builders, who would let Europe fend for itself. Austria, the "bulwark of Europe," became dependent upon the goodwill of her neighbouring rivals. It would be increasingly difficult for her to demonstrate the benefits of a dynastic, culturally diverse state.

The national impulse eventually proved irresistable. The partial German solution – a centralised northern German national state – became the dominant solution; the idea of an old Reich was revived once more by the losers at the Congress of Vienna.

In the process, Metternich's own tenets of policy became increasingly rigid. "The true merit of a statesman," he commented late in his life, after hearing a British Peelite defend the need to make concessions, "consists of governing so as to avoid a situation in which concessions become necessary." It was not a policy that a weak power could indefinitely maintain. But it did help Metternich hide Austria's weaknesses for more than a generation.

Metternich was forced to resign at the outbreak of the Revolutions of 1848. "For thirty-nine years I played the role of a rock, from which the waves recoiled," he said, persisting in his idea that the laws of good government were eternal; "On 14 March [1848], nothing happened save the elimination of one man." He warned the liberal opposition that Vienna was not Paris, that they would never be able to create a centralised national capital out of the *Residenzstadt*; that their parliaments would never have the authority of the House of Commons or the Chamber of Deputies. Yet the great Austrian multicultural experiment managed to continue for another seventy years.[30]

Emma, Lady Edgcumbe, who had become Countess Brownlow through marriage, met Metternich when he came to England immediately after his resignation. "Though age had told upon him," she said, "flashes of his former brilliancy at times shone forth." The new Austrian government allowed him to retire to his summer villa on the Rennweg. Count Hübner visited him there on 25 May 1859, when Metternich was eighty-six years old. "I was a Rock of Order," he repeated to the Count, as he sat at his writing desk, erect, cold, proud, and distinguished – not so very different from the way he had sat in the *salons* of Dresden and Paris fifty years earlier. Vienna's sun shone low into the room, picking out the gilted ornaments of his century. "A Rock of Order," he mumbled again. Three weeks later, he was dead.[31]

Castlereagh's Europe

One with no taste for universal theories was the man Napoleon damned on his deathbed as the emblem of "English oligarchy," Lord Castlereagh. Castlereagh had always considered himself a pragmatist, the inheritor of Pitt. The aim of the policy was a "just equilibrium" of power in Europe; no fancy ideas were needed to understand it. It had always been Britain's policy: constant opposition to the development of any single Power's dominance on the continent. But Castlereagh had gradually transformed an old island policy into a European policy – and the closer he came to achieving his goal, the more he found he had to explain himself. Theory and "principle" lay around the corner.

Pitt had initially designed his scheme for an island at war: it consisted of building up coalitions, as the occasions arose, to oppose the dominant Power, the source of hostility. No theory there. Castlereagh, on the other hand, had to devise a policy for a continent at peace: his responsibility was to avoid accidents and preserve a European equilibrium that had been purchased at a heavy price. His "principle" was, as he had told Samuel Whitbread in March 1815, "to effect great practical objects for the general security of Europe." General security implied stability; stability implied a system. Pitt, always at war, didn't need to worry about systems. Castlereagh, faced with a general peace, was obliged to. But that was not a way of thinking to which the British were accustomed. Castlereagh's defence of his European system brought him into conflict with "public opinion," with the press, with some of the most cherished beliefs in parliament, and with his own government.

The origin of Castlereagh's new system lay in the need to guarantee the peace. The Final Act of the Congress of Vienna had redrawn the political frontiers of most of Europe; the second Treaty of Paris, signed in November 1815, had done the same for France. But no guarantee was written into either of these treaties. It would have been the height of irresponsibility not to worry about this.

The philosophy in Britain was that no formal guarantees were needed. There was a feeling that, with the conclusion of peace, the great changes in Europe had come to an end, the drama of its history was over, and that the mechanical balance of power now achieved on the continent would somehow maintain itself; Britain could at last put her own house in order and, protected by the Channel, pursue greater glories elsewhere. Alexander's Holy Alliance represented the opposite opinion: it offered an absolute guarantee by imposing an ideological conformity thoughout Europe – which was exactly why Castlereagh so vigorously resisted it.

Castlereagh, as always, found himself in the middle. He rejected Alexander's "sublime piece of mysticism and nonsense," but he could not accept British disinterest in guarantees either. The Allies, he had reminded Whitbread, had resorted to arms to "preserve *the whole of Europe* from subjugation." Here he was alluding to another of Pitt's principles: that a just equilibrium could only be achieved in Europe if supported by an "overwhelming force." Translated into the terms of a European peace this meant military commitment. After the treaties were signed in 1815, there were those in Britain who thought such a commitment could be abandoned. Castlereagh was convinced it could not. That, in the end, was the cause of Castlereagh's own tragedy.

Some of Castlereagh's most articulate statements of "principle" –

eloquence was not his greatest quality – had been forced out of him in his debates with Whitbread. The news of his opponent's death was announced in Paris during the first week of the Allied occupation. Castlereagh was reportedly very moved. Thomas Creevey, the Whig diarist, met him at a ball given by the Duke of Wellington, who was now living at the Hôtel de la Reynière. Castlereagh had approached him to ask him if he were not greatly surprised at Whitbread's death and "the manner of it." Creevey noted, "we had a good deal of conversation on the subject."[32]

There were many balls, dinners, and suppers held in Paris during the summer and autumn of 1815. In this respect, Paris was a re-enactment of the Congress. Lady Castlereagh's *soirées* in the Borghese Palace had the same reputation for tedium as they had had in Vienna. Friedrich Gentz, who arrived in Paris in August, has left a record of how he prepared for them: "Accompanied Schulenburg to the *bordel*, then, at 10.30, to a *soirée* and ball at Lady Castlereagh's"; or, "Off for a round of *libertinage* in the faubourg Saint-Denis, then a dinner at Lord Castlereagh's." Yet there would be princes and archdukes present, along with English nobles and Scottish lairds, and a fair number from Britain's literary establishment, like Mr Jeffrey of the *Edinburgh Review*, Shelley, Lady Caroline Lamb, as well as Sir Walter Scott.

It was not long after news of Whitbread's death spread through town that Scott attended one of Lady Castlereagh's suppers. Her husband, with extreme gravity, astonished his guests with a ghost story.[33]

Castlereagh described a night he had spent in Ballyshannon, a small town in the west of Ireland where he had been billeted as a young lieutenant-colonel in the Londonderry Militia more than twenty years earlier. Preparation were being made for a possible French invasion. It was winter, Castlereagh had spent a long day on exercise with his company, he was tired and in low spirits. A fire of wood and peat blazed in the large fireplace that warmed his room. With a feeling of solitude, he watched it from his pillow before falling asleep. Some hours later he awoke. The embers in the hearth were still aglow. Then suddenly they flared up and, according to sombre Castlereagh, a naked male child stepped into the room and approached his bed. With every step it took, it grew larger, until "it had assumed the appearance of a ghastly giant with a bleeding wound on the brow and eyes glaring with rage and despair." Castlereagh jumped out of bed and "confronted the figure in an attitude of defiance": it retreated, reassumed its childlike form, and disappeared into the fire. Castlereagh returned to bed.

There was an obvious image in that story of the growth of menace, and menace defied.

The greatest menace to the peace of Europe in the summer and autumn of 1815 came from Prussia. This was in part a child of Castlereagh's own policy of "bringing Prussia forward" to the Rhine. Britain was wholly unconscious of the new danger. Castlereagh suddenly became aware of it during his first week in Paris, the week he learned of Whitbread's death.

On their entry into the capital the Prussians demanded that the city pay a hundred and ten million francs as a war indemnity and, in addition, provide equipment and lodging for a hundred and ten thousand men. They then announced they were going to blow up the pont d'Iéna (one of Napoleon's two new bridges that was named after the battle of 1806). Louis XVIII immediately sent notice that he was going to install himself on the bridge and "they can blow me up if they want to." Britain and Russia managed to stall Prussia on her financial demands while the bridge problem was resolved by changing its name.[34]

But that was only the beginning of difficulties. Wellington warned Castlereagh on 14 July that the behaviour of Prussian troops, "now imitated by the Bavarians," could lead to a kind of national war similar to the Spanish struggle he had witnessed against the French. "We are getting into a very critical state," he cautioned, "and you may depend upon it that, if one shot is fired in Paris, the whole country will rise in arms against us." Words of admonishment were not enough. By mid-August, Prussia had poured over a quarter of a million troops into France; the Bavarians lost no time in forwarding their own army "from Munich to the Loire in waggons"; Württemburgers, Nassauers, and Badeners started staking out their claims. "The fact is," lamented Castlereagh, "we have now before us demands from every State, however feeble, that either borders or approaches France, desiring to have some portion." The main problem to be resolved in Paris was not "between us and France: it is, in truth, a question much more between us and our Allies."[35]

The Cabinet in London, however, still concentrated on the French menace. They sought an absolute security against their old enemy and had little concern for the new threat. Indeed, the dispatches from London throughout the summer of 1815 showed a lot of sympathy for the demands of the neighbouring countries. Bathurst, for example, pointed out that the Prussians had suffered grievously in the previous wars and he thought they had a strong argument for "a more vigorous policy." Liverpool reported to Castlereagh that the prevailing idea in Britain was that "we are fairly entitled to take back from France the principal conquests of Louis XIV."

London's challenge induced Castlereagh to articulate a policy in collaboration with his old diplomatic partner, the Duke of Wellington: first, a policy on France and, second, on the whole future of Europe.

Just as during the October crisis of the preceding year, when Castlereagh faced the opposition of his own government over his policy on Saxony and Poland, Wellington proved again, in the summer of 1815, to be a crucial source of support. The two men worked for the cooperation of Russia, a "remote Power," to curb the demands on France from the "limitrophe Powers." The Tsar proved to be most cordial. If his mind, in 1814, appeared to focus on conquest and dominion, this year – remarked Castlereagh – "he is disposed to found his own glory upon a principle of *peace* and *benevolence*." Late in July the British government received a Russian note (heavily edited by Wellington and Castlereagh) that firmly opposed any permanent reduction of French territory.[36]

Meanwhile Castlereagh, again with Wellington's support, emphasised in his dispatches to London the need of strengthen King Louis XVIII's authority. "The justice of a demand for any great cession is doubtful," noted Wellington in early August. Castlereagh added the point – that would not be fully comprehended by Liverpool's Cabinet – that "the European Alliance can be made powerfully instrumental to [the King's] cause." Castlereagh was already advancing his European system.[37]

Later that month, Wellington and Castlereagh attacked directly the problem of dismembering France. They argued that Prussian demands went both too far and not far enough. What was the purpose of annexing a few fortresses? asked Wellington. That August, Napoleon's troops were still holding on to a number of frontier fortresses; it didn't provide them with much power. "If the policy of the united Powers of Europe is to weaken France, let them do so in reality," said Wellington. "Let them take from that country its population and resources as well as a few fortresses." Either they suppress France, or they pursue a policy of proportion and allow the King to "take his fair share in the concerns of Europe"; the third, middle, alternative would be a policy of permanent war. Wellington argued for the temporary occupation of north-eastern France to allow time for the neighbours to build up defensive barriers and for the King to consolidate his authority. Castlereagh then added another European point: the temporary occupation of France would "preserve Europe in a continued state of alliance," while permanent cessions of territory "would be melted down into sovereignties."[38]

Liverpool's Cabinet never understood what Castlereagh was actually driving at. Late in August, Castlereagh's brother, Charles Stewart, who was not the grandest diplomat, came over to London to urge on the Cabinet the idea of a temporary occupation. Liverpool thought the policy "entirely novel" and involved "serious inconveniences." But the Cabinet endorsed the policy without fully realising the principle that lay behind it.[39]

Castlereagh was determined not to let the neighbouring Powers seize any of the old Bourbon territories because this would undermine the King's authority and almost certainly lead to another war. He led a vigorous campaign against Prussian demands for Lille, Alsace-Lorraine, and "all the great places of the monarchy." But in September, the old borders of 1790 were finally breached when Prussia successfully negotiated the cession of Sarrelouis, an area that had been occupied by Louis XIV in 1680. It was not a sizable stretch of territory, but, within decades, it would develop into one of the most important centres of Europe's iron and coal industry; contention over Sarrelouis, or the Saarland as it came to be known, would poison Franco-German relations until the late 1950s. Talleyrand resigned over the issue of ceding "ancient territories," and the King's authority was for a while looking shaky until a new government was formed under the duc de Richelieu, descendent of the famous cardinal and a man close to the Tsar.[40]

Besides Sarrelouis, the inroads made into the old Kingdom of France were, fortunately for Castlereagh, not enormous: Condé and Givet were incorporated into the United Netherlands, the Prussians received the fortress of Landau in northern Alsace, a few rectifications were made to the Swiss frontier, and most of Savoy, in the south-east of France, was handed over to the King of Sardinia. The indemnity was settled at seven hundred million francs (Prussia had been demanding twelve hundred million) and the occupation force was limited to a hundred and fifty thousand men posted in frontier zones for a period of five years. There was a great outcry in Paris when the Louvre was emptied of the artworks looted by the French in the previous two decades. But the new Treaty of Paris was signed on 20 November. It could hardly be regarded as a punitive peace.

That very same afternoon, Ministers of the Four Allies – Britain, Austria, Prussia, and Russia – assembled in the British Embassy to sign a treaty that created what came to be known as the Quadruple Alliance. Castlereagh presented this to his own Cabinet as a renewal of the Treaty of Chaumont. But Chaumont had been a treaty against France; this was something else. The first articles, it is true, were aimed at protecting the arrangements made in the second Treaty of Paris, and that is what the British Cabinet concentrated upon. But the final article outlined a new European system of regular exchange between the Allies, a new form of diplomacy by conference. It was agreed that periodic meetings would be held "by the high contracting Parties . . . for the consideration of the measures which shall be considered the most salutary for the repose and prosperity of nations . . . and the peace of Europe."[41]

This would have institutionalised the Congress system as it had evolved in Vienna, it would have recreated, through regular conferences, a "Europe without distances": it would have placed the Continent under the tutelage of the Great Powers. This was Castlereagh's answer to the Holy Alliance. He had excluded its moral elements, dismissed the attempt to mould Europe's identity after one man's will, and had introduced in its place a collegial system. Castlereagh was transforming Pitt's old war expediency of the "balance of power" into a system of peace; a "great machine of European safety," he called it. "The treaty of Alliance that was signed in Paris between the Courts of London, St Petersburg, Vienna, and Berlin," he announced in a circular to all British ambassadors on 1 January 1816, "will prove to you the intimate union that subsists between Sovereigns and Allies for the preservation of the peace and independence of Europe."[42]

His natural ally was Metternich, who had initially rejected the idea of the Holy Alliance for the same reasons as Castlereagh and also saw Europe as a collection of sovereignties organised in conference – a cabinet diplomacy.[43]

Little of this was understood in London. Castlereagh's correspondence with his government colleagues never once mentioned the famous Sixth Article of the Quadruple Alliance. Was he deliberately misleading them? Silences do not necessarily tell a lie. Castlereagh – like all of Britain's diplomats on the continent – was isolated, aware of problems that no one saw in Britain, and unable to communicate because of that.

As long as France remained occupied, the pretence could be maintained that the essential purpose of the Alliance was to guard against the resurgence of French aggression. But in 1818 France, with help from Barings Bank, paid off her indemnity and the last of the foreign troops were withdrawn. A Congress was called at Aix-la-Chapelle (or Aachen), in the new Prussian lands on the Belgian frontier, not only to discuss the withdrawal but also to invite France to join the Alliance. The delusion both Castlereagh and his government had been harbouring for three years was broken for good. Aix-la-Chapelle was the first European conference Castlereagh had attended since Paris; it also proved to be his last.

At the conference, Tsar Alexander presented another of his grand schemes, an *Alliance Solidaire*. Castlereagh fought it tooth and nail. But having won his battle (thanks largely to Metternich's collaboration), Castlereagh boasted in a letter to Bathurst of "a new discovery in the European government," which gave "to the counsels of the Great Powers the efficiency and almost the simplicity of a single state."

A European state? Liverpool wrote to Castlereagh to warn him of the new parliament elected that year; it was not "accustomed to discussing foreign affairs," he cautioned. But a more immediate problem was the return to government of Castlereagh's old rival, George Canning. Bathurst, in his reply to Castlereagh, reported that there was real opposition within the Cabinet to his policies now. Canning not only denounced the idea of periodic meetings between Allies, he opposed the whole system. It got Britain too entangled in Europe's affairs. Britain's true policy, argued Canning, was never to intervene in Europe except in moments of real emergency. Canning had parliament behind him, as well as the press.[44]

From that time on, Castlereagh pushed the "principle of non-interference" to the fore. This was not entirely inconsistent with his policy, which was still essentially that of a mechanical balance of sovereign states, even if supposedly held together by his conference system. But the idea of regular conferences was abandoned.

Castlereagh, like all his colleagues, became preoccupied with grave domestic issues – themselves a product of the war. The more Britain withdrew into her shell, the more rigid became the Alliance system that she was so determined to ignore. The Alliance's actions became illiberal. Castlereagh himself denounced its efforts to stifle constitutional movements in Spain and in Italy. He began to distinguish between the "representative" governments within the Alliance (Britain and France) and the "more purely monarchic" governments (Austria, Prussia, and Russia). It was true, a division was appearing within Europe – a division for which Britain bore a heavy responsibility.

In the spring of 1821 Alexander Ypsilanti, a Greek who had spent his life in the Russian army and had been a friend of Emperor Alexander, led a band of soldiers from Russia into Turkish Rumania and made a call for Greek independence. The idea that part of the Ottoman Empire might become Greek, under the control of the Russians, was not something that Metternich liked to contemplate. He was suddenly converted to the "principle of non-interference" and appealed to Alexander not to support the Greeks in their call for independence. Castlereagh made the same plea. The old bond between Castlereagh and Metternich was thus revived, the old combination between Britain and Austria's multinational empire was restored, and for a moment it appeared that Castlereagh's European system might get a new life.

In October 1821, George – no longer Regent but King – accompanied Castlereagh to Hanover to meet the Austrian Emperor and his Chancellor; he was so delighted with his visit that he asked Castlereagh to be his Prime Minister, an offer Castlereagh declined out of loyalty to Liverpool. A Congress was promised the following year at Verona.

On 29 June 1822, a week before parliament was adjourned for the summer, Castlereagh wrote to Metternich to confirm that he would be attending the Congress; he would leave around 15 August, pass through Paris and then Vienna, before heading for Verona. "You will be informed by my brother and Prince Esterhazy of the opinion that we have here of recent events," he concluded, "but the consequences will require a deep and anguished examination when we see each other." The writing was more cursive than usual and suggested traces of strain.[45]

Princess Lieven, the Russian Ambassador's wife, was seeing a lot of Castlereagh at that time; she met him regularly in Kensington Gardens before he went down to the House of Commons. She wrote to the man who had been her lover since the Congress of Aix-la-Chapelle – Prince Metternich – to tell him about her encounters. Castlereagh, she reported, looked "ghastly" and had "aged five years in a week. . . one can see he is a broken man."[46]

The day after parliament was adjourned for the summer, the Cabinet held a meeting to discuss Castlereagh's trip to Verona. It was Wednesday, 7 August. Liverpool read the instructions. Castlereagh said not a word. "He appeared very low, out of spirit, and unwell," remarked Wellington, who was present. Liverpool, on the other hand, didn't notice anything in particular; he later reported that Castlereagh was "very well."

When the meeting was done, Wellington accompanied Castlereagh across St James's Park to his home. Castlereagh clung to the Duke's arm; he was "remarkably low and silent."[47]

The end of the beginning

In 1811, Castlereagh had taken a life lease on a small property just outside London and not very far from the Dover Road. After 1815, the hordes of cross-Channel travellers could read in their guidebooks that North Cray Farm was the residence of the famous Foreign Secretary, who had negotiated the peace of Europe. There was a small gate at the entrance and the path up to the front door was screened by thick laurel bushes. Lady Castlereagh was normally to be found in the garden in a muslin dress, a large straw hat on her head, an apron round her waist, a pair of scissors in her hand, cutting away dead flowers. Otherwise she would be in the greenhouses or the menagerie, at the back of the house, where she kept antelope, kangaroos, emus, ostriches, and a tiger that had been brought over from India for Wellington, who then passed it on to his friend.[48]

The property had a magnificent view of the rolling hills of northern Kent. Castlereagh used to enjoy taking a saunter in his gardens after an early dinner, or riding out in the evening into the adjoining fields. Castlereagh had a taste for the country because he was raised in the country; at North Cray he would often think of Ireland. At the foot of the property ran a narrow river: it was hardly Strangford Lough. His private secretrary, Hamilton Seymour, found him here on Thursday, 8 August 1822. He was walking at a heavy lifeless pace, at one moment fixing his eyes on the ground, at another, gazing towards heaven. Seymour went down to join him. "I hope your lordship is looking forward with pleasure to our Continental trip," he said in an effort to cheer him up. Castlereagh drew his hand across his forehead and answered very slowly, "At any other time I should like it very much, but I am quite worn out *here*." He kept his hand on his forehead. "Quite worn out here," he repeated, "and this fresh load of responsibility now put upon me is more than I can bear."

Ministers and ambassadors would visit Castlereagh at North Cray. He would show them around his six-room house. On the ground floor was a dining-room and a drawing room, which combined as a study for the Minister. Upstairs were two bedrooms. The Castlereaghs' room opened into a corridor, on either side of which was a dressing-room, Lady Castlereagh's on the right, his lordship's on the left, separated from the bedroom by a thin partition. Castlereagh's dressing-room was not, in fact, much more than a corridor itself. At the end of it, opposite the door, was a window and his lordship's washing-stand – with a drawer, in which he kept his toilet articles.

Entertainment at North Cray was about as exciting as it had been on the Minoritenplatz or at the Borghese Palace. Princess Lieven tells how, at one ball, all the guests went out for a stroll in the garden, with the exception of "little girls, dancers of the calibre of my husband and the master of the house, a few old women, and myself." Some of the all-male parties went better. One of them was held on Saturday, 3 August 1822, just before the adjournment of parliament.

Many of the members of the government were present, including the Duke of Wellington, Charles Arbuthnot, John Wilson Croker, William Huskisson, and Sir Robert Horton Wilmot. Wellington recorded that he had never seen Castlereagh "more decided or more clear in his mind." Croker noted in his journal that he appeared so happy, so aimiable, so contented with all about him; "we all congratulated him on having so well recovered from the fatigues of the [parliamentary] session." Arbuthnot called out a toast to Castlereagh. Castlereagh suddenly stood to his feet with a grave look on his face as though something very serious was about to happen. It was just the wine, he explained. Wellington noted that he had been drinking more than usual.

After the dinner, Castlereagh, Wellington, and Arbuthnot discussed several anonymous letters that threatened to expose an adulterous affair between Harriet Arbuthnot and Wellington. Wellington was not the sort of person who could be easily blackmailed. The author

North Cray Farm, on the Dover Road, Kent

had already been identified, a certain Mr Jennings, who had been seeking public employment for some years. Strangely, it was Castlereagh who was most upset about the letters. He appeared to think the accusations were aimed at him.

Castlereagh had lost his father the preceding year, just, in fact, as the Greek rebellion was getting under way. He had always been in correspondence with his proud father. "What are all the feelings and rejoicings of others," wrote old Lord Londonderry in December 1815, when he heard of Castlereagh's return from Paris, "when compared with the parental exaltation and transport I experience when I reflect on the goodness of Providence in blessing me with such a son."[49] In April 1821, Castlereagh became the second Marquess of Londonderry. In history, however, he remained Lord Castlereagh.

For his enemies, he likewise remained Lord Castlereagh. "Allow me to present to you Viscount Castlereagh," announced "Orator" Hunt from the hustings at Covent Garden, where Castlereagh had turned up to support the Tory candidate. Castlereagh and his companion had to seek refuge in a shop on St Martin's Lane. His friend managed to seek help from the police at Bow Street, and Castlereagh was then escorted by the police, followed by the mob, until he disappeared into the Admiralty. Just before slamming the door, he turned round, took off his hat, and smiled to the jeering mob, "Gentlemen, I thank you for your escort!"

It was the war that had created the economic difficulties, not Castlereagh. Public finances were in a chaotic condition, heavy borrowing was required, the disbandment of the armed forces led to growing unemployment, bad weather destroyed the crops, and there was a decline in demand for manufactured products. There were rural riots in East Anglia and industrial troubles in the Midlands and the north. In Manchester the crowds wore the tricolour cockade. Parliament suspended *habeas corpus* for several months. Castlereagh supported the measure, arguing in the Commons that a "conspiracy exists in the country for the subversion of the Constitution." But he showed sympathy for the eleven who died in the panic of "Peterloo" (which developed when Manchester's local yeomanry charged a crowd of eighty thousand) and was no enthusiast for the Six Acts that were subsequently passed by parliament. This did not convince the Cato Street conspirators, who wanted to "avenge the innocent blood shed at Manchester" by murdering the whole Cabinet. The conspirators were at blows over who should dispose of Castlereagh; "Everybody wanted the honour of cutting his throat," Princess Lieven reported to Metternich. Perhaps that failed conspiracy did mark the end of Radicalism in Britain, as Castlereagh confirmed to both Metternich and Hardenberg in March 1820; but the words "conspiracy" and "traitors" had become a part of his vocabulary and, henceforth, Castlereagh always carried a pair of loaded pistols in his breeches whenever he took his walks down the Mall.[50]

The Cato Street conspiracy had been revealed less than a month after the Prince Regent succeeded to the throne of his father. George III ceased to speak of his hazy visions on 27 January 1820 and died two days later in the same room at Windsor where he had been confined for nine years. The succession brought new problems to Castlereagh. The Prince Regent had been one of his closest political allies and a European at heart. When George became King, he wanted to divorce his Queen, still wandering around Italy. The government, especially Castlereagh, advised against it. Eventually it was agreed not to bring charges against the Queen unless she returned to England. Caroline landed at Dover on 5 June 1820 and entered London the next day to the enthusiasm of the mob. She was shown a long list of possible residences and chose a house that neighboured Castlereagh's in St James's Square. The crowds proved so violent that Castlereagh had to move out to the Foreign Office; his bed was in the same room where he received ministers and ambassadors. "To be reduced to that!" commented Princess Lieven to Metternich.

The trial of Queen Caroline was conducted in the House of Lords and Castlereagh, who continued to sit in the Commons, had nothing directly to do with it. But it was Castlereagh who had first presented the famous Green Bag, filled with incriminating documents, to the House of Commons, and it was upon Castlereagh's shoulders that all the odium of the Queen's treatment fell. He was hooted and hissed whenever he was recognised.[51]

Louis XVIII's new Ambassador to the Court of St James, in the year 1822, was Chateaubriand. He was surprised to be invited to Castlereagh's house at an unusually early hour on the day parliament was prorogued, Tuesday, 6 August. Castlereagh was equally surprised to see him. He had forgotten the invitation and was putting on his ceremonial robes for the joint session when the French Ambassador stepped into his dressing-room. Chateaubriand, searching desperately for something to say, congratulated Castlereagh for the approaching end of the session. "Yes, it has to finish, or I'm finished," answered Castlereagh curtly.[52]

On his way to Parliament he dropped in to see Harriet Arbuthnot, who had been deeply concerned by what he had had to say in a meeting the previous day regarding Mr Jennings's "anonymous" letters. Mrs Arbuthnot found Castlereagh looking very handsome in his dress clothes. "It does me good to see him," she noted in her diary.

The King was present at the ceremony. The King, it so happened, had been a source of one of Castlereagh's greatest problems. Until their happy reconciliation at Hanover the previous November (orchestrated by Metternich), he had refused to address a word to Castlereagh, even over matters of state. This was not simply due to Castlereagh's reluctance to pursue the divorce proceedings against Queen Caroline. On succeeding to the throne, George had cast aside his old mistress, the Marchioness of Hertford, Castlereagh's aunt, in favour of Lady Conyngham, who was, by all accounts, not a very cultivated woman – she had, said Princess Lieven, "not an idea in her head, not a word to say for herself; nothing but a hand to accept pearls and diamonds, and an enormous balcony to wear them on." Lady Conyngham and Lady Castlereagh became bitter rivals.

Despite the reconciliation between the King and his Minister, Lady Conyngham continued to refuse to invite Lady Castlereagh to her royal receptions. But Lord and Lady Castlereagh were inseparable.

The crisis came to a head in May 1822, when the King proposed a dinner in honour of a visit from the Crown Princess of Denmark. Lady Conyngham refused to invite Lady Castlereagh. After the dinner had been cancelled and reordered three times, it was eventually agreed – thanks to Princess Lieven's intervention – to invite both the Foreign Secretary and his wife. At a reception held the day after the dinner, Princess Lieven explained what had happened. Castlereagh exploded in anger. "Things cannot go on like this," he exclaimed. He threatened to resign and would not represent Britain at the forthcoming Congress of Verona. "Let the King give orders to Wellington or whoever he pleases," he rattled on – the Princess was horrified at Castlereagh's strange new appearance and his wild way of talking. He mentioned the Duke's name several times and implied that there was a conspiracy against him in the Cabinet. Wellington, he thought, coveted his post; the King was involved in the plot; "And you," he turned on the Princess, "you are also a traitor!"

"Well, either I am mad or he is," remarked the Princess's cuckolded husband as the Russian couple boarded their carriage.

Castlereagh became quite obsessed with this idea about Wellington. He bickered with his wife over Lady Conyngham. By now he had returned to St James's Square. He would rise at two or three in the afternoon, just in time to go to the Commons; and then return late in the evening to his home, where he was often seen weeping. Whenever he saw two people speaking together, he would say, "There is a conspiracy laid against me." His tone became bitter and ironical. His servants described him as "severe," as "bad," as "very incorrect," which was so unusual for mild-mannered Castlereagh. He spoke a great deal about his "position," about his "honour" and "pride" – "both are more wounded than I can say," he told Princess Lieven. Like his secretary, Seymour, she would try and calm him by talking about his continental trip in August. "In August, I shall no longer be the King's Minister," he grimly replied.

One thing in particular triggered his final "wildness." During the last weeks of the parliamentary session, London's press had hooked on to a new scandal. It had nothing to do with politics or, ostensibly, with Lord Castlereagh. The Right Reverend Percy Jocelyn, the Bishop of Clogher, member of an Irish aristocratic family with estates in County Down (Castlereagh's home county), was caught *in flagrante delicto* committing "a crime not to be named" with a private of the 1st Regiment of the Guards in a room of the White Hart in St Alban's Place, Westminster. The soldier was gaoled. The Bishop, who had been charged with the same crime eleven years earlier, jumped bail and fled to Edinburgh, where he lived out his long life as a butler under an assumed name.

Mr Jennings's letters, produced after the dinner at North Cray on Saturday, 3 August, provoked a link in Castlereagh's mind. At his meeting with Harriet Arbuthnot the following Monday, the day before parliament's adjournment and two days before his last Cabinet meeting, he confessed that he also had committed a "crime not to be named" and had been threatened with letters from someone who had witnessed this in an "improper house." Nobody has ever produced hard evidence of this. But in a book of recollections, privately printed 1855 for its author, the Right Reverend J. Richardson, it is told that Castlereagh, on returning home after the evening sessions at the Commons, would occasionally stop off at a brothel; he was being watched by Mr Jennings and seven fellow scoundrels. One night, in 1819, he accompanied a young lady to her room and watched as she undressed until, to his horror, he realised she was a boy. At that moment, doors were flung open and in rushed the villains.

Castlereagh fled, leaving all the money he had on him.[53]

Day by day the extortioners stood by the iron railings of St James's Square to let him know that they had not forgotten the scene. Richardson claims that Castlereagh eventually confided with the Duke of Wellington "and another nobleman" (probably his cousin, Lord Clanwilliam). Wellington advised him to admit all and take the blaggards to court. This Castlereagh could not bring himself to do, out of respect for his wife – for the Lord and his Lady were inseparable.

But, in the week parliament adjourned in 1822, Castlereagh confessed to several people that he had committed the same crime as the Bishop of Clogher. One of those witnesses was his former friend and ally, King George IV.

Early on Friday morning, 9 August, Castlereagh drove with his wife back to London to report to the King on his instructions for the Congress of Verona. He was expected to leave for the continent at the end of the following week. Hamilton Seymour was already convinced that something was seriously amiss with his master.

Before calling on Carlton House, Castlereagh went out to stroll in the streets. It was his last walk in London. Many people noticed him because he had so very an abstract manner and he was badly dressed; the top of one of his boots had slipped over his ankle, although he seemed unaware of the fact. He wandered along Pall Mall and then up Cockspur Street, where he made a scene with a head waiter for not finding an acquaintance of his. From there he was seen striding down St James's Street and on into Piccadilly. He mingled for a while amongst the crowd in front of the White Horse Cellar and approached a boy selling cheap knives on a tray; Castlereagh pocketed a small penknife with a white handle and tossed the boy a shilling.

Off he walked again, just as agitated, to Carlton House. He stood there a while and then strode away, with a quick and hurried pace, to St James's Square. Three times he returned to Carlton House before finally deciding to go in.

The King received him in one of his private apartments. Castlereagh at once seized his arm and inquired, "Have you heard the news, the terrible news?"

"No, what is it?" replied King George.

"Police officers are searching for me to arrest me," panted Castlereagh, wide-eyed.

"Come, come," smiled the King, who at first thought he was joking. "What nonsense! Why should they be?"

"Because I am accused of the same crime as the Bishop of Clogher." Castlereagh was dead serious.

"You must be crazy."

But Castlereagh shook his head and insisted. The warrant had already been issued, he had called up his horses from North Cray, and he would escape by the little gate at the back of the King's garden: "I shall go to Portsmouth and there sail for France. I can no longer live in England."

The King thought the conversation had gone quite far enough. Yet Castlereagh went on about the Bishop and his own flight from justice. "Everyone hates and shuns me," he said. "When I walk down the street, people take the opposite side to avoid meeting me." Then he broke into tears. "I am mad," he admitted, "I know I am mad. I have known it for some time, but no one has any idea of it."

The King, knowing something of the subject, recommended that he immediately see a doctor and have himself bled. "Remember the old times!" he said to comfort him. "Do you think you have a better friend than I?" And to lighten the conversation he brought up the subject of Castlereagh's next trip to the Continent.

"Sire," responded Castlereagh with renewed gravity, "the time has come to say good-bye to Europe. You and I alone have known Europe, and together we have saved her. There is no one left after me with any knowledge of Continental affairs."

As Castlereagh walked out, with mad purpose, the King had a premonition of tragedy. He was leaving for Scotland the next day – the voyage had been deliberately organised by the Government to prevent him from joining Castlereagh on the Continent. Before setting sail from Woolwich, he sent for Liverpool and told him that Castlereagh was "mad, quite mad, and if he is not watched, he is capable of making an attempt on his life." Liverpool thought that George was once again exaggerating and simply sent a short, noncommittal note to Lady Castlereagh.

On Tuesday, 13 August, the Royal Yacht was forced, through a violent storm, to take shelter in Berwick Bay. The King took the occasion to send his own note to Castlereagh: "Let me entreat you," he wrote, "not to hurry your Continental journey until you feel yourself quite equal to it. Remember of what importance your health is to the country, and above all things to me." But it was too late to save Lord Castlereagh.[54]

After leaving the King, Castlereagh had returned to his home in St James's Square. His distraught wife called out of a window to Wellington, who just happened to be riding by. Wellington found Castlereagh in a state of delirium. "Poor human nature! How little we are after all!" wrote Wellington to Mrs Arbuthnot the next day from Calais – he was on his way to inspect the frontier forts of Belgium.

Wellington had called in Doctor Charles Bankhead, a Doctor of Physic, who had served Castlereagh since his first election to the Irish parliament in 1790. Bankhead drew seven ounces of blood from the nape of Castlereagh's neck. It was "as thick as glue," reported

Bankhead; "it resembled jelly," said Lady Castlereagh. Castlereagh said he was considerably relieved after the operation; he drank two dishes of tea and then set off with his wife for North Cray Farm.

He remained in bed all Saturday in a state of considerable agitation. When Bankhead arrived in the early evening he found Castlereagh "labouring under a mental illusion": he asked Bankhead if he had "anything unpleasant to tell him," he spoke of conspiracies and hoped that Bankhead was not involved in them, and he expressed constant anxiety about his European trip. Bankhead slept in the guest's room at the end of the corridor. He spent all Sunday with Castlereagh, whose speech was incoherent for most of the time. That morning he had expressed "a forced and unnatural desire to shave."

The razors! Lady Castlereagh personally locked up the razors. The pistols! She closed them firmly in their red case and hid them on a high shelf. The knives! She combed the house and concealed every sharp instrument she could find. She ordered the maid to check the dressing-room: Mrs Robinson scoured the shelves, looked under the wash-basin, and pulled out the drawer of the wash-stand – but she missed the small penknife with the white handle Castlereagh had hidden in the dressing-case.

Bankhead eventually left Castlereagh at midnight. Lady Castlereagh continued to sleep with her husband. He got up twice during the night, once to wash his face, another time to scrub his teeth. At seven o'clock, Monday morning, Mrs Robinson brought in the breakfast. Castlereagh, sharp and severe, complained there was no butter; the butter was on the tray in front of him. At 7.30 he rang the bell and asked if Bankhead had come in from town. Mrs Robinson replied that he had slept in the next door bedroom. Castlereagh asked to see him. Lady Castlereagh followed the maid out of the room on the way to her dressing-room; as they spoke, Castlereagh accused them of conspiring together.

Once Lady Castlereagh had retired, he rushed past the bedroom door to his own dressing-room, passing the maid as he went. "Mrs Robinson," he ordered sternly, "I will not be watched. Go and send Doctor Bankhead to me instantly."

Bankhead was there in an instant. As he stepped into the dressing-room he could see Castlereagh standing, his front towards the window, his eyes gazing at the ceiling. "Bankhead," he said without turning, "let me fall upon your arm. 'Tis all over!"

Bankhead ran towards him as Castlereagh fell, still clasping at the bloodied white handle of his penknife. Bankhead could not support him, and laid him towards the window on his face, in his dressing gown, his head wrapped in a handkerchief.

Castlereagh, recorded the coroner's verdict that same afternoon, 12 August 1822, did "cut and stab himself on the carotid artery; and gave himself one mortal wound of the length of one inch and the depth of two inches." The wound was inflicted with anatomical precision. Bankhead gave evidence that death must have followed within a twinkling of an eye; "three quarts of blood flowed from him in one minute."[55]

The blood of Europe ran in Lord Castlereagh, the blood of twenty-five years of war, and the blood of many wars to come.

APPENDIX A

MAPS

Europe 1812

▬▬▬ Boundary of the
Confederation of the Rhine

SCOTLAND

NORTH
SEA

• Edinburgh

DENMARK-NORWAY *united until 1814*

Christian

SWE

Copenha

IRELAND

UNITED KINGDOM

Dublin •

WALES

ENGLAND

London •

Amsterdam

Hamburg •

Bremen •

Ber

English Channel

Brussels •

Cologne •

BERG

WESTPHALIA

ATLANTIC
OCEAN

Seine

Paris •

Pra

Rhine

CONFEDERATION
OF THE
RHINE

Loire

FRANCE

Berne •

HELVETIA

Inn

Lyon •

• Milan

ITALY

Garonne

Turin •

PORTUGAL

Ebro

Pyrenees

Rhone

Adria

Duero

Florence •

TUSCANY

Lisbon •

Tagus

Madrid •

CATALONIA

Corsica

PAPAL
STATES

SPAIN

Rome •

Guadiana

Balearic Is.

Naples •

SARDINIA

Gibraltar
(to Br.)

MEDITERRANEAN SEA

Palermo •

SIC

MOROCCO

ALGIERS

TUNIS

Malta
(to Br.)

Europe 1815

—— Boundary of the
German Confederation

NORWAY

Christian

S W E D

DENMARK

Copenha

NORTH
SEA

SCOTLAND

• Edinburgh

UNITED KINGDOM

IRELAND
Dublin

WALES

ENGLAND
London •

Hamburg •

KINGDOM OF THE NETHERLANDS

Bremen •

HANOVER

Berl

Amsterdam •

WEST-
PHALIA

P R U

Brussels •

Cologne •

SAXON

Pra

English Channel

LUX

ATLANTIC
OCEAN

Seine

Paris •

PAL

Rhine

BADEN

WÜRTTEM-
BERG

BAVARIA

Loire

FRANCE

Lyon •

Berne •
SWITZERLAND

Inn

ILLYRIA

SAVOY

Milan •

Turin •

LOMBARDY-VENETI

Adria

Garonne

Rhone

PIEDMONT

PARMA

MOD

PORTUGAL

Duero

Ebro

Pyrenees

LUCCA

Florence •

TUSCANY

PAPAL
STATES

Lisbon •

Tagus

Madrid •

SPAIN

Guadiana

Corsica

Rome •

Naples •

Balearic Is.

SARDINIA

Gibraltar
(to Br.)

MEDITERRANEAN SEA

Palermo •

K. OF T

MOROCCO

ALGIERS

TUNIS

Malta
(to Br.)

The major states and provinces of Europe
1814-1815

Austrian Empire was a new hereditary Empire founded by the Habsburgs in August 1804 after it became clear that their dynasty had lost control of the electoral college of the Holy Roman Empire. It consisted of the Habsburg German lands, Hungary, and Galicia (in southern Poland).

Belgium was, until the Revolutionary Wars, the Habsburg province of the "Austrian Netherlands." Between 1792-4, it exchanged hands between France and Austria. In 1794, it was incorporated into the French Republic. The Allies, in 1814, agreed to its unification with the Dutch Netherlands.

Confederation of the Rhine – a group of thirty-six southern German states placed under Napoleon's "protection" by a treaty of July 1806. One month later, the Holy Roman Empire was dissolved.

France had been a Kingdom until 1792 and a Republic until 1804, when she became an Empire. Coins were still being minted in 1809 that had France an Empire on one side and a Republic on the other. The First Treaty of Paris of 30 May 1814 reduced French frontiers to those of 1 November 1792, with important exceptions that added 170 square miles to her "ancient" territory.

Germany did not exist as a political entity. Castlereagh would refer to German-speaking Europe as the "intermediary system" between Russia and France. At the Congress of Vienna a German Committee (consisting initially of Austria, Prussia, Bavaria, Württemberg, and Hanover) was set up to discuss its organisation following the collapse of the Napoleonic Confederation of the Rhine.

Holy Roman Empire was described by Voltaire as neither Holy, Roman, nor an Empire; but then Voltaire did not entirely understand the German word "*Reich.*" The Empire's origin can be traced back to Charlemagne. Within its frontiers lay most of German-speaking Europe. The Empire was dissolved by an Austrian imperial decree on 6 August 1806. Germans would refer to it, somewhat nostalgically, as *das alte Reich*.

Italy, as Metternich put it in a memorandum of 2 August 1814, was "a mere geographical expression."

Naples – an ancient Kingdom of southern Italy, which in the eighteenth century came under the personal rule of the Spanish Bourbons. Napoleon drove the Bourbons out of Naples in 1805 and gave the Kingdom first to his brother, Joseph, and then to his brother-in-law, Joachim Murat.

Poland had disappeared from the map with the last partition, between Austria, Prussia, and Russia, in 1795. In 1807, after the Treaty of Tilsit with Russia, Napoleon recreated a state in the area that he called the "Grand Duchy of Warsaw." The future of Poland was one of the main items of contention at the Congress of Vienna.

Russian Empire – Tsar Paul I, son of Catherine the Great, was assassinated in 1801. His son and successor, Alexander I, had probably participated in the conspiracy.

Saxony was initially a German "Electorate," that is, a state whose Sovereign was a member of the electoral college of the Holy Roman Empire. Because of its strategic position, Saxony suffered terrible damage during the wars of the seventeenth and eighteenth centuries. In 1806, Napoleon turned the Electorate of Saxony into a Kingdom, so that his close ally, Elector Frederick Augustus III, became King Frederick Augustus I.

Spain – Philip V, grandson of Louis XIV of France, inaugurated the reign of the Spanish Bourbons when he became King in 1700. The Bourbons were deposed in 1808 and Napoleon attempted to impose his brother, Joseph, as King. But the French invasion of that year brought on insurrection and war. Wellington's victories in the Peninsula finally led to the restoration of the Bourbons in 1813. It was not an enlightened regime.

United Kingdom of Great Britain and Ireland – By the Act of Union of 1800, the Parliament of Dublin was united to that of Westminster, thus creating the United Kingdom of Great Britain and Ireland.

United Netherlands – This Kingdom, which united Belgium with the Dutch Netherlands, was created by an accord between the Allies at London in June 1814 and confirmed at the Congress of Vienna. The Sovereign Prince William of Orange was declared King William I on 17 March 1815.

Chronology

1814		London	Paris	Vienna	General
4	March				Treaty of Chaumont (Britain, Russia, Prussia, Austria)
31	March		Paris capitulates		
6	April		Napoleon abdicates		
4	May				Napoleon lands in Elba
30	May		First Treaty of Paris		
6	June	Arrival of Allied Sovereigns			
16	June			Kaiser Franz enters	
27	June	Departure of Allied Sovereigns			
1st	Aug	Grand National Jubilee			
26-8	Aug		Castlereagh visits Paris		
14	Sept			Castlereagh's arrival	
3-21	Oct	Parliament's autumn session			
9	Oct			Hardenberg's note on Saxony	
10	Nov			The Lainz hunt	
13	Nov			General Assembly of the "Congress" declared indefinitely postponed	
29	Nov			Beethoven's Concert	Prussian occupation of Saxony

1815	London	Paris	Vienna	General
3 Jan			"Secret" Treaty (Britain, Austria, France)	
21 Jan		Louis XVI's remains interred at St Denis		
23 Jan		Wellington's departure		
1st Feb			Wellington's arrival; Castlereagh's departure	
15 Feb				Fleury de Chaboulon's arrival in Elba
1st March	Castlereagh's arrival			Napoleon lands at Golfe Juan
4 March				
13 March			Allied Declaration on Napoleon	
20 March	Corn Law Act	Napoleon's entry		
25 March			Treaty of Chaumont renewed	
29 March			Wellington's departure	
30 March				Louis XVIII enters Ghent
4 April				Wellington arrives in Brussels
22 April		Promulgation of *Acte additionnel*		
30 April			Alexander proclaimed "King of Poland"	
2–3 May				Battle of Tolentino
8–22 May		Legislative elections		
12 May	Income Tax Act			
23 May	Parliament declares war			Naples surrenders
25 May				
1st June		Champ de Mai		
9 June			*Bundesakte* creates "Confederation of Germany"	

	London	Vienna	Paris	General
16 June				Battles of Ligny and Quatre Bras
18 June				Battle of Waterloo
19 June		Final Act		
22 June	Parliament informed of Waterloo		Napoleon's abdication	Louis XVIII leaves Ghent
28 June				Proclamation of Cambrai
30 June	Policy Memorandum			
1st July			Siege begins	Armistice conference at Haguenau
2 July	Castlereagh's departure		Capitulation	
3 July	Whitbread's suicide		French army evacuated	
6 July			Entry of Allied armies	
7 July			Entry of Louis XVIII	
8 July				
15 July				Napoleon, at Rochefort, boards HMS *Bellerophon*
9 Aug				HMS *Northumberland* sails for St Helena
14-22 Aug			Election of *Chambre introuvable*	
10-11 Sept			Festival, Plateau de Vertus	
26 Sept			Holy Alliance	
17 Oct				Napoleon lands on St Helena
20 Nov			Second Treaty of Paris	

Notes

ABBREVIATIONS

AF   Fournier, August, ed. *Die Geheimpolizei auf dem Wiener Kongress: Eine Auswahl aus ihren Papieren.* Vienna and Leipzig: F. Tempsky and G. Freytag, 1913.

BD   Webster, C.K., ed. *British Diplomacy, 1813-1815: Select Documents dealing with the Reconstruction of Europe.* London: G. Bell, 1921.

CC   Castlereagh, Viscount (Robert Stewart, Second Marquess of Londonderry). *Correspondence, Despatches, and Other Papers of Viscount Castlereagh.* Ed. Charles William Vane, Third Marquess of Londonderry. Vols. IX, X, and XI. London: John Murray, 1853.

MHW   Weil, Commandant M.H., ed. *Les Dessous du Congrès de Vienne d'après des documents originaux des Archives du Ministère impérial et royal de l'intérieur à Vienne.* 2 vols. Paris: Payot, 1917.

T&L   Talleyrand and Louis XVIII. *Correspondance inédite du Prince de Talleyrand et du Roi Louis XVIII pendant le Congrès de Vienne.* Ed. G. Pallain. Paris: Plon, 1881.

WD   Wellington, Field Marshal Arthur, Duke of. *The Dispatches of Field Marshal the Duke of Wellington during His Various Campaigns.* Vol. XII: *France and the Low Countries, 1814-15.* Ed. Lieut. Col. Gurwood. London: John Murray, 1831.

WSD   Wellington, Field Marshal Arthur, Duke of. *Supplementary despatches and memoranda.* Vols. IX, X, and XI. London: John Murray, 1862.

LONDON, Spring 1814

1 J.P. Malcolm, *First Impressions, or Sketches from Art and Nature, Animate and Inanimate* (London, 1807), 7, 21, 30; Madame d'Avot, *Lettres sur l'Angleterre, ou Mon séjour à Londres en 1817 et 1818, Par Mme M.D.* (Paris, 1819), 3-4; *St James's Chronicle*, 9-12 April 1814.

2 One generally did not consider the "late compulsory visit" of the exiled French Bourbons as a royal visit. See *The Examiner*, 22 May 1814.

3 Ibid.

4 Ibid.

5 *St James's Chronicle*, 31 May-3 June 1814.

6 Ibid., 7-9 June 1814.

7 Ibid., 2-4 June 1814.

8 *The Sunday Monitor*, 5 June 1814; *St James's Chronicle*, 2-4 June 1814.

9 John Brooke, *King George III* (London, 1972), 79, 390.

10 Ibid., 284-7, 386; Paul Johnson, *The Birth of the Modern: World Society, 1815-1830* (London, 1991), 450-1.

11 Louis Simond, *Journal of a Tour and Residence in Great Britain during the years 1810 and 1811 by A French Traveller* (Edinburgh, 1815), 24 March 1811, II, 115.

12 *The Times*, 6 June 1814.

13 Ida Macalpine and Richard Hunter, *George III and the Mad-Business* (London, 1991), 143-71.

14 Most of these comments are from the last parliamentary committee hearing on the King's health, in January 1812,

quoted in ibid., 165.

15 *The Times,* 9 June 1814.

16 Brooke, *George III*, 70-2, 301, 316, 348, 351; John Van der Kiste, *George III's Children* (London, 1992), 6-9; W.M. Thackeray, *The Four Georges and the English Humorists* (London, n.d. [ca. 1910]), 97.

17 Princess de Lieven, *Mémoires*, in *Correspondance de l'Empereur Alexandre Ier avec sa sœur, la Grande-Duchesse Catherine*, ed. Grand-Duc Nicolas Mikhaïlowitch (Saint Petersburg, 1913), 236; Christopher Hibbert, *George IV* (Harmondsworth, Mx., 1976), 61, 146, 397-8.

18 Ibid., 61-6, 244, 257; Johnson, *Birth*, 448.

19 Celina Fox, "A Visitor's Guide to London World City, 1800-40", in *London: World City, 1800-1840*, ed. Celina Fox (New Haven, Conn., 1992), 13-15; John Summerson, *Georgian London* (London, 1978 [1st ed., 1945]), 239-40; Iorwerth Prothero, *Artisans and Politics in Early Nineteenth-Century London* (Baton Rouge, La., 1979), 132-3.

20 Brooke, *George III*, 88; Valerie Cumming, "Pantomime and Pageantry: The Coronation of George IV," in *London*, ed. Fox, 39-40.

21 Hibbert, *George IV*, 195, 275-6, 287-8, 297, 412-14; Macalpine and Hunter, *Mad-Business*, 249; and Flora Fraser's recent biography, *The Unruly Queen: The Life of Queen Caroline* (London, 1996). These titles are my principal sources for the following paragraphs.

22 Hibbert, *George IV*, 194-206, 216.

23 Macalpine and Hunter argue, with powerful evidence, that the whole family suffered from porphyria, *Mad-Business*, 172-5, 244-5; Hibbert, *George IV*, 266, 425-6, 430, 436.

24 Ibid., 426-7.

25 Ibid., 415-17.

26 Ibid., 318-19, 416, 428.

27 Ibid., 432-6.

28 *The Times,* 3 March 1814. The "Tories" of 1814 had, in fact, sprung from a Pittite faction of Whigs and would have hotly denied any relationship with Irish Papist outlaws, Jacobites, and the royalist opponents of the Glorious Revolution of 1688.

29 Johnson, *Birth*, 461-2, 509-10; Hibbert, *George IV*, 421, 424-5, 439.

30 R. Fulford, *Samuel Whitbread, 1764-1815* (London, 1967), 297-8; *Dictionary of National Biography* (London, 1900), LXI, 24-8.

31 Brooke, *George III*, 294-9; *The Times,* 3 June 1814.

32 Hibbert, *George IV*, 422; Clancarty to Castlereagh, The Hague, 10 May 1814, in CC, X, 24-5.

33 The King had, in fact, refused to receive her at court.

34 *St James's Chronicle*, 28-31 May 1814; *The Times*, 31 May 1814; *The Examiner*, 5 June 1814.

35 Simon Heffer, *Moral Desperado: A Life of Thomas Carlyle* (London, 1995), 121; R.G. Thorne, *The House of Commons, 1790-1820* (London, 1986), I, 333-4; Peter Jackson, *George Scharf's London* (London, 1987), 130-2.

36 The account the parliamentary debates which follows is based on *The Times,* 4, 10, 13, 14, 17, 24 June 1814, and *The Examiner*, 26 June 1814.

37 *The Examiner*, 5 & 26 June 1814; *The Sunday Monitor*, 26 June & 3 July 1814.

38 M.K. Dziewanowski, *Alexander I: Russia's Mysterious Tsar* (New York, 1990), 101.

39 Liverpool to Castlereagh, undated but probably 1 May 1814, Public Record Office of Northern Ireland (PRONI), D.3030/4148.

40 Daria Olivier, *Alexandre Ier: Prince des Illusions* (Paris, 1973), 53

41 Ibid., 50-7, 172.

42 Francis Ley, *Alexandre Ier et sa Sainte-Alliance, 1811-1825* (Paris, 1975), 30-3; Dziewanowski, *Alexander I*, 119.

43 Alexander to Kochubey, 10 May 1796, in Ley, *Alexandre Ier*, 36, see also 18-19; Dziewanowski, *Alexander I*, 58.

44 Olivier, *Alexandre Ier*, 179-80.

45 Lieven, *Mémoires*, 241.

46 Alexander to Catherine, Brzezt 27 September 1805, Poulavy 2 October 1805, Poulavy 6 October 1805, 5 September 1809, in Nicolas Mikhaïlowitch, ed., *Correspondance*, 3-7 (all dates converted to western Gregorian calendar).

47 Harold Nicolson's description of the Grand Duchess as "an ugly little woman with a squat Kalmuck nose" has been repeated a thousand times, cf. Nicolson, *The Congress of Vienna* (London, 1946), 109; *The Times*, 1 April 1814; Lievin, *Mémoires*, 227-8.

48 Nicolas Mikhaïlowitch, ed., *Correspondance*, xxiv; Ley, *Alexandre Ier*, 49.

49 Alexander to Catherine, Saint Petersburg 19 September 1812, in Nicolas Mikhaïlowitch, ed., *Correspondance*, 84.

50 See the preface by the Grand Duke Nicolas Mikhaïlowitch Romanov (grand-nephew of Alexander I, first cousin of Alexander III and father of the last tsar, Nicolas II, he was a major historian murdered by the communists in 1917), in ibid., xxii; Olivier, *Alexandre Ier*, 194-208.

51 Ley, *Alexandre Ier*, 48; Alexander to Catherine, 5 September 1812, 2 January 1813, Catherine to Alexander, 18 September 1812, in Nicolas Mikhaïlowitch, ed., *Correspondance*, 82, 84, 113-14.

52 Alexander to Catherine, 19 & 30 September 1812, in ibid., 84, 86; Ley, *Alexandre Ier*, pp 55-60.

53 Ibid, 48, 54.

54 Catherine to Alexander, London 11 April 1814, Alexander to Catherine, Paris 20 April 1814, in Nicolas Mikhaïlowitch, ed., *Correspondance*, 184-5.

55 "*Il est assommant*" ["He bores me senseless"], Catherine to Alexander, London 4 April 1814, Rotterdam 25 March 1814, London 1 April 1814, in ibid., 176-9; Castlereagh's remarks are to be found in a letter from the Duke of Clarence to the Prince Regent, 23 March 1814 (*Windsor Archives*), quoted in C.K. Webster, *The Foreign Policy of Castlereagh* (London, 1931), I, 288, n. 1; see also letter of Castlereagh to his wife, Chaumont 12 March 1814, in ibid., I, 508.

56 *The Sunday Monitor*, 3 April 1814; Catherine to Alexander, London 1, 4 and 8 April 1814, in Nicolas Mikhaïlowitch, ed., *Correspondance*, 178-82.

57 Lieven, *Mémoires*, 229; there seem to be some inaccuracies in Harold Nicolson's account, cf, Nicolson, *Congress*, 109.

58 Lieven, *Mémoires*, 229, 242; Nicolson, *Congress*, 110-11.

59 Catherine to Alexander, London 4 April 1814, in Nicolas Mikhaïlowitch, ed., *Correspondance*, 180.

60 Catherine to Alexander, 9 May 1814, 4 April 1814 in ibid, 178-9, 189; *St James's Chronicle*, 7-9 April 1814.

61 *The Times*, 4 June 1814.

62 Hibbert, *George IV*, 439; Catherine to Alexander, 25 March, 1 & 8 April 1814,

in Nicolas Mikhaïlowitch, ed., *Correspondance*, 176-7, 182; Lieven, *Mémoires*, 232-4.

63 Lieven, *Mémoires*, 243; Nicolson gets his dinners mixed up, cf. Nicolson, *Congress*, 111.

64 Catherine to Alexander, 4 April 1814, in Nicolas Mikhaïlowitch, ed., *Correspondance*, 180.

65 *The Times*, 8 June 1814; *St James's Chronicle*, 4-7 June 1814; *The Examiner*, 12 June 1814.

66 Catherine to Alexander, 1 & 25 April 1814, in Nicolas Mikhaïlowitch, ed., *Correspondance*, 183, 187; Joseph Farington, *The Farington Diary*, ed. James Grieg (London, 1927), 7 June 1814, VII, 255.

67 Olivier, *Alexandre Ier*, 141, 296; Lieven, *Mémoires*, 237; Ley, *Alexandre Ier*, 17, 19, 21; Dziewanowski, *Alexander I*, 166, 198-9.

68 Lieven, *Mémoires*, 235.

69 Ibid, 225; Catherine to Alexander, 11 April 1814, in Nicolas Mikhaïlowitch, ed., *Correspondance*, 183.

70 Farington, *Diary*, 7 July 1814, VII, 262.

71 Simond, *Journal*, I, 84, II, 116; J.A. Anderson [A.A. Feldborg], *A Dane's Excursions in Britain* (London, 1809), I, 7, 11; Richard Rush, *A Residence at the Court of London* (London, 1833), 28, 53; Don Manuel Alvarez Espriella [Robert Southey], *Letters from England* (London, 1807), I, 75-6, 123; [John Feltham], *The Picture of London for 1815* (London, 1815), 60, 69, 100-1.

72 Summerson, *Georgian London*, 125-9.

73 Simond, *Journal*, I, 43; *The Times*, 3 January 1814.

74 Malcolm, *First Impressions*, 7.

75 Espriella [Southey], *Letters*, I, 75; Simond, *Journal*, I, 26-7; Rush, *Residence*, 51.

76 Ibid., 55; Summerson, *Georgian London*, 67, 82-3; Feltham, *Picture*, 70-1, 222-3; Johnson, *Birth*, 709.

77 Simond, *Journal*, I, 24, 28-30.

78 M. Dorothy George, *London Life in the Eighteenth Century* (London, 1925), 18-19, 68-9, 82-3; Mme d'Avot, *Lettres*, 205-8.

79 Prothero, *Artisans*, 20, 62-6.

80 Charles Dickens, *A Tale of Two Cities* (London, 1952), 179; Espriella [Southey], *Letters*, I, 74; Rush, *Residence*, 49-50; Simond, *Journal*, I, 28, 37; *The Times*, 13 January 1814.

81 Feltham, *Picture*, 208; George, *London Life*, 2; though dealing with a later

period Timothy B. Smith has some interesting comments to make about the archaic administrative structure of the City, "In Defense of Privilege: The City of London and the Challenge of Municipal Reform," *Journal of Social History*, XXVII (1993), 59-83; see also H.T. Dickinson, "Radical Culture," in *London*, ed. Fox, 209-24; for a brief assessment of the "popular" politics of the City Corporation in the eighteenth century, see George Rudé, *The Crowd in History, 1730-1848* (New York, 1964), 51-2.

82 Ibid., 60-4, 73-7, for the artisan make-up of the London "mob" in the eighteenth century; E.P. Thompson, *Making of the English Working Class* (New York, 1963), 240-68, 451-71, 611-19; and Prothero, *Artisans*, 36, 45, 85-8.

83 For examples see *St James's Chronicle*, 4-6, 8-11 January, 17-19 February, 16-19 April 1814; *The Sunday Monitor*, 8 May, 5 June 1814.

84 Simond, *Journal*, I, 28; Feltham, *Picture*, 80-6; Espriella [Southey], *Letters*, I, 66; Mme d'Avot, *Lettres*, 205-8.

85 Francis Place quoted by George, *London Life*, 4.

86 Ibid., 17; Simond, *Journal*, I, 183-8; *St James's Chronicle*, 23-6 April 1814.

87 Ibid., 30 December 1813 - 1 January 1814, 20-22 January 1814.

88 Ibid., 5-8 April, 28-31 May 1814; *The Times*, 4 April 1814; *The Examiner*, 5 June 1814; *The Sunday Monitor*, 3 April, 5 June 1814.

89 See Richard D. Altick, *The Shows of London* (Cambridge, Mass., 1978), 3.

90 Feltham, *Picture*, 55; *The Times*, 26 January, 1-7 February 1814; *St James's Chronicle*, 3-5, 5-8, 10-12 February 1814.

91 Farington, *Diary*, 7 & 8 June 1814, VII, 255-6.

92 *The Sunday Monitor*, 26 June 1814; *The Examiner*, 26 June; Lieven, *Mémoires*, 243.

93 Espriella [Southey], *Letters*, I, 95; *The Times*, 10 June 1814.

94 Ibid.

95 Farington, *Diary*, 9 June 1814, VII, 257.

96 *The Times*, 10 June 1814.

97 Illustrations of old St James's Square in F.W.H. Sheppard, ed., *Survey of London* (London, 1960), XXX, 130-1; description of former Number 18, Castlereagh's house, in ibid, XXIX, 159-61.

98 On Mount Stewart see *Mount Stewart* (London,1978); Wendy Hinde, *Castlereagh* (London, 1981), 15; Anne de Courcy, *Circe: The Life of Edith, Marchioness of Londonderry* (London, 1992), 34, 89, 153-4. But nothing is a substitute for a visit.

99 Hinde, *Castlereagh*, 33; H. Montgomery Hyde, *The Strange Death of Lord Castlereagh* (London, 1959), 164; for the father's delightful letters, PRONI, D.3030/H.

100 Hyde, *Strange Death*, 155-9; Hinde, *Castlereagh*, 13-14; *Mount Stewart*, 30-1.

101 Hinde, *Castlereagh*, 13; Hyde, *Strange Death*, 157-8; for Charles Stewart's correspondence with his half-brother see especially PRONI, D.3030/P.

102 Hyde, *Strange Death*, 156-7, 165; Hibbert, *George IV*, 323-36, 378.

103 Hinde, *Castlereagh*, 214-15; Johnson, *Birth*, 462, 578; Henry Kissinger, *A World Restored* (Boston, n.d.), 30; Hyde, *Strange Death*, 77, 89; Webster, *Foreign Policy*, I, 11-14, 49; II, 31-3; Nicolson, *Congress*, 87.

104 Hyde, *Strange Death*, 76, 90, 170-1; Webster, *Foreign Policy*, I, 50, 509; Kissinger, *World Restored*, 300.

105 Hyde, *Strange Death*, 163-6; Webster, *Foreign Policy*, I, 164-5.

106 *The Times*, 14 & 22 June 1814.

107 *St James's Chronicle*, 4-7 June 1814; Londonderry to Castlereagh, Mount Stewart, 12 June 1814, PRONI, D.3030/H/27.

108 J. Steven Watson, *The Reign of George III, 1760-1815* (Oxford, 1960), 434.

109 Brooke, *George III*, 307-9.

110 Webster, *Foreign Policy*, I, 54-5; Nicolson, *Congress*, 52; Olivier, *Alexandre Ier*, 97-9; Dziewanowski, *Alexander I*, 168-71.

111 For the actual text delivered to London, dated 11 September 1804, see Ley, *Alexandre Ier*, 40; also Webster, *Foreign Policy*, I, 54-5.

112 Ibid., 56-62.

113 Ibid., 57.

114 Ley, *Alexandre Ier*, 63-4; Olivier, *Alexandre Ier*, 267; Castlereagh to Cathcart, 8 April 1813, in Webster, *Foreign Policy*, I, p.125.

115 Olivier, *Alexandre Ier*, 267, 277; Hinde, *Castlereagh*, 203.

116 Webster, *Foreign Policy*, I, 199-200.

117 Kissinger, *World Restored*, 13.

118 Farington, *Diary*, 24 February 1814,

VII, 219; see also his comments on the "Balance of Power in Europe," 22 March 1814, ibid., 226; Kissinger, *World Restored*, 124.

119 Ibid., 131-2; Castlereagh to Liverpool, Paris, 20 April 1814, in CC, IX, 478.

120 Clancarty to Castlereagh, The Hague, 25 April 1814, in ibid, 500-7.

121 Clancarty to Castlereagh, The Hague, 10 & 13 May, 7 June 1814, ibid, X, 21-5, 31-5, 52.

122 This and following paragraphs: Hibbert, *George IV*, 439-49; *The Times*, 16, 21, 24 June 1814; *The Examiner*, 19 & 26 June 1814; *The Sunday Monitor*, 3 July 1814.

123 Hibbert, *George IV*, 447; Clancarty to Castlereagh, The Hague, 28 June 1814, in CC, X, 62-4.

124 Castlereagh to Clancarty, St James's Square, 26 June 1814, in ibid, 60-1; Webster, *Foreign Policy*, I, 297-305; Hinde incorrectly places this accord after the rupture, though many must have been aware, by 14 June, of the problems of the proposed marriage (the accord was signed on 14 June, while the Sovereigns were in Oxford, the rupture was on 16 June), Hinde, *Castlereagh*, 218-19.

125 Castlereagh to Clancarty, 26 June 1814, in CC, X, 61; Creevey to his wife, 21 June 1814, in Thomas Creevey, *The Creevey Papers*, ed. Herbert Maxwell (London, 1903), I, 197.

126 Farington, *Diary*, 7 July 1814, VII, 265-6.

127 Samuel Whitbread to Creevey, Dover Street, 1 July 1814; H.R.H. Princess of Wales to Samuel Whitbread, Connaught House, 30 June 1814; Brougham to Creevey, Temple, 1 & 4 July, 9 August 1814 – in Creevey, *Papers*, I, 198-204.

128 Farington, *Diary*, 25 June 1814, VII, 257-8.

129 Ley, *Alexandre Ier*, 80; *The Times*, 15-17 June 1814.

130 Ley, *Alexandre Ier*, 76-83; *The Times*, 22 June 1814.

131 *Sunday Monitor*, 26 June 1814; *The Times*, 29 June 1814.

132 E.C.C. Corti, *Metternich und die Frauen* (Zurich, 1948), I, 456.

133 Lieven, *Mémoires*, 246; *Sunday Monitor*, 3 July 1814; *The Times*, 29 June 1814; *The Examiner*, 3 July 1814.

134 Olivier, *Alexandre Ier*, 304-5.

135 Summerson, *Georgian London*, 177-90; Jackson, *London*, 20-32, 70-6, 126-38;

Donald J. Olsen, *The City as a Work of Art: London, Paris, Vienna* (New Haven, Conn., 1986), 9-34.

136 There were also the elaborate extensions made at Carlton House; these had been constructed to communicate with the new gothic conservatory and were designed so that the Regent's guests would be able to watch, in private, the peace festival on St James's Park. See *St James's Chronicle*, 31 May - 2 June, 1814.

137 Lieven, *Mémoires*, 241; various descriptions of the preparations in *The Times, The Examiner*, and *The Sunday Monitor*, months of May, June, and July 1814.

138 *The Times*, 28 & 30 June 1814.

139 Ibid.

140 Farington, *Diary*, 1 August 1814, VII, 274; *The Sunday Monitor*, 24 July, 7 August 1814; *The Times*, 2 August 1814 – for this and following paragraphs.

PARIS, Summer 1814

1 "All the powers engaged on either side in the present war shall, within the space of two months, send Plenipotentiaries to Vienna, for the purpose of regulating in general Congress the arrangements which are to complete the provisions of the present Treaty" – Article XXXII of the "Definitive Treaty of Peace and Amity between His Britannic Majesty and His Most Christian Majesty, Signed at Paris, 30 May 1814," in WSD, IX, 129.

2 *Sunday Monitor*, 12 June, 10 July 1814; *St James's Chronicle*, 9-12 April 1814.

3 C.K. Webster, *The Foreign Policy of Castlereagh* (London, 1931), 1, 287-8, 295-6; Harold Nicolson, *The Congress of Vienna* (London, 1946), 116-17.

4 Webster, *Foreign Policy*, I, 296.

5 *Souvenirs* of Mme von Freistett, quoted at length in Francis Ley, *Alexandre 1er et sa Sainte-Alliance* (Paris, 1975), 85.

6 A high judicial post that dated back to the old German Reich.

7 Jung Stilling to Professor Schwarz of Bâle, 15 July 1814, Juliette de Krüdener, *Journal, 1814*, and Comtesse d'Edling (Mlle Stourdza), *Mémoires*, in Ley, *Alexandre 1er*, pp 86-9.

8 Ibid., 92; Daria Olivier, *Alexandre 1er* (Paris, 1973), 307-9.

9 Nicolson, *Congress*, 119; Henry A.

Kissinger, *A World Restored* (Boston, n.d.), 149; Mr George Jackson to Castlereagh, Berlin, 19 August 1814 in CC, X, 97; see also Duke of Wellington to Clancarty, Courtrai, 20 August 1814, in ibid., 98; and on a threat by Alexander to publish his liberal views on the slave trade, William Wilberforce to Castlereagh, 13 August 1814, PRONI, D.3030/4178.

10 Henry Houssaye, *1814* (Paris, 1918), 258; Webster, *Foreign Policy*, II, 209.

11 Nicolson, *Congress*, 119; Castlereagh to Clancarty, London, 14 August 1814, CC, X, 85

12 Leo Tolstoy, *War and Peace* (London, 1978), 1339-44.

13 Georges Lacour-Gayet, *Talleyrand* (Paris, 1990), 757-9; *St James's Chronicle*, 7-9 April 1814.

14 Talleyrand to duchesse de Courlande, 16 February 1814, in C.M. de Talleyrand-Périgord, *Talleyrand intime d'après sa correspondance avec la duchesse de Courlande* (Paris, 1891), 123.

15 "Definitive Treaty...," in WSD, IX, 120-31; Kissinger, *World Restored*, 140-3; Nicolson, *Congress*, 98-100; Webster, *Foreign Policy*, I, 273-7; Lacour-Gayet, *Talleyrand*, 814-23.

16 Castlereagh to Bathurst, Paris, 20 May 1814, Major-General H. Fane to Wellington, London, 22 July 1814, in WSD, IX, 96 & 164.

17 Talleyrand to duchesse de Courlande, 31 May 1814, in *Talleyrand intime*, 271.

18 According to estimates made by contemporaries the number of people reading a single newspaper could range from six to eighty, though the average seems to have been between ten and thirty. It has been calculated that in 1820 one per cent of the adult population in Britain read newspapers, not perhaps a very large proportion by today's standards, but it would have been significantly higher than anywhere on the continent at that time. Moreover, these crude estimates don't take into account the way news and political opinion were spread by word of mouth; the people who crowded the Dover Road in early June 1814 were not all newspaper readers, any more than were the "mob" of London. See essays by Raymond Williams and Ivon Asquith in *Newspaper History from the Seventeenth Century to the Present Day*, eds., G. Boyce, J. Curran and P.

Wingate (London, 1978), esp. 42-3, 46-7, 99-101.

19 *The Times*, 7 June 1814; Castlereagh to Talleyrand, London, 16 July 1814, in WSD, IX, 162.

20 Castlereagh to Sir Henry Wellesley, London, 1 August 1814, in CC, X, 73; Wellington to Sir Henry Wellesley, London, 29 July 1814, in WSD, IX, 165.

21 Talleyrand to Castlereagh, Paris, 26 May 1814, in ibid, 111; Wellington to J.D. Villiers, Paris, 31 August 1814, in WD, XII, 91.

22 C.M. de Talleyrand-Périgord, *Mémoires, 1754-1815* (Paris, 1982), 667-9; Lacour-Gayet, *Talleyrand*, 819-21; Jean Orieux, *Talleyrand ou le sphinx incompris* (Paris, 1970), 593-4.

23 The account of Talleyrand's conversations with Stuart are based on five dispatches from Stuart to Castlereagh, dated 1, 8 and 9 August 1814, in WSD, IX, 180-5.

24 *Gazette de France*, 3 and 9 August 1814.

25 Ibid., 9, 15 and 18 August 1814.

26 Ibid., 13 August.

27 Castlereagh to Wellington, London, 14 August 1814, at night, in WSD, IX, 186.

28 Castlereagh to Charles Stuart, London, original dated 13 August, Castlereagh's copy dated 14 August, in ibid, 185, and CC, X, 91-2; Castlereagh to Wellington, London, 7 August 1814, in ibid, 76-8; Castlereagh to Wellington, London, 14 August, in WSD, IX, 186.

29 Wellington to Castlereagh, Mons, 18 August 1814, in CC, X, 93-4.

30 Castlereagh to Bentinck, Paris, 7 May 1814, in ibid, 18.

31 Elizabeth Longford, *Wellington* (London, 1969), I, 457.

32 Wellington to Bathurst, Courtrai, 20 August 1814, in WSD, IX, 187; see also Wellington to Clancarty, Courtrai, 20 August 1814, in CC, X, 98.

33 Longford, *Wellington*, I, 447.

34 For Wellington's early life see the first volume of ibid. and Neville Thompson, "The Uses of Adversity," in *Wellington: Studies in the Military and Political Career of the First Duke of Wellington*, ed. Norman Gash (Manchester, 1990), 1-10.

35 The occasion was that of Sir Brent Spencer's replacement at second-in-command of the Peninsular army in 1811 by General Graham, which,

Pakenham wrote, "may induce our friend [Wellington] to indulge himself a little more, although he has proved Himself near an Iron man." Longford, *Wellington*, I, 324.

36 Alan Schom, *One Hundred Days: Napoleon's Road to Waterloo* (London, 1993), 222.

37 Talleyrand to duchesse de Courlande, 5 May 1814, in *Talleyrand intime*, 245.

38 John K. Severn, "The Wellesleys and Iberian diplomacy, 1808-12," in *Wellington Studies*, ed. N. Gash, 34-65.

39 Details on this Wellesley system of diplomacy can be found in Severn's essay, Charles J. Esdaile, "The Duke of Wellington and the Command of the Spanish Army, 1812-14," and Donald D. Horward, "Wellington as a Strategist, 1808-14," in ibid., 34-116.

40 Longford, *Wellington*, I, 268.

41 Ibid., 261.

42 WD, XII, 125-9.

43 *Gazette de France*, 16-31 August 1814.

44 John Scott, *A Visit to Paris in 1814* (London, 1815), 6-7.

45 J. Regnault, "L'Empereur et l'opinion publique, 1813-1814," *Revue historique de l'Armée*, XIII (1957), 29-5; François René de Chateaubriand, *Mémoires d'outre-tombe.* (Paris, 1973), II, 295-6.

46 *Gazette de France*, 25 August 1814.

47 Ibid., various issues of July and August 1814; Longford, *Wellington*, I, 450.

48 Philip Mansel, *The Court of France, 1789-1830* (Cambridge, 1988), 98, 102-5.

49 Castlereagh's presence was signalled by a one-line statement in the *Gazette de France*, 29 August 1814: *"Lord Castlereagh est arrivé avant-hier [*26 August*] dans cette capitale."*

50 Wellington to W. Hamilton, Paris, 29 August 1814, see also Wellington to Sir Charles Stuart, London, 13 July 1814 and Wellington to W. Hamilton, Paris, 12 September 1814, in WD, XII, 76, 88-9, 108-9; the *Gazette de France* reports the purchase of the Borghese Palace and also rumours purchase of *"un terrain considérable"* near Morfontaine *"pour y faire des courses de chevaux,"* 19 & 26 August 1814.

51 Ibid., 24 August 1814; Wellington to Castlereagh, Paris, 25 August 1814, in WD, XII, 83; Mansell, *Court*, 102.

52 The Rev. Burroughs T. Norgate, *Paris and the Parisians the Year after Waterloo* (London, 1831), 26. Years later the Duke was having dinner with

Lord Stanhope in Apsley House when he pointed out the portraits of Louis XVIII and Charles X (Monsieur in 1814); "How much better after all," he said with a smile, "these two look with their *fleur-de-lis* and *Saint-Esprits*, than the two corporals behind, or the fancy dress in between." The corporals were Emperor Alexander and King Frederick William of Prussia; the man in fancy dress was the Prince Regent in Highland kilt and bonnet. Longford, *Wellington*, I, 46-7.

53 The general instructions given formally by the Regent opened with the words "Instructions for our Right Trusty and Right entirely Beloved Cousin and Councillor Arthur, Duke, Marquess, and Earl Wellington, Marquess Douro, Viscount Wellington of Talavera and of Wellington, and Baron Douro of Wellesley..." and thus went on for thirteen tight printed lines; Castlereagh to Wellington, Paris, 13 April 1814, and "General Instructions," in WSD, IX, 142, 168-71.

54 *Gazette de France*, 26 August 1814; Mansel, *Court*, 112.

55 *Journal de Paris*, 2 July 1814.

56 Mansel, *Court*, 101-6; Chateaubriand, *Mémoires*, II, 294.

57 Mansel, *Court*, 111; Sydney Owenson, Lady Morgan, *La France* (Paris and London, 1817), I, 150.

58 *Gazette de France*, 29 & 31 July, 4, 8, 9, 14, 16-17 August 1814; *The Sunday Monitor*, 14 August 1814; Christopher Hibbert, *George IV* (London, 1976), 456-7.

59 Norgate, *Paris*, 1-4; Benjamin Haydon, *Life of Benjamin Robert Haydon* (London, 1853), I, 223-5.

60 Scott, *A Visit*, 14.

61 Ibid., 16; Haydon, *Life*, I, 225; Norgate, *Paris*, 5.

62 Scott, *A Visit*, 17-18; *St James's Chronicle*, 30 April - 3 May 1814; Norgate, *Paris*, 6.

63 Haydon, *Life*, I, 226; Scott, *A Visit*, 112.

64 Norgate, *Paris*, 15; Scott, *A Visit*, 32-3.

65 Haydon, *Life*, I, 227; Morgan, *France*, I, 58-60; *The Times*, 20 June 1814; Scott, *A Visit*, 34; Norgate, *Paris*, 14-17.

66 Scott, *A Visit*, 20-3, 34; Norgate, *Paris*, 12.

67 Ibid., 20-1; Scott, *A Visit*, 50.

68 For complaints about the delays, the fraud and the inconveniences of the

tolls in London and on the Dover Road see, for example, *St James's Chronicle*, 5-7 May 1814, or Madame D'Avot, *Lettres sur l'Angleterre* (Paris, 1819), 4. The barrières only came down in 1860; Paris had simply burst beyond their seams. Jacques Hillairet, *Dictionnaire historique des rues de Paris* (Paris, 1985), I, 307; G. Dallas, *At the Heart of a Tiger: Clemenceau and His World* (London, 1993), 18-23,103.

69 Quoted in Hillairet, *Dictionnaire*, I, 22.

70 Jules Michelet, *Histoire de la Révolution française* (Paris, 1979), I, 31-2; to get an idea of the physical appearance of Paris in 1814, a visit to three rooms of paintings in the Musée Carnavalet is useful, but not the museum's catalogues with their postage stamp reproductions; the best published collection of paintings and prints is in Jean Tulard, *Nouvelle histoire de Paris: Le Consulat et l'Empire, 1800-1815* (Paris, 1983).

71 *Exposé de la situation de l'Empire au Corps législatif*, 24 August 1807 quoted in Tulard, *Paris*, 189, see also 204-5; Thomas Carlyle, *The French Revolution* (Oxford, 1989), I, 335, and II, 276; Gaspard Gourgaud, *Mémoires*, in *Napoléon à Sainte-Hélène*, ed. Jean Tulard (Paris, 1981), p. 493.

72 J.S.C. de Saint-Albin, *Voyages de Paul Béranger dans Paris après 45 ans d'absence...*, (Paris, 1819), I, xviii-xix; Louis Prudhomme, *Voyage descriptif et philosophique de l'ancien et du nouveau Paris* (Paris, 1814), II, 198; Norgate, *Paris*, 35; Victor Hugo, *Les Misérables* (Paris, 1951), 975-9.

73 Morgan, *France*, I, 54-5; Haydon, *Life*.

74 Carlyle, *French Revolution*, I, 10; Norgate, *Paris*, 22; Louis Chevalier, *Laboring Classes and Dangerous Classes in Paris During the First Half of the Nineteenth Century* (Princeton, N.J., 1973), 108-10; Saint-Albin, *Voyage descriptif*, I, 107.

75 La Chaise, *Topographie médicale*, quoted in Tulard, *Paris*, 191.

76 Carlyle, *French Revolution*, II, 294; Scott, *A Visit*, 96.

77 Lady Morgan, *Passages from My Autobiography* (London, 1859), 164-5; Haydon, *Life*, I, 232; Scott, *A Visit*, 111.

78 Ibid., 67, 111-12; Haydon, *Life*, I, 232.

79 Saint-Albin, *Voyage descriptif*, I, 12-13; Norgate, *Paris*, 28; Scott, *A Visit*, 113-

14; for a general history of bathing see Georges Vigarello, *Concepts of Cleanliness: Changing Attitudes in France Since the Middle Ages* (Cambridge, Eng., 1988) and my own review in *Journal of Social History*, XXIV (1990), 157-9.

80 Norgate, *Paris*, 56-7; Morgan, *France*, I, 285-90.

81 Scott, *A Visit*, 146-71; Morgan, *Autobiography*, 59, 148; Saint-Antoine, *Voyage descriptif*, 122-6; *Gazette de France*, 25 August 1814.

82 Norgate, *Paris*, 104-5.

83 William Sewell argues that the noble language of artisan labour was part of an old corporate identity, and he is undoubtedly right; but Sewell, like many labour historians, who limit themselves to organised labour, ignores the chestnut-vendor. See William H. Sewell, *Work and Revolution in France: The Language of Labor from the Old Regime to 1848* (Cambridge, 1980).

84 Scott, *A Visit*, 84-6.

85 Louis Prudhomme, *Miroir historique, politique et critique de l'ancien et du nouveau Paris et du département de la Seine* (Paris, 1807), II, 107, quoted in Tulard, *Paris*, 53; René Sédillot, *Le Coût de la Révolution française* (Paris, 1987), 151-254; Chevalier, *Laboring Classes*, 181-5.

86 Tulard, *Paris*, 92-5; Balzac quotation in David H. Pinkney, *Napoleon III and the Rebuilding of Paris* (Princeton, N.J., 1958), 11.

87 Scott, *A Visit*, 111.

88 Since 1811 a slump in industrial activity had affected all trades and, though a recommitment by the government to public works in 1812 had won some sympathy, that was all lost in the defeats of the following two years. Parisian workers longed for peace and a return of prosperity. It was said that Napoleon, at the end of the French campaign in 1814, had marched eastwards to Saint-Dizier and Vitry rather than on Paris because he could not count on the support of his capital. "Let's drink to the *last* victory of the Emperor's!" was the toast one heard in the cafés and coffee shops. Houssaye, *1814*, 4.

89 Wellington to Liverpool, Paris, 28 August 1814, in WD, XII, 88; *Gazette de France*, 6, 9, 13 July, 21 August 1814.

90 Carlyle, *French Revolution*, II, 65;

André Castelot, *Fouché* (Paris, 1990), 225.

91 Tulard, *Paris*, 191.

92 Talleyrand to duchesse de Courlande, 1 March 1814, in Talleyrand, *Talleyrand intime*, 130-1.

93 Talleyrand had passed through Brunn in December 1805, two weeks after the Battle of Austerlitz. "Brunn is a horrible place," he wrote to his secretary, d'Hauterive; "there are at this moment four thousand wounded here. Every day there are a large number of deaths. Yesterday the odour was foul." Quoted in Lacour-Gayet, *Talleyrand*, 557.

94 Talleyrand to duchesse de Courlande, 3, 10 February, 2, 15, 27 March 1814, in Talleyrand, *Talleyrand intime*, 67, 77, 133-4, 155, 187.

95 Houssaye, *1814*, 33-44

96 Ibid., 449-56; Tulard, *Paris*, 381-6.

97 For a long time historians speculated on whether Charlotte was his natural daughter. In 1951 Michel Missoffe discovered documents in colonial and police archives proving that she was in fact born to Marie-Jeanne Beaugeard, *née* d'Hugues, in London in October 1799 (when Talleyrand was a minister in Paris). In London, Madame Beaugeard had befriended Talleyrand's future wife, Madame Grand. Charlotte lived with the Talleyrands for many years before she was formally adopted in 1807 following secret negotiations with Madame Beaugeard in Madrid, where she was living. From that date onwards, Madame Beaugeard received a life pension of 4,800 francs annually from Talleyrand. Michel Missoffe, *Revue des Deux Mondes*, 15 September 1951, 331 ff.; quoted in Talleyrand, *Mémoires*, 616, n. 61. See also Lacour-Gayet, *Talleyrand*, 492-4.

98 Talleyrand to duchesse de Courlande, Paris, 10 February 1814, in *Talleyrand intime*, 69, 77; L.J. Arrigan quotes a source suggesting that by the summer of 1814 the Duchesss was renting a house from Madame Walther, a war widow, see Arrigan, *Une amie de Talleyrand: la duchesse de Courlande* (Paris, 1946), p. 51.

99 Talleyrand to duchesse de Courlande, 21 January, 19, 23 February, 1, 26 March 1814, *Talleyrand intime*, 106, 115, 131, 185.

100 Talleyrand to duchesse de Courlande, 25 January, 6 February 1814, ibid.

101 Lacour-Gayet, *Talleyrand*, 294.

102 Napoleon said of Talleyrand, "He is of a great House, and that erases all." Gourgaud, *Mémoires*, p. 534.

103 Lacour-Gayet, *Talleyrand*, 632, 635.

104 The sister of Queen Louise of Prussia, one of the figureheads of German resistance to Napoleon.

105 For Erfurt Conference and the marriage of Talleyrand's nephew, Edmond, to Dorothée, later duchesse de Dino, see Olivier, *Alexandre Ier*, 180-5; Lacour-Gayet, *Talleyrand*, 626-50; Evelyne Lever, *Louis XVIII* (Paris, 1988), 235-93; Gaston Palewski's preface to Talleyrand-Périgord, *Le Miroir de Talleyrand: Lettres inédites à la duchesse de Courlande* (Paris, 1976), 13-17; and duchesse de Dino, *Souvenirs* (Paris, 1908), 97-107, 169-253.

106 Talleyrand to Alexander, Paris, 24 March 1809, in Lacour-Gayet, *Talleyrand*, 648-9.

107 Ibid, 661-2.

108 Armand de Caulaincourt, *Mémoires* (Paris, 1986), 252, 257; Talleyrand, in fact, denied that he ever would have been able to help Napoleon, arguing that each time the Emperor had the slightest military victory "he would have disavowed my signature," ibid, 600.

109 Napoleon to Joseph, Nogent, 8 February 1814, in Lacour-Gayet, *Talleyrand*, 729.

110 Ibid, 724-35; Houssaye, *1814*, 439-49; Talleyrand, *Mémoires*, 599; Abbé de Pradt, *Récit historique sur la restauration de la royauté en France, le 31 mars 1814* (Paris, 1822), 31-8.

111 *Talleyrand intime*, 169; Talleyrand, *Mémoires*, 636.

112 Lacour-Gayet, *Talleyrand*, 123.

113 Houssaye, *1814*, 519-20; Comtesse de Boigne, *Mémoires* (Paris, 1979), I, 215-17.

114 Pradt, *Récit*, 55.

115 Houssaye, *1814*, 500-18.

116 Ibid., 523-34; Lacour-Gayet, *Talleyrand*, 750-53; Talleyrand to duchesse de Courlande, 31 March 1814, *Talleyrand intime*, 201.

117 Talleyrand, *Mémoires*, 630.

118 Napoleon was riding into Fontainebleau at that very moment. He had missed his appointment.

119 Houssaye, *1814*, 534-9; Lacour-Gayet, *Talleyrand*, 753-5.

120 Boigne, *Mémoires*, I, 217;

121 The Austrian Emperor had remained

behind in Dijon with Metternich and Castlereagh.

122 Houssaye, *1814*, 558-64; Tulard, *Paris*, 388.

123 It is indeed recorded that Alexander's first words were, "Monsieur de Talleyrand." Why not the "Prince de Bénévent"? Could it be that the victor refused to recognise a title bestowed on Talleyrand by the usurper. Before Talleyrand left for Vienna in September 1814, he dropped the "Prince de Bénévent" to become the "Prince de Talleyrand." Lacour-Gayet, *Talleyrand*, 759-62; Houssaye, 564-7; Nicolson, *Congress*, 84-5.

124 Proclamation of Calmar, 2 December 1804, in Lever, *Louis XVIII*, 285-7. Philosophically the question of what makes authority *legitimate* can be traced at least as far back as Rousseau's *Contrat social*.

125 Talleyrand, *Mémoires*, 632.

126 Lacour-Gayet, *Talleyrand*, 644-5; see also comments in Orieux, *Talleyrand*, 592.

127 Lacour-Gayet, *Talleyrand*, 388-9.

128 Talleyrand, *Mémoires*, 34-5. Madame Récamier, the famous salon hostess, said, "What determined the character of Monsieur de Talleyrand were his feet" – in Benjamin Constant, *Œuvres* (Paris, 1957), 967.

129 Jacob-Nicolas Moreau, *Mes Souvenirs*, (Paris, 1898), I, 7.

130 Lacour-Gayet, *Talleyrand*, 310.

131 Ibid., 234

132 Ibid., 296, 484, 583, 718, 738.

133 Talleyrand, *Mémoires*, 35. "We will be singing on Sunday [19 September] a *Te Deum* for the great successes that the Emperor had on the 26th and 27th [of August] at Dresden," Talleyrand wrote to the Duchess, confiding hope and sharing a moment of anxiety. "I spend my time correcting what I wrote, while taking waters, on the periods I had known so well that preceded the Revolution... It is a form of work that has something quite captivating about it, and, in all, is an activity needed to keep one's mood [*la disposition d'humeur*] sober." Talleyrand to duchesse de Courlande, ca. 18 September 1813, in Lacour-Gayet, *Talleyrand*, 717. Lacour-Gayet (p. 20) argues that the *Mémoires* were written in 1816, but this letter, which he later cites, would seem to contradict him, at least where the earlier passages are con-

cerned. Lacour-Gayet had access to the "Archives Talleyrand" at the Château de Valençay, which have since been sold off to collectors.

134 Talleyrand, *Mémoires*, 36.

135 *Mémoire sur les rapports actuels de la France avec les autres Etats de l'Europe* (London, 25 November 1792), quoted at length in Lacour-Gayet, *Talleyrand*, 172-4; on Austria and Poland, see ibid, 547-58, 590-7.

136 Mémoires de Madame de Rémusat, III, 667-70, quoted at length in Lacour Gayet, *Talleyrand*, 611-13.

137 Etienne Dumont, *Souvenirs sur Mirabeau*, in ibid, 159; Sir Samuel Romilly, "Diary of a Journey to Paris", in *The Life of Sir Samuel Romilly written by himself, with a selection from his correspondence* (London, 1842), I, 414; Longford, *Wellington*, I, 469; John Wilson Croker, *The Croker Papers* (London, 1884), I, 65.

138 *Mémoire sur les relations commerciales des Etats-Unis avec l'Angleterre*, 15 Germinal, An V (4 April 1797); Lacour-Gayet, *Talleyrand*, 174, 207-8.

139 Castlereagh to Metternich, Brussels, 22 August 1822, quoted in Webster, *Foreign Policy*, I, 323.

140 *Gazette de France*, 19 August 1814.

141 Benjamin Constant to Talleyrand, Paris, 3 April 1814; *Mémoires de Barras*, IV, 251-4, in Lacour-Gayet, *Talleyrand*, 776-7, 796-7; *Gazette de France*, 21 July 1814.

142 Wellington to Liverpool, Paris, 28 August 1814, in WD, XII, 88; Castlereagh to Liverpool, Paris, 28 August 1814, in WSD, IX, 193; Webster, *Foreign Policy*, I, 322.

143 Wellington to Castlereagh, Mons, 18 August 1814, in CC, X, 94.

144 Two dispatches from Castlereagh to Wellington, London, 6 August 1814, in WSD, IX, 167-8, 174-6; Wellington to Castlereagh, Paris, 25 August 1814, Wellington to Talleyrand, Paris, 26 August 1814, in WD, XII, 85-7, 91-2; Liverpool to Wellington, London, 23 September 1814, in CC, X, 132-4.

145 Castlereagh to Wellington, London, 7 August 1814, in ibid, 76-8.

146 Wellington to Castlereagh, Paris, 12 September 1814, in CC, X, 114-15.

147 Webster, *Foreign Policy*, I, 322-3; Talleyrand to duchesse de Courlande, 9 September 1814, in Lacour-Gayet, *Talleyrand*, 823, 1387n.

148 Talleyrand quotes the *Instructions* in

full in his *Mémoires*, 669-86 – they are dated "August 1814."

149 Louis Madelin, *Fouché* (Paris, 1903), I, 122-39; Stefan Zweig, *Fouché* (Paris, 1969), 45-64; Joseph Fouché, *Les Mémoires* (Paris, 1992), 51.

150 Ibid., 70-1; Schom, *Hundred Days*, 115.

151 Balzac, *Une ténébreuse affaire*, in Zweig, *Fouché*, 11-12.

152 Fouché, *Mémoires*, 418.

VIENNA, Autumn 1814

1 Robert Liston to Lord Castlereagh, Constantinople, 26 September 1814, in CC, X, 134-5.

2 See, for example, *The Examiner*, 26 June 1814.

3 HMS *Lady Castlereagh* was launched in London's docks in the spring of 1814 and joined the China and East Indies fleet in Bengal. The departure of the East Indies Fleet spelt economic disaster for many of London's ship-wrights and was a major cause for the resurgence of Radicalism that summer, an ironic development for a ship named *Lady Castlereagh*. See *St James's Chronicle*, 5-8 March 1814 and I.J. Prothero, *Artisans and Politics in Early Nineteenth-Century London: John Gast and his Times* (Baton Rouge, La., 1979), 62.

4 Wendy Hinde, *Castlereagh* (London, 1981), 35; C.K. Webster, *The Foreign Policy of Castlereagh* (London, 1931), I, 7-8; Comtesse de Boigne, *Mémoires* (Paris, 1979), I, 400.

5 Webster, *Foreign Policy*, I, 503-9.

6 "I find that I am in danger of committing the intolerable barbarism of writing a love-letter to my wife," Castlereagh confessed to Emily, when separated during his Irish trip in 1821. They had been married for twenty-seven years. See H. Montgomery Hyde, *The Strange Death of Lord Castlereagh* (London, 1959), 74-6

7 Lady Bessborough's comments were made in 1808, quoted in ibid, 73-4; and Webster, *Foreign Policy*, I, 8.

8 Stratford Canning to Castlereagh, Geneva, 17 September 1814, with enclosure of an address by Frédéric-César La Harpe to the inhabitants of the Pays de Vaud, PRONI D.3030/4237-8; Friedrich von Gentz, *Tagebücher* (Leipzig, 1873), I, 300-5.

9 What Britain meant by maritime rights was her right, in time of war, to visit and search neutral vessels on the high seas. Given her dominance of the seas, it could hardly be contested by the continental Powers in 1814. The issue was closely linked with the negotiations on Abolition of the slave trade. It was also the main cause of the squabble with America.

10 Henry A. Kissinger, *A World Restored* (Boston, n.d.), 147. Talleyrand at the time spoke of France as a "conserving Power."

11 George Jackson to Edward Cooke, Berlin, 26 September 1814, and Wellington to Castlereagh, Paris, 27 September 1814, in CC, X, 136-7.

12 Castlereagh to Emily, undated [January 1814], and Frankfurt, 15 January 1814, PRONI D.3030/T, reproduced in Webster, *Foreign Policy*, 503-4.

13 Germaine de Staël, *De l'Allemagne* (Paris, 1968), I, 115-16; Ludwig Hevesi, "Wien: Stadtbild, Festlichkeiten, Volksleben", in *Der Wiener Congress*, ed. Eduard Leisching (Vienna, 1898), 75; Gräfin Elise von Bernstorff, *Ein Bild aus der Zeit von 1789 bis 1835 aus ihren Aufzeichnungen* (Berlin, 1896), I, 126.

14 De Staël, *De l'Allemagne*, I, 99; James Sheehan, *German History, 1770-1866* (Oxford, 1989), 72.

15 For an account in English of the impact of the French Revolution on Germany, G.P. Gooch's *Germany during the French Revolution* (London, 1920) is still worth reading. Sheehan's *German History* provides an excellent update.

16 Sheehan, *German History*, 14-24.

17 Its most famous resident had been Mozart, who had rented the top flat there for a year, composed *Die Entführung aus dem Serail*, and married the landlady's daughter. Volkmar Braunbehrens, *Mozart in Vienna, 1781-1791*, trans. Timothy Bell (New York, 1989), 48, 63-4.

18 The transfer took a little over a week. See Hager Report, 17-18 September 1814, and Siber to Hager, 27 September 1814, in MHW, I, 84, 128; Webster, *Foreign Policy*, I, 332; Harold Nicolson gets his streets and houses confused, *The Congress of Vienna* (London, 1946), 126.

19 Webster, *Foreign Policy*, I, 329-31; Gentz, *Tagebücher*, I, 320, 324, 327, 356.

20 This meant that the Austrian services got no information from couriers going out. There were however occasions when couriers coming into the Legation were intercepted, as on 8 November 1814 when the Minister of Police victoriously announced to his Emperor that 56 letters and packets addressed to Castlereagh had been successfully intercepted. Hager Report, 8 November 1814, in MHW, I, 490. On the difficulty of surveying the British Legation see AF, 25.

21 De Staël, *De l'Allemagne*, I, 85, 129.

22 *Berliner Zeitung*, 26 October 1813, reprinted in *Österreichisch-Kaiserlichen priviligirten Wiener-Zeitung*, 5 November 1813, and reproduced in *Der Wiener Kongress in Augenzeugen berichten*, ed., Hilde Spiel (Düsseldorf, 1965), 31-2; Jean de Bourgoing, *Vom Wiener Kongress* (Vienna & Munich, 1964), 28.

23 Hevesi, "Wien," 75-6; M.F. Perth, *Wiener Kongresstagebuch* (Vienna & Munich, 1981), 23 September 1814, 36.

24 Hevesi, "Wien," 78; Joseph Richter, *Die Eipeldauer Briefe, 1799-1813* (Munich, 1918), II, 237; Bourgoing, *Wiener Kongress*, 83.

25 Robert Messner, *Die Leopoldstadt im Vormärz* (Vienna, 1962), 42-5; de Staël, *De l'Allemagne*, I, 83.

26 Nicolai, *Beschreibung einer Reise durch Deutschland* (1785), quoted in Marcel Brion, *La Vie quotidienne à Vienne au temps de Mozart et de Schubert* (Paris, 1959), 76, 80; de Staël, *De l'Allemagne*, I, 85; Robert Waissenberger, "Die Mentalität des Biedermeier," in *Wien, 1815-1848*, ed. R. Waissenberger (Vienna, 1986), 72.

27 Richter, *Eipeldauer*, II, 179 (letters dated 1804); Hevesi, "Wien," 80.

28 Beethoven, "Programme of the Concert of 22 December 1808…" in H. C. Robbins Landon, ed., *Beethoven: His Life, Work and World* (London, 1992), 152.

29 Adalbert Stifter, *Wien und die Wiener* (1844), in Messner, *Leopoldstadt*, 47; Hevesi, "Wien," 78-80; Richter, *Eipeldauer*, II, 392-6; de Staël, *De l'Allemagne*, I. 84-6.

30 Perth, *Kongresstagebuch*, 5 September 1814, 33.

31 Richter, *Eipeldauer*, II, 179-80 (Letters of 1804). For a brief general survey of Vienna's development in this period see Elisabeth Lichtenberger, *Vienna* (London, 1993), 14-36.

32 Waissenberger, "Mentalität," 51-70; Alois Brusatti, "Wien 1814-15," in *Wiener Kongress, Ausstellung* (Vienna, 1965), 233; Renate Banik-Schweitzer, *Wien in Vormärz* (Vienna, 1980).

33 Carl Bertuch, *Bertuchs Tagebuch vom Wiener Kongress*, ed. Hermann Freiherr von Egloffstein (Berlin, 1916), in Spiel, ed., *Wiener Kongress*, 115-16.

34 Johann Pezzl, "Sketch of Vienna," in H.C. Robbins Landon, *Mozart and Vienna* (London, 1991) 127; Joseph Farington, *The Farington Diary* (London, 1927), VII, 272, 23 July 1814; La Garde-Chambonas in Spiel, ed., *Wiener Kongress*, 115; Varnhagan von Ense and Seume in Bourgoing, *Wiener Kongress*, 28.

35 Pezzl, "Sketch," 118-19; Hevesi, "Wien," 78.

36 Perth, *Kongresstagebuch*, 1-2 September 1814, 32-3; Richter, *Eipeldauer*, II, 255; Waissenberger, "Mentalität," 72; Brion, *Vie quotidienne*, 62, 74-5; Richter, *Eipeldauer*, II, 387.

37 Ibid, 385; Bernstorff, *Ein Bild*, I, 129-30.

38 *Der Freimüthige*, 26 December 1805, and F.A. von Schönholz, *Traditionen zur Charakteristik Oesterreichs* (Munich, 1914) in Robbins Landon, *Beethoven*, 130, 160-1; Richard Kralik, *Histoire de Vienne* (Paris, 1932), 305-19; Brusatti, "Wien," 233-4.

39 Richter, *Eipeldauer*, II, 384 (1812 letters); Sheehan, *German History*, 280; de Staël, *De l'Allemagne*, I, 77-8; Brusatti, "Wien," 233.

40 Brion, *Vie quotidienne*, 52-4.

41 Hermann Broch, *Création littéraire et connaissance* (Paris, 1966), particularly in his essay "Hofmannsthal et son temps," 86-108.

42 The Nazis did not make trustworthy historians. They called their regime the Third Reich, but actually it was the Fourth. Those who, like Dr Conor Cruise O'Brien, worry about the possible emergence of a new German Reich may comfort themselves with the knowledge that the First Reich, founded by Charlemagne on Christmas Day, A.D. 800, lasted 1,006 years; the Second Reich, founded by Kaiser Franz in 1804, lasted 115 years; Bismarck's Third Reich, founded in 1871, lasted forty-seven years; Hitler's Fourth Reich lasted just twelve. A

43 Quotations from Jean Gabriel Eynard, Marie Therese von Sachsen, and Archduke Johann (on the Emperor in Paris) in Spiel, ed., *Wiener Kongreß*, 210-12; G. de Bertier de Sauvigny, *Metternich* (Paris, 1986), 136. A good detailed portrait of Kaiser Franz can be found in Heinrich Ritter von Srbik, *Metternich: Der Staatsmann und der Mensch* (Munich, 1954), I, 443-50.

44 Spiel, ed., *Wiener Kongreß*, 210.

45 C.L.W. von Metternich, *Mémoires, documents et écrits* (Paris, 1880),I, 128-30.

46 Enno E. Kraehe, *Metternich's German Policy* (Princeton, N.J., 1963), I, 292-3; Guillaume de Bertier de Sauvigny, "Sainte-Alliance et Alliance dans les conceptions de Metternich," *Revue historique*, ccxxii (1960), 260-1.

47 Metternich, *Mémoires*, I, 133.

48 Quoted in Sheehan, *German History*, 34.

49 Bertier de Sauvigny, *Metternich*, 202.

50 *"Vertraute höheren Standes"* should be translated literally as "confidants of a superior *Stand,"* the *Stand* being one's rank in the corporate order of the old Reich; the phrase makes a bit of a mouthful in English. The decree of 1806 is reproduced in AF, 8. For this and following paragraphs, ibid, 1-90; Spiel, ed., *Wiener Kongress*, 24-7, 195-204; MHW, I, vii-xxiv.

51 Hager's reviews, the intercepted letters and dispatches, the reports from the army of agents, along with Kaiser Franz's own marginalia were revealed to the public one hundred years later, during the First World War (see AF and MHW). They provide a detailed account of developments in Vienna in the year of the Congress. Baron Hager himself would die, like the younger Pitt, of exhaustion in 1816 at the age of fifty-six.

52 "I begin by saying to you that I do not like Vienna, that I have never liked it. Perhaps I will like it one day – but that will not be because of Vienna." Metternich to the Duchess von Sagan, Fribourg, 27 December 1813, in Clemens von Metternich and Wilhelmine von Sagan, *Ein Briefwechsel*, ed. M. Ullrichová (Graz & Cologne, 1966), 146.

53 For the following paragraphs on Metternich's early life I use Srbik, *Metternich*, particularly good on formative ideas; Alan Palmer, *Metternich* (London, 1971); Bertier de Sauvigny, *Metternich*; Kraehe, *German Policy*, which, in two volumes, goes far further in its general European analysis than its title might suggest; and Metternich's own *Mémoires*, which include papers and correspondence.

54 For a recent analysis of this "third Germany," see Peter Burg, *Die deutsche Trias in Idee und Wirklichkeit* (Stuttgart, 1989).

55 For his services in London, Count Lieven was made a prince in 1816.

56 Srbik, *Metternich*, I, 80-2; E.C.C. Corti, *Metternich und die Frauen* (Vienna and Zurich, 1948), I, 17-19, 30-46; Bertier de Sauvigny, *Metternich*, 83, 85.

57 Ibid, 39-41; Kraehe, I, 14, 62-70.

58 Srbik, *Metternich*, I, 237. See also Kissinger's comments on the peace of 1809, *World Restored*, 19.

59 Srbik, *Metternich*, I, 122.

60 Kraehe, *German Policy*, II, 119.

61 Ibid, I, 150; Sheehan, *German History*, 320.

62 Kraehe, *German Policy*, II, 80-4, 98-101.

63 For Metternich on the "society of states," see Metternich, *Mémoires*, I, 30-2.

64 Notably: "The real and permanent balance of power in Europe shall be regulated at the Congress upon principles *determined by the Allied Powers amongst themselves.*"

65 Palmer, *Metternich*, 112; Srbik, *Metternich*, I, 168; Metternich, *Mémoires*, I, 17, 181.

66 Metternich to Sagan, Baden, 15 September 1814, in Metternich and Sagan, *Briefwechsel*, 262-3.

67 Oddly enough, both Bagration's and Sagan's leases were due to expire in June 1815 – a significant date, as it turned out. Sagan was hoping that Bagration would leave for Italy so that the whole palace would come into her possession; this was wishful thinking. Metternich to Sagan, Frankfurt, 19 November 1813; Sagan to Metternich, Prague, 25 November 1813; Metternich to Sagan, Bâle, 13 January 1814; Sagan to Metternich, Vienna, 20 January 1814, in ibid, 112, 124, 168, 187.

68 Corti, *Frauen*, I, 8; AF, 21-2; Srbik, *Metternich*, I, 237-41; Bertier de Sauvigny, *Metternich*, 86-9.

simple statistical regression on this suggests that a Fifth Reich would survive, at the most, a few months.

69   Metternich to Sagan, Freiberg, 27-28 December 1813, in Metternich and Sagan, *Briefwechsel*, 146-8.

70   Metternich to Sagan, Géra, 23 October 1813, ibid, 85. Metternich hated the sight of war, a fact which undoubtedly accounted for the intensity of his feelings. During the war of 1813, the effect a remembered place could have on him was almost Proustian. For example, after he had crossed the appalling battlefield at Leipzig ("covered with dead," he said), he entered the town in a shaken state. There he had an important meeting with Hardenberg. He discovered the Prussian Chancellor in a house he had known ten years earlier: "I visited today your friend Chancellor Hardenberg and I found he had set himself up in the room where I met your mother and where I had first encountered Jeanne [Sagan's sister]." He found it odd to be reminded – amidst such horror, such carnage – of the enchantments of peace and the memory of Sagan and her family: "Leipzig had to be taken by assault for me to rediscover the circumstances which brought me close to you and your family." Standing in a room filled with pictures, furniture, and the curtains he had once touched, Metternich was overcome with old scenes and remembrances; "I am sure I only said stupidities to the Chancellor." "I cannot tell you the sensation I felt!" he scrawled excitedly late into the night. "Ten years were spread beneath my eyes – I went over the past – the present – I shuddered at the future! Three years of a peaceful and sweet pleasure were served, full of charm, to my eyes. My life, I said to myself, has flowed by unintentionally." Metternich to Sagan, Leipzig, 20, 21 October 1813, in ibid., 82-4.

71   The mother of Prince Adam Czartoryski, Alexander's tutor, minister, and friend – the same Czartoryski who had drafted the Russian programme for a European "league of states" in 1804 that provided the basis of the Pitt Plan, the basis also of Castlereagh's whole policy in Europe.

72   Clementine Bagration was acknowledged as Metternich's child even by his wife, Eleonore. She was brought up by the Metternichs in Baden and eventually married an Austrian general, Count Otto Blume. She died in childbirth in

1829. Corti, *Frauen*, I, 68-72; Palmer, *Metternich*, 36; and for a contemporary portrait, A. de La Garde-Chambonas, *Souvenirs du Congrès de Vienne, 1814-1815* (Paris, 1904), 88.

73   Evidently the blood of Baron von Armfeld was unacceptable to a man of Rohan's rank (the motto on his coat of arms was "*Roy ne puys, Duc ne daygne, Rohan suys*" – "Kings cannot, Dukes dare not, Rohans are"); Wilhelmine was forced to travel in concealment to Hamburg where she gave birth to Gustava, or "Vava," who would then be presented in public as her "adopted daughter." This appears to be the only child she ever had.

74   Corti, *Frauen*, I, 72-5; Bertier de Sauvigny, *Metternich*, 58-60.

75   Quoted in ibid, 60.

76   Corti, *Frauen*, I, 81-2, 124.

77   Ibid., I, 318 -23.

78   Young Alfred von Windischgrätz had made a brave contribution to Archduke Charles's campaign of 1809 but, unhappily, most historians would remember him as the old slaughterer of students and workers in the Revolution of 1848 – Metternich's final revenge on his rival.

79   Quoted in Bertier de Sauvigny, *Metternich*, 148.

80   Gentz to Pilat, Ratiborzitz, 14 June 1813, in Corti, *Frauen*, 376-7; Metternich to Sagan, Prague, 22 July 1813; Sagan to Metternich, 11 June 1813, in Metternich and Sagan, *Briefwechsel*, 23, 34.

81   Metternich to Sagan, Prague, 16, 17, 19, 20 August 1813 in ibid, 38-41.

82   Metternich to Sagan, Teplitz, 17 September 1813; Chemnitz, 12 October 1813, in ibid, 65-6, 80. Bertier de Sauvigny misquotes Metternich with "*Mon amie et l'Europe, l'Europe est mon amie,*" which rather distorts Metternich's original point. See Bertier de Sauvigny, *Metternich*, 169.

83   Sagan to Metternich, Prague, 21 October 1813; Ratiborzitz, 31 August 1813; Prague, 4 November 1813, in Metternich and Sagan, *Briefwechsel*, 52-4, 84, 96.

84   Metternich to Sagan, Teplitz, 22 September 1813, in ibid., 66.

85   Sagan to Metternich, Prague, 15 September 1813; Metternich to Sagan, Teplitz, 17 September 1813, in ibid, 63.

86   Metternich to Sagan, Frankfurt, 17 November 1813, and Freiburg, 27

December 1813, in ibid., 111, 148.

87 Kaiser Franz had honoured Metternich with the title of "Prince" immediately after the victory at Leipzig in October 1813.

88 Gentz to Metternich, 5 February 1814 in Corti, *Frauen*, I, 449-50.

89 Ibid., 450.

90 Sagan to Metternich, Vienna, 20 April 1814, in Metternich and Sagan, *Briefwechsel*, 250.

91 Metternich to Sagan, London, 8 June 1814, in ibid, 257.

92 Gentz, *Tagebücher*, 24 July 1814, I, 285

93 Guillaume de Bertier de Sauvigny states that "on Monday the 25th, [the Duchess von Sagan] went round to the Ballhausplatz to spend the night there with her lover. It is then, it seems, that [Metternich] extorted from her the most strange, and vain, of pacts: she promised to be exclusively faithful to him for six months." The professor does not cite his sources. The correspondence of Metternich, Sagan, and Gentz of the time all suggest that the "night" (if it took place at all) was short, bitter, and that Metternich was in no position to extort anything from Sagan at all. Bertier de Sauvigny, *Metternich*, 218.

94 Metternich to Sagan, Vienna, July 1814, in Metternich and Sagan, *Briefwechsel*, 258.

95 Sagan to Metternich, Baden, July 1814, in ibid.

96 Gentz to Metternich, Baden, 24 July 1814, in ibid., 258-9; Corti, *Frauen*, I, 472-3; Gentz *Tagebücher*, 24 July, 12 August, I, 285, 292.

97 Ibid.; Gentz, *Tagebücher*, 12 August 1814, I, 292; Metternich to Sagan, Baden, 15 September 1814, in Metternich and Sagan, *Briefwechsel*, 262-3.

98 Metternich to Sagan, Persenbeug, 14 August 1814, in ibid., 260. Divorce was not, in fact, wholly unacceptable in the Austrian Court at this time. Kaiser Franz himself, following the death of Maria Ludovika in 1816, married Caroline, daughter of King Maximilian Joseph of Bavaria and divorced wife of the King of Württemberg.

99 That is, the wife of his nephew, Edmond de Périgord.

100 Georges Lacour-Gayet, *Talleyrand* (Paris, 1990), 238; Talleyrand, *Mémoires*, 665.

101 Duchesse de Dino, *Souvenirs* (Paris,

1908), 110; L.-J. Arrigon, *Une amie de Talleyrand* (Paris, 1946), 47-53.

102 Lacour-Gayet at least claims that this is Lady Yarmouth (*Talleyrand*, 675); Arrigon, who quotes in the original English, cites this as a letter from Talleyrand's old friend, Montrond, to Flahaut, October 1812 (*Une amie*, 146).

103 Talleyrand had been married by civil authorities in the Tenth Arrondissement of Paris on 10 September 1802 under pressure from Napoleon; no religious ceremony ever took place. See Bibliothèque Nationale, Salle des Manuscrits, N.A.F. 24346; André Billecocq, *La Séparation aimiable du prince et de la princesse de Talleyrand* (Paris, 1987).

104 An *émigrée*, the former Mme Grand was immediately suspected of conspiring with the English when she returned to France in 1797. Convinced she was being pursued, she knocked at the gates of the Ministry of Exterior Relations and requested asylum. Talleyrand, perceiving "a woman in tears, with the most beautiful blond hair that perhaps ever existed," took her in, offered her a bed, breakfast, a dinner, a bed again, plus breakfast and dinner... "*Mme Grand ne sortit plus de l'hôtel,*" a contemporary of Talleyrand's reported. In Lacour-Gayet, *Talleyrand*, 312-13.

105 Ibid, 308-14, 469-82, 715.

106 Dino, *Souvenirs*, 155.

107 Metternich to Sagan, Paris, 23 April 1814, in Metternich and Sagan, *Briefwechsel*, 253.

108 Dino, *Souvenirs*, 126, 128, 138.

109 Lacour-Gayet, *Talleyrand*, 648; Arrigon, *Amie*, 121, 148-50.

110 Quoted in ibid, 152.

111 Talleyrand, *Mémoires*, 664-6; Lacour-Gayet, *Talleyrand*, 826.

112 Talleyrand, *Mémoires*, 664; Talleyrand to Caulaincourt, 28 August 1814, reproduced in ibid, 700.

113 Talleyrand to duchesse de Courlande, Strasbourg, 18 September 1814, in Talleyrand, *Le Miroir de Talleyrand: Lettres inédites à la duchesse de Courlande pendant le Congrès de Vienne*, ed. Gaston Palewski (Paris, 1976), 31; Talleyrand to Louis XVIII, Vienna, 25 September 1814, in T&L, 1. On the diplomatic tension between Britain and France over the Princess of Wales's presence in France, see Wellington to Liverpool, Paris, 9 and

12 September 1814, in WSD, IX, 234, 240-1.

114 Talleyrand, *Mémoires*, 701.

115 "Turkish music" was what somebody like Perth called the loud strains of the Austrian military bands. It probably had its origins in the Turkish siege of 1683. Elements of it can be heard in Haydn and Mozart, and particularly the famous final movement, *alla turca, allegretto,* the "Turkish March" of Sonata K. 331 (1779).

116 Perth, *Kongresstagebuch*, 19-24 September 1814, 33-7, 125; ** to Hager, 20 September 1814, in MHW, I, 92.

117 Nota to Hager, 25 September 1814, in ibid, 110.

118 La Garde-Chambonas, *Souvenirs*, 28-9; Gentz, *Tagebücher*, 18 - 23 September 1814, I, 307-10.

119 Metternich to Eleonore, Vienna, 19 September 1814, in Corti, *Frauen*, I, 471; Metternich to Sagan, Vienna, 19 September 1814, in Metternich and Sagan, *Briefwechsel*, 264; Gentz, *Tagebücher*, 19 September 1814, I, 307-8.

120 Kraehe, *German Policy*, II, 121-4.

121 The pertinent details of which are told P.G. Thielen's *Karl August von Hardenberg, 1750-1822: Eine Biographie* (Cologne, 1967).

122 Gentz, *Tagebücher*, 18 September 1814, I, 307; Kraehe gives the best account of the meeting in the Chancellery, *German Policy*, II, 124-5; Nicolson's discussion of procedural problems, though inaccurate, provides useful insights, *Congress*, 134-9.

123 The "protocol," or formal record of the diplomatic conferences, was one of the major innovations made during the Congress of Vienna. As Metternich noted in his memoirs "Two innovations in diplomacy date from this period: that of memoranda…, and that of simple protocols having the form and value of definitive conventions… They made the dispatching of business so much easier…" The need for brief memoranda and protocols arose from the fact that all the major Sovereigns and diplomats of Europe were to be found in one place. "Many affairs," explained Metternich, "which in other circumstances would have developed only slowly, were settled in a morning." Like business today done on the telephone, transactions at Vienna were done with speed but often went unrecorded. Metternich left a useful hint for historians: "During the whole duration of the Congress of Vienna, Lord Castlereagh and the plenipotentiaries of England and of France never ceased corresponding with their governments." Metternich, *Mémoires*, I, 136-7.

124 Nesselrode to Alexander, 25 September 1814, in Kraehe, *German Policy*, II, 127.

125 Kraehe, *German Policy*, II, 128-30; *Le Congrès de Vienne et les traités de 1815* (Paris, 1863), ed, comte d'Angeberg, I, 249-51; Nicolson, *Congress*, 140; Webster, *Foreign Policy*, I, 338.

126 Ibid.

127 AF, 120; Bourgoing, *Wiener Kongress*, 81; see also Nota to Hager, Vienna, 28 September 1814, in MHW, I, 156; Kraehe, *German Policy*, II, 127.

128 Ibid., II, 127, 131-2; Francis Ley, *Alexandre Ier et sa Sainte-Alliance* (Paris, 1975), 91.

129 Kraehe, *German Policy*, II, 133-6.

130 Ley, *Alexandre Ier*, 91; Grand Duchess Catherine to the Crown Prince of Württemberg, Franzensbrunn, 5 August 1814, in Corti, *Frauen*, I, 457; Nota to Hager, Vienna, 27 September 1814, in MHW, I, 129.

131 Kraehe, *German Policy*, II, 133.

132 Bourgoing, *Wiener Kongress*, 81. For the entry of Emperor Alexander and King Frederick William into Vienna see ibid, 81-3; Bernstorff, *Ein Bild*, I, 154; Perth, *Kongresstagebuch*, 25-6 September 1814, 37-41; La Garde-Chambonas, *Souvenirs*, 5-6.

133 Bourgoing, *Wiener Kongress*, 82.

134 Hager to Emperor, Vienna, 25-6 September 1814, in MHW, I, 106; Perth, *Kongresstagebuch*, 25 September 1814, 38.

135 Ibid.; Bernstorff, *Ein Bild*, I, 154; Talleyrand to Louis XVIII, Vienna, 25 September 1814, in T&L, 5.

136 Perth, *Kongresstagebuch*, 25 September 1814, 39; Metternich to Sagan, Vienna, 25 September 1814, 3 h 1/2, in Metternich and Sagan, *Briefwechsel*, 265.

137 Sagan to Metternich, Prague, 2 November 1813, in ibid., 96.

138 For intercepted letters on the Grand Duchess's relationship with the Archduke Charles and the Crown Prince of Württemberg, see MHW, I, 70-3, 98. See also Empress Dowager of

Russia to the King of Württemberg, Pawlowskoïé, 27 August 1814 (western Gregorian calendar), in ibid., 62-4.

139 Bernstorff, *Ein Bild*, I, 154; Hevesi, "Wien," 85.

140 Perth, *Kongresstagebuch*, 25 September 1814, 37, 39.

141 Report to Hager, 29 September 1814, in MHW, I, 160; other reports, intercepted letters, etc., for September in ibid, 66-8, 113, 125, 156-7.

142 Rosenbaum, *Tagebuch*, quoted in Hevesi, "Wien," 82.

143 Comtesse d'Edling (de Stourdza), *Mémoires* (Moscow, 1888), 197-8, in Ley, *Alexandre Ier*, 94.

144 Kraehe, *German Policy*, II, 131; Nota to Hager, 28 September 1814, in MHW, I, 156; Talleyrand to Louis XVIII, 29 September 1814, in T&L, 7-8.

145 Talleyrand to Louis XVIII, 25 September 1814, in ibid, 4.

146 Arrigon, *Amie*, 161; Talleyrand to duchesse de Courlande, 25 September 1814, in Talleyrand, *Miroir*, 35.

147 AF, 22.

148 Report to Hager, 27 September 1814; Bellion to Prince of Wallachia, 27 September 1814, in MHW, I, 133-4, 150; Talleyrand to Louis XVIII, 29 September 1814, in T&L, 7-8.

149 Talleyrand to Louis XVIII, 25 September 1814, in ibid, 3.

150 Letters reproduced in Talleyrand, *Miroir*, 38, and Nicolson, *Congress*, 143.

151 Ibid., 138-40; Kissinger, *World Restored*, 149-51.

152 Accounts of the ministerial conference in Gentz, *Tagebücher*, 30 September 1814, I, 312; Talleyrand, *Mémoires*, 704-6; Talleyrand to Louis XVIII, 4 October 1814, in T&L, 12-20; Kraehe, *German Policy*, II, 137-8.

153 Talleyrand, *Mémoires*, 705.

154 Talleyrand to Louis XVIII, 4 October 1814, in T&L, 16; Gentz, *Tagebücher*, 30 September 1814, I, 312.

155 Talleyrand, *Mémoires*, 705.

156 Gentz, *Tagebücher*, 30 September 1814, I, 312. Description of works in Metternich's gardens in "Fête de la Paix – Programme," reproduced in Metternich, *Mémoires*, I, 268-70.

157 Talleyrand to Louis XVIII, 4 October 1814, in T&L, 16-20.

158 *"Mais il faut que chacun y trouve ses convenances"* or literally "But each one must find there what is *suitable* to him." Similarly Alexander says, *"Les*

convenances de L'Europe sont le droit." The dialogue, recorded by Talleyrand less than a week later, bears the literary imprint of its French author. Here there is a play on words, for *"convenances"* can also mean "agreements" or "accords," just as the word *"droit"* (like *"Recht"* in German) means both "law" and "right," even "privilege." This ambiguity, even if Talleyrand embroidered his account, strikes me as true to the character of Alexander. Ibid.

159 Gentz, *Tagebücher*, 30 September 1814, I, 312.

160 Kraehe, *German Policy*, II, 138-9; Webster, *Foreign Policy*, I, pp, 339-40.

161 Metternich to Sagan, undated, but probably 2 or 3 October (or perhaps preceding the *soirée* of 30 September?) 1814, in Metternich and Sagan, *Briefwechsel*, 266.

162 Talleyrand to duchesse de Courlande, 2 October 1814, in Talleyrand, *Miroir*, 40.

163 Schmidt to Hager, 17 October 1814, in AF, 191.

164 Wellington did not specify to whom this letter was addressed, Wellington to Castlereagh, 27 September 1814, in CC, X, 137.

165 Wellington to Castlereagh, 9 October 1814, in ibid., 160-1.

166 For examples, see Kraehe, *German Policy*, II, 141, 193-4.

167 Bernstorff, *Ein Bild*, I, 156; Perth, *Kongresstagebuch*, 6-8 October 1814, 48-50; La Garde-Chambonas multiplies the number of disabled veterans present at the *Volksfest* by a factor of ten, *Souvenirs*, 78-80.

168 Kraehe, *German Policy*, II, 124, 142-3; ** to Hager, 10? October 1814, and Report, 8 October 1814, in AF, 167-70; Talleyrand to Louis XVIII, 9 October, in T&L, 39-44; Gentz, *Tagebücher*, 8 October 1814, I, 316. "It took a battle against your Prussians to introduce the phrase *public law*, because they love the usurpatory law of Bonaparte and all they seek is its success," Talleyrand wrote to the duchesse de Courlande on 13 October, *Miroir*, 55. Behind "the principles of public law," of course, Talleyrand saw his "sacred principle of legitimacy."

169 Gœhausen to Hager, 22 October 1814, in AF, 181; Bernstorff, *Ein Bild*, I, 168-9.

170 Ibid.; ** to Hager, 15 October 1814, in AF, 196; Varnhagen and Nostitz in

Bourgoing, *Wiener Kongress*, 83; La Garde-Chambonas, *Souvenirs*, 192-3.

171   Castlereagh to Wellington, 25 October 1814, in CC, X, 173-5. This letter contains one of the clearest and most concise statements on Castlereagh's foreign policy; it is significant that it should be addressed to Wellington and not to any member of the British Cabinet.

172   The English translation of Article VI – "The German States shall be independent, and united by a federal league" – is notably less ambiguous than the French version.

173   Kraehe, *German Policy*, II, 144-86; Bernstein, *Ein Bild*, I, 152; Gœhausen to Hager, 22 October, Anonymous report, 22 October, and Bartsch to Hager, 25 October 1814, in AF, 196-8, 202-3.

174   Talleyrand to Louis XVIII, 17 October 1814, in Talleyrand, *Mémoires*, 727-8.

175   O to Hager, 11 & 19 October 1814, in AF, 173-4, 192; Bernstorff, *Ein Bild*, 152.

176   Anon, 20 October 1814, in AF, 192.

177   Perth, *Kongresstagebuch*, 5 October 1814, 47; Hevesi, "Wien," 85.

178   ** to Hager, 4 October 1814, in AF, 156; Bernstorff, *Ein Bild*, I, 155-7.

179   Nota to Hager, 6 & 12(?) October 1814, in AF, 159, 175.

180   Roxandre Stourdza to Jung Stilling, Vienna, 17 October 1814; Krüdener to Stourdza, Strasbourg, 27 October 1814, in Ley, *Alexandre Ier*, 95-6. Baroness von Krüdener's prediction of Napoleon's return is reported in Mme Parquin (Louise Cochelet), *Mémoires* (Paris, 1836), II, 72-3, and *Mémoires de la Reine Hortense* (Paris, 1927), II, 272, and is confirmed in a letter written by the Baroness to Louise Cochelet in Strasbourg on 19 October 1814. But, as with all reported predictions of this kind, one must admit there is room for questioning.

181   Kissinger, *World Restored*, 156-60.

182   Kraehe, *German Policy*, II, 162, 193; Bertier de Sauvigny, *Metternich*, 233-4; Srbik, *Metternich*, I, 186-7.

183   Metternich to Sagan, 28 September 1814, *"au soir,"* in Metternich and Sagan, *Briefwechsel*, 266.

184   Metternich to Sagan, Vienna, 9 October 1814, in Sagan and Metternich, *Briefwechsel*, 267.

185   Nota to Hager, 2 October 1814, in AF, 149.

186   Nota to Hager, 3, 6 October, and

Hager Report, 16 October 1814, in ibid, 151, 158-9, 187-8.

187   Report, 14 October 1814 (Hager's official reports were regularly dated one day later than their compilation), in AF, 187; Talleyrand to Louis XVIII, 17 October 1814, *Mémoires*, 728-9; Kraehe, *German Policy*, II, 193-4.

188   Nota to Hager, 1st October 1814, in AF, 142-3.

189   D'Angeberg, ed., *Congrès*, II, 1936-9; Kraehe, *German Policy*, 158-9.

190   WSD, IX, 332-6.

191   Perth, *Kongresstagebuch*, 18 October 1814, 59; Kralik, *Histoire*, 325; Richter, *Eipeldauer*, II, 135. For a general history of war commemoration see George L. Mosse, *Fallen Soldiers* (Oxford, 1990).

192   Perth, *Kongresstagebuch*, 18-19 October 1814, 56-60; La Garde-Chambonas places this ceremony on the Glacis rather than the Jägerzeil, a fact contradicted by Perth and the enormous distance the troops would have to have covered to get to the feast that followed at the Lusthaus, *Souvenirs*, 22-5.

193   Perth, *Kongresstagebuch*, 18 October 1814, 58-9.

194   Bernstorff, *Ein Bild*, I, 148, 158-9.

195   Gentz, *Tagebuch*, 19 October 1814, I, 321.

196   Talleyrand to duchesse de Courlande, in *Miroir*, 58.

197   Gentz, *Tagebücher*, 20 October 1814, I, 321.

198   Hager's agents thought Julie Zichy was a wonderful alternative to the scheming Sagan, for Zichy was "too religious and virtuous to let anything at all unfavourable develop." See Hager Report, 14 October 1814, in AF, 187.

199   Metternich to Sagan, 21 October 1814, in *Briefwechsel*, 267-9.

200   Corti, *Frauen*, I, 476.

201   Gentz, *Tagebücher*, 22 October 1814, I, 322; Kraehe, *German Policy*, II, 205; text of Metternich's memorandum in Bourgoing, *Wiener Kongress*, 362-5.

202   Talleyrand to Louis XVIII, 25 October 1814, in Talleyrand, *Mémoires*, 729-30.

203   Gentz, *Tagebücher*, 24 October 1814, I, 323.

204   Talleyrand to Louis XVIII, in Talleyrand, *Mémoires*, 730-1; Metternich to Kaiser Franz, 24 October 1814, in Corti, *Frauen*, I, 477-8; Hegardt to Engeström, 12 November 1814, in AF, 280-1.

205 Gentz, *Tagebücher*, 25 October 1814, I, 323.

VIENNA, Winter 1814-1815

1 Metternich to Kaiser Franz, 24 October 1814, in E.C.C. Corti, *Metternich und die Frauen* (Vienna and Zurich, 1948), I, 477-8.

2 "The subject of this quarrel is not known, but the fact is incontestable," Hager Report, 31 October 1814, in MHW, I, 436-7. For the Sovereigns' visit to Buda, see ** to Hager, 6 November 1814, in AF, 239; and Talleyrand to Louis XVIII, 31 October 1814, in T&L, 87-8.

3 Metternich to Kaiser Franz, 2 November 1814, in E.E. Kraehe, *Metternich's German Policy* (Princeton, N.J., 1983), II, 232; Hardenberg to Castlereagh, 7 November 1814, in *Le Congrès de Vienne et les traités de 1815*, ed. comte d'Angeberg (Paris, 1863), I, 406-8; Castlereagh to Liverpool, 11 November 1814, in BD, 230; Talleyrand to Louis XVIII, 12 November 1814, in T&L, 109-10.

4 Talleyrand to Louis XVIII, 6 & 12 November 1814, in ibid., 97-8, 109-10; Castlereagh to Liverpool, 21 November 1814, in BD, 240; Kraehe, *German Policy*, II, 236-7.

5 Castlereagh to Liverpool, 5 November 1814; Emperor of Russia to Castlereagh, 21 November 1814; Castlereagh to Liverpool, 21 November 1814, in BD, 222-4, 239, 243-4.

6 Talleyrand to Louis XVIII, 31 October, 30 November 1814, in T&L, 90-1, 156; ** to Hager, 5 November 1814, in MHW, I, 473.

7 Talleyrand to Louis XVIII, 17 November 1814, in T&L, 132-3; Castlereagh reported the same meeting and virtually the same dialogue in a letter to Liverpool, 21 November 1814, in BD, 241.

8 Hager Report, 1 November 1814, in MHW, I, 434; ** to Hager, 9 November 1814, in AF, 305; A. de La Garde-Chambonas, *Souvenirs du Congrès de Vienne, 1814-1815* (Paris, 1904), 191-2.

9 Castlereagh to Liverpool, 11 & 21 November 1814, in BD, 230-3, 240.

10 Liverpool to Castlereagh, London, 14 & 28 October, 2, 18 & 25 November; Liverpool to Wellington, London, 26 November 1814; Bathurst to Castlereagh, London, 27 November 1814, in ibid, 210-11, 219-22, 235-6, 244-8.

11 Liverpool to Castlereagh, London, 18 & 25 November, in ibid, 235-6, 246.

12 Castlereagh to Wellington, Vienna, 25 October 1814, in CC, X, 173-5; Castlereagh to Liverpool, Vienna, 24 & 25 October 1814, in BD, 213, 217; Wellington to Castlereagh, 5 & 7 November, in ibid, 227-9; Louis XVIII to Talleyrand, and Blacas to Talleyrand, Paris, 9 November 1814, in T&L, 104-7.

13 Castlereagh to Wellington, 21 November 1814, in BD, 241.

14 Talleyrand to Louis XVIII, 17 & 25 November 1814, in *T&L*, 134, 142.

15 "Protestation du Roi de Saxe," Friedrichsfeld, 4 November 1814, in Angeberg, ed., *Congrès de Vienne*, I, 401-3.

16 **, Nota, and Goehausen to Hager, 1, 2, 3 & 9 November 1814, in AF, 234-6, 242-3.

17 Kraehe, *German Policy*, II, 241-4; Metternich to Hardenberg, n.d., 9 & 12 November 1814, in Angeberg, ed., *Congrès de Vienne*, I, 379-80, 406-8, 418-19.

18 See, for example, entries for 7-10 November 1814, Friedrich von Gentz, *Tagebücher* (Leipzig, 1873), I, 327-9.

19 6, 11, 13 November 1814, ibid, 327-30.

20 Hager Report and Nota to Hager, 1 November 1814, in AF, 233-5. Another story was that Alexander had been the cause of a breach in the budding relations between Metternich and the virtuous Julie Zichy. At one great *soirée* Alexander had approached the Countess and, within the hearing range of many, had said, "I know from Metternich himself that you have accorded him your favours." The virtuous Countess exploded into tears and from that evening on would accept from Metternich no excuse; she swore she would never listen to him again. See Hager Report, 1 November 1814, in ibid., 234.

21 Ibid.

22 ** to Hager, 4 & 6 November 1814, in MHW, I, 469, 480; Metternich to Sagan, 31 October - 28 November 1814, in Clemens von Metternich and Wilhelmine von Sagan, *Ein Briefwechsel*, ed. M. Ullrichová (Graz & Cologne, 1966), 269-74. This last let-

ter from Sagan to Metternich is actually dated 7 November (quoted in G. de Bertier de Sauvigny, *Metternich* [Paris, 1986], 229-30), but corresponds to the hostile attitude, reported by police, that she adopted towards Metternich throughout November.

23 Pozzo di Borgo, a Corsican who acted as Russia's Ambassador to Paris and who arrived in Vienna in November, had been trying since August to arrange a Franco-Russian entente. This provided Talleyrand with a useful threat to Austria.

24 ∗∗ to Hager, 3 November 1814, in AF, 237-8.

25 "Article semi-officiel sur la marche des travaux du Congrès de Vienne pendant le mois d'octobre 1814," n.d. (ca. 2 November 1814), in Angeberg, ed., *Congrès de Vienne*, I, 362-5.

26 Mavrojeni to Prince of Moldavia, Vienna, 2 November 1814, in AF, 276; Gentz, *Tagebücher*, 29 October 1814, I, 324.

27 Talleyrand to Louis XVIII, 31 October, 2 & 25 November 1814, in T&L, 94, 96-7, 99-101, 143; Löwenhjelm to Engeström, Vienna, 5 November 1814, in AF, 277-9; Kraehe, *German Policy*, II, 230-2.

28 "Troisième Protocole de la séance du 13 novembre 1814 des Plénipotentiaires des huit Puissances signataires du Traité de Paris," in Angeberg, ed., *Congrès de Vienne*, I, 424-7.

29 Kraehe, *German Policy*, II, 244-50; ∗∗ to Hager, 31 October 1814, in AF, 232.

30 Talleyrand actively encouraged the talk of war. At dinner one evening, when the Prince Eugène de Beaharnais was on the other side of his table, he jested with the pun, "Well the dinner will soon be over and I very much fear that there'll be only *coups de canon* for dessert." Ibid, 233; ∗∗ to Hager, 28 October 1814; Nota to Hager, 1 November 1814; Hager Report, 3 November 1814, in MHW, I, 424, 445, 458.

31 M.F. Perth, *Wiener Kongresstagebuch* (Vienna & Munich, 1981), 22 November 1814, 68, 156.

32 Ibid, 10 & 13 November 1814, 66-8.

33 "Déclaration du prince de Repnin," Dresden, 8 November 1814; "Publication des Gouverneurs généraux prussiens," Dresden, 10 November 1814, in Angeberg, ed., *Congrès de Vienne*, I, 413-14.

34 *"Ebullition, en Médicine, se dit de Toute espèce d'éruption passagère qui survient à la peau;* 'il a une ébullition par tout le corps.'" *Dictionnaire de l'Académie française* (Paris, 1820).

35 Perth, *Kongresstagebuch*, 18 November 1814, 68, 236; Talleyrand to duchesse de Courlande, 30 November 1814, in Talleyrand, *Le Miroir de Talleyrand: Lettres inédites à la duchesse de Courlande pendant le Congrès de Vienne*, ed. Gaston Palewski (Paris, 1976), 76-7, 81; Talleyrand to Louis XVIII, 17 November 1814, in T&L, 135; Castlereagh to Liverpool, 25 November 1814, in BD, 243. Hager's police put about the rumour that the Tsar had contracted a venereal disease. Talleyrand, on the other hand, dismissed Alexander's sickness as "a slight indisposition." Professor C.K. Webster, writing in the 1920s, claimed that the Tsar was suffering from "erysipelas" (popularly known as "St Anthony's fire" or "the rose") on one of his legs, *The Foreign Policy of Castlereagh* (London, 1931), I, 355. Daria Olivier, writing in the 1970s, claims that the symptoms of erysipelas only appeared in 1824, in the last year of the Tsar's life. See D. Olivier, *Alexandre Ier* (Paris, 1973), 427.

36 Talleyrand reserved his harshest comments for Castlereagh. Castlereagh's note of 11 October to Hardenberg, the full text of which was only now revealed to Talleyrand, filled him with repugnance; "it would be difficult for the neglect, if not contempt, for principles and the commonest ideas of healthy policy could be pushed further than in this note by Lord Castlereagh," he commented. Metternich's approach to the Saxon question was, he felt, more nuanced. Even allowing for Talleyrand's own prejudices, one has to admit that the French Minister had a point. Talleyrand to Louis XVIII, 17 November 1814, in T&L, 130-4.

37 Kraehe, *German Policy*, II, 236-56.

38 Hegardt to Engeström, 19 November 1814, in AF, 282; Talleyrand to Louis XVIII, 6 November 1814, in T&L, 97-8.

39 Talleyrand to Louis XVIII, 12, 17, 25 November 1814, in ibid, 110-11, 128, 148-9; Münster to Prince Regent, 27, 28, 30 November 1814, in Webster, *Foreign Policy*, 551-9; Castlereagh to Liverpool, 21 November 1814, in BD,

240; Kraehe, *German Policy*, II, 241.

40 ** to Hager, 11 November 1814, in AF, 248-9.

41 Gentz, *Tagebücher*, 21 November 1814, 332; ** to Hager, 12 & 14 November 1814, in MHW, I, 508, 525; Hegardt to Engeström, 19 November 1814, in AF, 282.

42 Münster to Prince Regent, 27, 30 November 1814, in Webster, *Foreign Policy*, 553-4, 558; Talleyrand to Louis XVIII, 12 November 1814, in T&L, 111.

43 ** to Hager, 11 November 1814, in AF, 248.

44 Hager Report, 6 November 1814, in MHW, I, 471-2; Talleyrand to Louis XVIII, 25 November 1814, in T&L, 144-7.

45 Münster to Prince Regent, Vienna, 30 November 1814, in Webster, *Foreign Policy*, 558; Louis XVIII to Talleyrand, 22 November 1814, in T&L, 136.

46 Metternich to Hardenberg, 20 November 1814, in Kraehe, *German Policy*, II, 257. On Vienna's hopes for peace in late November, see Countess Richberg to her father, 23 November 1814, and Mavrojéni to the Prince of Moldavia, 26 November 1814, in AF, 283-4.

47 La Garde-Chambonas, *Souvenirs*, 16; Talleyrand to Louis XVIII, 6 November 1814, in T&L, 103.

48 For an excellent collection of primary sources on Beethoven, see H. C. Robbins Landon, ed., *Beethoven: His Life, Work and World* (London, 1992), my principal source for the following paragraphs.

49 Reviews reproduced in ibid., 78, 81, 84, 108, 112, 178, etc..

50 AF, 288.

51 La Garde-Chambonas, *Souvenirs*, 41.

52 Ibid., 148-62; Gräfin Elise von Bernstorff, *Ein Bild aus der Zeit von 1789 bis 1835 aus ihren Aufzeichnungen* (Berlin, 1896), I, 160; Perth, *Kongresstagebuch*, 25 November 1814, 69-70; Talleyrand to duchesse de Courlande, 24 November 1814, in *Miroir*, 74.

53 Ibid; La Garde-Chambonas, *Souvenirs*, 161.

54 Kraehe, *German Policy*, II, 257-9.

55 Metternich to Sagan, 28 November 1814, "At Night," in *Briefwechsel*, 274.

56 Kraehe, *German Policy*, I, 259.

57 Descriptions of the Concert in Robbins Landon, ed., *Beethoven*, 174-6.

58 On Beethoven's conducting, ibid., 149-50, 173, 203-4, 214.

59 Metternich to Sagan, 27 November 1814, in *Briefwechsel*, 273; La Garde-Chambonas, *Souvenirs*, 197-203; Gentz, *Tagebücher*, 6 December 1814, 337; Talleyrand to duchesse de Courlande, 7 December 1814, in *Miroir*, 79.

60 Ibid., 75, 84; AF, 251, 281, 314; MHW, 445-6.

61 Perth, *Kongresstagebuch*, 1 December 1814, 70-1.

62 Hardenberg, *Note verbale*, 2 December 1814, in Angeberg, ed., *Congrès de Vienne*, II, 1941-52; Castlereagh to Liverpool, 5 December 1814, in BD, 248-51; Kraehe, *German Policy*, II, 260-1.

63 Ibid, 262; Castlereagh to Liverpool, 5 & 7 December 1814, in BD, 251-7.

64 Metternich to Hardenberg, 10 December 1814, and "Mémoire de Frédéric de Gentz," 12 February 1815, in C.L.W. von Metternich, *Mémoires, documents et écrits* (Paris, 1880), II, 485-6, 503-9.

65 Castlereagh to Liverpool, 17 December 1814, in BD, 257-9; Kraehe, *German Policy*, II, 264-71; Hager Report, 16 December 1814, in AF, 303.

66 Hager Report, 16 December 1814, and ** to Hager, 22 December 1814, in ibid, 304, 308; Castlereagh to Liverpool, 25 December 1814, in BD, 272. Even Württemberg backed down from its usual pro-Russian stance and expressed willingness to join an anti-Prussian League; Grand Duchess Catherine, engaged to the King's first born, was persuaded to make an appeal to her brother.

67 Kraehe, *German Policy*, II, 270, 283-4; Hager report, 22 December 1814, 308.

68 Kraehe, *German Policy*, II, 284; Henry A. Kissinger, *A World Restored* (Boston, n.d.), 166. Friedrich Gentz, reviewing two months later the policies of each major Power at the Congress, said that France's was "the most beautiful and the simplest of them all." See Gentz, "Mémoire," in Metternich, *Mémoires*, II, 480.

69 Talleyrand to Metternich, 19 December 1814, in ibid., 509-14.

70 Castlereagh to Liverpool, 24 December 1814, in BD, 269-70.

71 Liverpool to Castlereagh, 23 December 1814, in ibid., 265-7.

72 Castlereagh to Liverpool, 17 December

1814, in ibid., 259; Kraehe, *German Policy*, II, 270-1; Bartsch to Hager, 22 December 1814, in AF, 309-10.

73 ** to Hager, 23 December 1814, in ibid, 312-14; Castlereagh to Liverpool, 24 December 1814, in BD, 268-71.

74 ** to Hager, 26 December 1814, in AF, 315.

75 Chevalier Freddi to Hager, 26 December 1814, in ibid, 316.

76 ** to Hager, 26 December 1814, in ibid., 315; Castlereagh to Liverpool, 24-5 December 1814, in BD, 272-3.

77 Kraehe, *German Policy*, II, 287-8.

78 **, an anonymous agent, and O to Hager, 26, 28, 29 December 1814, in AF, 315, 319-21; Castlereagh to Liverpool, 1 January 1814, in BD, 277.

79 Kraehe, *German Policy*, II, 288-91; Jean de Bourgoing, *Vom Wiener Kongress* (Vienna & Munich, 1964), 231-6; Castlereagh to Liverpool, 1 January 1815, in BD, 277-8.

80 Perth, *Kongresstagebuch*, 31 December 1814 - 1 January 1815, 79-80; La Garde-Chambonas, *Souvenirs*, 241-2.

81 Bernstorff, *Ein Bild*, I, 169-70; Joseph Richter, *Die Eipeldauer Briefe, 1799-1813* (Munich, 1918), II, 236-7; Richard Kralik, *Histoire de Vienne* (Paris, 1932), 324.

82 Gentz, *Tagebücher*, 1 January 1815, I, 346.

83 Metternich to Sagan, 31 December 1814 ("Night, 11 o'clock"), in *Briefwechsel*, 274-5.

84 Gentz, *Tagebücher*, 31 December 1814 - 5 January 1815, I, 344-7.

85 Metternich to Sagan, 3 January & 21 March 1815, in *Briefwechsel*, 275-6, 279.

86 Castlereagh to Liverpool, 5 January 1815, in BD, 283. News of the Treaty of Ghent, signed Christmas Eve 1814, reached Vienna before the United States, where it arrived too late to save the life of Wellington's brother-in-law, Edward Pakenham; he died at the head of his troops in a useless little battle at New Orleans on 8 January. Thus the war ended on the same tragic note as it had begun – over a misunderstanding due to the delay in trans-Atlantic communications.

87 Castlereagh to Liverpool, 1st January 1815, in ibid, 277-8; Kraehe, *German Policy*, II, 292-3.

88 Ibid., 294-8; Castlereagh to Liverpool, 2-5 January 1815, in BD, 280-3; Talleyrand to Louis XVIII, 4 January

1815, in Talleyrand, *Mémoires*, 737-8; Talleyrand to duchesse de Courlande, 6 January 1815, in *Miroir*, 94.

89 Perth, *Kongresstagebuch*, 7 January 1815, 81.

90 La Garde-Chambonas, *Souvenirs*, 187; Bernstorff, *Ein Bild*, I, 138, 180-1.

91 Ibid., 174-5; Talleyrand to duchesse de Courlande, 8-9 February 1815, in Talleyrand, *Mémoires*, 739-40; Metternich to Sagan, 8 February 1815, in *Briefwechsel*, 277-8; ** to Hager, 5 February 1815, in AF, 381; Corti, *Frauen*, I, 481.

92 Wendy Hinde, *Castlereagh* (London, 1981), 227; Kissinger, *World Restored*, 170-4; Harold Nicolson, *The Congress of Vienna* (London, 1946), 179-80.

93 Nota to Hager, 3 February 1815, ** to Hager, 5 February 1815, in AF, 380-1; Bernstorff, *Ein Bild*, I, 162, 182.

94 Kraehe, *German Policy*, II, 325-6.

95 Metternich, *Mémoires*, I, 204-5.

ELBA and PARIS, Winter 1814-1815

1 Napoleon to Dalesme, aboard HMS *Undaunted*, 3 May 1814, in Louise Laflandre-Linden, *Napoléon et l'Ile d'Elbe* (Castel, 1989), 91.

2 Armand de Caulaincourt, *Mémoires* (Paris, 1933), III, 316-34.

3 Ibid., 158.

4 Guillaume Bertier de Sauvigny, *Metternich* (Paris, 1986), 196; Neil Campbell, *Napoleon at Fontainebleau and Elba* (London, 1869), 162-8, quotes in full, in French and English, the text of the Treaty of Fontainebleau as well as some of Castlereagh's correspondence with London.

5 *The Times*, 15 June 1814.

6 Caulaincourt, *Mémoires*, III, 247-9, 314-15, 341-2.

7 Ibid, 346, 358; Marie-Louise to Napoleon, Angerville, 12 April 1814, quoted in Vincent Cronin, *Napoleon* (London, 1994), 369.

8 Castlereagh to Liverpool, Paris, 13 April 1814, in Caulaincourt, *Mémoires*, III, 342, and Campbell, *Napoleon*, 102.

9 Castlereagh to Campbell, Paris, 16 April 1814, in ibid., 154-5; Katharine MacDonogh, "A Sympathetic Ear: Napoleon, Elba and the British," *History Today* (February 1994), 34.

10 Campbell, *Napoleon*, 103, 156-60. On Napoleon's suicide attempt, Caulaincourt, *Mémoires*, III, 357-66.

11 For a history of Elba see Laflandre-Linden, *Elbe*. André Pons de L'Hérault, *Souvenirs et anecdotes de l'Ile d'Elbe* (Paris, 1897) is an important record, by the administrator of the iron ore mines at Rio Marina, both of life in Elba and of Napoleon's stay.

12 Duval in Laflandre-Linden, *Elbe*, 82.

13 Ibid.

14 Reports of plague in Elba reached the British press, see *St James's Chronicle*, 31 May - 2 June 1814. Neil Campbell reports that the quarantine was eventually lifted on 31 July 1814 after it had been determined that no infection had spread, *Napoleon*, 272.

15 Ibid., 230; Laflandre-Linden, *Elbe*, 97-101.

16 Campbell, *Napoleon*, 217, 233; Laflandre-Linden, *Elbe*, 152-60.

17 Henry Houssaye, *1815: La Première Restauration, le Retour de l'Ile d'Elbe, les Cent Jours* (Paris, 1920), 155; Fernand Beaucour, *Napoléon à l'Ile d'Elbe* (Paris, 1991), 2-3; Laflandre-Linden, *Elbe*, 151-2, 160-8.

18 Campbell, *Napoleon*, 233, 243-9.

19 Houssaye, *Première Restauration*, 157.

20 E. Tangye Lean, *The Napoleonists* (London, 1970), 12-17, 126-48.

21 Campbell, *Napoleon*, 212, 240-1.

22 Ibid., 280 (entry for 3 August 1814); Viscount Ebrington, *Memorandum of two conversations...* (London, 1823), 19, 23; Fernand Beaucour, *Une visite à Napoléon...* (Paris, 1990), 3; MacDonough, "Sympathetic Ear," 31.

23 Beaucour, *Une visite*, 3; Campbell, *Napoleon*, 317.

24 F. R. de Chateaubriand, *Mémoires d'outre-tombe.* (Paris, 1973), II, 259-60, 428.

25 Emmanuel-Dieudonné Las Cases, *Mémorial de Sainte-Hélène*, in Jean Tulard, ed., *Napoléon à Sainte-Hélène* (Paris, 1981), 128-9. On Napoleon's style of dictation and his poor spelling see comments of his private secretary during the Hundred Days, Fleury de Chaboulon, *Mémoires* (London, 1820), I, 286. For the following paragraphs on Napoleon, I use Cronin, *Napoleon*, Jean Tulard, *Napoléon ou le mythe du sauveur* (Paris, 1977), J.M. Thompson, *Napoleon Bonaparte* (Oxford, 1988), and Georges Lefebvre, *Napoleon, from Tilsit to Waterloo* (New York, 1969); also see essays in *L'Europe de Napoléon*, ed. Jean Tulard (Paris, 1989).

26 Campbell, *Napoleon*, 302-3; Ebrington, *Memorandum*, 7.

27 There seems to be some disagreement over when and where Napoleon actually wrote his *"Discours sur le bonheur."* I take his comment, "liberty conquered after twenty months of energy," as an indication that he was writing in March 1791, twenty months after the fall of the Bastille. The essay was presented for a prize at the Academy of Lyon. In November 1791 the examining committee decided that no prize would be given until 1793. Napoleon, "Discours sur le bonheur," in Napoleon Bonaparte, *Œuvres littéraires* (Paris, 1888), I, 21-44; see also Cronin, *Napoleon*, 52-3; and Las Cases, *Mémorial*, 44.

28 On St Helena, Napoleon would explain to Las Cases what were the duties of a ruling prince: "The first duty of a prince, without doubt, is to do what the people wants; but what the people wants is almost never what it says: its will, its needs are to be found less in its mouth than in the heart of the prince." Las Cases was astonished at what little he – Las Cases – knew about how the institutions under Napoleon worked, and he listened with great interest to Napoleon's explanations. Las Cases's ignorance was not at all unusual; very few Frenchmen knew how the institutions of the people worked and they certainly had no idea of what was going on within them. Ibid., 60, 117.

29 Cronin, *Napoleon*, 143.

30 For a general evaluation of French losses under Napoleon, see René Sédillot, *Le Coût de la Révolution française* (Paris, 1989); on Spain, see J.R. Aymes, "La guerre au Portugal et l'affaire espagnole," in Tulard, ed., *L'Europe*, 428-36; on Russia, Monika Senkowska-Gluck, "La campagne de 1812," in ibid., 469-70.

31 For a balanced assessment of Napoleon's Continental System, Tulard, *Napoléon*, 371-83; Sédillot, *Coût*, 201-22; François Crouzet, "Wars, blockade and economic change in Europe," *Journal of Economic History*, XXVII (1964), 567-88; on Amsterdam, André Palluel-Guillard, "Les Pays-Bas face à l'impérialisme français," in Tulard, ed., *L'Europe*, 262-3.

32 Sidney Pollard, *Peaceful Conquest* (Oxford, 1981), 87-94.

33 Las Cases, *Mémorial*, 28-9 November 1815, 102-5.
34 Campbell, *Napoleon*, 304, 318-19, 343; Houssaye, *Première Restauration*, 167.
35 Norman Mackenzie, *The Escape from Elba* (Oxford, 1982), 150-2.
36 Campbell, *Napoleon*, 319, 344; Laflandre-Linden, *Elbe*, 167.
37 Ebrington, *Memorandum*, 5-7; Campbell, *Napoleon*, 313-17, 347-8.
38 *Journal des Débats*, 11 & 13 December 1814.
39 Houssaye, *Première Restauration*, 160-9; ** to Hager, 24 October 1814, in AF, 200-1.
40 Wellington the diplomat, like Wellington the military commander, was a man of detail. "I assure you that during the course of the Congress and your absence a less eminent man [than Wellington] would not have been at all convenient," the comte de Jaucourt (at the Ministry of Foreign Affairs) wrote to Talleyrand on 2 October; "the little details seem to take up as much space in his head as the great and they occupy him as much" – in T&L, 141. On Wellington in Paris, see Elizabeth Longford, *Wellington* (London, 1969), I, 449-65.
41 Wellington to Dumouriez, Paris, 26 November 1814, in WD, XII, 192-3. Further comments on the growth of "public employment" and its effects can be found in Wellington to Castlereagh, 20 October 1814, in ibid., 152; Wellington to Castlereagh, 4 October 1814, in WSD, IX, 314-16.
42 Wellington to Prince of Orange, 21 October 1814, in ibid, 364-5; Wellington to Hereditary Prince of Orange, 11 December 1814, Wellington to Henry Wellesley, 17 December 1814, Wellington to Bathurst, 18 January 1815 in WD, XII, 210-11, 218-19, 247-8.
43 Fouché to Talleyrand, Ferrières, 25 September 1814, in T&L, 138-9; Joseph Fouché, *Mémoires* (Paris, 1992), 424, 426-9.
44 Dennis Wood, *Benjamin Constant* (London, 1993).
45 Ibid., 205-6; Benjamin Constant, *Œuvres* (Paris, 1957), 983-1096.
46 For a general review of French regions at this time, see A. Jardin and A.J. Tudesq, *La France des notables, 1815-1848* (Paris, 1973), especially vol. II; also R.S. Alexander, *Bonapartism and the Revolutionary Tradition in France: The Fédérés of 1815* (Cambridge, 1991).

47 Fouché, *Mémoires*, 140; Wellington to Castlereagh, 4 October 1814, in WSD, 314; Wellington to Castlereagh, 5 December 1814, WD, 205; Jaucourt to Talleyrand, 8 October & 29 November 1814, in T&L, 139-40.
48 Guillaume de Bertier de Sauvigny, *La Restauration* (Paris, 1955), 65-7; David Hamilton-Williams, *The Fall of Napoleon* (London, 1994), 154-5. The Ministers were so worried about what some of their colleagues might get up to that they presented a bill to the two Chambers demanding "pain of death against any Minister who threatened the security of the person of the King, who threatened the interior or exterior security of the state by practising intelligence with the enemies of France, or who threatened to overturn the royal authority, the order of succession to the Crown, or the constitutional power of either of the two branches of the legislature." For several days the bill was debated in the Chamber of Deputies in secret session and was eventually passed on 16 December 1814. *Journal des Débats*, 3, 10, 17 December 1814.
49 Ebrington, *Memorandum*, 8-9.
50 *Gazette de France*, 6 June 1814; Houssaye, *Première Restauration*, 43-51, 106-7; on the veterans, see Isser Wolloch, *The French Veteran from the Revolution to the Restoration* (Chapel Hill, North Carolina, 1979), esp. 295-6.
51 Wellington to Castlereagh, 4 October 1814, in WSD, IX, 314; Wellington to Castlereagh, 13 October 1814, in WD, XII, 146-7.
52 Through the autumn and winter 1814-15 the campaign on the way people should dress stepped up in the French press and the English replied in kind. *Journal de Paris*, 21 January 1815; *Le Nain Jaune*, 20 December 1814; Joseph Farington, *The Farington Diary* (London, 1927), 28 October 1814, VII, 283.
53 Ibid., 11 October 1814, 281.
54 Wellington to Liverpool, 23 October 1814, in WSD, 368-9; Wellington to Liverpool, 3 December 1814, in WD, XII, 202. On the hounds, Jaucourt to Talleyrand, 19 & 27 November 1814, in T&L, 141-2; on the royal gift, *Journal de Paris*, 11 January 1815.
55 Liverpool to Wellington, London, 13 November 1814, Wellington to Liverpool, Paris, 16 & 18 November

56 Jaucourt to Talleyrand, 3 December 1814, in T&L, 140; Wellington to Liverpool, 3 December 1814, and Wellington to Castlereagh, 5 December 1814, in WSD, XII, 202-5.

57 Louis XVIII to Talleyrand, 4 December 1814, in T&L, 159.

58 *Le Nain Jaune*, 5 January 1815.

59 Wood, *Constant*, 212; Fouché, *Mémoires*, 430.

60 Joseph Lainé had been an outspoken opponent of Napoleon in the Corps Législatif, where he had attacked high taxes, conscription, and the "unspeakable misery" caused by "a barbarous, purposeless war." In the years to come he would be one of the leading liberal lights of France.

61 *Journal des Débats*, 31 December 1814.

62 *Journal de Paris*, 2 January 1815.

63 Alexander, *Bonapartism*, 117-18; Houssaye, *Première Restauration*, 87-9; Wellington to Castlereagh, 19 January 1815, in WD, XII, 250-1.

64 Ibid.; Jaucourt to Talleyrand, 20 January 1815, in T&L, 262-3; *Journal de Paris*, 17 February 1815; Houssaye, *Première Restauration*, 93-5.

65 Ibid, 96; *Journal de Paris*, 22 & 24 January 1815.

66 He only received the invitation the night before the ceremony (as he explained ingenuously in a note to the comte de Jaucourt) and since no prior note had been received from the King's Secretary he had assumed that diplomats were not supposed to attend – so he had made no provisions for the 21st. In other words, Britain was keeping a low profile. Wellington to Jaucourt, 21 & 22 January 1815, in WD, XII, 252.

67 *Journal de Paris*, 8 February 1815; *Le Nain Jaune*, 10 February 1815.

68 Ibid., 15 & 25 February 1815; *Journal de Paris*, 16, 20, 28 February 1815.

69 Ibid., 26 & 27 February 1815; Baron de Vitrolles, *Mémoires* (Paris, 1951), II, 91.

70 Ibid., 81-2; "Souvenirs du Lieutenant Général Vicomte de Reiset" in *The Hundred Days*, ed. Antony Brett-James (London, 1964), 3-4.

71 Louis-Philippe d'Orléans, *Mon Journal* (Paris, 1849), I, 6-13.

72 Ibid.

73 Houssaye, *Première Restauration*, 269-74, 286-92; Tulard, *Napoléon*, 429; Constant *Journaux intimes*, 4, 5 & 6 March 1815, in *Œuvres*, 774-5.

74 Hippolyte Carnot, "Mémoires sur Carnot," in Brett-James, ed., *Hundred Days*, 12-13; Jules Michelet, *Ma Jeunesse* (Paris, 1884), 115-34.

75 Hortense de Beauharnais, *Mémoires de la Reine Hortense* (Paris, 1927), II, 310-13, 321-2.

76 Houssaye, *Première Restauration*, 235-50; and a contemporary account in Jacques Berriat Saint-Prix, *Napoléon à Grenoble* (Grenoble, 1861), 66-79.

77 "Journal du Général Fantin des Odoards" in Brett-James, ed., *Hundred Days*, 4-5.

78 Las Cases, *Mémorial*, 140-3; *Le Moniteur Universel*, 21 & 22 March 1815; Houssaye, *Première Restauration*, 301-2; Alan Schom, *One Hundred Days* (London, 1993), 28.

79 Vitrolles, *Mémoires*, II, 95-103, 110; Louis-Philippe, *Journal*, 58-61, 81, 88-91.

80 Benjamin Constant, *Mémoires sur les Cent-Jours* (Paris, 1961), 44-9, 70-88; Barrot's motion of 18 March 1815 reproduced in ibid., 115-16; Jaucourt to Talleyrand, Paris, 8 March 1815, in T&L, 316-17.

81 Fouché, *Mémoires*, 434-6.

82 Louis-Philippe, *Journal*, 126-9; Edmund Walcot in Brett-James, ed., *Hundred Days*, 11; Constant, *Mémoires*, 47-9, 119; Chateaubriand, *Mémoires*, II, 314-15.

83 "Discours du Président de la Chambre des députés, le 16 mars 1815," in Constant, *Mémoires*, 111-14.

84 Houssaye, *Première Restauration*, 305-26.

85 Louis-Philippe, *Journal*, 107-16.

86 Vitrolles, *Mémoires*, II, 91-6, 116-23.

87 Ibid.; Alexandre de Laborde, *Quarante-huit heures de garde au Château des Tuileries pendant les journées des 19 et 20 mars 1815* (Paris, 1816), 8-16.

88 Chateaubriand, *Mémoires*, II, 323.

89 Walcot in Brett-James, ed., *Hundred Days*, 12. John Cam Hobhouse, an English Whig who arrived in Paris a few weeks later, was told that Paris on the 20th had been "mournful." "The shops were all shut and no one appeared at the windows," a witness informed him. "There was no noise nor any acclamations." See J.C. Hobhouse, *The Substance of Some Letters written by an Englishman Resident at Paris* (London, 1816), I, 178-80.

90 Laborde, *Quarante-huit heures*, 20; Antoine-Marie, comte Lavalotte,

Mémoires et souvenirs, in Brett-James, ed., *Hundred Days*, p.14.

91 Goehausen to Hager, 11 March 1815, in MHW, II, 316. Alexander was on the point of leaving for St Petersburg. See, Talleyrand to duchesse de Courlande, Vienna, 3 March 1815, in Talleyrand, *Le Miroir de Talleyrand*, ed. Gaston Palewski (Paris, 1976), 130-1; Talleyrand to Louis XVIII, 3 March 1815, in *T&L*, 316.

92 Metternich, *Mémoires, documents et écrits divers* (Paris, 1981), I, 205-6, 328-9.

93 Friedrich von Gentz, *Tagebücher* (Leipzig, 1873), 7 March 1815, I, 363; Talleyrand to Louis XVIII, 7 March 1815, T&L, 135.

94 Today Bratislava, capital of Slovakia.

95 Kraehe, *German Policy*, II, 327-8.

96 Gräfin Elise von Bernstorff, *Ein Bild aus der Zeit von 1789 bis 1835 aus ihren Aufzeichnungen* (Berlin, 1896), I, 178; A. de La Garde-Chambonas, *Souvenirs du Congrès de Vienne, 1814-1815* (Paris, 1904), 433-6; Clancarty to Castlereagh, Vienna, 11 March 1815, in CC, X, 264; Gentz, *Tagebücher*, 7 March 1815, I, 363.

97 Talleyrand to the duchesse de Courlande, 8 March 1815, in Talleyrand, *Miroir*, 135-6.

98 Talleyrand to Louis XVIII, Vienna, 7 & 12 March 1815, in T&L, 321-6; Wellington to Castlereagh, Vienna, 12 & 18 March 1815, in Wellington, WSD, IX, 580-90, 603-4.

99 On the general political indifference in Vienna, La Garde-Chambonas, *Souvenirs*, 436; Bernstorff, *Ein Bild*, I, 178. On the weather in March, Talleyrand to the duchesse de Courlande, 3 March 1815, in *Miroir*, 130; M.F. Perth, *Wiener Kongresstagebuch* (Vienna & Munich, 1981), 4 March 1815, 92; Gentz, *Tagebücher*, 26 & 31 March 1815, I, 367-8. On Sagan and Bagration, Duchess von Sagan to Lord Stewart (intercepted letter), 7 March 1815, ** to Hager, 11 March 1815, in MHW, II, 304, 317.

100 Grand Duchess Maria to Grand Archduke of Weimar, Vienna, 16 March 1815, in AF, 434; Wellington to Castlereagh, Vienna, 12 March 1815, in BD, 312; Talleyrand to Louis XVIII, 19 & 23 March 1815, in T&L, 357, 359-62; Kraehe, *German Policy*, II, 327-30.

101 Castlereagh, writing instructions from

London on the 12th, said he hoped there would be a "joint declaration" announcing a "determination to maintain inviolable the Peace of Paris." But it had already been made by the time the dispatch arrived in Vienna. See Castlereagh to Wellington, London, 12 March 1815, in BD, 309. On Talleyrand's attitude, see Talleyrand to Louis XVIII, Vienna, 14 March 1814, in T&L, 319. On British caution, see Castlereagh to Wellington, London, 14 March 1815, in Wellington, WSD, IX, 596. Metternich wrote to Sagan, "The Bourbons seem to me morally sick as are old bodies" – Metternich to Sagan, undated, but references in the text place the letter between 11 and 21 March 1815; in Clemens von Metternich and Wilhelmine von Sagan, *Ein Briefwechsel*, ed. M. Ullrichová (Graz & Cologne, 1966), 279. Gentz, in April, would actually develop some sympathy for Bonaparte, see Kraehe, *German Policy*, II, 330.

102 "Each state may have as its enemy only other states and not men," said J.-J. Rousseau in the *Contrat social*, repeating a principle long established by the classical jurists of war and peace in Europe. That the diplomats at Vienna were aware of this is demonstrated in Gentz's article. By incorporating the Declaration into the formal protocol of the meeting of 13 March, the Five Powers reduced its status to that of a statement of policy as opposed to a formal Allied manifesto – an important fact in the legal minds of its authors. For an analysis of the classical jurists, see Raymond Aron, *Peace and War* (New York, 1973), 99-102.

103 "*Declaration*" and "*Article de la Gazette de Vienne du 16 Mars 1815. Traduit de l'Allemand*", PRONI D3030/4453 & 4454. On the drafting of the Declaration and the Talleyrand to Jaucourt, 16 March 1815; to Louis XVIII, 19 March 1815; to duchesse de Courlande, 16 March 1815; in T&L, 347-9, 354.

104 Talleyrand to Jaucourt, 16 March 1815; to Louis XVIII, 19 March 1815; to duchesse de Courlande, 16 March 1815; in T&L, 347-9, 354.

105 Gentz, *Tagebücher*, 17 March 1815, 365.

106 Wellington to Castlereagh, Vienna, 12 March 1815, in BD, 312.

107 Castlereagh to Wellington, London, 16

March 1815, in BD, 313-14, 320; Castlereagh to Wellington, London, 26 March 1815, and Castlereagh to Clancarty, London, 8 April 1815, in CC, X, 285, 301-2; Talleyrand to Louis XVIII, 23 March 1815, Talleyrand to Jaucourt, 19 April 1815, in T&L, 359-62.

108 Kraehe, *German Policy*, II, 332-8; Wellington to Castlereagh, 25 March 1815, in BD, 316-17; Stein to Plessen, 21 March 1815, in AF, 436.

109 Castlereagh to Wellington, London, 26 March 1815, in CC, X, 286; Wellington to Castlereagh, Vienna, 25 March 1815, in BD, 316-17.

110 Castlereagh to Wellington, London, 26 March 1815, in CC, X, 285-6.

111 *Examiner*, 5 March 1815; Goltz to Hardenberg (intercepted letter), Paris, 27 February 1815, in MHW, II, 308.

112 *The Parliamentary Debates*, ed. T.C. Hansard (London, 1815), 6 March 1815, XXX, 27-38.

113 American readers should note that "corn," in British English, refers to all grains *excluding* maize, which was not grown anywhere in Europe at this time, save northern Spain and a south-western corner of France.

114 Hansard, ed., *Debates*, 27 February 1815, XXIX, 1050-83.

115 Ibid., 21 February 1815, 993-8.

116 Ibid., 2 March 1815, 1173-5.

117 Ibid., 27 February 1815, 1082-3.

118 Ibid., 6 March 1815, XXX, 13-15.

119 Ibid., 27-39.

120 *Examiner*, 12 March 1815.

121 Hansard, ed., *Debates*, 8 March 1815, XXX, 78-81.

122 *Examiner*, 12 March 1815; Hansard, ed., *Debates*, 10 March 1815, XXX, 113-14. The Bill passed through the Lords on 20 March and the royal assent was given on the 23rd, the day before Good Friday.

123 *Times, Morning Post, Morning Herald, Morning Chronicle*, 11 March 1815; *Examiner*, 12 March 1815.

124 Hansard, ed., *Debates*, 20 February 1815, XXIX, 846-9; *Examiner*, 5 March 1815.

125 Lean, *Napoleonists*, 90-103.

126 Castlereagh to Wellington, London, 14 March 1815, in WSD, IX, 595-6.

127 Castlereagh to Wellington, London, 12 March 1815, in BD, 309-10.

128 Hansard, ed., *Debates*, 16 March 1815, XXX, 228-31. *The Examiner* of 26 March reported, "Lord Castlereagh's late indisposition, it is said, attacked him on the very day the news of Bonaparte's arrival in France reached London. The particular nature of it was not mentioned; but report has it, that it affected his Lordship in rather an odd manner; for when any of his friends mentioned the word 'Congress,' a visible agitation was observed in his whole frame: when the name of Bonaparte was uttered, his face exhibited a deadly paleness; and on 'the Deliverance of Europe' being touched upon, a convulsive twitch was immediately perceivable."

129 Hansard, ed., *Debates*, 20 March 1815, XXX, 265-82.

130 Ibid., 282-303; PRONI D.3030/4463 for original version, with revisions.

131 On Cabinet doubts about the authenticity of the Declaration, see Vansittart's declaration to the Commons, in ibid., 3 April 1815, 352. For Castlereagh's relevent papers, see PRONI D3030/4453 & 4454. English translation of Declaration and text of Message in the *Examiner*, 9 April 1815. Wellington commented on the poor translation of the Declaration in Wellington to W. Wellesley Pole, Brussels, 5 May 1815, in WD, XII, 351.

132 On the grounds that the recent events in France were "in direct contravention of the engagements concluded with the Allied Powers at Paris" and were "highly dangerous to the tranquillity and independence of Europe," the Regent's Message ordered an increase in Britain's land and sea forces. It also announced that Britain would be entering "a concert as may most effectually provide for the general and permanent security of Europe." For the text of the Message and the ensuing parliamentary debate, see Hansard, ed., *Debates*, XXX, 7 April 1815, 373-463.

133 See Castlereagh to Wellington, 8 April 1815, in CC, X, 300; and comments in *Examiner*, 9 April 1815, that a war against Napoleon "will not, it cannot succeed."

134 Wood, *Constant*, 213-14; Constant, *Journaux intimes*, 18 March - 14 April 1815, in *Œuvres*, 777-80, 1576.

135 Fleury, *Mémoires*, I, 261.

136 Hobhouse, *Letters*, I, 210-11.

137 Houssaye, *Première Restauration*, 392-437.

138 Constant, *Mémoires*, 167-9.

139 Ibid., 171-2.

140 Fleury, *Mémoires*, II, 1, 21; Fouché,
     Mémoires, 437, 442.
141 Ibid., 439-40.
142 Hobhouse, *Letters*, I, 154-9.
143 Fleury, *Mémoires*, I, 342-4; Hortense,
     Mémoires, II, 343-7, III, 5-9; Fouché,
     Mémoires, 441; Houssaye, *Première
     Restauration*, 441-2.
144 Napoleon to the Sovereigns, 4 April
     1815; Caulaincourt to the Foreign
     Ministers, 4 April 1815, French texts in
     Hobhouse, *Letters*, II, 370-2.
145 Fouché, *Mémoires*, 441; Fleury,
     Mémoires, I, 345-7.
146 Ibid., 347-71.
147 Ibid., 379-98; Hobhouse, *Letters*, vol.I,
     21-2, 36; Hortense, *Mémoires*, II, 331-
     8.
148 Ibid., 359.
149 A *jacquerie* is a peasant revolt. It takes
     its name from a famous rising of peas-
     ants, or *jacques*, in the Beauvaisis,
     north of Paris, in 1358.
150 Constant, *Mémoires*, 132-6.
151 Constant, *Mémoires*, 139. Text of the
     *Acte additionnel aux Constitutions de
     l'Empire*, Palais de l'Elysée, 22 April
     1815, in Frédéric Bluche, *Le Plébiscite
     des Cent-Jours* (Geneva, 1974), 129-35.
152 Hobhouse, *Letters*, I, 198-204;
     Constant, *Mémoires*, 163-4; Constant,
     Œuvres, 781-3. For Constant's belief
     that a popular consultation might
     reveal the truths of a text, see ibid.,
     142-4. Constant was convinced that if
     he had stood up to Napoleon and
     imposed an absolutely new constitu-
     tion, France would have won the war.
     According to Constant, France was
     defeated in June 1815 not for military
     reasons but because the country had
     been paralysed by a misunderstanding
     of the Act. Constant showed the same
     kind of constitutionalist faith, almost
     religious in nature, that prevented the
     Chamber of Deputies from taking
     effective military measures as
     Napoleon approached Paris in March.
153 Bluche, *Plébiscite*, 15-25.
154 Ibid., 36-51, 81-7; Bluche, *Le
     Bonapartisme* (Paris, 1980), 107-16.
155 *Journal de Paris*, 19 April, 27, 28, 29
     May 1815; Hortense, *Mémoires*, II,
     357; Hobhouse,   *Letters*, I, 401-4;
     Fleury, *Mémoires*, I, 263.
156 A most detailed study of the *Fédérés*
     can be found in Alexander,
     Bonapartism.
157 *Journal de Paris*, 15 May 1815;
     Hobhouse, *Letters*, I, 221-2; Fleury,

     Mémoires, II, 79-83. Fouché started to
     advise Napoleon to retire to the United
     States of America and let someone else
     do the job of governing the ungovern-
     able French, see *Mémoires*, 450.
158 Many historians have the sun shining
     on the Champ-de-Mai, drawing their
     accounts from Henry Houssaye (*La
     Première Restauration*, 598-610), for
     whom the sun shone from Napoleon's
     landing at Golfe Juan to the very day
     of Waterloo. In fact, the sunny week-
     end of 27-8 May came to an end with a
     thunderstorm on the 29th and for the
     whole of June there was cloud cover
     and periodic torrential rains. The
     Observatoire recorded, for 1 June, that
     the sky was "covered" at four a.m.,
     "very cloudy" at noon, and still "very
     cloudy" at 4.30 p.m.. The temperature
     was 12.4° C at dawn and reached 20° C
     in the afternoon, *Journal de Paris*, 2
     June 1815.
159 Hobhouse, *Letters*, I, 401, 408-25;
     Michelet, *Ma Jeunesse*, 134; Fleury,
     Mémoires, II, 96-106; Hortense,
     Mémoires, III, 11; Fouché, *Mémoires*,
     450.

WATERLOO, Spring 1815

1 Baron de Vitrolles, *Mémoires* (Paris,
   1951), II, 118; M.A. Reiset, *Souvenirs*
   (Paris, 1902), 120-4, 173-5; J.E.J.A.
   Macdonald, *Souvenirs* (Paris, 1892),
   367-8. Reiset recounts that thirty hackney coaches had to be hired on the second day of the *Maison's* march to carry
   "equipment and the sick."
2 Macdonald, *Souvenirs*, 369-71, 376.
3 Louis-Philippe d'Orléans, *Mon Journal*
   (Paris, 1849), I, 189-91.
4 Macdonald, *Souvenirs*, 370-1.
5 Ibid., 371-4; Reiset, *Souvenirs 125-7;
   Orléans, *Mon Journal*, I, 211-19.
6 Ibid, 220-64; Macdonald, *Souvenirs*,
   374-80.
7 Reiset, *Souvenirs*, 126-34.
8 Louis XVIII to Talleyrand, 26 March
   1815, in T&L, 485; "Memorandum by
   Lord Harowby of his interview with
   Louis XVIII," Brussels, 7 April 1815,
   in WSD, X, 39-40.
9 Cavalié Mercer, *Journal of the Waterloo
   Campaign* (London, 1870), I, 30;
   Jaucourt to Talleyrand, Ostend, 27
   March 1815 and Talleyrand to Louis
   XVIII, Vienna, 5 April 1815, in T&L,
   356, 374-5; Blacas to Castlereagh,
   Ostend, 25 March 1815, in CC, X, 283-4.

10 Reiset, *Souvenirs*, 182-4; Harrowby, "Memorandum", in WSD, X, 39.

11 Chateaubriand to Talleyrand, 28 April 1815, in T&L, 395; Jean-Claude Beugnot, *Mémoires du comte Beugnot, 1779-1815* (Paris, 1959), 297-303; François Guizot, *Mémoires pour servir à l'histoire* (Paris, 1858), I, 84.

12 Jaucourt to Talleyrand, Ghent, 24 April, 2 & 11 May 1815, in T&L, 411-12, 419. Wellington, within a week of his arrival was recommending to Castlereagh that the duc d'Orléans be considered as a candidate for the French throne; Wellington spoke of Orléans as the "only acceptable middle term between Buonaparte, the army, and the Jacobins on the one hand, and the King and the violent émigrés on the other." See Wellington to Castlereagh, Brussels, 11 April 1815, in WSD, X, 60-2. Fouché had established contact with Ghent through Monsieur Gaillard, a former seminarist and intimate friend of Fouché, who appeared in the Flemish capital in April, cf. Chateaubriand, *Mémoires*, II, 342-3.

13 Jaucourt to Talleyrand, Ghent, 24 April 1815, in T&L, 378; Reiset, *Souvenirs*, 176; Chateaubriand, *Mémoires*, II, 362; and Guizot, *Mémoires*, I, 84, on the limited power of the "reactionaries" at Ghent.

14 On the attitude of the Dutch King, Sir Charles Stuart to Castlereagh, Brussels, 28 March 1815, in WSD, IX, 630-1. On the attitudes of the "men of business" and Talleyrand, Beugnot, *Mémoires*, 309-10; Talleyrand to Jaucourt, Vienna, 19 April 1815, in T&L, 361; Duc d'Orléans to Louis XVIII and to Talleyrand, both London, 25 April 1815, in Orléans, *Mon Journal*, II, 7-18, 25-6. Description of Berry's equipage and of Alost in John Scott, *Paris Revisited in 1815, by way of Brussels* (London, 1816), 58-9, 101-2.

15 Ibid., 42.

16 Chateaubriand, *Mémoires*, II, 334-5, 338; Reiset, *Souvenirs*, 191-4; Beugnot, *Mémoires*, 307-8.

17 Ibid., 304-5.

18 John Cam Hobhouse (who travelled to Paris via Brussels in early April 1815), *The Substance of Some Letters written by an Englishman Resident at Paris* (London, 1816), I, 14-16.

19 Wellington to Gneisenau, 5 April 1815, in WD, XII, 288; Scott, *Paris Revisited*, 76-7, 107.

20 Thomas Creevey, *The Creevey Papers* (London, 1903), I, 225. Jaucourt wrote to Talleyrand from Ostend on Easter Monday to say that everybody was impatiently awaiting the arrival of Lord Wellington to reassure the English, who "were all in flight," Jaucourt to Talleyrand, Ostend, 27 March 1815, in T&L, 356. See also Sir Charles Stuart to Wellington, Brussels, 30 March 1815, in WSD, X, 7.

21 Major-General Sir H. Torrens to Earl Bathurst, Ghent, 8 April 1815, in ibid., 43. Wellington received his Dutch commission on 3 May (Wellington to Bathurst, Brussels, 6 May 1815, in WD, XII, 356).

22 Wellington to Bathurst, 21 April, and to Torrens, Brussels, 22 May 1815, in ibid, 319, 416; Scott, *Paris Revisited*, 77-8. For a general outline of the problems faced by Wellington in Brussels, see Jac Weller, *Wellington at Waterloo* (London, 1992), 30-44.

23 Creevey, *Papers*, I, 228.

24 Clancarty to Wellington, with enclosures, Vienna, 1 April 1815, in WSD, X, 13-14; Wellington to Duke of Brunswick (10 April), Bathurst (12 April), Prince of Nassau (2 May), Hardenburg (3 May), Captain Frennat (19 May), Sir Henry Hardinge (24 May), in WD, X, 298-302, 340, 345, 401; Clancarty to Castlereagh, Vienna, 26 & 28 April 1815, in PRONI D.3030/4528-9.

25 Earl of Harrowby to Castlereagh, Brussels, 7 April 1815, in WSD, X, 32; Wellington to Stuart, 13 May 1815, in WD, XII, 381-3.

26 Wellington to Prince of Orange, Ostend, 17 April 1815, and Memorandum, Brussels, 23 April 1814, in WD, X, 312-13, 324-6. Hobhouse, *Letters*, I, 17-18.

27 One suspects that either B or C was the famous English spy, Lieutenant-Colonel Colquhoun Grant. Cf. Weller, *Wellington*, 42.

28 J. Frissel to Castlereagh, Brighton, 7 April, Correspondent B, Brussels, 9 April, and Correspondent C, Paris, 9 & 12 April 1815, in WSD, X, 28-31, 55-9, 68. See also report by Sir John Sinclair, "The State of France," 21 April 1815, in PRONI, D.3030/4480. On the expected "Republick," see Creevey, *Papers*, I, 215; Wellington to Blücher, Brussels, 23 April 1815, in WD, XII, 324.

29 Louis XVIII to Talleyrand, Ghent, 9
    April 1815, in T&L, 377; Wellington to
    Clancarty, Brussels, 10 April 1815, in
    WD, XII, 297.

30 Louis XVIII to Talleyrand, 9 April,
    Jaucourt to Talleyrand, Ghent, 10 & 23
    April 1815, in T&L, 376-8, 387-9;
    Wellington to duc de Berry, Brussels, 9
    May 1815, WD, XII, 365-6.

31 Orléans, *Mon Journal*, I, 269-70, II, 25-
    6. Letters of particular interest in
    Castlereagh's papers are Louis XVIII
    to duc d'Orléans, Ghent, 10 May 1815,
    duc d'Orléans to Louis XVIII,
    London, May 1815, Wellington to duc
    d'Orléans, Brussels, 6 June 1815, and
    duc d'Orléans to Wellington, London,
    12 June 1815, in PRONI D.3030/4548-
    9, 4576/2, 4581/2. Count Lieven,
    Russia's Ambassador to London,
    reported to Count Nesselrode, the
    Russian Minister in Vienna, that
    Orléans was not initially welcomed in
    England; he even had to make his
    crossing in a Dutch vessel because the
    British refused to provide one. See
    Lieven to Nesselrode, London, 2 & 7
    April 1815, in MHW, II, 460, 489-90;
    also Liverpool to Canning, London, 13
    June 1815 in WSD, X, 464-5.

32 Castlereagh to Sir Charles Stuart,
    London, 24 April, Wellington to
    Castlereagh, Brussels, 24 April,
    Castlereagh to Clancarty, 29 April,
    Castlereagh to Stuart, 8 May [2 letters],
    Castlereagh to Wellington, 9 May,
    Clancarty to Castlereagh, Vienna, 19
    May, Castlereagh to Stuart, 20 May,
    Clancarty to Castlereagh, 26 May,
    Castlereagh to Stuart, 7 June 1815, in
    PRONI D.3030/4522-77. See also
    Wellington to Castlereagh, Brussels, 11
    April, Castlereagh to Wellington,
    London, 16 April 1815, in WSD, X, 60,
    80-1.

33 "Secret Memorandum for Prince of
    Orange, Earl of Uxbridge, Lord Hill &
    Quarter Master General," Brussels,
    n.d., Wellington to Castlereagh (2
    May), to Bathurst (2 May), to Stuart (3
    May), to Prince of Orange (3 May
    1815), in WD, XII, 337-8, 343-5. The
    Prussian Minister in Ghent also
    warned that Napoleon was poised to
    attack in the Ardennes rather than in
    Belgium, Goltz to Hardenberg, Ghent,
    ca. 5-6 May 1815, in MHW, II, 577-8.

34 F.C.F. von Müffling, *Aus meinem
    Leben* (Berlin, 1851), 201-12; Hardinge
    to Wellington, Liège, 4 May 1815, in

WSD, X, 219-21; Castelalfer (not
"Castlereagh", as Weil identifies corre-
spondent) to Saint-Marsan, Berlin, 20
May 1815, in MHW, II, 586-7.

35 Wellington to Clancarty (3 May) and
    to Hardinge (Brussels, 5 May 1815), in
    WD, XII, 346, 349-50; Müffling,
    Leben, 211-12.

36 This was perhaps not the only mutiny
    in the Allied Armies that spring. *The
    Examiner* (7 May 1815) reproduced a
    letter from Brussels, dated 27 April,
    that spoke of "Belgic soldiers who
    were brought, wounded, in waggons,
    from the frontiers to the military hos-
    pital in this city, last Sunday evening
    (23 April)." There were also "some
    Dutch troops, likewise, who came
    maimed, and mingled with the Belgic
    soldiers, but not many." Rumour was
    that, after two Belgian regiments
    attempted to desert to the French, a
    conflict broke out with British troops,
    "in which the killed and wounded took
    place according to the report first
    received" [*sic*]. The same issue of the
    Examiner reproduced a proclamation
    by William, King of the Netherlands,
    which warned that "all those who shall
    shew themselves to be the partizans or
    instruments of a foreign power...shall
    be punished according to the extent of
    the crime." Punishments included
    "exposure in the pillory from one hour
    to six, by degradation, by brand, by
    imprisonment from one year to ten,
    and fine from 100 to 10,000 francs." If
    the offense involved "troubling the
    public repose," those found guilty
    "shall be condemned, besides the fine,
    to hard labour, and to brand, without
    being relieved from the pain of death, if
    the case shall require it." Reports on
    the Saxon mutiny appeared in the
    Examiner of 14 & 21 May 1815.

37 Weller, *Wellington*, 36-7; Wellington to
    Clancarty, Brussels, 3 May 1815, in
    WD, XII, 346.

38 Wellington to Prince of Orange (11
    May), to Stewart (Brussels, 8 May
    1815), in ibid., 358, 375-6.

39 *Examiner*, 23 April 1815.

40 *The Parliamentary Debates*, ed. T.C.
    Hansard (London, 1815), 1 May 1815,
    XXX, 1014-24; 10 May 1815, XXXI,
    232-8. Despite the fears expressed that
    the Income Tax had returned forever, it
    was abolished in 1816. It was finally
    revived by another Tory, Sir Robert
    Peel, in his famous budget of 1842 and,

after that date, was never again repealed. By way of contrast, France only introduced income tax – again as a temporary war measure – in 1916; it only became a serious charge on citizens after the Second World War.

41 Christopher Hibbert, *George IV* (London, 1976), 466-9; Hansard, ed., *Debates*, 8 May 1815, XXXI, 198-207.

42 Ibid.; *The Examiner*, 7 May 1815. For an account of George Canning's much criticised mission to Lisbon, see Wendy Hinde, *Canning* (London, 1989), 268-76.

43 Hansard, ed., *Debates*, 27 April 1815, XXX, 891-939, 944.

44 Ibid., 876-86.

45 Ibid., 28 April 1815, 960-98.

46 *The Examiner*, 7, 21, 28 May 1815; Hibbert, *George IV*, 466.

47 In a report to Nesselrode (Russian Minister in Vienna), Count Lievin gives some detail of Castlereagh's consultations with the diplomatic corps in London following publication of the Treaty. By May, Castlereagh was "so badgered" by Parliament that he "hardly had the time to concentrate on office work." Lievin to Nesselrode, London, 24 April, 9 May 1815, in MHW, II, 530-1, 573.

48 Hansard, *Debates*, 22, 23, 25 May 1815, XXXI, 285-7, 295-302, 371, 391; Joseph Farington, *The Farington Diary* (London, 1927), 21-6 May, 8 June 1815, VIII, 1-3, 7.

49 *Examiner*, 7, 14, 21, 28 May 1815.

50 The duc d'Enghien, son of the prince de Condé, was kidnapped from his exile in Ettenheim in Baden by a squadron of Napoleon's troops, carried to Paris, and, after a night in the fort of Vincennes, was summarily executed on 21 March 1804. He was suspected, probably wrongly, of participating in a plot to assassinate the Emperor. Enghien's execution became one of the *causes celebres* of the wars that followed.

51 *Examiner*, 18 June 1815.

52 ✳✳ to Hager, Vienna, 12 May 1815, in MHW, II, 555.

53 ✳✳ to Hager, 9 May; J. de Carro to Rochemont, Vienna, 7 June 1815, in ibid, 545, 623.

54 Castlereagh to Stewart, London, 9 June 1815, in CC, X, 378-80.

55 Henry Houssaye, *1815: La Première Restauration, le Retour de l'Ile d'Elbe,*

les Cent Jours (Paris, 1920), 464-73.

56 Marescalchi to Guidicini, Vienna, 8 May 1815, in MHW, II, 547.

57 Clancarty to Humboldt, 29 April 1815, in ibid, 521; E.E. Kraehe, *Metternich's German Policy* (Princeton, N.J., 1983), II, 341-3.

58 Talleyrand to duchesse de Courlande, 20 April 1815, in Talleyrand, *Le Miroir de Talleyrand: Lettres inédites à la duchesse de Courlande pendant le Congrès de Vienne*, ed. Gaston Palewski (Paris, 1976), 183; Talleyrand to Clancarty, 13 April, Stackelberg to Phull, 25 April 1815, in MHW, II, 463, 508.

59 Czartoryski to Anstett, 29 April, Hager Report, 4 May 1815, in ibid., 518, 538-9.

60 An old enemy, Turkey, was also causing some nervousness among the Russians. ✳✳ reported in May that the latter had encouraged the Serbs, on the frontiers of the Ottoman Empire, to organise a massacre of Turks to "keep them busy" while the French campaign lasted (✳✳ to Hager, 29 May 1815, in ibid, 599). It was only in June that the Turks joined the Allies in the war against Napoleon – for whom Turks had no special fondness (they had not forgotten the French Egyptian expedition of 1799). "Thus civilised or not," wrote Talleyrand to the duchesse de Courlande on hearing the news, "the whole world is against Buonaparte," 7 June 1815, in Talleyrand, *Miroir*, 210.

61 Hager Report, 15 April 1815, in MHW, II, 466-7; Francis Ley, *Alexandre Ier et sa Sainte-Alliance* (Paris, 1975), 100-5.

62 ✳✳ to Hager, 24 April & 12 May 1815, in MHW, II, 505, 555.

63 ✳✳ to Hager, 10 June 1815, in ibid, 638; Münster to the Prince Regent, 3 June 1815, in C.K. Webster, *The Foreign Policy of Castlereagh* (London, 1931), I, 561-2.

64 Compare Clancarty's report of his conversation with Alexander on 13 April (Clancarty to Castlereagh, 15 April 1815, in BD, 327-9), to Talleyrand's analysis of the situation in France in Talleyrand to Louis XVIII, 23 April 1815, in T&L, 399-400.

65 Ibid., and also Talleyrand to Jaucourt, 22 April 1815, in ibid, 404-5. (These two letters were written in the 48 hours that preceded Montrond's reported departure.) Jaucourt to Talleyrand, Ghent, 27 May 1815, in ibid., 408;

Dalberg to Baron Cotta, 10 April 1815 in Talleyrand, *Miroir*, 201; Wellington to Castlereagh, Brussels, 24 April 1815, in WSD, X, 146-7; Chevalier Freddi, to Hager, Vienna, 13 April 1815, in MHW II, 462; Clancarty to Castlereagh, Vienna, 26 May 1815 (on Talleyrand's supposed hostility to Louis XVIII), in PRONI D.3030/4567

66 Casimir, the comte de Montrond, had been one of Talleyrand's three "courtiers" (along with Théophile Cazenove and Roux de Laborie) in the Ministry of Exterior Affairs during the Consulate and Empire. Talleyrand used Montrond, for instance, to negotiate money from the United States in 1798. Talleyrand, in fact, always negotiated for money and Montrond was often the man who actually accomplished this. See Georges Lacour-Gayet, *Talleyrand* (Paris, 1990), 249, 295-6, 441, 454, 486-7.

67 This was also Henry Houssaye's impression, see *La Première Restauration*, 450-1.

68 Auguste de Talleyrand to Dalberg, Zurich, 30 April 1815, in MHW, II, 550-4.

69 Metternich's instructions to Offenfels (pseud. Henry Werner), Vienna, 9 April 1815, and Metternich to Fouché, Vienna, 9 April 1815, in C.L.W. von Metternich, *Mémoires, documents et écrits* (Paris, 1880), II, 514-16. Prince Richard von Metternich, the editor, noted that the latter letter was unsigned and was written in invisible ink. Fleury de Chaboulon, *Mémoires* (London, 1820), II, 1-43, provides details on his exchange with "Herr Werner."

70 Münster to the Prince Regent, Vienna, 3 June 1815, in Webster, *Foreign Policy*, I, 562; Hager Report, 28 April 1815, in MHW, II, 516.

71 "Quinzième Protocole de la séance du 12 mai des Plénipotentiaires des huit Puissances," in *Le Congrès de Vienne*, ed. comte d'Angeberg (Paris, 1863), II, 1181-8.

72 The Metternichs' youngest daughter, Hirminie, was born on 1 September 1815; so she was conceived in early December, 1814, a week or so after the Prince's rupture with Sagan.

73 Friedrich von Gentz, *Tagebücher* (Leipzig, 1873), 15-28 May 1815 I, 380-2. Gentz notes that most of his entries for May and June were a backlog of events not recorded at the time.

74 Kraehe, *German Policy*, II, 366-7; d'Angeberg, *Congrès*, II, 1218-20. Baron von Gagern represented the United Netherlands on the German Committee, Count von Bernstorff represented Denmark.

75 Stackelberg to Phull, Vienna, 24 May; Official Reports, 26, 31 May; Anon.,**, Nota to Hager, 27, 29 May, 8, 19 June, 2 July 1815, in MHW, II, 585, 595-6, 600, 609, 625, 658, 670.

76 ** to Hager, 6 June 1815, in ibid., 616; Kraehe, *German Policy*, II, 368-99; James Sheehan, *German History, 1770-1866* (Oxford, 1989), 401-4.

77 C.M. de Talleyrand-Périgord, *Mémoires, 1754-1815* (Paris, 1982), 717.

78 Gärtner to Solms-Laubach and the Count of Westphalia, Vienna, 9 June 1815, in MHW, II, 641.

79 ** to Hager, 11 June 1815, in ibid., 645.

80 "Acte final du Congrès de Vienne, 9 juin 1815," in d'Angeberg, *Congrès*, II, 1386-1433.

81 Spaen to Nagell, Vienna, 25 May & 22 June 1815, in MHW, II, 590, 662; Gentz, *Tagebücher*, 9-19 June 1815, vol I, 385-6.

82 Talleyrand to duchesse de Courlande, 1st - 8 June 1815, in *Miroir*, 199-213; Official Report, 11 June 1815, in MHW, II, 643. Gentz reports Talleyrand's departure on 11 June, *Tagebücher*, I, 385.

83 Hager Reports, 29 May - 11 June, 20 July 1815, in MHW, II, 601, 611, 613-15, 620, 624, 642, 684-6.

84 Nota to Hager, 8-22 June 1815; ** to Hager, 11-25 June 1815, in ibid, 626, 644-52, 663, 666.

85 Gentz, *Tagebücher*, 12 June 1815, I, 385.

86 Ibid., 25 June 1815, I, 388.

87 Third Canto of "Childe Harold's Pilgrimage", stanzas 21-5, in Lord Byron, *The Complete Poetical Works* (Oxford, 1980), II, 84-5; W.M. Thackeray, *Vanity Fair* (London, 1968), 341-6.

88 Lady De Lancey, *A Week in Waterloo*, ed. B.R. Ward (London, 1906), 45; Müffling, *Aus meinem Leben*, 230.

89 Ibid.; "Diary of Lieut.-Colonel Sir William Verner," in *The Hundred Days*, ed. Antony Brett-James (London, 1964), 40.

90 Ibid., 39, 43.

91 De Lancey, *Week*, 39-40; B. Jackson, *Notes and Reminiscences of a Staff Officer* (London, 1903), 6-9; Longford,

Wellington, I, 495-7.

92 Müffling, *Aus meinem Leben*, 228; "Memorandum on the Battle of Waterloo," signed Wellington, 24 Sept 1842 (written in answer to the unjust criticisms of Karl von Clausewitz), in WSD X, 513-31 (esp. 522-5).

93 "Napoleon has *humbugged* me, by God!" Wellington is supposed to have exclaimed to the Duke of Richmond, who for some strange reason reported to Captain George Bowles of the Coldstream Guards, who reported to the Earl of Malmesbury. The only trouble I have with the story is that Wellington *never* referred to Napoleon as "Napoleon" – he was always the Corsican upstart, "Buonaparte." Cf. Brett-James, ed., *Hundred Days*, 44.

94 Creevey, *Papers*, I, 223, 229.

95 B.R. Wood provides some evidence of this in his edition of De Lancey, *Week*, 106.

96 Napoleon's orders to Ney do not seem to be as clear as some historians claim. The crucial evidence against Ney comes from a second-hand source. "Go and push the enemy up the road to Brussels and take up your position at Quatre-Bras," Napoleon is supposed to have told Ney on the morning of the 15th, before Charleroi. In his written orders, Napoleon refers to Quatre-Bras as "Quatre-Chemins." Cf. Henry Houssaye, *1815: Waterloo* (Paris, 1924), 122-3; Napoleon to Ney, Charleroi, 16 June 1815, in

97 The principal sources for my account of the Waterloo campaign are Houssaye, *Waterloo*; Weller, *Wellington*; David G. Chandler, *Campaigns of Napoleon* (New York, 1966); John Keegan, *The Face of Battle* (New York, 1977); and Alan Schom, *One Hundred Days* (London, 1993).

98 Müffling, *Aus meinem Leben*, 204-5.

99 Quoted in Houssaye, *Waterloo*, 270-1.

100 Wellington to duc de Berry, Waterloo, 18 June 1815, 3 a.m., in WD, XII, 476-7.

101 Wellington to the Governor of Antwerp, Waterloo, 18 June 1815, 3 a.m., in ibid., 478.

102 Wellington to Stuart, Waterloo, 18 June 1815, 3 a.m., in ibid., 476.

103 Wellington to Lady Frances W. Webster, Waterloo, 18 June 1815, 3 a.m., in WSD, X, 501.

104 *The Capel Letters*, in Brett-James, ed., *Hundred Days*, 123.

105 Chateaubriand, *Mémoires*, II, 362-3; Wood's edition of De Lancey, *Week*, 48, 108.

106 Creevey, *Papers*, I, 229-31; Jackson, *Notes*, 16-17, 34-6; Mrs Charlotte A. Eaton [Waldie], 'Days of Battle,' in Brett-James, ed., *Hundred Days*, 126-8.

107 Chateaubriand, II, 361-6; Reiset, *Souvenirs*, 204-14

108 Creevey, *Papers*, I, 231-4; Jackson, *Notes*, 38-9.

109 Ibid., 48-9; Keegan, *Face*, 139-43, 156-7. For general sources on the battle, see above, note 97.

110 Private John Lewis, 8 July 1815, in Brett-James, ed., *Hundred Days*, 136; Wellington to Sir John Sinclair, Cambrai, 13 April 1816, in WSD, X, 507.

111 Prince Jerome's attack on Hougoumont, a château with a walled garden and orchard (i.e. a fortress) to the west of the Charleroi road, began at 11.50 a.m. Napoleon intended it to be a diversion on Wellington's centre right in preparation for the main offensive that he launched at 1.30. A very expensive diversion it proved to be: it absorbed two French divisions against just four companies of the Coldstream Guards, who, although sorely tried, managed to hold on to the farm during the entire day. A vicious "battle within a battle," this episode is but a footnote to the Battle of Waterloo.

112 Keegan, *Face*, 154, 180, 192-5.

113 Houssaye, *Waterloo*, 438.

114 Ibid., 439-49; J.M. Thompson, *Napoleon Bonaparte* (Oxford, 1988).

115 Houssaye, *Waterloo*, 450-2; Houssaye, *1815: La Seconde Abdication, La Terreur Blanche* (Paris, 1918), 13-15.

116 Ibid., 22.

117 Ibid., 348-402; Thompson, *Napoleon*, 384-88; Victor Cronin, *Napoleon* (London, 1994), 405-7.

118 *The Times*, 8 August 1815.

119 *Morning Post*, 8 August 1815; *Morning Chronicle*, 27 July - 9 August 1815; *The Times*, 2-11 August 1815.

PARIS, Summer 1815

1 Christopher Hibbert, *George IV* (London, 1976), 463-4, 474-80; John Van der Kiste, *George III's Children* (London, 1992), ix, 100-9.

2 It houses today the East India and Devonshire Club.

3 Julian Charles Young, *A Memoir of*

Charles Mayne Young (1871) and
Melesina Trench, *The Remains of the
late Mrs Richard Trench* (1862) in *The
Hundred Days*, ed., Antony, Brett-
James (London, 1964), 190-2; Emma
Sophia, Countess Brownlow [Emma,
Lady Edgcumbe] *Slight Reminiscences
of a Septuagenarian* (London, 1867),
116-20.

4 Wellington to Bathurst, Waterloo, 19
   June 1815, in WD, XII, 482;
   Brownlow, *Reminiscences*, 119.

5 Burdett criticised Castlereagh for
   speaking of the war as "the most just
   of all causes" and he reminded the
   House that only two days earlier they
   had been debating a Mutiny Bill
   designed to abolish the inhumane practice of flogging. This was no idle concern. Mr H.G. Bennet, a close associate
   of Whitbread, reported to the House
   on 21 June that "the inhabitants of
   Brussels had complained that their ears
   were stunned with the cries and groans
   of our brave warriors smarting under
   the lash" (House of Commons, 21 June
   1815, in *The Times*, 22 June).
   Wellington's own correspondence and
   general orders indicate that he took a
   very tough stand against deserters and
   the spreaders of false rumour, partly,
   no doubt, because of the mutinies of
   May, partly because of the panics of
   March, May, and June. See, for example, his General Order, Nivelles, 20
   June 1815, in WD, XII, 493-4; and
   WSD, X, 538-40.

6 House of Commons, 22-3, 28 June
   1815, in *The Times*, 23-9 June; E.
   Tangye Lean, *The Napoleonists*
   (London, 1970), 100.

7 House of Commons, 28 June 1815, in
   The Times, 29 June; Castlereagh to G.
   Canning, London, 22 June 1815, in
   CC, X, 383.

8 Elizabeth Longford, *Wellington*
   (London, 1972), II, 14-15.

9 Bathurst to Wellington, London, 26
   June 1815; Provisional Government of
   France to Castlereagh, Paris, 25 June
   1815; Bathurst to Wellington, London,
   29 June 1815, in WSD, X, 586, 593,
   625.

10 Liverpool to Castlereagh, London, 30
   June 1815, in BD, 339-41.

11 Cathcart to Castlereagh, Heidelberg,
   21 June 1815, in CC, X, 383.

12 Castlereagh to Wellington, Bavay, 4
   July 1815, in WSD, X, 654.

13 Francis Phippen, *An Authentic Account

of the Late Mr. Whitbread* (London,
1815) reproduces a number of original
documents. Roger Fulford, *Samuel
Whitbread, 1764-1815* (London, 1967),
297-316, is especially good on
Whitbread's finances.

14 Phippen, *Account*, 23-6.

15 Fulford, *Whitbread*, 305-6; House of
   Commons, 4 July 1815, in *The Times*, 5
   July; *The Examiner*, 9 July 1815.

16 Phippen, *Account*, 19-23 (reproduction
   of the Coroner's Inquest).

17 Wellington to Bathurst, Waterloo, 19
   June; Wellington to Earl of Uxbridge,
   Le Cateau, 23 June 1815, in WD, XII,
   482, 500; Wellington to Bathurst,
   Brussels, 19 June 1815, in WSD, X,
   531-2.

18 Wellington to Aberdeen, WD, XII,
   488; "The Diary of Frances Lady
   Shelley" 1787-1817, in Brett-James, ed.,
   Hundred Days, 215

19 General Order, Nivelles, 20 June 1815,
   in ibid, 538-40; General Order,
   Joncourt, 25 June 1815, in WSD, X,
   579.

20 Wellington to Bathurst, Joncourt, 25
   June 1815, in WD, XII, 509.

21 Henry Houssaye, *1815: La seconde
   abdication, la Terreur blanche* (Paris,
   1918), 112-16; Marc Blancpain, *La Vie
   quotidienne dans la France du Nord
   sous les occupations* (Paris, 1983), 8-9,
   15, 18; Proclamation, Malplaquet, 22
   June 1815, in WD, XII, 494-5.

22 Boldero MS in Brett-James, ed.,
   Hundred Days, 205-6.

23 Wellington to Uxbridge, Le Cateau, 23
   June 1815, in WD, XII, 499-500.

24 Henry Houssaye, *1815: Waterloo*
   (Paris, 1924), 455-83; Houssaye,
   Seconde abdication, 105-12.

25 Colquhoun Grant to Wellington, Le
   Cateau, 23 June 1815, in WSD, X, 569.

26 Wellington to duc de Feltre (2 letters,
   Nivelles, 20 June), duc de Berry
   (Nivelles, 20 June), Feltre (Le Cateau,
   22 June) and Talleyrand (Le Cateau, 24
   June 1815), in WD, XII, 492, 495-6,
   502; Lieut. Gen Baron Vincent to
   Wellington, Brussels, 22 June 1815, in
   WSD, X, 559.

27 "With the usurper, declared enemy of
   humankind, there can be neither peace
   nor truce... All those who are absent
   from their homes after [our] entry into
   France... will be consided as his adher-
   ents and as enemies." Proclamation,
   Malplaquet, 22 June 1815, in WD, XII,
   494-5.

28 General Order, Nivelles, 20 June 1815, in WSD, X, 539. On fortified towns see the example of Péronne, where the King's representatives were even invited to issue the summons for surrender, ibid, 595. On negotiations to put French Commissioners in charge of Allied requisitions (which failed largely because of the rush of events but also because of Metternich's opposition), see Jean-Claude Beugnot, *Mémoires du comte Beugnot, 1779-1815* (Paris, 1959), 312-13.

29 Lieut.-Gen Colville to Wellington, Cambrai, 25 June 1815, in WSD, X, 581-2. "I cannot command such officers," wrote Wellington, on learning of the duel. "I have been long enough a soldier to know that plunderers, and those who encourage them, are worth nothing before the enemy; and I will not tolerate them." Wellington to Chassé, Vermand, 28 June 1815, in WD, XII, 513-15.

30 George Farmer in Brett-James, ed., *Hundred Days*, 207-8; Blancpain, *Occupations*, 33-43, 50-1.

31 Houssaye, *Seconde abdication*, 97-8; Wellington to French Commissioners, Joncourt, 26 June 1815, in WD, XII, 512.

32 Wellington to Charles Stuart, Orvillé, 28 June 1815, in ibid, 516; Blücher to his wife, Compiègne, 27 June 1815, in Brett-James, ed., *Hundred Days*, 207.

33 T&L, xxx; F.R. de Chateaubriand, *Mémoires d'outre-tombe* (Paris, 1973), II, 375-6.

34 Baron Vincent, (Brussels, 22 June), General Waltersdorff (Brussels, 22 June), and Talleyrand (Mons, 25 June 1815) to Wellington, in WSD, X, 559-61, 587. This last letter suggests that it was also in Brussels that Talleyrand prepared his first draft of a "Proclamation" that he wanted Louis to publish on entering France.

35 Talleyrand to duchesse de Courlande, Brussels, 23 June 1815, in G. Lacour-Gayet, *Talleyrand* (Paris, 1990), 839.

36 Vicomte de Reiset, *Souvenirs*, (Paris, 1902), 214-17.

37 Wellington to duc de Feltre, to duc de Berry, and to Bathurst, Nivelles, 20 June 1815, in WD, XII, 492-3.

38 Charles Stuart to Castlereagh, Grammont, 22 June 1815, in WSD, X, 564-5.

39 C.M. de Talleyrand-Périgord, *Mémoires, 1754-1815* (Paris, 1982),

751-2.

40 Chateaubriand, *Mémoires*, II, 376-8; Beugnot, *Mémoires*, 315-16; Stuart to Castlereagh (Mons, 23 June), Stuart to Wellington (Mons, 23 June 1815), in WSD, X, 563-5.

41 Beugnot, *Mémoires*, 317.

42 Reiset, *Souvenirs*, III, 219-20; "Proclamation," Cateau-Cambrésis, 25 June 1815, in WSD, XII, 580-1.

43 Wellington to Talleyrand, Le Cateau, 24 June 1815, in WD, XII, pp 502-3; Beugnot, *Mémoires*, 318-19.

44 Wellington to Stuart and to Bathurst, Joncourt, 25 June 1815, in WD, vol XII, 507-8; Reiset, *Souvenirs*, III, 221-5.

45 Talleyrand, *Mémoires*, 753; Talleyrand to duchesse de Courlande, Mons, 26 June 1815, in Talleyrand, *Le Miroir de Talleyrand* (Paris, 1976), 225.

46 "My Proclamation was ready; I would have liked it to have been drafted with you so that it would appear only after your approval," Talleyrand wrote to Wellington, regretting he had not yet had an interview with the Duke, Mons, 25 June 1815, in WSD, X, 587.

47 "Proclamation du Roi: Le Roi aux Français," Cambrai, 28 June 1815, in ibid, 615-16.

48 Talleyrand, *Mémoires*, 753.

49 Beugnot, *Souvenirs*, 321-3.

50 Stuart to Wellington, Cambrai, 28 & 29 June 1815, in WSD, X, 614, 625-6.

51 Beugnot, *Souvenirs*, 324.

52 Daria Oliver, *Alexandre Ier* (Paris, 1973), 331.

53 More exactly, one should say both men and women. Alexander's attachment to Prince Eugène de Beauharnais had been a great scandal in Vienna and one suspects that more was involved here than the link this represented with Napoleon. While heterosexual intrigue was the talk of the town, homosexuality was just not discussed in Vienna, and this included Baron von Hager's secret dossiers. To reinforce one's suspicions, one might consider a letter Alexander wrote to Jung Stilling on 10 July 1814 at the moment of his spiritual marriage to Roxandre de Stourdza: "There was however something good about Gustavus Adolphus (King of Sweden, overthrown by a *coup d'état*). But now he has lost all; a terrible fall! That God protect me from such a fall!" King Gustavus Adolphus was a notorious homosexual. Quoted in Ley,

Alexandre Ier, 118.

54 Alexander to Catherine, Heilbronn, 3 June 1815 (western Gregorian), in *Correspondance de l'Empereur Alexandre Ier avec sa sœur la Grande-Duchesse Catherine, Princesse d'Oldenbourg, puis Reine de Wurtemberg, 1805-1818*, ed. Grand-Duc Nicolas Mikhaïlowitch (Saint Petersburg, 1910), 194-5. Grand Duke Nicholas claims this was Julie von Krüdener, but the date makes this impossible. Grand Duchess Catherine finally left Vienna on 6 June, after a trip to Hungary. On Gabrielle Auersperg, see especially Nota to Hager, Vienna, 22 October 1815, in MHW, II, 722.

55 Comtesse Edling [Roxandre de Stourdza], *Mémoires*, in ibid, 116.

56 H.S. Harris, *Hegel's Development* (Oxford, 1983), quoted in James J. Sheehan, *German History* (Oxford, 1989), 350.

57 Ley, *Alexandre Ier*, 90-113.

58 Ibid, 111.

59 The journal is quoted at length by Ley, a direct descendent of the Krüdeners. See ibid, 112-13; Olivier, 332-5.

60 Most of this dialogue is drawn from H.L. Empaytaz (one of Krüdener's closest collaborators), *Notice sur Alexandre* (Paris & Geneva, 1840) in Ley, *Alexandre Ier*, 115-16. As Ley demonstrates, it is supported by accounts left by Roxandre de Stourdza, recorded in Julette von Krüdener's journal, and even reported by Alexander himself.

61 Humboldt (circular) to Ambassadors, Vienna, 12 June 1815, in MHW, 649-50.

62 Charles Stewart to Frances Lady Londonderry, Heidelberg, 21 June 1815, in PRONI D.3030/Q2/2.

63 Alexander to Wellington, Heidelberg, 23 June 1815, in WSD, X, 562; Wellington to Alexander, Louvres, 30 June 1815, in WD, XII, 524; Metternich to Marie, Heidelberg, 22 June 1815, in in C.L.W. von Metternich, *Mémoires, documents et écrits* (Paris, 1880), II, 517-18.

64 Marie von Metternich to her father, Baden, 15 June and Metternich to Marie, Heidelberg, 24 June 1815, in E.C.C. Corti, *Metternich und die Frauen* (Vienna & Zurich, 1948), I, pp 516-18; Gentz to Metternich, Vienna, 20 June 1815, Friedrich von Gentz,

Briefe (Munich & Berlin, 1913), III/1, 307-9.

65 Houssaye, *Seconde abdication*, 120-1.

66 Proclamation (signed by Schwarzenberg but composed, on his own admission, by Metternich), Heidelberg, 23 June, and Metternich to Talleyrand, Mannheim, 24 June 1815, in Metternich, *Mémoires*, II, 519-21; Metternich to Wellington, Heidelberg, 24 June 1815, in WSD, X, 575-6.

67 Juliette von Krüdener, *Journal*, 24 June 1815, in Ley, *Alexandre Ier*, 123; Alexander to Catherine, Mannheim, 26 June 1815, in Nicolas, *Correspondance*, 197; Metternich to his wife, Mannheim, 24 June 1815, in Guillaume de Bertier de Sauvigny, *Metternich* (Paris, 1986), 268.

68 Prince Metternich and Count Nesselrode to Wellington, Mannheim, 26 June, and Stewart to Castlereagh, Mannheim, 26 June 1815, in WSD, X, 592, 639-40.

69 "Ouverture faite par les Commissaires des trois Cours...," Haguenau, 1 July, and Stewart to Wellington, Haguenau, 1st July 1815, in ibid, 639, 652

70 Metternich to Marie, Sarrebourg, 2 July 1815, in Metternich, *Mémoires*, II, 522.

71 E. Lebretonnière, *Macédoine. Souvenirs du Quartier Latin* (Paris, 1863), 268-9; *Moniteur universel*, 19 June 1815; John Cam Hobhouse, *The Substance of Some Letters* (London, 1817), II, 79-80.

72 *Moniteur universel*, 21-2 June 1815.

73 Ibid, 23 June 1815; General Lauberdière to Davout, Rouen, 26-7 June 1815, in Houssaye, *Seconde abdication*, 70-1.

74 *Moniteur universel*, 22-3 June 1815.

75 Labretonnière, *Souvenirs*, 165, 221-3, 239; *Journal des Débats*, 11 July 1815.

76 *Journal de l'Empire*, 25 June 1815.

77 Typical of the difficulties in the way of a social analysis of Paris crowds at this time is the story of the rapid rise and fall of the *Fédérés*. Who were the *Fédérés*? There were at least three groups: The Paris *Fédération* (a political organisation that held meetings in a hall on the corner of rues Saint-Honoré and Grenelle, near the Halles), the *Fédérés tirailleurs* who claimed to be affiliated with the National Guard, and the *Fédérés tirailleurs* who would have nothing to do with the National Guard. They all probably overlapped. Dr R.S. Anderson argues that the

Fédérés tirailleurs "were almost entirely lower class." Using a register that he has discovered in the archives of the Prefecture of Paris he shows that at the end of June there were 13,725 *Fédérés tirailleurs*, of which only two were "students." E. Bretonnière, on the other hand, speaks of signing up, in the Luxembourg Gardens, to the 11th Batallion of *Fédérés tirailleurs*, which was made up entirely of students from the Latin Quarter; cf. R.S. Anderson, *Bonapartism and Revolutionary Tradition in France* (Cambridge, 1991), 204-7; Labretonnière, *Souvenirs*, 239; and (for more contradictions on social origins) K.D. Tönnesson, "Les Fédérés de Paris pendant les Cent-Jours," *Annales historiques de la Révolution Française*, LIV (1982), 393-415. Arguments over whether the Parisian *Fédération* existed or not were presented in the Parisian press during the last week of June; see, for example, *Gazette de France*, 24 June; *Journal de Paris*, 25 & 28 June 1815.

78 Ibid, 23, 29 June & 1st July 1815; Hobhouse, *Letters*, II, 125, 155.

79 *Journal de l'Empire*, 30 June.

80 Labretonnière, *Souvenirs*, 273; Hobhouse, *Letters*, II, 155.

81 "Rapport à S.M. Empereur par S.E. le duc d'Otrante, ministre de la police générale," *Journal de Paris*, 18 June 1815.

82 Henry Houssaye, *Seconde abdication*, 29.

83 Louis Madelin, *Fouché, 1759-1820* (Paris, 1910), II, 402-5.

84 Fouché, *Mémoires*, 452-7; Houssaye, *Seconde abdication*, 221-8.

85 *Journal de l'Empire*, 25 June 1815; Houssaye, *Seconde abdication*, 84-6, 170-4.

86 Davout to Fouché, and Fouché to Davout, Paris, 27 June 1815, in WSD, X, 611-12.

87 *Journal de l'Empire*, 30 June & 1st July 1815; *Journal de Paris*, 30 June 1815; Hobhouse, *Some Letters*, II, 152-3. One finds in this last article the source of old revolutionary tensions between countrymen and citizens. These tensions have been analysed in detail in the grand works of Richard Cobb. Like most Jacobins, Joseph Fouché, the merchant's son from Nantes, was no lover of peasants.

88 *Journal de Paris*, 28 June 1815; Labretonnière, *Souvenirs*, 274-5.

89 Alexander, *Bonapartism*, 202; *Journal de Paris*, 28 June 1815; Labretonnière, *Souvenirs*, 252-4.

90 Houssaye, *Second abdication*, 252-3.

91 *Journal de Paris*, 29-30 June 1815.

92 Ibid, 1 July 1815; *Journal de l'Empire*, 1 July 1815; Hobhouse, *Letters*, II, 165-7.

93 Wellington to Bathurst, Gonesse, 2 July 1815, in WD, XII, 532; Houssaye, *Seconde abdication*, 247, 259-61.

94 Ibid, 263-73.

95 *Journal de l'Empire*, 3 July 1815; Hobhouse, *Letters*, II, 187-9.

96 Gneisenau to Wellington, Versailles, 2 July 1815, in WSD, X, 651; Wellington to French Commissioners, to Earl of Uxbridge, to Blücher, to Bathurst, Gonesse, 1-3 July 1815, in WD, XII, 525-9, 532-9; Houssaye, *Seconde abdication*, 281-96.

97 Wellington to Bathurst, Gonesse, 2 July 1815, in WD, XII, 538.

98 Chateaubriand, *Mémoires*, II, 381.

99 Beugnot, *Mémoires*, 324-6.

100 Chateaubriand, *Mémoires*, II, 382; Lacour-Gayet, *Talleyrand*, 856.

101 Talleyrand to duchesse de Courlande, Roye, 3 July 1815, in Talleyrand, *Miroir*, 321; Beugnot, *Mémoires*, 325.

102 Ibid, 328.

103 Ibid, 329-30; Chateaubriand, *Mémoires*, II, 385-8; Madelin, *Fouché*, II, 419-23; Houssaye, *Seconde abdication*, 184-5.

104 *Journal de L'Empire*, 7 July 1815.

105 Ibid, 4-5 July 1815; Wellington to Blücher (Gonesse, 2 July) and to Bathurst (Gonesse, 2 & 4 July 1815), in WD, XII, 526-7, 537-8, 541-2.

106 Fouché to Wellington, Paris, 3 July 1815, in WSD, X, 652-3; Wellington to Fouché, "Head Quarters", 4 July 1815, in WD, XII, 541. Beugnot claims the meeting took place "at Poissy, in a country house belonging to the mother of a former Minister of the Emperor"; but this does not accord with others, see Beugnot, *Mémoires*, 329.

107 Houssaye, *Seconde abdication*, 314-15.

108 Hobhouse, *Letters*, II, 190-4.

109 Alexander, *Bonapartism*, 208-9; *Journal de l'Empire*, 6 July 1815.

110 Wellington to Bathurst, Gonesse, 2 July, in *WD*, XII, 538.

111 *Journal de l'Empire*, 7 July 1815.

112 *Journal des Débats*, 8 July 1815; Wellington to Blücher, Gonesse, 1st July 1815, in WD, XII, 527; Hobhouse, *Letters*, II, 216-24; Houssaye, *Seconde*

abdication, 325-31. The King's two Proclamations of Cateau-Cambrésis and Cambrai were published in Paris on 7 July.

113 Ibid, 321; Madelin, *Fouché*, II, 445-6.
114 Beugnot, *Mémoires*, 332-4.
115 *Journal des Débats*, 8 July 1815.
116 Chateaubriand, *Mémoires*, II, 386-7; Beugnot, *Mémoires*, 334.
117 *Journal des Débats*, 8 July 1815; Labretonnière, *Souvenirs*, 284; Madelin, *Fouché*, II, 447.
118 *Journal des Débats*, 10 July 1815.
119 Hobhouse, *Letters*, II, 245-7; Labretonnière, *Souvenirs*, 285-6; Chateaubriand, *Mémoires*, II, 388; Houssaye, *Seconde abdication*, 336; Lacour-Gayet, *Talleyrand*, 858-9.
120 Madelin, *Fouché*, II, 447-8.
121 *Journal de Paris*, 10 July 1815.

EUROPE, EUROPE

1 Gaspard Gourgaud, "Mémoires," in *Napoléon à Sainte-Hélène*, ed. J. Tulard (Paris, 1981), 541.
2 Georges Lacour-Gayet, *Talleyrand* (Paris, 1990), 1251; André Castelot, *Fouché* (Paris, 1990), 379-82.
3 Henry Houssaye, *1815: La Seconde Abdication, la Terreur Blanche* (Paris, 1918), 403-37.
4 G. de Bertier de Sauvigny, *La Restauration* (Paris, 1955), 119.
5 Castlereagh to Liverpool, Paris, 11 September 1815, in BD, 377.
6 E.A.D. Las Cases, "Mémorial," in Tulard, ed., *Sainte-Hélène*, 156, 383, 399-400.
7 Las Cases, "Mémorial," C.T. de Montholon, "Récits de Sainte-Hélène," and Grand Maréchal Bertrand, "Les Cahiers de Sainte-Hélène," in Tulard, ed., *Sainte-Hélène*, 122, 587, 628, 657.
8 Las Cases, "Mémorial," 303, 329, 380.
9 Ibid, 397.
10 Ibid, 248.
11 Ibid, 325-8, 341-5, 409-24.
12 Ibid, 203-4; Gourgaud, "Mémoires," 449, 533; Montholon, "Récits," 594-8, 652-3.
13 Bertrand, "Cahiers," 685-94, 722.
14 Alexander to Catherine, Void, 7 July (new style) 1815, in Grand-Duc Nicolas Mikhaïlowitch, *Correspondance de l'Empereur Alexandre Ier avec sa sœur la Grande-Duchesse Catherine* (St Petersburg, 1910), 200.
15 Francis Ley, *Alexandre Ier et sa Sainte-Alliance* (Paris, 1975), 127-31.

16 Julie von Krüdener to Alexander, Paris, ca. 28 July 1815, in ibid, 129.
17 Ibid, 136-9; Emma Sophia, Countess Brownlow, *Slight Reminiscences of a Septuagenarian* (London, 1867), 149-61.
18 Nesselrode to his wife, Paris, 16 September 1815; H.L. Empaytaz, *Notice sur Alexandre* (Geneva, 1840); Juliette von Krüdener, *Journal*, in Ley, *Alexandre Ier*, 109, 139-40.
19 C.L.W. von Metternich, *Mémoires, documents et écrits* (Paris, 1880), I, 209-12.
20 "Holy Alliance" – original text, Metternich's corrections, and final version in ibid, 149-53.
21 Castlereagh to Liverpool, Paris, 28 September 1815, in BD, 382-4.
22 Ley, *Alexandre Ier*, 144-7, 149-53.
23 Alexander to Catherine, Brussels, 1 October [ns] 1815, in Mikhaïlowitch, *Correspondance*, 203; Ley, *Alexandre Ier*, 159.
24 Daria Olivier, *Alexandre Ier* (Paris, 1973), 432-60.
25 Henry Kissinger, *A World Restored* (Boston, n.d.), 200.
26 G. de Bertier de Sauvigny, *Metternich* (Paris, 1986), 19.
27 Metternich to Marie (daughter), Paris, 13 July 1815, in Metternich, *Mémoires*, II, 524-5; Gentz, *Tagebücher*, I, 400, 404.
28 Bertier de Sauvigny, *Metternich*, 276, 279.
29 Ibid, 278.
30 Kissinger, *World Restored*, 195-6.
31 Brownlow, *Slight Reminscences*, 140; Harold Nicolson, *Congress of Vienna* (London, 1946), 276-7.
32 H. Montgomery Hyde, *The Strange Death of Lord Castlereagh* (London, 1959), 167.
33 Gentz, *Tagebücher*, 21 August & 5 September 1815, I, 401, 406; Brownlow, *Some Reminiscences*, 129-34; Walter Scott repeated Castlereagh's ghost story to the Irish poet Tom Moore, cf. Montgomery Hyde, *Strange Death*, 161-2 .
34 C.M. de Talleyrand-Périgord, *Mémoires* (Paris, 1982), 756; *Journal des Débats*, 10 July 1815.
35 Wellington to Castlereagh (Paris, 14 July), Castlereagh to Liverpool (14 July, 17 & 24 August, 4 September), Castlereagh to Clancarty (4 September 1815), in BD, 342-4, 363-5, 370-6.
36 Castlereagh to Liverpool, Paris, 24 & 29 July, 28 September 1815, in ibid,

350-4, 384.

37 Castlereagh to Liverpool (Paris, 17 July, 17 August 1815), Wellington to Castlereagh (Paris, 11 August 1815) in ibid, 347-9, 358, 362.

38 Wellington to Castlereagh (Paris, 11 August), "Memorandum of Lord Castlereagh," 12 August 1815, in ibid, 357-9, 361.

39 Liverpool to Castlereagh, London, 23 & 28 August, in ibid, 368-9, 372-3.

40 Richelieu had not seen France in twenty-five years and had been Governor of Sebastopol, in the Crimea, for the last decade. "He's the man of France who knows Crimea the best!" commented Talleyrand to the duchesse de Courlande on 27 September, in Lacour-Gayet, *Talleyrand*, 880. On Castlereagh's concern over Talleyrand's departure, see Castlereagh to Liverpool, Paris, 21 & 25 September 1815, in BD, 379-80.

41 C.K. Webster, *The Foreign Policy of Castlereagh* (London, 1925), II, 54-6.

42 Antoine d'Arjuzon, *Castlereagh* (Paris, 1995), 422-3.

43 Hyde, *Strange Death*, 90.

44 Kissinger, *World Restored*, 222; d'Arjuzon, *Castlereagh*, 431-2

45 Ibid, 463; Hyde, *Strange Death*, 174.

46 Ibid, 96.

47 Ibid, 45-7, 65.

48 Most of this section is drawn from documents reproduced *in extenso* in Hyde, *Strange Death*. On North Cray Farm, see also F.R. de Chateaubriand, *Mémoires d'outre-tombe* (Paris, 1973), II, 516.

49 Londonderry to Castlereagh, Mount Stewart, 4 December 1815, in PRONI D.3030/H/31.

50 D'Arjuzon, *Castlereagh*, 415-20; Hyde, *Strange Death*, 84, 134-40.

51 Ibid, 132.

52 D'Arbuzon, *Castlereagh*, 458; Hyde, *Strange Death*, 3, 41-2.

53 Rev. J. Richardson, *Recollections of the Last Half Century*, and William Toynbee, *Glimpses of the Twenties*, in ibid, 183-7.

54 Ibid, 49-54, 70.

55 In a recent study of Members of the House of Commons between 1790 and 1820, R.G. Thorne notes that at least nineteen Members committed suicide; seven cut their throat. Thorne furthermore notes that thirty-five Members either verged on insanity or were insane. See R.G. Thorne, *The House of Commons, 1790-1820* (London, 1986), I, 330-2.

Bibliography

BOOKS AND ARTICLES

Alexander, R.S. *Bonapartism and the Revolutionary Tradition in France: The Fédérés of 1815.* Cambridge: Cambridge University Press, 1991.

Altick, Richard D. *The Shows of London.* Cambridge, Mass.: Belknap, Harvard University Press, 1978.

Anderson, J.A. [A.A. Feldborg]. *A Dane's Excursions in Britain.* 2 vols. London: Mathews & Leigh, 1809.

Angeberg, d' [Léonard Chodze]. *Le Congrès de Vienne et les traités de 1815.* 2 vols. Paris: Amyot, 1863.

Arjuzon, Antoine d'. *Castlereagh.* Paris: Tallandier, 1995.

Aron, Raymond. *Peace and War: A Theory of International Relations.* Trans. Richard Howard and Annette Baker Fox. New York: Doubleday, 1973.

Arrigon, L.-J. *Une amie de Talleyrand: La Duchesse de Courlande, 1761-1821.* Paris: Flammarion, 1946.

[Avot, Madame d']. *Lettres sur l'Angleterre, ou Mon séjour à Londres en 1817 et 1818, Par Mme M.D.* Paris: Germain Mathiot, 1819.

Banik-Schweitzer, Renate. *Wien in Vormärz.* Vienna: Verein für Geschichte der Stadt Wien, 1980.

Beauharnais, see Hortense de Beauharnais.

Beaucour, Fernand. *Napoléon à l'Ile d'Elbe.* Paris: C.E.N., 1991.

_____. *Une visite à Napoléon à l'Ile d'Elbe d'un membre du Parlement anglais.* Paris: C.E.N., 1990.

Bernstorff, Gräfin Elise von. *Ein Bild aus der Zeit von 1789 bis 1835 aus ihren Aufzeichnungen.* 2 vols. Berlin: Mittler, 1896.

Berriat Saint-Prix, Jacques. *Napoléon à Grenoble: histoire du 7 mars 1815.* Grenoble: Maisonville & Jourdan, 1861.

Bertrand, Grand Maréchal. *Les Cahiers de Sainte-Hélène.* In *Napoléon à Sainte-Hélène,* ed. Jean Tulard, pp. 611-756.

Bertier de Sauvigny, G. de. *Metternich.* Paris: Fayard, 1986.

_____. *La Restauration.* Paris: Flammarion, 1955.

Beugnot, Jean-Claude. *Mémoires du comte Beugnot, 1779-1815.* Ed. Robert Lacour-Gayet. Paris: Hachette, 1959.

Billecocq, André. *La Séparation amiable du prince et de la princesse de Talleyrand.* Paris: Clavreuil, 1987.

Blancpain, Marc. *La Vie quotidienne dans la France du Nord sous les occupations (1814-1944).* Paris: Hachette, 1983

Bluche, Frédéric. *Le Bonapartisme: aux origines de la droite autoritaire*

(1800-1860). Paris: Nouvelles Editions Latines, 1980.

_____. *Le Plébiscite des Cent-Jours*. Geneva: Droz, 1974.

Boigne, Comtesse de. *Mémoires de la comtesse de Boigne, née Osmond: récits d'une tante*. Vol. I: *Du règne de Louis XVI à 1820*. Paris: Mercure de France, 1979.

Bourgoing, Jean de. *Vom Wiener Kongress*. Vienna & Munich: Herold, 1964 (1st ed. 1943).

Boyce, George, James Curran and Pauline Wingate, eds. *Newspaper History from the Seventeenth Century to the Present Day*. London: Constable, 1978.

Braunbehrens, Volkmar. *Mozart in Vienna, 1781-1791*. Trans. Timothy Bell. New York: Grove Weidenfeld, 1989.

Brett-James, Antony, ed.. *The Hundred Days: Napoleon's Last Campaign from eye-witness accounts*. London: Macmillan, 1964.

Brion, Marcel. *La Vie quotidienne à Vienne au temps de Mozart et de Schubert*. Paris: Hachette, 1959.

Brooke, John. *King George III*. London: Constable, 1972.

Brownlow, Emma Sophia, Countess. *Slight Reminiscences of a Septuagenarian, from 1802 to 1815*. London: John Murray, 1867.

Brusatti, Alois. "Wien, 1814-15". In *Der Wiener Kongress, 1. Sept 1814 bis 9 Juni 1815, Ausstellung, 1 Juni bis 15 Oktober 1965*. Vienna: Bundesministerium, Verein der Museumsfreunde, 1965, pp. 233-5.

Burg, Peter. *Die deutsche Trias in Idee und Wirklichkeit: von alten Reich zum Deutschen Zollverein*. Stuttgart: Franz Steiner, 1989.

Byron, Lord. *The Complete Poetical Works*. Vol II: *Childe Harold's Pilgrimage*. Ed. Jerome J. McGann. Oxford: Clarendon Press, 1980.

Campbell, Neil. *Napoleon at Fontainebleau and Elba, being a Journal of Occurrences in 1814-1815*. Ed. Archibald Neil Campbell MacLachlan. London: John Murray, 1869.

Carlyle, Thomas. *The French Revolution*. 2 vols. Oxford: Oxford University Press, 1989.

Castelot, André. *Fouché*. Paris: Perrin, 1990.

Castlereagh, Viscount. (Robert Stewart, Second Marquess of Londonderry). *Correspondence, Despatches, Despatches, and Other Papers of Viscount Castlereagh*. Ed. Charles William Vane, Third Marquess of Londonderry. Vols. IX, X, and XI. London: John Murray, 1853.

Caulaincourt, Armand de. *Mémoires*. Ed. Jean Hanoteau. 3 vols. Paris: Plon, 1933.

Chandler, David G. *Campaigns of Napoleon*. New York: Macmillan, 1966.

Chateaubriand, François René de. *Mémoires d'outre-tombe*. 3 vols. Paris: Livre de Poche, 1973.

Chevalier, Louis. *Laboring Classes and Dangerous Classes in Paris During the First Half of the Nineteenth Century*. Trans. Frank Jellineck. Princeton: Princeton University Press, 1973.

Clark, J.C.D. *English Society 1688-1832: Ideology, Social Structure and Political Practice during the Ancien Regime*. Cambridge: Cambridge University Press, 1985.

Comte-Sponville, André. *Petit traité des grandes vertus*. Paris: P.U.F., 1995.

Constant, Benjamin. *Mémoires sur les Cent-Jours*. Ed. O. Pozzo di Borgo.

Paris: J.J. Pauvert, 1961.

_____. *Œuvres*. Ed. Alfred Roulin. Paris: Gallimard (Pléiade), 1957.

Corti, Egon Cäsar Conte. *Metternich und die Frauen*. Vol. I: *Von der Französischen Revolution bis zum Wiener Kongress, 1789-1815*. Vienna and Zurich: Europa-Verlag, 1948.

Courcy, Anne de. *Circe: The Life of Edith, Marchioness of Londonderry*. London: Sinclair-Stevenson, 1992.

Creevey, Thomas. *The Creevey Papers*. Ed. Sir Herbert Maxwell. 2 vols. London: John Murray, 1903.

Cronin, Vincent. *Napoleon*. London: HarperCollins, 1994 (1st ed., 1971).

Crouzet, François. "Wars, blockade and economic change in Europe." *Journal of Economic History*, 27 (1964), pp. 567-88.

Cumming, Valerie. "Pantomime and Pageantry: The Coronation of George IV". In *London: World City, 1800-1840*. Ed. Celina Fox, pp. 39-50.

Daunton, Martin. "London and the World". In *London: World City, 1800-1840*. Ed. Celina Fox, pp. 21-38.

De Lancey, Lady. *A Week at Waterloo in 1815*. Ed. Major B.R. Ward. London: John Murray, 1906.

Delon, Michel, and Daniel Baruch, eds.. *Paris le jour, Paris la nuit*. Paris: Robert Laffont, 1990.

Dickens, Charles. *A Tale of Two Cities*. London: Collins, 1952.

Dickinson, H.T. "Radical Culture". In *London: World City, 1800-1840*. Ed. Celina Fox, pp. 209-24.

Dino, Dorothée de Courlande, comtesse Edmond de Périgord, duchesse de. *Souvenirs de la duchesse de Dino*. Paris: Calmann-Lévy, 1908.

Dziewanowski, M.K. *Alexander I: Russia's Mysterious Tsar*. New York: Hippocrene Books, 1990.

Ebrington, Viscount. *Memorandum of two conversations between the Emperor Napoleon and Viscount Ebrington at Porto Ferrajo, on the 6th and 9th of December, 1814*. London: James Ridgeway, 1823.

Esdaile, Charles J. "The Duke of Wellington and the Command of the Spanish Army, 1812-14". In *Wellington: Studies in the Military and Political Career of the First Duke of Wellington*. Ed. Norman Gash, pp. 66-86.

Espriella, Don Manuel Alvarez [Robert Southey]. *Letters from England*. 3 vols. London: Hurst, Rees and Orme, 1807.

Farington, Joseph. *The Farington Diary*. Ed. James Grieg. 7 vols. London: Hutchinson, 1923-1927.

[Feltham, John.] *The Picture of London for 1815*. London: Longman, 1815.

Fleury de Chaboulon, P.A. Edouard. *Mémoires pour servir à l'histoire de la vie privée, du retour et du règne de Napoléon en 1815*. 2 vols. London: Longman, Hurst, Bees, etc, 1820.

Fouché, Joseph. *Mémoires de Joseph Fouché, Duc d'Otrante*. Ed. Michel Vovelle. Paris: Imprimerie Nationale, 1992.

Fournier, August, ed. *Die Geheimpolizei auf dem wiener Kongress: eine Auswahl aus ihren Papieren*. Vienna and Leipzig: F. Tempsky and G. Freytag, 1913.

Fox, Celina, ed. *London: World City, 1800-1840*. New Haven, Conn.: Yale University Press, 1992

_____. "A Visitor's Guide to London World City, 1800-40". In *London: World City, 1800-1840*. Ed. Celina Fox, pp. 11-20.

Fraser, Flora. *The Unruly Queen: The Life of Queen Caroline*. London: Macmillan, 1996.

Fulford, Roger T.B.. *Samuel Whitbread, 1764-1815: A Study in Opposition*. London: Macmillan, 1967.

Gentz, Friedrich von. *Briefe von und an Friedrich von Gentz*. Eds. F.C. Wittichen and E Salzer. 3 vols. Munich and Berlin: Oldenbourg, 1913.

_____. *Tagebücher*. 4 vols. Leipzig: Brockhaus, 1873-4.

George, M. Dorothy. *London Life in the Eighteenth Century*. London: Kegan Paul, Trench, Trubner, 1925.

Gooch, G.P. *Germany during the French Revolution*. London: Longman, 1920.

Gourgaud, Gaspard. *Mémoires*. In *Napoléon à Sainte-Hélène*, ed. Jean Tulard, pp. 443-552.

Guizot, François. *Mémoires pour servir à l'histoire de mon temps*. Vol. I. Paris: Michel Lévy, 1858.

Hamilton-Williams, David. *The Fall of Napoleon: The Final Betrayal*. London: Arms and Armour, 1994.

Hansard, T.C., ed. *The Parliamentary Debates from the Year 1803 to the Present Times*. Vols. XXIX & XXX. London: Hansard, 1815.

Haydon, Benjamin Robert. *Life of Benjamin Robert Haydon, Historical Painter from His Autobiography and Journals*. Ed. Tom Taylor. 3 vols. London: Longman, Brown, Green and Longmans, 1853.

Heffer, Simon. *Moral Desperado: A Life of Thomas Carlyle*. London: Weidenfeld and Nicolson, 1995.

Hevesi, Ludwig. "Wien: Stadtbild, Festlichkeiten, Volksleben". In *Der Wiener Congress: Culturgeschichte, die Bildenden und das Kunstgewerbe, Theater, Musik, in der Zeit von 1808 bis 1825*. Ed. Eduard Leisching. Vienna: Artaria, 1898, pp. 75-93.

Hibbert, Christopher. *George IV*. Harmondsworth, Mx: Penguin, 1976.

Hillairet, Jacques. *Dictionnaire historique des rues de Paris*. 2 vols. Paris: Editions de Minuit, 1985.

Hinde, Wendy. *Canning*. Oxford: Blackwell, 1989 (1st ed. 1973).

_____. *Castlereagh*. London: Collins, 1981.

Hobhouse, John Cam. *The Substance of Some Letters written by an Englishman Resident at Paris during the Last Reign of the Emperor Napoleon*. 2 vols. London: Ridgways, 1816 (at times using 1817 edition).

Hortense de Beauharnais, Queen. *Mémoires de la Reine Hortense*. Ed. Jean Hanoteau. 3 vols. Paris: Plon, 1927.

Horward, Donald D. "Wellington as a Strategist, 1808-14". In *Wellington: Studies in the Military and Political Career of the First Duke of Wellington*. Ed. Norman Gash, pp. 87-116.

Houssaye, Henry. *1814*. Paris: Perrin, 1918.

_____. *1815: La Première Restauration, le Retour de l'île d'Elbe, les Cent Jours*. Paris: Perrin, 1920.

_____. *1815: Waterloo*. Paris: Plon, 1924.

_____. *1815: La Second Abdication, la Terreur Blanche*. Paris: Plon, 1918.

Hugo, Victor. *Les Misérables*. Paris: La Pléiade, Gallimard, 1951.

Hyde, H. Montgomery. *The Strange Death of Lord Castlereagh*. London: Heineman, 1959.

Jackson, Lieut.-Col. Basil. *Notes and Reminiscences of a Staff Officer chiefly relating to the Waterloo Campaign*. Ed. R.C. Seaton. London: John Murray, 1903.

Jackson, Peter. *George Scharf's London: Sketches and Watercolours of a Changing City, 1820-50*. London: John Murray, 1987.

Jardin, A., and A.J. Tudesq. *La France des notables, 1815-1848*. 2 vols. Paris: Seuil, 1973.

Johnson, Paul. *The Birth of the Modern: World Society, 1815-1830*. London: Weidenfeld and Nicolson, 1991.

Keegan, John. *The Face of Battle: A Study of Agincourt, Waterloo and the Somme*. New York: Vintage, 1977.

Kissinger, Henry A. *A World Restored: Metternich, Castlereagh and the Problems of Peace, 1812-1822*. Boston: Houghton Mifflin, n.d.

Kraehe, Enno E.. *Metternich's German Policy*. 2 vols. Princeton, N.J.: Princeton University Press, 1963, 1983.

Kralik, Richard. *Histoire de Vienne*. Trans. André Jundt. Paris: Payot, 1932.

E. Labretonnière. *Macédoine. Souvenirs du Quartier Latin*. Paris: Marpon, 1863.

Laborde, Alexandre, comte de. *Quarante-huite heures de garde au Château des Tuileries pendant les journées des 19 et 20 mars 1815*. Paris: Nicole et la Normant, 1816.

Lacour-Gayet, Georges. *Talleyrand*. Paris: Payot, 1990 (1st ed., 1928-31).

Laflandre-Linden, Louise. *Napoléon et l'Ile d'Elbe*. Castel: La Cadière d'Azur, 1989.

Las Cases, E.A.D. *Mémorial*. In *Napoléon à Sainte-Hélène*, ed. Jean Tulard, pp. 31-439.

La Garde-Chambonas, Comte Auguste de. *Souvenirs du Congrès de Vienne, 1814-1815*. Paris: Emile-Paul, 1904 (1st ed., 1820).

Langford, Paul. *A Polite and Commercial People: England 1727-1783*. Oxford: Oxford University Press, 1989.

Lefebvre, Georges. *Napoleon, From Tilsit to Waterloo, 1807-1815*. Trans. J.E. Anderson. New York: Columbia University Press, 1969.

Le Gallo, Emile. *Les Cent-Jours*. Paris: Plon, 1923.

Lever, Evelyne. *Louis XVIII*. Paris: Fayard, 1988.

Ley, Francis. *Alexandre Ier et sa Sainte-Alliance, 1811-1825*. Paris: Fischbacher, 1975.

Lichtenberger, Elisabeth. *Vienna*. Trans. Dietlinde Mühlgassner and Craig Reisser. London: Belhaven, 1993.

Lieven, Dorothea Benkendorff, Daria Christoforovna, Princess de. *Memoirs*. In *Correspondance de l'Empereur Alexandre Ier avec sa sœur, la Grande-Duchesse Catherine*. Ed. Grand-Duc Nicolas Mikhaïlowitch, pp. 225-46.

Louis-Philippe d'Orléans. *Mon Journal*. 2 vols. Paris: Michel Lévy, 1849.

Longford, Elizabeth. *Wellington*. 2 vols. London: Weidenfield & Nicolson, 1969-72.

Macalpine, Ida, and Richard Hunter. *George III and the Mad-Business*.

London: Pimlico, 1991 (1st ed. 1969).

Macdonald, J.E.J.A. *Souvenirs du maréchal Macdonald*. Ed. Camille Rousset. Paris: Plon, 1892.

MacDonagh, Katharine. "A Sympathetic Ear: Napoleon, Elba and the British." *History Today* (February 1994), pp. 29-35.

Mackenzie, Norman. *The Escape from Elba: the Fall and Flight of Napoleon, 1814-1815*. Oxford: Oxford University Press, 1982.

Madelin, Louis. *Fouché, 1759-1820*. 2 vols. Paris: Plon, 1910.

Malcolm, J.P. *First Impressions, or Sketches from Art and Nature, Animate and Inanimate*. London: Longman, 1807.

Mansel, Philip. *The Court of France, 1789-1830*. Cambridge: Cambridge University Press, 1988.

_____. *The Eagle in Splendour: Napoleon and His Court*. London: George Philip, 1987.

Mercer, General Cavalié. *Journal of the Waterloo Campaign, kept throughout the Campaign of 1815*. 2 vols. London: Blackwood, 1870.

Mercier, Louis Sébastien. *Le nouveau Paris*. In *Paris le jour, Paris la nuit*. Eds. M. Delon & D. Baruch, pp. 373-479.

_____. *Tableau de Paris*. In *Paris le jour, Paris la nuit*. Eds. M. Delon & D. Baruch, pp. 25-372.

Messner, Robert. *Die Leopoldstadt im Vormärz: historisch-topographische Darstellung der nordöstlichen Vorstädte und Vororte Wiens auf Grund der Kadastralvermessungen*. Vienna: Verlag Notring der wissenschaftlichen Verbände Österreichs, 1962.

Metternich, Prince Clemens Lothar Wenzel von. *Mémoires, documents et écrits*. Ed. Prince Richard von Metternich. Vols. I - II: *1773-1815*. Paris: Plon, 1880.

_____ and Wilhelmine von Sagan. *Ein Briefwechsel, 1813 - 1815*. Ed. Maria Ullrichová. Graz and Cologne: Hermann Böhlaus Nachf, 1966.

Michelet, Jules. *Histoire de la Révolution française*. 2 vols. Paris: Robert Laffont, 1979.

_____. *Ma Jeunesse*. Paris: Calmann Lévy, 1884.

Mikhaïlowitch, see Nicolas Mikhaïlowitch.

Montholon, C.T. de. *Récits de Sainte-Hélène*. In *Napoléon à Sainte-Hélène*, ed. Jean Tulard, pp. 557-606.

Moreau, Jacob-Nicolas. *Mes Souvenirs*. 2 vols. Paris: Plon, 1898-1901.

Morgan, Sidney Owenson, Lady. *La France*. 2 vols. Paris and London: Treuttel et Würtz, 1817.

_____. *Passages from My Autobiography*. London: Richard Bentley, 1859.

Mosse, George L. *Fallen Soldiers: Reshaping the Memory of the World Wars*. Oxford: Clarendon Press, 1990.

Mount Stewart. London: The National Trust, 1978.

Müffling, Friedrich Carl Ferdinand, Freiherr von. *Aus meinem Leben*. Berlin: E.S. Mittler, 1851.

Myerly, Scott Hughes. "'The Eye Must Entrap the Mind'": Army Spectacle and Paradigm in Nineteenth-Century Britain." *Journal of Social History*, XXVI (1992), pp. 105-31.

Nicolas Mikhaïlowitch [Romanov], Grand-Duc. *Correspondance de l'Empereur Alexandre Ier avec sa sœur la Grande-Duchesse Catherine,*

Princesse d'Oldenbourg, puis Reine de Wurtemberg, 1805-1818. Saint-Petersburg: Manufacture des Papiers de l'Etat, 1910.

Nicolson, Harold. *The Congress of Vienna*. London: Constable, 1946.

Norgate, The Rev. Burroughs T. *Paris and the Parisians the Year after Waterloo; being observations made during a visit to Paris in the year 1816*. London: London Literary Society, 1831.

Olivier, Daria. *Alexandre Ier: Prince des Illusions*. Paris: Fayard, 1973.

Olsen, Donald J.. *The City as a Work of Art: London, Paris, Vienna*. New Haven, Conn.: Yale University Press, 1986

Orléans, see Louis-Philippe d'Orléans.

Palmer, Alan. *Metternich*. London: Weidenfeld & Nicolson, 1972.

Pezzl, Johann. "Sketch of Vienna". Trans. in H.C. Robbins Landon, *Mozart and Vienna*, pp. 53-191.

Phippen, Francis. *An Authentic Account of the Late Mr. Whitbread*. London: Hone, 1815.

Pinkney, David H. *Napoleon III and the Rebuilding of Paris*. Princeton, N.J.: Princeton University Press, 1972.

Pollard, Sidney. *Peaceful Conquest: The Industrialization of Europe, 1760-1970*. Oxford: Clarendon Press, 1981.

Pons de L'Hérault, André. *Souvenirs et anecdotes de l'Ile d'Elbe*. Paris: Plon, 1897.

Pradt, Abbé de. *Récit historique sur la restauration de la royauté en France, le 31 mars 1814*. Paris: Rosa, 1822.

Prothero, I.J. *Artisans and Politics in Early Nineteenth-Century London: John Gast and his Times*. Baton Rouge, La.: Louisiana State University Press, 1979.

[Prudhomme, Louis.] *Voyage descriptif et philosophique de l'ancien et du nouveau Paris: miroir fidèle*. Paris: Chez l'auteur, 1814.

Pückler-Muskau, Prince. *A Regency Visitor: The English Tour of Prince Pückler-Muskau Described in his Letters, 1826-1828*. Trans. Sarah Austin. London: Collins, 1957.

Regnault, J. "L'Empereur et l'opinion publique, 1813-1814". *Revue historique de l'Armée*, XIII (1957), pp. 29-50.

Reiset, Marie-Antoine. *Souvenirs du lieutenant-général Vicomte de Reiset (1814-1836)*. Paris: Calmann-Lévy, 1902.

Richter, Joseph. *Die Eipeldauer Briefe, 1799-1813*. Vol. II. Munich: Georg Müller, 1918.

Robbins Landon, H.C., ed. *Beethoven: His Life, Work and World*. London: Thames & Hudson, 1992.

_____. *Mozart and Vienna*. London: Thames and Hudson, 1991.

Romilly, Sir Samuel. "Diary of a Journey to Paris". In *The Life of Sir Samuel Romilly written by himself, with a selection from his correspondence*. London: John Murray, 1842, vol. I, pp. 407-24.

Rosenthal, Harold, and John Warrack. *Guide de l'Opéra*. Trans. and eds., Roland Mancini and J.J. Rouveroux. Paris: Fayard, 1974.

Rudé, George. *The Crowd in History, 1730-1848*. New York: John Wiley, 1964.

Rush, Richard. *A Residence at the Court of London*. London: Bentley, 1833.

Saint-Albin, J.S.C. *Voyages de Paul Béranger dans Paris après 45 ans d'ab-*

sence. 2 vols. Paris, Dalibon, 1819.

Schom, Alan. *One Hundred Days: Napoleon's Road to Waterloo.* London: Michael Joseph, 1993.

Scott, John. *A Visit to Paris in 1814; being a review of the moral, political, intellectual and social condition of the French capital.* London: Longman, Hurst, Rees, Orme, and Brown, 1815 (at times using 1816 edition).

_____. *Paris Revisited in 1815, by way of Brussels: including a walk over the field of battle at Waterloo.* London: Longman, Hurst, Rees, Orme, and Brown, 1816.

Sédillot, René. *Le Coût de la Révolution française.* Paris: Perrin, 1989.

Severn, John K. "The Wellesleys and Iberian Diplomacy". In *Wellington: Studies in the Military and Political Career of the First Duke of Wellington.* Ed. Norman Gash, pp. 34-65.

Sewell, William H. *Work and Revolution in France: The Language of Labor from the Old Regime to 1848.* Cambridge: Cambridge University Press, 1980.

Sheehan, James J. *German History, 1770-1866.* Oxford: Clarendon Press, 1989.

Sheppard, F.W.H. *Survey of London.* Vols XXIX and XXX. London: The Athlone Press, University of London, 1960.

Shroeder, Paul W. *The Transformation of European Politics, 1763-1848.* Oxford: Clarendon Press, 1994.

[Simond, Louis]. *Journal of a Tour and Residence in Great Britain during the years 1810 and 1811 by A French Traveller.* 2 vols. Edinburgh: A. Constable, 1815 (& 2nd ed. 1817).

Smith, Timothy B. "In Defence of Privilege: The City of London and the Challenge of Municipal Reform". *Journal of Social History*, XXVII (1993), pp. 59-83.

Southey, Robert. See Espriella, Don Manuel Alvarez.

Spiel, Hilde, ed. *Der Wiener Kongreß in Anzeugen berichten.* Düsseldorf: Karl Rauch, 1965.

Staël, Germaine de. *De l'Allemagne.* 2 vols. Paris: Flammarion, 1968.

Summerson, John. *Georgian London.* London: Penguin, 1978 (1st ed., 1945).

Talleyrand-Périgord, C.M. de. *Mémoires, 1754-1815.* Eds. Paul-Louis and Jean-Paul Couchaud. Paris: Plon, 1982.

_____. *Le Miroir de Talleyrand: Lettres inédites à la duchesse de Courlande pendant le Congrès de Vienne.* Ed. Gaston Palewski. Paris: Perrin, 1976.

_____. *Talleyrand intime d'après sa correspondance avec la duchesse de Courlande: La Restauration en 1814.* Paris: Ernest Kolb, 1891.

_____. and Louis XVIII. *Correspondance inédite du Prince de Talleyrand et du Roi Louis XVIII pendant le Congrès de Vienne.* Ed. G. Pallain. Paris: Plon, 1881.

Tangye Lean, E. *The Napoleonists: A Study in Political Disaffection, 1760-1960.* London: Oxford University Press, 1970.

Thackeray, W.M. *The Four Georges and the English Humorists.* London: Collins, n.d. (ca. 1910).

Thielen, Peter Gerrit. *Karl August von Hardenberg, 1750-1822: Eine*

Biographie. Cologne: Grote, 1967.

Tolstoy, Leo. *War and Peace*. Trans. Rosemary Edwards. London: Penguin, 1978.

Thompson, E.P. *The Making of the English Working Class*. New York: Random, 1963.

Thompson, J.M. *Napoleon Bonaparte*. Oxford: Blackwell, 1988 (1st ed., 1952).

Thompson, Norman, ed. *Wellington: Studies in the Military and Political Career of the First Duke of Wellington*. Manchester: Manchester University Press, 1990.

Thorne, Roland G. *The House of Commons, 1790-1820*. 5 vols. London: Secker and Warburg, 1986.

Tönnesson, K.D. "Les Fédérés de Paris pendant les Cent-Jours". *Annales historiques de la Révolution Française*, LIV (1982), pp. 393-415.

Tulard, Jean. *Napoléon ou le mythe du sauveur*. Paris: Fayard, 1977 (occasionally using expanded 1993 edition).

_____. *Nouvelle histoire de Paris: Le Consulat et l'Empire, 1800-1815*. Paris: Hachette, 1983.

_____. ed. *Napoléon à Sainte-Hélène*. Paris: Laffont, 1981.

_____. ed. *L'Europe de Napoléon*. Paris: Horvath, 1989.

Van der Kiste, John. *George III's Children*. London: Alan Sutton, 1992.

Vigarello, Georges. *Concepts of Cleanliness: Changing Attitudes in France Since the Middle Ages*. Trans. Jean Birrell. Cambridge: Cambridge University Press, 1988.

Vitrolles, Eugène d'Arnauld, baron de. *Mémoires de Vitrolles*. Ed. Pierre Farel. 2 vols. Paris: Gallimard, 1950-1.

Walks through Kent. London: Sherwood, 1827.

Watson, J. Steven. *The Reign of George III 1760-1815*. Oxford: Oxford University Press, 1960.

Webster, C.K. *The Foreign Policy of Castlereagh, 1812-1815: Britain and the Reconstruction of Europe*. London: G. Bell, 1931.

_____. *The Foreign Policy of Castlereagh, 1815-1822: Britain and the European Alliance*. London: G. Bell, 1925.

_____. ed., *British Diplomacy, 1813-1815: Select Documents dealing with the Reconstruction of Europe*. London: G. Bell, 1921.

Weil, Commandant M.H., ed.. *Les Dessous du Congrès de Vienne d'après des documents originaux des Archives du Ministère impérial et royal de l'intérieur à Vienne*. 2 vols. Paris: Payot, 1917.

Weller, Jac. *Wellington at Waterloo*. London: Greenhill, 1992.

Wellington, Field Marshal Arthur, Duke of. *The Dispatches of Field Marshall the Duke of Wellington during His Various Campaigns*. Vol. XII: *France and the Low Countries, 1814-15*. Ed. Lieut. Col. Gurwood. London: John Murray, 1831.

_____. *Supplementary despatches and memoranda*. Vols. IX, X, and XI. London: John Murray, 1862.

Williams, Raymond. "The Press and Popular Culture: An Historical Perspective". In *Newspaper History*, eds. George Boyçe, James Curran and Pauline Wingate, pp. 41-50.

Wolloch, Isser. *The French Veteran from the French Revolution to the*

Restoration. Chapel Hill, NC: University of North Carolina Press, 1979.

Wood, Dennis. *Benjamin Constant: A Biography*. London: Routledge, 1993.

Woodward, Llewellyn. *The Age of Reform 1815-1870*. Oxford: Clarendon Press, 1962 (1st ed. 1938).

Ziegler, Philip. *Addington: A Life of Henry Addington, First Viscount Sidmouth*. London: Collins, 1968.

_____. *The Duchess of Dino*. London: Collins, 1962.

Zweig, Stefan. *Fouché*. Trans. Alzir Hella and Olivier Bournac. Paris: Grasset, 1969 (1st ed., 1929).

NEWSPAPERS

London: *The Courier   The Examiner   Morning Post   St James's Chronicle   The Sun   The Sunday Monitor   The Times*

Paris: *Le Censeur   Gazette de France   Journal des Débats   Journal de l'Empire   Journal de Paris   Journal universel   Moniteur universel Le Nain Jaune*

Ghent   *Moniteur de Gand*

DOCUMENTS

Public Record Office of Northern Ireland (PRONI), Belfast

— D.3030	*The Castlereagh Papers* (deposited by the National Trust, Mount Stewart)
/3925 – 4740	The main run of the papers of Viscount Castlereagh, 1814-1815
/T 2,3 & 4	Letters from Castlereagh to his wife
/H/1-44	Letters of the First Lord Londonderry
/Q2/2	Letters of condolance to 3rd Marquess of Londonderry on brother's (Castlereagh's) death
/NN	Letters of Tsar Alexander to Frances Anne, Lady Londonderry, bound in red velvet (an interesting insight into Alexander's fears and sentimentality)

Illustration credits

The author and publishers wish to thank the following for permission to reproduce illustrations:

AKG, London, pages 123, 143, 180-1, 215, 250, 329, endpapers.

Apsley House, Wellington Museum/Bridgeman Art Library, London, 29, 83.

Bibliothèque Nationale, Paris 99.

Bridgeman Art Library, London, 211, 255, 387.

British Library/Bridgeman Art library, London, 61.

Christies/Bridgeman Art Library, London, 378-9 *above*.

Mary Evans Picture Library, London, 395.

Guildhall Library, Corporation of London Bridgeman Art Library, London, 1.

Heeresgeschichtliches Museum, Vienna/AKG, London, 415.

Historisches Museum der Stadt, Vienna/AKG, London, 198, 244.

Louvre, Paris/Bridgeman Art Library, London 107.

Mansell Collection, London, 11, 43, 153, 265, 290, 295, 367, 433.

Musée Carnavalet/Bulloz, Paris, 399.

Musée Carnavalet/Roger-Viollet, Paris, 115.

Musée National du Château de Versailles/Roger-Viollet, Paris, 100, 324-5.

National Maritime Museum, Greenwich, 384-5.

Petworth House, Sussex/National Trust Photographic Library, London, 56.

United Services Club/Bridgeman Art Library, London, 378-9 *below*.

Maps designed by Rodney Paul.

Index

Note: page numbers in *italic* refer to illustrations